Women in Management Worldwide

An ageing workforce, potential talent shortages, an increasingly competitive international environment and the need to utilize the talents of the best-qualified people, regardless of gender: these are some of the unprecedented challenges faced by organizations today. More women than men, in many cases, are graduating from universities and gaining the requisite experience to qualify for advancement to higher levels of management.

In this expanded and revised third edition, Professors Burke and Richardsen, together with a list of international contributors, address women's progression in the workforce and into the upper echelons of management. They cover a range of professions and a geographically dispersed territory, thereby advancing the understanding of women in management within a traditional context and making a substantial contribution to the literature for both an academic and practitioner audience. The broader regional perspective offers a comprehensive overview of the challenges and opportunities facing women in the workplace, and promotes the ongoing analysis of the interface between women's career aspirations and societal and organizational norms, assumptions and values. Following the same format as the previous edition, the country-by-country analysis allows for the data between countries and regions to be compared, for the differences to be addressed and a more holistic picture of the situation in a given country to be assessed.

Women in Management Worldwide will appeal to researchers, policy-makers in a range of countries interested in workforce issues, talent management and gender equality, as well as consultants working with international organizations on HRM and organizational effectiveness challenges.

Ronald J. Burke is an Emeritus Professor of Organizational Studies at the Schulich School of Business, York University, Canada.

Astrid M. Richardsen is Professor of Organization Psychology at BI Norwegian Business School, Norway.

An excellent book that details the progress, or lack of, being made for women in management worldwide. It includes a wealth of statistical and academic support and is a must for all of those involved in this area. Congratulations editors!

Dr Sandra Fielden, Honorary Senior Lecturer in Organisational Psychology,
Manchester Business School, University of Manchester, UK

This book is amazing in its breadth and scope, covering many countries in a meaningful way. It explains the journey for women's equitable representation across the globe in key areas of legislative, economic, educational, social and organizational change. I heartily recommend it.

Isabel Metz, Melbourne Business School, University of Melbourne, Australia

Women in Management Worldwide

Signs of progress

Third edition

Edited by
Ronald J. Burke and Astrid M. Richardsen

Routledge
Taylor & Francis Group

LONDON AND NEW YORK

First published 2004 by Routledge

2 Park Square, Milton Park, Abingdon, Oxfordshire OX14 4RN
52 Vanderbilt Avenue, New York, NY 10017

Routledge is an imprint of the Taylor & Francis Group, an informa business

First issued in paperback 2019

British Library Cataloguing in Publication Data
A catalogue record for this book is available from the British Library

Library of Congress Cataloging in Publication Data
Names: Burke, Ronald J., editor. | Richardsen, Astrid M., editor.
Title: Women in management worldwide : signs of progress / edited by Ronald
J. Burke and Astrid M. Richardsen.
Description: Third edition. | Abingdon, Oxon ; New York, NY : Routledge,
2017. | Includes bibliographical references and index.
Identifiers: LCCN 2016009882| ISBN 9781472462718 (hardback) | ISBN
9781315546742 (ebook)
Subjects: LCSH: Women executives--Cross-cultural studies.
Classification: LCC HD6054.3 .W66 2017 | DDC 331.4--dc23
LC record available at https://lccn.loc.gov/2016009882

ISBN: 978-1-4724-6271-8 (hbk)
ISBN: 978-0-367-88659-2 (pbk)

Typeset in Bembo
by FiSH Books Ltd.

Contents

Figures

Tables

Contributors

Jouharah M. Abalkhail is Assistant Professor of Business Administration and Management, and the Director of Research and Consulting, Department of Business Administration, Institution of Public Administration, Riyadh, Saudi Arabia. She received her PhD in 2012 from the University of Hull, UK. Her research has examined mentoring and networking among managerial and professional women in Saudi Arabia and the UK.

Zeynep Aycan is Professor of Psychology and Management at Koc University. Her PhD is from Queen's University, Canada and her postdoctoral work at McGill University. She has published in *Science*, *Journal of Applied Psychology*, and *Journal of International Business Studies*. Her book, *Organizations and Management in Cross-cultural Context* (Sage), received the CMI Book of the Year Award in Management in 2014.

María Jose Bosch is Director of the Work and Family Research Center and Assistant Professor in the Department of Organizational Behavior at ESE Business School in Chile. She holds a PhD and MSc from IESE, Universidad de Navarra, and a BS from Pontificia Universidad Catolica de Chile. Her areas of interest are work–life balance, women in leadership, leadership competencies, organizational behavior, and work motivations across different cultures.

Ronald J. Burke (PhD, University of Michigan) is Emeritus Professor of Organizational Studies at the Schulich School of Business, York University in Toronto. His research interests include work and health, the aging workforce, women in management, the sandwich generation, and creating healthier workplaces.

Carlos Cabral-Cardoso (PhD, University of Manchester, UK) is Professor of Management in the Faculty of Economics, University of Porto, Portugal. Currently, he is the Director of the Doctoral Program in Business and Management Studies. His main research interests involve issues of diversity ethics, careers, and workplace privacy.

Jan Cambopiano is Senior Vice President of Research and Chief Knowledge Officer at Catalyst. She holds a Bachelor's degree in American History and a Master's degree in Women's History from the State University of New York at Binghampton. She is responsible for overseeing the development of breakthrough research and insights that empower leaders and organizations to create inclusive workplaces.

Fang Lee Cooke (PhD, University of Manchester, UK) is Professor of Human Resource Management and Asia Studies at the Monash Business School, Monash University. Her research interests are in the areas of employment relations, gender studies, diversity management, strategic HRM, knowledge management and innovation, outsourcing, Chinese HRM, employment of Chinese migrants, and HRM in the care sector.

Cynthia Emrich is Vice President and Leader of the Catalyst Center for Career Pathways – a center that exposes the root causes of gender gaps in the classroom to the board room. She has written on the lack of senior women leaders in corporations and gender bias in performance appraisals. She earned both her PhD and Master's degrees in Industrial and Organizational Psychology from Rice University and her honors BA cum laude from the University of South Florida.

Marc Grau is a doctoral candidate in Social Policy at the University of Edinburgh. He holds an MBA from ESADE and an MA in Political and Social Sciences from University Pompeu Fabra. Marc serves as a collaborator at the International Center for Work and Family (IESE Business School) and as a researcher at Universitat International de Catalunya.

Neera Jain (PhD) is Associate Professor and Area Chair, Business Communication at the Management Development Institute, Gurgaon, India. Her areas of interest include leadership communication and women leaders in India, organizational communication, cross-cultural communication, and negotiation skills. She has published her research papers and cases in reputed international journals.

Kety Jauregui is Associate Professor of Human Resource Management and Corporate Social Responsibility, Department of Administration, and Director of the Masters Program in People, Organization and Management at the Graduate School of Business, University of ESAN, Lima, Peru.

Hayat Kabasakal is Professor at the Management Department of Boğaziçi University. Her PhD is from the University of Minnesota. Her research focuses on leadership, culture, employee attitudes, and gender. She has published in the *Journal of Strategic Management, Journal of Applied Psychology: An International Journal, Journal of World Business*, and *International Journal of Human Resource Management*.

Fahri Karakaş is Lecturer in Business and Leadership at Norwich Business School at the University of East Anglia (Norwich, UK). He received his PhD in 2010 in Organizational Behavior from McGill University. His thesis on benevolent leadership was selected as the winner of the 2010 Emerald/EFMD Outstanding Doctoral Research Award.

Rekha Karambayya (PhD, Northwestern University) is Associate Professor in Organization Studies at the Schulich School of Business, York University, Toronto, Canada. Her interests are in gender and race in the workplace, individual identity, power and conflict, and work and non-work issues. She wrote the Canadian chapters in the 2004 and 2011 volumes.

Ronit Kark is Senior Lecturer of Organizational Studies in the Department of Psychology, and the founder of the graduate program Gender in the Field at Bar-Ilan University in Israel. She is also an Affiliated Scholar of the Center for Gender in Organizations (CGO) at Simmons

College, Boston. Her research is focused on leadership and on gendered dynamics in organizations.

Mireia Las Heras is Professor at IESE Business School, University of Navarra, Spain, where she serves as Research Director of the International Center for Work and Family. She is an industrial engineer by training, holds an MBA from IESE Business School and a Doctorate in Business Administration from Boston University.

Jacqueline Laufer, a sociologist, is Emeritus Professor at HEC-Paris, France. Her research interests concern gender and organizations, equal opportunity between women and men, glass ceiling phenomena in organizations, and legal and sociological dimensions of diversity policies. For several years she has been Assistant Director of MAGE (Marche du travail et genre), an international and multidisciplinary research network dealing with the situation of women in the labor market and in society. She is a member of the Editorial Board of *Travail: Genre et Society*, and a member of the Steering Committee of GID (Genre, Inegalities, Discrimination) project in the Île de France region.

Ceyda Maden is Assistant Professor of Management in Istanbul Kemerburgaz University, Department of International Trade, Turkey. Her research interests focus on person–environment fit, work engagement, and employee proactivity. She has published in different academic outlets such as the *International Journal of Human Resource Management*, the *Services Industry Journal*, and *Personnel Review*.

Babita Mathur-Helm is Senior Lecturer in Organizational Transformation and Development, Diversity Management, Leadership and Gender Studies at University of Stellenbosch Business School (USB) in Cape Town, South Africa. She is also Research Head for USB's Small Business Academy. Her research interests are in the areas of management of multicultural and gender diversity, leadership, social entrepreneurship, and women in management and leadership. She had published several book chapters and journal articles.

Shoma Mukherji (PhD) teaches business communication, international HRM, cross-cultural management and intercultural communication. She has over 30 years' corporate experience in HR, general management, and transactional logistics. She is Associate Professor at Delhi School of Business and Visiting Faculty at Shiv Nadar University and Management Development Institute, Gurgaon, India.

Julie Nugent, Vice President and Center Leader, Catalyst Research Center for Corporate Practice, examines organizational diversity efforts, change models, career experiences, and perceptions of women and men professionals across various levels and industries. She holds her MA in Industrial/Organizational Psychology from New York University and received her BA in Psychology and English from Ohio University,.

Nancy Papalexandris is Professor of Human Resource Management and Academic Coordinator of the MSc Program in Human Resource Management of the Athens University of Economics and Business. She has served as Vice-Rector for Academic Affairs and Personnel of her university. She is President of the Greek Association of Women University Professors.

Jeanine Prime is Senior Vice President and co-lead of Catalyst's research programs. Her expertise includes gender in organizations, stereotyping, implicit bias, change management, and leadership effectiveness. She received her PhD in Social Psychology from Cornell University, an MBA from the State University of New York at Binghampton, and a BA in Psychology from Spelman College.

Astrid M. Richardsen is Professor of Organization Psychology at BI Norwegian Business School. Her main research interest is occupational health, specifically relationships between individuals and work characteristics, job stress, engagement, and work outcomes. She has also published work on women in management. A recent focus of her research is work motivation and motivational climate at work.

Anna Roberts is currently a PhD student in Organization Studies, Schulich School of Business, York University, Toronto. Previously she led the West Coast Regulatory Practice Area at Gerson Lehrman Group. She graduated magna cum laude from Rice University and was the sole recipient of the Muhammad Yunus Commencement Award for Humanitarian Leadership.

Serena G. Sohrab (PhD, York University) is Assistant Professor of Organizational Behavior at the University of Ontario Institute of Technology, Oshawa, Ontario, Canada. Her research focuses on gender and diversity, as well as the study of team effectiveness. Serena's research has been presented and published in various international outlets, including the Canada chapter in the Davidson and Burke 2011 collection.

Phyllis Tharenou is Executive Dean of the Faculty of Social and Behavioral Sciences at Flinders University, following other senior management roles in academia and government. Her research interests are careers, including women's managerial advancement, with publications in that area in the *Academy of Management Journal, Journal of Organizational Behavior*, and *Organizational Behavior and Decision Processes*.

Kea G. Tijdens is Research Coordination at the University of Amsterdam and Professor of Women's Work at the Erasmus University, Rotterdam. She studied Sociology and Psychology at Groningen University and obtained her PhD in Sociology in 1989. Her main research interests focus on women's labor market re-entry and part-time work, wage setting, occupational segregation, measurement of occupations, and web-survey methodologies.

Laura E. Mercer Traavik is Associate Professor at BI Norwegian Business School, Oslo, Norway. Her research and teaching interests include diversity, inclusion, and negotiations. She received her PhD and Master's degrees from the Norwegian School of Economics and Business Administration, Bergen, Norway and a Bachelor's degree in Psychology from the University of British Columbia, Vancouver, Canada.

Ronit Waismel-Manor holds a PhD in Organizational Behavior from the School of Industrial and Labor Relations at Cornell University. She is Lecturer at the School of Behavioral Sciences at the Netanya Academic College, Israel. Waismel-Manor's work focuses on the intersection of gender inequality and organizations.

Fiona M. Wilson is currently Professor of Organizational Behavior in the Business School, University of Glasgow, Scotland. She has published about 45 articles in journals such as *Sociology, Work, Employment and Society*, and *Organization and Human Relations*. Her current interests are focused mainly on gender and disadvantage at work.

Gina Zabludovsky is a tenured Professor Researcher and member of the Board of Governors at the Universidad Nacional Autonoma de Mexico (UNAM). Her main research areas are sociological theory, intellectual history, and woman managers and business owners in Mexico. She has written several books and articles on the latter. She is also part of the Expert Group on Women in Management coordinated by international organizations such as the United Nations, APEC, OCDE, and Catalyst.

Acknowledgements

I first want to acknowledge my colleague Marilyn Davidson for thinking of and helping to develop this series over ten years ago. Astrid Richardsen did a terrific job linking with our authors and Gower. I have worked with her for about 25 years and have managed to involve her in more things than she might like. Here in Toronto, Carla D'Agostino managed to keep me on track – no small feat. I thank our international contributors for their work, some of them for the third time. I truly believe there are signs of progress, but still wide country differences.

Ronald J. Burke
Toronto

1 Women in management worldwide

Progressing slowly[1]

Ronald J. Burke

This volume, *Women in Management Worldwide: Signs of Progress* (2016), is the third edition in our Women in Management Worldwide series. Marilyn Davidson and I concluded in 2003 that it would be useful to take stock of the status of women in the workforce, in management and professional jobs, country legislation supporting women's advancement, and company initiatives supporting the development of qualified women. We thought it made sense to examine this in a sample of countries, both developed and developing. We asked authors from 21 countries to indicate the status of women in their workforces, in the professions, and in management, by considering common areas such as women in education, women in entrepreneurship, and country legislation related to women and work. We hoped this would provide benchmark data to permit analyses of changes over time and allow comparisons across countries. These data might also shed light on ways country cultural values shape women's work experiences and career progress.

We invited contributors from countries in all major regions of the world. Some of our initial contributors declined our invitation to take part as their countries did not systematically collect information of the kind we desired. Contributors from 20 countries did take part, resulting in the first edition.

Women in Management Worldwide: Facts, Figures, and Analysis (2004)

Countries were allocated to seven regions as follows: European Union countries: Greece, Belgium, Ireland, the Netherlands, Portugal, and the United Kingdom (UK); other European countries: Norway, Poland and Russia; North and Central America: Canada, Mexico, and the United States; Australasia: New Zealand and Australia; Asia: China, Malaysia, Turkey and Israel; South America: Argentina; and Africa: South Africa.

Although this is getting ahead of our journey, there are likely several countries, as this is being written in late 2015, where the collection of such data is either given a very low priority or is non-existent. Ongoing wars, sectarian conflicts, and terrorist activities make women in the workforce and in management concerns of low priority or may even contribute to women's plight (e.g. Afghanistan, Yemen, Nigeria, Palestine, and Somalia).

Our objectives for this volume were:

- to understand more about the status of women at work and women in the professions and management in a number of countries throughout the world;
- to begin a process for collecting common information in a variety of countries to capture both trends over time and support comparisons across countries;

- to collect baseline information to provide background data, indicating the current status of women in management;
- to facilitate more cross-cultural research in this area;
- to encourage the exchange of research findings as well as company "best practice" efforts;
- to shed some light on the roles of country culture on women's career advancement and international career assignments;
- to encourage more research in these areas, and more collaborative research across countries. Sadly research on gender issues in organizations is still seen as a marginal research activity by most academics;
- to raise issues of utilizing the best talent available for organizational success.

Although the availability of relevant information varied from country to country, authors noted barriers experienced by women in management, supportive country legislation, and suggestions for reducing these obstacles. More women were getting education, more women were in the workforce, there were increases in the numbers of women in management, more women were becoming entrepreneurs, and more countries had enacted legislation (e.g. pay and gender equality, maternity and paternity leaves). But improvements were small.

Women in Management Worldwide: Progress and Prospects (2011)

Six years later Marilyn and I decided, in 2009, to update the 2004 volume, asking some of the original contributors to update their earlier chapters to identify possible/anticipated changes that took place in the intervening six or seven years. We also invited contributors from three new countries, replacing four countries from the 2004 volume. Our objectives for the second edition were similar to those mentioned above. Sixteen countries appeared in both editions, eight countries appeared once, four in each of the two editions. Chapters reported on labor force characteristics, women pursuing education, women in management, women entrepreneurs, country legislation, organizational initiatives, and their thoughts on the future.

Nineteen countries were allocated to the same seven regions as follows: European Union countries: France, Greece, the Netherlands, Portugal, Spain, and the UK; other European countries: Norway and Russia; North and Central America: Canada, Mexico and the USA; Australasia: Australia and New Zealand; Asia: China, Israel, Lebanon, and Turkey; South America: Argentina; and Africa: South Africa. Again, modest gains were present in most countries in some of these areas. It should be noted that countries were selected because there were individuals in these countries researching and writing about women in management and these countries were most likely to be making efforts to support professional and managerial women. As in the first edition, there was considerable variation among countries in these indicators. But there were positive features in the 20 countries, along with some worrisome aspects. The rate of progress and change was again slow; women continued to face bias and barriers, with some indictors remaining essentially unchanged. Achieving gender balance and gender equality is very difficult. If gender balance and gender equality were easy, they would have happened already.

Women in Management Worldwide: Signs of Progress (2016)

Building on the success of these two volumes, Gower, our publisher wondered if we would produce a third edition. Both Marilyn and I had retired, becoming Emeritus Professors. Lyn decided not to take part as she was having lots of fun doing other things (not that working together wasn't fun – just less fun). I agreed to consider this offer. When my friend and colleague, Astrid Richardsen, agreed to collaborate and co-edit this collection, we decided to move forward.

Our objectives for this updated collection were generally similar to those that guided our first volume (see above). In addition we invited some of our original contributors as well as adding some new countries and authors. This edition includes 20 countries, with a new region, the Middle East, added to accommodate our country chapters. Countries came from all regions of the world and included both developed and developing nations. Five new countries were added for the first time: Chile, Peru, Saudi Arabia, Iran, and India. Most of these first-time countries have received little previous research attention in these areas. Thirteen countries have appeared in each of the three volumes, seven countries appeared once, three in the first edition, four in the second, and five in the third. As in our earlier collections, we asked contributors to address some areas in common (e.g. women in education, women in the workforce, country legislation, etc.).

Several of our objectives for this series were being realized, though we do not claim credit for this. Research on women in management is increasing in general, including in many regions and countries that have historically been relatively ignored. Several other research and consulting organizations (McKinsey, Catalyst, Dell, Twenty First, International Labour Organization) have collected data in several countries simultaneously for comparison purposes. More research has included measures of cultural norms and values to help position and explain findings.

Why advancing women matters

Schwartz (1992) suggests that supporting the advancement of qualified women means that organizations have the best people in leadership roles, giving senior-level men the experience of working with capable senior-level women. It also indicates to women employees, clients, and customers that women can succeed, serve as role models for junior-level women, and given the "war for talent" supporting the advancement of qualified women offers a competitive advantage. Most importantly, women can utilize their talents and develop their full potential. Shriver (2009) notes that the increasing numbers of women in the workforce will change women, men, families, organizations, and societies. Women have now become an important economic force (Silverstein and Sayre, 2009a, 2009b).

Tarr-Whelan (2009) identifies several benefits to organizations from having more women in senior-level jobs: better performance, more risk aversion, less destructive competition, contributions to individuals and societal health in terms of better integration of work and family and a higher quality of life for both men and women, higher levels of individual and corporate responsibility, and better management practices such as teamwork and participative decision making more in touch with twenty-first-century values. There is strength in the differences women and men bring with them (Annis and Gray, 2013).

Women are entering the workforce in increasing numbers in almost every country. The rate of women's advancement into higher levels of management continues to be slow, with some writers concluding that improvements have stopped. Women continued to gain the necessary education and experience but fell short in their advancement. Women were still paid less than men, still faced bias and discrimination, and shouldered more responsibility for home and family functioning than did men.

*Advancing women – not only the right and the smart thing for
organizations and societies to undertake*

Gonzales *et al.* (2015), in a Staff Discussion Note prepared by the International Monetary Fund (IMF), examined the role of gender-based legal restrictions on female labor force participation rates. Obstacles such as restrictions on women's rights to inheritance and property, and impediments to opening a bank account, or choosing professions reduce women's labor force participation rates. Wright (2015), reviewing the recent 2015 IMF report, notes that countries that make it difficult for women to enter the workforce incur lost productivity and poorer economic performance. Countries that close this gender gap can increase gross domestic product (GDP) by 15 to 35 percent. The IMF study found that almost 90 percent of countries had at least one legal restriction with 28 countries having ten or more legal restrictions (e.g. limits on women's property rights, laws prohibiting women from pursuing particular occupations, laws allowing husbands to prevent their wives from working) (Wright, 2015). Productivity losses ranged from 15 percent in Greece, Italy, and Japan to 35 percent in Iran, Qatar, and the United Arab Emirates (Wright, 2015).

The Organization for Economic Co-operation and Development (2014) observed that G20 countries would experience economic growth and increased citizen welfare by increasing labor force participation of females. While these gender differences are slowing shrinking, barriers to women's participation rates still remain.

Two studies undertaken by international consulting firms showed that having more women in the workforce and more women on corporate boards of directors have large economic benefits. McKinsey (2015a) reported that if every country matched the progress toward gender equality of its nearest neighbor, the power of parity, it would add US$12 trillion to global GDP by 2025. A study of the financial performance of organizations in the US, UK, and India undertaken by Grant Thornton (2015) reported that boards having female directors outpace the male-only boards by $655 billion.

Increasing the participation rates of women in the workforce is important to address a shrinking workforce due to both an aging population and lower fertility rates, as well as the need to utilize the best talent available. In addition to increasing women's labor force participation rates, however, efforts must also be made to reduce/eliminate barriers to women's development and advancement. Among G20 countries, the gender gap in labor force participation rates ranges from 7 percent in Canada to over 50 percent in India and Saudi Arabia, with a gap of greater than 10 percent in 15 of the G20 countries.

Barriers women face

Catalyst (1998) identified the following important barriers to women's career advancement, all of which are still alive and well in 2016:

- Negative assumptions in executive ranks about women, their abilities, and their career commitment.
- Perceptions that women don't fit with the organizational culture.
- Lack of career planning and the variety of job experiences needed to meet the future staffing needs of the organization.
- Lack of important opportunities for women who have management potential.
- Belief that women won't relocate for career advancement.
- Failure to make managers accountable for the advancement of women.

- No or limited succession planning.
- Reluctance to give women important line experiences (in bottom-line jobs).
- Lack of mentoring and exclusion from informal career networks.
- Different criteria for women and men in appraisal and pay systems.
- Discrimination and sexual harassment.
- A culture that values long hours over tangible performance, has limited work–family support, and little interest in diversity.

Catalyst (2002, 2007), in surveys of the US and 20 European countries, found that gender stereotypes and assumptions about women's roles emerged as the top barriers. In a later survey of 110 US companies, gender biases and stereotypes again emerged as the number one barrier, particularly in succession planning processes. Only a small minority of managerial and professional women see their organizations as meritocracies. While 75 percent of companies say that gender diversity is a priority of the chief executive officer (CEO), few women and men (about one third) say advancing women's equality was high on their CEO's list of priorities.

Wells (2015), accessing the world's largest data base on male and female salaries at work, found that male supervisors/managers had a 23 per cent larger salary while higher level male executives had a 33 percent higher salary than their female counterparts.

Think manager, think male

Schein introduced the notion of "think manager, think male" in the early 1970s, and research has since then been carried out in several countries. Her early work (1973, 1975) indicated that women were seen by both male and female managers as unlikely to have the characteristics associated with successful managers. More recent data (Schein, 2007) have shown that males still hold these views but women in many countries no longer hold them. It is important to continue addressing the "think manager, think male" belief however through legal pressures, addressing the long work hours culture, the masculine nature of organizational culture, and investing in the training and development of qualified women.

Women and the economic crisis

Karamessini and Rubery (2014) consider the consequences of the recent 2008 worldwide economic recession for women and men, observing that while there were again wide country differences, women tended to be more adversely affected than men. They also believe these effects will slow down progress towards gender equality. The chapters by Nancy Papalexandris on Greece and Mireia Las Heras and Marc Grau and on Spain in this volume bear this out.

Women's experiences in countries in economic and political transition

Metcalfe and Afanassieva (2005a) organized a special issue for the Women in Management Review on the effects of the economic and political transitions taking place in Russia and countries in the former Soviet Union on managerial and professional women. Research and writing showed that the transition from a command to a market economy was having negative effects on the work experiences and careers of women in Russia (Metcalfe and Afanassieva, 2005b; Posadskaya, 1994; Zavyalova and Kosheleva, 2010) and possible beneficial effects for women in both Estonia and Belarus (Alas and Rees, 2005; Rees and Mezhevich, 2005).

National cultural values and women's work experiences

Hofstede (1980) identified four cultural values in his pioneering work, one of which was masculinity-femininity (MF). Countries higher on masculinity have higher values for work centrality and a smaller percentage of women in professional and technical jobs. House *et al.* (2004) divide Hofstede's MF measure into two, assertiveness and gender egalitarianism, and measure both of these at organizational and societal levels, as well as these at current levels and how respondents believed they should be. Data were collected in 62 countries from almost 17,000 female and male middle managers. They found that countries scoring higher on gender egalitarianism had a higher percentage of women in the workforce, more women in higher education, higher levels of psychological health, higher levels of gross national product (GNP) per capita, greater women's purchasing power, and more women in government. Countries scoring low on gender egalitarianism believed that their countries should have more of it.

Management itself is a masculine concept developed in masculine countries (e.g. UK, USA). Hofstede and Hofstede (2005) note some differences related to MF are likely to influence women's work and non-work experiences:

- Feminine societies: job choice based on intrinsic interest, men and women study the same subjects, conflicts dealt with by compromise and negotiation, rewards equality, work to work less, work to live, more leisure time over money, careers are optimal for both women and men, and more women are in high-level management jobs.
- Masculine societies: job choice based on career opportunities, men and women study different subjects, conflict dealt with by fighting, stress results and reward equity, want to work more, live to work, more money over leisure, career compulsory for men, optional for women, and few women in top-level management jobs.

The role of culture and religion

An innovative meeting held in Seoul in 2011 by the Asia Chapter of the Academy of Human Resource Development asked researchers from eight countries to discuss prospects for women in management in their countries (Cho *et al.*, 2015). The countries were China, India, Japan, Korea, Malaysia, Sri Lanka, and Thailand. All these countries ranked below 60 in the World Economic Forum (WEF) (2014) *Gender Gap Report.* In all eight countries social values and religious beliefs (Confucianism, Buddhism) limited women in management. Social values included patriarchy, stereotyped gender roles, male dominance, gender-divided family structures, men preferring to hire men, and gendered division of labor with women undertaking domestic responsibilities. Culture and religion shaped values, perceptions, models for male and female leadership behaviors, and the role of work and family. Some of these countries also have low rates of female labor force participation and low numbers of women in higher education.

Glavin (2015) writes that the emancipation of women around the world remains "the most important freedom struggle in human history." The emancipation of women, he argues is the most promising solution for the world's major problems such as poverty, illiteracy, decent work, public health, economic vitality and growth, and inter-state conflicts. Countries need to do away with forced labor slavery and human trafficking, eradicate child, early forced marriages, and female genital mutilation.

Modernization theory

Inglehart and Welzel (2005) describe the effects of societal modernization on its effects on the economic, political, and social capabilities of countries. Modernization, in their theory, changes two dimensions: the traditional versus secular, and the rational and survival versus self-expression values. A study of the influence of modernization theory on work-related attitudes and values in 88 countries and territories at various stages of human development (Yeganeh, 2015) found that in first-phase countries (lower levels of modernization), more discrimination against women existed than in countries in the second phase of development (higher modernization). Countries high on modernization included Norway, Sweden, the Netherlands, Finland, and Switzerland, among others; countries low on modernization included Turkey, Bangladesh, Mexico, Russia, and Zimbabwe, among others.

Differences across countries and cultures

It is clear that some countries and cultures do better than others in advancing women's careers (Burke, 2009). It has been suggested that a country's culture, wealth, values, and practices influence women's advancement to leadership positions. Toh and Leonardelli (2013, 2012) propose instead that a culture's tightness (or looseness) is a significant factor in this regard. Cultural tightness refers to the strength of its norms and values. Cultural tightness produces resistance to changing cultural values and practices, thus reducing women's advancement to leadership roles. Toh and Leonardelli (2012, 2013) identified two leadership-influencing practices. First, individuals emerge as leaders by fitting the factors that inform what leaders act and look like. When women are seen as "leaderlike" more women will advance to leadership roles. Second, women may be less likely to seek leadership roles feeling that men are more "leaderlike" than women are. Using national-level data from 32 countries, they found that egalitarian practices were associated with a higher percentage of women leaders when cultural tightness was high and there was a significant negative relationship between cultural tightness and women in leadership positions when gender egalitarian practices were low. Tight cultures can influence the numbers of women leaders if their values support this (e.g. greater gender egalitarianism).

Hori and Kamo (2014), using a 2002 data base involving 33 countries and 15,199 respondents, examined the relationship of country-level indicators of gender equality and gender norms with individual-level indicators of work and family well-being separately for women (wives) and men (husbands). Women scored significantly lower than men on psychological well-being in about half the countries, with these differences typically appearing in more conservative European, Asian, and developing countries. In addition, traditional female roles had a more negative impact on women in more egalitarian countries. Finally, women and men with egalitarian attitudes in traditional countries reported lower psychological well-being, while women and men with egalitarian attitudes in egalitarian countries indicated higher levels of psychological well-being. The same negative and positive effects were noted among women and men having traditional attitudes in egalitarian and traditional countries (misfit and fit).

Similarities across countries and cultures

Although country cultural values are likely to influence women's prospects in their workplaces, there may well be similarities across cultures as well, given common needs of both women and men across cultures (e.g. for respect, fairness, dignity). Burke (2009) found that particular work experiences (e.g. mentoring, training, and development acceptance) were associated with favorable work outcomes in a number of countries; in addition, managerial and professional women in several countries defined themselves as having a career-family priority as opposed to a career primary priority; and though men differed from women on several personal and work situation characteristics (e.g. salary, organizational level) women and men in several countries reported similar levels of work satisfaction and engagement.

There are also wide differences. North American organizations undertake more initiatives to advance qualified women; the imposition of quotas is a non-starter here while Scandinavian countries rely on quotas more than other regions to advance qualified women.

Sex or culture – which has the strongest effect?

Cordano *et al.* (2002), collecting data from men and women in two countries with different cultures (Chile and US), found that sex had a significantly stronger effect than cultural values on attitudes towards women as managers. In addition, the likelihood of women experiencing negative attitudes towards them as managers was increased or decreased as a function of country culture. They suggest that women should be aware of potential problems with men in some cultures, and that human resource (HR) managers need to address these issues facing women.

Women in various sectors – a status report

Women in politics worldwide

Thames and Williams (2013) examined increases in women's political participation in 159 democratic countries from 1945 to 2006. They reported increases as well as considerable country variation. Thus in 2006, women comprised 47 percent of Sweden's legislation but only 5 percent in Sri Lanka. Countries having more women were better off economically, women had the right to vote for a longer period of time, and there were more women in the labor force. The percentage of women in legislatures was also associated with having more female party executives.

Women entrepreneurs

There is considerable evidence that women are increasingly engaging in entrepreneurship worldwide (Brush *et al.*, 2014). But there is considerable variability in support for female entrepreneurship activities across countries. Terjesen and Lloyd (2015) report the results of a seven-country study of female entrepreneurship undertaken by the Global Entrepreneurship and Development Institute. The top ten countries for female entrepreneurship were (from the top downward) the US, Australia, UK, Denmark, Netherlands, France, Iceland, Sweden, Finland, and Norway. Unfortunately 44 of the 77 nations ranked low and need to reduce barriers female entrepreneurs face. The bottom ten countries were Pakistan, Malawi, Bangladesh, Uganda, Iran, Ethiopia, Guatemala, India, Ghana, Angola, and Algeria (from lowest upwards). Country per capita GDP was a strong but less than perfect predictor of levels of support for female entrepreneurship. Some regions ranked relatively low: Sub-Saharan Africa, Southeast Asia, South Asia, and parts of the Middle East and South America. Not surprisingly, level of women's education was positively related to levels of female entrepreneurship. Women entrepreneurs continue to face structural constraints that limit growth of their enterprises. In addition, women in family businesses (daughters) continue to be less likely to succeed the founder than are men (sons) (Blackburn *et al.*, 2015).

Women in STEM careers

Increasing the numbers of women in science, technology, engineering, and mathematics (STEM) is important in improving organizational and country productivity and innovation and providing a competitive advantage (Bilimoria *et al.*, 2014). Several developed countries have made efforts to increase the numbers of women in STEM careers. National governments, industries, organizations, and academic institutions have undertaken initiatives here As is the case in other areas of women's advancement, progress has been slow.

Bilimoria and Lord (2014) review obstacles facing women in STEM careers (a glass obstacle course; a leaky pipeline), women's experiences in STEM careers, organizational efforts to advance women in STEM careers, and changing the discussion about women in STEM careers (e.g. engineering is gendered). To attract young girls to science, the University of Toronto has invited girls and boys in grades 3 and 4 (nine and ten year olds) to spend a few hours on weekends learning about science. York University, also in Toronto, offers classes for girls in which they teach science using superhero characters; the University of Waterloo has a program for girls as young as six (Casey, 2015).

The experiences of women in international management

Career advancement in large multinational organizations sometimes requires working in another country for a period of time. It has been suggested that the low number of women expatriates reflects more women than men having difficulty in relocating, company reluctance to send women abroad, and discrimination faced by women in their host countries (Caligiuri and Cascio, 1998; Caligiuri and Tung, 1998; Tung, 2004; Vance *et al.*, 1999). Adler (1984) found that women want expatriate experiences, companies want to send women to other countries, and that host countries' prejudice against women was a relatively small factor in their experiences and job performance. In a study of India and the US as host countries, Varma *et al.* (2006) found that female expatriates from the US were not only less discriminated against but in fact were preferred to male expatriates in the Indian host country.

To be successful in international assignments both women and men have to tailor their leadership to fit local norms. Unfortunately in many countries (e.g. China, India, Russia) women and men have to meet different standards. Men must be assertive; women must be reserved yet authoritative. Organizations need to develop cross-cultural training programs that equip both women and men with this information.

Women on corporate boards of directors

Thomson Reuters (2014), using data from over 4000 global public companies worldwide, reported more than half of these companies had 10 percent or more women on their boards, noting this as slow but steady progress. This figure becomes significantly lower when small and medium-sized businesses are included. Governments have attempted to support women's appointments to corporate boards of directors and to executive ranks by requiring organizations to "comply or explain." Compliance requires the submission of a formal plan to advance women with the setting of performance targets or goals. A majority of Canadian organizations have then adopted a "comply or explain" policy regarding their efforts to advance women. Firms had to indicate the numbers of women on their boards of directors, in executive ranks, and their plans for advancing more women (Flavelle, 2015a). If they did not provide this information they had to explain why in public filings. Only 14 percent of these organizations indicated a formal plan for promoting women to their boards, and only 7 percent had specific targets. Those having no plans said they believed targets were inefficient or arbitrary and they preferred to promote on merit. So much for "comply or explain."

Does having more women on corporate boards of directors improve board performance and contribute to higher levels of firm performance? The evidence on these questions has produced mixed results. Post and Byron (2015) undertook a meta-analysis of 146 studies of these questions. First, they found that the relationship between female board representation and market performance was near zero; but the relationship was positive in countries with greater gender parity and negative in countries with low gender parity. Female board representation was positively related to performance of two important board responsibilities: monitoring and strategy involvement.

Women faculty at American business schools

American business schools are also making slow progress in their number of women faculty. The American Association of Collegiate Schools of Business (AACSB) reported in March 2015 that females comprised 31.2 percent of faculty and males 68.8 percent, with a higher percentage of women at instructor than professor levels (39.7 percent versus 20.1 percent). There were also wide variations in the percentages of women in various disciplines (e.g. 63.2 percent in business communication, 44 percent in human resources management, 17 percent in real estate, and 18 percent in logistics). The percentage of women faculty increased from 29 percent in 2010–2011 to 31 percent in 2014–2015. While their numbers are still very small, the number of female deans of AACSB schools has also slightly increased. New female doctorate hirings were slightly higher in female-led than male-led business schools (39 percent versus 33 percent, respectively).

Contributions of international consulting firms – some international statistics

Over the past decade, an increasing number of international management consulting firms have undertaken research on women and professionals in management. Their work has increased our understanding of international country comparisons, bringing resources to this work that exceeds those of individual researchers. Increasing interest in the experiences of women managers and professionals has resulted in more research on women's representation on corporate boards of directors and in senior management in several regions of the world. Some of their findings are presented in Tables 1.1 and 1.2.

McKinsey (2011a) notes that Asia has a lower percentage of women on boards and women on executive committees than European countries; 18 percent versus 6 percent, and 10 percent versus 8 percent respectively. Asian executives do not see gender, specifically the development of more women, as a strategic priority (70 percent do not).

Increasing academic and trade publishing efforts

There continues to be both recent academic books (Hutchings and Michailova, 2014; Kumra *et al.*, 2014; Vinnicombe *et al.*, 2013), books indicating how organizations might go about

Table 1.1 Percentage of women on executive committees and percentage change by country

Country	Percentage (% change)
Sweden	21 (8)
Norway	15 (3)
UK	11 (9)
Belgium	11 (4)
Netherlands	8 (3)
France	8 (4)
Czech Republic	9 (0)
Italy	6 (1)
Germany	3 (2)
European Union	10 (6)

Source: McKinsey (2012) based on 2011 data

Table 1.2 Percentage of women on boards and percentage of women on executive committees by country

Country	Percentage of women on boards	Percentage of women on executive committees
Australia	13	13
Hong Kong	9	11
China	8	9
Taiwan	8	9
Singapore	7	15
Malaysia	6	5
Indonesia	6	5
India	5	3
South Korea	1	2
Japan	2	1

Source: McKinsey (2011a)

achieving a gender balanced workforce (Wittenberg-Cox, 2010; Wittenberg-Cox and Maitland, 2008) as well as more popular trade books (Sandberg, 2013; Slaughter, 2012, 2015) targeted at professional and managerial women. These efforts have continued to place advancing women on the front burner, hopefully leading to a tipping point in spurring organizational action. There is also more women in management research being undertaken in more countries (see Burke, 2009, for a sample of these works).

In addition more men, particularly younger men, are voicing their dissatisfaction with the "rat race," joining some of their women peers (see the Amazon stories of the last month). These women and men want a better balance in their lives, becoming allies of their female colleagues.

Signs of progress – some good news

Signs of progress include:

- More business school efforts are being made to recruit female students, there are more clubs, and more support. But "gender courses" are in low demand; course content does not include adequate female representation. Business schools still are not women friendly.

- Three women received the Nobel Peace Prize in 2011: Tawokkul Karman, Leymah Ghowee, and Ellen Johnson Sirleaf. Malalal Yousafzai, a young Afghan girl, received the Nobel Peace Prize in 2014. Twelve other women have been awarded this prize since 1901.
- More women have been elected to the US Congress and Senate than ever before.
- Mary Barra became CEO of GM, now having to deal with the "mess" left to her by previous male CEOs.
- The European Union launched the "Science is a girl thing" campaign.
- Women in Saudi Arabia were given the right to vote in 2015 and to run for office in municipal elections.
- The Foote Foundation in the US – a group of companies and business schools – holds one-day events for women offering information, advice, networks, and access to 36 MBA schools in Canada, Europe, and the US.
- Gender Summits have been held in various parts of the world.
- Business schools line up MBA alumni with non-profit or service board of directors appointments so they might build experience and expertise for corporate board appointments.
- The Rotman School of Management in Toronto started the Judy project, specifically designed for high potential women (250 have gone through the program). It is a week-long tough and entertaining educational effort. A graduating group leaves connected to all other participants, potential sources of advice, and mentoring.
- The *Financial Post* publishes an annual list of Canada's most powerful top 100 women including women from the public, private, and nonprofit sectors. These women achieve both a profile and signs of acknowledged competence.
- Female candidates are running for US president in 2016 (Hilary Clinton for the Democrats and Carli Fiorina for the Republicans).
- In the first ever election in Saudi Arabia held on December 12, 2015 in which women ran for local offices with about 2100 seats up for election, 20 women won seats (1 percent of the total seats) with almost 1000 women up for election. It was also the first time women were allowed to vote.
- The *Financial Post* (2015) in Canada published material developed by the Canadian Board Diversity Council with pictures and names of 50 potential board candidates (42 women) to help organizations identify qualified women directors.
- Kolinda Kitardvic was elected the first female president of Croatia.
- The Church of England appointed its first female bishop, Rev. Libby Lane, in 2014. Besides appointing female bishops for the first time, the Church of England plans to rewrite the official liturgies to refer to God as female. God may be female.
- Admiral Michelle Howard became the first woman in the US to be made a four-star admiral in 2014.
- British Prime Minister David Cameron included more women in his cabinet to change a composition the media termed "male, pale and stale." Eight women, not all ministers, became part of his 33-member cabinet.
- Japanese Prime Minister Abe made good on his promise of moving more women into positions of power, and appointed 5 women to his 18-member cabinet in 2014.
- The newly elected prime minister of Canada, Justin Trudeau, made good on his 2015 promise to have gender parity in his cabinet, appointing 15 women and 15 men. A national survey a week after his cabinet was announced indicated that 74 percent of Canadians were pleased with the gender-balanced cabinet.
- Five of the premiers of Canada's ten provinces were women in 2015.

- Sally Blount, became Dean of the Kellogg School of Management, a top-rated US school of management.
- More women are in professional schools (law, business, engineering).
- The are more courses being offered to increase women holding corporate director appointments. In Canada, about 35 percent of the graduates are women, but it is still too early to know if these courses will make any difference.
- The National Science Foundation in the US started the ADVANCE Institutional Transformation Program to provide financial support to academic institutions to increase the participation and advancement of women in academic STEM careers.

But are we really making enough progress?

Carter and Silva (2010a), respectively vice president of Research and director of Research at Catalyst, one of the world's largest research and advisory groups on women's advancement, write that we have made very little progress towards women's advancement. Based on data from more than 4000 MBA graduates from elite business schools who graduated between 1996 and 2007, they reported the following: women start their careers at lower levels than men, women advance slower and earn less pay than men throughout their careers, men who left business careers to pursue nontraditional careers fared better on their return to traditional business careers than did women, men changed jobs more than women did for career growth, and while women changed jobs more than men because of "bad" bosses, men at all managerial levels were more satisfied with their careers than women, and earned more income; women earned $4600 less than men in their first jobs, with this gap increasing over time.

Using these same data, Carter and Silva (2010b) conclude that women and men were equally likely to get mentoring, mentoring provided greater benefits to men than to women, men had mentors at higher organizational levels than did women, men were more likely to have informal mentors while women more likely had formal mentors as part of a mentor program, and men were more likely than women to have mentors serving as sponsors.

In comparing statistics for a few countries in our 2004 volume with those in our 2011 volume (e.g. Canada, US, Norway) we noted small gains in women in the workplace, women in management, women in executive positions, and women serving on corporate boards of directors: typically gains of 5 percent or less – again a sign of slow progress.

Authors of at least five of the eight countries represented in the Cho *et al.* (2015) collection noted some progress in women's advancement (India, Japan, Malaysia, Taiwan, Thailand); three country authors did not address this directly in their writings. However slow progress was noted across all eight countries when similarities across them were considered.

The International Labour Office (2004) noted that women's labor force participation has increased but there were wide country differences: 83 women for every 100 men in East Asia, and 40 women for every 100 men in the Middle East. Female unemployment rates were higher than men's, women were more likely than men to work part-time, and women earned less pay.

The World Economic Forum's (2014) *Gender Gap Report* notes improvements in gender equality in four areas (health, education, economy, political participation) in a study of 142 countries. The top five countries were Iceland, Finland, Norway, Sweden, and Denmark; the bottom five countries were Yemen, Pakistan, Chad, Syria, and Mali. The gender pay gap has decreased by 3 percent over the past decade, stalling after the 2008 world economic downturn. Unfortunately it will take several decades at this pace for this gap to close completely (Flavelle, 2015b).

Wirth (2001, with a 2004 update), using data from 48 countries, reported that women increased their share of legislative, senior official, and managerial jobs between 1 and 5 percent in 26 countries between 1990 and 2001–2002. Some countries showed large increases (Costa Rica, 24 percent) while others showed decreases (Ireland, 6 percent, Canada, 4 percent). The International Labour Organization (2015), using data from almost 1300 private sector firms from 39 countries, noted increasing numbers of women moving into managerial and professional jobs, but women were often concentrated in specific management functions (e.g. human resources, marketing), with few at the CEO level.

May (2015) reports results of a study by Marika Morris and Pauline Rankin of female leadership in the Canadian public service which showed that women held more that 55 percent of all jobs and 45 percent of executive titles below deputy minister. In 1990 women held only 14 percent of these executive positions. Ironically, these women now have less power and responsibility to initiate change because of increased economic constraints, job cuts, rigid rules and structures, and less risk taking. Women's management styles were also at odds with rigid hierarchies, traditional forms of accountability, and a culture of fear.

There are several reasons why progress has been slow. It is difficult and time consuming to change organizational cultures; but there are signs that more organizations are embarking on such changes. It is difficult and time consuming to change societal and cultural values; some societies resisting any change. There have also been macro-economic and political events that have hampered change. These include the worldwide economic recession beginning in 2008, continuing economic difficulties in some countries (e.g. Greece, Spain) associated with high rates of youth unemployment reaching 25 percent, international tensions (e.g. Russia and the Ukraine, Israel-Palestine in the West Bank, ISIS in the Middle East, the failure of the Arab Spring in Egypt). On the positive side, supportive changes have occurred among younger women and men: women are increasingly being educated and gaining necessary work experience, more young men want a balanced life and are supportive of initiatives that benefit both women and men, and families are having fewer children, making it easier to have enriched work and family lives.

Women have made undeniable progress. There are a lot of firsts, but these are necessary as women occupy more prominent positions worldwide. One might expect progress to be even more marked in the next decade. So we still have a long way to go and much to do. And we might have expected better after two decades or more of indicating why supporting the advancement of qualified women makes good business sense.

Most of the research on women in management has been undertaken in developed Western countries. This Western context is very different from those in a host of countries in other parts of the world. For example, there is relatively little women in management research conducted in South America, Africa, and the Arab Middle East. In these relatively conservative countries, women must understand the important role of Islamic values, cultural characteristics, and the historical basis of gender relevant to current country economic, social, and educational development goals.

Changes involving the status of women in some Middle Eastern countries are now occurring more rapidly than the changes that took place in North America from the 1950s to the 2010s. This is particularly true in the areas of education (e.g. UAE, Qatar, Bahrain, Kuwait, Oman, Jordan).

Starting with the context as it exists

It would be wonderful if all societies had in place attitudes, values, programs, and practices necessary for the advancement of women. Unfortunately countries differ widely on these.

Thus one must start with the situation as it exists. Metcalfe (2008) advocates this view and uses realities in the Middle East to address institutional and cultural barriers facing women. She offers suggestions on what governments can undertake (legislation, entrepreneurship support, development and training support), what organizations can do (support women's networks, diversity and equality policies), and what women can do (engage in lifelong learning, join women's networks).

Using quotas to increase women's presence on corporate boards of directors and in senior management

Behren and Staubo (2013) report that since Norway's legislated requirement of 40 percent women's representation on boards of directors applied to particular types of organizational forms, some organizations in these categories have actually changed their forms or structures to bypass this requirement. The Norwegian government is not considering applying this requirement to other types of organizational forms as well. Brunzell and Liljebloom (2014) in a study of board chairmen from Nordic countries (98 percent male) found that they were significantly less satisfied with female than male board members. These chairmen, for whatever reasons, perhaps including the imposition of quotas, had a bias against women directors. These findings should be treated with caution since their sample constituted only a 20 percent response rate.

The Canadian government will ask organizations to increase the percentage of women board directors from the current average of 15 percent to 30 percent by 2020. Companies will set targets but not have quotas imposed. Compliance will be voluntary, using moral persuasion. Companies would have to "comply or explain" results or non-results. Unfortunately, companies can always find "explanations" for not reaching their targets. The chair of the Ontario Securities Commission expressed disappointment in early company responses to appoint more women to corporate boards under these terms, explaining that legislation may be needed (Shecter, 2015). Companies were required to disclose and explain their process for increasing their women board members, most efforts being "technically compliant." The UK had earlier adopted a similar "comply or explain" approach.

There has been increasing support for the use of quotas, not surprising given the slow pace of change. But quotas are non-starters in North American (Canada, US), for example. An interesting question then becomes why do some countries embrace quotas and others avoid them? Toh and Leonardelli (2011) write that quotas are more likely to be introduced in countries with "tight" cultures as opposed to "loose" cultures. "Tight" cultures are those with clear cultural norms and these reinforced by sanctions from authorities. Quotas fly in the face of particular cultural norms (e.g. everyone has an equal opportunity). Grant Thornton (2014) indicates regional support for the introduction of quotas for women in executive boards of large limited companies (the percentage of businesses supportive). This is shown in Table 1.3

Eight countries have passed legislation mandating a fixed percentage of women on boards of directors. For example, Norway was 40 percent in 2008 and Germany 30 percent in 2016. At least eight other countries have set non-binding targets, for example the UK at 25 percent in 2015 and the Netherlands at 30 percent in 2016.

An important question, but difficult to answer today, is whether increasing women's presence on corporate boards of directors adds to corporate performance and innovativeness. Early writing reviewed by Burke and Mattis (2000), without much evidence, claimed that more women on boards increased organizational performance. More recent research (Ahern and Dittmar, 2012), using Norwegian data, concluded that having more women on boards of

Table 1.3 Percentage of support for the introduction of quotas for women in executive boards of large limited companies, by region

Region	Percentage
Asia Pacific (excluding Japan)	71
Latin America	69
South East Asia	55
Southern Europe	46
Global	45
Eastern Europe	43
European Union	41
North America	30
Nordic	21

Source: Grant Thornton (2014)

directors yielded younger boards, less competent boards, and lowered organizational performance. There is also no evidence that imposing quotas increases the representation of women on boards of directors beyond having gender as a factor for nominating committees.

Learning from affirmative action plans

The use of quotas, as with the use of affirmative action quotas, has a potential downside. The US instituted affirmative action plans (AAPs) in the 1960s for certain occupations (e.g. police officers, fire fighters), with little success. Leslie *et al.* (2014), using meta-analysis, found that others viewed AAP targets as less competent and less warm, and exhibited lower levels of job performance, while the recipients of AAP reported greater stereotyping by others, lower levels of perceived self confidence, and lower levels of positive affect. These factors reduced levels of target job performance. Leslie *et al.* offer some practical implications of their findings. Organizations need to publicize the qualifications of their women, stress the fact that increasing diversity will benefit everyone in the organization and the organization itself, let women themselves know they are qualified, and let others know of the qualifications of these women. My school created a specialization in management in the mining sector, a sector that has very few women working in it. These women chose to enter the mining sector; the mining sector was not forced to hire more women. These women jokingly refer to themselves as "Women that rock." Organizations in the mining sector can learn from the difficulties in affirmative action programs to introduce these women in more positive and productive ways.

Why organizational initiatives supporting women matter

India has a very small percentage of women in senior professional and managerial jobs, perhaps less that 5 percent. The Indian Center for Social Research (2009), based on a survey of both women and HR mangers in a sample of firms, reported that India lagged behind many other countries in the numbers in managerial jobs finding that 72 percent of the firms in their study had no policies or programs to support women's advancement, with HR managers stating that women lacked the ambition to advance.

Karam (2014) offers some examples of organizational efforts to support women's advancement in the Arab Middle East, looking at 13 Arab countries. These included: Saudi Aramco offering financial help to business projects for women in Saudi Arabia; Dolphin Energy recruiting women for the energy sector in Quatr and the United Arab Emirates (UEA); and Zain Communications supporting women's projects in telecommunications in Saudi Arabia. She also describes various government efforts to help employers support and advance women (e.g. making the business case for women in management, equal opportunity policies, networking with women business associations, and identifying strategies to promote more women in management).

Although women and men enter organizations in managerial and professional jobs in roughly the same numbers in many countries, the subtle biases that exist at entry levels, compounded as one advances up the organizational hierarchy, produces all male CEOs and executive teams. Fortunately, a small decrease in biases against women at entry level will, over time, also disproportionately increase the percentages of women at more senior levels.

The hard work of changing organizational cultures

More organizations are now struggling to embrace an increasingly diverse workforce. To be successful in today's challenging times organizations need to employ the best talent available. This requires culture change within organizations – not slogans but values, policies, and structures that support the attraction, retention, and development of women and men. Supporting qualified women is not the "right thing to do" or the "nice thing to do" but is necessary for organizational success. Women and men need to have the same opportunities and access to development and support.

Changing organizational cultures takes commitment, determination, time, and resources. Individuals and teams must be held accountable for progress. The establishment of concrete, measurable, but realistic long-term goals is vital. Men have a large role to play in supporting women. Key activities include mentoring, sponsorship, and succession planning. In the last of these, for each executive position ideally three candidates should be in the development pipeline with one being different from the other two, ensuring diversity though not a quota.

A useful first step is for an organization to determine the numbers of women on the work teams at the top three or four organizational levels (CEO teams, CEO direct reports teams, their teams' direct reports etc.). This would make these data available to women and men at the top, available to potential women recruits to see where the top women are or aren't, available to potential investors, and perhaps put more pressure on organizations to do more.

Yee (2014) suggests organizations consider five questions in thinking about how they take action:

1   Where are the women in our talent pipeline? An accurate picture of where women are is a good start in identifying barriers.
2   What skills are we helping women build? Developing women's networks helps, but organizations need to build skills in women to help them succeed – confidence, resilience, and grit.
3   Do we provide sponsors as well as role models? Sponsorship opens up higher-level presence and opportunities.
4   Are we rooting out unconscious biases? Uncovering these biases opens up an opportunity to discuss, challenge, and reduce them.
5   How much are our policies helping?

CEOs need to lead their organization's efforts to increase the presence of qualified women on their top teams (perhaps on all teams), make the case why this is a business imperative, and provide resources to increase the skills of women and men to work effectively with each other. Wittenberg-Cox (2014a) argues that efforts must be focused on changing the mindsets of organizational leadership rather than "fixing the women." She argues for use of the words "gender balance," since there are only two genders, instead of gender diversity. Management teams are either balanced or unbalanced. Gender balance then becomes a potential competitive advantage instead of a problem to be fixed (Wittenberg-Cox, 2014b).

McKinsey (2015b), noting the slow progress here, attributes it to the fact that advancing qualified women is not a top business priority. It is a difficult to change organizational cultures on a number of fronts simultaneously because of the complexities of gender issues, the years it takes to bring about successful change, and because of larger issues around gender in the wider social environment. Too many corporate cultures and leadership styles create workplace expectations of a 24/7 commitment, resulting in little work–life balance (McKinsey, 2014). There is also little support from men.

To be successful, initiatives require a passionate leader at the top prepared to make an intense emotional commitment to advancing qualified women (McKinsey, 2011b). In addition, the top team, the HR function, and all levels of management need to embrace this challenge, making a complete commitment to a culture of inclusion. Having more women serving on one's board of directors will also help (McKinsey, 2013). Slaughter (2015) writes that the problem is not with women but with work, using Hilary Clinton's phrase "quarterly capitalism" to capture this. Thus it is important to change both women's roles and men's roles for these changes to be successful.

"Because it's 2015"

Newly elected Canadian prime minister, Justin Trudeau, indicated that he would have a gender balanced cabinet, a promise he delivered on. When asked why he would do this he said "Because it's 2015." This phrase might provide support for increasing the numbers of women in elected office, on corporate boards of directors, and in senior managerial jobs as it tackles the false distinction between gender and competence. Women can aspire to and be considered for these roles as they are competent.

Taking stock

There are some similarities across many of the counties in this volume, as well as in countries in the two previous volumes. Areas of commonality include:

- More women are now in their workforces.
- More women are now receiving education with more women than men typically receiving higher levels of education. But in some countries gender segregation in terms of areas of study is evident (fewer women in science, engineering).
- There is an increasing number of women in professional and managerial jobs. Again, examples of gender job segregation are present, and women are relatively rare at higher management levels or on boards of directors. In some countries women fare better in the public sector than in the private sector.
- There is a suggestion that the pace of progress for women may be slowing in some countries (e.g. U.S., Canada).

- There is evidence that race and ethnicity still affect women's progress in some countries (e.g. South Africa, US, Canada).
- A significant pay gap still is present in every country.
- There are generally increases in women pursuing entrepreneurship.
- There are modest gains in numbers of women holding elected offices but few women are at top levels.
- An increasing number of countries have legislation supporting women in the workplace, almost all countries having some forms of legislation in various areas, but too often it makes little difference as it is not well implemented nor monitored, and violations of the legislation go unpunished in some countries.
- A small number of countries have adopted the use of quotas to increase women's representation, and this number may be modestly growing; but quotas will never be implemented in most other countries.
- Private sector organizational initiatives to support the advancement of women are being undertaken in only a minority of countries (e.g. US, Canada) and rarely in others (Turkey, Iran).
- External forces such as the 2008 worldwide economic recession, and the breakup of the former Soviet Union, have influenced the work and career experiences of managerial and professional women, typically in negative ways.
- Although we selected among the best countries in advancing women, the pace of change is slow across all countries in all three volumes. Important statistical data are not being collected, even in some of our best countries.

Increasing the pace of women's advancement

Given the wide range of barriers women face, the persistence of the glass ceiling and glass walls, the impact of the larger economic, cultural and political environment, and mixed country progress to date, a multi-pronged approach is critical. Here is a sample of what is needed:

- From governments – enact, support, monitor, and reward/punish favorable/unfavorable outcomes, disseminate the virtues of gender-balanced workplaces in terms of performance, support training in entrepreneurship and management more generally for women, and build networks of organizations to help each other develop ways of changing cultures into more women-friendly places. Governments in the developed world, along with international research organizations (International Labour Organization, World Economic Forum) need to make resources available to countries just beginning the journey of empowering women.
- From organizations – build top executive support, reduce barriers to the career progress of women, develop policies and programs more supportive of a gender-balanced workplace, develop succession planning processes that include women, develop clear promotion criteria, identify where women employees currently reside in the organization, set targets of progress and monitor developments, address flexible work arrangements, maternity leave, training and development, and executive coaching opportunities. Organizations making progress should make their experiences available to others interested in such initiatives.
- From women – participate in training and development activities, seek out mentors and sponsors, get a wide range of work experiences including line management and in

positions having bottom-line impact, ask for things that would enhance your work and your work–family responsibilities, and look for successful female role models.
- From men – there is evidence from some countries that more men, especially younger men, Millennials, are now in the process of change in their own priorities, particularly men with daughters, making it more likely that they will be allies and advocates of women's progress.

Postscript

We believe that slow progress is being made in some parts of the world in addressing women's advancement. We anticipate continuing and hopefully greater progress will be evident in our fourth volume in 2023.

Note

1   Preparation of this chapter was supported in part by York University.

References

Adler, N. J. (1984) Women do not want international careers: And other myths about international management. *Organizational Dynamics*, 13, 66–79.

Ahern, K. R. and Dittmar, A. K. (2012) The changing of the boards: The impact on firm evaluation of mandated female board representation. *Quarterly Journal of Economics*, 127, 137–197.

Alas, R. and Rees, C. J. (2005) Estonia in transient: Exploring the impact of change on women managers. *Women in Management Review*, 20, 446–460.

American Association of Collegiate Schools of Business (2015) *Business school faculty: Focusing on gender reported for full-time faculty*. Tampa, Fla.: American Association of Collegiate Schools of Business.

Annis, B. and Gray, J. (2013) *Work with me*. New York: Palgrave MacMillan.

Behren, O. and Staubo, S. (2013) *Does mandatory gender balance work? Changing organizational form to avoid board upheaval*. Oslo: Norwegian Institute of Management.

Bilimoria, D. and Lord, L. (2014) *Women in STEM careers: International perspectives on increasing workforce participation, advancement and leadership*. Cheltenham: Edward Elgar.

Bilimoria, D., Lord, L. and Marinelli, M. (2014) An introduction to women in STEM. In Bilimoria, D. and Lord, L., *Women in STEM careers: International perspectives on increasing workforce participation, advancement and leadership*. Cheltenham: Edward Elgar, pp. 3–15.

Blackburn, R., Hytti, U. and Welter, F. (2015) *Context, process and gender in entrepreneurship*. Cheltenham: Edward Elgar.

Brunzell, T. and Liljeboom, E. (2014) Charimen's perceptions of female board representation: A study of Nordic listed companies. *Equality, Diversity, and Inclusion: An International Journal*, 33, 523–534.

Brush, C. G., Greene, P. G., Balachandara, L. and Davis, A. E. (2014) *Women entrepreneurs 2014: Bridging the gender gap in venture capital*. Boston: Babson College.

Burke, R. J. (2009) Cultural values and women's work and career experiences. In R. S. Bhagat and R. M. Steers (eds) *Culture, organizations, and work*. Cambridge: Cambridge University Press, pp. 418–440.

Burke, R. J. and Mattis, M. (2000) *Women on corporate boards of directors*. Dordrecht, NL: Kluwer.

Caligiuri, P. and Cascio, W. F. (1998) Can we send her there? Maximizing the success of western women on global assignments. *Journal of World Business*, 33, 394–416.

Caligiuri, P. and Tung, R. L. (1998) Comparing the success of male and female expatriates from a U.S.-based multinational company. *International Journal of Human Resource Management*, 10, 763–782.

Carter, N. M. and Silva, C. (2010a) Women in management: Delusions of progress. *Harvard Business Review*, March, 19–21.

Carter, N. M. and Silva, C. (2010b) *Mentoring: Necessary but not sufficient for advancement*. New York: Catalyst.

Casey, L. (2015) U of Toronto magnets to attract girls to science. *Toronto Star*, March 2, A6.

Catalyst (1998) *Advancing women in business: The Catalyst guide*. San Francisco, CA: Jossey-Bass.

Catalyst (2002) *Women in leadership: European business imperative*. New York: Catalyst.

Catalyst (2007) *Expanding opportunities for women and business: Women in management global comparison*. New York: Catalyst.

Cho, Y., McLean, G. N., Amornpipat, I., Chang, W.-W., Hewapathirana, G. I., Horimoto, M., Lee. M. M., Li, J., Manikoth, N. N., Othman, J. and Hamzah, S. R. (2015) Asian women in top management: Eight country cases. *Human Resource Development International*, 18, 407–428.

Cordano, M., Scherer, R. F. and Owen, C. L. (2002) Attitudes towards women as managers: Sex versus culture. *Women in Management Review*, 17, 51–60.

Davidson, M. J. and Burke, R. J. (2004) *Women in management worldwide: Facts, figures and analysis*. Surrey: Gower.

Davidson, M. J. and Burke, R. J. (2011) *Women in management worldwide: Progress and prospects*. Surrey: Gower.

Financial Post (2015) Diversity 50: Canada's most diverse board candidates. October 15, FP6.

Flavelle, D. (2015a) Business doing poor job promoting women: Survey. *Toronto Star*, September 29, A2.

Flavelle, D. (2015b) Gender wage parity could be a century away. *Toronto Star*, November 20, S9.

Glavin, T. (2015) When women are held back, humanity remains enchained. *National Post*, August 7, A8.

Gonzales, C., Jain-Chandra, S., Kochhar, K. and Newiak, M. (2015) *Fair play: More equal laws boost female labor force participation*. IMF Discussion Note. Paris: International Monetary Fund.

Grant Thornton (2014) *Women in business: From classroom to boardroom*. Grant Thornton.

Grant Thornton (2015) *Women in business: The value of diversity*. Grant Thornton International Limited.

Hofstede, G. H. (1980) *Culture's consequences: International differences in work-related values*. Beverly Hills, CA: Sage Publications.

Hofstede, G. H. and Hofstede, G. J. (2005) *Cultures and organizations: Software of the mind*. New York: McGraw-Hill.

Hori, M. and Kamo, Y. (2014) A multi-level analysis of psychological well-being related to work and family in 33 countries. *Contemporary Perspectives in Family Research*, 8B, 1–25.

House, R. J., Hanges, P. J., Javidan, M., Dorfman, P. W. and Gupta, V. (2004) *Culture, leadership and organizations: The GLOBE study of 62 societies*. Thousand Oaks, CA: Sage.

Hutchings, K. and Michailova, S. (2014) *Research handbook on women in international management*. Cheltenham: Edward Elgar.

Indian Center for Social Research (2009) *Women managers in India: Challenges and opportunities*. Visant Kunj: Center for Social Research.

Inglehart, R. and Welzel, C. (2005) *Modernization cultural change, and democracy: The human development sequence*. New York: Cambridge University Press.

International Labour Office (2004) *Breaking through the glass ceiling: Women in management*. Geneva: International Labour Office.

International Labour Organization (2015) *Women in business and management: Gaining momentum*. Geneva: International Labour Organization.

Karam, C. M. (2014) Employer attitudes to promoting women. Paper presented at the Annual Meeting of the Academy of Management. Philadelphia. August.

Karamessini, M. and Rubery, J. (2014) *Women and austerity: The economic crisis and the future for gender equality*. London: Routledge.

Kumra, S., Simpson, R. and Burke, R. J. (2014) *The Oxford handbook of gender in organizations*. Oxford: Oxford University Press.

Leslie, L. M., Mayer, D. M. and Kravitz, D. A. (2014) The stigma of affirmative action: A stereotyping-based theory and meta-analysis: Test of the consequences for performance. *Academy of Management Journal*, 57, 964–989.

May, K. (2015) For women bureaucrats, clout lags rank: Canada's public service executives 50 percent female target: report. *National Post*, February 23, A6.

McKinsey (2011a) *Women matter: An Asian perspective*. New York: McKinsey.

McKinsey (2011b) *Changing companies' minds about women.* News York: McKinsey.

McKinsey (2012) *Women matter 2012. Making the breakthrough.* New York: McKinsey.

McKinsey (2013) *Lessons from the leading edge of gender diversity.* New York: McKinsey.

McKinsey (2014) *Why gender diversity at the top remains a challenge.* New York: McKinsey

McKinsey (2015a) *The global gender issue.* New York: McKinsey.

McKinsey (2015b) *How advancing women's equality could add $12 trillion to global growth.* New York: McKinsey Global Institute.

Metcalfe, B. D. (2008) Women, management and globalization in the Middle East. *Journal of Business Ethics,* 83, 85–100.

Metcalfe, B. D. and Afanassieva, M. (2005a) Gender, work, and equal opportunities in Central and Eastern Europe. *Women in Management Review,* 20, 397–411.

Metcalfe, B. D. and Afanassieva, M. (2005b) The woman question? Gender and management in the Russian Federation. *Women in Management Review,* 20, 429–445.

Organization for Economic Co-operation and Development (2014) *Achieving stronger growth by promoting a more gender-balanced economy.* Geneva: Organization for Economic Co-operation and Development.

Posadskaya, A. (1994) *Women in Russia: A new era of Russian feminism.* London: Verso.

Post, C. and Byron, K. (2015) Women on boards and firm financial performance: A meta-analysis. *Academy of Management Journal,* 58, 1546–1571.

Rees, C. J. and Mezhevich, G. (2005) The emerging identity of women managers in post-soviet Belarus. *Women in Management Review,* 20, 412–428.

Sandberg, S. (2013) *Lean in: Women, work and the will to lead.* New York: Alfred Knopf.

Schein, V. E. (1973) The relationship between sex role stereotypes and requisite management characteristics. *Journal of Applied Psychology,* 57, 95–100.

Schein, V. E. (1975) Relationship between sex role stereotypes and requisite management characteristics among female managers. *Journal of Applied Psychology,* 60, 340–344.

Schein, V. E. (2007) Women in management: Reflections and perceptions. *Women in Management Review,* 22, 6–18.

Schwartz, F. N. (1992) *Breaking with tradition: Women and work: The new facts of life.* New York: Warner.

Shecter, B. (2015) OSC floats gender laws for boards. *National Post,* June 11, FP1, FP2.

Shriver, M. (2009) *The Shriver Report: A women's nation changes everything.* Washington, DC: Center for American Progress.

Silverstein, M. J. and Sayre, T. K. (2009a) The female economy. *Harvard Business Review,* 87, 46–53.

Silverstein, M. J. and Sayre, T. K. (2009b) *Women want more: How to capture your share of the world's largest market.* New York: HarperCollins.

Slaughter, A. M. (2012) Why women still can't have it all. *Atlantic,* August, 85–102.

Slaughter, A. M. (2015) *Unfinished business: Women, men, work and family.* New York: Random House.

Tarr-Whelan, L. (2009) *Women lead the way: Our guide to stepping up to leadership and changing the world.* San Francisco: Berrett-Koehler.

Terjesen, S. and Lloyd, A. (2015) *The 2015 Female Entrepreneurship Index.* Washington, DC: Global Entrepreneurship and Development Institute.

Thames, F. C. and Williams, M. S. (2013) *Contagious representation: Women's political representation in democracies around the world.* New York: New York University Press.

Thomson Reuters (2014) *Climb to the top: Tracking gender diversity on corporate boards.* New York: Thomson Reuters.

Toh, S. M. and Leonardelli, G. (2012) Cultural constraints on the emergence of women leaders: How global leaders can promote women in different cultures. *Organizational Dynamics,* 42, 191–197.

Toh, S. M. and Leonardelli, G. (2013) Cultural constraints on the emergence of women as leaders. *Journal of World Business,* 42, 604–611.

Tung, R. L. (2004) Female expatriates: The model global manager? *Organizational Dynamics,* 33, 243–253.

Vance, C. M., Paik, Y. and Semos, W. (1999) Biggest obstacles to career success of female American expatriates: Selection bias at home? Paper presented at the Annual Meeting of the Academy of Management. Chicago. August.

Varma, A., Toh, S. M. and Budhwar, P. (2006) A new perspective on the female expatriate experience: The role of host country categorization. *Journal of World Business*, 41, 112–120.

Vinnicombe, S., Burke, R. J., Blake-Beard, S. and Moore, L. L. (2013) *Handbook of research on promoting women's careers*. Cheltenham: Edward Elgar.

Wells J. (2015) Female executives endure a bigger pay gap. *Toronto Star*, November 11, S8.

Wirth, L. (2001) *Breaking through the glass ceiling: Women in management*. Geneva: International Labor Office.

Wittenberg-Cox, A. (2010) *How women mean business: A step-by-step guide in profiting from gender balanced business*. New York: John Wiley.

Wittenberg-Cox, A. (2014a) *Stop trying to fix women*. Boston, MA: Harvard Business Review Press.

Wittenberg-Cox, A. (2014b) *Seven steps to leading a gender-balanced business*. Boston, MA: Harvard Business Review Press.

Wittenberg-Cox, A. and Maitland, S. (2008) *Why women mean business: Understanding the emergence of our next economic revolution*. New York: John Wiley.

World Economic Forum (2014) *The global gender gap report 2014*. Geneva: World Economic Forum.

Wright, L. (2015) Female labor key to healthy economy, IMF says. *Toronto Star*, February 24, A10.

Yee, L. (2014) *Fostering women leaders: A fitness test for your top team*. New York: McKinsey and Company.

Yeganeh, H. (2015) *Cultural modernization and work-related values and attitudes*. College of Business, Winona State University. Minnesota.

Zavyalova, E. K. and Kosheleva, S. V. (2010) Gender stereotyping and its impact on human capital development in contemporary Russia. *Human Resource Development International*, 13, 341–349.

PART I
Women in management
European Union countries

2   Women in management in France

Jacqueline Laufer

Given their progress in higher education, women represent an increasing share of *cadres*, professionals and managers in France. For some years now, several researchers (Laufer, 2005) and governmental reports (Conseil économique et social, 2007) have shed light on societal and organisational factors accounting for the glass ceiling phenomenon which characterizes, in France as elsewere, the situation of women professionals and managers.

Following the development of the parity movement aimed at reducing the scarcity of women in the highest elective positions in the political sphere, and the legal instauration, in 2011, of compulsory women quotas in boards of large firms and public organisations (Laufer and Paoletti, 2015), the focus of attention has now shifted more specifically to include the situation of those women executives in top positions and decision-making functions. After a review of statistics concerning the situation of women in education, the labour force and in management and entrepreneurial activities, we shall review briefly the main dimensions of the glass ceiling, which women still come up against despite some progress. The legal and institutional framework of equal opportunity and of quota policies for women on boards will be given central attention as these convey important cultural and institutional changes which have been taking place in France concerning the status of women in top positions in all sectors of activity. Companies' initiatives concerning the situation of women in management will also be presented. The extent to which, according to some analysts, those evolutions and initiatives concerning 'women at the top' could take place at the expense of the progress of equal opportunity for all women will also be examined.

Women pursuing education

In France, girls have better results in school than boys: in 2013, 89.2 per cent of girl candidates succeed at the baccalaureat, or high school degree, while only 84.6 per cent of boys succeed. However, gender differences remain in the field of studies: during their last year in high school, girls do not select the same fields of study. They are a great majority in humanities (78.8 per cent) and in economic and social issues (60.5 per cent) but they are not at parity in sciences (45.9 per cent). While the share of girls among the candidates at the scientific baccalaureat exam is only 45.6, while the share of boys is 54.4, the rate of success of girls is 92 per cent against 91 per cent for boys. In higher education, girls represened 55 per cent of students, but 74.1 per cent were in languages, 70 per cent in literature, 64 per cent in law and political sciences, 62 per cent in health and medicine, 65 per cent in pharmacy, 75 per cent in veterinarian schools, but only 25 per cent in the sciences. In the more selective *classes préparatoires* (intensive two-year courses preparing candidates for competitive entrance exams to France's most prestigious higher educational institutions), girls represented only 30 per cent in mathematics and sciences, 54 per cent in economics and 74 per cent in literature. In engineering schools, girls represent only 28.2 per cent of students (Ministére de la santé et des droits des femmes, 2015).

Labour force characteristics

In 2013, nearly half of the working population were women (47.75 per cent), the workforce participation of women aged 20 to 64 being 74.1 per cent, against 83.8 per cent for men. While women are more often salaried than men (93 per cent against 86 per cent), they are also more often employed in the public sector: women make up 61 per cent of the public sector and 44 per cent of private sector employees. While women are more often white-collar employees or clerks (45.6 per cent) and men are more often manual workers (32 per cent), French women's employment is gender segregated: half of the jobs occupied by women are concentrated in 12 of 87 identified jobs and professions: domestic services, administrative and secretarial jobs, sales, care, education and health. Women represent 99 per cent of child-caring jobs, 66.5 per cent of social workers, 86.8 per cent of nurses and they also make up 69 per cent of teachers. Other jobs such as construction, industrial qualified workers, maintenance or electronics technicians include less than 10 per cent of women. Furthermore, 27.3 per cent of all jobs occupied by women are not qualified, while this is the case for only 15 per cent of men. While gender diversity progresses in qualified jobs, it does not decrease in less-qualified jobs (Maruani, 2011; Ministére de la santé et des droits des femmes, 2015).

Women also constitute 82 per cent of part-time workers. In 2013, 30.6 per cent worked part time, against only 7.2 per cent of men. In 2013, 36 per cent of women working part-time worked at least 80 per cent of a full-time job, against only 20 per cent of men. However 36 per cent worked at the most half time, against 53 per cent of men. Since 2000, the share of part-time work in the employment of women has stabilised, while it has increased for men (up by 2.1 per cent between 2002 and 2013). While more than 45 per cent of economically active women with at least three children work part time, women who work part time are more likely to wish to work more: 9.7 per cent of employed women are in a situation of under employment (i.e. they work part time and would like to work more), against only 2.8 per cent of employed men. Women are also slightly more likely to occupy temporary and short-term contracts: 13.9 per cent against 13.1 per cent for men (Ministére des Droits des Femmmes, Chiffres clés, 2012).

Furthermore, pay differentials between men and women persist. In 2012, the mean net monthly salary for women working full time in the private and semi-public sector was 19.2 per cent lower than for men. In public service and especially in state administration, differences are smaller and amount to 14.8 per cent. Among managers, pay differentials are the highest, with female managers earning 22.3 per cent less than male managers in the private or semi-public sector, and 15.2 per cent less in the state civil service (Ministère des droits des femmes, 2012).

Women in management in firms and public service

In 2013, 15 per cent of women in employment occupied a job in a cadre, as a manager or highly qualified professional, against 20 per cent for men. In administrative, managerial and professional occupations, the proportion of women has increased. Women now account for 56.4 per cent of professors and scientific professions and 43.1 per cent of cadres and managers in the public sector. In business firms, 45 per cent of firms' business administration and sales executives and 21.7 per cent of engineers and technical executives are women.

In 2011, the percentage of women among the chief executive officers (CEOs) of firms was 18.1 per cent, with a variation between different sectors: 7.4 per cent in construction, 12.7 per cent in industry, 19.9 per cent in commerce and 20.9 per cent in services. The share of women heads of firms decreases as the size of firm increases: they represent 40 per cent of those working alone in their firm, 28 per cent in those firms employing up to four employees, 16 per cent in firms employing 20 to 49 employees and 14 per cent for firms employing more than 50 employees. The return on investment in the firms headed by women is EU€182,000 against €294,000 for men.

In 2013, in large companies belonging to France's CAC 40 stock index, women represented 7.9 per cent of CEOs, 8.5 per cent of directors, 7.9 per cent of executive committee members and 24 per cent of board members with a sharp rise in the share of women board members thanks to the quota policy (see below) (Capitalcom, 2013).

In the French public administration and civil service, although women make up the majority of employees (61 per cent), in the state administration they account for only 19 per cent of those top jobs appointed by the government and 27 per cent of other senior managerial jobs. In the decentralised regional public sector, women hold 33 per cent of senior management jobs and 41 per cent of local administrators jobs. In the third branch of the French civil service, the hospital service, which employs 77 per cent of women, 40 per cent of heads of hospitals are women.

Women entrepreneurs

Among entrepreneurs, 28 per cent of firms in industry and services were created by women. The rate of company creation has been rising recently, thanks, among other causes, to the creation, in 2011, of a simpler legal status of micro-entrepreneur. Out of 550,700 firms started in 2014, 70 per cent of them registered as 'personal firms', and 38 per cent of these personal firms were started by women.

A recent poll (Barométre des femmes entrepreneures, Caisse d'épargne, 2014) of 723 entrepreneurs (360 women and 363 men having started their firm for at least a year) showed that women entrepreneurs had higher educational qualifications than their male counterparts: 71.4 per cent have the baccalaureat, compared to 57.2 per cent of men. However, they have less professional experience: 16.5 per cent of women entrepreneurs had no professional activity before creating their company, against 8.7 per cent of men. While 49 per cent of firms created by women were in commerce, transport and catering, only 41 per cent of those started by men were. In services the rates were of 38 per cent of women, but 26 per cent of men, and in industry and construction: 12 per cent of women, but 31 per cent of men.

Women more often benefit from some kind of support while launching their project: 34.2 per cent of women entrepreneurs were helped by their husbands (16.9 per cent of men were helped by their wives) and 30.6 per cent of women were helped by a specialised agency. As to the likelihood that the firm is still in activity three years after its creation, this depended more upon the activity sector than upon the gender of the entrepreneur.

Breaking the glass ceiling

The various factors and obstacles which characterize the career development of French women professionals and managers and the glass ceiling they are faced with have now been well identified (Laufer and Fouquet, 2001; Laufer, 2011): vertical and horizontal segregation, both in the private and public sectors; women managers being concentrated in a much smaller number of occupational sectors (health, education, social services, administration, communications and human resources); under-representation of women in operational functions and management of large teams; stereotypical representations of social and organisational roles which emphasise women's difficulties in accessing leadership roles and functions; weight of organisational cultures and norms and career development policies that are supposedly 'neutral' but in fact result in gender inequalities for those women who do not fit the model; detrimental impact for women of the 'total availibility model' when it comes to having access to top jobs; smaller attention given by women managers to the development of networks; greater difficulties for women to cope with conflict between professional and family roles than their spouses or partners. Indeed, under the influence of the norm of equal opportunities for women, career development policies are becoming more gender neutral in early-stage career management, but this is not sufficient to eliminate the influence of 'male' organisational norms. In fact, many women managers pursue career development but withdraw from power competition when it comes to reaching top executive jobs, therefore leaving the dominant organisational norms unchanged. This leads to the scarcity of women in the upper echelons of organisations (Belghiti-Mahut, 2004; Fortino, 2002; Guillaume and Pochic, 2007; Landrieux-Kartochian, 2005; Laufer, 2005, 2011; Laufer and Fouquet, 1998).

In recent years, research has also been focused on those few women in France who have been able to go beyond the glass ceiling and have reached top executive positions in firms of various sizes (Benquet and Laufer, 2016). In recent research on a sample of 42 top women executives, the diversity of their profiles (with most having graduated from prestigious *grandes écoles* while some had graduated from university), the various types of strategies they used to become visible, to build networks and to refuse assigned 'feminine' careers with little decision making and leadership power, were issues under scrutiny. While many of these top executives were able to develop their careers in very large French or international firms, displaying therefore 'internal' mobilities, some of them experienced a great number of mobilities *between* firms. The great majority of these women were able to reconcile career and family: 81 per cent of them were living with a spouse and 67 per cent had two or more children. However, it was not obvious that supposedly 'family friendly' policies of firms played a great role in the career development of those women executives. Instead, for those women who were willing and able to pursue a typically 'male' career pattern, it appeared that the notion of 'career friendly families' could characterise the way in which the husband and the children did play their part in the career development of those women top executives. Indeed, spouse and children were flexible enough to adapt to the availability or mobility constraints of those women concerned who had often the 'leading career' in the family (Laufer *et al.*, 2014).

Legislation, policies and social actors supporting women, and women in management

Since the passage of the law on 'professional equality' in 1983, the legal framework for gender equality has evolved in France in three directions. One is the development of a more compelling legal and administrative framework concerning gender equality at work, with a strong emphasis given to collective agreements. The second has to do with the implementation of the principle of gender parity, both in the political sphere and at the top of organisations both public and private. The third direction concerns the implementation of 'real equality' as an integrated objective throughout all public policies (according to the logic of mainstreaming) on such diversified issues as work equality, reconciliation of work and family issues and parental leave, violence against women, women's rights in the field of health, gender parity in political and professional responsibilities, sexism and stereotypes, with each new law or policy being evaluated as to its potential impact on gender equality (Laufer, 2014).

The French law on gender equality in the workplace that was passed on 13 July 1983 imposed a three-fold obligation on business firms with over 300 employees: to implement equal treatment and equal opportunity between men and women, to carry out a diagnosis on the comparative employment situation of women and men in order to identify workplace inequalities, and eventually to open negotiations with social partners on the issue of gender equality. Such negotiations were optional in the 1983 law but became mandatory under the May 2001 law (Laufer, 1992, 1998, 2000, 2014).

Given the slow progress of the number of agreements negotiated with social partners on equality measures, and the low efficiency of measures taken to eradicate inequalities, in spite of government action to develop and publicise expertise as to gender equality policies (Conseil Supérieur de l'Égalité Professionnelle, 2002), legislation introduced in March 2006 required firms to negotiate measures to eliminate differences in compensation by the end of 2010. It also introduced a mechanism to offset the effect of maternity on employee pay: the law grants employees on maternity or adoption leave pay increases equal to the general increase, plus the average individual pay increase awarded during the leave period to employees in the same professional category. In the 2014 law, measures have been taken to simplify the negotiation process on professional equality: each year, businesses must open a negotiation with social partners including both differences in compensation and other types of measures to improve equal treatment and equal opportunity.

These laws, in addition to more stringent controls and sanctions for firms that do not comply, have produced an increase in the number of agreements on gender equality. Since 2007, the share of collective agreements which include gender equality measures or are dedicated to this objective have increased from 0.7 per cent in 2004 to 12 per cent in 2011 (Laufer, 2014). The majority of large firms have negotiated an agreement on professional equality, including a vast array of measures based on qualitative and quantitative diagnostics concerning various dimensions of women's status and career, and various dimensions of human management policies: hiring, career opportunities, training, compensation and work–life balance concerning both parents (Laufer and Silvera, 2006).

In 2009, 70 per cent of the firms of the CAC 40 had an agreement on professional equality. The situation is indeed more favourable in those larger firms staffed with a greater number of HR professionals and therefore better able to elaborate organisational diagnosis and action plans on gender equality. The situation is very different in small and medium-sized firms which employ a greater proportion of the female labour force in which management and unions experience more difficulties to meet the demands of such diagnosis and action plans (Laufer, 2014). As negotiation with social partners on the topic of professional equality is compulsory only in firms employing more than 50 employees, only 46.2 per cent of the female salaried population were covered by those agreements (Fete, 2012, 2013). In 2013, an agreement was passed between the minister of women's rights and 28 large firms which pledged to support small subcontractors and providers in their definition and implementation of an equal opportunity policy.

Beyond this legislative evolution and the increase in the number of signed collective agreements, which testify to the increasing legitimacy of professional equality measures, one must emphasise the role played by the development of diversity policies, particularly for female managers. The issue of diversity policies has been widely debated in France (Bender, 2004; Bereni, 2009; Laufer, 2009; Garner-Moyer, 2012). Some considered that the notion of diversity euphemises the anti-discrimination approach detailed in the law of 2001 that, following European directives, defines the concept of discrimination and lists the various grounds for discrimination (Halde, 2011). The risk of weakening the objective of gender equality because of the many issues included in diversity policies has been also discussed. Companies however, have still developed diversity policies, supported by the research evidence, on the benefits of the employment of women as contributing to economic performance, particularly female managers (Landrieux-Kartochian, 2005; Laufer and Paoletti, 2010). They increased the numbers of women holding managerial positions that were supported by mentoring practices, encouraging women to join networks, training aimed at increasing awareness about stereotypes and by developing high potential policies geared to a better selection of women (Laufer, 2005). Addressing gender stereotypes appears to be especially important (Commissariat général à la stratégie et à la prospective, 2013; Chaintreuil and Epiphane, 2013), for example in recruiting or through assigning women to certain 'feminine' jobs or 'feminine' leadership styles or because of women's tendency to exclude themselves from leadership positions and to lack self-confidence. The potential difference in self-confidence levels between men and women in the workplace induces expectations that are more modest amongst women. According to recent surveys, differences in self-confidence levels between men and women could explain up to 4.5 of the 25 percentage points of salary gap. Men are nine times more inclined to ask for a wage raise than women (Dejouany, 2012).

Concerning reconciliation policies, while parental leave was introduced in 1977 for both men and women, the detrimental impact of such leave concerning the careers of women who constitute the great majority (97 per cent) of beneficiaries of parental leave, has long been debated in France (Meurs *et al.*, 2010). The rate of activity of mothers drops according to the number of children, while it increases for men. In 2013, the workforce participation rate for women aged 20–64 years was 81.6 per cent with one child, 66 per cent with two children and 41.1 per cent with three children (Fagnani and Letablier, 2005; Jenson and Sineau, 1998; Ministére de la santé et des droits des femmes, 2015). To encourage the sharing of family responsibilities, the law of 21 December 2001 gave fathers, whether employed or self-employed, access to 11 days of paternity leave in the four months following the birth or adoption of a child. In 2010, two thirds of new fathers benefited from this paid leave, full pay being now more frequent in several large firms. To encourage the sharing of parental responsibilities, the law of 4 August 2014 on 'real equality' between men and women stipulates that for parents of two children the length of the leave and of the allowance will be maintained for three years if the second parent (generally the father) takes at least six months of the leave. The objective of this new policy is to reach 25 per cent of fathers taking the leave by 2017.

Other initiatives were undertaken by large companies which address the balance between domestic and professional work, for example the comitment to the *Charte de la parentalité*, supported by the Observatoire de l'équilibre des temps et de la parentalité and the Ministére des Droits des Femmes, in favour of equal sharing of domestic and professional work that promotes a more flexible managerial culture that respects the private life of all employees and that takes their personal constraints into account. The companies that signed this charter, in accordance with the 15 commitments, can adapt the content of the charter to the reality of their organisations, one example being the scheduling of meetings to minimise their impact on family responsibilities. More than 500 companies have already signed the charter (Charte de la parentalité, 2008).

Among the new actors promoting gender equality and anti-discrimination policies, the mission of the Défenseur des droits is to provide information, support and expertise for those people who think that they are discriminated against on one or several grounds included in the 2001 law againt discrimination (Laufer, 2014). In this context, it is important to mention those (few) cases of direct and indirect discrimination concerning women managers which have been recently taken to court, a practice that is not as frequent in France as it is in Anglo-Saxon countries but that proved to play an important role for several types of actors (business firms, researchers and experts on gender equality) in raising awareness as to the scope of the equal treatment or equal pay principle and as to the role of the law and of trials to enforce these principles; however, for the time being, such cases concern only a few women who have the necessary support and resources to engage in such trials. Indeed, the much publicised case of Ms X allowed the full appreciation of the scope of this principle of equal treatment as it applies to the rights of mothers (concerning job and position, access to training or the level of pay) when they return from maternity or parental leave. These cases lead to the realisation that while a method had been devised by a major union to analyse the career delays of male union members, leading to significant financial compensation, the same method of analysis of career delays could also be applied to female executives and managers (Lanquetin, 2010). Another significant case concerns Ms Z and the principle of 'work of equal value'. Ms Z was an HR manager in a middle-sized firm but her level of compensation was not equivalent to the rest of the male members of the executive committee (commercial, financial directors etc.). She was the only one in the executive comittee of the firm not to have the title of director. The court estimated that her work and responsibilities should be given equal compensation to that of the other directors (Silvera, 2011).

From equality to parity

While collective agreements on gender equality have included actions to improve the career development of women and have increased the awareness of the obstacles facing women's and mothers' career development, they have not dealt specifically with the issue of women's access to power positions and decision-making functions at the top of public and private large organisations, an issue which was better adressed following the establishment of the parity principle concerning the access to women in power positions in the political sphere (Bereni, 2009).

The first law on parity of 6 June 2000 was designed to increase the access of women to electoral mandates and elective functions. It compels political parties to present an equal number of women and men candidates for local (in cities larger than 3500), regional, senate and European elections and it provides for a penalty for those parties which do not comply with this rule in national elections. The law of 31 January 2007 extends this first law. The law of 23 July 2008 modifies article 1 of the French constitution and extends the equal access principle to professional and social responsibilities. The law of 4 August 2014 increases the public subsidy withheld from political parties that do not follow the parity rule for candidates.

Concerning the economic sphere, the law of 27 January 2011 set up a quota policy for women on boards for firms of more than 500 employees (250 since 2014) and €500 million (€50 million since 2014); those must include at least 20 per cent of each sex in 2013 and 40 per cent in 2018. The law also applies to public firms. The sanctions which apply concern director's fees and cancelled nominations. In large business firms, the results have been very positive, with the share of women tripling in three years. In 2014, the boards of the firms belonging to the SB120 French stock index included 30 per cent women board members, reaching 33.3 per cent in 2015, with some firms being now well beyond the target of 40 per cent (Laufer and Paoletti, 2015).

One of the major benefits of quotas for women on boards is the potential positive effects on executive committees of large firms. Though these are outside the scope of the law on quotas, several firms came to favour the setting of voluntary numerical targets concerning the share of women in executive comittees and the share of women on the list of candidates to be examined concerning access to these top positions. In firms of the CAC 40, the share of women in these committees has increased from 8 per cent to 10.6 per cent. Moreover, 35 per cent of the women who are members of executive committees were in operational functions, and not just in support functions such as communication and HR.

Concerning public administration, the law of 12 March 2012 sets up quantitative objectives concerning the top jobs in the public sector but also in other types of public service organisations (Jacquemart *et al.*, 2016). The law of 22 July 2013 concerns universities and research and the existence of quantitative objectives for women in university bodies. Since 2008, the law also favours equal access of women to top jobs in unions, in national cultural and sport associations and in media organisations. The 4 August 2014 law extends the role of quantitative objectives for top positions in sport and cultural organisations. Figures on the share of women at the top of all of these organisations have been widely reported to justify the policies. For example, if women are a large majority among TV programme presenters, they are only 38.5 per cent of developers of specific topics. They are also only 4 per cent among conductors and 25 per cent of theatre directors.

Beyond these legal developments, other governmental initiatives have also been put in place. In order to encourage firms to increase the proportion of women in executive positions, a 'success list' of those top firms having the highest rates of women in boards, executive ranks and among the 100 first top directors, established by the consulting firm Ethics and Boards and supported by the Ministry of Women's Rights, was first published in 2013. It has been published each year since then. Additionally, various media and other groups have published figures on firms, for example those firms having a very high ratio of women in their workforce and among managers, but having none in their executive comitees. In 2013, the Ministry of Women's Rights signed agreements with 27 firms committing themselves to increasing the proportion of women in their top jobs and executive comitees. This has encouraged well-known women's networks to promote women candidacies to fill these positions in boards and executive committees.

Concerning public service, after a long series of reports followed by little action (Le Pors and Milewski, 2005), the 12 March 2012 law introduced an annual report on gender equality in the workplace (recruitment, promotion, training, working conditions, etc.) and reported, as of 1 January 2013, that the nominations of new top managers in central government, local governent and hospitals counted at least 20 per cent of members of each gender. This rate will go up to 30 per cent in 2015 and to 40 per cent in 2018. Interestingly, these objectives were surpassed and in 2013, women represented 32 per cent of new nominations in top management against 27 per cent in 2012. To guarantee that these changes last, additional actions were planned: the rule imposing three applicants, including a member of each sex for each nomination for the top jobs named in a cabinet meeting, was made systematic. As concerns reconciliation, it planned that time charts enhancing a better articulation of professional and private lives be set up in each ministry and that the rules imposing geographical mobility that slow down women's advancement or promotion be revised. The minister of public service, a woman, has started negotiations with trade unions for that purpose. On 8 March 2013, the first global agreement on professional equality was signed with the trade unions and the representatives of employers.

Concerning the development of entrepreneurship, in recent years a lot has been done to favour the increase of the share of women among new entrepreneurs. The French start-up aid agency, APCE, joined the action led by the Ministry of Women's Rights to enhance female entrepreneurship by creating an internet site with three objectives:

- To promote female entrepreneurial vocations by broadcasting testimonies of women who created or took over companies of all sizes;
- To answer women's questions about their personal situation and provide them with methods and tools to succeed in their project;
- To steer them towards the existing networks where they can find support.

Beyond these governmental initiatives, one must underline the role played by other actors in the development of a climate favourable to women's access to managerial and top managerial positions. Indeed, over the past 15 years, an important number of female managers' networks have developed inside companies, within public service, among alumni of major business and engineering schools, among female entrepreneurs and among employers' organisations. These networks have greatly contributed to end the discretion that long characterised female managers in France and have shed light on what is at stake in female careers by making good use of numerous studies and surveys on the obstacles female managers face in the course of their careers. These publications have been issued by such consulting firms as McKinsey or by non-government organisations such as Catalyst, or issued in France by such organisations as Accenture, or produced by the French Economic, Social and Environmental Council. In parallel to these publications, consulting and training activities have been developed that aimed at supporting not only companies, but also public sector organisations. This development of networks and consulting activities raises the question of women's commitment to activities that are in line both with a form of feminism, since women's status in society is at stake – even if the word feminism is rejected by a vast number of women concerned – and with the claim for an affiliation with the world of economic power, and therefore with a feminism of 'rich women' (Blanchard *et al.*, 2013).

The focus over the few past years on the question of women's access to power in the economic sphere leads us to wonder whether the attention that is granted to female managers and top managers is not detrimental to the attention given to other issues in the field of professional equality. An example of this fact is the difficult renegotiation of collective agreements in order to reevaluate lower qualified female professions and make progress towards equal pay (Defenseur des Droits, 2012; Lemière and Silvera, 2010). One can also note how difficult the employment and positive action policies are for women who hold precarious and unqualified jobs. Several reports (for example, Lemière, 2013) have revealed that firms' professional equality policies and collective agreements in France do not take sufficient account of the problems that face women who have difficult access to the employment market. These policies tend to only take into account the situation of women who already are employed, mostly in big companies and hence holding stable jobs.

References

Belghiti-Mahut, S. (2004) Les determinants de l'avancement hiérarchique des femmes cadres, *Revue Française de Gestion*, 30(151): 145–160.

Bender, A.-F. (2004) Égalité professionnelle ou gestion de la diversité. Quels enjeux pour l'égalité des chances?, *Revue Française de Gestion*, 30(151): 205–218, juillet–août.

Benquet, M. and Laufer, J. (Dir) (2016) Femmes dirigeantes, Travail, *Genre et Sociétés*, 35: 19–27.

Bereni, L. (2009) Quand la mise à l'agenda ravive les mobilisations féministes. L'espace de la cause des femmes et la parité politique (1997–2000), *Revue française de science politique 2*, 59: 301–323.

Blanchard, S., Boni, I. and Rabier, M. (2013) Une cause de riches? L'accès des femmes au pouvoir économique, *Sociétés contemporaines*, 1(89): 101–103.

Capitalcom (2013) Sondage *Le Monde*, www.Capitalcom.fr, March 8.

Chaintreuil, L. and Epiphane, D. (2013) Les hommes sont plus fonceurs mais les femmes mieux organisées: quand les recruteurs parlent du sexe des candidates, *Bref*, 315, octobre, CEREQ.

Charte de la parentalité (2008) Observatoire de l'équilibre des temps et de la parentalité en entreprise, www.observatoire-equilibre.com/.

Commissariat général à la stratégie et à la prospective (2013) *Lutter contre les stéréotypes filles-garçons: un enjeu d'égalité et de mixité dès l'enfance*, Commissariat général à la stratégie et à la prospective.

Conseil Économique et Social (2007) *La place des femmes dans les lieux de décision: promouvoir la mixité*, rapport présenté par Monique Bourven. Conseil Économique et Social.

Conseil Supérieur de l'Égalité Professionnelle (2002) *Guide d'appui à la négociation au sein des entreprises et des branches*. Service des Droits des Femmes et de l'Égalité.

Défenseur des Droits (2012) *Guide pour une évaluation non discriminante des emplois à prédominance féminine*, coordonné par Becker M., Lemière S., Silvera R., Défenseur des Droits.

Dejouany, L. (2012) *Les femmes au piège de la négociation salariale – Ou comment demander de l'argent à son patron sans le fâcher*, L'Harmattan.

Fagnani, J. and Letablier, M.T. (2005) La politique familiale française, in Maruani, M. (Dir) *Femmes, genre et sociétés, l'état des savoirs*. Paris, La Découverte.

Fete (2012) *Égalité professionnelle et syndicats en Bourgogne*. www.fete-bourgogne.org.

Fete (Femmes Égalité Emploi) (2013) *Focus sur l'égalité professionnelle dans les entreprises en Bourgogne*. www.fete-bourgogne.org.

Fortino, S. (2002) *La mixité au travail*, La Dispute.

Garner-Moyer, H. (2012) *Réflexions autour du concept de diversité: Éclairer pour mieux agir*, Association française des managers de la diversité, juin.

Guillaume, C. and Pochic, S. (2007) La fabrication organisationnelle des dirigeants, *Travail, Genre et Sociétés*, 17: 79–105.

Halde (2011) Rapport annuel (High authority on the fight against discrimination and for equality), Halde.

Jacquemart, A., Le Mancq, F. and Pochic, S. (2016) Femmes hautes fonctionnaires en France, L'avénement d'une égalité élitiste, *Travail genre et sociétés*, 35, avril, 27–45.

Jenson, J. and Sineau, M. (1998) *Qui doit garder le jeune enfant? Modes d'accueil et travail des mères dans l'Europe en crise*, Éditions LGDJ.

Landrieux-Kartochian, S. (2005) Femmes et performance des entreprises, l'émergence d'une nouvelle problématique, *Travail et Emploi*, 102, avril–juin, 11–20.

Lanquetin, M.T. (2010) Maternité et discrimination dans la carrière, *Le Droit Ouvrier*, 746, septembre.

Laufer, J. (1992) L'entreprise et l'égalité des chances – Enjeux et démarches. *La Documentation Française*.

Laufer, J. (1998) Equal opportunity between men and women: the case of France, *Feminist Economics*, 4(1): 53–69.

Laufer, J. (2000) *Promoting gender equality at the work place: the case of France*, report to the Fondation européenne pour l'amélioration des conditions de vie et de travail, Dublin.

Laufer, J. (2005) La construction du plafond de verre : le cas des femmes cadres à potentiel, *Travail et Emploi*, 102: 31–44.

Laufer, J. (2009) L'égalité professionnelle entre les hommes et les femmes est-elle soluble dans la diversité?, *Travail, genre et sociétés*, 21: 29–54.

Laufer, J. (2011) Women in management in France, in M.J. Davidson and R.J. Burke (eds) *Women in management worldwide, Progress and prospects*, Gower.

Laufer, J. (2014) *L'égalité professionnelle entre les femmes et les hommes*, Paris, La Découverte, Collection Repéres.

Laufer, J. and Fouquet, A. (1998) Le plafond de verre est toujours là, *Revue française de gestion*, 119: 110–112.

Laufer, J. and Fouquet, A. (2001) Les cadres à l'épreuve de la feminisation, in P. Bouffartigue (ed.) *Cadres: la grande rupture*, Paris, La Découverte, 249–268.

Laufer, J. and Paoletti, M. (2010) Controverse sur les spéculations sur les performances économiques des femmes, *Travail Genre et Sociétés*, avril, 23: 167–170.

Laufer, J. and Paoletti, M. (2015) Controverse: Quotas en tous genre, *Travail, Genre et Société*, 23: 167–170.

Laufer J. and Silvera, R. (2006) *Les accords d'entreprise sur l'égalité professionnelle*, La Documentation française, coll. Regards sur l'actualité.

Laufer, J., Perrin-Joly, C., Mascova, E. *et al.* (2014) *Femmes dirigeantes en entreprise: des parcours aux leviers d'action*. AFMD, HEC-Paris.

Lemière, S. (Dir.) (2013) *L'accès à l'emploi des femmes: une question de politiques*, rapport remis à la Ministre des Droits des Femmes.

Lemière, S. and Silvera, R. (2010) *Comparer les emplois entre les femmes et les hommes: de nouvelles pistes pour réduire les inégalités de salaires*, Halde, La Documentation Française.

Le Pors A. and Milewski, F. (2005) *Vouloir l'égalité*. Troisiéme rapport du comité de pilotage pour l'égal accés des femmes et des hommes aux emplois superieurs de la function publique et de la Réforme de l'Etat. La Documentation française.

Maruani, M. (2011) *Travail et emploi des femmes*, La Découverte, coll. Repères, Paris, 4ème édition.

Meurs, D., Pailhié, A. and Ponthieux, S. (2010) Enfants, interruptions d'activité des femmes et écarts de salaire entre les sexes, *La Revue de l'OFCE*, 114, juillet.

Ministère des droits des femmes (2012) *L'égalité entre les femmes et les hommes*. Chiffres clés.

Ministére de la santé et des droits des femmes (2015) *Vers l'égalité réelle entre les femmes et les hommes*, Chiffres clés.

Silvera, R. (2011) Inégalités salariales: un nouveau film en 3D, *La Pensée*, 367: 115–125.

3 Women in management in Greece

Nancy Papalexandris

Introduction

Following 2009, Greece entered a severe economic crisis that had dramatic effects on employment, income of the population and labour market characteristics. Women and young people have suffered most from this situation. Although attitudes towards the ability of women to move ahead are improving, the economic situation limits available opportunities and favours the equality gap.

In this chapter we will first briefly present the overall economic crisis and its impact on the labour market, focusing on the existing situation for women in employment, in education and in politics. Then we will describe the role of women in decision making and in entrepreneurship. We will discuss obstacles that limit higher participation of women at the top and present initiatives that aim at supporting women in their journey towards equality.

The Greek economic crisis

Most of the industrialised world entered a deep recession in 2008–2009 as the financial crisis that began in the USA evolved to a global recession with multiple economic, employment and social implications. Despite measures taken by governments worldwide, unemployment, poverty, inflation and national debts rose in an unprecedented manner (Eurostat, 2009; World Bank, 2009). Southern Europe has been affected the most. As a result, the European Union (EU) reacted with harsh anti-crisis austerity policies, creating growing unemployment, falling real wages, cuts in the social security system, erosion of the collective agreement system and privatisation of public property (Busch *et al.*, 2013).

In Greece, the economy deteriorated, with sharp contractions of gross domestic product (GDP) reaching 25 per cent between 2009 and 2015. Since the start of the crisis, poverty rates have increased to record levels. By the end of 2009, the Greek economy faced its most severe debt crisis. This was due to the fact that Greece, like many other European countries, was borrowing money beyond its means. In 2010 Greece's ability to repay its sovereign debt was questioned and high borrowing rates effectively prohibited access to the financial markets. In May 2010, the International Monetary Fund, the European Commission and the European Central Bank (together known as the Troika) agreed to a rescue package. To secure this funding Greece was required to sign two consecutive memoranda and to adopt harsh austerity measures and reforms to bring its deficit under control (Stavrou-Costea and Papalexandris, 2015).

In 2014 a small growth in GDP was evident due to the austerity measures and the growth in the tourist sector. However, this was interrupted by the change in government. The Greek government elected in January 2015 came to power after declaring that it would stop austerity measures and negotiate new terms with the Troika. Negotiations were very slow and led to further deterioration of the economy and the signing of a third memorandum. New elections took place in September 2015, where the same party was re-elected. At present the economy is at a standstill awaiting reforms and further agreements with lenders.

Labour force characteristics

This being the overall picture, there is, however, a part of the population for whom the impact of the economic policies imposed by the loan agreements and memoranda is even harder, i.e. women, whose position is getting worse on a number of issues. The most serious problem women face is unemployment. Starting in 2010 unemployment rates increased dramatically as can be seen in Table 3.1. The latest figures show a general unemployment rate of 25.2 per cent with a rate of 23.5 per cent for men and 30.6 per cent for women.

The employment rate for the active population, i.e. persons in the 15–64 age group, was the lowest in EU, with Greece reaching 49.4 per cent for men in 2014, from 61.4 per cent in 2008. At the same time women's employment rate fell to 40.1 per cent in 2014 from 49 per cent in 2008 due to the previously mentioned reasons. At the same time the average EU rate for women's employment rate is 58.8 per cent, with Sweden showing the highest rate of 72.8 per cent (Eurostat, 2014).

As described in the *Greek League for Women's Rights Journal*, 70 per cent of unemployment is long term (at least 12 months), with the female long-term unemployment rate at 15.9 per cent and male at 10.4 per cent. A large part of women have joined the ranks of 'discouraged workers' who are not accounted for in the statistics. It should be noted that the monthly unemployment allowance is currently at €360 per month, and is paid for a maximum of 400 days. Thus it does not cover the long-term unemployed and, due to strict conditions, only about 160,000 persons receive it. As a result, unemployed women are more likely to miss out on this support. A woman who is unemployed because she lost her job or cannot find one when trying to enter the labour market, not only loses her financial means, but becomes dependent on others; if she stays home to care for the other members of the family (children, ailing, elderly) she loses health and pension insurance coverage, and is expected to go back to traditional housewife duties (*Greek League for Women's Rights Journal*, 2014).

At the same time, budget cuts affect care services and benefits for children (only 10 per cent of children aged 0 to 2 years and only 61 per cent of children aged 3 to 6 years are covered),

Table 3.1 Unemployment in Greece

Year	Total (%)	Men (%)	Women (%)
2002	10.3	6.8	15.7
2004	10.5	6.6	16.2
2006	8.9	5.6	13.6
2008	7.7	5.1	11.1
2010	12.7	9.7	15.7
2012	26.1	23.2	30.2
2014	26.5	23.8	30.9
2015	25.2	23.5	30.6

Source: Hellenic Statistical Authority (2015)

for the elderly, the sick and disabled. As a result, care lies now more heavily on families, particularly on women.

Women mostly occupy the less-well-paid positions in the hierarchy and receive smaller pensions when retired. The estimated pay gap is 22 per cent for women and the pension gap 25.1 per cent (European Commission, 2014). Salary and pension cuts deepen the feminisation of poverty (women make up 60 per cent of the poor), and make things very difficult indeed for elderly and pregnant women, for those who live alone or try to sustain a single parent family.

Furthermore, twice as many women are employed on a part-time basis. While this is also the case in other European countries where much higher differences between men and women exist in part-time employment, the Greek situation is quite different. Very few of the women working part time have asked for it for reasons of work/family balance, as in most countries of the north. The very low pay for part-time jobs makes them highly unappealing. However, due to the high unemployment rate and in the absence of alternative solutions, women are forced to accept them.

By observing Table 3.2, which shows the unemployment rate for different age groups, we notice that the highest unemployment rate is recorded among young people in the age group of 15 to 24 years (51.9 per cent). For young females, the unemployment rate is 57.0 per cent.

It is true that while southern EU countries have very high unemployment rates for the general population, their youth unemployment rates are unprecedentedly high. These levels are partly attributed to their being considered as 'rigid' labour markets, where employers are reluctant to hire because of high hiring costs or difficulties in dismissal stemming from high rates of unionisation or universal statutory severance payments (Stavrou-Costea and Papalexandris, 2015). Especially for the young, this rigidity is detrimental as, even though they may be more qualified than older generations of workers, those who entered the labour market during the period of growth between the 1960s and 1990s are protected as 'insiders', making it harder for new entrants to get in. This is particularly true for Greece, as can be seen in Table 3.2.

As regards the educational attainment level, Greece, according to the Organization for Economic Co-operation and Development (OECD), ranks third among country members in graduation rates, as 94 per cent of its young people are expected to complete upper secondary education in their lifetime (OECD, 2012). The unemployment rate is higher among persons with lower qualifications. The lowest unemployment rates are observed among persons who have completed post-graduate studies or have a doctorate (12.9 per cent), and among those

Table 3.2 Unemployment rate (%) by gender and age group

Age group	First quarter						
	2014				2015		
	Males	*Females*	*Total*		*Males*	*Females*	*Total*
Total	25.0	31.4	27.8		23.5	30.6	26.6
15–24	52.6	61.5	56.7		47.5	57.0	51.9
25–29	40.7	44.2	42.4		36.7	43.0	39.7
30–44	23.4	30.8	26.7		21.9	30.1	25.7
45–64	18.5	22.7	20.3		18.4	23.2	20.4
65+	14.4	7.9	12.6		12.3	3.6	9.3

Source: Hellenic Statistical Authority (2015)

who have completed university studies (19.8 per cent). However, the preference for hiring men is evident in all levels of education (see Table 3.3).

The following figures, appearing in Table 3.4, are taken from the Gender Equality Index, which measures gender equality taking into consideration various indicators among EU countries and is prepared by the European Institute for Gender Equality (2015). Greece shows a gap due to gender differences in full-time equivalent employment and duration of working life. Women and men graduates appear in equal ratios. However, there is a concentration in the caring professions which, although evident in most EU countries, appears higher for Greece. With reference to the gap in working life duration, this is due to the fact that women were encouraged by legislation especially in the public sector to get a pension at an early age in order to care for family obligations. While this provision no longer exists, in the past it also kept many women from seeking or being considered for posts of higher responsibility.

Compared to the EU-28 average a very high difference exists when we look at the time spent by women caring for children and undertaking household tasks. This shows that despite educational attainment, women still serve traditional roles, with little assistance from men. There is also a gap in the number of graduates with a degree in humanities, where women show increased participation. It appears that despite the contemporary success of young women with university degrees, there is a global, distinct gap between the humanities and technology-based studies.

To bridge this gap, only recently the European Commission (EC) launched a campaign to promote increased participation of women and to reduce the gender gap, within the science, technology, engineering and maths (STEM) fields.

The only figure where Greece appears to be above the EU average is in life expectancy, partly due to the good weather and the Mediterranean lifestyle.

Summarising the above we can conclude that the main problem effecting women in Greece is the high unemployment rate, which is also a major problem for the whole population. Figure 3.1, taken from the 2014 report on equality prepared by the EC, shows the seriousness of the situation, with Greece lagging behind all remaining EU countries. It is evident that strong austerity measures and high taxation have led to that closing of many business firms and loss of jobs. Unless more funds are given to the economy, jobs will not be created and women's position will continue to deteriorate.

Table 3.3 Unemployment rate (%) by gender and educational level

Level of education	Unemployment					
	2014			2015		
	Males	*Females*	*Total*	*Males*	*Females*	*Total*
Total	*25.0*	*31.4*	*27.8*	*23.5*	*30.6*	*26.6*
Postgraduate studies, PhD	15.6	14.9	15.3	9.2	17.2	12.9
University	16.1	21.0	18.7	17.3	22.0	19.8
Tertiary vocational educational, post-secondary vocational education	23.8	35.0	29.2	22.6	31.9	27.2
Secondary education	26.8	37.2	31.1	24.4	36.7	29.3

Source: Hellenic Statistical Authority (2015)

Table 3.4 Indicators included in the Gender Equality Index for the year 2012

Indicators	Greece		EU-28	
	Women (%)	*Men (%)*	*Women (%)*	*Men (%)*
Full time equivalent employment (15+ population)	29.8	47.2	38.8	55.7
Employment of country nationals (15–64 corresponding population)	41.8	60.3	59.2	69.6
Duration of working life	27.8 years	36.0 years	32.2 years	37.6 years
Employed people in education, human health and social work activities (15–64 employed)	22.0	8.3	29.8	8.1
Graduates of tertiary education (15–74 population)	21.1	21.0	24.1	22.8
Tertiary students in the fields of education, health and welfare, humanities and arts	39.4	17.9	45.0	22.0
Workers doing cooking and housework, every day for one hour or more (15+ workers)	52.6	17.4	44.6	27.4
Workers caring for and educating their children or grandchildren every day for one hour or more (15+ workers)	77.8	9.3	77.1	27.0
Life expectancy in absolute value at birth	83.4	78.0	83.1	77.5

Source: European Institute for Gender Equality (2015)

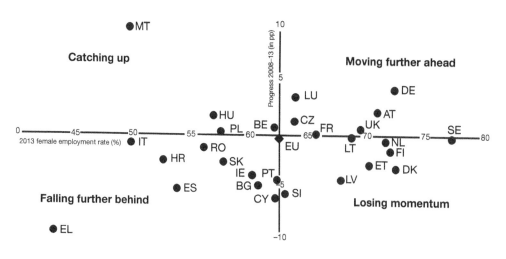

Figure 3.1 Women's employment rate in 2013 (%) and progress between 2008 and 2013
Source: Eurostat (2014)

Women in decision making

In Greece there have been several initiatives to promote women in decision making, including mandatory quotas and sets of recommendations but mainly in the state sector and in public life. Mandatory measures have aimed at areas controlled by the state where public interest is involved. Specifically, in order to promote women's participation in decision-making bodies since 2000, legislative measures took place aiming at the increase of female participation in politics and in state-appointed committees for research and technology. This legislation, which included a mandatory quota of a third for each gender, was necessary because women in Greece are still underrepresented in politics, in Parliament, in local government and in research bodies. At present, a third of the candidates on election lists for Parliament, local community representatives as well as a third of board members of public agencies and a third of members in promotion committees for administrative employees of ministries and state-controlled entities (universities, hospitals, public utilities etc.) have to be women.

With reference to participation in politics, as can be seen from Table 3.5, women's participation in the Greek Parliament has steadily increased since 2000.

However there is still a considerable gap from the EU-28, especially in ministerial positions. In 2014, only 5 per cent of active government members were women. This number rose to 15 per cent in the September 2015 government which includes 7 women within a total number of 46 ministerial posts. A good sign was the appointment in August 2015, for the first time in Greece, of a woman as interim prime minister for 20 days, who was responsible for preparing the country for the forthcoming elections. Top Supreme Court judge, Vassiliki Thanou, was appointed to this honorary post and this was considered as a very good step towards gender equality.

Figure 3.2 shows the situation in the EU with Greece (EL) holding one of the lowest percentages for women in the government though with a higher showing in Parliament.

Considering women's qualifications, better scores are feasible given the fact that over the past 20 years the percentage of women in higher and post-graduate education has increased considerably, having reached a point where more women than men are now holders of university degrees in the total population. Among people studying at present, women amount to 60 per cent of the student population at the undergraduate and 55 per cent at the graduate levels (Hellenic Statistical Authority, 2015).

However, women's careers in higher education and in research are characterised by strong vertical segregation, with only a very low proportion of women occupying the highest academic posts and the number of female researchers being still significantly lower than that of men (ELEGYP, 2012).

Table 3.5 Female participation in the Greek Parliament

Year	Total members	Women members	Percentage of women members
2000	300	31	10.3
2004	300	39	13.0
2007	300	48	16.0
2009	300	52	17.3
2014	300	63	21.0
2015	300	69	23.0

Source: General Secretariat for Gender Equality (2015)

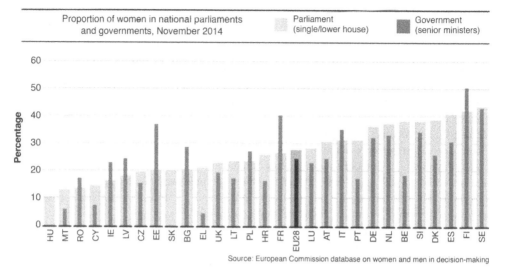

Figure 3.2 Proportion of women in national parliaments and governments, November 2014
Source: European Commission (2014)

An area where women's participation in higher-level jobs has increased spectacularly, without any particular measures, is public administration. Administrative jobs in the public sector is an area where entry systems favour women's participation since entry was as a rule through national exams and qualified women had many chances of gaining access. These women have gradually moved to higher positions. Furthermore, women show greater preference for the public sector where working conditions and tenure is in favour of a work–life balance. Table 3.6 shows women's participation in decision-making posts in the public sector.

A major issue concerning women in decision making is female participation in the boards of listed companies. The predominance of men in the boardroom is a reality worldwide. According to a 2014 report by Grant Thornton, companies with diverse executive teams outperform competitors run by men only. Their analysis suggests that the profit lost or opportunity cost by the companies with male-only boards is an impressive US$655 billion across the economies of the UK, USA and India. The impact of moving to mixed boards for companies on the S&P 500 and FTSE 350 could raise GDP by around 3 per cent (Grant Thornton, 2014).

The one third quota requirement for state-appointed positions on boards applies only to the state or semi-state sector in Greece and it has not reached private listed companies, where 8.9 per cent of board members were women in 2014 against an EU-28 average of 20.2 per cent (European Commission, 2014) (see Figure 3.3).

Table 3.6 Percentage of women in administrative posts (2012)

	Ministries	*State-owned companies*	*Local community organisations*
General directors	40.0	69.6	36.7
Directors	35.5	39.4	45.7
Department heads	46.4	76.3	44.0

Source: Ministry of Internal Affairs (2012)

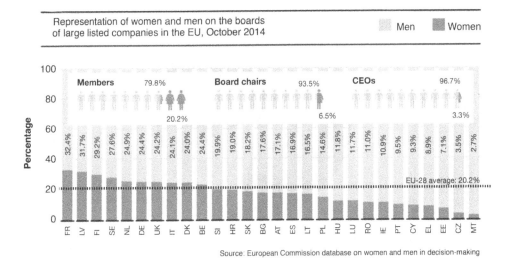

Figure 3.3 Representation of women and men on the boards of large listed companies in the EU, October 2014
Source: European Commission (2014)

According to these data France ranks first, with 32.4 per cent of women in board participation, closely followed by Latvia. Greece holds the twenty-fifth position, with Czech Republic and Malta holding the last positions. The 8.9 per cent Greek percentage of board membership is not necessarily a valid indication as many companies are family owned and female family members are offered seats without real decision-making power. Therefore this rate is even lower than it appears.

Women entrepreneurs

Women in Greece have been attracted to entrepreneurship due to the greater work flexibility it offers and the opportunity to fight unemployment (Petrakis-Kottis, 1996). Figure 3.4 shows the proportional distribution of employed persons in Greece by occupational status in 2015. The unpaid family workers are largely women. Entrepreneurs can be found both in the employers and the self-employed category.

According to a European survey (Ioannidis, 2007), 12 per cent of women in Greece had a business or were in the process of starting a new one. However 40 per cent of women engaged in entrepreneurial activity because they did not have other options. Also in many cases their companies belonged to men, mainly their husbands, who for various reasons had not registered their enterprises under their names.

According to Michaelidis (2012), women start their business not out of sheer opportunity but mainly driven by financial need or as a second or third profession. Many of them have experienced a considerable amount of dissatisfaction with their previous careers working for others, difficulty in combining professional and family life, and lately, loss of job. Most of them have high educational degrees. Once becoming business owners, women usually tend to be more satisfied and content with their personal and professional life. In addition, because of their previous careers, early retirement, etc., women entrepreneurs enter the business world later on in life, at around 40 to 60 years old. Their main problem is to achieve a life-work balance as sometimes they run their business from home.

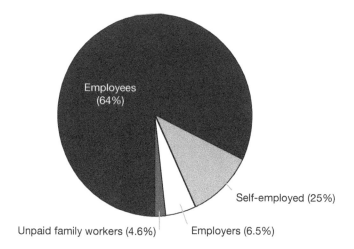

Figure 3.4 Proportional distribution of employed persons by occupational status, December 2015
Source: Hellenic Statistical Authority (2015)

Other problems women entrepreneurs face relate to the small size of their firms. Twenty-one per cent of female-owned firms do not have any employees and only 3 per cent employ between five and ten employees. This is due mainly to lack of funding, lack of role models, lack of networking and lack of entrepreneurial experience. An encouraging sign comes from startups, where more women (40.8 per cent) than men (30.4 per cent) are using innovation (Sarri and Trichopoulou, 2012).

In the recent past, various programmes to boost women's entrepreneurship have been proposed or implemented in higher education, in professional associations, in women's organisations and in state agencies responsible for gender equality. Apart from the major problem of providing funds these programmes include:

- Training for female entrepreneurship
- Use of successful women entrepreneurs as role models
- Work–life balance counselling
- Guidelines for reaching funding.

Emphasis is also given to young women's entrepreneurship, with annual contests taking place in universities or funding agencies, where the best business plans are selected and supported during their initial implementation stages. Young women students or young women graduates are strongly encouraged to participate in these contests, together with their male colleagues, and results so far show a strong interest on the part of young women (Papalexandris, 2015).

Initiatives supporting women in employment

As mentioned by Petrakis-Kottis and Ventoura (2011), the existing legislation for promoting gender equality is based on the State Constitution of 1975 and its 2001 revision. Being an EU member, Greece has included all rules and regulations for the promotion of gender equality in its legislation.

Various sets of recommendations and positive action programmes have been introduced under the initiative of the General Secretariat of Gender Equality and several non-governmental organisations. As described in the Seventh National Report of Greece to the United Nations Committee for the Elimination of Discrimination against Women, by the General Secretariat for Gender Equality (2011), most legislative measures taken for gender equality aim at assisting women facing difficult situations arising from having to raise their children alone, from having three or more children, falling victim to trafficking or intra-family violence, facing unemployment or needing extra time off from their job due to parental obligations. Such measures include extra pay or extra days of paid leave. Unfortunately at present, allowances for mothers of three or more children have been reduced and are even at risk due to the economic crisis.

In addition, certain initiatives have taken place mainly to sensitise public opinion in favour of increased women's participation in employment, decision making and entrepreneurship. Some examples of good practices are the following:

- The General Secretariat for Gender Equality has planned and implemented a National Programme for Gender Equality (2010–2013) with four strategic targets: protection of women's rights (especially for poor and underprivileged groups), prevention from various forms of violence against women, support for women's employment situation and support for promoting women in decision making. Although many steps have taken place, these targets have been partially met due to the financial crisis and the limited funds available for meeting them.
- The Center for Research in Gender Equality Issues has participated in several European and nationally funded programmes aiming at promoting women's participation in political, public and economic life in towns throughout Greece outside the capital Athens. The programmes included research on local problems, counselling sessions to promote employment and entrepreneurship, the organisation of conferences and published material, with best practices from other European countries. Also the Center has conducted an extensive programme throughout Greece to train high-school educators in promoting and applying gender equality in their teachings.
- Several Greek universities have established both undergraduate and post-graduate study programmes for equality issues and programmes for female entrepreneurship.
- Several Greek ministries (Ministry of National Defense, Ministry of Merchant Marine, Ministry of Education, Ministry of Tourism) have organised seminars against gender stereotyping and have introduced positive measures to encourage female students in applying for studies in traditionally male professions (i.e. the merchant marine).
- The Greek Association of University Women has organised seminars to encourage girls in secondary high schools to follow university studies in science and technology and for young women graduates to find employment or continue in post-graduate and doctoral studies. Furthermore online counselling services are offered to young women graduates to help them plan their career or seek employment.

Apart from the initiatives mentioned above, the question of women's participation in private economic decision making is at the centre of debate by university researchers in business schools, by associations of managers and by large corporations under their programmes of diversity or social corporate responsibility.

In the Athens University of Economics and Business, books and papers have been published in relevant journals showing among others the limited percentage of women in top jobs and ways to overcome existing obstacles (Vakola and Apospori, 2007).

The problem of the glass ceiling facing women managers as well as the issue of attitudes towards women in management and differences between the two genders in leadership, supervisory and decision-making styles have been subjects of academic research over the years (Papalexandris and Bourantas, 1990, 1991; Galanaki *et al.*, 2007). Results have shown an improvement in attitudes towards women in management and an improved rate of acceptance. However many respondents believe that women are not very interested in becoming leaders. Research has also shown that respondents who have experience with women top managers are more favourably disposed as they are no longer influenced by stereotypes about women's inability to serve in top jobs (Galanaki *et al.*, 2009).

With reference to women's leadership style it was found that it is more dependent on their individual personality than their gender, and acceptance by their subordinates is not influenced by gender as it has to do with various behavioural traits that are equally distributed between the two genders (Papalexandris and Galanaki, 2014). All these findings have been discussed extensively in women's conferences, managers' forums and various events organised by women professionals, where young female leaders are asked to talk about their careers and serve as role models.

An encouraging sign is the fact that, despite the low percentage of women top managers, a considerable percentage of middle managers or department heads in private corporations are women, especially in the functions of human resource management, marketing, communications, public relations and advertising. Lower percentages are found in finance and information technology departments, something that is also common among corporations across Europe. A desirable goal is to support talented women in middle management to apply for promotion when the opportunity comes as often women lack the self-confidence to move ahead.

The general awareness created by research and other activities has produced some encouraging results, especially among larger corporations. Policies favouring family–work balance, diversity, corporate social responsibility and positive measures for women's advancement in the corporate hierarchy are now in use. Company bosses believe that in order to promote their company's reputation and improve their image as a good employer, an ethical business partner and a good corporate citizen, they should deal with women's participation in higher jobs.

Many large and medium-sized companies take part in various annual prizes such as 'Best Workplace', 'European Foundation of Quality Management', 'Investors in People' and 'Business Ethics Network', where they receive awards for policies and practices favouring women's participation in economic decision making. These contests help in an indirect way to promote equality and sensitise corporate members about the potential benefits of female leadership.

With reference to participation in boards of listed companies, as is well known, Vivien Redding, the EU's Justice Commissioner, proposed in November 2012 a directive setting as a minimum objective 40 per cent of the underrepresented sex in non-executive board member positions by 2020. France, Italy and Belgium have enacted fully fledged quota legislation with sanctions. The Netherlands and Spain have passed laws without sanctions but with recommendations for a 'comply or explain' approach. In other countries voluntary targets have been set.

As already mentioned, in Greece quotas can be imposed in the public sphere, as is the case with a third of candidates for national and local community elections being women. This, however, does not mean that the persons actually elected follow these quotas and there has been serious criticism against imposing quotas. Reality has shown that laws and regulations cannot necessarily change the existing situation. For instance, the one third quota imposed by law for state-appointed members of scientific committees for research in science and technology has not yet been implemented, with the excuse that not enough women have the appropriate expertise to occupy such posts. We can assume that state officials responsible for appointing members are very reluctant to enforce the quota that would mean leaving out some well-established men scientists. Given the experience from the public sector, we can conclude that quotas in the private sector hardly have any chance for success. It appears that inviting corporations to commit themselves on a voluntary basis to gender diversity and women's participation on supervisory boards could work better. At present there is a commitment by large companies listed in the Athens Stock Exchange under guidelines by the Council for Corporate Governance to promote gender equality but also to improve talent management, pay transparency and change in the workplace for better corporate effectiveness. Listed companies are encouraged to apply the 'comply or explain' approach by monitoring and reporting their progress.

The future

Women's position in Greece is highly dependent on the economic situation. Unemployment, poverty and lack of opportunity are unfortunately evident for both genders and these conditions further increase the gender gap. Women, however, are contributing a lot in overcoming the present crisis in ways such as: supporting their family and all their dependents, starting small businesses and pursuing higher education and working to improve their qualifications.

According to the chief executive officer of a major opinion polling company in Greece (Mavros, 2015), the economic crisis has strengthened the role of women in Greek society. Women participate more in family, political or social decisions and they have a stronger voice in proposing solutions to the existing situation.

We believe that when the present economic crisis is over, women will face a smaller gender gap. The following give us room for hope:

- Various legislative measures have updated the existing legal framework for women's rights.
- The improved level of education and professional skills of younger women is actually equal or even higher to that of men.
- There is growing awareness about women's capabilities and an increased rate of positive attitudes towards women as decision makers.
- There is an improved level of self-confidence among women and an awareness among women of their need to realise their full potential and seek positions with higher responsibility or engage in entrepreneurial activities.
- Programmes are already in action by large companies to promote diversity and women's participation in executive and supervisory boards.
- Women's involvement in university and educational institution programmes is raising awareness about gender equality and demonstrating the benefits of increased women's involvement.

To conclude, we believe that there is positive growing belief among members of Greek society that in order to meet and exit from the existing crisis, all existing talent available must be utilised. It seems that people in leading posts have realised that no talent can be spared in politics, in business, in science and in administration. Talent is equally distributed between the two genders. By mobilising all available talent, women can prove to be the driving force for fighting the crisis and establishing gender equality.

References

Busch, K., Hermann, C., Hinrichs, K. and Schulten, T. (2013). *Euro Crisis, Austerity Policy and the European Social Model. How Crisis Policies in Southern Europe Threaten the EU's Social Dimension.* Friedrich-Ebert-Stiftung International Policy Analysis.

ELEGYP (Greek Association of University Women) (2012). *Women in Greek Academic Institutions, Research Study*, ELEGYP, Athens.

European Commission (2014). *Report on Equality between Women and Men*, EC.

European Institute for Gender Equality (2015). Gender Equality Index.

European Parliament (2015). Committee on Women's Rights and Gender Equality. European Parliament.

Eurostat (2009). *Europe in Figures: Eurostat Yearbook 2009*, Eurostat.

Eurostat (2014). *Labour Force Survey*, Eurostat.

Galanaki, E., Papalexandris, N. and Bourantas D. (2007). Acceptance and leadership style of women managers in Greece. In M. Vakola and E. Apospori (eds), *Women and Management*, Sideris.

Galanaki, E., Papalexandris, N. and Chalikias J. (2009). Revisiting leadership styles and attitudes towards women as managers in Greece: 15 years later, *Gender in Management: An International Journal*, Vol. 24, Numbers 7 and 8.

General Secretariat for Gender Equality (2011). *Seventh National Report of Greece to the United Nations Committee, Athens.* General Secretariat for Gender Equality.

General Secretariat for Gender Equality (2015). *Information Bulletin.* General Secretariat for Gender Equality.

Grant Thorton (2014). *Women in Business: The value of diversity.* Grant Thornton.

Greek League for Women's Rights Journal (2014). Issue 91.

Hellenic Statistical Authority (2015). *Labour Force Survey.* Hellenic Statistical Authority.

Ioannidis, S. (2007). *Women Entrepreneurs in Greece.* Institute of Economic and Industrial Studies.

Mavros, D. (2015). Women's role in the Greek economic crisis, in *Women Managers' Bulletin*, Greek Management Association.

Michailidis A. (2012). *Reflections on Women in Entrepreneurship and ICT.* Militos Emerging Technologies & Services,.

Ministry of Internal Affairs (2012). Statistical bulletins. Ministry of Internal Affairs.

OECD (Organization for Economic Co-operation and Development) (2012). *Greece, Key Facts–Education at a Glance 2012.* OECD.

Papalexandris, N. (2015). Women in Leadership. Paper presented at the 2nd Annual HR Minds Forum, Frankfurt, 29–30 January 2015.

Papalexandris, N. and Bourantas, D. (1990). Sex differences in leadership: Leadership styles and subordinate satisfaction, *Journal of Managerial Psychology*, Vol. 5, Number 4.

Papalexandris, N. and Bourantas, D. (1991). Attitudes towards women as managers: The case of Greece, *International Journal of Human Resource Management*, Vol. 2, Number 2.

Papalexandris, N. and Galanaki E. (2014). Does gender of employees influence their preference for leadership behaviors? An empirical study among firms in Greece. Paper presented at the 5th LAEMOS Colloquium 'Constructing Alternatives: How can we organize for alternative social, economic, and ecological balance?', Havana, Cuba, 2–5 April 2014.

Petrakis-Kottis, A. (1996). Women in management and the glass ceiling in Greece, *Women in Management*, Vol. 11, Number 2.

Petrakis-Kottis, A. and Ventoura, Z. (2011). Women in management in Greece. In M. Davidson and R.J. Burke (eds), *Women in Management Worldwide*, Gower Press.

Sarri K. and Trichopoulou A. (2012). *Greek Entrepreneurship: Approach to Greek reality*, Rossili Publishing House.

Stavrou-Costea, E. and Papalexandris, N. (2015). Mediterranean HRM: Key trends and challenges. In M. Dickmann, C. Brewster and P. Sparrow (eds), *International HRM: Contemporary issues in Europe* (3rd edition), Edward Elgar Publishers.

Vakola, M. and Apospori, E. (eds) (2007). *Women and Management: Obstacles, Myths and Expectations*, Sideris.

World Bank (2009). *Global Development Finance 2009: Outlook Summary*, World Bank.

4 Women in management in the Netherlands

Kea G. Tijdens

Introduction

This chapter highlights the current labor force characteristics in the Netherlands, including an overview of the changes over the past 10 to 20 years. It extends the conclusions of a similar chapter for the 1970s and 1980s, for the 1990s and for the early 2000s (Tijdens, 1993; 2004; 2011). First, this chapter details the labor force characteristics of women, followed by a review of women pursuing education, and the focus then changes to women in management. This broad category is sub-divided into women in managerial occupations, women in supervisory jobs, women on corporate boards of directors, and women holding elected offices in local and national government. The following section draws attention to women entrepreneurs, notably self-employed women, assisting members of the family, and professional women. The final sections highlight legislation in the Netherlands, the initiatives to support the advancement of women, and predictions about the future.

Labor force characteristics

During the post-war period, Dutch women were supposed to contribute to the rebuilding of society by starting a family. Many of them did, as the baby boom in the late 1940s and early 1950s shows. Women overwhelmingly left the labor market on the day of their marriage to become full-time, permanent housewives. The breadwinner system was firmly established in industrial relations and in wage policies, as well as in general attitudes towards gender roles. Male workers were supposed to earn a family wage in a 48-hour working week, and nearly all men were able to do so, thanks to a non-dispersed wage distribution. Women spent on average far more than a 48-hour week on their household chores. In this period, women's paid work was predominantly girls' labour (Pott-Buter and Tijdens, 1998).

Due to a steady decline in household time due to improved household appliances, new materials, and better housing, due to increasing education levels, and due to the growth of the service sector at the cost of the agricultural and manufacturing industries, women's participation rates have grown, particularly since the 1970s (Tijdens, 2006). Prime-age women became predominantly the core of the female labor force. Female participation rates in the age group 15–64 grew from 34 percent in 1982 to 62 percent in 2003 to 68 percent in 2014.[1]

The Netherlands is well known for the highest part-time rate of female workers in the European Union (Portegijs and Keuzenkamp, 2008). In 2003, almost 46 percent of the working women had a 20–34 hours' job. Eleven years later, in 2014, this had increased to 51 percent. In the same period, the share of women in jobs of less than 20 hours has decreased from 33 to 28 percent, whereas the share of women in jobs of 35 hours and over remained stable at 21 percent.[2] The more children women have, the more likely they are to work in a part-time job or to have no paid job (CBS, 2009a).

Part-time jobs facilitate the reconciliation of work and family life, once women have started or anticipate starting a family of their own. In the past decades, the Netherlands has opted for regulating and equalizing part-time employment as a main strategy for policies concerning reconciliation of work and family life (Pott-Buter and Tijdens, 1998). These policies have influenced employers, as they tend to set the starting and finishing times of work and they have transferred the prerogative of the number of working hours to the employee. Taken into account the very high percentages of part-timers, the Netherlands is unique in Europe, both with respect to women's and to men's labour.

The part-time employment policies consist of three options. First, employees' legal right to adjust their own working hours. Second, working hours can be adjusted in one's own job, and therefore do not imply any job changes. Third, all discriminatory clauses based on working hours have been removed. These policies are integrated in both national legislation and regulation, and collective bargaining (Pott-Buter and Tijdens, 1998). Over the years, these policies have largely prevented part-time jobs from marginalization and in general, part-time jobs of more than 12 hours per week do not differ greatly from full-time jobs with respect to hourly wages and other working conditions. For the large majority of households, an income based on one full-time and one part-time working partner is sufficient for a decent living. The average working week of women living in a couple with minors is 24.4 and that of men 40.2 hours (Merens and Van den Brakel, 2014).

Although husbands' and wives' working hours are not equal, their leisure time is. According to Merens and Hermans (2008) women's total working and household hours are converging over time, and were, in 2005, one hour less than that of men's. The Netherlands is the only country in the European Union where women have as much leisure time as men. In all other European countries, men have more leisure time than women (Breedveld and Van den Broek, 2001). In addition, partly because of the opportunities to adjust working hours, women increasingly have a continuous working career (Portegijs and Keuzenkamp, 2008).

Women pursuing education

During the twentieth century, participation rates in education grew steadily, the boys mostly a step ahead of the girls. In 1950, almost 70 percent of boys aged 14 and 15 were in full-time education, as opposed to 60 percent of girls. It was not until 1975 that girls closed this gap with almost 100 percent of the boys and girls in this age group being in full-time education (Pott-Buter and Tijdens, 1998). Similar patterns can be seen for older girls and boys and by 1985, 17-year-old girls had closed the gap with participation rates of nearly 90 percent. By 2006, girls' overall education attainments were generally better than those of boys.[3]

Although increasingly females are opting for subjects and disciplines that have traditionally been a male preserve, gender-based differences in subject choices still remain (Pott-Buter and Tijdens, 1998). In particular, few males choose traditionally female educational courses, although in the 2000s the gender segregated patterns are slowly decreasing (Merens and Van den Brakel, 2014). In secondary education, boys are much more likely to opt for subjects in science, chemistry and advanced maths, whereas girls are still more likely to choose French language, German language and biology. With regard to subjects such as economics or introductory maths, the gender gap is small. Yet, the share of women in the male-dominated science, technology, engineering and mathematics (STEM) subjects is slowly increasing, from 11 percent in 2003/04 to 18 percent in 2013/14 (Merens and Van den Brakel, 2014). In universities, most studies have kept constant their sex typing over time, but some faculties have not and it is interesting to note that subject areas such as medicine, law and psychology have faced a feminization.[4] Women's share among the STEM subjects is slowly increasing, from 20 percent in 2003/04 to 26 percent in 2013/14 (Merens and Van den Brakel, 2014).

In 2013, 32 percent of women aged 25 to 65 years had at least a higher education level compared to 34 percent of men (Merens and Van den Brakel, 2014). In the 35–44 age group men and women have virtually the same level of education, but in the younger age groups women have higher educational levels than do men.[5] Perhaps not surprisingly, compared to higher-educated women, lower-educated women are more likely to choose being a homemaker as a career (Portegijs and Keuzenkamp, 2008). As well, non-western ethnic minorities are clearly less educated than indigenous persons, and this gap rises with age. However, among the non-western ethnic minorities aged under 35, women are comparatively better educated than men, whereas the reverse holds for those aged over 35 years.[6] Generally speaking the labor market prospects for training courses predominantly taken by girls are good, although many of these courses offer few career opportunities and are generally not as well paid. More men than women take part in education at a later age. Furthermore, the men are more often concerned with obtaining professional qualifications (Merens and Hermans, 2008).

Women in management

In this section, the focus is firstly on women in managerial positions. Table 4.1 reveals that both the number of men and the number of women in managerial positions has increased from 2003 to 2014. Here, managerial positions are defined as managerial occupational groups.[7] Expressed as a percentage of the male and female workforce, however, the share in managerial positions has slightly decreased over time from 9.9 to 9.0 percent for the males and from 3.9 to 3.6 percent for the females.

Table 4.1 Labor force and managerial positions for men and women, 2003–2014

	Labor force (men)	Labor force (women)	Labor force total	Women (%)	Managers (men)	Managers (women)	Male managers in male labor force (%)	Female managers in female labor force (%)
	x 1000	x 1000	x 1000		x 1000	x 1000		
2003	4399	3384	7783	43.5	434	131	9.9	3.9
2004	4360	3401	7761	43.8	352	112	8.1	3.3
2005	4375	3443	7818	44.0	337	99	7.7	2.9
2006	4421	3518	7939	44.3	369	119	8.3	3.4
2007	4520	3649	8169	44.7	394	137	8.7	3.8
2008	4599	3760	8359	45.0	410	148	8.9	3.9
2009	4569	3792	8361	45.4	415	157	9.1	4.1
2010	4492	3786	8278	45.7	425	176	9.5	4.6
2011	4466	3814	8280	46.1	395	160	8.8	4.2
2012	4488	3842	8330	46.1	379	152	8.4	4.0
2013	4444	3822	8266	46.2	409	132	9.2	3.5
2014	4442	3772	8214	45.9	401	134	9.0	3.6

Source: Statistics Netherlands, www.cbs.nl/statline, accessed 11.12.2015

Having a closer look at the characteristics of women in supervisory positions compared to men, the 2014 data of the WageIndicator web-survey present a detailed comparison of male and female supervisors, using multivariate analyses.[8] Regarding job characteristics, the two groups differed significantly with respect to their personal and household characteristics. The female supervisors were less likely to be living with a partner or having one or more children, compared to their male counterparts. Female supervisors are slightly younger than male supervisors (35 versus 38 years of age). The female supervisors were far less likely to work long hours (35 versus 43 hours per week). They had on average a slightly higher education level than the male supervisors. In terms of pay, females' hourly earnings were almost a quarter less than males. They supervised fewer employees (12 versus 20 employees) and they worked in smaller companies. The largest differences, however, were found with regard to segregation by gender. The supervisors in female-dominated firms (80–100 percent females) were very likely to be women, and the supervisors in male-dominated firms (0–20 percent females) were even more likely to be men. Compared to their male counterparts, female supervisors were twice as likely to be in work environments where most of their colleagues in similar positions were women (34 percent of female supervisors report that co-workers are predominantly male versus 84 percent of male supervisors). Therefore, these data point to the continued existence of gendered structures in organizations in relation to supervisory positions.

Turning our attention to the elite network of the stock exchange, it still firmly remains an "old boys network," but women are more present than ever before. The proportion of women on boards in the top companies has slightly increased in the past decade. In 1999, there were no women on the boards of executive directors of the 25 largest companies quoted at the stock exchange, but in 2009 it had increased to 5.6 percent (Sociaal en Cultureel Planbureau en Opportunity in Bedrijf, 2011). Moreover, the gender composition of the board of governors in these companies increased from 8.1 percent to 14.4 percent during this time period.

When it comes to women holding elected offices in national government, women's share in Parliament grew steadily up from one-quarter in the 1980s to one-third in the 1990s (Merens and Hermans, 2008). In 2012, it had further increased to 39 percent.[9] The percentage of female mayors also shows an upward movement since the 1980s, rising steadily from 4 percent in 1984 to 19 percent 25 years later (Merens and Hermans, 2008). In 2014, 22 percent of all Dutch mayors were female.[10]

A study explaining the share of women in managerial, higher academic, and elected positions showed a strong relationship between women's labor force participation rates and their share in elected positions in 15 European countries (De Wilde, 2007). Nevertheless, hardly any correlation was shown regarding women's participation rates and their share in managerial and higher academic positions. Presumably, more factors than women's participation rates only are at stake when explaining women's advancement in management across countries (De Wilde, 2007).

Although the Netherlands has no legislation on quotas, and contract compliance is rarely included in equal opportunities programs, during the 1990s there was definitely increasing government pressure and policies towards stimulating women's participation in decision-making bodies. However, this pressure became less intense in the 2000s. Nevertheless, there appears to be a growing awareness in the electorate for supporting female candidates and the majority of the political parties are aware of the importance of having women on their list of candidates (Leyenaar, 2007).

Women entrepreneurs

The category of female entrepreneurs ranges from freelancers, who have no employees, to managers or owners of large companies, employing tens of thousands of employees. In our review of women entrepreneurs, we utilized data from Statistics Netherlands.[11] In 1992, the self-employed working at least 12 hours a week in their business totalled 627,000 individuals, of which 28 percent were female. In 2008, the number had increased to 982,000, and the share of women amounted to 31 percent. In 2014, the number had increased further to 1,138,000 individuals, of which 33 percent were women (Merens and Van den Brakel, 2014). Compared to men, women more often have a single-person company. Their companies typically offer services such as beautician, care worker, translator or business consultant, or they may offer products, for example through web shops. Women more often perceive their success rate of establishing entrepreneurial activities lower than men do, they are more often afraid of failures and they often think that they do not possess the right skills for these activities. Both self-employed women and men are slightly older compared to the employed. It may be that they perceive better opportunities due to longer work experience, but it may also be the case that they perceive fewer opportunities for finding a new job in case they are dismissed. Research shows that the latter assumption is hardly relevant for the Netherlands (Bosch *et al.*, 2012). Until 2012 only 6 percent of the female self-employed and 9 percent of the male self-employed had started their enterprise because they were unable to find a job or other income-generating activities. Hence, the vast majority of self-employed do so from free will (Kelly *et al.*, 2013). It may be the case that in recent years this share has decreased due to the economic crisis but unfortunately no recent figures are available.

Compared to women in wage employment, self-employed women more often live with a partner and more often have children (Merens and Van den Brakel, 2014). A better work–life balance is a frequently mentioned argument for women to start their own company. The female self-employed more often work part-time hours compared to their male counterparts. In the 2000s, however, the share of female entrepreneurs working part time has not increased. In 2003 62 percent of them worked part time and in 2014 this had decreased to 58 percent.[12]

When it comes to women assisting members of the family in running their own business, the focus traditionally is primarily on the agricultural sector (Pott-Buter and Tijdens, 1998). However, in the 2000s, their numbers have shown a sharp decline. In 2003 the Dutch labor force included 38,000 female assisting members, but in 2014 their numbers had declined to 30,000. The share of part-time workers in this group has increased from 71 percent to 78 percent, indicating an even steeper decline of this group.[13]

Country legislation

The feminist and women's movement in the late 1960s and early 1970s made it very clear that government needed to respond to changes in society, particularly women's demands not to spend their whole adult life as housewives and to attain equal rights. In 1974, an Equal Opportunities Commission was set up as an advisory body and since 1978 the government has made funds available to stimulate equal rights policy throughout society. Subsequently other measures were to follow, which were increasingly aimed at women in paid employment.[14] In legislation, the issue of reconciling work and family life has received substantial attention throughout the 1980s, 1990s, 2000s, and 2010s. A few of the major policies will be summarized here.

In the Netherlands, maternity leave is 16 weeks and a 100 percent replacement rate applies, paid according to the Sickness Benefits Act.[15] Self-employed women are entitled to paid maternity leave, though here conditions of insurance apply.[16] The Parental Leave Act entitles both women and men in waged employment to unpaid parental leave of 26 weeks of leave each, though in some collective agreements clauses for payment during leave apply.[17] The leave arrangements are not transferable between parents.

Women's rising participation rates in paid employment, particularly of women with young children, have caused a growing demand for day care (Pott-Buter and Tijdens, 1998). From the 1970s onwards, the state used to finance playgroups for children aged from 2–4 years, where they could play for a few hours a day. During the 1980s, regardless of the severe pressure from women's organizations, trade unions, tripartite bodies and others, the government retained its view that the care for children was solely the parents' responsibility. It was expected that private day care centers would come into being, because the demand for child care was estimated to be high. However, this did not happen as only a small minority of couples could afford the high child care costs (Tijdens and Lieon, 1993). It was not until 1989 that the government changed its view and decided to subsidize child care, under the condition that both employers and parents took part in the costs. A substantial increase in day care facilities followed. The capacity of child care facilities, and especially out-of-school child care, increased further in the 2000s, although it is still the more highly educated women who predominantly use formal child care, with the middle- and less-educated women relying on informal child care such as relatives (CBS, 2009b). In 2012 government subsidies for child care decreased, as did the number of children in day care, predominantly because of parents' rising child care costs (Portegijs *et al.*, 2014). Parents, and particularly mothers, reduced their number of working hours to be able to care more for their children or, to a lesser extent, grandparents substituted formal child care arrangements.

As far back as 1951, the International Labour Organization (ILO) agreed on equal pay for equal work for male and female employees. Typical of the Netherlands, the government did not take action until the social partners had agreed upon the principle, which took more than two decades. In 1971, when all wage inequality had been removed from collective agreements, the government ratified the ILO convention and in 1975 Parliament passed the Equal Pay Act. In 1976 and 1980, the Equal Pay Act was followed by two acts prescribing equal treatment at work in the public and private sectors. According to these laws, women as well as men, be it individually or as a group, can submit complaints to the Equal Treatment Commission if they believe they have been treated unfairly at work or paid unequally. The 1975 legislation on equal pay and the 1980 legislation on equality were integrated into the 1994 legislation on equal treatment. However, in the 2000s, it became clear that equal pay legislation would not solve the gender wage gap, which by 2005 was still 18.3 percent according to Statistics Netherlands, and the government changed its policy towards raising awareness rather than improving legislation (Van Klaveren *et al.*, 2007). In a reply to questions from members of parliament, the minister of social affairs said that he would continue to support awareness raising activities, such as websites and campaigns.[18]

Initiatives supporting women in the workforce

In this section, attention is drawn to three initiatives to support the advancement of women in employment. By 1995, the Ministry of Home Affairs established a national information center on positive action to consult with municipalities, provinces and water control boards for advice. By then, 30 percent of all employees in central government had to be female. The center developed into E-Quality, a knowledge center for gender, family, and diversity issues. It collects and analyses facts, figures, research data, and practical examples for advising governments, politicians, and public organizations. E-Quality aims at stimulating equal treatment, individual growth, and equal development of all people. In 2012 the center merged with an institute for women's history and the joint organization was renamed Atria.[19]

In 1983, female teachers and students of polytechnic schools set up a foundation to promote the advancement of women in technical studies, called VHTO, an abbreviation for the Dutch National Expert Organization on Girls/Women and Science/Technology. At that time only 1.7 percent of students were female. It was awarded a start-up subsidy to support counselling of these female students, in addition to encouraging girls into choosing technical education. VHTO also set up a network of women engineers. Over the years the foundation has become a center of expertise in the field of girls/women and science/technology/IT, focusing on the schooling system as well as on the labor market and the foundation has taken a wide range of initiatives to promote its aims.[20] VHTO has been building up knowledge and experience of the participation of girls and women in the world of science, technology and IT and deploying this expertise in areas such as education. In 2015, VHTO received a Google RISE Award for their DigiVita program to increase the participation of girls in computer science (CS). In the Netherlands girls and women are highly underrepresented in CS and IT jobs. The DigiVita program aims to increase the participation of girls in CS, encouraging girls aged 8–18 to code in extracurricular DigiVita code events.

In 1996 Opportunity in Bedrijf[21] (OIB) was established. It was shaped after the UK's Opportunity 2000 that in 1991 was launched by a business association and backed by the prime minister. Although originally initiated by the Ministry of Social Affairs and Employment, from the very beginning OIB was meant to become an independent consultancy, predominantly financed by the members' fees. An increasing number of firms, particularly large firms, joined OIB.[22] It has developed into a national network of businesses and organizations that aim towards a balanced workforce and as a center of expertise for its members.[23] OIB initiated a private consultancy, Opportunity Advies, aiming to support organizations to promote talented women's careers and to arrive at a more gender-balanced middle and senior management.

The future

This chapter on women in management in the Netherlands has shown the dynamics in the female workforce over the past decades. Prominent findings include the rapid increase in female participation rates in the workforce, the decrease of homemaker careers among young women, the huge increase and acceptance of part-time employment (the highest in Europe), and the slowly rising share of women in managerial and entrepreneurial positions. Nevertheless, the chapter also highlights that when it comes to the highest hierarchical levels and to senior decision-making positions, women's progress has been very slow and there is still a long way to go.

It is also evident that, in the Netherlands, there is still massive gender segregation in the workplace. Both self-selection by potential employees and selection by the organization play a role in a continuation of a masculine organizational culture, particularly in senior managerial positions. As regards future developments, women's increased participation in the labor force and women's increasing purchasing power may force male-dominated organizations with predominantly masculine organizational cultures to adopt feminine values.

In general, segregation by gender is assumed to have a large impact on women's careers. Even in female-dominated occupations, proportionally men still dominate senior positions and the majority of female supervisors are supervised by males. In the future it is more likely that this hierarchical gender balance will be changed more in female-dominated organizations than in male-dominated ones. This may lead to better career possibilities for women in these female-dominated organizations. However, breaking through the thick walls in male-dominated organizations will definitely require more time, and more effort. To conclude, gendered organizational structures and career structures are quite likely mutually interlocked. Further research is necessary on how gendered organizational structures coincide with unequal attributions of power, including, for example, the allocation of budgets, internal career opportunities, managerial commitment, authority, and contacts within and outside the organization.

Notes

1   See www.cbs.nl/statline, Centraal Bureau voor de Statistiek, Den Haag/Heerlen, accessed 11.12. 2015.
2   See www.cbs.nl/statline, Centraal Bureau voor de Statistiek, Den Haag/Heerlen, accessed 11.12. 2015.
3   See www.cbs.nl/statline, Centraal Bureau voor de Statistiek, Den Haag/Heerlen, accessed 11.12. 2015.
4   See www.vsnu.nl/Universiteiten/Feiten-Cijfers/Onderwijs/Downloadbare-tabellen-onderwijs. htm, accessed 01.10.2009.
5   See www.cbs.nl/statline, Centraal Bureau voor de Statistiek, Den Haag/Heerlen, accessed 11.12.2015.
6   See www.cbs.nl/statline, Centraal Bureau voor de Statistiek, Den Haag/Heerlen, accessed 11.12. 2015.
7   These are codes 051 to 055 in the occupational classification scheme of Statistics Netherlands, including managing directors; managers in administrative and commercial services; production managers and specialized goods; managers of hospitality, retail and other services; and managers not specified.
8   Author's analyses on the dataset of www.wageindicator.org (English) or www.loonwijzer.nl (Dutch).
9   See www.allesoverdeverkiezingen.nl/daling-aantal-vrouwen-in-kamer/, accessed 11.12.2015.
10 See www.parlement.com/id/vh8lnhrr6zzm/vrouwelijke_burgemeesters , accessed 11.12.2015.
11 See www.cbs.nl/statline, Centraal Bureau voor de Statistiek, Den Haag/Heerlen, accessed 11.12.2015.
12 See www.cbs.nl/statline, Centraal Bureau voor de Statistiek, Den Haag/Heerlen, accessed 11.12.2015.
13 See www.cbs.nl/statline, Centraal Bureau voor de Statistiek, Den Haag/Heerlen, accessed 11.12.2015.
14 Stimuleringsregeling Positieve Actie, Tweede Kamer, 1987–1988, 20 343, nr. 1.
15 See www.rijksoverheid.nl/onderwerpen/zwangerschapsverlof-en-bevallingsverlof, accessed 11.12.2015.
16 See www.rijksoverheid.nl/actueel/nieuws/2008/05/29/zwangerschapsverlof-zelfstandigen-4-juni-van-start, accessed 11.12.2015.
17 See www.rijksoverheid.nl/onderwerpen/ouderschapsverlof, accessed 11.12.2015.
18 See file:///C:/Users/ACER/Documents/Downloads/beantwoording-kamervragen-over-het-bericht-dat-vrouwen-minder-verdienen-dan-mannen.pdf, accessed 11.12.2015.
19 See www.atria.nl/atria/content/318504/geschiedenis_e-quality, accessed 11.12.2015.
20 See www.vhto.nl/over-vhto/english/, accessed 11.12.2015.

21   Bedrijf is Dutch for "business."
22   See www.ambassadeursnetwerk.nl/images/stories/netwerkvijf/Inzicht%20Uitzicht%20OiB10jr_
Omslag%20DEF.pdf, accessed 11.12.2015.
23   See www.opportunity.nl/, accessed 11.12.2015.

References

Bosch, N., G. Roelofs, D. van Vuuren and M. Wilkens (2012) *De huidige en toekomstige groei van het aandeel zzp'ers in de werkzame beroepsbevolking [Current and future growth of the share of self-employed in the labour force]* (The Hague: Centraal Planbureau).

Breedveld, K. and Van den Broek, A. (2001) *Trends in de Tijd [Trends over Time]* (The Hague: Social Cultural Planning Office).

CBS (Central Bureau voor de Statistiek) (2009a) *Steeds meer Moeders met Grotere Deeltijdbaan [Growing Number of Mothers with Large Part-time Jobs]* (The Hague: Statistics Netherlands, Webmagazine).

CBS (2009b) *Hoogopgeleide Moeders Maken meer Gebruik van Kinderopvang dan Laagopgeleide Moeders [More Highly Educated Mothers use Childcare Facilities More Often than Less Educated Mothers]* (The Hague: Statistics Netherlands, Webmagazine).

De Wilde, L. (2007) De Weg Naar de Top! Een Onderzoek naar Vrouwen in Topposities in EU15 [The Road to the Top! A Study on Women in Higher Level Jobs in 15 Countries of the European Union] (Rotterdam: Master Thesis Sociology, Erasmus University, Rotterdam).

Kelly, D. J., Brush, C. G., Greene, P. G., Litovsky, Y. and Global Entrepreneurship Research Association (GERA) (2013) *Global Entrepreneurship Monitor 2012; Women's Report*. Accessed at: www.gemconsortium.org/report.

Leyenaar, M. (2007) De Last van Ruggespraak [The Trouble with Feedback] (Inaugural lecture, Nijmegen: Radboud Universiteit).

Merens, A. and Hermans, B. (eds) (2008) *Emancipatiemonitor 2008 [Monitoring Women's Progress 2008]* (The Hague: Social Cultural Planning Office and Statistics Netherlands).

Merens, A. and Van den Brakel, M. (eds) (2014) *Emancipatiemonitor 2014 [Monitoring Women's Progress 2014]*. (The Hague: Social Cultural Planning Office and Statistics Netherlands).

Portegijs, W. and Keuzenkamp, S. (2008) *Nederland Deeltijdland. Vrouwen en Deeltijdwerk [The Netherlands is a Part-time Country. Women and Part-time Jobs]* (The Hague: Social Cultural Planning Office).

Portegijs, W., Cloïn, M. and Merens, A. (2014) *Krimp in de kinderopvang. Ouders over kinderopvang en werk [Shrinkage in childcare. Parents on childcare and work]* (The Hague: Social Cultural Planning Office).

Pott-Buter, H. A. and Tijdens, K. G. (1998) *Vrouwen, Leven en Werk in de Twintigste Eeuw [Women, Their Lives and Work in the Twentieth Century]* (Amsterdam: Amsterdam University Press).

Sociaal en Cultureel Planbureau en Opportunity in Bedrijf (2011) *De Feiten: Toptelling v/m 2011 [The Facts: Topcount F / M 2011]* (The Hague: Sociaal en Cultureel Planbureau en Opportunity in Bedrijf).

Tijdens, K. G. (1993) Women in business and management – The Netherlands. In M. J. Davidson and C. L. Cooper (eds) *European Women in Business and Management* (London, UK: Paul Chapman Publishing, pp. 79–92).

Tijdens, K. G. (2004) Women in management – the Netherlands. In M. J. Davidson and Burke, R. J. (eds) *Women in Management Worldwide* (Aldershot, UK: Ashgate Publishing, pp. 68–82).

Tijdens, K. G. (2006) Een Wereld van Verschil: Arbeidsparticipatie van Vrouwen 1945–2005 [A World of Differences: Women's Labour Participation Rates 1945–2005] (Inaugural lecture, Erasmus University, Rotterdam).

Tijdens, K. G. (2011) Women in management in the Netherlands. In Davidson, M. and Burke, R. J. (eds) *Women in Management Worldwide, Progress and Prospects* (Aldershot, UK: Ashgate Publishing, pp. 55–68).

Tijdens, K. G. and Lieon, S. (1993) *Kinderopvang in Nederland. Organisatie en Financiering [Childcare in the Netherlands Organisation and Finances]* (Utrecht: Jan van Arkel).

Van Klaveren, M., Sprenger, W. and Tijdens, K. G. (2007) *Dicht de Loonkloof! Verslag van het CLOSE (Correctie LOonkloof in SEctoren) Onderzoek voor de FNV, ABVAKABO FNV en FNV Bondgenoten [Close the Gender Pay Gap. Report of the CLOSE Project. Research fot the FNV, ABVAKABO FNV and FNV Bondgenoten]* (Eindhoven/Amsterdam: STZ Advies & Onderzoek/Universiteit van Amsterdam).

5 Women in management in Portugal

Carlos Cabral-Cardoso

Women in Portugal are now the best-educated segment of the labour force and the majority of the members in many professions. In terms of managerial positions in general, women remain below the one-third threshold. When it comes to the very top management positions and despite some recent progress, women's representation is still at the 10 per cent level. This chapter examines the situation of women in the labour force and reflects on recent developments and challenges to women's access to management positions in Portugal.

The major statistical sources used to describe the characteristics of the Portuguese labour force were the Office for National Statistics (INE, 2015) and Pordata (2015), a database organised and developed by the Francisco Manuel dos Santos Foundation. The latter also includes a wide range of European sources that allow for a comparative analysis between Portugal and other European countries. Unless otherwise stated, the data referred to were collected from either INE or Pordata sources and refer to the year 2014. Whenever relevant, current figures and percentages are compared to similar indicators from previous years (sometimes from previous decades) to illustrate the dynamics of those indicators and provide a better understanding of what has been changing in Portuguese society. Besides these two comprehensive databases, other sources of statistical information used were the general indicators in education, from the Ministry of Education and Science (DGEEC, 2015), Eurostat (2015) and the International Labour Organization (ILO, 2015). Both Eurostat and ILO sources were mainly used for comparative purposes. Other institutions such as the Commission for Equality in Labour and Employment (CITE) also provided useful information about the situation of men and women in the Portuguese labour market. Different coding and methodologies adopted by the various sources do not always make the comparisons meaningful but, taken together, they contribute to depict an accurate picture of the situation in Portugal.

Social and demographic changes

In 2014, and according to the Pordata (2015) dataset, the resident population in Portugal was about 10.4 million, of whom about 5.5 million (52.5 per cent) were women. The major demographic change in recent decades was the considerable increase in the size and proportion of the elderly population, due to the combined effect of a significant decline in fertility and an increase in life expectancy. The total fertility rate has been declining since the 1960s to reach only 1.23 in 2014 (2.25 in 1980). Since the year 2000, the total fertility rate has been consistently below 1.50 and in 2013 it reached 1.21, the lowest rate in Europe in that year. As a result of persistent low fertility indicators, the 'under 15 years of age' group reached about 1.5 million individuals in 2014 (14.5 per cent of the resident population), which compares to over 2.5 million in 1980 (25.8 per cent of the resident population). At the other extreme of the age distribution, the 'over 65' group has grown to over 2 million in 2014 (20.1 per cent of the resident population), which compares to only about 1.1 million in 1980 (11.3 per cent of the resident population). Life expectancy at birth in 2013 was 80.2 (77.2 for men, 83 for women).

The social relevance of these demographic changes is best illustrated by the old-age dependency ratio, that is, the ratio of the number of individuals aged 65 and over, generally economically inactive, to the number of individuals of working age (15 to 64 years old). The old-age dependency ratio that was 18 per cent in 1980 has since then climbed to an all-time high of 30.7 per cent in 2014. Comparing to the other 28 EU countries (2013 figures), the Portuguese old-age dependency ratio (29.9) was the fifth highest, only below Italy (32.9), Germany (31.4), Greece (31.2) and Sweden (30.2).

The ageing of the population has significant economic and social implications. And due to gender differences in life expectancy, the ageing of the population means there is a growing proportion of women in the population, particularly among the elderly. The sex ratio (number of males per 100 females) in Portugal was only 90.5 in 2014. In 2013, only the Baltic countries had lower sex ratios: Estonia (87.6), Lithuania (85.4) and Latvia (84.5). When age groups are considered, gender balance is only achieved in the 'below 30 years of age' group. In the '30 to 34 years' group the ratio drops to 94.7, and continues to decline gradually to reach 90.1 in the '55 to 59 age' group. Above that age, the sex ratio declines steadily: 83.2 at the retirement age (65 to 69 years of age) and down to 46.2 in the '85 or more' age group.

Other indicators with employment and gender equality implications are related to the provision of childcare. Childcare remains to a large extent women's responsibility, despite the growing involvement of men. In fact, women were in 2014 more than eight times more likely than men to be beneficiaries of leave for the care of children, provided by social security. Excluding parental leave after birth (a statutory requirement), 86.5 per cent of employed women claimed in 2010 they never benefited from workload reductions to look after their children (CITE, 2014). And only 17.0 per cent of women admitted in the same survey to have interrupted their careers for at least one month for childcare reasons (excluding parental leave after birth), against 2.8 per cent of men who claimed to have done that, a difference that illustrates the persistent gender gap in childcare provision. And yet, the CITE (2014) report acknowledges the growing proportion of men benefiting from parental leave after birth, a benefit that the father and the mother can share to some extent. In 2013, 28.3 per cent of fathers with an employee status shared parental leave after birth with the mothers, up from 0.5 per cent in 2005, which is a remarkable social progress and shift in family values.

In 2014, the foreign population with regular residence made up about 3.8 per cent of the total resident population. That percentage compares to only 0.5 per cent in 1980 but it also represents the lowest proportion of foreign population since 2001. The financial crisis that has hit Portugal severely in recent years, associated with high unemployment rates, has led many migrants to return to their home countries or to move elsewhere, bringing down the proportion of foreign population with regular residence in Portugal to the level of the pre-Euro times.

Labour force characteristics

The active population (15 to 64 years of age) in 2014 was about 5.2 million, 2.5 million of them (48.7 per cent) women. By gender, the active population was made up in 2013 of 81.6 per cent of the population of men of active age, and 72.5 per cent of the population of women of active age. These figures compare to 77.8 per cent of the population of men of active age in the EU28, and 65.6 per cent of the population of women of active age in the EU28 in 2012.

Some gender differences are apparent when 2014 activity rates are compared: 64.3 per cent for men and 53.8 for women. But while the activity rate for men has been declining in the last decades (75.0 in 1990), the activity rate for women has remained relatively stable (51.8 in 1990) in the same period. In both cases, however, activity rates are in line with the EU28 average in 2014: 64.4 for men and 51.3 for women.

In terms of employment rate, 50.6 was the ratio between the employed population and the population aged 15 or more in 2014, but that ratio was 55.6 for men and 46.1 for women. In other words, although the proportion of women employed in the overall employed population has been increasing from 38.8 per cent in 1980 to 48.4 per cent in 2014, the participation of women in the employed population remains below that of men. However, when it comes to the younger and more educated segment of the employed population gender differences tend to fade away. In fact, looking at the 'employment rate of recent graduates', a Eurostat indicator of the employability of young people and measured by the proportion of individuals aged 20 to 34 and having attained at least upper secondary education that are currently employed, the data show that rate in Portugal to be 69.7 for women and 69.0 for men, both rates below the EU28 average (74.2 for women, 77.9 for men) for that age cohort.

The Portuguese economy has become highly dependent on the service sector in recent decades, a sector that accounts now for 67.5 per cent of the overall employment, against just 8.6 per cent accounted for by the primary sector. This represents a significant shift since the mid-1970s when the primary sector still accounted for 35 per cent of overall employment, against less than 32 per cent accounted for by the service sector. This shift is strongly associated with women's access to the labour market that took place in this period. In 2014, the service sector employed 78.7 per cent of the population of women employed, against 56.9 per cent of the population of men employed. Sex segregation is even stronger in the other two sectors, with 32.2 per cent of employed men working in industry, against only 15 per cent of employed women working in this sector.

No significant gender differences were detected in the nature of the employment contract: 78.3 per cent of male employees and 78.8 per cent of female employees had a permanent contract in 2014. The proportion of employees under temporary work contract is an indicator of the level of job precariousness. The figures available suggest a significant level of job precariousness in the Portuguese labour market. According to Eurostat (2015) data, the percentage of female employees in Portugal with temporary work contracts was 21.1 in 2015, well above the EU28 average of 14.4 per cent, and only below Poland (28 per cent), Spain (24.6 per cent), Cyprus (24.4 per cent) and the Netherlands (22 per cent). Job precariousness is even more apparent when it comes to male employees. The percentage of male employees in Portugal with temporary work contracts was 21.6 in 2015, also well above the EU28 average of 13.6 per cent, and only below Poland (28.5 per cent) and Spain (23.6 per cent).

Gender differences become more apparent when the characteristics of the employment contract, such as the effective weekly hours of work and payment, are taken into consideration. In 2014, women had on average 33 effective weekly hours of work, against 37 hours for men. In the same year, 11.5 was the percentage of employed men working part time, against 14.8 per cent women. This percentage is well below the EU28 average of 32.9 per cent employed women working part time and only compares to what is found in most Eastern European countries. The explanation for the small proportion of women working part time is likely to be associated with the traditional characteristics of the Portuguese economy as a low-wage economy, further stressed by the financial crises in recent years. In fact, the cumulative impact of the international financial crisis that started in the US in 2008, and the debt crisis that followed and hit Portugal in 2011, has produced a significant decline in the standards of living of the employed population, both men and women, making it almost impossible to survive on a part-time job salary.

Women also seem to be the most affected by unemployment. Eurostat data show that the unemployment rate in 2014 was 14.5 for women, slightly higher than the men's rate of 13.8, and long-term unemployment was 8.5 per cent for women and 8.4 per cent for men. In both cases, Portuguese figures are well above the European average (10.3 female unemployment rate in the EU27, and 5.1 per cent female long-term unemployment in the EU 28). 2015 data show that the rate of young people aged between 15 and 34 years old neither in employment nor in education and training is also higher for women: 15.1 per cent women in that age group are in that situation, compared to 12.5 per cent men in the same age group. In terms of the more qualified segment of the workforce, the unemployment rate of active population with higher education completed was in 2014, 11.2 for women and 8.1 for men. In other words, regardless of the way the data are looked at, women seem more likely to face unemployment than men, including in the most educated segment of the population. Such differences seem consistent across the board. Women also made 57.7 per cent of the discouraged job-seekers aged 25 or more in 2014, according to the ILO (2015) dataset. And more propensity to become unemployed normally means higher risk of poverty. In fact, the Eurostat database also indicates that 28.1 per cent of Portuguese women were considered in 2014 at risk of poverty or social exclusion (26.7 per cent for Portuguese men), above the 25.2 per cent figure for the EU27 average. That condition is further stressed by the single-parent status of a considerable number of women. In 2014, INE (2015) data show that there were seven times as many women living in lone-parent private households than men.

In 2014, the number of employees earning the national minimum wage was 19.6 per cent of the employed population, which compares to only 4.0 per cent in 2002. Moreover, while 15.1 per cent men employed full time in 2014 earned the national minimum wage, the proportion of women employed full time covered by minimum wage was 25 per cent. In other words, one in four women (against nearly one in seven men) employed full time in 2014 only earned the minimum wage.

In terms of the average monthly wage of employees in 2013, the average basic remuneration was €993 for men and €816 for women, and the average earnings, €1209 for men and €958 for women. In other words, the average monthly earnings of female employees was just about 79.2 per cent of their male counterparts. However, the gender earnings gap widens when it comes to senior personnel, i.e., senior staff members and technicians operating in managerial, commercial or production areas, for whom the average monthly earnings of women was just about 72.9 per cent of their male counterparts. When the economic sector is considered, the widest gender gaps in average monthly earnings were found in the health and social work (average monthly earnings of female employees 70.5 per cent of their male counterparts), manufacturing (71 per cent) and financial activities (75.7 per cent). In public administration, the largest employer of qualified workers in the country, the average monthly earnings of female employees was 106 per cent of their male counterparts in 2013.

In general, the disparity in terms of the average monthly earnings between male and female employees widens with the academic qualifications of the employee. In 2012, the disparity in the average monthly earning between male and female employees with an educational level equal or below the lower secondary education was 13.5 per cent, but this figure increases to 18.2 per cent when employees with a higher education level are considered. Similarly, the disparity in the average monthly earnings between male and female employees in less qualified occupations was 9.6 per cent, but that figure rises to 14.1 per cent when the most qualified occupations are considered.

The gender pay gap, that is to say, the difference between average hourly earnings of male paid employees and female paid employees as a percentage of average hourly earnings of male paid employees, was in Portugal 13 per cent in 2013. This figure compares positively with other EU countries, including those usually considered more egalitarian (e.g., 19.7 in the UK, 15.2 in Sweden, 16 in the Netherlands, 16.4 in Denmark). Even so, the gender pay gap has been widening considerably in Portugal since the start of the financial crisis. For instance, in 2007, the year immediately before the crisis, the gender pay gap was only 8.5 per cent, illustrating the profound social impact of the financial crisis including on issues such as the gender pay gap.

Despite the promotion of business initiatives and entrepreneurship as a way out of the unemployment status that took place during the worst period of the financial crisis, the proportion of the employed population who are actual employees has grown by about 5 per cent since 2007, the year before the financial crisis. Some gender differences account for that growth. In 2014, 75.7 per cent of employed men were actual employees, a slight increase from the 73.5 per cent in 2007. But 85.1 per cent of employed women were employees in 2014, up from 77.1 per cent in 2007.

In 2014, 3.1 per cent of employed women were actually employers, against 7.1 per cent of employed men who were employers. In 2007, the proportion of employers among the employed population was 3.5 per cent for women and 7.4 per cent for men. In other words, the financial crisis had some impact in the destruction of businesses, and that impact was felt by men and women employers in very much the same way.

Differences in the employed population are accounted for by gender differences in the self-employed population, particularly by the proportion of self-employed women. In 2014, 16.7 per cent of employed men were self-employed, down from 17.9 per cent in 2007. For women, the percentage of self-employed in the employed population decreased quite significantly from 17.5 per cent in 2007 to 11.2 per cent in 2014. These figures are not that far away from the EU28 average of 19.1 per cent for men and 10.4 per cent for women in 2014, but show an important change in terms of the employment of women, suggesting a move away from self-employment to employee status.

Portuguese women have traditionally been less likely to be involved in entrepreneurial activities than men and that pattern has not been reversed in recent years (GEM, 2015). Women also appear to be driven by different motivational factors when engaging in entrepreneurial activities. According to the GEM (2015) survey, men seem to be more driven than women by the sense of opportunity, either because they identified a business opportunity or started the business because they want to earn more money or be more independent. Women, by contrast, seem to start a business venture more often out of necessity than men, possibly because they had no better options to obtain resources for living. The current Fifth National Plan for Gender Equality, Citizenship, and Non-discrimination 2014–2017 includes the development of entrepreneurialism among women as one of the objectives as a means to mobilise women towards active economic lives and to promote self-employment among women.

Education and the professions

Despite the important progress made in the last 25 years, Portugal still compares poorly with other European countries in terms of education. In 1992, only 19.9 per cent of the population aged 25 to 64 had completed at least upper secondary education. In 2014, that percentage more than doubled to 43.3 per cent. However, when compared to other European countries, that percentage represents a poor record, only above Malta's 42.2 per cent. In terms of the nature of the employment, 26.2 per cent of employees hold a higher-education degree. That figure compares to 15 per cent of the self-employed and 22.4 per cent of employers holding a higher-education degree. These percentages mean that in relative terms and as far as higher education is concerned, employees in Portugal tend to be better educated than employers.

When gender is taken into account, it is observed that the progress achieved in education is mainly due to women's efforts. In fact, the percentage of the male population aged 25 to 64 that had completed at least upper secondary education increased in the period 1992 to 2014, from 20.5 to 38.8 per cent, whereas the female population increased from 19.5 to 47.5 per cent. These data mean that women are the most educated segment of the Portuguese population. The higher education rate of the resident population aged between 25 and 64 years old was 21.7 per cent in 2014, with 25.9 per cent for women and 17.2 per cent for men. In 2014, women made up 61.4 per cent of the population aged 15 or more holding a higher-education degree, and that represents a pattern that has been evident for quite some time. In 1998, women were already 58.9 of the resident population holding a higher-education degree.

Female students enrolled in higher education have been the majority since 1985. In 2015, they were 53.6 per cent of the students enrolled, down from an all-time high of 57 per cent in 2001. In 2014, 59.1 per cent of the students who graduated in that year were women, but the gender gap in terms of graduations has been evident for some time and has been fairly consistent. In 2001, for instance, 67.1 per cent of the graduates in that year were women (DGEEC, 2015). Some level of gender imbalance remains according to subject area: women are 80.7 per cent of the students enrolled in education; 58.7 per cent in arts and humanities; 58.6 per cent in social sciences, business, and law; 76.7 per cent in health related subjects; 47.8 per cent in sciences, mathematics and computing; but only 26.2 per cent in engineering. These percentages are, broadly speaking, in line with other EU member states. The exceptions are basically limited to the arts and humanities in which the proportion of female students enrolled in Portugal is one of the lowest in Europe; and the subject areas of sciences, mathematics and computing in which Portugal has the second largest proportion of female students enrolled in Europe.

Nevertheless, disparities in the educational level appear to be considerably wider among women than among men. In other words, the remarkable educational achievements of the most educated segment of the female population co-exist with the overrepresentation of women among the least educated segment of the population. In fact, while being the majority of the most educated segment of the workforce, women also make up the largest proportion of unqualified workers. 2014 data show that overall, 11.2 per cent of the Portuguese workforce was considered 'unqualified', of which 8 per cent were female and the remaining 3.2 per cent male.

In the professions, women often represent the majority of its members, as indicated by 2014 data: judges (58.4 per cent); public prosecutors (61.5 per cent); lawyers (53.3 per cent); solicitors (62.2 per cent); court officials (62.2 per cent); medical doctors (52.9 per cent); and teachers (ranging from 99.1 per cent at pre-school level to 71.2 at the secondary level). Gender parity was found among researchers in higher-education institutions (50 per cent when measured in terms of full-time equivalent). However, when top jobs in each profession are seen in isolation, the proportion of women tends to decline. For instance, according to Iberian Lawyer (2015), only 26 per cent of partners at major law firms in Portugal are women. And although women were 58.4 per cent of the judges in 2014, that proportion is reduced to slightly over 15 per cent when only Supreme Court judges are considered.

In the professions where women already make up the majority of members this trend is likely to be further reinforced in the foreseeable future, bearing in mind the proportion of female students with the required degrees to access those professions. In the health sector, for instance, women are 67.6 per cent of the students enrolled in medicine and 83.6 per cent of students enrolled in nursing and caring degrees. This trend is apparent regardless of the higher-education study cycle, with women making up 70.1 per cent of the Master's students and 69 per cent of the PhD students in health-related subject areas.

The positive representation of women in the professions is challenged when it comes to the most prestigious segments and high-rank positions. Women tend to be the minority in these high-rank positions despite being the majority in the profession as a whole. For instance, despite being the large majority in the teaching profession as a whole, women become the minority when the focus is on higher education alone, in which they make up 44.4 per cent of the teaching staff. A similar pattern was found in the judicial profession. Although they make up the majority of the judges taken together, they become a clear minority when the Supreme Court is considered, as pointed out above. And although close to gender balance, judges in the Constitutional Court are 46.2 per cent female. In other more high-status sectors, gender balance is further away from parity. For instance, in the media industry, only 28 per cent of the workforce employed in 2009 in this sector were women (EIGE, 2014), despite the fact that 69 per cent of the graduates in journalism and information in the same year were women.

The gender picture becomes more unbalanced when political appointments and elected bodies are considered. In these cases, the proportion of women is generally limited and nearly residual in some circumstances. For instance, currently only one out of 14 vice-chancellors of public universities is female; only 9.8 per cent of the ambassadors are women; only 7.5 per cent of the city councils presidents are women. Women members of Parliament rose to 33 per cent in the 2015 election, an all-time high, but gender balance remains a long-term goal in politics.

In the regulators, women also tend to be underrepresented. There are no women among the board members of the Portuguese central bank, and the same happens in the health regulation authority, and in the energy services regulatory authority. The board of the regulator of the communications sector is currently close to parity with 40 per cent women, including a female chair. And in the media regulatory authority, 40 per cent of the board members were women in 2012, a per centage that was then above the EU27 average (31 per cent) (EIGE, 2014).

In sum, substantial progress has been made in the access of women to the professions, often outnumbering men in prestigious careers such as the judicial system and the medical professions. However, the underrepresentation of women at the top levels remains an issue. The access of women to these positions also appears to remain particularly problematic in what could be described as political appointments and elected bodies. In these positions, gender balance is far from parity.

Women in management

The ILO (2015) dataset shows that the proportion of women employed in senior and middle-level management positions in Portugal was 31.8 per cent in 2014, up from 27.6 per cent the previous year. Due to redefinition of the measure and changes in the statistical series implemented in recent years, conclusions about progress in the access of women to managerial positions should be made with care. However, it is safe to say that some progress towards parity has been made in the last 20 years, but that such progress has been rather slow. Since 1997, the proportion of women employed in senior and middle-level management positions has varied from 21.6 per cent in 1998, the lowest figure, to 35.7 per cent in 2010, the highest proportion on record. During this period, the figures have remained within this range, with a slight trend upwards. An international comparison based on the same database shows that the Portuguese figures in 2014 compare with those of Belgium (31.3 per cent), Australia (32.3 per cent), France (31.9 per cent), Ireland (30.8 per cent), Switzerland (31.3 per cent) and the UK (32.9 per cent). They are below Sweden's figures (37.4 per cent), but above Denmark's (26.2 per cent), Germany's (27.8 per cent), Spain's (29.4 per cent) and Italy's figures (21.9 per cent). In sum, the proportion of women employed in senior and middle-level management positions in Portugal is around the one-third range and appears to be in line, broadly speaking, with most other European countries.

A more detailed analysis shows some variations worth referring to. In general, and similar to what has been found elsewhere, the representation of women seems to decrease as the decision-making level goes up. As pointed out by ILO (2015, p. 7), "the larger the company or organisation, the less likely the head will be a woman". When it comes to the top executive positions in the largest companies in Portugal, the representation of women decreases to almost a token level. In 2012, women accounted for 6.9 per cent of non-executive directors and 9.6 per cent of executive directors in the largest publicly listed companies in Portugal (EU, 2013). Data from the EU Commission quoted by CITE (2014) indicate that the percentage of board seats held by women in 2013 in Portugal was 9 per cent. In 2014, only 14 out of 218 (6.4 per cent) members of executive boards of PSI20 companies (companies with the largest market capitalisation and the most actively traded stocks in the Euronext Lisbon exchange) were women, down from 7.4 per cent the previous year. And in 2015, the European Commission (EU, 2015a) reported that women on the boards of PSI20 companies reached 11 per cent, the fifth lowest percentage among the EU28 countries. When senior executives and non-executives members are counted separately, the EU (2015b) data show that the percentage of women drops to 10 per cent among the senior executive members and rises to 12 per cent among the non-executives, though the latter seems to be currently increasing due to policy measures recently adopted.

Other datasets provide figures that are, broadly speaking, in line with the official EU indicators. Based on data compiled by Bloomberg Intelligence, Charlton (2014) claims that 'Portugal has the lowest proportion of female board members of any European country', locating the country in the 5 per cent range of women on boards of the country's companies included in the Stoxx Europe 600 Index. Catalyst (2014a) data, further discussed in ILO (2015), present the proportion of board seats held by women in Portugal at 3.7 per cent, and in another report (Catalyst, 2014b), women's share of board seats in Portuguese companies listed in the European stock index is said to be 7.9 per cent. Only three publicly listed companies seem to have a percentage of women on board above the EU28 average (15.8 per cent). In 2014, the company with the largest percentage of women on board in that year was Mota-Engil, a building company (ACEGIS, 2014), curiously from a sector with a strong underrepresentation of women in the workforce (below 9 per cent). And according to this report, seven publicly listed companies had not a single woman on boards in 2014. In state-owned companies, the picture is somewhat better. Women on the boards reached 23.1 per cent in 2014, and 9.4 per cent of board chairs were women. The same applies to non-listed corporations in which 20.9 per cent of the board seats were occupied by women (Dun & Bradstreet, 2015).

As expected, some variation is found in the figures available for the percentage of women in top management positions, depending on the sample and data collection procedures adopted, but even so, the data seem very consistent: when it comes to the top of business organisations, only about one in ten members are women. Women seem almost confined to token status. And such a picture becomes even clearer if the focus is on the very top. When it comes to board chairs, the representation of women decreases even further. Catalyst (2014a) data show that in 2014 not a single listed company in Portugal had a woman board chairperson. EU (2015a) data confirmed that this remained the case in 2015. In sum, despite some variations according to the dataset, it is apparent that the percentage of women board members is merely residual and remains one of the lowest representations in Europe.

Obviously, when the aggregate broadens and also includes positions and occupations at lower management ranks, the picture changes considerably. According to the ILO (2015) dataset, and regarding the broad aggregate of 'managers, professionals and technicians', the proportion of women was 53.5 per cent in 2014, up from 50.3 per cent a decade before (2004), though not so different from the 1997 figures (52.2 per cent). As pointed out above, these comparisons should be made with care given the breaks in the series, but a very slight move upwards seems to emerge from the data when a broader concept of "manager" is considered. In terms of the mean weekly hours actually worked per individual, the ILO (2015) dataset for the aggregate of 'managers, professionals and technicians' indicates that women worked 39.1 hours per week, against 41.4 hours worked by their male counterparts.

The management function also plays a part in the representation of women. Dun & Bradstreet (2015) point towards 24.9 per cent of women playing some kind of leadership role in business organisations. When the management function is taken into account, the data show that the percentage goes up to 62.6 per cent for quality/technical directors, 47.8 per cent for human resource directors, 33.5 per cent for financial directors, and it goes down to 17.9 per cent for purchasing and logistics directors, 13.4 per cent for sales/commercial directors, and 12.6 per cent for IT directors. Even worse, the percentage of women is only 8.2 per cent for chief executive officers.

Using a more inclusive concept of organisation (business companies, public or private, and cooperatives), the Dun & Bradstreet (2015) study found in 2014 that 44.9 per cent have a management team that is entirely male; 12.2 per cent entirely female; and 55.1 per cent have at least one female manager. Overall, only 42.9 per cent of organisations have a mixed gender management team. In other words, more than half of Portuguese organisations have a single sex management team. Organisational size also appears to be unfriendly to women. In the 500 largest companies, 6.2 per cent have women in some kind of leadership role, but when the largest 1000 companies are considered that percentage raises to 14.3 per cent (Dun & Bradstreet, 2015). If size is measured in terms of sales volume, a similar conclusion can be drawn. In 34.6 per cent of companies with a sales volume up to €2 million, women can be found in the management team. However, that percentage decreases to 25.3 per cent when companies with a sales volume between €2 million and €10 million are considered, and to 18.8 per cent in companies with a sales volume between €10 million and €50 million. That percentage decreases even further to merely 11.5 per cent in companies with a sales volume above €50 million. By sector, the largest proportion of companies with women in the management team is found in cloth manufacturers (46.3 per cent of the companies have women directors), a sector with a workforce also predominantly female (86.4 per cent).

Public administration, the largest employer of qualified workers, provides another good illustration of the gender gaps that prevail in Portugal. Overall, women made up about 56.2 per cent of the workforce in public administration in 2013. At the middle management level, women occupied 57.2 per cent of these positions. However, when the more senior manage-ment positions are considered, the percentage of women decreases to 33.6 per cent (CITE, 2014). These figures seem to reflect the political dimension involved in the appointment. In middle management positions, technical expertise is likely to be a decisive factor and, therefore, being the most educated segment of the workforce is likely to contribute to a proportion of women holding middle management positions that is actually higher than in the overall workforce. However, when it comes to senior management positions, political (among other) criteria are likely to become more relevant, overtaking technical expertise as the most relevant factor in those appointments.

A not so different picture can be found in many other sectors. In the media industry, for instance, despite the growing number of women employed in this sector, senior staff placed in decision-making positions are still predominantly male. In 1995, only 8 per cent of executive producers, the level at which decisions about media content are made, were women (EIGE, 2014). Given the influential nature of the media industry informing public opinion, the way gender-related content is created and produced is particularly relevant. In a 2012 survey, EIGE (2014) found no woman as chief executive officer or chief operating officer in this sector, but overall 26 per cent of the senior staff at the directorship level were women. That percentage rises to 33 per cent when the public sector is considered separately, suggesting that women are more likely to be recruited or promoted to strategic positions in the public sector than in the private sector. However, when the figures pertaining to women's participation in decision-making are disaggregated by management rank it becomes clear that such a participation is higher at the more junior managerial positions (EIGE, 2014).

Legislation and policy initiatives

Most surveys and official reports worldwide on the issue of women in management conclude that a slow but steady rise is observed in female board representation (e.g., MSCI, 2014). But although admitting that the proportion of women on boards has risen in recent years, a careful look at the data also show that the pace of change is by no means conducive to gender parity in the foreseeable future, and Portugal is no exception. 'The overall change represents an average increase of 0.4 percentage points per year. At this rate of change boards with at least 40 per cent of each gender would not be seen for at least 75 years', concluded the European Commission referring to the Portuguese case (EU, 2013).

Following the objective set by the European Union of a 40 per cent presence of the underrepresented sex among non-executive directors of companies listed on stock exchanges by 2020, the Portuguese government has passed legislation (Resolution 19/2012 of 8 March 2012) obliging state-owned companies to adopt gender equality plans aiming to promote gender balance in management and executive positions. According to this legislation, state-owned companies are to design, implement and monitor the implementation of these plans; state-owned companies also have to report the progress achieved to the government every six months. The same legislation also recommends publicly listed companies take similar measures, while exempting small and medium-sized enterprises (SMEs), the vast majority of the Portuguese business community. At the national level, progress is to be monitored through the indicators defined in the Fifth National Plan for Gender Equality, Citizenship, and Non-discrimination 2014–2017, including indicators such as the 'number of state-owned companies that have adopted equality plans', and the 'board representation of women in state-owned companies'.

The legislation itself is more likely to be effective at the symbolic level and by adding visibility to this important issue rather than promoting actual change in the short term. Several reasons contribute to this cautious assessment of the effectiveness of this particular piece of legislation. On the one hand, it does not apply to SMEs and SMEs make up over 99 per cent of the firms in Portugal (OECD, 2015). On the other hand, the measures are obligatory in state-owned companies but there are very few state-owned companies left after the latest privatisation programme conducted recently. Furthermore, it does not apply to non-listed companies. Excluding SMEs, state-owned and non-listed companies, the EU (2013) estimates that approximately 50 listed companies in Portugal are likely to be affected by the legislation. But with regard to publicly listed companies, these measures are simply 'recommendations' with no direct penalty attached for non-compliance. Failure to adopt gender equality plans by publicly listed companies can only be perceived as leading to some kind of penalty if that is taken into account when public subsidies and state contracts are awarded.

In the aftermath of this legislation, an interesting debate has taken place in the media (newspapers, TV channels, blogs and social networks) as to whether compulsory targets and some kind of a quota system should be set up and also applied to publicly listed companies (e.g. TSF, 2015). The arguments on both sides were the usual ones involved in the debate on affirmative action initiatives, with very few new arguments on either side. On the quota supporters' side, the arguments put forward tended to emphasise that merit should prevail as the board recruitment criterion, rather than gender, but that leaving out half the population (and the better educated half at that) was a tremendous waste of resources. A view supported by many businesswomen with little sympathy with the idea of having quotas admitted they were prepared to accept the quotas as a pragmatic way to change the status quo, as long as the quotas were seen as temporary. On the opponents' side, the arguments were mainly that the quota system meant an unjustified interference of the government in the way private businesses are run – 'if there are economic advantages in having a more gender balanced board as supporters claim to be the case, it is then up to the shareholders to realise it and take advantage of recruiting more women to the boards' was a typical comment. A second line of argument was that quotas are patronising and ultimately detrimental to women. The president of Euronext Lisbon added a different argument: by imposing a quota system to publicly listed companies, though not to non-listed ones, companies would not be competing on a level playing field and fair competition would be at stake (TSF, 2015).

Being an advocate of business self-regulation, the Portuguese government at the time was reluctant to adopt a more directive approach that would imply imposing some kind of quota system for women on boards of private companies, instead favouring initiatives geared towards raising awareness among the business community of the relevance of having a more gender-balanced composition of the boards. A 'carrot and stick' approach was adopted in this case, involving incentives for companies to change their board appointment practices while threatening them with the imposition of quotas if the companies did not do so voluntarily.

On 5 March 2015, the government announced its intention to start negotiations with publicly listed companies in order to get their commitment to the target of 30 per cent women on boards by 2018. To put additional pressure on the companies, the secretary of state for equality, announcing these measures, also added that the companies had in their own hands the solution to the problem of the underrepresentation of women on boards while avoiding the imposition of quotas. But such an imposition would not be discarded if the companies did not comply voluntarily with that target (e.g. Dinheiro Vivo, 2015).

On 30 June 2015, a 'voluntary agreement' was signed between the government and 13 publicly listed companies, nine of which are part of the PSI20 index and that all together represent about 70 per cent of market capitalisation and currently employ about 95,000 employees. The group of companies that signed the agreement was mainly composed of the recently privatised utilities in which government influence was still considerable. Other publicly listed companies joined the agreement at a later date. Under this agreement and according to the popular press, the companies commit themselves to the target of 30 per cent women on boards by 2018 (e.g. Público, 2015). This agreement was also backed by a media campaign launched by the Commission for Equality in Labour and Employment (CITE) to raise public awareness of the relevance of these issues.

In an interview with a business newspaper on the same date the agreement was signed, the secretary of state admitted that the 46 publicly listed companies in Portugal had been approached but only 13 accepted the agreement, adding that 'this was a difficult process; some companies simply ignored our contact; others sent a "no" answer straight away and we realised it would be a waste of time to try to negotiate with companies with such a backward mindset' (Diário Económico, 2015). In the same interview, the member of government blamed the recruitment made in closed and mainly male circuits for the current state of affairs and hoped self-regulation would work. She also acknowledged that women who have already made it to the boards have often shown little awareness of the difficulties faced by other women accessing top positions.

Additional measures have been adopted in various domains with a view to putting pressure on companies to change their culture with regard to gender balance issues. For instance, in accordance with the Fifth National Plan for Gender Equality, Citizenship, and Non-discrim-ination 2014–2017, the legislation that regulates the access to European funds determines that candidates to the European-funded 'Portugal 2020' programme are informed that in case of candidates with the same score, the preference will be given to the company with the larger representation of women on board and other executive positions, and to companies with the lowest gender pay gap.

Another important piece of legislation with significant implications for the gender balance in top positions is Law n° 67/2013 (Regulators framework). This legislation establishes that the mandates of the board chairs of the regulators should rotate between men and women, and in all cases the boards should have at least a 33 per cent gender representation. In practice, the full effects of this legislation have yet to be seen.

A look ahead

In 2014, the situation of women in Portugal could be illustrated with some simple figures: women make up 52.5 per cent of the population; 48.4 per cent of the employed population; 61.4 per cent of the population aged 15 or more holding a higher-education degree; 31.8 per cent of the individuals in senior and middle-level management positions; but only 11 per cent of the board members of publicly listed companies included in the PSI20 index. In other words, despite being the most educated segment of the population for some time now, the representation of women tends to decline and it does so quite dramatically, as the analysis approaches the top positions in the largest business organisations in Portugal. A not so different picture could be drawn if the analysis had focused on the political structure rather than the economy.

However, it is fair to say that some progress has been made, as shown by most indicators, and that slowly but steadily the participation rate of women in management has been increasing. Moreover, policy measures adopted in recent years appear to be making an impact, namely the ones derived from the EU proposed legislation with the aim of attaining a 40 per cent objective of the underrepresented sex in non-executive board member positions in publicly listed companies by 2020. The Portuguese government seems to have adopted a 'carrot and stick' approach in order to implement the 'recommendation' to publicly listed companies that they should commit themselves to the target of 30 per cent women on boards by 2018. Although the direct imposition of quotas was discarded, publicly listed companies were put under pressure to agree on voluntary commitments to reach that target. While negotiating with the listed companies on this matter, the message was explicitly passed through the media that the imposition of quotas would be reconsidered if progress was not made in due course. So far, the strategy of the government seems to be producing some results and more publicly listed companies have been announcing their agreement to participate in the demographic reconfiguration of their boards.

These developments raise some interesting questions for the near future: will the affirmative measures taken recently succeed in changing the traditional state of affairs and particularly, will the 'carrot and stick' approach work? And more importantly, what will be the visible consequences of the demographic reconfiguration of the boards of publicly listed companies? The consequences can be assessed in different ways. The two most obvious ones are the performance of the companies, namely financial performance, and the role of women on boards as promoters of the access of other women to management positions.

It is difficult to establish a direct relationship between the gender composition of the management team and performance, given the wide range of factors that influence the outcome of the company. The suggested explanatory mechanism is that having more women in top management positions can contribute to a working environment more receptive to diversity and one that incorporates different perspectives, thus leading to more balanced decisions that ultimately improve company performance. The study of the relationship between women on boards and financial performance of the companies has attracted considerable attention and there is now a wide body of literature examining that relationship. The empirical evidence available 'is decidedly mixed', as concluded by Post and Byron (2015) in their meta-analysis. In the literature, studies can be found showing that female directors may lead to better performance (e.g. Singh *et al.*, 2001), to lower performance (e.g. Minguez-Vera and Martin, 2011) and may have little impact on performance (e.g. Carter *et al.*, 2010). In other words, the performance argument in this debate is perhaps misleading, and the actual reasons to support or challenge the idea of having a more gender balanced management team have to be found elsewhere.

In the Portuguese context, the evidence about the relationship between the gender composition of the management team and the performance of the company is scarce and just as inconclusive as found elsewhere. In 2013, 46.1 per cent of the companies led by men grew in terms of sales volume and 18 per cent in terms of jobs, a better performance than the 43.6 per cent of the companies led by women that grew in terms of sales volume and 15.9 per cent in terms of jobs (Dun & Bradstreet, 2015). When the largest 1000 SMEs are considered, companies led by women seem to do slightly better in terms of sales volume (6.6 per cent against 6.4 per cent in companies led by men) and employment (4.1 per cent against 3.0 per cent in companies led by men), but companies led by men appear to have a better performance in terms of exports (10.7 per cent against 5.7 per cent in companies led by women).

With regard to the positive impact of women in top management positions in the promotion of a more gender-balanced management demographic, the picture is also far from clear. The Dun & Bradstreet (2015) study on Portugal found that the gender of the chair is somewhat related with the gender balance of the management team. Management teams led by men seem more likely to be predominantly male, whereas management teams led by women appear to have a more gender-balanced composition. According to the Dun & Bradstreet (2015) study, 58.8 per cent of the management teams led by men are exclusively male, though 60.3 per cent of management teams led by women have both men and women members. These findings seem to suggest that female leadership in the management team may have a positive impact in the promotion of other women to senior positions. This evidence fuels the quota debate and seems to render support to the advocates of the quota system. But this represents a simplistic view of the question. In fact, the evidence available in the literature recommends that such conclusions are made with care. Numerous studies show than the relationships between women in organisations are more complex and contradictory that is assumed by believers in the direct positive relationship (e.g. Mavin *et al.*, 2014). In their study, Mavin *et al.* (2014) show how top women leaders often lead to negative workplace interpersonal relations between women that ultimately undermine the prospects of other women.

In another study, Elsesser and Lever (2011), using a large sample of male and female subordinates, found that men judged their female bosses more favourably and women judged male bosses more favourably, and nearly half of the participants reported preferring male over female bosses by more than a 2:1 ratio, which they explain through role congruity theory. From this viewpoint, women managers tend to act in ways that are more frequently associated with the male gender role, adopting a 'think manager – think male' approach, thus becoming incongruent with their expected sex role. And according to role congruity theory, role incongruity leads women managers to receive greater scrutiny and criticism than men, and to be evaluated more negatively (Eagly and Karau, 2002). In other words, though it might appear that having more women on boards would facilitate the access of other women to more senior positions, it is not at all clear that the more junior women would share that view and see it as a necessary and desirable scenario. The implications for the women who have actually broken through the glass ceiling and reached the upper echelons of management are no less relevant. They might appear to have been placed in more precarious leadership positions than men, in a position that Ryan and Haslam (2007) label 'glass cliffs' and this also deserves further attention. In sum, the assumption that there is a positive contribution of the preferential recruitment of women to boards to a significant shift in the current gender-unbalanced composition of management teams is not entirely supported empirically and clearly deserves further research, and research that takes into account contextual and cultural features.

It is acknowledged that differences between men and women in the workplace can be attributed, to a considerable extent, to the different roles they play in the family and in society in general. Despite the obvious progress already achieved and reported in this chapter, the major conclusions drawn in the previous edition of *Women in Management Worldwide* (Cabral-Cardoso, 2011) remain valid. Entrenched gender stereotypes, the long hours work culture and family-unfriendly work arrangements and, above all, the gender roles in the family have to be challenged and reconsidered before sustainable changes can be expected in terms of the proportion and role of women in senior management positions in business organisations.

References

ACEGIS (2014) Equilíbrio de Género nos Conselhos de Administração: As Empresas do PSI 20 – relatório 2014 (Gender balance in the boards: The PSI20 companies) <www.cig.gov.pt/wp-content/uploads/2014/03/ACEGIS_Equilibrio_genero_empresas_PSI20.pdf> (Accessed 4 December 2015).

Cabral-Cardoso, C. (2011) Women in management in Portugal. In M.J. Davidson and R.J. Burke (eds), *Women in Management Worldwide: Progress and Prospects* (2nd edition, pp. 69–84). Farnham, Surrey: Gower Publishing.

Carter, D.A., D'Souza, F., Simkins, B.J. and Simpson, W.G. (2010) The gender and ethnic diversity of U.S. boards and board committees and firm financial performance. *Corporate Governance: An International Review*, 18, 396–414.

Catalyst (2014a) Quick take: Women on boards <www.catalyst.org/knowledge/women-boards> (Accessed 4 December 2015).

Catalyst (2014b) 2014 Catalyst census: Women board directors report <www.catalyst.org/knowledge/2014-catalyst-census-women-board-directors> (Accessed 10 December 2015).

Charlton, E. (2014) Portugal has Europe's fewest women on boards: Chart of the day <www.bloomberg.com/news/articles/2014-08-18/portugal-has-europe-s-fewest-women-on-boards-chart-of-the-day> (Accessed 19 August 2014).

CITE (Comissão para a Igualdade no Trabalho e no Emprego) (2014) Relatório sobre o progresso da igualdade entre mulheres e homens no trabalho, no emprego, e na formação profissional – 2013. (Progress Report on Equal Opportunities for Men and Women at Work, in Employment and Vocational Training). Lisboa, Portugal: Comissão para a Igualdade no Trabalho e no Emprego.

DGEEC (Direcção-Geral de estatísticas da Educação e Ciência) (2015) <http://w3.dgeec.mec.pt/dse/eef/indicadores/Indicador_5_8.asp> (Accessed 16 November 2015).

Diário Económico (2015) 13 empresas portuguesas vão ter mais mulheres na administração (13 companies are going to have more women on board) <http://economico.sapo.pt/noticias/13empresas-portuguesas-vao-ter-mais-mulheres-na-administracao_222328.html/-1> (Accessed 30 June 2015).

Dinheiro Vivo (2015) Governo quer 30% de mulheres até 2018 nas empresas cotadas (The government wants 30 percent women in publicly listed companies by 2018) <www.dinheirovivo.pt/economia/governo-quer-30-de-mulheres-ate-2018-nas-empresas-cotadas/#sthash.ZL9tJyrT.dpuf> (Accessed 6 March 2015).

Dun & Bradstreet (2015) Onde páram as mulheres? Presença feminina nas organizações em Portugal 2015 (5ª edição) (Where are the women? Female presence in organisations in Portugal). Lisbon: Informa.

Eagly, A.H. and Karau, S.J. (2002) Role congruity theory of prejudice toward female leaders. *Psychological Review*, 109(3): 573–598.

EIGE (European Institute for Gender Equality) (2014) *Review of the implementation of the Beijing Platform for Action in the EU Member States. Advancing gender equality in decision-making in media organisations: Portugal.* Luxembourg: Publications Office of the European Union.

Elsesser, K.M. and Lever, J. (2011) Does gender bias against female leaders persist? Quantitative and qualitative data from a large-scale survey. *Human Relations*, 64(12), 1555–1578.

EU (European Union) (2013) National factsheet: Gender balance in boards <http://ec.europa.eu/justice/gender-equality/files/womenonboards/womenonboards-factsheet_pt_en.pdf> (Accessed 16 November 2015).

EU (European Commission – Justice) (2015a) Board members <http://ec.europa.eu/justice/gender-equality/gender-decision-making/database/business-finance/supervisory-board-board-directors/index_en.htm> (Accessed 16 November 2015).

EU (European Commission – Justice) (2015b) Executives and non-executives <http://ec.europa.eu/justice/gender-equality/gender-decision-making/database/business-finance/executives-non-executives/index_en.htm> (Accessed 16 November 2015).

Eurostat (2015) Database <http://ec.europa.eu/eurostat/data/database> (Accessed 16 November 2015).

GEM (Global Entrepreneurship Monitor) (2015) Global Entrepreneurship Monitor 2014 Global Report. London: Global Entrepreneurship Research Association.

Iberian Lawyer (2015) Women twice as well represented at firms in Portugal than in Spain. <www.iberianlawyer.com/index.php/news/4528-women-twice-as-well-represented-at-firms-in-portugal-than-in-spain?utm_source=Mondaq&utm_medium=syndication&utm_campaign=View-Original> (Accessed 4 December 2015).

ILO (International Labour Organization) (2015) *Women in business and management: Gaining momentum, Abridged Version of the Global Report.* Geneva: International Labour Office <www.ilo.org/ilostat/faces/oracle/webcenter/portalapp/pagehierarchy/Page137.jspx?locale&_afrLoop=44618024502055&clean=true#%40%3Flocale%3D%26_afrLoop%3D44618024502055%26clean%3Dtrue%26_adf.ctrl-state%3Dulxyiww64_9> (Accessed 16 November 2015).

INE (Instituto Nacional de Estatística) (2015) *Portuguese Official Statistics.* Lisboa, Portugal: Instituto Nacional de Estatística <www.ine.pt/xportal/xmain?xpid=INE&xpgid=ine_base_dados&context o=bd&selTab=tab2 > (Accessed 16 November 2015).

Mavin, S., Grandy, G. and Williams, J. (2014) Experiences of women elite leaders doing gender: Intra-gender micro-violence between women. *British Journal of Management,* 25, 439–455.

Minguez-Vera, A. and Martin, A. (2011) Gender and management on Spanish SMEs: An empirical analysis. *International Journal of Human Resource Management,* 22, 2852–2873.

MSCI (2014) Governance issue report 2014: Survey of women on boards <http://30percentclub.org/wp-content/uploads/2014/11/2014-Survey-of-Women-on-Boards-1.pdf> (Accessed 4 December 2015).

OECD (Organization for Economic Co-operation and Development) (2015) *Financing SMEs and Entrepreneurs 2015: An OECD scoreboard.* Paris: OECD Publishing.

Pordata (2015) The database of contemporary Portugal <www.pordata.pt/en/Portugal> (Accessed 16 November 2015).

Post, C. and Byron, K. (2015) Women on boards and firm financial performance: a meta-analysis. *Academy of Management Journal* 2015, 58(5), 1546–1571.

Público (2015) Treze cotadas comprometem-se a ter 30% de mulheres em cargos de administração (Thirteen listed companies commit themselves to 30 percent women on board) <www.publico.pt/economia/noticia/doze-cotadas-comprometemse-a-ter-30-de-mulheres-em-cargos-de-adminis-tracao-1700493> (Accessed 30 June 2015).

Ryan, M.K. and Haslam, S.A. (2007) The glass cliff: Exploring the dynamics surrounding the appointment of women to precarious leadership positions. *Academy of Management Review,* 32(2), 549–572.

Singh, V., Vinnicombe, S. and Johnson, P. (2001) Women directors on top UK boards. *Corporate Governance: An International Review,* 9, 206–216.

TSF (2015) Quotas para mulheres nas empresas, sim ou não? <www.tsf.pt/economia/interior/quotas-para-mulheres-nas-empresas-sim-ou-nao-4445004.html> (Broadcast on 10 March 2015).

6 Women in management in Spain

Mireia Las Heras and Marc Grau

Spain: the country and its context

Geographically Spain is at the crossroads. It is between Europe and Africa. It lies between the Mediterranean Sea and the Atlantic Ocean. From the year 200 BC to AD 19 the Romans conquered the peninsula, which had previously been conquered by the Phoenicians and Carthaginians, among others. It was a few centuries after the Roman settlement, in AD 711, that the Moors invaded and settled. They ruled for almost 800 years. It was after the Christian armies ended the reconquering of the territories, in 1492, that the recently reunified Spain, composed of several kingdoms, became a world power. From then on Spain dominated Europe and maintained a vast overseas empire until it lost most of its territories during the eighteenth and nineteenth centuries. The last territories over which Spain ruled were Cuba and the Philippines, which got their independence in 1898. The beginning of the twentieth century was very turbulent in Spanish politics, and culminated in the Civil War (1936–1939), which deterred it from being involved in either the First or the Second World Wars. The country was then ruled by General Franco for almost four decades, between 1939 and 1975. In 1975, after Franco's death, it peacefully transitioned to a monarchic democracy, in which Juan Carlos I became the first king. Since then, left- and right-wing parties have alternated in ruling the country, following peaceful elections. In June 2014, Felipe VI, Juan Carlos' and Sofia's son, became the second king of the democracy after the dictatorship.

In recent years, Spain has changed quite dramatically. The Spanish economy was one of the most dynamic in the European Union during the late 1990s and the beginning of the twenty-first-century. However, tourism, housing and the construction industry were hit hard by the global economic crisis of 2008–2009. The bursting of the housing bubble pushed Spain into a severe recession and by the spring of 2013 unemployment had risen to a peak of 27.2 per cent. Most worrisome was the youth unemployment rate, which at its peak reached a 55.8 per cent in April 2013. Indeed the dissatisfaction and distrust of the youth had already been expressed in 2010 by young people in Spain in political protests, such as the anti austerity movements known as 15m (International Labour Organization, 2013).

Nonetheless, the Spanish economy began to turn around by the end of 2013, and the country saw stronger than expected growth the following year, with overall unemployment falling back to 21.18 per cent in August 2015, and youth unemployment falling to 48.8 per cent in August 2015 (Trading Economics, 2015).

Women in the labor force. From the beginning of the crises 2008, until 2015

At an early stage of the crisis in Spain, 2008–2009, the high degree of vertical gender segregation in the Spanish labour market led to a closing of the gender gap in unemployment rates due to a massive reduction in male employment. At this stage of the crisis construction and automotive industries, male-dominated sectors, were most severely hit. However, in a second phase of the crisis, which ran from mid-2009 to mid-2011, the crisis spread to the entire Spanish economy but with a more moderate growth in unemployment due to some expansionary economic policies. At this stage, increases in male and female unemployment rates were similar. In a third phase, which started in the third quarter of 2011, austerity measures accelerated unemployment again. In this third phase unemployment rates for women grew again at a higher rate. In fact, the gender gap in unemployment increased, from a minimum of 0.14 in the second quarter of 2012 to 1.17 in the third quarter of 2013, with a male unemployment rate of 25.5 per cent and a female rate of 26.67 per cent.

Female employment tends to recover later from the economic crises due to higher 'social tolerance' of female unemployment. Supposedly 'gender-blind' expansionary policies tend to focus on male-dominated industries, and the negative effect of austerity policies tend to affect female-dominated sectors, such as social services, education or health. In the second quarter of 2013, in which unemployment fell for the first time in Spain since the start of the crisis, the number of unemployed decreased by 161,900 for men and only 63,300 in women. One of the most negative impacts on women's employment has been caused by a huge drop in public employment of 12 per cent from 2011, exceeding the fall in employment in the private sector, as three out of four public jobs destroyed were occupied by women.

Women in management: an overview

In 2014, Spanish women occupied 22 per cent of management positions, up from 21 per cent the previous year. This situates Spain below the world average of 24 per cent and below the European Union, which has an average of 25 per cent (Eurozone 35 per cent). This figure translates to 37 per cent of companies with more than 100 employees not having any women in its top management. Moreover, 63 per cent of Spanish companies oppose the establishment of quotas for women on boards of directors, and only 5 per cent plan to increase the percentage of women on their management boards.

We know that worldwide companies with strong links to the public sector are most likely to have women in their leadership teams. Indeed, 41 per cent of education and social services as well as healthcare around the world report having women in senior management. Companies in service sectors such as hospitality (33 per cent), food and beverages (27 per cent), financial services (25 per cent) and professional services (24 per cent) also have relatively higher proportions of women in senior roles. Women are more poorly represented in primary sector businesses such as mining (12 per cent), agriculture and energy (both 16 per cent) (Grant Thorton, 2015).

In Spain, although women account for 51 per cent of graduates and 44 per cent of the workforce of the country, they only hold 21 per cent of management positions in medium and large companies (those over 100 employees). In 2013 the percentage of women managers in Spain dropped three points, compared to previous years when it stood at 24 per cent. Thus, in 2015 it had returned to the levels of 2009 (Grant Thorton, 2014).

The figure for 2013 interrupted a clear trend of increase in the number of women in managerial positions. That trend had shown an increase since 2004. Still Spain is slightly ahead of the US and the UK regarding the percentage of women in managerial positions, with the US having 20 per cent and the UK 19 per cent. Spain is still below the world average (24 per cent) and the average in the European Union (25 per cent). In Spain there has been an increase in the percentage of companies that do not have any women on their management teams, reaching 37 per cent, five points higher than in the previous year of 2012 (Grant Thorton, 2014).

Most women managers tend to be in human resources (HR) and other staff departments. In fact, women account for 47.05 per cent of all HR managers in Spain. Spanish women in managerial positions are often in financial services management, in which they make up for 43.94 per cent of the HR positions. However, they only make up 14.80 per cent of general management positions (chief executive officers – CEOs), while 21.68 per cent are sales directors and 14.16 per cent chief information officers (Grant Thorton, 2014). However, while the percentage of women in management in Spain increases overall, the percentage of companies without any women on their management teams reached 37 per cent in 2013. The average in the Eurozone stands at 35 per cent. The picture is reproduced in Spanish companies: 39 per cent do not have female representation on their boards of directors and the situation, rather than improving, has deteriorated dramatically since the percentage has increased 15 percentage points from 24 per cent in 2012. Among listed companies, the situation is better if we analyse only the IBEX 35 where that percentage drops to 12 per cent.

Women on boards of directors

Few women in management lead to even fewer women on boards of directors: 39 per cent of public listed companies do not have female representation on their boards of directors. In the IBEX 35 (the 35 biggest companies in Spain), 17.32 per cent of board seats are held by females (IESE, 2015). Out of 462 seats in the IBEX 35, 80 are occupied by women. Five of these women sit on two boards, and one sits on three. Thus, in total, there are 73 women with seats on IBEX M35 Boards (IESE, 2015). Among those there is only one company, Red Eléctrica Española (REE), in which half of the seats are held by female executives (Gender Map, 2015). REE is a previously state-owned company that is practically a monopoly in the country as even though it is a part of a deregulated market, the idiosyncrasy of the company makes it very tough for competitors to enter the market. REE is exclusively involved in the operation of the electricity system. In 2015 there were 12 companies among the 35 in the IBEX 35 with either just one woman on their boards or none (IESE, 2015).

Adding to the lack of women in boards in Spain, it has been demonstrated that there is a gender gap in pay in the boards of firms listed on the Spanish Stock Exchange (Pucheta-Martínez and Bel-Oms, 2015). According to the authors, female directors suffer pay discrimination mostly in large firms and when those are profitable (i.e. those with the highest return on assets). Also discrimination occurs when firms have large boards. In contrast, the gender pay gap narrows when female independent directors are graduates, when the female board members have between two and four years of seniority and in firms operating in the financial services and property sectors. Thus, equality does not exist, which should incentivise regulators and politicians to push for changes that guarantee the elimination of male–female compensation discrimination at all levels.

Women in education

Although women make up the majority of the labour force in the educational system in Spain, gender bias in school management has evolved in recent years (CNIIE, 2012). In 2012 women made up 98 per cent of the teachers in kindergartens (ages 3 to 5), 79 per cent in primary education (ages 6 to 12) and 55 per cent in secondary education (ages 13 to 16). Women also make up 94 per cent of management positions in kindergartens, but only 63 per cent in primary education and 40 per cent in secondary education (CNIIE, 2012). Thus, in primary education, as well as in secondary education, the gap between the proportion of female teachers and female managers is 16 and 15 percentage points, respectively.

Moreover, the lowest percentage of female participation occurs in the position of headteachers, and females tend to hold positions as 'heads of study' and 'secretaries'. This is not the case in kindergartens, in which the presence of women in the three posts is very similar. However, in primary schools under public ownership the presence of women headteachers is only 53.3 per cent, while the number of secretaries and heads of study remains higher, at around 60 per cent and 70 per cent, respectively. Ownership of the educational centre is a variable to consider, for in private centres female participation is, for all profiles considered (teachers, principals, secretaries and heads of study), slightly higher (CNIIE, 2012).

In secondary education, the percentage of women in management teams and also their presence as teachers is reduced. As already stated, women make up around 55 per cent of teachers, but only 30 per cent run the centres. Participation rates as secretaries and heads of study rise above this figure, approaching 45 per cent. In private centres, the number of women taking leadership positions is higher than in public schools: principals (41 per cent) and secretaries (64 per cent).

The female gap is even more persistent regarding university-level education. Women enter research at a higher rate than men (graduate and postgraduate students, for example), where entrance is determined by competitive criteria (48 per cent of PhDs are women). However, women represent less than 14 per cent in the category of full professors in public and private universities, and less than 17 per cent in public research centres (European Commission, 2010). The proportion of women in all university positions has increased in Spain. In public universities in 2015 they made up 40 per cent of professors and 20 per cent of full professors. In 2015 there were only ten female presidents among 75 in public and private universities in Spain, which represents a total of 13 per cent of all university presidents in the country.

Women in entrepreneurship

Entrepreneurial activity decreased with the beginning of the crisis, from 2008 to 2010. However, it increased again from 2011 to 2013, reaching a modest 5.2 per cent (Global Entrepreneurship Monitor, 2014). Entrepreneurial activity among men varied between 5.4 per cent and 9.2 per cent between 2004 and 2013. In that same period entrepreneurial activity varied between 2.9 per cent and 6.0 per cent among women. Thus, it is quite evident that Spanish women still lag behind their male counterparts in terms of entrepreneurship activity. The percentage of entrepreneurs who launch businesses motivated by a lack of access to the labour market has been increasing in recent years (Global Entrepreneurship Monitor, 2014). These new firms, in many cases, are not very competitive when it comes to extending their business beyond the critical first five years of existence. Their owners lack ambition, and often the capacity and skills, to expand their businesses.

Although firm size does not seem to increase much during the early stage of new ventures (averaging one to three employees), new businesses do tend to make it into the marketplace. Spain's business discontinuation rate is lower than that found in other advanced economies (Global Entrepreneurship Monitor, 2014).

Developed Europe has highly educated women entrepreneurs, who are more likely than their male counterparts and non-entrepreneurial women to have a college degree. The internationalisation of the services they offer is high among women entrepreneurs in Spain and developed Europe, although not as high as in developing Europe (which is about 50 per cent higher) and nor is it as high as their male equivalents. Perhaps more surprising is the low growth aspirations among women entrepreneurs in Spain: only 14 per cent projected to add six or more employees in the next five years, lower than their male counterparts and little more than half that of women in developing Europe.

In Spain, the Women's Institute (Instituto de la Mujer), an organisation operating under the Ministry of Health and Social Affairs, promotes women's entrepreneurship through a variety of initiatives. For example, at the university level, the 'Woman-Emprende' programme highlights success stories of women entrepreneurs, offering training and networking opportunities for women.

In a resolution adopted on 13 September 2011 the European Parliament highlighted that women entrepreneurship is key for increasing female employment rates. It also highlights that women play a decisive role in the growth process of countries. The same resolution recognises that men and women still do not have equal opportunities when it comes to managing and developing companies, and urges member states to promote national measures to support female entrepreneurship action and to facilitate access to financial instruments, such as microfinance.

Addressing women's entrepreneurship in Spain will likely require a combination of broader efforts and more targeted ones. Spain would benefit overall from efforts such as providing better access to business education, and these efforts would enhance entrepreneurial activity. Some wide-ranging initiatives, like promoting societal role models in the media and education, might also be necessary.

Women in politics

Women's political participation is a critical component of democratic dialogue and social cohesion. Spain has improved its female to male ratio in parliament and is among the top ten best countries in the world on this variable (World Economic Forum, 2015). However, Spain has dropped in the political empowerment sub index since 2006, largely due to a drop in the female to male ratio of women in ministerial positions. In 2006 women made up 50 per cent of all ministerial positions, compared to 31 per cent in 2014 (World Economic Forum, 2015).

In September 2014, the percentage of women in executive positions in the seven most relevant political parties in the country was 34.0 per cent. In 2014, only two of these seven parties met the criterion of a balanced presence of men and women recommended (either gender should not exceed 60 per cent representation) by the 2007 Equality Act. However, two of these seven parties had just 18 per cent and 23 per cent female representation.

As regards the participation of women in government, it should be noted that following the general elections of November 2011, four women hold ministerial portfolios in the government of the Popular Party, giving a female presence in the Council Ministers of 30.77 per cent. The ministerial portfolios headed by women are: the Ministry of Presidency, the Ministry of Health, Social Services and Equality, the Ministry of Development, and the Ministry of Employment and Social Security.

It is noteworthy that Spain is the European country with more women in parliaments and regional governments and, until the election of December 2015, the second highest female representation in its central executive. However, with regards to the representation in the highest courts and in the diplomatic services, Spain does not exceed the European average.

Country legislation supporting women in management

Spain introduced many legislative changes regarding men and women in the workforce between the 1970s and the late 1990s. The equality principle was highlighted in Article 14 of the Spanish Constitution of 1978, which clearly prohibited discrimination on the grounds of gender. The Workers' Statute Act of 1980 (amended several times since then) established in Article 28 wage equality for work of equal value. The third Plan for Equal Opportunities for Men and Women (1997–2000) recognised the persistence of unjustifiable wage inequalities for women already working. To palliate this unfair situation, a number of actions were taken under the Plan to provide women with real access to employment with full social and economic rights by encouraging structural changes and transformations that favoured this purpose.

In 2015 in Spain there are three legislative frameworks for equal opportunities:

1   The Activity Plan for Employment (with a special emphasis on gender equality), passed in 1998;
2   The EU Strategy Plan for Gender Equality, started in June 2000;
3   Act 3, 'The Equality Act', of 22 March 2007, for effective equality between women and men, which in its Article 5 also highlights that wage equality has to prevail between men and women.

These efforts have had a positive impact mainly on discrimination in the public sector where today, one can hardly find a pay gap anymore (Aláez-Aller *et al.*, 2011).

Spanish law has followed the pattern of Norway, the first country in the world to establish a gender quota of 40 per cent on boards, and this law also forced companies to reach a gender quota of 40 per cent by 2015. De Anca (2008) argues that this percentage is not a high target, given the high level of rotation among board members in Spanish listing firms. However, the progress made is still too slow to meet the government's 2015 target, and for this reason, González-Menéndez and Martínez-González (2012) recommend that stronger government sanctions, combined with more effective equality plans within companies, are required for the quota to be met (Pucheta-Martínez and Bel-Oms, 2015). There is an important debate, both among academics as well as politicians, about the use of female quotas in politics and business. Recent empirical studies suggest that female quotas in politics increase not only female leadership and policy outcomes (Pande and Ford, 2011), but also lead to better electoral results (Casas-Arce and Saiz, 2015). According to the review of Pande and Ford (2011) on gender quotas and female leadership, the board quota evidence is more mixed than the gender quotas for political parties. As the authors argue, the gender quota for corporate boards seems to have a negative impact on short-run profits, but a positive long-term impact due to changing management practices.

On 31 January 2014, large Spanish companies and the government, in their effort to increase the presence of women in management positions, signed an agreement pledging to ensure a minimum of 20 per cent of women in corporate management. It is also important that of the 31 companies that have signed the pact, 11 of them are in the IBEX 35. It is a small step that, if met, could encourage other companies to follow. However, there is still a long way to go until it reaches a point where companies do not have to consider under their sole discretion that they must have a minimum of women in their management.

Work and family in Spain

According to the European Working Conditions Survey (2010), only one third of Spaniards are satisfied with the way they combine their family and work responsibilities. There are several reasons explaining this lack of satisfaction between work and family, such as lack of family policies (Delgado *et al.*, 2008), economic crisis (Grau-Grau, 2013) or the rise of dual-earner couples (García Román, 2012). However, there are other significant factors negatively influencing the lack of work–family balance in Spain such as the culture of presentism and the long-working day in Spain. Today, different civic, political and academic actors are working to reverse this situation.

The IESE Family-Responsible Employer Index (IFREI) aims to examine the work–family balance level of different organisations. IFREI analyses the implementation level of flexibility and work–family reconciliation policies in companies, their effect on employees and on the organisation itself. The International Center for Work and Family (ICWF) of IESE Business School developed in 1999 the IFREI 1.0, evaluating the implementation of policies aimed to reconcile work, family and personal life in 19 countries. The questionnaire collected information from CEOs or HR managers and focused its study on policies, culture, brakes and drivers. In 2010, a new version of the questionnaire was developed. The IFREI 1.5, addressed to all employees of a company, measures the impact that policies, the supervisor and culture have on organisational and individual results. It has involved more than 30,000 people in 23 countries, and specifically more than 300 in Spain (in 2015). According to the Spanish results in 2015, two thirds of the sample reported that they have access to flexible schedules, with no significant difference between men and women (62 per cent and 63 per cent, respectively). Regarding culture, only one third of men (33 per cent) and one quarter (25 per cent) of women reported that they work in a culture that allows a good balance between work and family responsibilities. The average number of working hours in the office per week was 45.8 for men and 43.07 for women. Moreover, the participants in this study reported that they work five hours more per week from home (5.7 men and 4.8 women), resulting in more than 50 total working hours per week for men and 48 working hours for women.

In a context such as Spain, the role of the supervisors is crucial. Table 6.1 shows the preference for servant leadership for male and women. Servant leaders are those who create the conditions for people to trust them by putting their interests and needs in first place, that is, by serving them (Greenleaf, 1977). Servant leaders display behaviours that instill in their followers 'the self-confidence and desire to become servant leaders themselves' (Liden *et al.*, 2008, p. 162). As we can observe the preference for servant leadership is relatively high, more than 5 points in a 7-point Likert scale, with no special differences between men and women, although there is higher rate of women with a woman as a supervisor, and the lower rate of men with a man as a supervisor. However, if we examine the rating for the actual servant leadership (Table 6.2), we can observer a considerable gap between preferences and real ratings. For example, while the preference of servant leadership for men is 5.1 (male supervisor) and 5.2 (female supervisor), the real rating for actual servant leadership is 3.7 and 3.6, respectively. We found similar results for women, as Table 6.2 shows. Thus, supervisors, who have an important impact on employee's work–family balance, have room to improve in their leadership style.

Table 6.1 Preference for servant leadership

	Male (supervisor)	Female (supervisor)
Men (employee)	5.1	5.2
Women (employee)	5.3	5.4

Source: IESE Family Responsible Employer Index (IFREI) 2016. Developed by the ICWF at IESE Business School. For more information about IFREI visit: http://ifrei.iese.edu/en

Table 6.2 Rating of actual servant leadership

	Male (supervisor)	Female (supervisor)
Men (employee)	3.7	3.6
Women (employee)	3.8	3.8

Source: IESE Family Responsible Employer Index (IFREI) 2016. Developed by the ICWF at IESE Business School. For more information about IFREI visit: http://ifrei.iese.edu/en

Challenges for women to advance to higher managerial positions in Spain

Women are seen, and expected, to be primary carers of children and older people. Women tend to do most of the caring work, such as cooking, cleaning and shopping, and it is mostly around activities related to playing and sports that men share the responsibilities to an even extent.

The results of IFREI Survey (2015) show this clearly. There is an important difference in the number of hours per day devoted to children between men and women (Figure 6.1). As Figures 6.1 to 6.5 show, the participants have been categorised in four different environments depending on the policies, culture and supervisor of their organisations. An A environment (enriching) means that people have access to flexible policies, work in a culture that allows work–family balance and they have family-supportive supervisors. In contrast, people in a D environment (polluted) work in an environment that systematically hinders work–family balance. According to that classification, the first conclusion is that women devote more time to their children regardless of the working environment they are in. The second conclusion is that the working environment clearly affects the number of hours devoted to children under 14 years old by fathers and mothers. We can see this same trend in the data related to the number of times men and women have dinner with their children, play with them or read to them (Figures 6.2, 6.3 and 6.4).

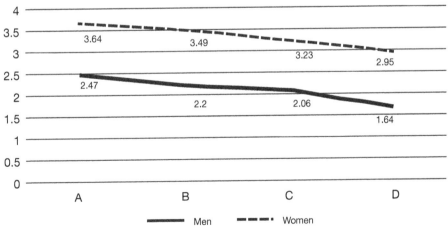

Figure 6.1 Number of hours per day devoted to children under 14 years old
Source: IESE Family Responsible Employer Index (IFREI) 2016. Developed by the ICWF at IESE Business School. For more information about IFREI visit: http://ifrei.iese.edu/en

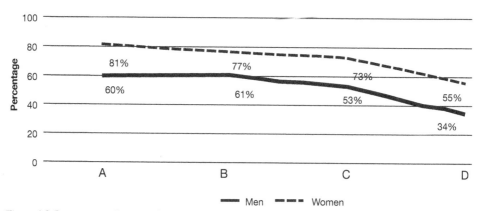

Figure 6.2 Percentage of men and women who have dinner more than four times per week with their children under 14

Source: IESE Family Responsible Employer Index (IFREI) 2016. Developed by the ICWF at IESE Business School. For more information about IFREI visit: http://ifrei.iese.edu/en

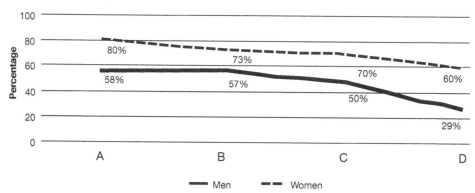

Figure 6.3 Percentage of men and women who play more than four times per week with their children under 14

Source: IESE Family Responsible Employer Index (IFREI) 2016. Developed by the ICWF at IESE Business School. For more information about IFREI visit: http://ifrei.iese.edu/e

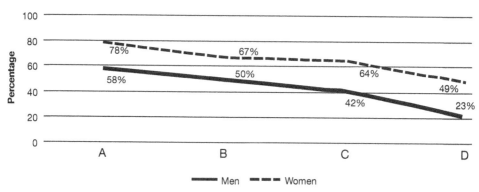

Figure 6.4 Percentage of men and women who read more than four times per week with their children under 14

As Figure 6.5 shows, the working environment not only has an impact on children but also on elderly parents who are in need. In this particular case, we see only a positive impact of the A environment, but not with the rest of the environments. So, in this case, only working in a very good environment has a positive impact on the attention devoted to parents who are in need.

This problem is exacerbated by the number of divorces that has led to an increase in the number of households headed by single (and or divorced) mothers. Women who raise their children without the support of their partners are held to a double standard: they are, on the one hand, expected to provide extremely dedicated care to their children; and on the other hand, they are scrutinised to see whether they are excellent workers who merit having a job.

All these barriers result in a greater proportion of women leaders, than men leaders, with no family responsibilities. Indeed, women in higher positions are more likely to be divorced and to have fewer and older children than are men.

How to unleash the economic power and potential of women

In Spain there is clearly a need to facilitate flexibility both for men and women and not only for family reasons, but for productivity reasons, health reasons, and to unleash the potential that new technologies allow and demand. A substantial number of changes is needed to make more gender-balanced managerial representation feasible. Among them we highlight three necessary changes:

1   Managers' mindset: organisational decision makers should understand that long office hours are no longer necessary or beneficial. A mindset that favours long hours in Spain translates into the organisational culture of 'presentism', low productivity and low work–family balance.
2   A more flexible job market, in which men and women can exit and re-enter in a smooth and painless manner: to date the job market is so inflexible that women who exit it for family reasons are most likely to never re-enter again. As a result:
  a)   Many women leave the job market and can never return, or do so accepting a much lower managerial ranking than they should otherwise have;
  b)   Many women do not exit the job market for family reasons, yet they avoid having the number of children they would ideally like to, resulting in an extremely low birth rate in the country;

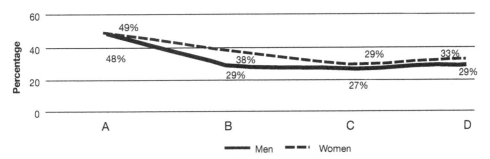

Figure 6.5 Percentage of men and women who help elderly parents in need with two or more
      activities (e.g. doctors, social needs, etc.)
Source: IESE Family Responsible Employer Index (IFREI) 2016. Developed by the ICWF at IESE Business School.
      For more information about IFREI visit: http://ifrei.iese.edu/en

c)   Many women refuse to accept promotions because those promotions are incompatible with caring for family.

Full development of organisational, family and social roles. As an example, Table 6.3 shows the number of children that people have and the ideal number of children they would like to have. According to Table 6.3, people want to have more children than they have and one potential barrier is the way they balance work and family responsibilities.

Conclusion: how to foster women's advancement

We suggest that promoting women's leadership would be beneficial for society in general. The goal is to have a more humane society and business world, which as a consequence will allow men and women from different ethnic and other backgrounds to thrive, flourish and perform to their optimal capacity.

Furthermore, we also suggest that the work that is required to make this a reality should be done by the government, businesses and society at large. Only by changes articulated at these three levels will Spain facilitate equal opportunities for both men and women. These changes require a mindset that is more pro-family, more pro-female and more flexible.

We propose that governments should support women in the workforce with policies such as: fostering a higher involvement of men at home, implementing new and strong family policies (parental leave, universal work service cheque), offering benefits for those companies with pioneering initiatives on work–family balance, and implementing legislation that allows a balance between work and family for men and women.

Business organisations have also an important role to play in supporting women in the workforce. As a suggestion, we propose that they: measure the beneficial effects of having people involved in family matters, since the home environment is where people develop soft skills that are required in the twenty-first century; encourage talented women in the business by offering the necessary training and mentoring opportunities; and review their current evaluation process and make an extra effort to measure the performance and competences of their employees.

Spain is still far from offering an environment, both for men and women, where people can fully thrive professionally and personally. There is a need to have governmental policies that facilitate a flexible yet, to some extent, secure environment. Such a legislative environment should facilitate a higher employment and re-employment rate. It should foster a work environment that both men and women can enter, exit and re-enter easily, gaining in employability with each change. It should facilitate couples to have the number of children they ideally would like to, thus achieving the necessary workforce replacement rate. There is

Table 6.3 Desired number of children

Actual number of children	Desired number of children
0	2.35
1	2.30
2	2.56
3	3.52
4	4.33

Source: IESE Family Responsible Employer Index (IFREI) 2016. Developed by the ICWF at IESE Business School. For more information about IFREI visit: http://ifrei.iese.edu/en

a need for organisations to facilitate more humane environments that foster employees' contributions and diversity. In such environments, managers should value employees' contributions more than they value their hours of physical presence. Last but not least, there is a need for a shift in mindset among employees. They should be able to proactively manage their careers so that they retain their employability, demand and offer flexibility, and contribute to their companies.

There is still a long road ahead for Spain to offer the best possible environment for men and women to develop their careers. However, a lot has been accomplished and the efforts among academics, business members and political groups have resulted in great improvements.

References

Aláez-Aller, R., Longás-García, J. C. and Ullibarri-Arce, M. (2011). Visualising gender wage differences in the European Union. *Gender, Work & Organization*, *18*(s1): e49–e87.

Casas-Arce, P. and Saiz, A. (2015). Women and power: unpopular, unwilling, or held back? *Journal of Political Economy*, *123*(3), 641–669.

CNIIE, I.D.L.M. (2012). Mujeres en cargos de representación del sistema educativo II. www.inmujer.gob.es/areasTematicas/educacion/programas/docs/MujeresCargosRepresentacion.pdf (last visited 5 October 2015).

De Anca, C. (2008). Women on corporate boards of directors in Spanish listed companies. In S. Vinnicombe, V. Singh, R. J. Burke, D. Bilimoria and M. Huse (eds), *Women on Corporate Boards of Directors: International Research and Practice* (pp. 96–107). Cheltenham: Edward Elgar.

Delgado, M., Meil, G. and Zamora, F. (2008). Short on children and short on family policies. *Demographic Research*, *19*, 1059–1104.

European Commission (2010). *Mapping the Maze: Getting more women to the top in research*. Brussels: EC.

García Román, J. (2012). El Uso del tiempo en las parejas de doble ingreso. (Doctoral Thesis). Universitat Autònoma de Barcelona, Spain.

Gender Map (2015). Gender map. www.gender-map.com/#/economy/country/Spain/sortBy/ratio (last visited 5 October 2015).

Global Entrepreneurship Monitor (2014). Informe GEM España 2013. file:///C:/Users/mlasheras/Downloads/1396885660GEM_Spain_2013_Report.pdf (last visited 27 October 2015).

González Menéndez, M. C. and Martínez González, L. (2012). Spain on the Norwegian pathway: Towards a gender-balanced presence of women on corporate boards. In C. Fagan, M. C. González Menéndez and S. Gómez Anson (eds), *Women on Corporate Boards and in Top Management: European trends and policy* (pp. 169–197). Chippenham, UK: Palgrave-MacMillan.

Grant Thorton (2014). Presencia de mujeres en puestos directivos: retroceso en España. www.grantthornton.es/publicaciones/estudios/Grant-Thornton-Estudio-IBR-2013-mujer-en-puestos-directivos.pdf (last visited 5 October 2015).

Grant Thorton (2015). Women in business: the path to leadership. www.grantthornton.be/Resources/IBR-2015-Women-in-Business.pdf (last visited 5 October 2015).

Grau-Grau, M. (2013). Clouds over Spain: Work and family in the age of austerity. *International Journal of Sociology and Social Policy*, *33*(9/10), 579–593.

Greenleaf, K. R. (1977). *Servant Leadership*. Mahwah, NJ: Paulist Press.

IESE (2015). Tercer informe de las mujeres en los Consejos del IBEX-35. http://blog.iese.edu/nuriach-inchilla/files/2015/03/Informe-Mujeres-2015-FINAL.pdf (last visited in 23 October 2015).

International Labour Organization (2013). *Global Employment Trends for Youth 2013. A generation at risk*. Geneva: ILO.

Liden, R. C., Wayne, S. J., Zhao, H. and Henderson, D. (2008). Servant leadership: Development of a multidimensional measure and multi-level assessment. *Leadership Quarterly*, *19*(2): 161–177.

Pande, R. and Ford, D. (2011). Gender quotas and female leadership: A review. Background paper for the *World Development Report on Gender*. Unpublished.

Pucheta-Martínez, M. C. and Bel-Oms, I. (2015). The gender gap in pay in company boards. *Industrial and Corporate Change, 24*(2): 467–510.

Trading Economics. (2015). Spain. http://es.tradingeconomics.com/spain/unemployment-rate (last visited 22 October 2015).

World Economic Forum (2015). *The Global Gender Gap Report 2014.* http://reports.weforum.org/_static/global-gender-gap-2014/ESP.pdf (last visited 20 October 2015).

7 Women in management in the United Kingdom

Fiona M. Wilson

Introduction

The number of women in management in the UK has grown, and continues to grow, so that the proportion of women among UK managers is 34.8 per cent, slightly higher than the European Union average of 33.5 per cent (ONS, 2013). However the lack of equality that women managers face is quite striking. There is particularly a lack of female managers in the most senior positions. The top positions are largely filled by white able-bodied men (Gatrell and Swan, 2008). Less than one third of the UK's most influential jobs are held by women. For example the armed forces has just 1.3 per cent of women in top posts whereas the judiciary has 13.2 per cent (Holt, 2012). A good deal of concern has been expressed about women's lack of success in breaking through the 'glass ceiling', not least by women themselves who believe that the barriers to them progressing in their careers have not diminished (ILM, 2011). Equal pay is also an issue, as are attitudes towards women in management. The slow progress towards equality is a concern. Before we look in more detail at women in management, let's look at the labour force characteristics to tease out whether there are fundamental differences between men and women's employment.

Labour force characteristics

The number of women in employment in the UK has gradually risen over the last 40 years; more women are either seeking work or are in work than was the case in the past (ONS, 2013). This trend has been accompanied by a fall in the number of men employed, mainly due to the demise of shipbuilding, mining and manufacturing where men's jobs dominated. A vast amount of literature has charted the rise in women's employment, particularly that of mothers, in the last four decades. While only a half of women were in or seeking any sort of work in 1971, around 67 per cent of women aged 16 to 64 were in work in 2013 (ONS, 2013). The number of men in work full time was 15.3 million; for women the figure was 13.4 million. The full-time men worked an average of 44 hours a week while women worked 40 hours (ONS, 2013). In 2013 there were 2.1 million men and 5.9 million women in part-time employment (ONS, 2013). There has been little change in these figures for the last ten years. Marriage or cohabitation and children now make little difference to whether or not women work. For example the employment rate for mothers in a couple is 80 per cent and for lone mothers is 74 per cent (ONS, 2013). There are over 2.4 million women who are not in work but want to work and over 1.3 million who want to increase the number of hours they work (Women's Business Council, 2013). However females continue to be segregated into certain jobs and sectors. Women are far more likely to be in the low paid jobs (around 17.2 per cent of men in work are low paid compared with 28 per cent of women workers) (TUC, 2012). The most common occupation for women is nursing while the most common for men is as programmers and software development professionals (ONS, 2013). Women dominate employment within caring and leisure, accounting for 82 per cent of these jobs; 77 per cent of administrative and secretarial jobs are done by women. Men tend to be in higher skilled jobs and professional occupations associated with higher levels of pay. Why does this happen? Research on gender stereotyping shows that men are preferred for male-dominated jobs (Koch *et al.*, 2015). Some research in the UK has focused on women managing in male-dominated professions such as construction (Ness, 2012; Watts, 2009a) and fire fighting (Woodfield, 2015). That research shows that men have an embodied competence that women do not have (Woodfield, 2015). Men are seen as the 'ideal type' of manager or worker whereas women are the 'wrong' sex (Hatmaker, 2013). Those who take up a management position on a part-time basis or with flexible working time are viewed with suspicion and as less than fully committed to their jobs. It is assumed that senior management can only be a full-time commitment involving very long hours (Watts, 2009b). Yet research has shown how flexible work arrangements (e.g. flexible start and finishing times, working from home, working compressed hours, job sharing) can lead to significantly higher feelings of balance, job satisfaction and professional progression for both men and women (Wichert, 2014) and so should be supported by employers.

Women in the labour force face inequality and it is still women, rather than men, who take time out of paid work when they have children and who then suffer the 'parenthood penalty' on their return to work (Scott *et al.*, 2008). However, highly educated women are more likely to return to full-time paid work earlier, often to the same employer and do not suffer the parenthood penalty as much as less educated women (Li *et al.*, 2008). Research also shows that being a parent is not a significant predictor of seniority. There is no statistically significant difference in the number of promotions between women with children and women without children. Taking time out to have a family appears to have a marginal but not significant impact of women's career progression (KPMG, 2014).

The vast majority of unpaid domestic work is provided by women. Research consistently shows the high levels that they contribute. For example Ben-Galmin and Thompson (2012) found that 77 per cent of married women do more housework than their husbands. Just one in ten married men do an amount equal to their wives.

One may think that because women have a higher share of childcare responsibilities and household duties, research might show that their work commitment is less than that of men. On the contrary, research has indicated that women's work commitment is typically stronger than men's and that work commitment is stronger among the more highly educated and higher social classes (Esser, 2009). That commitment may lead (at least in part) to female managers being childless. Research has also shown that 41 per cent of the women managers surveyed were childless compared with 28 per cent of men (ILM, 2011).

Despite women's higher commitment and the Equal Pay Act (1970), women in the UK face a high gender pay gap. This pay gap is significantly lower in the public sector, where it is half that of the private sector (TUC, 2012). The overall pay gap in the UK stands at 19.1 per cent (2014) measured by median gross hourly pay (ONS, 2014a). Whilst the gap has fallen significantly from 27.5 per cent in 1997, this figure is still above the EU 2014 average of 16.4 per cent (Eurostat, 2014). Income inequality has risen faster in the UK than any other country in the Organization for Economic Co-operation and Development (OECD) and today women earn on average £140,000 less than men over their working careers (Player, 2013). A male graduate can expect to earn 20 per cent more than a female one (ONS, 2011). Between

20011 and 2012, the average male in an executive role earned a basic salary of £40,325 compared to £30,265 for a female in the same type of role. Based on current pay levels, an average female executive would earn £423,390 less than a male executive on a similar career path (Chartered Management Institute and XpertHR, 2012). Data from the Chartered Management Institute show that discrepancies in salaries widen at the higher levels of management and particularly affect female managers over the age of 40 who earn 35 per cent less than men (Goodley, 2014). There is also a bonus pay gap so that the average bonus for a female director stands at £41,956, while for male directors the average bonus is £53,010. Certainly there are good reasons for women to pursue higher education, to try to avoid the lower paid lower status jobs.

Women pursuing education

Participation in higher education is expanding, particularly for women. There has been a 550 per cent change in the percentage of females in higher education in the last three decades (Scott *et al.*, 2008). Women now outnumber men as registered students in the UK. A higher proportion of female students (56.2 per cent) than male students (43.8 per cent) were studying in higher education in the UK in 2013 (HESA, 2013). In 2015 this amounted to nearly 58,000 more women entering university than men. Women also achieved higher marks, as 72 per cent received at least an upper second class degree compared with 68 per cent of men (Grove, 2015). While women outnumber men in the majority of university subjects studied (including law, social science, medicine and education), there are some subjects where men are more numerous. These include computer science and engineering. In business and administrative studies, women comprise half the students (Universities UK, 2012). At MBA level 32 per cent of students were female in 2012, an increase of around 20 per cent since the 1990s (Finn, 2012). Recognising the under-representation of women pursuing MBAs, some business schools (such as London and Saïd) offer scholarships for female candidates.

Women in management

The number of women occupying management positions is greater than it has ever been. The number of female managers has grown. For example women in management roles more than trebled between 1994 and 2005 (Chartered Management Institute, 2009). However women's representation in more senior management positions is still low. Women make up only 33 per cent of managers, directors and senior officials and only 13.3 per cent of FTSE 250 board members (Sealy and Vinnicombe, 2013). Only four companies in the FTSE 100 have female chief executive officers (CEOs) (Smith, 2014). A man is 4.5 times more likely to make it into an executive committee role on the board of directors of an organisation than a woman starting out at the same time; senior women are two times less likely to be promoted than their male peers (KPMG, 2014). While the UK government has called on the eight FTSE 100 companies with men-only boards to improve their diversity, and asked UK companies to disclose the proportion of men and women in senior executive positions and in their boardrooms, they have not introduced quotas so the gender imbalance remains (Neville and Treanor, 2012). There are good reasons for companies to increase the numbers of women in senior posts, for example companies with more women in their executive committees have better financial performance (McKinsey, 2010). A UK business school reports that having at least one female director on the board appears to cut a company's chances of becoming insolvent by about 20 per cent, while having two or three female directors lowers the risk even more (Wilson and Altanlar, 2009). However all the studies show a continuing problem for women who aspire to top management positions. The glass ceiling (a term coined in 1986 to describe the invisible barrier preventing women moving up the corporate ladder) continues to be firmly in place (Weyer, 2007). Women are not seen to have the necessary characteristics for leadership in senior or middle management positions compared to men. Not only do women face a glass ceiling, there is also a 'glass cliff' (Ryan *et al.*, 2011) where it is suggested women are more likely than men to be appointed as leaders in times of poor company performance. Women then find they are overwhelmingly restricted to lower levels of management (Lyness and Heilman, 2006; Brannan and Priola, 2012). Successful managers are perceived to possess those characteristics attitudes and temperament more commonly ascribed to men than to women (Schein, 1973; Harris, 2002). Female stereotypical attributes, including communal qualities of warmth and niceness, tend to be inconsistent with the attributes believed to be required for success in many organisations. What results from the mismatch between the group stereotype (women) and a job role (manager) is negative performance expectations, which in turn produce biased evaluations (Heilman and Eagly, 2008). Schein's (1973) adage "think manager, think male" appears to still apply well in the UK. Not only are the characteristics held by a manager seen as similar to the conceptions of men, but also those who select managers are likely to see men as more plausible candidates for managerial jobs (Schein *et al.*, 1998; Harris, 2002). Gender stereotypes have shown little change over the last 50 years; there may even be an increase in sex typing, especially regarding the stereotypes and self concepts focusing upon the personality traits of women (Lueptow *et al.*, 2001).

What other explanations are there as to why the proportion of women in top management has remained so small? Powell (2000) goes as far as to argue that women's presence at top levels of management violates the norm of male superiority. This is one explanation as to why women are likely to be sexually harassed; men are hostile to women who compete with them for jobs and can demonstrate that hostility in the form of sexual harassment. Women as a minority encounter difficulties in adjusting to and fitting into male managerial cultures. They become 'tokens', their behaviour taken as an example of 'women's' behaviour and always in the spotlight. They face an unsupportive environment, the 'old boys' network, an unwillingness by those in power to confront and eliminate sexism and being assigned less influential projects (Nelson and Burke, 2000).

How do women in management perceive their situation? Women managers perceive that the glass ceiling exists. Of nearly 3000 managers questioned in a survey for the Institute of Leadership and Management (ILM, 2011), 73 per cent of women agreed that the glass ceiling exists while only 38 per cent of men did. Alongside well-known obstacles to advancement such as maternity and childcare-related issues, the findings revealed that women managers are also impeded by lower ambitions and expectations. Compared with men, the female respondents tended to lack self belief and confidence and so followed a less straightforward career path. The higher expectations and confidence of male managers propelled them forward in more senior posts earlier than the women. To increase the female representation on boards, some 47 per cent of women but only 24 per cent of men backed quotas for female executives as a way of bringing about greater equality (BBC, 2011). These findings are supported by other studies, for example Sealy (2010) who found that the women executives she interviewed intuitively were not in favour of any kind of affirmative action to bring about greater equality.

It may be that we have to question whether and how women might be choosing to opt out of striving for the highest managerial positions. It may be, for example, that women are not defining their career success by considering that as a place on the corporate board (Cornelius and Skinner, 2008). It may be that women seek a better work–life balance than is offered by the top jobs in management and are rejecting jobs where they are required to subordinate home and family for company and career (Collinson and Collinson, 2004). Perhaps women would want and flourish in top management jobs if they were given the freedom to work flexible hours instead of having to adhere to the 'presenteeism' that is often deemed requisite for a successful career (Sealy, 2010). Perhaps women, despite being as committed to progression as men, find that their lack of promotion means they do not reach the top management (KPMG, 2014).

Would part-time working help female managers? While part-time work is increasing, paradoxically excessively long working hours for managers have become the norm. This is due in part to work intensification and partly because long working hours have come to be an indicator of commitment. Work intensification has come about, in part, due to restructuring and downsizing and more recently due to the economic recession. Evidence of increasing managerial workloads is widespread. Recently research has shown an alarmingly high level of concern amongst managers about how their health is being negatively affected by the long hours they work. Around half the managers surveyed by Worrall *et al.* (2008) linked personal health problems to the long hours they worked. Forty five per cent believed their productivity at work was disadvantaged by the long hours spent at work; it also impacted on social lives and personal relationships. As a result of long working hours, men and women have to make a stark choice between work and families. The UK has a particularly long hours working culture which increases occupational downgrading amongst mothers and can encourage the gender division of paid work and childcare, with fathers working long hours and mothers working part time and providing care (Metcalf and Rolfe, 2010).

What about managers from ethnic backgrounds? How do they fare in management? There may still be a colour bar to management jobs in the UK. One in ten employed people are from black, Asian and minority ethnic (BAME) backgrounds but only 1 in 16 of top management positions and 1 in 13 management positions are held by BAME people and there has been virtually no ethnicity change in top management positions between 2007 and 2012 (Race for Opportunity, 2012). While fewer than 1 per cent of white managers indicate that racial discrimination had been a barrier to their progression, one third of Asian and 20 per cent of black managers indicate that this is a barrier for them (Wilton, 2008).

Women managers can also suffer from age discrimination. Research in the UK has shown that women experience more age discrimination than men (Duncan and Loretto, 2004; Granleese and Sayer, 2005). Managers are expected to have knowledge and experience that come with age. This is often naturally associated with older men, whereas women's knowledge is not valued as much (Jyrkinen and McKie, 2012).

Women entrepreneurs

Women's entrepreneurship can be seen as a means of escaping the persistent inequalities and the occupational confines of the labour market. There are, however, fewer women defined as entrepreneurs than men and the identity of entrepreneur is gendered masculine (Lewis, 2013). While 9 per cent of men are engaged in entrepreneurial activity in the UK, the figure stands at just 4 per cent for women (Global Entrepreneurship Monitor, 2010). Despite the numbers of self-employed being higher than at any point in the last 40 years and the number of self-employed women increasing at a faster rate than men so that between 2008 and 2011 women accounted for an unprecedented 80 per cent of the new self-employed (ONS, 2013; Prowess, 2015), women constitute just 32 per cent of the self-employed (ONS, 2014b) and 17 per cent of business owners (Prowess, 2015). These higher rates of start ups may be balanced by high rates of closure. Women attribute their business exits less to failure and more to personal reasons, especially amongst the 25–34 age group (Marlow *et al.*, 2012).

In focusing on sex as a variable in the entrepreneurship literature, certain differences have been highlighted and others obscured. Female entrepreneurs can be portrayed as lacking or 'lesser'. For example one Global Entrepreneurship Monitor report says that women 'are less likely to know an entrepreneur, less likely to be thinking of starting a business, less likely to think they have the skills to start a business, less likely to see business opportunities and more likely to fear failure than their male counterparts' (Harding, 2007: 3 7). Women are more likely to own firms which are operated from home, are part time and in lower order services with low growth trajectories (Marlow *et al.*, 2012). Yet research also shows that once in business, few gender-related performance differences are evident amongst the self-employed or small firm owners. In fact women-owned firms outperform those owned by their male counterparts when firm characteristics are controlled for (business age, sector, size) as well as the attributes of the individual (education, age, income) (Marlow *et al.*, 2012). Both men and women show a strong appetite for growing their businesses (CFE, 2015). It is clear then that we need to research this topic of women running their own businesses in a sensitive manner to explore and uncover some of the myths that have arisen about women–owned businesses (Marlow and McAdam, 2013; Lewis, 2013). A new UK government initiative has created mentoring events for female entrepreneurs to encourage them (Government Equalities Office, 2015).

Country legislation

In Britain there have been three major complementary pieces of legislation to impact on the employment of women and promote greater equality. These were the Equal Pay Act 1970 that prohibited any less favourable treatment between men and women in terms of pay, and the Sex Discrimination Act 1975 that promoted equality and opportunity between men and women. The third, the Employment Protection Act 1975 made it illegal to sack a woman due to pregnancy and introduced statutory maternity provision. This domestic framework of legislation enacts various requirements in European law and continues to be profoundly influenced by rulings of the European Court of Justice. The Sex Discrimination Act covered discrimination on grounds of gender, marital status and gender reassignment. The provisions of the Act applied to women, men and married persons. In 1970 the Equal Pay Act enshrined the principle that women and men doing the same or comparable work should be paid the same amount. The Act asserts the principle that men and women should receive equal pay for equal work, including redundancy pay, pensions, severance pay, sick pay and paid leave. The legislation requires a comparator that can be 'like work', 'work rated as equivalent' and 'work of equal value'. However while the full-time gender pay gap was reduced by about 20 percentage points between 1970 and 2010, four decades later we are still waiting for the rhetoric of equal pay to fully become reality (Bailey, 2013). There appears to be renewed political pressure to reduce the pay gap with the introduction of the Equality Act 2010. The Equality Act 2010 makes some important changes in relation to equal pay. For example it requires public bodies to report on unequal pay and to comply with the Equality Duty and bans employment secrecy clauses that prevent people discussing their own pay.

Positive discrimination is not permitted under British sex discrimination law but positive action is allowed. Under-represented groups can be encouraged to apply for posts, and an organisation can set targets for the number of women to be recruited. Family friendly measures such as career breaks, flexible working time and assistance with childcare help individuals carry the double load of paid work and domestic commitments. (From the end of June 2014 every employee has the statutory right to request flexible working after 26 weeks of employment service.) Access to single sex training can allow women to overcome earlier educational and training disadvantage and encourage them to move up the management hierarchy.

Further legislation has strengthened the existing legislation to extend women' rights. For example, there have been extensions of the maternity leave period, with a widening of coverage to more women as well as increases in the paid maternity leave entitlement and the introduction of paid paternity leave to fathers. The Equality Act 2010 brought together a number of pieces of equality legislation. If section 28 of the Act was activated, it would require companies to report on their pay gap. However the British government has indicated that it is not minded to commence these provisions. It is easy to conclude that legislation has consistently fallen short of protecting women from sex discrimination (Smith, 2014).

Initiatives to support the advancement of women

There appears to be renewed political pressure to reduce the pay gap with the introduction of the Equality Act 2010 and a government initiative launched in September 2011 – \Think, Act, Report', a Government Equalities Office campaign, which encourages companies to think about gender equality in the workplace and disclose differences in pay. The Equality Act 2010 makes some important changes in relation to equal pay, as mentioned above.

A UK nationwide voluntary business campaign, established in 1991, called 'Opportunity Now', set key goals for tackling inequality through a broad-based, business-driven policy approach (www.opportunitynow.org.uk). Senior managers were asked to drive change from the top, be seen as role models in leading equal opportunities, and develop and address the issues as part of their business strategy. They were asked to make an investment, change behaviour, communicate and share ownership in developing new working methods to enhance business performance. Members of Opportunity Now are required annually to demonstrate how they have met their goals. Opportunity Now currently boasts a membership of 350 employers from the UK's largest organisations in the private, public and education sectors 'who wish to transform their workplaces by insuring inclusiveness for women' (www.opportunitynow.org.uk). They work with Catalyst, based in the US, to collaborate in research on women's advancement in management. Another government initiative called POWERful women showcases female leadership potential in the UK's energy sector, where only 12.8 per cent of jobs are held by women and 12.5 percent of directors on energy boards are female (www.gov.uk/government/news/fuelling-the-pipeline-of-female-talent-in-the-uks-energy-sector). Similarly the 30% Club was launched in the UK in 2010 supported by the Department for Culture, Media and Sport, with a goal of achieving 30 per cent women on FTSE 100 boards by the end of 2015. They say that there are five factors that bring results: 1) a measurable goal with a defined timetable; 2) political consensus that the status quo is unacceptable; 3) change driven by those in power; 4) openness to collaborate; and 5) a concerted and consistent series of actions and programmes from schoolrooms to boardrooms (see http://30percentclub.org). Organizations such as Ernst and Young are founding members.

The issue of diversity at board level has been given close attention in the UK (Higgs, 2003; Davies, 2011; Department for Business, Innovation and Skills, 2013; Mercer, 2014) and a business case has been made repeatedly. However there are still barriers preventing women for reaching top positions and progress has been 'glacial' (ILM, 2011). The pace of change is so slow that the Financial Reporting Council is considering amending the UK Corporate

Governance Code to require listed companies to establish a policy concerning boardroom diversity, including measurable implementation objectives (Davies, 2011).

Equal opportunities polices have been part of employment policy and business practice since the early 1980s. To further enhance these policies, the Gender Equality Duty came into force in April 2007; this duty requires all public sector bodies to eliminate discrimination and harassment and to promote equality of opportunity between women and men (www.equali-tyhumanrights.com). It was introduced in recognition of the need for a radical new approach to equality – one that places more responsibility with service providers to think strategically about gender equality, rather than leaving it to individuals to challenge poor practice. The public sector has been regarded as leading the way in the development of equal opportunities policy. Results in both the private and public sector have been very mixed. Research has found that line managers play an important role in either challenging or reproducing inequality (Kirton and Greene, 2000).

Management and leadership development can support women's career progression. Research based in the UK (McBain *et al.*, 2012) has found that men and women report different types of development as being most effective. While business school and professional bodies' qualifications were among the top five most effective routes for both sexes, coaching (either by the line manager or an external source) was ranked the most effective development by women, but not by men. Mentorship and sponsorship can help women's career development (Chartered Management Institute and Women in Management, 2013).

Government initiatives to help employees reconcile work and family responsibilities have been introduced since the late 1990s. These have included enhanced maternity leave and pay, the introduction of paid paternity leave and unpaid parental leave (Teasdale, 2013). The policies are more likely to be found in large organisations such as those in the public sector. However these work–life policies are not widely accessed and many men and women working in management and the professions feel that they are not able to pursue flexible working (Fagan, 2009). Three times more women than men make requests for flexible working. However individuals are concerned about the adverse career implications of flexibility, particularly where commitment is equated with long working hours (Watts, 2009b) and work penalties (Tomlinson and Durbin, 2010).

The future

The model of the successful manager is male and while these stereotypes remain, they succeed in perpetuating the dominant place for men in management. Management cultures are described as masculine, characterised by long work hours, bullying and harassment and lacking in family friendly polices. While the traditional male career model of a full-time career is the norm and some women and very few men (Burnett *et al.*, 2013) step off the fast track to meet family responsibilities, women will continue to be seen as at a competitive disadvantage. Organisational initiatives relating to family friendly policies and flexible working have been directed at both men and women and positioned as gender neutral. However it is mainly women with dependent children who are most likely to pursue such working arrangements (Teasdale, 2013) and men may feel less entitled or fear there will be adverse pay and career implications if they use them (Gambles *et al.*, 2006). Changes in flexible working alone will not bring about equality for women in management in Britain. A quantum leap towards achieving greater equality in management and organisation is needed for women in the UK. We need to recognise how difficult it will be to change the stereotypes and conventions that underlie so much gender inequality in management.

References

Bailey, A. (2013) BIS: Government must match rhetoric with action on equal pay, *Guardian*, 20 June.

BBC (2011) Female managers say glass ceiling intact-survey, *BBC Business News*, 21 February. www.bbc.co.uk/news/business-12518277

Ben-Galmin, D. and Thompson, S. (2013) *Who's breadwinning? Working mothers and the new face of family support*, London: IPPR.

Brannan, M. and Priola, V. (2012) 'Girls who do boys like they're girls': Exploring the role of gender in the junior management of contemporary service work, *Gender, Work and Organization*, 19(2): 119–141.

Burnett, S. B., Gatrell, C. J., Cooper, C. L. and Sparrow, P. (2013) Fathers at work: a ghost in the organizational machine, *Gender, Work and Organization*, 20(6): 633–646.

CFE (2015) *Shattering stereotypes: women in entrepreneurship*, Centre for Entrepreneurs and Barclays Bank, April. www.centreforentrepreneurs.org/images/centreforentrepreneurs/Shattering_Stereotypes_Women_in_Entrepreneurship.pdf

Chartered Management Institute (2009) *Managers pay in the UK. Figures from the National Management Salary Survey*. www.managers.org.uk

Chartered Management Institute and XpertHR (2012) National management salary survey. www.managers.org.uk./news/women -hit-£40000-gender-paygap-over-course-careers

Chartered Management Institute and Women in Management (2013) *Women in leadership*, White Paper, March, London: CMI.

Collinson, D. L. and Collinson, M. (2004) The power of time: Leadership, management and gender, in C. F. Epstein and A. L. Kalleberg (eds) *Fighting for time: Shifting boundaries of work and social life*. New York: Russell Sage Foundation.

Cornelius, N. and Skinner, D. (2008) The careers of senior men and women – a capabilities theory perspective, *British Journal of Management*, 19: S141–S149.

Davies, M. (2011) *Women on boards*, London: Department for Business Innovation and Skills. www.gov.uk/government/uploads/system/uploads/attachment_data/file/31480/11-745-women-on-boards.pdf

Department for Business, Innovation and Skills (2013) *BIS Occasional paper 4: The business case for equality and diversity; a survey of the academic literature*, BIS/13/556.

Duncan, C. and Loretto, W. (2004) Never the right age? Gender, age-based discrimination and employment, *Gender, Work and Employment*, 11(1): 95–115.

Esser, I. (2009) *Has welfare made us lazy? Employment commitment in different welfare states*, British Social Attitudes, the 25th report, London: Sage.

Eurostat (2014) *Gender pay gap statistics*. ec.europa.eu/eurostat/statistics-explained/index.php/Gender_pay_gap_statistics

Fagan, C. (2009) *Working time in the UK – development and debates. Working time – in search of new research territories beyond flexibility debates*, Japanese Institute for Labour Policy and Training International Seminar on Working Time, 21–23 January, Tokyo.

Finn, W. (2012) MBA women: breaking down barriers at business schools, *The Telegraph*, 22 November. www.telegraph.co.uk/education/educationadvice/9683856/MBA-women-breaking-down-barriers-at-business-school.html

Gambles, R., Lewis, S. and Rapoport, R. (2006) *The myth of work–life balance: The challenge of our time for men, women and societies*, Chichester: John Wiley and Sons.

Gatrell, C. and Swann, E. (2008) *Gender and diversity in management: A concise introduction*, London: Sage.

Global Entrepreneurship Monitor (2010) *Global Entrepreneurship Monitor women's report 2010*. www.espae.espol.edu.ec/images/FTP/2010_GEM_Womens_Report.pdf

Goodley, S. (2014) Gender pay gap: female bosses earn 35 per cent less than male colleagues, *Guardian*, 19 August. www.theguardian.com/business/2014/aug/19/gender-pay-gap-women-bosses-earn-35-percent-less-than-men

Government Equalities Office (2015) Government funds new speed mentoring events for female entrepreneurs to nurture talent across the nation. www.gov.uk/government/news/government-funds-new-speed-mentoring-events-for-female-entrepreneurs-to-nurture-talent-across-the-nation

Granleese, J. and Sayer, G. (2005) Gendered ageism and 'lookism': a triple jeopardy for female academics, *Women in Management Review*, 21(6): 500–517.

Grove, J. (2015) Gender gaps among students revealed by UCAS, *Times Higher*, 21 January. www.times highereducation.co.uk/news/gender-gaps-among-students-revealed-by-ucas/2018113.article

Harding, R. (2007) *State of women's enterprise in the UK*, Norwich: Prowess Ltd.

Harris, H. (2002) Think international managers, think male: why are women not selected for international management assignments? *Thunderbird International Business Review*, 44(2): 175–203.

Hatmaker, D. M. (2013) Engineering identity: gender and professional identity negotiation among women engineers, *Gender, Work and Organization*, 20(4): 382–396.

Heilman, M. E. and Eagly, A. H. (2008) Gender stereotypes are alive, well and busy producing workplace discrimination, *Industrial and Organizational Psychology*, 1: 393–398.

HESA (2013) Student population statistics. www.hesa.ac.uk/intros/stuintro1213

Higgs, D. (2003) *Review of the role and effectiveness of non-executive directors*, January, London: Department of Trade and Industry. www.ecgi.org/codes/documents/higgsreport.pdf

Holt, G. (2012) Women hold fewer than one third of the top jobs – BBC research, *BBC News*, 29 May. www.bbc.co.uk/news/uk-18187449

ILM (Institute of Leadership and Management) (2011) *Ambition and gender at work*, London: ILM. www.i-l-m.com/About-ILM/Research-programme/Research-reports/Ambition-and-gender

Jyrkinen, M. and McKie, L. (2012) Gender, age and ageism: experiences of women managers in Finland and Scotland, *Work, Employment and Society*, 21(1): 61–77.

Kirton, G. and Green, A.M. (2000) *The dynamics of managing diversity*, Oxford: Butterworth-Heinemann.

Koch, A. J., D'Mello, S. D. and Sackett, P. P. (2015) A meta analysis of gender stereotypes and bias in experimental simulation of employment decision making, *Journal of Applied Psychology*, 300(1): 128–161.

KPMG (2014) *Cracking the code*. www.kpmg.com/UK/en/IssuesAndInsights/ArticlesPublications/Documents/PDF/About/Cracking%20the%20code.pdf

Lewis, P. (2013) The search for an authentic entrepreneurial identity: difference and professionalism among women business owners, *Gender, Work and Organization*, 20(3): 252–266.

Li, Y., Devine, F. and Heath, A. (2008) *Equality group inequalities in education, employment and earnings*, EHRC Research Report 10, Manchester.

Lueptow, L. B., Garovich-Szabo, L. and Lueptow, M. B. (2001) Social change and the persistence of sex typing, 1974–1997, *Social Forces*, 80(1): 1–32.

Lyness, K. and Heilman, M. (2006) When fit is fundamental: performance evaluation and promotions of upper-level female and male managers, *Journal of Applied Psychology*, 9(14): 777–785.

Marlow, S., Hart, M., Levie, J. and Shamsul, M. K. (2012) *Women in enterprise: a different perspective*, RBS Group, UK.

Marlow, S. and McAdam, M. (2013) Gender and entrepreneurship: advancing debate and challenging myths; exploring the mystery of the under-performing female entrepreneur, *International Journal of Entrepreneurial Behaviour and Research*, 19(1): 114–124.

McBain, R., Ghobadian, A., Switzer, J., Witton, P. Woodman, P., and Pearson, G. (2012) *The business benefits of management and leadership development*, London: Chartered Management Institute and Penna.

McKinsey (2010) *Women matter*. www.mckinsey.com/features/women_matter

Mercer, M. (2014) *Diversity at senior team and board level*, IES Perspectives on HR 2014, Member paper 95, London: Institute for Employment Studies.

Metcalf, H. and Rolfe, H. (2010) *Women's choices in the labour market*, National Institute of Economic and Social Research, London.

Nelson, D. L. and Burke, R. J. (2000) Women, work stress and health, in M. J. Davidson and R. J. Burke (eds) *Women in Management: current research issues*, Vol II, London: Sage.

Ness, K. (2012) Constructing masculinity in the building trades: 'Most jobs in the construction industry can be done by women', *Gender, Work and Organization*, 19(6): 654–676.

Neville, S. and Treanor, J. (2012) Research highlights lack of women in executive roles, *Guardian*, 12 December. www.theguardian.com/business/2012/dec/12/research-lack-women-executive-roles

ONS (Office for National Statistics) (2011) *Economic and Labour Market Review*, 5, 4.

ONS (2013) *Full report – women in the labour market*. www.ons.gov.uk/ons/dcp171776_328352. pdf

ONS (2014a) *Annual survey of hours and earnings 2014, provisional results*, December. www.ons.gov.uk/ons/rel/ashe/annual-survey-of-hours-and-earnings/2014-provisional-results/stb-ashe-statistical-bulletin-2014.html#tab-Gender-pay-differences

ONS (2014b) *Why has the number of self employed increased?* www.ons.gov.uk/ons/rel/lmac/self-employed-workers-in-the-uk/2014/sty-self-employed.html

Player, A. (2013) Gender inequality: why women are still held back, *Guardian*, 6 December. www.theguardian.com/business/economics-blog/2013/dec/06/gender-equality-women-stereotypes-stop-progress

Powell, G.N. (2000) The glass ceiling: explaining the good and bad news, in M. J. Davidson and R. J. Burke (eds) *Women in management: current research issues*, vol. II, London: Sage.

Prowess (2015) UK female entrepreneurship: key facts. www.prowess.org.uk/facts

Race for Opportunity (2012) *Race at the top: a review of BAME leadership in the UK*. http://raceforopportunity.bitc.org.uk/system/files/research/rfo_race_at_the_top_-_exec_summary_0.pdf

Ryan, M. K., Haslam, S. A., Heresby, M. D. and Bongiorno, R. (2011) Think crisis – think female: The glass cliff and contextual variation in think manager–think male stereotype, *Journal of Applied Psychology*, 96: 470–484.

Schein, V. (1973) The relationship between sex role stereotypes and requisite management characteristics, *Journal of Applied Psychology*, 57(2): 95–100.

Schein, V., Mueller, R., Lituchy, T. and Liu, J. (1998) Think managers – think male: a global phenomenon? *Journal of Organizational Behaviour*, 17(1): 33–41.

Scott, J., Dex, S. and Joshi, H. (2008) *Women and employment: Changing lives and new challenges*, London: Edward Elgar.

Sealy, R. (2010) Changing perceptions of meritocracy in senior women's careers, *Gender in Management: An International Journal*, 25(3): 184–197.

Sealy, R. and Vinnicombe, S. (2013) *Female FTSE Board Report 2013: false dawn of progress for women on boards?* London: Cranfield School of Management.

Smith, S. (2014) *Limitations to equality: gender stereotypes and social change*, IPPR. www.ippr.org/juncture/limitations-to-equality-gender-stereotypes-and-social-change

Teasdale, N. (2013) Fragmented sisters: The implications of flexible working policies for professional women's workplace relationships, *Gender, Work and Employment*, 20(4): 397–412.

Tomlinson, J. and Durbin, S. (2010) Female part-time managers: Work–life balance, aspirations and career mobility, *Equality, Diversity and Inclusion*, 29(3): 255–270.

Universities UK (2012) *Patterns and trends in UK higher education*, London: Universities UK.

TUC (2012) *Women' pay and employment update: a public/private sector comparison*, report for Women's Conference. www.tuc.org.uk/sites/default/files/tucfiles/womenspay.pdf

Watts, J.H. (2009a) Leaders of men: Women managing in construction, *Work, Employment and Society*, 23(3): 512–530.

Watts, J.H. (2009b) Allowed into a man's world. Meanings and work–life balance: perspectives of women civil engineers as 'minority' workers in construction, *Gender, Work and Organization*, 16(1): 37–56.

Weyer, B. (2007) Twenty years later: explaining the persistence of the glass ceiling for women leaders, *Women in Management Review*, 22(6): 482–496.

Wichert, I. (2014) How flexible working is good for you – and for your career, *Guardian*, 24 April. www.theguardian.com/women-in-leadership/2014/apr/24/flexible-working-career-progression-work–life-balance

Wilson, N. and Altanlar, A. (2009) *Director characteristics, gender balance and insolvency risk: An empirical study*, 30 May. http://ssrn.com/abstract=1414224

Wilton, P. (2008) *Management recruitment: understanding routes to greater diversity*, June, Report for Chartered Management Institute, London.

Women's Business Council (2013) *Maximising women's contribution to future economic growth*, Government Equalities Office. www.gov.uk/government/publications/womens-business-council-report-maxi mising-womens-contribution-to-future-economic-growth

Woodfield, R. (2015) Gender and the achievement of skilled status in the workplace: the case of women leaders in the fire and rescue service, *Work, Employment and Society*, 22 May (online first).

Worrell, L., Lindorff, M. and Cooper, C. (2008) *Quality of working life 2008: a survey of organizational health and employee well-being*, London: Chartered Institute of Management.

PART II

Women in management

Other European countries

8   Women in management in Norway

Laura E. Mercer Traavik and Astrid M. Richardsen

Introduction

In 2015 Norway was placed number one in the UN's ranking of the best country to live in (UN, 2015) and second in the *Global Gender Gap Report* on gender equality (World Economic Forum, 2015). Since the *Gender Gap Report* began in 2006, Norway has placed in the top three countries. In 2003 Norway was the first country to legislate that corporate boards of directors should contain at least 40 per cent women for both public and private sector companies, and Norway is known globally as a pioneer for achieving gender balance in these boards (Huse, 2013). Today the prime minister of Norway is a woman, Erna Solberg, and the national cabinet comprises 47 per cent women. With these amazing achievements, Norway is often viewed as a country in which women have reached equality, yet unfortunately, this is not the case. Norway represents a country with groundbreaking legislation and virtually unsurpassed gender equality, yet inequities, discrimination and gender segregation in both education and the labour market still exist.

In the spring of 2015 a heated debate erupted in the Norwegian media regarding the paucity of women in top leadership positions. Several chief executive officer (CEO) appointments were made in Norway's largest companies and not one woman was hired. One side was arguing that there were no qualified women, and the other side was claiming discrimination. Then, in the autumn, the Norwegian newspaper *Verdens Gang* uncovered that Telenor, one of Norway's largest companies, who had hired a male CEO, had not even interviewed any female contenders. *Verdens Gang* reported that the chairman of the board, Svein Aaser, had misled key stakeholders into thinking they had included women in the interview process and had even contacted the qualified Telenor female candidates requesting that they give statements that they had been involved in the hiring process (DN, 2015). The women refused; they had not been included. At the end of 2015 headlines in another important leadership newspaper, *Ukeavisen Ledelse,* read '44 top leader appointments, 0 women' (Myklemyr, 2015). In 2015 in Norway, true gender equality has not been achieved and open discrimination continues. Among Norway's largest companies there are currently no women occupying the CEO position (Svanemyr and Lorch-Falch, 2015).

Norway has a population of over 5.2 million people, and life expectancy in 2014 was 80 years for men and 84 years for women (Statistics Norway, 2015). The average number of children per woman is approximately 1.8, and although it has declined in recent years, Norway remains a country with one of the highest fertility rates in Europe. In 2013, 90 per cent of children between the ages of one and five had either daycare, pre-school or kindergarten places (Statistics Norway, 2015). Thirteen per cent of the population is foreign born, with the largest number of immigrants coming from Poland, Sweden and Lithuania (Statistics Norway,

2015). Although Norway is a relatively homogeneous country, the pattern is changing and with the recent wave of refugees in 2015 ethnic and cultural diversity will not be diminishing.

Single parents are eligible for substantial government support (NAV, 2015), and Norway has laws that ensure women's right to have an abortion on demand. Norwegian culture prioritises family life and children, which is reflected in working hours and national holidays. The overall standard of living is one of the highest in the world, and as mentioned, Norway ranked first in the 2015 UN Human Development Index (UN, 2015). In this country of high living standards and equality, we examine the current situation for women in management, and investigate arenas where Norway is leading and where inequalities persist.

Labour force characteristics

Norway has a long history of female participation in the workforce, and in 2014 had the second highest participation rates in the Organization for Economic Co-operation and Development (OECD) (OECD, 2015a), yet there remain occupational segregation, wage disparity and a high percentage of women working part time. In this section, we outline both general labour market trends and the current situation for women in the workforce in Norway.

Although Norway has not been seriously affected by the recent economic crisis in Europe, Norway's long-term unemployment has increased continuously since 2012 (OECD, 2015b) and is the highest among the Nordic countries. The OECD report identifies two problems that Norway needs to tackle in order to maintain economic success: 1) integration of the growing number of migrants and 2) reduction of people claiming sick leave and collecting disability benefit. Even with these challenges, Norway demonstrates a strong growth in average incomes, low income inequality, employment rates well above the OECD average and high labour market participation rates compared to other OECD countries (OECD, 2015b).

Examining women in Norway we find that participation in the workforce rose from below 50 per cent in the 1970s to 77 per cent in 2013 (Statistics Norway, 2015). In 2015 men's participation was 83 per cent (Statistics Norway, 2015). Currently women make up 47 per cent of the Norwegian workforce (Statistics Norway, 2015), although many of them work part time (34 per cent in 2014). This trend of working part time has stabilised, and between 2014 and the third quarter of 2015 the number of women in full-time employment increased by 19,000 while part-time work participation remained the same. There has been a recent change where there are more women and fewer men in full-time employment, and an increasing number of men in part-time work. These trends are being attributed to the redundancies in the oil and gas sector, a sector traditionally dominated by men. Even with this positive shift for women, Norway continues to have a rate of women working part time above the EU average (Eurostat, 2015). In 1990 48 per cent of women were working part time, whereas in 2014 this had fallen to 34 per cent (Statistics Norway, 2015). The number of men working part time has increased from 9 per cent in 1990 to 15 per cent in 2015 (Statistics Norway, 2015). A research report, *Work Life Barometer*, from 2015, asked a representative sample of the employed population what was their most important reason for working part time (Bergene *et al.*, 2015). For women the reason most frequently given for choosing part-time work was health (29 per cent), and in second place (16 per cent) were three reasons: (1) caring for children/family, (2) finding full-time employment was difficult and (3) wanting more free time. For men, the number one reason (26 per cent) for working part time was to collect a pension in addition to their regular salary, and a close second reason (25 per cent) was due to health reasons. Only 6 per cent of men stated that caring for children and family was the reason they chose part-time work (Bergene *et al.*, 2015). In the same study the researchers asked who takes more responsibility at home. This subjective evaluation showed strong trends from 1989 until the present day that more men and women are reporting that they share work at home equally with their partner. From 2012, 23 per cent of men assert they do most of the work at home whereas 63 per cent of women claim they contribute the most (Bergene *et al.*, 2015). Statistics Norway (Egge-Hoveid and Sandnes, 2013) found that from 1971 to 2010 the average time per day spent on paid work went up for women and down for men. Fathers with children up to two years of age use one hour less a day on paid work than they did in 1990, and they have increased the amount of time they spend on household work. Mothers have gone in the opposite direction, using more time on paid work and less time on household work, however these changes are less than for fathers. These trends have been attributed to the improved availability of day care, and the parental leave opportunities for fathers as well as mothers (Egge-Hoveid and Sandnes, 2013).

Norway does not have specific statistics on minority women; however, there are data available on immigrants and their descendants. This group makes up approximately 15.6 per cent of the Norwegian population. For immigrants born outside of Norway, labour market participation is often lower and varies greatly depending on country of origin, length of time in Norway and reason for immigration (IMDi, 2015). Across all regions of origin men have a higher participation rate in the labour market than women. Registered unemployment among immigrants in the third quarter of 2015 was 7.6 per cent, compared to 2.3 in the rest of the population. Registered unemployment for both men and women is about the same, 7.3 and 7.8 respectively, whereas in the rest of the population men have higher unemployment (2.5) than women (2.0) (Statistics Norway, 2015). For the Norwegian with parents born in other countries, the pattern of employment is very similar to the majority population (Olsen, 2015), however unemployment is slightly higher than in the population without an immigrant background (men 4.7 per cent and women 4.5 per cent in the third quarter of 2015). Since 2007, the largest group of immigrants to Norway is those seeking work rather than family unification or asylum, although this could change with the recent refugee crisis.

From these labour market statistics it is clear that women have a strong presence in the Norwegian workforce, however all women continue to work less than men and their participation in the labour market is influenced by their family situation and their country of origin.

When we examine *where* these women work, stark gender differences emerge. Many professions continue to be dominated either by men or by women. As reported by Statistics Norway (2015) men and women continue to choose traditional career paths. Women made up an overwhelming majority (over 80 per cent) of pre-school teachers and nurses in 2014, whereas men dominated engineering and building (Statistics Norway, 2015). However, in other professions, such as human resource managers or mail carriers, it is more balanced. In 2013, 70.5 per cent of those employed in the public sector were women compared to 36.5 per cent in the private sector (Statistics Norway, 2015).

The proportion of women among academic and research staff continues to be low, although signs are that it is slowly improving. In Norway, postgraduate work is often funded through scholarships and women are taking postgraduate studies and qualifying for academic careers in record numbers (Statistics Norway, 2015). However there continues to be a striking gender imbalance in research and research funding, and the Norwegian Research Council devoted 40 million NOK in 2013 to the project 'Gender balance in senior positions and research management' (BALANSE) (NFR, 2015). Statistics from the Committee for Gender Balance and Diversity in Research state that in 2013 women accounted for only 25 per cent of full professors, with medical and health science and humanities having the largest share of female professors (34.9 per cent and 30.5 per cent respectively). In the technology field, only 10 per cent of full professors were women in 2013 (Kifinfo, 2015).

The data clearly demonstrate that gender segregation in the labour market continues to be pronounced, and when we review the statistics on educational choices later in the chapter, the future continues to look traditional.

Perhaps the unexpected labour force characteristic found in Norway, given its ranking on gender equality, is the persistent difference between men and women's incomes and salaries. Women continue to have an average gross income that is 33 per cent below that of their male counterpart (Statistics Norway, 2015). Examining salaries for similar work, Norway is doing very well relative to other countries and has risen from placing 42nd to 2nd place in the *Gender Gap Report* (from 2006 to 2015). However, parity between men and women has not been achieved, and in 2014, women only earned 86.4 per cent of what a man makes (Statistics Norway, 2015). In the financial services, women earn only 71 per cent of a man's wage, however in education, equity is almost achieved with women making 95 per cent of what men make (Statistics Norway, 2015). A report from 2013 (Barth *et al.*, 2013) examined salary differences between men and women in the period 2001 to 2011. When the researchers examined men and women working in the same industries and occupations in 2011, the gender wage gap reduced from 14.1 to 7.1 per cent. These findings indicate that half of the gap can be explained by the gender segregated labour market in Norway (Barth *et al.*, 2013). However, differences between men and women continue even after controlling for occupation and education and this gap matters. Barth *et al.* (2013) found in the younger cohorts that the wage differential begins to develop at the beginning of their career, and in older cohorts that gap narrows slightly. For women, having children is detrimental to wage level (although it decreases over time), while for men, children are related to better earnings (Barth *et al.*, 2013). In Norway there have been many policy initiatives and political discussions, yet this difference has remained relatively stable over time. Recent years show improvements, however the segregation in the labour market remains strong.

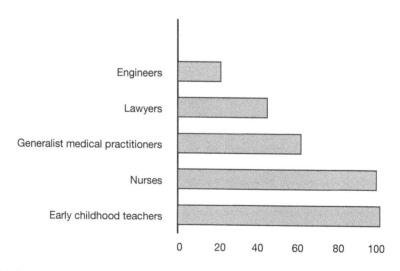

Figure 8.1 Percentage of women in selected professions, 2014
Source: Statistics Norway (2015)

The overall picture of the Norwegian labour market is that women are participating in increasing numbers, however they work less than men; they are not obtaining the same salary levels as men; they are not entering into traditionally male-dominated professions or jobs; and they are not increasing their numbers in the private sector. The Norwegian woman continues to face challenges.

Women pursuing education

Trends in higher education in Norway send a mixed message. The good news is that women have entered higher education in droves and since the mid 1980s female students have outnumbered male students. In 2014 women accounted for 61 per cent of university and college graduates and the majority of PhD students in 2015. In 2014, 50 per cent of doctorate degrees were awarded to women (Statistics Norway, 2015). The bad news is that the gender segregation found in the labour market is still present in the educational choices of both Norwegian men and women. Women comprise almost 80 per cent of all students in health, welfare and sport studies, and men account for almost 70 per cent of all students in the natural science, vocational and technical fields.

The traditional gender divide of men as engineers and women as nurses and pre-school teachers persists, and these gender differences have remained relatively constant over the years. There are positive exceptions, such as in the study of medicine. In this field the number of women has risen from 12 per cent in 1970 (NOU, 2008) to approximately 65 per cent in 2015 (Den norske legeforening, 2015). Also in economics and administration, women have increased their representation from 25 per cent in 1980 to over 50 per cent today (Statistics Norway, 2015). In Norway, the title of civil economist is a professional title that has traditionally paved the route to top leadership positions in Norwegian business. The oldest and most prestigious business school, the Norwegian School of Economics and Business Administration, has increased the proportion of female students in this programme from 29 per cent women in 2005 to 48 per cent in 2013 (Sommerstad, 2013). At the other business school, which is the largest business school in Norway, BI Norwegian Business School, 51.8 per cent of the students were women in 2015 (NSD, 2015). Across educational institutions, female students comprise 54.5 per cent of business and administration studies students, reflecting gender balance in this field. In the field of education, women represent 75 per cent of the students. In the humanities, social sciences and law, women also make up the majority.

When we examine the immigrant population, in 2014, Norwegian-born women with foreign parents had a rate of participation in higher education of almost 48 per cent, which is substantially more than the Norwegian national average of 34 per cent, and more than women in the total population (41 per cent). However, when this group is combined with all the immigrant women the rate of participation drops to 20 per cent (Statistics Norway, 2015). Among the immigrant population and Norwegian-born people with immigrant parents, similar gender divides are found that exist in the general population, however, there are some interesting variations. The statistics indicate that there is more gender balance in female-dominated studies such as healthcare and early education than in the non-immigrant population (Egge-Hoveid and Sandnes, 2015). It also appears that Norwegian-born women with immigrant parents choose more male-dominated areas of study than women without an immigrant background (Egge-Hoveid and Sandnes, 2015). Statistics from 2013 indicate that representation in engineering is more balanced in the immigrant populations than in the rest of the population. Also, immigrant men choose nursing more often than men without an immigrant background (Egge-Hoveid and Sandnes, 2015). Generally female immigrant women with immigrant parents achieve better results at school than men, and immigrants in general are contributing slightly to the reduction of the gender divide in some areas of study (Egge-Hoveid and Sandnes, 2015).

The data on education show that while women are making great progress in many fields, as well as in the sheer percentages actually obtaining higher education, there continues to be dramatic differences in choices of study, indicating that women and men continue to choose gender-stereotyped fields.

Women in management

In this section, we give an overview of the general progress of women in management and leadership in Norway. A positive trend is that the number of female managers is increasing across Norwegian municipalities in 2013 (Statistics Norway, 2015), and there was a 10 per cent increase in the proportion of female managers between 2000 and 2012 in Norway (ILO, 2015). In addition, Norway continues to be a world leader with the proportion of women on corporate boards. However, the picture is complex. Juxtaposed to these positive developments is the fact that today in Norway there is not one woman leading any of the largest companies; 100 per cent of these leaders are men and men continue to dominate top leadership positions (ILO, 2015). Although placing second in the overall ranking of the *Global Gender Gap Report*, Norway only ranked 43 for legislators, senior officials and managers (World Economic Forum, 2015). In this section, we provide an overview of both the noteworthy developments and the challenges that continue in Norway for women in management and leadership.

In 2015, women made up 40 per cent of the members of the national parliament, and 47 per cent of the cabinet. Women occupy powerful ministerial roles: the prime minister, the minister of finance, the minister of trade and industry and the minister of defence (Government of Norway, 2015). At the municipal level women represent 38 per cent of the councils (Remen and Nerum, 2015) and at the city level 23 per cent of the mayors are women (Amundsen, 2015). These numbers show that continued inequality between men and women still exists at the regional and local levels of government. Also within the civil service there continue to be challenges. The percentage of senior female civil servants was 22 per cent in 2012, which is quite low compared to Sweden with 42 per cent (ILO, 2015). The number of women in politics showed a sharp increase from the 1970s into the 1990s as a result of a proactive strategy from the Socialist left party and the Liberal party. These political parties initiated voluntary gender quotas in the 1970s, and today almost all parties use gender quotas to ensure female nominees (Ministry of Children and Equality, 2009). However, in 2015, there were 43 per cent women nominated for the municipal elections but only 38 per cent were elected, the same percentage as in 2011.

In the public sector women account for 70.5 per cent of all employees, whereas in the private sector they account for 36.5 per cent. Within the public sector we find that women are more often employed in local government and men are equally represented in both local and central government (Statistics Norway, 2015). Although there has been a continual increase in the number of female managers over the last years, the majority of these positions are in middle management rather than in top management. Overall women make up 35.7 per cent of the leaders (Statistics Norway, 2015). However, upon closer inspection there are several salient inequalities. A recent mapping of the 50 largest companies on the Oslo stock exchange showed that since 2009 all new top leaders recruited and hired were men – in total 44 (Myklemyr, 2015). In 2015, 15 per cent of general managers in private limited companies were women, and only 5.5 per cent in publicly listed companies, down from 7 per cent in 2008 (Statistics Norway, 2015).

After government legislation in 2003 and 2006 and the accompanying threat of government action, joint stock companies now have boards comprising 41 per cent women, up from 18 per cent in 2006 (Statistics Norway, 2015), however in private limited companies where there is no quota legislation women still account for only 18 per cent. In 2013 only 13 per cent of women were company chairs (ILO, 2015).

Overall it appears that quotas, voluntary or legislated, have helped propel Norway to more equality, however there remains large inequalities in senior and top management. Norway is both horizontally segregated in the labour market and vertically segregated in terms of top management.

Women entrepreneurs

According to the OECD (2015) women entrepreneurship is increasingly recognised as a key source of employment creation and innovation and is key for addressing inequalities. There are substantial gender differences in entrepreneurship in Norway, but these gender differences are often difficult to measure, complicating the evaluation of support policies for women entrepreneurs. While entrepreneurship and gender is quickly emerging as an area of growing research interest (Henry *et al.*, 2015a, 2015b), studies often have serious methodological limitations. First of all, there is little consensus on the definition of entrepreneurship (Berglann *et al.*, 2011). Definitions of an entrepreneur vary from someone who is self-employed or self-employed with employees (OECD, 2015c), individuals in early phase entrepreneurial activity (Alsos *et al.*, 2013), people who are owners of a company and individuals who devote their labour to that company (Berglann *et al.*, 2011). In addition, several authors criticise the proliferation of large-scale empirical studies focused on male–female comparisons (Henry *et al.*, 2015a), and call for studies with more contextual and business sector information as well as feminist critique of findings. In the following section we look at findings from available studies, notwithstanding some of the methodological weaknesses.

The latest research from the Global Entrepreneurship Monitor (Alsos *et al.*, 2013) calculates the total early phase entrepreneurial activity (TEA) (percentage of the population that attempts to start their own company) for women in Norway to be 4 per cent in 2007 and 5 per cent in 2008. Female involvement in early phase entrepreneurship fell somewhat in the years after 2008, and in 2013, only 3.6 per cent of women were involved in entrepreneurial activities (Alsos *et al.*, 2013). The corresponding number for men was 8.9 per cent, continuing the trend of men being more active in TEA (Bullvåg *et al.*, 2008). While no detailed country profile is available after 2013, the global report in 2014 indicated that the TEA for women in Norway had increased to 4 per cent, whereas the activity for men had decreased to 7.3 per cent. The most recent Norwegian report still shows that men continue to be more active than women in early stage entrepreneurship, but in 2013, women represented about one half of total entrepreneurial activity (Alsos *et al.*, 2013). There are some indications that new enterprise creations for women are somewhat higher than 2007 levels in 2015 (OECD, 2015c). Nevertheless, total early entrepreneurial activity in Norway has decreased since 2007, and while it is difficult to ascertain the reasons for this, one possible explanation is the Norway has a tight labour market where it is relatively easy to get salaried jobs (Alsos *et al.*, 2013; Singer *et al.*, 2014).

Looking at the proportion of women in new business ventures, the percentage of women establishing their own business increased from 25 per cent in 2004 to 33 per cent in 2007

(Kolvereid *et al.*, 2007). In 2008 the Norwegian government introduced an action plan for increasing entrepreneurship among women (Ministry of Municipal and Regional Development, 2008), and the expressed goal was that at least 40 per cent of entrepreneurs should be women by 2013. In an evaluation of this action plan and the initiatives to implement this goal, Spilling *et al.* (2011) conclude that while the action plan so far has been important for increasing gender equality in business and industry, it also has a number of weaknesses. These include unclear targets, a portfolio of initiatives that is too broad and a lack of clear leadership in the follow-up of the plan. The authors conclude that for these reasons one should have limited expectations for goal attainment (Spilling *et al.*, 2011), a fact confirmed by data from the Global Entrepreneurship Monitor (GEM) in 2013, which indicate that only 29 per cent of new business ventures were owned by women (Alsos *et al.*, 2013). Gender differences in entrepreneurial activities are not unique to Norway but exist in many of the countries included in the GEM (Singer *et al.*, 2014). However, among the 25 innovation-driven countries included in the GEM data, the results indicate that only two countries, the Czech Republic and Korea, had a lower proportion of women entrepreneurs than Norway (Alsos *et al.*, 2013).

Considering entrepreneurship in the OECD member countries (OECD, 2015c), Norway has the lowest number of women who report their status as self-employed or who report themselves as self-employed with employees. About 80 per cent of self-employed women have their activities in the services sector while only 5 per cent report activity in manufacturing and construction (OECD, 2015c). The distribution of Norwegian self-employed women by sector indicates that about 22 per cent have activities in agriculture, 5 per cent in industry, about 8 per cent in trade, hotels and transport, and the remaining 65 per cent have activities within public and social services, professional or other services (OECD, 2015c).

Several authors have focused on the reasons why there are so few female entrepreneurs in Norway (Berglann *et al.*, 2013; Raknerud and Rønsen, 2014; Rønsen, 2014). There seems to be some consensus in the literature that dissimilar education backgrounds and experience, access to capital and social and cultural factors may explain part of the gender gap (Raknerud and Rønsen, 2014; Rønsen, 2014). However, Berglann *et al.* (2013) found that in Norway, when controlling for factors such as age and calendar year, country of origin, place of residence, family situation, education, business sector and salary, most of the gender gap still remained. Some authors have identified social and cultural factors embedded in the family and household situation as potential explanations for the gender differences observed (Berglann *et al.*, 2013; Raknerud and Rønsen, 2014; Rønsen, 2014). This is based on the observation that despite the high degree of gender equality in Norway, a high proportion of women with small children work part time (Bø *et al.*, 2008), and women spend about 1.5 hours more per day on housework than men (Vaage, 2012). However, recent findings indicate that children are not a barrier to female self-employment but may in fact be an incentive (Raknerud and Rønsen, 2014, Rønsen, 2014). Other studies have found that women with young children are more inclined to switch from salaried jobs to entrepreneurship than women without children (Berglann *et al.*, 2011). Rønsen (2014) found that female entrepreneurship propensity was negatively related to the partner's working hours and positively related to the partner being self-employed himself. These studies indicate that there are still relationships to be explored in the efforts to find explanations for the large gender differences in entrepreneurship in Norway.

The typical Norwegian entrepreneur will have upper secondary education when setting up a company (Fjærli *et al.*, 2013), and there is no notable difference between male and female entrepreneurs. Education fields of entrepreneurs at start up are quite different for men and women. More than 65 per cent of female entrepreneurs have education in general programmes, business and administration, and programmes in health, welfare and sports; whereas over 80 per cent of male entrepreneurs have backgrounds in natural sciences, vocational and technical studies; as well as general programmes, and business and administration (Fjærli *et al.*, 2013). Over 40 per cent of male entrepreneurs have education in the field of natural sciences, whereas only 6 per cent of female entrepreneurs have such an educational background (Fjærli *et al.*, 2013).

Female businesses tend to be smaller than men's (Foss and Ljunggren, 2006) and men are more often involved in high-growth start ups (Bullvåg *et al.*, 2008; Ljunggren, 2008). When it comes to attitudes toward entrepreneurship, 64 per cent of the Norwegian population perceives that opportunities for business ventures are good where they live, and this percentage is much higher than most other countries assessed by GEM (Alsos *et al.*, 2013). However, while 70 per cent of Norwegian men respond positively to the idea of entrepreneurship, only 57 per cent of women were positive. Entrepreneurial activity may also depend on the knowledge and skills people perceive they have to start their own business, and in this regard there is a gender difference. While 46 per cent of men perceive that they have sufficient competence to start a business, only 22 per cent of women answer positively (Alsos *et al.*, 2013). GEM also monitors the extent to which fear of failure is a deterrent in starting a new business, and here the difference between men and women is marginal: for both genders 35 per cent indicate that this is a reason for hesitation. Ambitions for growth and innovation in new business ventures are not reported for men and women in the 2013 GEM data. Isaksen and Kolvereid (2005) found that although both men and women expected their new start ups to provide full-time employment, significantly more men (27 per cent) than women (18 per cent) aspired to having employees.

Furthermore, Skalpe (2006) reported in his study that only 7 per cent of companies had women as majority owners. Recent statistics show that in 2013, there were about 25 per cent women company owners (NHO, 2015a). Of these the majority of companies are sole proprietorships, while there are only between 10 and 15 per cent women owners in private (AS) and public (ASA) limited companies. There have been large discrepancies between men and women in terms of the type of industry in which registrations are made (Spilling, 2001). While 54 per cent of male start ups were in construction, primary industries and agriculture, producer services and transport, 64 per cent of female start ups were in wholesale and retail trade, and community and social services (Spilling 2001).

In summary, data indicate that women's enterprises in Norway tend to be small with one or two employees, and tend to be concentrated in two commercial sectors. As a rule, therefore, women-led enterprises are often operating in a local market economy and have only local competition. Women-led businesses are also more often sole proprietorships than businesses led by men, which more often tend to be limited companies.

Country legislation supporting women in the workforce

Norway prides itself on a strong social democratic tradition, which is based on the assumption that men and women should be treated equally and fairly. The Gender Equality Act was first passed in Norway in 1978 and put in practice in 1979 and has undergone many reformulations over the years, with the most recent taking place in 2013 (Lovdata, 2015). This Act provides the framework for ensuring that women have the same rights, obligations and opportunities as men and vice versa. The recent amendments (2005, 2013) to the law require a much more proactive approach from companies and organisations. The law states that public authorities, employers and enterprises must 'make active, targeted and systematic efforts to promote gender equality' (Lovdata, 2015). Companies that are required to prepare annual reports must include information on the current gender equality in the organisation, as well as plans for promoting gender equality. The law also allows for affirmative action and prevents job advertisements restricting applicants based on their sex. Norway has also set up institutions, such as the Equality and Anti-discrimination Ombudsman, to provide guidelines, information and to assist people in making discrimination complaints.

The other pioneering legislation mentioned above is laws requiring equal representation of women in important boards and committees in both public organisations and private companies. In 1981 the law requiring gender balance on all boards and committees in public sector organisations was enacted. Although this led to female participation in many important decision-making bodies, it did not have an impact on top leadership. In 2002 the law that there must be at least 40 per cent female representation on the boards of all publicly owned and privately owned publicly listed enterprises was introduced. The law was a result of cooperation between the Ministry of Children, Equality and Social Inclusion and the Ministry of Trade and Industry (Huse, 2013). The law was passed in 2003 and came into effect from 1 January 2004 for publicly owned enterprises. The law was not received positively by Norwegian businesses and the business community, and it created a lot of heated discussions in the media and also public debate (Bergstø, 2013; Huse and Seierstad, 2013). The business community argued that gender balance on boards could be reached through voluntary actions and soft regulations (Huse and Seierstad, 2013), and the Norwegian Parliament gave private companies two years to meet the objectives of the law. By July 2005 the percentage of women on boards in privately owned publicly listed companies was 16 per cent, showing clearly that companies had not achieved gender balance through voluntary actions (Huse and Seierstad, 2013). Private sector companies were given until January 2008 to comply with the new laws. The laws were incorporated into the Norwegian Companies Act, which meant that non-compliance with the regulation would lead to dissolution of the companies (Hoel, 2008; Huse and Seierstad, 2013). The legislation worked, in 2011 the percentage of women on boards of directors was 36 per cent, and has since remained between 36 and 40 per cent. Gender balanced boards also spread to companies where it was not enforced, and today the quota law has largely become a non-issue in Norway (Seierstad *et al.*, 2015). In addition, the example of Norway has led to many other countries around the world adopting similar gender quotas (Huse and Brogi, 2013). These laws have undoubtedly had a positive impact. The facts and figures in our earlier section on women in management show this legislation has led to the reality of gender parity in boardrooms.

The legislation directed at giving women equal status and rights has not been able to redress all the imbalances between men and women in the workplace. An example of where legislation is not having the desired effect is with the new proactive section of the law requiring firms to actively promote gender equality. Hovde (2008) found that only 24 per cent of 50 companies surveyed in central Norway were complying with the proactive section of the Gender Equality Act, and 22 per cent did not deem it necessary to have any measures or policies to promote gender equality. Possible explanations for this situation are that certain sections of the Gender Equality Act do not have the legal clout or ability to impose sanctions easily or in such a way as to act as a powerful deterrent. When there is a powerful deterrent, such as dissolving or fining companies not complying with the law, the legislation works (Hoel, 2008; Huse and Seierstad, 2013). Hovde (2008) also found that larger companies had the most proactive integrated policies and plans.

There are also examples of legislation which might have adverse effects on female advancement and equality. In 1999 the Christian Democratic government passed a bill to give families with children added financial support in order to provide parents with opportunities to spend more time at home with their children. An early study demonstrated a short-term negative effect on women's employment as more women chose to remove themselves from the labour market and receive the government benefit (Schøne, 2004). Still today, a large proportion of women with small children work part time, and the Confederation of Norwegian Enterprises (NHO, 2015a) is quite explicit in its recommendation to remove the financial support in order to increase women's participation in the private sector and stimulate advancement into leadership positions. The government should tailor policies for families and gender equality that allow both men and women to combine careers and family responsibilities.

Initiatives supporting women in the workforce

To address the paucity of women in higher management and the continued salary disparity, many initiatives have been launched over the years. In this section we highlight the projects assisting women in management and entrepreneurship, and comment on the roles of networks.

In Norway a very influential actor is the NHO, the Confederation of Norwegian Enterprises. This organisation is the most important representative body for Norwegian companies with a current membership of over 18,500 enterprises. In 1995, NHO began a mentoring programme with the goal of helping women obtain leadership positions and corporate board positions. At the end of the year 2008, they had had 900 participants (Anderson, 2008). The Confederation of Norwegian Enterprises also started the Female Future project in 2003 to mobilise and develop talent, and create a meeting place for women in order to move them into leadership positions (NHO, 2015b). Since its inception Female Futures has had over 1500 participants from 750 companies, and results from the last two years show that two out of every three participants have received offers of board work or have been promoted within six months of the programme (NHO, 2015b). A unique approach of the programme is that it is the businesses themselves that are the driving force behind it since they are responsible for recruiting women.

Innovation Norway is a state-owned company that promotes nationwide industrial development, Norwegian products and services internationally, and entrepreneurship. Women are a priority target group in the organisation and with the programme 'Women in focus', it seeks to strengthen the role of women in the private sector, in leadership and as entrepreneurs. The programme finances entrepreneurs, offers consultancy services and sponsors women-focused projects. In 2008 Innovation Norway contributed 1.4 billion Norwegian crowns to female projects and companies (Innovation Norway, 2009).

In order to counteract the 'old boys' network and its effects on important management decisions, a number of women in business have realised the need for women to create their own networks. New women's networks are growing fast, and many of these work actively to break the glass ceiling and help promote women in management. Women's networks have been established within politics, business, among students as well as in cultural areas, and they arrange a variety of activities, training and opportunities for sharing information. Examples are Women Innovation (http://kvinnovasjon.no/) for female entrepreneurs, and the Association of International Professional and Business Women (www.aipbw.no), a network for business women in Norway of international background. Common to all the fast-growing networks is a belief that not much will change unless women themselves take action and build networks and contacts the way men do.

Improvements

In order to assess the improvements for women in management in Norway we have to examine the role of women in the labour market. Norway is excellent in terms of female participation in the workforce, women on publicly listed company boards, and in obtaining higher education. There are more women in business and administration, law and medicine and an increasing number of women in management. We also note that women are spending more time in paid work and men are using more of their time sharing the work at home. However, these improvements go hand in hand with the continued gender segregation of the labour market, few women in top management and a high number of women in part-time employment.

The UN in 2012 listed several concerns and recommendations for Norway regarding equality for women (UN, 2012) in the coming years. First, they are concerned that equality is not well enough defined in the constitution and gender neutrality means that women are not sufficiently protected against discrimination and that minority women are especially vulnerable. They also mentioned their concern that the proportion of women in the municipal elections decreased in 2011, and that there are few female professors and judges (UN, 2012). Again there was an emphasis on minority women's underrepresentation. Not surprisingly, the UN flags the gender segregation in educational choices and recommends initiatives so that stereotypical educational choices are not made. Lastly, they point to the continued pay gap, high percentage of part-time work, discrimination against women who are pregnant and the new pension system in Norway which penalises those who take breaks in their careers (UN, 2012).

The UN observations highlight that the improvements for women in Norway are not uniform and that advances in some areas do not make up for the fact that Norwegian women still have not achieved full equality in the workplace. The report also emphasised the role that government has in addressing these inequalities. The review in this chapter also shows that when policies are put into action change occurs. Improvements in women's position in Norway will continue as long as the government stays active.

The future

Although Norway has enjoyed an excellent reputation for equality, the reputation hides the statistical truth that women still work in stereotypically female jobs, face discrimination, are paid less than men and do not reach top leadership positions. Considering the most recent statistics, one has to conclude that despite a number of political initiatives and social welfare policies that promote equality, Norway has failed to close the gender gap. The progress in Norway can be described as both being excellent and improving and at the same time being poor, not progressing and in some cases declining. The shadow of success, especially in comparison to other countries, can mask the continued injustices and lead to political stagnation or resignation. The recent media storm uncovering the discrimination in top leadership selection emerged at the same time Norway was placed as the number one country to live in and second in the *Global Gender Gap Report*. This situation highlights that Norway has come far, but still has far to go. What can be learned from the Norwegian experience?

Norway's biggest successes have been achieved through quotas, legislation and political pressure, which have had a snowballing effect on other countries that have adopted similar legislation (Machold *et al.*, 2013). Authorities are also doing more to encourage nontraditional choices in education (for example, offering extra points needed to get into studies that are currently underrepresented by women, such as engineering), and putting more muscle behind their policies. The changes in the Gender Equality Act have also shifted the pressure to companies who are now required to be proactive, rather than non-discriminatory, and to deliver policies and plans. The legislation has pushed Norwegian organisations to take responsibility.

A clear message from the Norwegian experience is that affirmative action, quotas and clear goals lead to increases in the number of women in boardrooms and in politics. Research assessing diversity management policies in the US concluded that it is the structural variables that are most important (Kalev *et al.*, 2006). Examining the situation of women on corporate boards we see that quotas led to 40 per cent women on boards in the publicly listed companies but in the privately listed companies with no quota the numbers remain extremely low at 18 per cent. Organisations that establish practices that assign responsibility for achieving change achieve the change they seek (Kalev *et al.*, 2006) and the same can be said of countries. In a land of equality, the values of same worth are in place, and the recent focus on goals and organisational accountability is promising. However, Norway still must address the gender segregated education system and the paucity of women in top leadership in the private sector. It is 2016; it is time that equality in one of the world's most egalitarian countries is achieved.

References

Alsos, G.A., Clausen, T. H., Isaksen, E. J., Åmo, B.W. and Bullvåg, E. (2013). *Entreprenørskap i Norge 2013: Global Entrepreneurship Monitor.* Bodø, Norway: Universitet i Nordland.

Amundsen, I. H. (2015). Slik bekles ordfører-Norge av menn. *Verdens Gang* 18.08.2015. www.vg.no/nyheter/innenriks/kommunevalget-2015/slik-bekles-ordfoerer-norge-av-menn/a/23507256/ [Accessed December 2015].

Anderson, H. A. (2008). *Ledere som utvikler seg sammen med ledere.* AFF. www.aff.no/AFF/lnnyhet.nsf/wPrId/8A387C80BC9ECDFCC1257443003B7C0B!OpenDocument [Accessed April 2009].

Barth, E., Hardoy, I., Schøne, P. and Misje Østbakken, K. (2013). Lønnsforskjeller mellom kvinner og menn: Hva har skjedd på 2000-tallet? *Institutt for samfunnsforskning.* www.samfunnsforskning.no/Publikasjoner/Rapporter/2013/2013-007#sthash.zJ3tL7gL.dpuf [Accessed December 2015].

Bergene, A. C., Brattbakk, I., Egeland, C. and Steen, A. H. (2015). Norsk arbeidsliv 2015: Det nye arbeidslivet: hvem, hva, hvor? *Arbeidslivsbarometer.* YS. www.ys.no/kunder/ys/mm.nsf/lupgraphics/Arbeidslivsbarometerrapport_2015.pdf/$file/Arbeidslivsbarometerrapport_2015.pdf [Accessed December 2015].

Berglann, H., Moen, E. R., Røed, K. and Skogstrøm, J. F. (2011). Entrepreneurship: Origins and returns. *Labour Economics, 18* (2), 180–193.

Berglann, H., Golumbek, R. and Røed, K. (2013). Entreprenørskap I Norge – mest for menn? (Entrepreneurship in Norway – mostly for men?). *Søkelys på Arbeidslivet, 01-02/2013,* 3–21.

Bergstø. K. (2013). Women mean business: Why and how Norway legislated gender balance on the boards of listed companies. In S. Machold, M. Huse, K. Hansen and M. Brogi (eds), *Getting women in to corporate boards: A snowball starting in Norway.* Cheltenham, UK: Edward Elagar Publishing.

Bø, T. P., Kitterød, R. H., Køber, T., Nerland, S. L. and Skoglund, T. (2008). *Arbeidstiden – mønstre og utviklingstrekk (Working time – patterns and trends).* Report 2008/12. Oslo-Kongsvinger: Statistics Norway.

Bullvåg, E., Jenssen, S.A., Kolvereid, L. and Åmo, B.W. (2008). *Global Entrepreneurship Monitor: Entrepreneurship i Norge 2008.* www.gemconsortium.org/document.aspx?id=891 [Accessed May 2009].

Den norske legeforening. (2015). *Den norske legeforening.* http://legeforeningen.no/Emner/Andre-emner/Legestatistikk/ [Accessed December 2015].

DN (2015). VG: Ble bedt om å bekrefte at hun ble verert-nektet. *DN Dagens Næringliv.* www.dn.no/nyheter/naringsliv/2015/12/08/0559/Telenor/vg-ble-bedt-om—bekrefte-at-hun-ble-vurdert-nektet [Accessed December 2015].

Egge-Hoveid, K. and Sandnes, T. (2013). Kvinners og menns tidsbruk i ulike livsfaser og familietype (45/2013). *Statistics Norway.* http://ssb.no/en/kultur-og-fritid/artikler-og-publikasjoner/_attachment/143501?_ts=141b700dc88. [Accessed December 2015].

Egge-Hoveid, K. and Sandnes, T. (2015). Innvandrere og norskfødte medinnvandrerforeldre i et kjønns- og likestillingsperspektiv (26/2013). *Statistics Norway.* www.ssb.no/befolkning/artikler-og-publikasjoner/_attachment/231261?_ts=14f975e12e8. [Accessed December 2015].

Eurostat (2015). Labour market statistics. http://epp.eurostat.ec.europa.eu/portal/page/portal/eurostat/home. [Accessed December 2015].

Fjærli, E., Iancu, D. and Raknerud, A. (2013). Facts about entrepreneurship in Norway. Who become entrepreneurs and how do they perform? Report 52/2013. www.ssb.no/en/virksomheter-foretak-og-regnskap/artikler-og-publikasjoner/facts-about-entrepreneurship-in-norway [Accessed October 2015].

Foss, L. and Ljunggren, E. (2006). Women's entrepreneurship in Norway. Recent trends and future challenges. In C. G. Brush (ed.), *Growth-oriented women entrepreneurs and their businesses.* Cheltenham: Edward Elgar Publishing.

Government of Norway (2015). www.regjeringen.no/en/id4/ [Accessed December 2015].

Henry, C., Foss, L. and Ahl, H. (2015a). Gender and entrepreneurship research: A review of method-ological approaches. *International Small Business Journal,* 1–25.

Henry, C., Foss, L., Fayolle, A., Walker, E. and Duffy, S. (2015b). Entrepreneurial leadership and gender: Exploring theory and practice in global contexts. *Journal of Small Business Management, 53*(3), 581–586.

Hoel, M. (2008). The quota story: five years of change in Norway, in S. Vinnicombe *et al.* (eds), *Women on corporate boards of directors: International research and practice,* Cheltenham: Edward Elgar Publishing.

Hovde, K. (2008). Bedrifters redegjørelse for likestilling – Undersøkelse av 50 bedrifter sin årsberetning for 2006. www.kun.nl.no/no/publikasjoner_fra_kun/rapporter/ [Accessed April 2009].

Huse, M. (2013). The political process behind the gender balance law. In S. Machold, M. Huse, K. Hansen and M. Brogi (eds), *Getting women in to corporate boards: A snowball starting in Norway.* Cheltenham, UK: Edward Elgar Publishing.

Huse, M. and Brogi, M. (2013). Introduction. In S. Machold, M. Huse, K. Hansen and M. Brogi (eds), *Getting women in to corporate boards: A snowball starting in Norway.* Cheltenham, UK: Edward Elgar Publishing.

Huse, M. and Seierstad, C. (2013). Getting women on to corporate boards: Consequences of the Norwegian Gender Balance Law. *The European Financial Review,* December 28. www.europeanfinancialreview.com/?p=572) [Accessed October 2015].

ILO (2015). *Women in business and management: Gaining momentum.* International Labour Organization, Geneva. www.ilo.org/wcmsp5/groups/public/—-dgreports/—-dcomm/—-publ/documents/publication/wcms_334882.pdf [Accessed December 2015].

IMDi (Directorate of Integration and Diversity Norway) (2015). *Imdi (2015). Fakta om sysselsetting.* www.imdi.no/Fakta-og-statistikk/Sysselsetting/ [Accessed December 2015].

Innovation Norway (2009). *Satser på kvinner.* www.innovasjonnorge.no/Satsinger/Kvinner-i-fokus/ [Accessed April 2009].

Isaksen, E. and Kolvereid, L. (2005). Growth objectives in Norwegian start-up businesses. *International Journal of Entrepreneurship and Small Business, 2*(1), 17–26.

Kalev, A., Dobbin, F. and Kelley, E. (2006). Best practices or best guesses? Assessing the efficacy of corporate affirmative action and diversity policies. *American Sociological Review, 71,* 587–617.

Kifinfo (2015). Committee for Gender Balance and Diversity in Research. http://kifinfo.no/c42711/seksjon.html?tid=42728 [Accessed December 2015].

Kolvereid, L., Bullvåg, E. and Aamo, B. W. (2007). *Global Entrepreneurship Monitor: Entrepreneurship i Norge 2007.* www.gemconsortium.org/document.aspx?id=701 [Accessed April 2009].

Ljunggren, E. (2008). *Kunnskapsbehov om entreprenørskap og kjønn i Norge (Knowledge requirements about entrepreneurship and gender in Norway).* NF-Arbeidsnotat No. 1031/2008. Bodø: Nordlandsforskning.

Lovdata (2015). Lov om likestilling mellom kjønnene (Gender Equality Act). https://lovdata.no/dokument/NL/lov/2013-06-21-59?q=likestillingsloven [Accessed October 2015].

Machold, S., Huse, M., Hansen, K. and Brogi, M. (eds) (2013). *Getting women in to corporate boards: A snowball starting in Norway*. Cheltenham, UK: Edward Elgar Publishing.

Ministry of Municipal and Regional Development (2008). Stortingsmelding nr. 25. *Lokal vekstkraft og framtidstru: Om distriks-og regionalpolitikken.* www.regjeringen.no/contentassets/e4fceff4dccf4b95b2 eeab11fd485e68/nn-no/pdfs/stm200820090025000dddpdfs.pdf [Accessed October 2015].

Myklemyr, A. (2015). Ingen kvinner blant 44 nye toppsjefer de siste syv årene. *Ukeavisen*,18. December. www.dagensperspektiv.no/2015/ingen-kvinner-blant-44-nye-toppsjefer-de-siste-syv-arene [Accessed December 2015].

NAV (2015). *Alene fra fødsel*. www.nav.no/no/Person/Familie/Enslig+mor+eller+far/Relatert+ informasjon/alene-fra-f%C3%B8dsel [Accessed December 2015].

NFR (2015). Norwegian Research Council. www.forskningsradet.no/en/Funding/BALANSE/ 1253985316903/p1184150364108?visAktive=false [Accessed December 2015].

NHO (2015a). *Kvinner i næringslivet.* www.nho.no/Politikk-og-analyse/Arbeidslivspolitikk/kvinner-i-naringslivet/ [Accessed October 2015].

NHO (2015b). The *Female Future programme.* www.nho.no/Prosjekter-og-programmer/Female-Future/ [Accessed October 2015].

NOU (2008). *Kjønn og lønn.* www.regjeringen.no/pages/2052468/PDFS/NOU200820080006000 DDDPDFS.pdf [Accessed April 2009].

NSD (2015). Norwegian Social Science Data Services. http://dbh.nsd.uib.no/ [Accessed December 2015].

OECD (2015a). *Labour force participation.* https://data.oecd.org/emp/labour-force-participation-rate.htm [Accessed December 2015].

OECD (2015b). *Employment outlook: Norway 2015.* www.oecd.org/norway/Employment-Outlook-Norway-EN.pdf [Accessed December 2015].

OECD (2015c). *Entrepreneurship at a glance 2015.* http://dx.doi.org/10.1787/entrepreneur_aag-2015-en [Accessed October 2015].

Olsen, B. (2015). Unge med innvandrerbakgrunn i arbeid og utdanning 2013. Eksklusive EØS-/EU-innvandrere. Report 2015/7. *Statistics Norway.* www.ssb.no/arbeid-og-lonn/artikler-og-publik asjoner/_attachment/217928?_ts=14b72d7bc20 [Accessed December 2015].

Raknerud, A. and Rønsen, M. (2014). *Why are there so few female entrepreneurs? An examination of gender differences in entrepreneurship using Norwegian registry data.* Discussion paper No. 790, Statistics Norway.

Remen, A. and Nerum, H. (2015). De nye kommunestyrene: MDG har flest kvinner, FrP har færrest. *NRK 26.10.2015.* www.nrk.no/norge/de-nye-kommunestyrene_-mdg-flest-kvinner_-frp-faerrest-1.12620935 [Accessed December 2015].

Rønsen, M. (2014). Children and family: A barrier or an incentive to female self-employment in Norway? *International Labour Review, 153* (2), 337–349.

Schøne, P. (2004). Kontantstøtten og mødres arbeidstilbud: Varig effekt eller retur til arbeid. *Norsk Økonomisk Tidsskrift, 118*, 1–21.

Seierstad, C., Huse, M. and Seres, S. (2015). *Lessons from Norway in getting women onto corporate boards.* http://theconversation.com/lessons-from-norway-in-getting-women-onto-corporate-boards-38338 [Accessed October 2015].

Singer, S., Amoros, J. E. and Arreola, D. M. (2014). *Global Entrepreneurship Monitor 2014: Global report.* http://gemconsortium.org/report [Accessed October 2015].

Skalpe, O. (2006). Kvinner leder små bedrifter i lite lønnsomme bransjer, *Magma*, 9(2), 51–59.

Sommerstad, H. (2013). NHH på søkertoppen, Paraplyen 4/13. http://paraplyen.nhh.no/ paraplyen/arkiv/2013/april/nhh-pa-sok/ [Accessed December 2015].

Spilling, O. R. (2001) Women entrepreneurship and management in Norway: A statistical overview, *Discussion Paper*, Norwegian School of Management BI.

Spilling, O. R., Lauritzen, T., Hagen, E. E. and Bjørnåli, E. S. (2011). *Evaluering av handlingsplan for mer entreprenørskap blant kvinner.* NIFU: Rapport 20/2011. www.nifu.no/files/2012/11/NIFUrapport 2011-20.pdf [Accessed October 2015].

Statistics Norway (2015) www.ssb.no.

Svanemyr, S. and Lorch-Falch, S. (2015). Syv av ti ledere i Norges største selskaper er menn. http://e24. no/jobb/syv-av-ti-ledere-i-norges-stoerste-selskaper-er-menn/23491382 [Accessed December 2015].

UN (2012). Convention on the elimination of all forms of discrimination against women: Norway. file:///C:/Users/fgl97113/Downloads/FNs%20konklusjon%20om%20Norge%20og%20kvinners% 20rettigheter%202012.pdf [Accessed December 2015].

UN (2015). *United Nations human development report.* http://hdr.undp.org/en/countries/profiles/ NOR [Accessed December 2015].

Vaage, O. F. (2012). *Tidene skifter: Tidsbruk 1971–2010 (Times change: Time allocation 1971–2010).* Statistical Analysis, No. 125. Oslo: Statistics Norway.

World Economic Forum (2015). *The global gender gap report 2015.* Geneva: World Economic Forum.

PART III

Women in management

North and Central America

9   Women in management in Canada

Anna Roberts and Rekha Karambayya

Introduction

In this chapter, we return to the status of women in management in Canada[1] in the wake of the global recession and at the possible advent of another. Our primary interest in this chapter is focus on changes in employment patterns since 2011, to share the experience of women in management, and tell the story behind the numbers. To set the stage we will offer an overview of national data on education, employment by sector and employment conditions, as well as salary and compensation. We will also take the time to assess national data on women's advancement within the workplace. In our look at women's progress up the hierarchy, we pay particular attention to obstacles to the advancement for middle managers and the state of women at the corporate and executive level. To conclude this section, we will also discuss some promising recent initiatives to improve the work lives, roles, and retention of women in management.

After a tour of the data, we provide contextual information about the current state of women and work in Canada, beyond pure statistics. Since 2011, women have been particularly harmed by the economic impact of the recession. Also, many parts of Canada – particularly high-density urban areas like Toronto and Vancouver – soon will have "minority majority" populations. Thus, the intersectionality of gender with other social identities and conditions is likely to be much more significant. However, this does make it more difficult to assess the state of women as a whole without speaking to the differences in women's experience of their gender arising out of race, immigrant status, and sexual orientation. As a result, we will discuss some data and issues related to how women's experiences in the workforce might be shaped by race and ethnicity. Unlike previous chapters, we will also devote attention to sexual orientation and include the experiences of lesbian women and transwomen. We will also discuss how immigrant and First Nations women are faring in the workplace and in management.

In this recent period, the nation's attention, sadly, was captivated by a number of high-profile cases of sexual harassment and assault of women at work. These cases may offer insight into not just the nature of such instances, but also the reporting of and responses to sexual harassment in the workplace. In this chapter, we will discuss the sexual harassment case against the Dalhousie dental students and the sexual harassment and assault cases against CBC Radio host Jian Ghomeshi and the Royal Canadian Mounted Police (RCMP). We suggest these cases could lead to an increased sensitivity to sexual harassment and assault of women in the workplace and hopefully redoubled efforts to end its harm and address its wide-ranging consequences.

We then conclude this chapter by taking stock on where and how women in management have progressed since 2011, where women have slipped back from earlier advancement, and the opportunities and challenges that await women in management in Canada. Advocates both within and outside of Canada like Anne Marie Slaughter, Arlie Hochschild, and Sheryl Sandberg are inspiring a renewed attention to the increasingly demanding workplace in Canada. The fostering of a culture of care instead of competition in the work environment could be one way to achieve work–life balance for both genders in Canada.

The statistics since 2011

While the labor force participation of men in Canada shows a marginal increase of about 0.5 percent year over year since 2011, that of women shows a larger marginal increase of 0.7 percent until 2013 and then a decline of 0.3 percent in 2014. Interestingly, the largest increase in labor force participation of over 4 percent year over year for both men and women is in the over 55 age group (Statistics Canada, 2015, Table 282-0002). Although the gap between men's and women's labor market participation continues to narrow, women's participation rate still trails that of men's (Statistics Canada, 2015, Table 282-0087). In 2014, the labor market participation rate for women over age 15 was 61 percent, compared to 70 percent for men of the same age (Milan, 2015). More Canadian women are working, but in lower paying jobs (Milan, 2015). Women were most likely to be employed in sales and service occupations (27 percent), business, finance, and administration (24.6 percent), and education, law, social, and government services (16.8 percent). In general, women's employment appears to be concentrated in the services sector, particularly in the healthcare and social services sectors in which they held over 80 percent of the jobs (see Table 9.1).

In the next sections, we discuss some key factors for why women continue to be trapped in lower paying jobs and how that influences the conditions for women in management. We particularly focus on how education shapes women's employment outcomes and the persistence of occupational segregation. We also discuss women who pursue management through self-employment and entrepreneurship. Finally, higher-status women – MBA graduates, corporate executives, and corporate board members – still face significant difficulties in achieving parity to men in management.

Table 9.1 Top 10 female-dominated Canadian occupations

Occupation	Total employees	Women's share of total employees (%)
Dental assistants	29,785	98.2
Medical administrative assistants	14,965	98.2
Dental hygienists and dental therapists	23,325	97.0
Early childhood educators and assistants	187,750	96.8
Office administrative assistants (general, legal, and medical)	381,275	96.3
Home childcare providers	62,610	95.5
Court reporters, medical transcriptionists, and related occupations	9,075	94.8
Receptionists	155,355	94.0
Dietitians and nutritionists	9,960	93.7
Audiologists and speech-language pathologists	9,020	93.7

Source: Statistics Canada, National Household Survey 2015

Education

Before delving into management education, we look broadly at women's educational attainment in Canada since 2011. During the 2012/2013 academic year, women accounted for 56.3 percent of total enrolments in university programs compared with 43.7 percent for men (Statistics Canada, 2015, November 30). These proportions have remained stable over the past decade. Female graduates represented 58 percent of the total number of graduates in 2012, continuing a long trend in which female graduates have outnumbered their male counterparts.

Business, management, marketing, and related support services in Canada remains the most common major for both college and university graduates across both genders (Statistics Canada, 2015, November 4). For instance, 20 percent of all bachelors' degrees awarded by universities in 2012 were in business and public administration, an increase from 15 percent in 1992. At the graduate level, women in Canada are slightly more likely than men to return to school for a post-secondary degree program (25 percent versus 22 percent for men) (Statistics Canada, 2015, November 4).

Women's enrollment in the MBA programs in Canada, however, follows a different story. Women constituted 38 percent of Canadian citizens who sat for the GMAT in 2014 (Graduate Management Admissions Council, 2015, March 15). However, it appears that some prospective women students are not making it to business school. Following some promising leaps forward over the past 15 years, recruitment of women into Canadian full-time MBA programs appears to have flatlined in the mid to low 30 percent range (Hansen, 2014). The top business schools in Canada report that women will represent 30–33 percent of their MBA graduating class of 2016. This compares with a global average of around 38 percent. There is some suggestion that the opportunity costs are higher for women because pursuing an MBA degree involves giving up an established career and incurring a sizable financial burden, all for a lower return on investment. The Rotman School at the University of Toronto has consciously redesigned its teaching model to encourage inclusivity. Other schools have tried to offer flexibility to students to switch between full-time and part-time programs to deal with work–life conflicts. Accelerated and shorter programs have also proved particularly attractive to women. For example, at the Schulich School of Business at York University, female enrollment in the one-year specialized master programs ranges between 45 percent and 65 percent (Hansen, 2014).

Attaining business degrees at the undergraduate and graduate level is often the first step towards women advancing in management. Yet, women are twice as likely as men in Canada to choose a non-corporate job post-MBA (Beninger, 2013). Clearly, the rise of university-educated women alone is not enough to create gender parity in management. In the next section, we discuss some specific gaps between women and men in employment trends and discuss how these gaps affect women's position, pay, and possibilities of advancement in the workplace.

Employment by sector: public/private sector, elected officials, non-traditional sectors

Looking broadly at Canadian women's employment and participation in the labor force, women represented nearly half (47.3 percent) of the labor force in 2014, compared to 37.1 percent in 1976 (Status of Women Canada, 2015). This represents an increase of close to 30 percent. The proportion of women grew in many occupations in Canada between 1991 and 2011, especially among university-educated workers (Statistics Canada, 2014, April 2). In 2012, 51 percent of professional business and financial positions were held by women (Statistics Canada, 2014, April 2). Specifically, the proportion of women in management-related occupations, including sales, marketing, and advertising managers, rose by 17 percentage points from 1991 to 2011 (from 35 percent to 52 percent) and the proportion of women as financial auditors and accountants rose by 14 percentage points (40.1 percent to 54.1 percent) (Uppal and LaRochelle-Côté, 2014). Nevertheless, this near parity in management demographics for some occupations belies significant gender disparity in corporate roles and opportunities for advancement. This gap only widens further as Canadian women make their way up the corporate ladder.

Progress up the hierarchy

High-potential women, in addition, face significant discrepancies in pay, position, and opportunities. A recent study by researchers from Carleton University and Deloitte found that women experience underrepresentation in senior leadership even in sectors in which they constitute a significant percentage of middle managers and dominate in terms of educational credentials (Rankin and Stewart, 2012). Thus, this is not just due to a lack of qualified women in the corporate environment. Those who enter the corporate sector post-MBA still face significance discrepancies in opportunities compared to their male peers, according to a 2013 report by Catalyst Canada[2] (Beninger, 2013). First, these high potential women are more likely to start their post-MBA careers in an entry-level position (Beninger, 2013). Second, female MBAs received fewer high visibility projects and mission critical roles, or "hot jobs" that predict advancement when compared to men (Beninger, 2013). Third, of the few international assignments made available to Canadians of both genders, men were significantly more likely than women to get those assignments (29 percent men versus 19 percent women) (Beninger, 2013). Therefore, even the attainment of an MBA does not translate into better roles and management opportunities for women.

This discrepancy in management opportunities for recent graduate and high-potential women produces unequal gender effects in Canada's executive suites, the nation's board rooms, and legislature. In 2009, the proportion of women on boards of listed companies in Canada was one of the lowest (6 percent) in the Organization for Economic Co-operation and Development (OECD) (10 percent), and a significant percentage of listed companies (42 percent) had no women on their boards (OECD, 2012). Not much has changed since 2009. Currently, there is only one woman serving as a head on the TSX 60: Dawn L. Farrell, TransAlta Corporation (Catalyst, 2015e). Women hold just 20.8 percent of board seats at Canadian Stock Index Companies (Mulligan-Ferry *et al.*, 2014; Catalyst, 2015a) (see Figure 9.1). The percentage of women directors compared to male directors in all FP500 companies is even lower, at 15.9 percent (Mulligan-Ferry *et al.*, 2014; Catalyst, 2015a). Looking at individual FP500 companies, 40 percent of the companies had no women directors in 2013 (Catalyst, 2015a). Some industries are further ahead of others in including women in their boards of directors (McFarland, 2014). In 2014, women accounted for almost one quarter of directors in the consumer staples, healthcare, and telecommunications industries. In contrast, natural resources companies, including energy, mining, and forestry firms, lag behind all other sectors for the proportion of women on their boards (see Table 9.2). In fact, a majority of energy companies in the S&P/TSX composite index have no female directors. Clearly, there is much work to be done at the highest corporate levels.

Women appear to fare better in the public sector. In 2013, women held more than 55 percent of federal public service jobs and 45 percent of executive positions (Status of Women

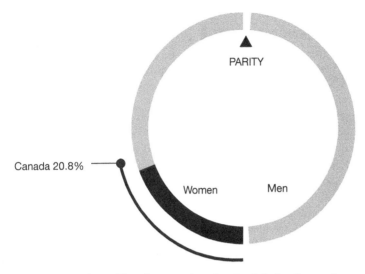

Figure 9.1 Women's share of board seats at Canadian Stock Index Companies
Source: Catalyst (2015a)

Canada, 2014). Yet, it is a different story at the leadership level of elected officials. For instance, women comprise just 38.6 percent of the Senate and 25.2 percent of the House of Commons (Women in National Parliaments, 2015). As of January 2014 women accounted for an average of 26.5 percent of elected members of provincial and territorial governments, representing a wide range from 32 percent in Yukon to 10.5 percent in the Northwest Territories. A study by the Federation of Canadian Municipalities (2012) found that women comprise only 28 percent of municipal councilors Canada-wide. The same study found that only 18 percent of municipal mayors Canada-wide are women.

The most recent election in October 2015 ushered in a dramatic change by electing a majority Liberal government, yet one thing remained virtually unchanged: the proportion of women who will serve. Of the newly elected members of parliament, 26 percent are women, up only one percentage point since the last election (Equal Voice, 2015). Yet, the conditions for women in public leadership in Canada are not entirely bleak. New Prime Minister Justin Trudeau recently appointed an equal number of men and women to his cabinet: 15 men and 15 women. Thus, 2015 marks the first time gender parity has been achieved among ministers at the federal level in Canada. The move represents a huge leap when it comes to the proportion of women represented in cabinet. Before this year's election, approximately one in four cabinet ministers were women.

Table 9.2 Women's share in male-dominated Canadian industries

Industry	Women's share of total industry (%)
Construction	11.5
Fishing, hunting, and trapping	14.2
Forestry and logging with support activities	18.4
Mining (including oil and gas extraction)	19.4
Utilities	23.8

Source: Statistics Canada, 2015, Table 282-0008

Salary and compensation

Women in Canada also face lower salaries and compensation packages than men in similar positions. In 2014, Canadian women earned almost $0.82 to every $1 earned by men (Statistics Canada, 2015, Table 282-0072). Improvement in the wage gap for full-time workers has been minor since 1977. In 1977, women made 77.2 percent of men's wages; in 2014, they made 82.4 percent men's wages (Statistics Canada, 2015, Table 282-0072). Women fare even worse when calculating the gender wage gap based on average weekly wages, rather than just calculating full-time workers' wages. Out of all workers in 2014 (including both full- and part-time workers), women earned just 75.3 percent compared to men (Statistics Canada, 2015, Table 282-0072). While this is slightly better than in the United States, this is not cause for celebration. The gender pay gap is much larger than that in many other developed countries. Some reports suggest that the global pay gap for women is $4000 a year, while the pay gap in Canada is just over $8000 a year (Zamon, 2015).

This wage gap is not erased when women are able to reach management and other higher positions within corporations. For instance, Catalyst Canada found that women in their first post-MBA job are making $8167 less than men (Beninger, 2013). One explanation for this wage gap is a difference in employment conditions faced by men and women. In the next section, we will discuss how the concentration of women in part-time work and causal work and the gender gap in pursuit of entrepreneurship affects women's employment conditions.

Employment conditions (part-time/full-time, entrepreneurship)

Another potential barrier to women's advancement in management is their concentration in part-time work. Women are more likely to be in part-time work and casual work. Nearly 70 percent of part-time workers in 2013 were women, a proportion that has not changed significantly over the past three decades (Status of Women Canada, 2015). While men tend to choose part-time work in order to further their education (35.5 percent, compared to 25.4 percent of women), many more women (15 percent) than men (2.6 percent) were choosing to work part-time to accommodate family needs (Statistics Canada, 2015, Table 282-0014). This concentration of women in casual and part-time labor is one plausible explanation for both the lack of women in senior management in corporations and the gendered wage gap.

Entrepreneurship could be one way for women to gain the flexibility to accommodate family needs and to overcome inequalities in opportunities and wages in the corporate sphere. A 2013 BMO Financial Group survey reveals that 36 percent of women in Canada are interested in starting their own business within the next ten years. Yet, self-employment rates in Canada remain substantially lower for women than for men and have changed little since the 1980s (Rybczynski, 2015). Of women who report an interest in entrepreneurship, 83 percent say that having role models and mentors would be critical to their success (Status of Women Canada, 2015). A recent study found that a major hurdle for women entrepreneurs is the number of children they have, whereas children improve survival rates for men (Rybczynski, 2015). Compared to men, women entrepreneurs tend to have less experience as business owners and spend less time on their business, often because of family commitments. This contributes to the 36 percent earnings gap between self-employed men and women, which is around the OECD average (OECD, 2012). Thus, societal obstacles for advancement still exist for self-employed women, even when they are not navigating a rise within a firm.

Government legislation and company initiatives

Recent government legislation in Canada aimed to increase representation of women on corporate boards has sparked some changes. The Province of Québec, for example, has made gender parity on the boards of its Crown corporations a statutory requirement (OECD, 2012). In June 2014, a government-created Advisory Council of leaders from the private and public sector recommended 30 percent of all governance positions to be held by women by 2019. The Council also endorsed a "comply or explain" approach to support board gender balance. This would require companies to indicate annually whether they have increased the representation of women on their boards, and if not, to provide a rationale. Some advocates say that this could be a good first step for increasing women on boards; others argue that "comply or explain" still fails to require companies to act.

Like other issues affecting women in the workplace, the gender parity for women in management has been difficult to address purely through governmental legislation. Several corporations recently profiled for diversity excellence appear to be targeting initiatives to level the playing field for women. For instance, *The Globe and Mail* and Mediacorp jointly publish a list of Canada's Best Diversity Employers (Mediacorp, 2015), highlighting corporate initiatives promoting diversity. One profiled company, Agrium, an agribusiness company, launched a company-wide mentorship program for women in 2011, pairing female employees with mentors for an 18-month period. Agrium also sponsors a "Women in Agribusiness" conference and participates in "Mentornet," a program that provides mentorship to female post-secondary students in the fields of science, technology, engineering, and math. Blakes, Cassels and Graydon, an elite law firm, has a network called Women@Blakes to provide mentorship, networking, and support to female employees.

The Bank of Montreal, one of the earliest winners of the Catalyst Award in recognition of its efforts to support female employees has introduced "Women in the Pipeline" sessions in which women share challenges in and strategies for navigating careers at the bank. In partnership with Catalyst, the bank has developed a training program to help build inclusive leadership skills among senior managers. BMO Nesbitt Burns, the brokerage division of the bank, has launched a campaign to attract more women into financial advising roles. The campaign seems to be paying off and BMO now reports that 16 percent of investment advisors are women, up from 1 percent in 2012 (Trichur, 2014).

In addition, Capgemini Canada has established the Women LEAD network to provide leadership opportunities for women and act as a liaison for the company's global gender diversity initiative, Women@Capgemini. Capgemini has recently launched a three-month leadership program for women, featuring sessions every four to six weeks and aligning participants with an executive sponsor who will help them navigate career issues and support movement up the hierarchy.

One employer, McMaster University in Hamilton, Ontario, took drastic steps to address the gender wage gap one employee at a time (Flaherty, 2015). A university-wide study found a 2 percent pay gap (amounting to $3515) between men and women that could not be explained away by discipline or rank. In order to address the pay gap, McMaster University announced in April 2015 that the difference of $3515 would be added to all full-time tenured female professors' paychecks.

The story behind the numbers

Clearly, the lack of gender parity in management cannot be explained purely by statistical analysis alone. Societal expectations and workplace culture still constitute significant barriers to women's participation in the workplace and ascent into senior leadership positions. Despite significant advances in gender equality, many women still confront societal expectations of senior leaders as male and stereotypes about working motherhood and women's role as caregivers (Rankin and Stewart, 2012). For example, over 60 percent of eldercare providers are women, who report high levels of physical and emotional strain arising out of those caregiving roles (Duxbury *et al.*, 2011). In addition, there has been a marked change in family roles with the number of stay-at-home parents declining in number from more than half in 1976 to less than a fifth in 2014. Only 11 percent of these stay-at-home parents were men in 2014 (Uppal, 2015). Women continue to assume a greater share of family responsibilities and that leaves many women in middle management wary of undertaking leadership posts (Rankin and Stewart, 2012).

On top of these broad societal pressures and stereotypes related to women's role in the workplace and the home, women in management in Canada have been uniquely affected by the recent global recession and unpredictable energy markets. The next section discusses the mixed impact of the recession on women in Canada, particularly unemployed women and recent female university graduates.

The impact of the recession

The recession has disproportionally affected women in management in a number of ways. Female-dominated industries, such as the retail and healthcare and social assistance sectors, experienced a decline in employment in 2013, and have not fully recovered to their pre-recession employment rates (DePratto, 2014). Single mothers with children under six saw the biggest increase (among parents) in their rate of unemployment during the recession: from 11 percent in 2007 to 17 percent in 2010 (McAnnruff, 2014a). Women who stayed in the workforce after age 65 doubled between 2007 and 2013 (McAnnruff, 2014a). Even if the recovery plan had risen Canada's economy back to 2007 conditions, women would have not necessarily been better off economically. Women had lower levels of employment and higher levels of poverty than men before, during, and after the recession (McAnnruff, 2014a).

Ostensibly "gender-neutral" economic policies implemented before and after the recession by Canada's conservative-led government actually produced disproportionately worse outcomes for women in the recession and slowed women's economic recovery. Feminist economists specifically fault the government's pre-recession benefits slashing, its hasty "repackaging" of previously implemented economic policies as stimulus measures in "Canada's Action Plan," and its removal of equality mandates from federal programs (Lahey and de Villota, 2013). For example, far fewer women fall into each of the successively higher income brackets that have benefitted from tax cuts.

Intersectionality

In addition to these pressures facing all women, the intersectionality of gender with other social factors means that there is no typical experience for women in management. Instead, parenthood, race, sexual orientation, immigration status, and First Nations membership and other social conditions shape the experience of women in very specific and differing ways. The *intersectionality* of *other* cultural patterns of oppression – such as race, class, and ethnicity – is not only interrelated to gendered patterns of oppressions, but these are bound together and influenced by each other. In this section, we take a closer look at the management and economic experiences of women of color, lesbian women, First Nations women, and immigrant women.

Women of color

Overall, Canadian women are becoming more diverse and will only continue to become more so (Catalyst, 2015d). As of 2011, 19 percent of all Canadian women and girls are people of color[3] (3.2 million). By 2031, Statistics Canada has predicted that women of color may be as high as 31 percent. Currently, women of color are 7.4 percent of the total labor force (Catalyst, 2012). Yet, women of color make up 35.9 percent (79,010) of people of color in management occupations and are 13.5 percent of all women in management in Canada (Catalyst, 2012). Furthermore, due to the intersectional nature of oppression, the pay gap is even larger for women of color in Canada. Women of color earn 17 percent less than white women and 25 percent less than men of color (McAnnruff, 2014b).

Sexual orientation

Fewer women are in senior positions in Canada and even fewer who openly identify as lesbian. Furthermore, many lesbian, gay, bisexual, transgender (LGBT) people are closeted, making it difficult to get an accurate population count in Canada. Best estimates place 1.3 percent of Canadians as gay or lesbian and an additional 1.1 percent as bisexuals (Catalyst, 2015b). Some scholars have suggested that gender and sexuality intersect in the workplace to provide a "double-glazed" glass ceiling for lesbian women. The participants in a qualitative small study of LGBT professionals in Canada certainly felt that their gender combined with their sexual orientation affected their professional opportunities (Bowring and Brewis, 2009). For instance, all women have difficulty being "appropriate" in behavioral terms due to the "double bind": women must be tough enough to achieve results and feminine enough to maintain and foster workplace relationships. Lesbian women have even more difficulty navigating these societal norms related to gender and management, particularly because they suffer from the absence of organizational role models (Bowring and Brewis, 2009). This study also found that those men and women who complied with social and gender norms were less organizationally vulnerable. However, our data do not allow us to remark further on this possibility.

Immigrant women

Statistics Canada's population projections predict that Canada could be home to 11.1 million immigrants in 2031 (Malenfant *et al.*, 2010). Of these, approximately 5.8 million (52.3 percent) would be women and girls. Immigrants would then constitute 27.4 percent of Canada's female population (Malenfant *et al.*, 2010). Immigrant women are also more likely be at the intersection of race, gender, and nationality. E. Joy Mighty (1997) describes these women as facing "triple jeopardy": immigrant, female, and of color. In fact, most female immigrants in 2011 belonged to a visible minority group (60.6 percent) (Hudon, 2015). Asia and the Middle East are the birthplace of more than half of recent immigrants (Hudon, 2015). In comparison, 19.3 percent of Canada's total female population belonged to a visible minority group (Hudon, 2015).

Over the last decade, a rising proportion of principal applicants in the economic class for permanent residency in Canada are female. In 2004, females comprised 30.4 percent of applicants admitted under this class (Hudon, 2015). In 2013, however, females accounted for 40.9 percent of principal applicants admitted under the economic class. Educational attainment also is higher among immigrant women compared to Canadian-born women. Yet, the overall labor force participation rate is lower among immigrant women (56.5 percent) compared to Canadian-born women (63.3 percent). Even in the core working age group of 25 to 54 year olds, 76.4 percent of immigrant women are labor force participants, compared to 83.6 percent of Canadian-born women. In the past, this gap in immigrant women's labor force participation has been attributed to source-country gender-role attitudes that persist following emigration to a new country. However, recent scholarship has shown when gender role attitudes are accounted for, source-country female labor force participation rate instead is a strong predictor of immigrant women's earnings in Canada (Frank and Hou, 2015). This suggests that although gender-role attitudes may be related to participation in the labor force, this relationship is mediated by source-country labor force participation to predict labor force participation in Canada.

Once in the labor force, immigrant women suffer employment disparities compared to Canadian-born women and immigrant men. For instance, immigrant women in Canada are more often underemployed. In 2011, 48.6 percent of working immigrant women with a bachelor's level education or higher were employed in positions that did not typically require a degree. In contrast, this was the case for 32.8 percent of Canadian-born women and 41 percent of male immigrants overall (Frank and Hou, 2015). Also, most immigrant women who work are wage earners and more immigrant women than Canadian-born women also work part-time. As a result, first-generation immigrant women overall earn 15 percent less than non-immigrant women and 25 percent less than immigrant men (McAnnruff, 2014b). Employment income becomes more similar to Canadian-born women with time spent in Canada. Canadian-born women are also slightly more likely (10.3 percent) than immigrant women (8.9 percent) to hold a management position (Frank and Hou, 2015).

First Nations/Aboriginal women

There has been some progress in Aboriginal women's incomes, but they still lag behind the incomes for non-Aboriginal women and Aboriginal men. For example, between 2005 and 2010, median total income for Aboriginal women aged 15 years and over increased from $17,044 to $19,289 (in constant 2010 dollars), even as a significant gap remains when compared to non-Aboriginal women ($24,842 in 2010) and Aboriginal men ($22,924 in 2010) (Status of Women Canada, 2013b). The progress of Aboriginal women as elected and appointed political leaders, however, has been mixed. As of August 2013, among the First Nations, which report to Aboriginal Affairs and Northern Development Canada (AANDC) on governance, women held 16 percent of band chief positions, down from 19.8 percent in 2012 (Status of Women Canada, 2014). Of 2669 reported First Nations band councilors, 755 (28 percent) were women, a drop from 800 reported in 2011 (Status of Women Canada, 2014). In the 41st Parliament, two of the six Aboriginal members of parliament were women: one Inuit and one Métis (Status of Women Canada, 2014). In November 2015, a female Aboriginal lawyer, Jody Wilson-Raybould, was appointed minister of justice and attorney general of Canada. Of the five Aboriginal senators, two are First Nations women (Status of Women Canada, 2014).

Sexual harassment: Jian Ghomeshi, Canadian Olympic Committee,
Dalhousie dental students, RCMP

Several cases of workplace sexual harassment have recently made national news in Canada. Jian Ghomeshi, a high-profile host of a radio show on the national broadcaster, CBC, has been accused of sexual assault by four women. Marcel Aubut, the chair of the Canadian Olympic Committee, resigned in disgrace in October 2015 after being accused by several female colleagues of inappropriate behavior. In 2014, several male dentistry students at Dalhousie university were accused of creating a Facebook page in which they sexually harassed their female colleagues. The RCMP, an iconic national law enforcement organization, stands accused by 400 women of decades of sexual harassment and discrimination.

These cases have drawn attention to the prevalence of sexual harassment and a culture of misogyny in a wide variety of Canadian workplaces and universities. Worse they have drawn attention to the inability or the failure of organizations to establish processes to address these incidents and protect the victims. A task force investigating the Dalhousie incidents revealed that the victims were often isolated and blamed while the perpetrators faced few consequences (Chiose, 2015). Other cases are now working their way through the court system. An independent inquiry into the Jian Ghomeshi case reported that CBC routinely ignored complaints from employees, often condoning Ghomeshi's abusive behavior at work (*The Toronto Star*, 2015). The complainants in the RCMP case are asking a judge in British Columbia to certify a class action lawsuit against their employer because they are alleging that the abuse they experienced is systemic and they cannot rely on their employer to address it.

Several experts have suggested that these cases represent a sea change in that they are forcing employers and the courts to pay attention to the definitions of sexual harassment and the importance of policies to address it (Flavelle, 2015). They also draw attention to the difficult workplace challenges faced by women and the tendency for organizations to either sweep them under the rug or blame the victim. The Province of Ontario is stepping up the fight against sexual violence by making it harder for bosses and schools to ignore sexual assault while attempting to define it in law. Legislation proposed by the government would force employers to respond to complaints and allow victims access to legal action (Ferguson, 2015).

Cultures of care, not competition

Definitions of good leadership have changed within many organizations; yet, women leaders continue to encounter gendered notions of leadership that reflects a traditional male model (Rankin and Stewart, 2012). Although public and private sector women and men alike agree that definitions of leadership have evolved to embrace "soft skills," such as the capacity to engage employees, reformulated ideas about leadership and leadership competencies have not resulted in significant changes in the expectations women leaders face (Rankin and Stewart, 2012). Women who "make it" to the top regularly face expectations of extended work hours, 24/7 availability, and ready mobility for travel (Rankin and Stewart, 2012). Leadership models that fail to take the realities of many women's lives into account can negatively impact women's experience in senior leadership positions and may affect the ability to retain women leaders (Rankin and Stewart, 2012). Existing Canadian organizations dedicated toward the advancement of women in the workplace have already existed historically in Canada, such as Women of Influence, Inc. and their RBC Canadian Women Entrepreneur Awards. In addition, recent years have been marked by an increasing attention to the incompatibility of the workplace with the realities of women's lives. Canadian women have been inspired by

Facebook Chief Operating Officer (COO) Sheryl Sandberg and her book *Lean In: Women, Work, and the Will to Lead* (2013). For instance, Lean In Canada was founded in 2013 to encourage fellow women be more fearless in their careers and overcome mental obstacles that may hold them back. Two years later, the organization had over 2000 members in various professions and hosted monthly meetings in Toronto, Montreal, Calgary, and Vancouver.

One outcome of all of this attention to women in the workplace has been a focus on the inhospitable nature of work and management to the human and social demands for care. Anne-Marie Slaughter's article "Why Women Still Can't Have It All" (2012) and her new book *Unfinished Business: Women Men Work Family* (2015a) described the increasing concerns that the world of work is toxic for everybody. The demands of the working world are almost impossible to manage for any male and female workers who aren't young, healthy, childless, and unencumbered by any outside needs or demands. To Slaughter, the problem is with the workplace, or more precisely, with a workplace designed for families of a bygone era in which one partner does all the work of earning an income and the other partner does all the work of turning that income into care. Slaughter argues that the division of income-generating and caring responsibilities in families is no longer so rigidly divided and as a result, our workplaces do not fit the realities of the caring demands of our lives.

Some Canadian organizations have recognized and responded to employees' needs around family care. For example:

- Ivanhoé Cambridge Inc., Montreal. Property management; 1301 employees. Supports full-time employees with compassionate leave top-up payments when called upon to care for a loved one, to 80 percent of salary for eight weeks.
- Trican Well Service Ltd., Calgary. Support for oil and gas operations; 2395 employees. Offers maternity and parental leave top-up payments for new mothers and adoptive parents to 100 percent of salary for 52 weeks, as well as parental top-up for new fathers to 100 percent of salary for 37 weeks.
- World Vision Canada, Mississauga. Social advocacy; 464 employees. Offers alternative work arrangements, including flexible hours, telecommuting, shortened and compressed work week options, and reduced summer hours.
- Accenture Inc., Toronto. Business consulting; 3623 employees. Offers a generous in-vitro fertilization (IVF) subsidy to employees requiring treatments, to a maximum of $15,000.

Taking stock

Looking back at our exploration of women in management in Canada it is clear that the evidence highlights some progress and several challenges. For example, improvement in the gender wage gap has been marginal since 1977, particularly when part-time workers are considered. Although the wage gap in Canada is marginally better than the gap in the United States, it is much larger than that in many other developed countries. Furthermore, the pay gap is much higher for women of color, Aboriginal women, and immigrant women. While the most common assumption attributes the pay gap to mothers taking time off to raise children, some evidence points to a pay gap of 6.6 percent between men and women just one year after graduation (Catalyst, 2015c). The Ontario Pay Equity Commission (2014) reports that approximately 10 to 15 percent of the pay gap may be attributed to discrimination. Pay equity legislation and training women to negotiate better wages may narrow the gender pay gap, but may not entirely erase it.

These main conclusions largely circle around women in management's stalled progress – if not slipping back – due to (1) lack of network and connections for advancement; (2) the intersectional nature of inequality; (3) workplace cultures of competition, not caring; (4) the persistence of gender roles in the home. First, high-potential women and university-educated immigrant women are not just experiencing a gap in pay, they also experience inequalities in position and opportunities (Beninger, 2013; Hudon, 2015). Second, Canada is facing several demographic shifts; thus, the experience of "women" in management in Canada can no longer be considered a singular and universal one. By 2031 nearly a quarter of the female population is projected to be aged 65 or older, up from 16 percent in 2010 (Status of Women Canada, 2013a). This might result in longer working lives for women. While women of color made up 19 percent of the female population, by 2031 that number is likely to be as high as 31 percent. Meanwhile the population of Aboriginal women grew at four times the rate of all Canadian women between 2006 and 2011 (Milan, 2015). We were surprised by the paucity of research on the special challenges faced by visible minority and immigrant women, despite the fact that some (see Mighty, 1997) have been drawing attention to the "triple jeopardy" faced by women from visible minority and immigrant groups. There is a pressing need to understand the work and life experiences of women who are particularly vulnerable because they are lesbian, single, recent immigrants, or belong to First Nations groups.

Third, Anne Marie Slaughter (2015b) has suggested that too much of career success is shaped by the standard of the "ideal worker": someone who is available at all hours, rises to the challenge of every workplace emergency, never gets sick, and is willing to travel at short notice. The emerging digital, gig economy may offer a more appealing, flexible option to women, particularly those with family care responsibilities, who are unable or unwilling to accede to the demands of 24/7 availability at the workplace. This is already evident in some occupations, such as law and medicine. However, Slaughter points out that gains for women in the gig economy are only possible with a portable social safety net, a benefits package that travels with the employee, and a culture that values care-giving as much as paid employment.

Finally, another troubling issue with huge implications for women and work is the slow pace of change in gender roles in the home. As Reeves and Sawhill (2015) point out in a recent article:

> So far the gender revolution has been a one-sided effort. Women have entered previously male precincts of economic and political life, and for the most part they have succeeded... But along the way something crucial has been left out. We have not pushed hard enough to put men in traditionally female roles–that is where our priority should lie now.

Legislation may be one way to reshape gender roles. In 2001 the Canadian federal government extended parental leave to about a year. While Canadian women have access to fairly generous parental leave policies, many do not qualify for maternity leave either because they have not worked long enough or are self-employed. The Province of Quebec had charted its own course in this arena by offering universal subsidized childcare and significantly modifying parental leave policies in 2006 to improve eligibility criteria, allowing special time for fathers that is not transferrable to mothers, and increasing flexibility by offering parents more options. Fathers in Quebec now have the option of taking three to five weeks of paternity leave, and parents have the option of taking a longer leave at a reduced pay rate or a shorter leave with higher pay. While only 10 percent of fathers in other Canadian provinces claim parental benefits, in Quebec that number increased sharply to 56 percent right after the new paternity leave policy came into effect (Marshall, 2008). While government legislation has the potential to change gendered roles to some extent, that may not be enough. We may need to change broadly held assumptions that commitment to caring is a burden that is incompatible with work commitment.

In conclusion, our review of women in management in Canada points to marginal progress and much work still to be done. We were unable to find much research or statistics on the increasingly important issue of intersectionality and its role in predicting women's progress and challenges. While Canadian corporations appear to be attempting to level the playing field for employees, they seem to be hampered by outdated perceptions and strongly held assumptions about gender roles that no longer reflect the reality of women's lives in the workplace and the family.

Notes

1　Unless specified, we use the phrase "women in Canada" and "Canadian women" interchangeably to refer to women residing in Canada. These phrases include both women who are citizens of Canada and women who are residents of Canada.
2　Founded in 1962, Catalyst is the leading non-profit membership and research organization working globally with businesses and the professions. With offices in the United States, Canada, and Europe, it aims to expand opportunities for women in business and to help corporations cultivate inclusive environments.
3　The Employment Equity Act in Canada defines visible minorities as "persons, other than Aboriginal peoples, who are non-Caucasian in race or non-white in colour." The visible minority population includes the following groups: Chinese, South Asian, Black, Filipino, Latin American, Southeast Asian, Arab, West Asian, Japanese, Korean, and Pacific Islander. Governmental statistics available from Statistics Canada use the term visible minorities.

References

Beninger, A. (2013). *High-Potential Employees in the Pipeline: Maximizing the Talent Pool in Canadian Organizations.* Toronto: Catalyst Canada.
BMO Financial Group. (2013). BMO poll: One-third of women interested in becoming business owners within the next decade. Retrieved from: http://newsroom.bmo.com/
Bowring, M. A. and Brewis, J. (2009). Truth and consequences: managing lesbian and gay identity in the Canadian workplace. *Equal Opportunities International,* 28(5), 361–377.
Catalyst. (2012). *Quick Take: Visible Minorities.* New York: Catalyst. Retrieved from: www.catalyst.org/knowledge/visible-minorities
Catalyst. (2015a). *2014 Catalyst Census: Women Board Directors.* New York: Catalyst. Retrieved from: www.catalyst.org/knowledge/2014-catalyst-census-women-board-directors
Catalyst. (2015b). *Quick Take: Lesbian, Gay, Bisexual & Transgender Workplace Issues.* New York: Catalyst. Retrieved from: www.catalyst.org/knowledge/lesbian-gay-bisexual-transgender-workplace-issues
Catalyst. (2015c). *Quick Take: Women's Earnings and Income.* New York: Catalyst. Retrieved from: www.catalyst.org/knowledge/womens-earnings-and-income#footnote7_wxl4wt6
Catalyst. (2015d). *Quick Take: Women in Canada.* May 6. New York: Catalyst. Retrieved from: www.catalyst.org/knowledge/women-canada
Catalyst. (2015e). *Women Heads of the TSX 60.* New York: Catalyst. Retrieved from: www.catalyst.org/knowledge/women-heads-tsx-60
Chiose, S. (2015). Dalhousie made string of errors in dentistry probe, report finds. *The Globe and Mail.* June 29. Retrieved from: www.theglobeandmail.com/news/national/report-says-dalhousie-did-not-treat-female-students-fairly-transparently-in-dentistry-scandal/article25174977/

DePratto, B. (2014). *Falling Female Labour Participation: A Concern.* October 24. Toronto: TD Economics. Retrieved from: www.td.com/document/PDF/economics/special/FemaleParticipation 2014.pdf

Duxbury, L., Higgins, C. and Smart, R. (2011). Elder care and the impact of caregiver strain on the health of employed caregivers. *Work: A Journal of Prevention, Assessment and Rehabilitation,* 40(1): 29–40.

Equal Voice. (2015, October 20). Press release: Despite dramatic results, no meaningful change in the percentage of women elected to Parliament. Retrieved from: http://eepurl.com/bDaTZL

Federation of Canadian Municipalities. (2012). *Women in Local Government: Getting to 30% by 2026.* Ottowa: Federation of Canadian Municipalities. Retrieved from: www.fcm.ca/Documents/reports/ Women/Getting_to_30_percent_by_2026_EN.pdf

Ferguson, R. (2015). New Ontario law targets sexual violence, harassment in workplaces, schools. *The Toronto Star.* October 27. Retrieved from: www.thestar.com/news/queenspark/2015/10/27/new-ontario-law-targets-sexual-violence-harassment-in-workplaces-schools.html

Flaherty, C. (2015). Levelling the Field: McMaster U addresses gender pay gap by giving $3,500 raises to female faculty members. *Inside Higher Ed.* Retrieved from: www.insidehighered.com/news/ 2015/04/30/mcmaster-u-addresses-gender-pay-gap-3500-raises-female-faculty-members

Flavelle, D. (2015). High-profile sexual harassment cases causing "sea change." *The Toronto Star.* October 10. Retrieved from: www.thestar.com/news/insight/2015/10/10/high-profile-sex-harassment-cases-having-impact.html

Frank, K. and Hou, F. (2015). Beyond culture: source country female labour force participation and the earnings of immigrant women. *Work, Employment & Society*: 1–26. DOI: 10.1177/09500170155 87874.

Graduate Management Admissions Council. (2015). Data to go: women and graduate management education. March 15. Retrieved from: www.gmac.com/market-intelligence-and-research/research-library/diversity-enrollment/women-in-graduate-management-education-2015.aspx

Hansen, D. (2014). How B-schools are responding to the persistent gender gap. *The Globe and Mail.* November 5. Retrieved from: www.theglobeandmail.com/report-on-business/careers/business-education/how-b-schools-are-responding-to-the-persistent-gender-gap/article21441117/

Hudon, T. (2015, October 21). Immigrant women. In *Women in Canada: A Gender-based Statistical Report (89-503-X).* Ottawa, ON: Statistics Canada. Retrieved from: www5.statcan.gc.ca/olc-cel/olc. action?ObjId=89-503-X201500114217&ObjType=47&lang=en

Lahey, K. A. and de Villota, P. (2013). Economic crisis, gender equality, and policy responses in Spain and Canada. *Feminist Economics,* (19)3: 82–107. DOI: 10.1080/13545701.2013.812267

Malenfant, É. C., Lebel, A. and Martel, L. (2010). *Projections of the Diversity of the Canadian Population, 2006-2031.* Catalogue no. 91-551-X. Ottawa, Ontario: Statistics Canada, Demography Division.

Marshall, K. (2008). Fathers' use of parental leave. *Perspectives on Labour and Income.* May 14. Statistics Canada.

McAnnruff, K. (2014a). *Ontario's Gender Gap: Women and Jobs Post-Recession.* Toronto: Canadian Centre for Policy Alternatives. Retrieved from: www.policyalternatives.ca/publications/reports/ontarios-gender-gap#sthash.cQk4mus2.dpuf

McAnnruff, K. (2014b). *Testimony to the Standing Committee on the Status of Women,* April 30. Toronto: Canadian Centre for Policy Alternatives. Retrieved from: www.policyalternatives.ca/publications/ reports/study-economic-leadership-and-prosperity-canadian-women

McFarland, J. (2014). Women on Boards: How Canadian industries stack up. *The Globe and Mail.* November 23. Retrieved from: www.theglobeandmail.com/report-on-business/careers/manage ment/board-games-2014/women-in-boardrooms/article21690107/

Mediacorp. (2015). *Canada's Best Diversity Employers, 2015 Winners.* Retrieved from: www.canada stop100.com/diversity/

Mighty, E. J. (1997). Triple Jeopardy: Immigrant women of color in the labor force. In P. Prasad, A. J. Mills, M. Elmes and A. Prasad (eds), *Managing the Organizational Melting Pot: Dilemmas of workplace diversity* (pp. 312–339). Thousand Oaks, CA: Sage Publications, Inc.

Milan, A. (2015). Female population. In *Women in Canada: A Gender-based Statistical Report (89-503-X).*

March 30. Ottawa, ON: Statistics Canada. Retrieved from: www5.statcan.gc.ca/olc-cel/olc.action?ObjId=89-503-X201500114152&ObjType=47&lang=en&limit=0.

Mulligan-Ferry, L., Bartkiewicz, M. J., Soares, R., Singh, A. and Winkleman, I. (2014). *2013 Catalyst Census: Financial Post 500 Women Board Directors*. New York: Catalyst. Retrieved from: www.catalyst.org/knowledge/2013-catalyst-census-financial-post-500-women-board-directors-0

OECD. (2012). Country facts: Canada. In *Closing the Gender Gap: Act Now*. Retrieved from: www.oecd.org/gender/closingthegap.htm

Ontario Pay Equity Commission. (2014). *Gender Wage Gap*. April. Retrieved from: www.payequity.gov.on.ca/en/about/pubs/genderwage/wagegap.php

Rankin, L. P. and Stewart, J. (2012). *Progress in Inches, Miles to Go: A benchmarking study of women's leadership in Canada* [electronic resource]. Toronto: Deloitte and Centre for Women in Politics and Leadership. Retrieved from: http://carleton.ca/cwppl/2012/progress-in-inches-miles-to-go-a-benchmarking-study-of-womens-leadership-in-canada-a-report/

Reeves, R. V. and Sawhill, I. V. (2015). Men's lib!. *The New York Times*. November 15. Retrieved from: www.nytimes.com/2015/11/15/opinion/sunday/mens-lib.html?_r=0

Rybczynski, K. (2015). What drives self-employment survival for women and men? Evidence from Canada. *Journal of Labor Research*, 36(1), 27–43.

Sandberg, S. (2013). *Lean In: Women, Work, and the Will to Lead*. New York: Alfred A. Knopf.

Slaughter, A. (2012). Why women still can't have it all. *The Atlantic*, July/August. Retrieved from: www.theatlantic.com/magazine/archive/2012/07/why-women-still-cant-have-it-all/309020/

Slaughter, A. (2015a). *Unfinished Business: Women Men Work Family*. New York: Random House.

Slaughter, A. (2015b). The gig economy can actually be great for women. *Wired*. October 23. Retrieved from: www.wired.com/2015/10/unfinished-business-women-men-work-family/

Statistics Canada. (2014, April 2). Occupational profile and over-qualification of young workers in Canada, 1991 to 2011. *The Daily*. Retrieved from: www.statcan.gc.ca/daily-quotidien/140402/dq140402a-eng.htm

Statistics Canada. (2015). Table 282-0072. Labour force survey estimates (LFS), wages of employees by type of work, North American Industry Classification System (NAICS), sex and age group, annually. CANSIM (database).

Statistics Canada. (2015, January 27). Table 282-0002. Labour force survey estimates (LFS), by sex and detailed age group, monthly. CANSIM (database).

Statistics Canada. (2015, January 28). Table 282-0087. Labour force survey estimates (LFS), by sex and age group, seasonally adjusted and unadjusted, monthly (Headline LFS data for employment and unemployment). CANSIM (database).

Statistics Canada. (2015, August). Table 282-0014. Labour force survey estimates (LFS), part-time employment by reason for part-time work, sex and age group, annual (persons x 1,000). CANSIM (database).

Statistics Canada. (2015, November 4). Education in Canada: Attainment, field of study and location of study, 2011. Retrieved from: www12.statcan.gc.ca/nhs-enm/2011/as-sa/99-012-x/99-012-x2011001-eng.cfm#a7

Statistics Canada. (2015, November 30). University enrolment. Retrieved from: www.statcan.gc.ca/tables-tableaux/sum-som/l01/cst01/educ71a-eng.htm

Status of Women Canada. (2015). *Fact Sheet: Economic Security*. February 25. Ottawa, ON: Status of Women Canada. Retrieved from: www.swc-cfc.gc.ca/initiatives/wesp-sepf/fs-fi/es-se-eng.html

Status of Women Canada (2014). *Fact Sheet: Leadership and Democratic Participation*. September. Ottawa, ON: Status of Women Canada. Retrieved from: www.swc-cfc.gc.ca/initiatives/wldp/wb-ca/fs-fi/dp-pd-eng.html

Status of Women Canada. (2013a). *Women in Canada at a Glance: Statistical Highlights*. September 30. Ottawa, ON: Status of Women Canada. Retrieved from: www.swc-cfc.gc.ca/rc-cr/stat/wic-fac-2012/glance-statistical-eng.pdf

Status of Women Canada. (2013b). *Fact Sheet: Women in Non-Traditional Occupations*. September 30.

Ottawa, ON: Status of Women Canada. Retrieved from: www.swc-cfc.gc.ca/initiatives/wesp-sepf/fs-fi/wnto-fetm-eng.html

Toronto Star (2015). CBC management needs shakeup after damning report on Ghomeshi affair: Editorial. *The Toronto Star.* April 17. Retrieved from: www.thestar.com/opinion/editorials/2015/04/17/cbc-management-needs-shakeup-after-damning-report-on-ghomeshi-affair-editorial.html

Trichur, R. (2014). Bank of Montreal wants to hire more female investment advisers: launches website to recruit women for brokerage division. *The Wall Street Journal.* July 10. Retrieved from: www.wsj.com/articles/bank-of-montreal-wants-to-hire-more-female-investment-advisers-1404964863

Uppal, S. (2015). Employment patterns of families with children. *Insights on Canadian Society.* June. Statistics Canada Catalogue no. 75-006-X.

Uppal, S. and LaRochelle-Côté, S. (2014). Overqualification among recent university graduates in Canada. *Insights on Canadian Society.* April. Statistics Canada Catalogue no. 75-006-X.

Women in National Parliaments. (2015). World Classification. Retrieved from: www.ipu.org/wmn-e/classif.htm

Zamon, R. (2015). The gender pay gap in Canada is twice the global average. *Huffington Post Canada.* June 5. Retrieved from: www.huffingtonpost.ca/2015/05/06/gender-pay-gap-canada_n_7223508.html

10 Women in management in Mexico[1]

Gina Zabludovsky

Introduction

The dramatic increase in the number of women working outside the home constitutes an unprecedented social change, one that has radically transformed societies over the past thirty years. The growing insertion of women is reflected in different areas of the economy, particularly in higher education, and in many professions. The following chapter analyzes women's participation in the Mexican labor force and the proportion of women holding leadership positions as managers, officers, members of boards of directors, and entrepreneurs. Thus, as we shall observe, the active presence of women has become evident in every environment.

Labor force characteristics

The increased participation of Mexican women in the nation's labor force has been one of the fastest-paced changes taking place in Latin America, increasing from 20.6 percent in 1970 to 37.8 percent in 2015 (in an economically active population of 50,336,088 in 2015, of which 16,027,016 were women and 31,309,072 men; INEGI, 2015) The aforementioned percentage is even higher in the urban areas of the country, where women comprise 41.2 percent (2015) of the total economically active population of 23,332,692. As shown in Table 10.1, over the last seventeen years, this percentage has been steadily increasing.

The majority of women (61.3 percent) work in the service sector, compared to 50.2 percent of men. Women have an especially important presence and outnumber men in such areas of business as social services (65 percent), hotels and restaurants (55 percent), and other services (54 percent). They also have a significant presence in commerce (48 percent). In contrast, females have an extremely low presence in traditionally masculine sectors, such as construction (6

Table 10.1 Male and female labor force (urban areas), 1991–2015

Year	Men (%)	Women (%)	Total (%)
1991	65.5	34.5	100
1997	63.4	36.6	100
2003	63.3	36.7	100
2008	59.46	40.5	100
2010	59.20	40.8	100
2015	58.77	41.2	100

Source: Developed by Gina Zabludovsky, data from INEGI, Encuesta Nacional de Empleo 1991–2011 and Encuesta Nacional de Empleo 2015

percent) and agriculture and livestock (14 percent), as well as in mining (15 percent) (INEGI, 2015). However, the percentage of females in the these traditional sectors has increased significantly in recent years (in 2000 women comprised only 6 percent of mine workers). The same holds true in the transportation and related services sector, where although women now comprise only 13 percent, this figure is significantly higher than in 2000, when women made up only 8.2 percent of the labor force in transportation and 12.6 percent in agriculture and livestock (INEGI, 2000, 2015) (see Figures 10.1 and 10.2).

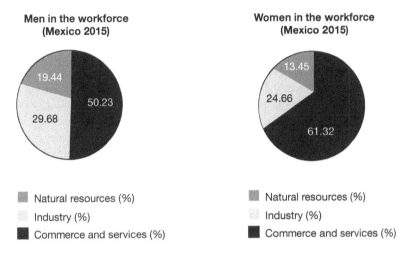

Figure 10.1 Distribution of men and women in the workforce by sector, 2015
Source: Developed by Gina Zabludovsky from INEGI (2015), Encuesta Nacional de Empleo

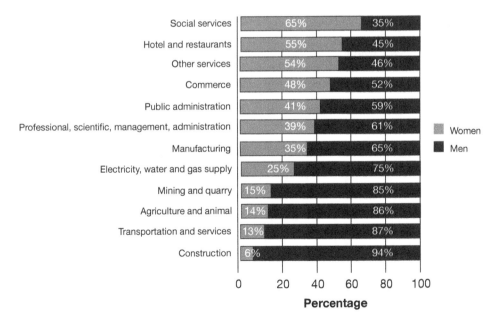

Figure 10.2 Male and female labor force by industry categories, 2015
Source: Developed by Gina Zabludovsky from INEGI (2015), Encuesta Nacional de Empleo

Despite women's growing presence in the labor force, it is interesting to note the inequalities that appear when comparing women's and men's earnings (Zabludovsky, 2004). Figure 10.3 shows that regarding the total workforce earning less than one minimum wage, the percentage of women reaches 64 percent, while, in contrast, the proportion of women in the areas of the labor force earning over three minimum salaries drops to 31 percent (INEGI, 2015).

This difference between men's and women's income appears in all the 32 states comprising the Mexican Republic, both in the nation's richest states, located in the north and thus closest to the United States, such as Baja California and Nuevo León, as well as in the poorer southern states, namely Oaxaca, Tlaxcala, and Guerrero. (The exception is Chiapas, the poorest state in Mexico, where men and women earn the same and their income falls within the lowest wage category.)

According to World Bank reports, the wage gap between men and women in Mexico was 80 percent in 2012 (Mendoza, 2012). In part, this difference could be explained due to unpaid family responsibilities. Women in Mexico spend up to forty-two hours a week on housework, while among men this number is only fifteen (INEGI, 2009c). Thus, as shown by some studies, the notable increase of women in the workforce has not led to a reassessment of responsibilities and duties of household members (Ariza and de Oliveira, 2006). In fact, a survey conducted in twenty countries in 2011, showed that 54 percent of Mexican women live under pressure because of their multiple responsibilities (Nielsen, 2011). In this regard, Mexican women were only surpassed by Indian women (Nielsen, 2011; Vargas, 2011; Zabludovsky, 2015).

Women pursuing education

In the 1990s, the percentage of women enrolled in higher education in many countries came to exceed that of men (Avelar and Zabludovsky, 1996). In line with these international trends, the number of women enrolled in higher education in Mexico has grown significantly and at an accelerated pace.

According to national statistics, in 2015, the proportion of males and females among college graduates in major cities was 50 percent men and 50 percent women. If we view the percentage distribution in higher education by sex, from 1970 significant changes can be observed, since the student population in that year was 19 percent female, increasing to 30 percent in 1980, 40 percent in 1990, 46 percent in 1998, and 50 percent in 2015 (see Figure 10.4) (ANUIES, 2015).

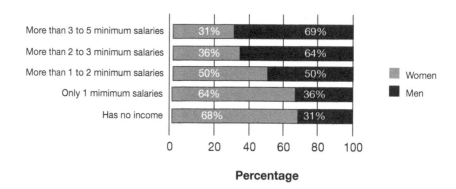

Figure 10.3 Male and female labor force in relation to salary, 2015
Source: Developed by Gina Zabludovsky from INEGI (2015), Encuesta Nacional de Empleo

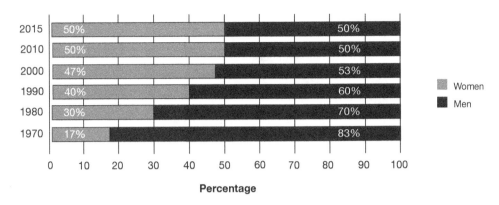

Figure 10.4 Percentage of men and women enrolled in higher education, 1970–2015
Source: Developed by Gina Zabludovsky from ANUIES, Anuarios estadisticos

Meanwhile, as shown in Figure 10.5 during the last two decades, there has been a significant increase in the participation of women in professions such as business administration and law, with 56 percent of female students. Their presence is also very important in the fields of marketing, education, communication, dentistry, and chemistry where they reach figures above 60 percent. Women constitute 65 percent of college students in the health professions. While it is true that in the latter sector a large number of them are dedicated to nursing, in recent years, enrollment in medical careers has taken a drastic turn and now the percentage of women students is similar to that of men (ANUIES, 2011; Zabludovsky, 2015, 2016).

However, women are far from achieving equality in all fields and occupations. While in professions related to education, women constitute 73 percent of students, in the areas of technology, the presence of women is still below 30 percent. In some particular fields such as automotive, civil, mechanical, and electronic engineering, women make up less than 25 percent of the total enrollment. In those considered as "female professions" such as education, nursing, nutrition, and psychology, at least three out of four students are women (ANUIES, 2015).

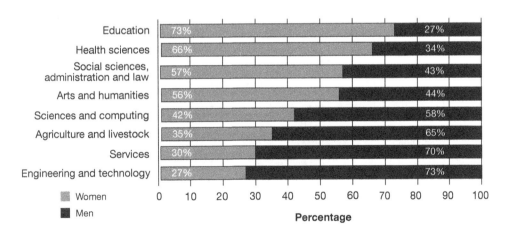

Figure 10.5 Percentage of men and women enrolled in different higher education sectors, 2014–2015
Source: Developed by Gina Zabludovsky from ANUIES, Anuarios estadisticos

Some of the reasons for the low participation of women in mathematics and other sciences have to do with the education paths of teachers and parents from an early age. As several studies have shown, they usually reproduce attitudes and stereotypes that do not promote women's interest in these areas of knowledge (Gunderson *et al.*, 2011).

Women in management

According to my own estimate based on national surveys, the percentage of women administrators in the private sector is 29 percent (INEGI, 2013), ten points below the ratio of women officers in governmental positions and the public sector.[2] However, if we take into account other sources of information such as business directories and indexes, the amount of women in middle management is barely 23 percent.[3] If we consider only the highest executive positions, the percentage of women as general directors in different areas[4] is only 13 percent, and a scarce 5 percent as chief executive officers (CEOs) (Conexión Ejecutiva, 2012; Expansión, 2012).

Apart from the vertical segregation, demonstrated by the larger number of women in the lower levels of the hierarchy, there is a high degree of horizontal segregation as well. Women executives are concentrated in a restricted number of fields such as marketing and communication (29 percent), human resources (21 percent), and public relations.[5] In contrast, the participation of women decreases notably in the areas of operations and research (8 percent), finances and administration (5 percent), and computers and systems (2 percent) (Zabludovksy, 2015) (see Figure 10.6).

The exclusion of women executives from certain areas is much more significant from a strategic standpoint than what is shown by mere numbers, since it often means that women are barred from the positions that confer functional responsibilities and offer more opportunities for ascending the administrative hierarchy (Hola and Todaro, 1992; Kanter, 1993).

Mexico is not unique as regards its profile of women directors. In fact, according to the *Latin American Business Chronicle*, only 1.8 percent of Latin American companies are run by a women.

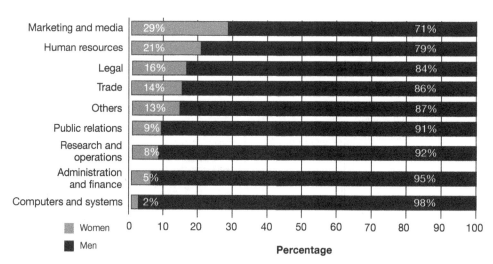

Figure 10.6 Percentage of male and female executives in top management positions, 2012
Source: Developed by Gina Zabludovsky with information from 227 of 500 of the biggest companies in Mexico (based on Expansion and Conexión Ejecutive magazine)

Just 15.4 percent of companies out of the top 500 in Latin America have a woman executive in upper management (Catalyst, 2012; Nambur and Calderon, 2012). The presence of women as directors of the production area is quite scarce, while, in contrast, their presence increases in the leading administration positions in commerce, sales, marketing, human resources, and finance (Maxfield, Cárdenas and Heller, 2008).

Women's segregation into certain occupations may be partially explained by differentiated socialization in early life that has a significant influence on the choice and practice of a profession and that leads women to be inclined towards certain occupational areas, while rejecting others (Bauman, 1994; Elias and Scottson, 1965; Kanter, 1993; Simmel, 1998; Zabludovsky, 2005). Expectations for academic and non-academic education related to the different patterns of success for men and women in traditional contexts have influenced the fact that certain positions of authority and leadership are considered as prototypically masculine. Consequently, it is not at all far-fetched to assume that women themselves, whether consciously or unconsciously, whether as the product of a rational decision or their own construction of their subjectivity, consider that some positions are not an option for them and therefore pursue job choices considered "more feminine" and limit their aspirations to holding less strategic positions, which do not include production areas.

However, apart from these general cultural patterns comprising a large portion of the differentiating axes of men's and women's "personalities" in Mexican society, there are also other factors in "corporate culture" where the distinct characteristics of "feminine" and "masculine" are reproduced exponentially (Albrow, 1997; Burell and Hearn, 1989; Mills, 1990; Sheppard, 1990; Zabludovsky, 2003). Organizations tend to replicate aspects of their social context, while considering that their own corporate culture is neutral and objective, although in practice it in fact corresponds to a masculine organization of power.[6]

As a result of assigning occupations based on gender, bureaucracies in the public and private sectors determine the distinct behaviors for men and women. Organizational life significantly contributes to the construct of what is "feminine" and what is "masculine," since the descriptions of job profiles for the different positions and ranks are based on presuppositions related to employees' general characteristics as determined by gender. These formal and informal practices are often not recognized but rather perceived as "natural" and consequently limit women's opportunities (Williams, 1995).

The absence of women in leading companies' most important directorship positions and their major presence in a limited number of areas can thus be explained by an organizational culture that exponentially reproduces the assignment of occupations in relation to social gender roles. This exclusion becomes more acute due to other features of corporate life, among which is the fact that the expected stance of unconditional loyalty to a company often means that officers cannot set a limit to working hours and that, on the contrary, they must be available and totally dedicated around the clock. These values can hardly be accommodated to women's social responsibilities. In practice, women face enormous obstacles to fulfilling their different roles and striving to carry out their family and professional duties (Serna Pérez, 2001; Zabludovsky, 2007).

In large corporations women's participation also varies in relation to the origin of the capital of the companies. Generally speaking, foreign companies operating in Mexico have a greater presence of women in executive positions than those of national capital. As shown in Figure 10.7, the percentage of women in middle management in Mexican companies is barely 18.1 percent, while in other corporations this rises to 29.2 percent. In the higher executive positions the percentage of women directors in Mexican companies is 10.4 percent as compared to 15.3 percent in the multinational companies in Mexico that have their main headquarters in another

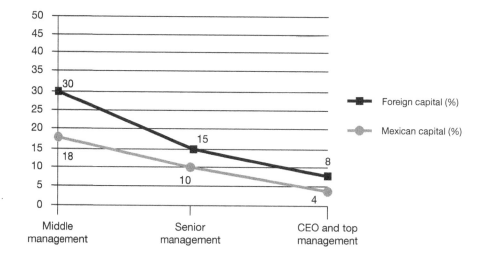

Figure 10.7 Women in management in Mexico's top 500 companies, 2012
Source: Developed by Gina Zabludovsky with information fromm 227 of 500 of the biggest companies in Mexico
    (based on Expansion and Conexión Ejecutive magazine)

country. In fact, among Mexican companies only 3.7 percent have a female president or CEO
(in contrast to 7.9 percent of foreign capital corporations in Mexico). This gap may be explained
by the policies introduced by foreign corporations in recent years. Many of them have launched
special programs to ensure the promotion and retention of female talent in Mexico and the
advancement of women through the hierarchy (Zabludovsky, 2015).

As far as women on "corporate boards" are concerned, a review of the boards of directors
of companies quoted at the Mexican Stock Exchange (Bolsa Mexicana de Valores, 2015) showed
that females have a significantly lower presence on boards than in other environments, with
women representing only 7 percent of the total positions on boards of directors. However, the
status of women on the boards varies greatly according to the business sector. In Mexico there
is not a single woman on the boards of the energy industries, while in the health industry the
participation of women reaches 20 percent (Bolsa Mexicana de Valores, 2015) (see Table 10.2).

Moreover, only one woman held the position of chairman of the board[7] and there are just
two women who are vice presidents. Both of them are part of a family firm and their brothers
are the chairmen of the board. In fact, several members of the board were found to have the
same surname. The companies with the largest percentage of women sitting on the board are
family-owned companies. In this regard, it is interesting to note that, as the author has indicated
in previous articles, the importance of women in family businesses in Mexico is not limited to
the companies quoted on the Stock Exchange but includes all sizes of women-owned businesses
(Grabinsky and Zabludovsky, 2001).

Women entrepreneurs

In addition to participating in the workforce as salaried employees, women in Mexico are also
entering the ranks of remunerated work as independent owners of small businesses. Women of
all ages and economic levels are running companies on their own, with their husbands or other
relatives (Grabinsky, 1996; Grabinsky and Zabludovsky, 2001).

Table 10.2 Men and women on boards of directors, 2015

	Men (%)	Women (%)
Health	80	20
Consumer products	92	8
Telecommunications	93	7
Manufactures	94	6
Raw materials	95	5
Energy	100	0

Source: Developed by Gina Zabludovsky based on Directorios de la Bolsa de Valores de Mexico, 2015

Concerning entrepreneurship, women represent 43 percent of the independent workers in the country (including self-employed workers and employers) (INEGI, 2015). The figure has increased in recent years, so that, while in 1991, the percentage of women was 25.3 percent, in 1995 it had reached 28.4 percent, and rose to 39 percent in 2015 (see Table 10.3).

Due to the major differences between employers and own-account workers, for purposes of the different surveys we have conducted in the country, we considered women entrepreneurs to be comprised solely of those women business owners who are employers, meaning that they hire at least one employee apart from themselves. This definition coincides with that adopted in Mexico's statistical instruments and allows us to make adequate comparisons. Under this classification women now comprise 23.5 percent of the total number of business owners, a percentage that has gradually increased in recent years, rising from 13.6 percent in 1991, to 15 percent in 1997, to 17 percent in 2000, to 19.7 percent in 2008, and to 23.5 percent in 2015.

Women entrepreneurs in Mexico are particularly important as the owners and directors of micro businesses with a small number of employees. In this respect, it is important to stress that this is not due to the fact that companies are highly sophisticated enterprises, where technology has replaced the number of employees. On the contrary, these establishments tend to be very simple. Usually, women owners get a very low income that they use for their subsistence and their family's daily needs.

Concerning the different sectors of activity, the percentage of women entrepreneurs shows sharp variations depending on the type of business. Generally speaking women do not participate at the construction industries and are highly involved in commerce and services, where their percentage rises to 31 percent. Currently, more women employers are occupied in a wide variety of sectors, including such industrial activities as durable manufacturing, a field where very few women were active up to just a few years ago. Table 10.4 shows how during the last decade, the percentages of women entrepreneurs has increased in commerce, services, and manufacturing.

Table 10.3 Self-employed men and women, 2015

	Men (%)	Women (%)
Self-employed (total) employers and self-employed workers	61	39
Employers	76	24
Self-employed workers	57	43

Source: Developed by Gina Zabludovky based on INEGI (2015), Encuesta Nacional de Empleo y Ocupación

Table 10.4 Employers by sector and gender, 2005–2015

		2015 (%)	2010 (%)	2005 (%)
Agriculture and ranching	Men	98	96	94
	Women	2	4	6
	Total	100	100	100
Construction	Men	99	99	99
	Women	1	1	1
	Total	100	100	100
Manufacturing	Men	79	84	83
	Women	21	16	17
	Total	100	100	100
Commerce	Men	69	68	71
	Women	31	32	29
	Total	100	100	100
Services	Men	69	72	77
	Women	31	28	23
	Total	100	100	100

Source: Developed by Gina Zabludovsky from INEGI (2015)

National legislation supporting women in the workforce

With respect to the actions taken by the legislative branch of government, the Chamber of Deputies and the Senate have had their own Equality and Gender Commission in place since 1997. They also organized the "Women's Parliament" to give impetus to a national legislative agenda intended to contribute to eliminating all forms of discrimination against the female sex, promoting government policies that fully ensure women's rights, and the implementation of programs to benefit them. Among the legislative results of these actions, various laws have been enacted and decrees implemented in line with the Beijing Action Plan and are centered especially on ways to prevent and prosecute acts of violence against women (PRONAM, 1999).

In relation to the Federal Labor Law, in matters of pregnancy, maternity, and breastfeeding, companies cannot oblige women to carry out activities that could endanger their health during pregnancy and companies are required to grant pregnant females a six-week leave prior to birth and another six-week leave after childbirth, as well as two extraordinary rest periods during the workday, while they are breastfeeding.

Some aspects of the Federal Labor Law were reformed in March 2014, and since then, women are allowed to ask for a maternity leave fourteen days before the child is born and seventy days after. Also, for the first time, men got five days of paid fathers' leave for the birth of their children.

Concerning women's presence in positions of authority and political power, in 2002 important changes were made to the Federal Electoral Code concerning gender, which required political parties to register a certain quota of women as candidates. This first decree forbade registering over 70 percent of candidates from the same gender, which in practice meant a 30 percent minimum of women candidates (Cámara de Diputados, 2009b). Later, this percentage was raised to 40 percent and in February 2014 it was elevated to a compulsory 50 percent of women candidates, which is now the rule. This decision had a direct impact on the number of women in the nation's legislative chambers. While women comprised 16 percent of the members of the Chambers of Deputies and the Senate in the 2000–2003 period, by the 2003–2006 period, they comprised 23 percent of legislators,[8] and by the 2012–2015, the percentage was 33.

The progress of women in the legislature contrasts with participation rates in other political positions. There have only been seven women governors in Mexican history. This situation is similar to that of municipal presidents, and since 2013 women have occupied only 8 percent of these positions. However, since 2014, new laws have been promoted in various states of the Mexican Republic to promote women candidates at the local level.

The presence of women has also been very low in presidential cabinets, since from 1981 until today their presence have never reached more than 15 percent. Their participation as secretaries of state has been concentrated in certain areas such as tourism (1994, 2000, 2006, 2012), social development (2000, 2006, 2012), comptroller general of the federation (1988, 1994), and foreign relations (1994, 2006, 2015).

Besides the important changes in the electoral regulations of the country, one of the most relevant recent laws is the General Law for the Equality of Men and Women (LGIMH) enacted in August 2006 and intended to ensure fairness and non-discrimination based on gender and to propose institutional guidelines and procedures that ensure equality and promote the "empowering" of women (Cámara de Diputados, 2009a). To achieve these objectives, the law proposes ensuring that budget planning should include a gender perspective, so as to encourage women's participation, achieve balanced political representation, promote equal access and women's full enjoyment of their social rights, and strive towards the elimination of gender stereotypes. The National Women's Institute is in charge of coordinating the program derived from this law, while the National Commission of Human Rights is responsible for evaluating and monitoring the results.

The law stresses the importance for federal budgets to allocate specific funding to achieve its objectives and also promote cooperative initiatives and policies in the economic sphere and in decision-making processes, including some compensation measures, such as affirmative action in social, cultural, and civic life. The law also prescribes that various authorities must take action to support parliamentary work from the gender viewpoint, create an awareness of the need to eliminate all forms of discrimination, and ensure that every level of education operates within a framework of equality for men and women (Cámara de Diputados, 2009b).

Initiatives supporting women in the workforce

Concerning work to strengthen equity in economic matters, the law calls for the inclusion of a gender perspective in public policies intended to reduce poverty. The author believes that funds should be allocated to raise awareness and promote equality at work and in production processes to avoid segregation, promote equality in leadership, and encourage access to work for people who are relegated to certain areas and levels based on their gender, especially with respect to directorship positions. To achieve these objectives, special programs should be implemented, such as incentives and certificates of equality to be granted yearly to those companies that have gender policies and practices in place (INMUJERES, 2010; INMUJERES and PNUD, 2007).

In 2001, state programs specifically addressed to women's issues achieved a new visibility in the government agenda, when the National Institute of Women (INMUJERES) was created as an autonomous, decentralized public sector agency, with its own legal status and funding (Diario Oficial de la Federación, 2001; INMUJERES, 2002; PRONAM, 1999). The

Institute has gained strength in recent years because of the important role it was assigned by the Law for the Equality of Men and Women to act as the coordinator of the actions and programs derived from that law.[9]

Concerning the pursuit of equal opportunities in the corporate world, in 2003, INMUJERES established a gender equity model (*modelo de equidad de género* – MEG), as a means of acknowledging the implementation of equity policies in public and private sector organizations and of enforcing top management's commitment to eliminating discrimination against women and their unequal treatment (INMUJERES and PNUD, 2007).

To promote these policies and attitudes, INMUJERES grants gender equity certification to those organizations that voluntarily elect to participate in and be evaluated on practices for promoting gender equity in the workplace. The award consists of a seal that may be affixed to the organization's products and used in its services and institutional image. By 2009, 132 organizations had been granted the gender equity seal, 93 of which were in the private sector and 39 in the public sector.[10] By 2015, there were 250 organizations granted the MEG seal.[11]

As to other public sector programs aimed at women business owners, during past governments some of them were specifically aimed at extremely small-sized businesses and were intended to reduce poverty levels. Within the Ministry of the Economy's sphere of influence, the two projects of this type are the Trust to Fund Micro-Financing to Rural Women (Fideicomiso del Fondo de Microfinanciamiento de Mujeres Rurales – FOMMUR) and the National Fund for Solidarity Enterprises (Fondo Nacional de Empresas de Solidaridad – FONAES).

FOMMUR supports impoverished women by providing micro-funding for their production projects. FONAES, in turn, spurs job creation by encouraging the generation, implementation, and consolidation of production projects related to commerce or services created by individuals, social organizations, or groups in rural areas, among the indigenous population, or low-income groups.

During recent years, the federal government has initiated several programs that go beyond support to women business owners at the microenterprise level and also target small and medium firms. These plans have been implemented through the National Institute of the Entrepreneur (Insituto Nacional del Emprendedor – INADEM), a centralized public body created in 2011 to support the creation and consolidation of companies of various levels.

Today INADEM has a joint program with INMUJERES that seeks to develop and consolidate companies of different levels led by women. Through this program, women entrepreneurs can have access to preferential financing and tools for enterprise development. INADEM also gives a national annual award to recognize a woman entrepreneur. Moreover, INADEM and the National Women's Institute, with the support of financial institutions and some local governments in Mexico, have launched a network of Small Business Development Centers providing access to resources, information, training, and other services to women entrepreneurs.[12]

Meanwhile, women involved in small, medium, and large enterprises have organized themselves on their own to create networks, form relationships, and fight for their rights. Some of the most important associations of this type are the Mexican Association of Executive Women (Asociación de Mujeres Ejecutivas – AMME) and the Association of Women Business Owners (Asociación de Mujeres Jefas de Empresa – AMMJE).

AMME groups women executives from all types of public or private companies, partnerships, institutions, or associations to create and project the image of women managers in the professional, intellectual, cultural, and social spheres. Its mission is to promote professional development and further the advancement of women executives to attain top management positions, while achieving a balance between their enjoying a high quality of life and fully achieving their professional objectives. AMME's objective is to bring women executives together and facilitate their access to directorship positions, create a fund for granting training scholarships, organize conferences and congresses, and convey its viewpoint on women-related matters to all public and private institutions (AMME, 2009).

Regarding AMMJE, the Mexican organization is part of a world association, Femmes Chefs D'Entreprises Mondiales, founded in France in 1946, which from the very beginning has encouraged and supported women's entrepreneurial activities in 42 countries. Some of the association's objectives are: to promote the exchange of information and the sharing of experience and knowledge; contribute to the development of professional skills through conferences, seminars, and workshops; expand communications and support networks; offer assessment on legal matters and promotional areas; create financial instruments and foster the development of its women business-owner members. AMMJE has grown significantly in recent years, increasing from eight city branches in 1998 to thirty-six at present, while the membership base of 400 in 1998 had risen to 4000 in 2009 (AMMJE, 2009). Today AMMJE has 54 branches that represent women entrepreneurs in 29 states of the Mexican Republic (AMMJE, 2015).

Also since 1997 women's associations have been founded within important business chambers, such as the women's business chamber in the Employers Federation of Chambers of the Mexican Republic (Confederación de Patronal de la República Mexicana – COPARMEX) and the Women Industrialists of the National Chamber of the Transformation Industry (Camara Nacional de la Industria de Transformación – CANACINTRA). These entrepreneurial women's associations have held several national conferences in different Mexican cities. Moreover, by making use of new technologies, some women business organizations, supported by INMUJERES, have created the National Network of Women Business Owners (Red de Mujeres Empresarias).

In recent years other women organizations have been created such as the European Association of Women Executives (CEDEA), founded by European and Mexican executives in February 2013 to promote women's networking, professional development, and leadership in organizations.

The future

During recent years there have been fundamental changes in Mexican laws to ensure gender parity in terms of political representation. Although in the corporate and entrepreneurial worlds, the changes have not been as drastic, women have also acquired an increasing visibility as corporate executives and business owners of their own firms.

The programs implemented by governmental offices and the organizations of women entrepreneurs and executives have helped create a greater awareness of the importance of providing equal opportunities for advancement to both men and women. In addition, women have achieved extraordinary advances in higher education and are entering a wide range of working environments, including business administration. However, the presence of women in areas of basic science and technology is still limited. Therefore, a serious attempt should be made from elementary school level onwards to avoid gender stereotypes to promote the presence of women in math and sciences.

In the business world, although we have observed important progress and major changes, women business owners have tended to be concentrated in micro-businesses, while in corporations, women directors solely hold positions linked to certain types of activities considered "feminine," which generally provide fewer opportunities for advancement.

To change the still prevalent stereotypes in the workplace, it is important to question the traditional separation of "feminine" and "masculine" positions, furthering the placement of men in positions in public relations and human resources and offering women more opportunities for entering the directorships of production and other strategic positions.

Moreover, the assumption still holds that the responsibility of running a home is considered to be primarily women's work, so that females must take on the burden of working the equivalent of double and triple shifts every day. Therefore, it is important to give impetus to revamping the assignment of responsibilities at home and in marriage. With the recent changes to the Federal Labor Law, for the first time men are allowed to take paid fathers' leave for a period of five days after their child is born. In the future this period should be extended and more efforts should be made to involve men in family and domestic responsibilities.

During recent years, many multinational companies that work in Mexico have implemented diversity policies, work–life balance initiatives, and other measures to promote the presence of women at every level of the companies. It would be desirable if in the coming years, we could also see more firms that are in Mexican ownership implementing these kinds of programs.

In relation to entrepreneurship, as we have seen in this chapter, during recent years new programs have been implemented to support women business owners. It will be important to follow up on their progress in the near future when there is information needed to evaluate their real impact on Mexican society.

Notes

1   The author appreciates the work of F. Daniel Mendoza Luna as a research assistant for this chapter.
2   Data estimated by the author based on data about officers and directors of public, private, and social sectors who earn more than five minimum wages (maximum level available through INEGI statistics) (INEGI, 2015).
3   Author's calculation based on business directories and indexes of 277 of the largest companies in Mexico (Expansion Magazine, Conexión Ejecutiva and others, 2012).
4   For Figure 10.6 I take into account the top executive positions as general directors of a certain area of the companies studied.
5   The presence of women executives is especially important as head of the newly created role of chief of public relations in many companies (Zabludovsky, 2008).
6   Because males are the sex that created art, industry, science, commerce, the state, and religion for centuries, women have been considered as "foreigners" or outsiders or intruders with no right to belong to the various environments of economic, scientific, political, and cultural leadership. Concerning the social construct of "foreigners" the following sources may be consulted: Elias and Scottson, 1965; Bauman, 1994; Kanter, 1993; Simmel, 1998; Zabludovsky, 2005.
7   The person in question is Cynthia Grossman of Grupo Continental, one of the largest Coca-Cola bottling companies in the world.
8   These percentages are similar to those in other Latin American countries and lower than those for Nordic countries, where women comprise up to 41 percent of the members of parliament. In contrast, the lowest percentages for women are in the Arab countries where women only comprise 9 percent of parliaments. See WLCA (2001) and UN (1999).
9   Since 2003, INMUJERES has become a major campaigner combating gender discrimination and promoting public policy with a gender perspective. In that year, the Mexican government and the World Bank signed the program on gender equality, Generosidad. This agreement may be considered the most important public policy to combat gender discrimination in the country's history.
10   In 2008, the MEG seal was awarded to various public and private sector organizations, including: Addition Human Resources; American Express; State of Guerrero General Auditing Department;

Best Day Travel; Chihuahua National Chamber of Commerce and Services; Campbell's de México; National Chamber of the Electronics, Telecommunications and Information Technology Industries; Casa Rufino; Chivagente; Chivas de Corazón; Combustibles de Oriente: Storage and Distribution Terminal, Corporate, Transportation; Federal Electricity Commission; Transmision Oriente Management; Puebla State Congress; and State of Jalisco Controllership.

11 Some of the companies that have MEG recognition are: Africam Safari, Comisión Federal de Electricidad (CFE), Grupo Gigante, Grupo Omnilife-Chivas, HP Hewlett-Packard de México, Instituto del Fondo Nacional de la Vivienda para los Trabajadores (Infonavit), Metlife, Pfizer, Volaris, Volkswagen de México, and Walmart de México y Centroamérica.

12 See www.org.mx/quienes-somos/

References

Albrow, M. (1997) *Do Organizations Have Feeling?* (London: Blackwell).

AMME (2009) www.amme.org.mx/tiendavirtual.cfm?ma68mtno=4012, accessed June 9, 2009.

AMMJE (2009) *Asociación Mexicana de Mujeres Empresarias, Asociación Civil*, www.ammjenacional.org/, accessed June 9, 2009.

AMMJE (2015) www.ammjenacional.org/, accessed December 10, 2015.

ANUIES (2011) *Anuario Estadístico de Educación Superior 2011*, www.anuies.mx/informacion-y-servicios/informacion-estadistica-de-educacion-superior/anuario-estadistico-de-educacion-superior, accessed August 1, 2013.

ANUIES (2015) Anuarios Estadísticos 2014–2015. In *Estadísticas de la Educación Superior*, www.anuies.mx/informacion-y-servicios/informacion-estadistica-de-educacion-superior/anuario-estadistico-de-educacion-superior, accessed November 30, 2015.

Ariza, M. and De Oliveira, O. (2006) Regímenes sociodemográficos y estructura familiar: los escenarios cambiantes de los hogares mexicanos, *Estudios Sociológicos*, Vol. xxiv, núm. 70, enero–abril (México: El Colegio de México).

Avelar, S. and Zabludovsky, G. (1996) Women's leadership and glass ceiling barriers in Brazil and Mexico. In Ana María (ed.), *Women's Leadership in a Changing World* (New York: UNIFEM).

Bamrud, J. and Calderon, G. (2012) Latin American: Few female CEOs, *Latin Business Chronicle*, March, http://latintrade.com/latin-america-few-female-ceos/ accessed November 1, 2015.

Bauman, Z. (1994) *Pensando Sociológicamente* (Argentina: Nueva Visión).

Bolsa Mexicana de Valores (2015) *Annual Financial Facts and Figures* (Mexico: BMV).

Burell, G.Y. and Hearn, J. (1989) The sexuality of organizations. In J. Hearn, D.L. Sheppard, P. Tancred and G. Burrell (eds) *The Sexuality of Organizations* (London: Sage Publications).

Cámara de Diputados (2009a) *Ley Federal del Trabajo* (2006), www.ordenjuridico.gob.mx/Federal/Combo/L-130.pdf, accessed November 30, 2015.

Cámara de Diputados (2009b) *Ley General para la Igualdad entre Mujeres y Hombres* (2006), www.cddhcu.gob.mx/LeyesBiblio/pdf/LGIMH.pdf, accessed November 30, 2015.

Catalyst (2012). *Catalyst Quick Take: Women in the Labor Force in Latin America.* (New York: Catalyst).

Conexión Ejecutiva (2012) *Directorio empresarial de los ejecutivos líderes de México*, www.conexionejecutiva.com/Default.aspx, accessed September 3, 2013.

Diario Oficial de la Federación (2001) *Ley del Instituto Nacional de las Mujeres*, http://cedoc.inmujeres.gob.mx/documentos_download/100199.pdf, accessed November 4, 2015.

Elias, N. and Scottson, J. (1965) *The Established and the Outsiders.* (London, Frank Cass).

Expansión (2012) *Las 500 compañías más importantes de México*, http://expansion.mx/rankings/2012/las-500-empresas-mas-importantes-de-mexico-2012, accessed September 3, 2013.

Grabinsky, S. (1996) Crisis in Mexico: Its Effects on the family-owned business, *Journal of Entrepreneurship Culture*, vol. 4, September, www.worldscinet.com/jec/jec.shtml, accessed November 30, 2015.

Grabinsky, S. and Zabludovsky G. (2001) *Mujeres, empresas y familias* (México: Del Verbo Emprender).

Gunderson E., Ramírez G., Levine S. and Beilock, S. (2011) *The Role of Parents and Teachers in the Development of Gender-Related Math Attitudes*, Department of Psychology, University of Chicago.

Hola, E. and Todaro R. (1992) *Los mecanismos de poder: hombres y mujeres en la empresa moderna* (Santiago de Chile: Grupo Editor Latinoamericano).

INEGI (2000) *Encuesta Nacional de Empleo* (México: Instituto Nacional de Estadística e Informática).

INEGI (2003) *Encuesta Nacional de Empleo 2002* (México: Instituto Nacional de Estadística e Informática).

INEGI (2005) *Encuesta Nacional de Empleo 2004* (México: Instituto Nacional de Estadística e Informática). www.inegi.org.mx/prod_serv/contenidos/espanol/bvinegi/productos/encuestas/hogares/ene/2004/ENE_2004.pdf, accessed November 30, 2015.

INEGI (2009a) *Consulta de Microdatos de la ENOE 2005–2008* 02/03/2009 www.inegi.org.mx/est/contenidos/espanol/soc/sis/microdatos/enoe/default.aspx?s=est&c=14439

INEGI (2009b) *Encuesta Nacional de Ocupación y Empleo 2008* (México: Instituto Nacional de Estadística e Informática).

INEGI (2009c) *Encuesta Nacional Sobre Uso del Tiempo, 2009* (México: Instituto Nacional de Estadística y Geografía e Informática).

INEGI (2013) *Encuesta Nacional de Ocupación y Empleo, 2013* (México: Instituto Nacional de Estadística y Geografía).

INEGI (2015) *Encuesta Nacional de Empleo y Ocupación 2015* (México: Instituto Nacional de Estadística e Informática).

INMUJERES (2002) *Propuesta del Instituto Nacional de las Mujeres para incorporar la perspectiva de género en la modernización de la ley laboral* (México: DF, INMUJERES).

INMUJERES (2010) *Compartiendo las mejores prácticas del Modelo de Equidad de Género*, http://cedoc.inmujeres.gob.mx/documentos_download/101189.PDF, accessed 9 November 2015.

INMUJERES and PNUD (2007) *ABC de Género en la Administración Pública*, http://cedoc.inmujeres.gob.mx/documentos_download/100903.pdf, accessed November 5, 2015.

Kanter, R. M. (1993) *Men and Women of the Corporations* (New York: Basic Books).

Maxfield, S., Cárdenas, M. and Heller, L. (eds) (2008) *Mujeres y vida corporativa en Latinoamérica, retos y dilemas.* (Colombia: Universidad de los Andes–Facultad de Administración).

Mendoza, V. (2012) *Falta de igualdad frena el desarrollo en cnn expansión*, www.cnnexpansion.com/economia/2012/01/12/falta-de-igualdad-merma-al-desarrollo, accessed January 20, 2013.

Mills, A. (1990) Gender, sexuality and organizations theory. In J. Hearn, D. L. Sheppard, P. Tancred and G. Burrell (eds) *The Sexuality of Organizations* (London: Sage Publications).

Nielsen (2011) "Women of tomorrow. a study of women around the world, www.nielsen.com/content/dam/corporate/us/en/reports-downloads/2011-Reports/Women-of-Tomorrow.pdf, accessed August 20, 2013.

PRONAM (1999) *Alianza para la igualdad, Informe de Avances de Ejecución* (Mexico: DF, PRONAM).

Serna Pérez, M. (2001) Empresarias y relaciones de género en dos ciudades de provincial, *Empresarias y ejecutivas, mujeres con poder* (Mexico: Colegio de Mexico).

Sheppard, D. (1990) Organizations, power and sexuality: the image and self-image of Women Managers. In J. Hearn, D. L. Sheppard, P. Tancred and G. Burrell (eds) *The Sexuality of Organizations* (London: Sage Publications).

Simmel, G. (1998) *Sobre la Aventura, Ensayos filosóficos* (Barcelona: Península).

UN (1999) *Inter-Parliamentary Union of Women in Public Life* (Geneva: UN).

Vargas, I. (2011) Los secretos de la mujer que triunfa, *CNN Expansión*, http://expansion.mx/mi-carrera/2011/08/23/los-secretos-de-la-mujer-que-triunfa, accessed June 20, 2013.

Williams, C. (1995) *Still a Man's World* (Berkeley and Los Angeles: University of California).

WLCA (2001) *Women and Power in the Americas, A Report Card, Inter-American Dialogue* (Washington: WLCA).

Zabludovsky, G. (2003) Burocracia y comportamiento organizacional, de la jerarquía moderna a la sociedad-red. In M. Guitián and G. Zabludovsky (eds) *Sociología y modernidad tardía: Entre la tradición y los nuevos retos /Sociology and Late modernity: Between tradition and the new challenges)* (México: Juan Pablos/UNAM).

Zabludovsky, G. (2004) Women in management in Mexico. In Davidson, M. J. and Burke, R. J. (eds) *Women in Management Worldwide* (Canada: York University).

Zabludovsky, G. (2005) Zigmunt Bauman and Norbert Elias, *Revista Anthropos*, Vol. 206, pp. 196–209.

Zabludovsky, G. (2007) México: mujeres en cargos de dirección del sector privado, *Revista Latinoamericana de Administración*, No. 38, Primer Semestre, pp. 9–26.

Zabludovsky, G. (2008) "Las mujeres en cargos de dirección en México" in Maxfield, S., Cárdenas, M. and Heller, L. (eds.) *Mujeres y vida corporativa en Latinoamérica, retos y dilemas*. (Colombia: Universidad de los Andes-Facultad de Administración).

Zabludovsky, G. (2015) Las mujeres en los ámbitos de poder económico y político de México, *Revista Mexicana de Ciencias Políticas y Sociales*, No. 223, enero–abril, pp. 61–94.

Zabludovsky, G. (2016) Mujeres, trabajo y educación en México. In K. Caplan (ed.) *Género es más que una palabra. Educar sin etiquetas* (Bueno Aires: Miño y Dávila).

11 Women in management in the United States

Jeanine Prime, Jan Combopiano, Cynthia Emrich and Julie Nugent

The outlook for women in US leadership is mixed, despite claims about the "end of men"

In her highly-acclaimed book, *The End of Men: And the Rise of Women*, author Hanna Rosin (2012) declared that the struggle for gender equality had been won. According to Rosin, Americans ha entered a new era, where women would routinely claim the advantages that once belonged to men. But as this chapter will show, the outlook is not quite as rosy as Rosin has described. There have been important gains but significant barriers still dampen US prospects for closing leadership gender gaps.

First, the good news: Americans have already made significant strides towards gender equality. This progress is marked by dramatic attitudinal shifts. For example, in 1977, a majority of Americans favored traditional, gender-based divisions of labor. Back then, the prevailing view was that women should focus on caregiving, leaving men to focus on breadwinning (Cotter *et al.*, 2014). Yet by 2012, this trend had completely reversed, with a significant majority of Americans supporting more fluid, and *progressive*, gender roles. In 2012, most Americans roundly rejected the notion that a woman's place was in the home (Cotter *et al.*, 2014). And by some accounts (Pew Research Center, 2010), Americans have now become almost unequivocal in their support of gender equality. In fact, as much as 97 percent of Americans agree that men and women *should* be treated equally under the law (Pew Research Center, 2010).

Just as attitudes have changed, so have behaviors and gender roles. Women's workforce participation rates are far greater than they were in the 1960s (Mosisa and Hipple, 2006). A majority of mothers—from all racial and ethnic backgrounds—are now combining caregiving with breadwinning (Mosisa and Hipple, 2006). There are more women in positions of power too—both in the public and private sectors. From 1995 to 2013, we saw the percentage of women on Fortune 500 corporate boards increase by 76 percent (Catalyst, 2014a). And for two recent presidential races (2008 and 2016), women have been among the top contenders.

Yet despite these gains, troubling gender gaps still persist in the US—casting doubt on Rosin's "end-of-men" thesis. Even when controlling for human capital differences and industry, women continue to lag men in compensation and promotion rates (Carter and Silva, 2010). Given their often-superior levels of education and preparation (National Center for Education Statistics *et al.*, 2014), women also remain grossly under-represented in business and political leadership (Catalyst, 2015a; CAWP, 2015a, 2015b). Even as women enter business and politics in larger and larger numbers (BLS, 1995, 2015; CAWP, 2015a, 2015b), they access positions of power and leadership in far lower numbers than men—not at all proportionate with their representation in feeder talent pools.

And what's more, there are signs that the rate of change has slowed (World Economic Forum, 2015). While many countries are making progress towards equality, there are indications that the US may in fact be regressing. According to the World Economic Forum's 2015 report, the US ranked 28th in the world on measures of gender equality, down 8 points from the previous year. The same report showed US rankings falling even more dramatically to 72nd, a loss of 18 points relative to the previous year, when measures of political equality were considered (World Economic Forum, 2015). And while the US had steadily made progress in closing the gender wage gap between the 1960s and 1990s, progress on this front has also slowed to a snail's pace in recent years (Hegewisch *et al.*, 2014).

Arguably, as women's visibility and prominence in public life has become more normative, Americans are less concerned about achieving equality than they once were. A significant proportion of Americans now believe that most of the changes needed to achieve equality have already been made (Pew Research Center, 2010). This growing complacency and lost momentum threatens to erode the hard-fought gains of previous decades.

As we'll show in the chapter, Rosin's claims about the end of men are premature. Taking stock of the relative status of women and men in the US, we take a realistic look at both the opportunities for catalyzing change and the hurdles that are impeding further progress in closing leadership gender gaps. Without intentional action on the part of American policy makers, employers, and the individuals throughout society, we contend that the gains of previous decades will likely be lost. We argue that engaging men in advocacy for gender equality and a focus on building more inclusive institutions are critical to turning the tide.

Trends that have fueled progress in closing US leadership gender gaps

The federal government led early efforts paving the path to parity

In the US, the path towards equality has been shaped to a large extent through legislation, regulation, and the courts. During the 1960s and 1970s, the US federal government helped dismantle significant barriers that kept women from accessing education and opportunities for paid work. For example, the first major piece of US legislation addressing gender inequity in employment was the Equal Pay Act of 1963, which made it illegal to pay women and men differently for doing the same work. It was a huge step forward, building upon the 1948 UN Declaration of Human Rights, which advocated equal pay for equal work (United Nations, 1948). The next year, the centerpiece legislation of President Johnson's Great Society, the Civil Rights Act of 1964, was signed into law:

> The 1964 Civil Rights Act, perhaps the most sweeping piece of social legislation ever enacted by any Congress … Title VII of the act carried a clear interpretation of affirmative action, and became the cornerstone of employment discrimination law prohibiting employment discrimination in areas such as selection, promotion, and training based on race, color, religion, gender, or national origin.
>
> (Elliott and Ewoh, 2000, pp. 212–213)

Indeed, this legal code became the foundation of most government efforts to end gender and racial discrimination in the US and create a more inclusive national culture.

Legislation was not the only approach the federal government took, however. Regulations operationalized the laws that Congress passed and the Supreme Court clarified what was acceptable practice and what was illegal under these new rules. In 1965, one of the most important bulwarks against discrimination, the Equal Employment Opportunity Commission, was "created … to give life to Title VII of the Civil Rights Act of 1964" (United States Equal Employment Opportunity Commission, 2015). It was this agency that would create the guidelines for companies to follow and which had the authority to sue employers to provide accountability for fair and equitable employment practices. President Johnson did not merely want to end discrimination, he wanted to address past injustice and ensure equal opportunities (Kovach *et al.*, 2004). This approach was manifested in 1965 with Executive Order 11246, which prohibited employment discrimination among federal contractors on the basis of race, religion, color, and national origin; and ultimately sex, which was added in 1968 in Executive Order 11375 (Kovach *et al.*, 2004). The Supreme Court also codified equal opportunities with landmark decisions ending sex-segregated job advertisements, discrimination against mothers and pregnant women (Brown, 2008).

As gender discrimination continued to be assailed through deliberate action by the executive branch and the courts, Congress did not remain idle. It continued to pass consequential legislation, including Title IX of the Educational Amendments of 1972, which forced colleges and universities that received federal funding to provide women and men with equal access to education and sports programs (Valentin, 1997). The last major piece of legislation during this period was the Pregnancy Discrimination Act of 1978, which made it illegal for employers to discriminate on the basis of pregnancy or the potential of pregnancy by treating pregnancy as a temporary disability (Mukhopadhyay, 2012). It was a government-sanctioned signal that women, regardless of parental status, belonged in the workplace.

In these ways, the federal government intentionally set key changes in motion that would propel the US on a path to equality. By making discrimination illegal and implementing affirmation action policies, the government enabled women to gain greater access to education and job opportunities. Further, by prohibiting discriminatory behavior, the government also played a role in shifting mindsets and attitudes about gender equality. Below we describe how women's enhanced access to education, high labor force participation, and progressive attitudes towards gender roles, continue to create the right conditions for closing leadership gender gaps.

Increasingly gender egalitarian norms and roles

Perhaps driven in part by the actions of the federal government, women's participation in the labor force has gained increasing acceptance among Americans since the 1960s (Bolzendahl and Myers, 2004; Cotter *et al.*, 2014). A recent study conducted by the Council on Contemporary Families reported that less than one-third of respondents felt that men should be breadwinners, leaving women to be homemakers and caregivers. In stark contrast, as much as 66 percent of respondents held that view in 1977 (Cotter *et al.*, 2014).

Further, in a recent survey of working fathers conducted by Boston College's Center for Work and Family, the majority (86 percent) reported that their children were their number one priority. Moreover, for these men, what it meant to be a good father went beyond providing financial support to their families (Harrington *et al.*, 2011). These men placed providing "love and emotional support" and being "involved and present" in their children's lives as top priorities—above providing financial security (Harrington *et al.*, 2011). Additionally, over one-half of the sample (53 percent) agreed that if money was a non-issue, they would "feel okay if I didn't work outside of the home" (Harrington *et al.*, 2011).

These dramatic attitudinal shifts have been mirrored by behavioral ones too. As Americans' attitudes have become increasingly gender egalitarian, so has the division of labor in American households. One of the most marked changes has been in the roles prescribed for husbands and wives. In 1972, as many as 41 percent of married couples with children under 18 were being supported solely by a male breadwinner. By 2012, that percentage had dropped significantly, with male breadwinners being the sole source of support for only 28.3 percent of households (Glynn, 2014). Today, an increasingly large majority of married couples with children under 18 are supported by *both* spouses (BLS, 2015; Glynn, 2014). And not surprisingly, unmarried mothers are even more likely than married mothers to be employed (BLS, 2014b). But just as women have added breadwinning to the roles they've traditionally played as primary caregivers and homemakers, the roles of men have changed significantly too, albeit at a slower pace. For example, although the number of stay-at-home dads is still relatively small, it has nearly doubled in recent decades. According to the Pew Research Center, there were 1.1 million stay-at-home dads in 1989—and that number rose to 2 million in 2012 (Livingston, 2014). This trend is encouraging as greater parental involvement among fathers predicts women's status in public life and their access to elite positions of authority (Coltrane, 1988, 2004).

Women are surpassing men in educational attainment

To close gender gaps in leadership, gender differences in human capital must also be attenuated. Fortunately, this is already happening. Particularly when it comes to educational attainment, American women have made tremendous strides within recent decades: "Improvements in women's education have been phenomenal. Also the same for women's work continuity, which has really improved for highly-educated women. But this means all the low-hanging fruit has been handled; we've now exhausted the things under women's control" (Jennifer Glass, Professor of Sociology, Barbara Pierce Bush Regents Professor of Liberal Arts, The University of Texas at Austin, personal communication).

In 1980, the National Center for Education Statistics of the US government began tracking who has earned, or as the government puts it, attained college degrees—both four-year undergraduate degrees (what are called "bachelor's" degrees in the US and "tertiary" degrees in many other parts of the world) and also master's degrees. At that time, a greater percentage of males (24.0 percent) than females (21.0 percent) earned bachelor's degrees (National Center for Education Statistics *et al.*, 2014). Since that starting point, however, females approached and, by 2000, eclipsed males' educational attainment. For example, in 2014, 37.2 percent of females but just 30.9 percent of males earned bachelor's degrees. The same trend holds true for master's degrees: females (6.2 percent) outstripped males (4.7 percent) beginning in 2000 and have continued to earn master's degrees in greater numbers than males, with 9.3 percent of US females and just 5.9 percent of males earning these degrees in 2014. Table 11.1 provides data for selected years of females' and males' educational attainment.

Table 11.1 represents good news with respect to gender equality in higher education—an important means through which individuals develop the human capital necessary to assume leadership roles in organizations.

Further, it is important to note that the rise in women's educational attainment rates has occurred across racial and ethnic lines. For example, even though a higher percentage of White females earn bachelor's degrees than Black and Hispanic females, the *rate* at which minority women have been gaining ground is comparable, if not more aggressive relative to White women. As shown in Table 11.2, the percentage of Black and White women earning bachelor's degrees from 1980 to 2014 increased 92 percent and 89 percent respectively. And during this same period, the percentage of Hispanic females earning bachelor's degrees grew most compared to all other groups—increasing by as much as 165 percent.

Table 11.1 Percentage of females and males earning bachelor's and master's degrees in the United States, 1980–2014

	Females earning bachelor's (%)	Males earning bachelor's (%)	Females earning master's (%)	Males earning master's (%)
1980	21.0	24.0	NA	NA
1990	22.8	23.7	NA	NA
1995	24.9	24.5	4.1	4.9
2000	30.1	27.9	6.2	4.7
2005	32.2	25.5	7.3	5.2
2010	35.7	27.8	8.5	5.2
2014	37.2	30.9	9.3	5.9

Source: National Center for Education Statistics *et al.*, 2014

Table 11.2 Percentage of females of different race/ethnicities earning bachelor's degrees in the United States, 1980–2014

	Black (%)	Hispanic (%)	American Indian/ Alaska Native (%)	White (%)
1980	12.4	6.9	NA	23.2
1990	11.9	9.1	NA	26.2
1995	13.7	10.1	NA	29.2
2000	17.4	11.0	NA	35.8
2005	20.5	12.4	NA	38.2
2010	23.3	16.8	18.4	42.4
2014	23.8	18.3	NA	43.9

Source: National Center for Education Statistics *et al.*, 2014

Women continue to enter the pipeline in large numbers

To close gender gaps in leadership, women and men must also gain comparable work experience and on-the-job training. One measure of this aspect of human capital is the workforce participation rate. The US has fallen in the rankings among countries of the Organization for Economic Co-operation and Development (OECD) with respect to women's labor force participation (LFP) over the past few decades (OECD, 2015). However, this overarching trend masks two important points regarding the current reality of LFP in the US. First, the realities of LFP are strikingly different for women and men. Men's LFP has been decreasing for 60 years, peaking at 86.4 percent in 1950 (Fullerton, 1999) and reaching an historic low of 69.7 percent in 2013 (United States Department of Labor, 2013). In contrast, women's LFP peaked much later, at 60 percent in 1999 and, since then, has declined more modestly to 57.2 percent in 2013 (BLS, 2014b). That brings us to the second important point regarding women's LFP: by historic standards, it remains high, despite the US's falling rank among OECD countries.

Given the very different trends or trajectories for women's versus men's LFP in the US, it is perhaps not surprising that very different factors are at work. Men's falling LFP has been attributed to two longer-term trends: greater access to social security benefits over the second half of the twentieth century and the shrinking (real) wages for lower-skilled workers. In contrast, a single, shorter-term factor wholly explains the more recent, modest decline in LFP among women: recent recessions, including the "Great Recession" (Van Zandweghe, 2012). This set of explanations—especially the differences among women and men—suggests that women's LFP will rise to and possibly even surpass its peak as the US economy expands. The fact that women's labor force attachment has risen dramatically over the past several decades provides further support for this assumption. Clearly parity with respect to the sheer representation of women in the US labor force is a necessary condition for women to achieve parity in leadership roles. Indeed as women's LFP has increased over the past several decades, there's been a concomitant increase in their representation in the managerial and professional ranks from which leaders emerge: women were in the clear minority in managerial and professional ranks in 1975 (34.8 percent) but had achieved near parity with men by 1995 (48.0 percent)— around the time their LFP peaked in the US (Wootton, 1997).

Trends that stymie progress in closing US leadership gender gaps

Although the above trends bode well for closing US leadership gender gaps, there are also some troubling ones which threaten progress. These include the government's increasingly anti-regulatory stance to closing gender gaps, modern sexism, and persistent institutional discrimination.

Gradual dialing back of federal action to close gender gaps

As noted earlier, the federal government played an instrumental role, starting in the 1960s, that helped put the US on a path towards gender equality. Unfortunately, this trend did not continue and support for taking federal action to promote equality waned increasingly over time (Leonard, 1989). This anti-regulatory stance flourished under the Reagan Revolution of the 1980s, but continues to this day with currently Republican-led Congresses. A core tenet of US political conservatism is limited governmental intrusion into the free market (Farmer, 2005), even if doing more would lead to ending institutional sexism. According to Cohen (2013, p. 1):

> That we lack anything resembling a twenty-first-century family policy is not an oversight. It is not because American society refuses to come to grips with the reality of working mothers. Rather, it is the result of a political hijacking so fabulously successful it wiped away virtually any trace of its own handiwork.

What had seemed like an orderly march toward progress in the 1960s—the Equal Pay Act, the Civil Rights Act, and the establishment of a government watchdog in the Equal Employment Opportunity Commission—started to encounter glitches under President Nixon. In 1971, the country was a presidential signature away from establishing a national childcare system. Republicans and Democrats in Congress had passed the Comprehensive Child Development Act, which would create a national network of local, comprehensive childcare centers, to provide quality education, nutrition, and medical services, but President Nixon vetoed it (Cohen, 2013). This lack of available childcare has had lasting effects for working women, as many continue to struggle with work–life issues to the current day (Cohen, 2013). The backlash to this defeat prompted a bipartisan majority in Congress to pass the Equal Rights Amendment (ERA) in 1972, sending it to the states, with the hopes that three-fourths (38 states) would ratify it (Blackerby, 2013; Cohen, 2013). This effort would take a decade and ultimately be defeated in 1982 (Blackerby, 2013), but the ERA would have enshrined gender equality in the Constitution and provided one of the strongest, if not the strongest ever, structural support for dismantling barriers. As Ruth Bader Ginsberg said during her testimony to Congress in 1978:

> Arbitrary gender lines still clutter the law books and regulations of the nation and states, the Supreme Court vacillates insecurely from one decision to the next, and is sometimes disarmed from reaching any decision, as it holds back doctrinal development and awaits the signal the Equal Rights Amendment would supply.
>
> (Quoted in Kay, 2004, p. 18)

The ERA has been re-introduced in every Congressional session since, but to no avail (Blackerby, 2013). It was also during this period that the Supreme Court became more conservative and shifted away from supporting efforts to end gender and racial discrimination (Elliott and Ewoh, 2000).

During the 1970s and 1980s, perhaps as a result of significant changes during the previous decade, a wave of conservatism swept the country. This did not bode well for continuing the significant dismantling of structural barriers by the federal government, as:

> the policies of the Reagan years had enormous but not always happy consequences for women. The gendered assumptions embedded in Reaganomics were part of an attempt to increase women's dependence on the patriarchal family, and the policies often worked to increase women's dependence on the state.
>
> (May and Stephenson, 1994, p. 535)

This turning away from government action has resulted in the US not keeping pace with the rest of the world. In 1993, Congress passed the Family and Medical Leave Act (FMLA), allowing employees to take unpaid leave for pre-determined family and medical reasons without fear of losing their jobs (United States Department of Labor, n.d.). This was the first national standard, but it remains an unpaid benefit more than 20 years later. Other countries have not stood still and are picking up the legislative/regulatory banner. As of 2015, the US is the only developed country that does not have mandatory paid medical leave (Frothingham, 2015).

It is not just ensuring mothers stay in (or return to) the workplace that is the focus of other countries' efforts. Some are trying to overcome stalled progress for women in business leadership by mandating women's representation on boards. According to the World Bank (2015, p. 10), "The principle of equity is at the core of arguments in favor of gender quotas. Quotas can enable a more equitable representation of women in leadership positions ... which may translate into more equitable representation of women's interests in decision making." In spite of many studies showing the correlation between companies with women on their boards and improved financial performance (Catalyst, 2004, 2011; Credit Suisse, 2012; Desvaux *et al.*, 2007), the average of women on S&P500 boards has yet to crack 20 percent (Catalyst, 2015b). While many advocate more progress in the US, there has been little beyond voluntary efforts, as "companies here tend to bristle at the idea that the government could tell them whom to hire" (Miller, 2014, p. B4). Because of that attitude, there are no legislative requirements for board diversity and the strongest regulation is the Securities and Exchange Commission (SEC) requirement that companies disclose information about whether they take diversity into account when nominating members of their boards (United States Government, 2009).

Over the past decade, countries in Europe, Asia, and Africa have taken a more proactive approach to increasing gender diversity on boards. The earliest legislated quota for a specific percentage of women on boards went into effect in Norway in 2006 and now there are at least 14 countries and provinces that have legislated or regulated quotas or targets for public companies and/or state-owned enterprises (Catalyst, 2014b; World Bank, 2015). In less than 10 years, three countries have outpaced the US—by 2013, Norway had more than double the percentage of women on boards than in the US (40.5 percent) (Statistics Norway, 2013); while Finland, France, and Sweden are close to 30 percent, though Sweden does not yet have a quota but might have one soon (Catalyst, 2015b; Local, 2015). And with legislated quotas in so many other countries, it would not be surprising to see many more countries make more progress than the US in having higher percentages of women on boards.

Institutional discrimination: men's career outcomes continue to exceed women's—even after controlling for human capital differences

Changing norms around gender and work—no doubt fueled, in large part, by females' educational attainment and increased LFP—indeed provide reason to be hopeful about the prospects for gender equality in the US workplace. Yet these factors combined likely will not be sufficient to close the gender gaps that persist in position and pay. Consider, for example, the fact that around the time women's educational attainment clearly eclipsed men's in 2005, Catalyst statistics began to flat-line with respect to women in senior leadership and boardrooms (Catalyst, 2014a). In addition to persistent gaps in leadership positions, we continue to see sizable gaps in pay: for example, in the *overall* working population in the US, women still today earn only 79 cents to a man's dollar. Among the most recent graduates— who presumably would benefit from women's advances in educational attainment and LFP over the past several decades—the situation isn't much rosier: these young women earn just 82 cents to their male peers' dollar one year after college graduation (Corbett and Hill, 2012). And it's important to remember that this gap may be as narrow as it gets for these (now) young women, because research from both Catalyst (Carter and Silva, 2010, 2011) and the American Association of University Women (Dey and Hill, 2007) demonstrates that the pay gap widens significantly over the course of women's and men's careers. In short, educational attainment doesn't appear to be the silver bullet to closing the gender gap in pay.

To better understand the root causes of these persistent gender gaps in the workplace, in 2008 Catalyst launched a longitudinal study of the careers of women and men who earned MBAs from leading schools around the globe. This project, which is still ongoing, has tracked the career experiences and outcomes of this group of so-called high-potential women and men and yielded a series of annual reports. Each one has discredited myths that attribute gender gaps in position and pay to women's qualifications or choices. The overarching story this research series tells is relatively straightforward, if discouraging: despite equivalent qualifications, experience *and* aspirations, highly-talented women trailed men in both position and pay from "Day 1" (Carter and Silva, 2010). And despite working as proactively as men to advance their careers, they have been unable to catch up (Carter and Silva, 2011). These women have as many mentors as do men, but they aren't as senior (Carter and Silva, 2010). Perhaps for this very reason, these women do not have the same access to the development opportunities so critical to advancement in the workplace—opportunities such as large and highly-visible projects, mission-critical roles, and international assignments (Silva *et al.*, 2012). We refer to these opportunities as "hot jobs" because of the critical role they play in helping high potentials to advance. Table 11.3 summarizes these findings from this research series,

Table 11.3 Myths and facts when it comes to obstacles to women's advancement in the workplace

Myth	Fact
"The pipeline of women eligible for leadership positions is robust"	Equally-qualified women lagged men in position and pay from their very first post-MBA jobs (Carter and Silva, 2010)
"Women don't aspire to the top the way men do"	Women were as likely as men to aspire to the top in their organizations (Carter and Silva, 2010)
"Women aren't as proactive in advancing their careers"	Women were as likely as men to be doing "all the right things" experts recommend to advance one's career, however, women's efforts did not pay off to the same extent as men's (Carter and Silva, 2011)
"Women lag men because they have too few mentors"	Women had as many mentors as men, however, their mentors were not as senior (Carter and Silva, 2010)
"Men and women receive the same development opportunities"	Women get fewer of the development opportunities that are critical to advancement – what Catalyst refers to as "hot jobs" (Silva *et al.*, 2012)

juxtaposing key myths versus facts with respect to gender gaps in the career experiences and outcomes of this group of highly-talented individuals.

These facts represent the global landscape of gender equality in the workplace for a unique sample of highly-educated and motivated women and men—the majority of whom work for large, global firms. One could argue that this landscape presents a best-case scenario, because these women (and men) already cleared substantial hurdles to gain entry to, and graduate from, premier graduate business schools in the US, Canada, Europe, and Asia. Yet gender gaps persist even among this group of women and men—gaps that could not be explained by women's qualifications or choices.

One study in this series focused exclusively on a subset of high-potential women and men working in the US (Thorpe-Moscon and Pollack, 2014). It confirmed that these women, like their counterparts around the globe, also faced a gender gap in position from "Day 1"—despite commensurate qualifications and experience. Like high-potential women in other parts of the world, they did not have the same access as their male peers to the senior mentors or hot jobs so critical to their advancement. And the picture for women who felt different from their peers based on their race and/or ethnicity was even more discouraging. For these women, the opportunity gaps were even wider than for women who did *not* report feeling different. It's important to note that these women who felt different based on race and/or ethnicity were no less qualified to lead. They received fewer opportunities and less support to do so, leaving them to feel less included in their workgroups and more discouraged about their career prospects. Specifically for racially/ethnically diverse women, progress in the workplace has been even slower. Racially/ethnically diverse women face more barriers in the workplace than men of color or white women. They are significantly more likely to report: dissatisfaction with supervisory support and comfort of manager interaction; dissatisfaction with distribution of major assignments and training opportunities; and a perceived lack of commitment from senior leadership towards bringing in a diverse workforce (Bagati, 2009; Giscombe, 2007). Overall, the pattern of findings from this research series suggests a vicious cycle in which gender gaps in access to career-making opportunities make it very difficult for even highly-educated, high-aspiring women to level the playing field with men. And for women who feel different from their peers due to their race and/or ethnicity, this cycle is an even more vicious one.

These findings point to institutional discrimination as a key barrier to women's career advancements. Even when we compare men and women with similar qualifications, ambitions, career advancement strategies, and parental responsibilities—men enjoy far better outcomes than women do. With similar inputs to "the system" men and women get very different outputs. Sociologists, such as Joan Acker (2006), attribute this fact to the highly gendered nature of US workplaces. Although apparently gender-neutral, work practices and structures systematically privilege men and disadvantage women—even though they were not designed with that outcome in mind (Acker, 2006; Martell *et al.*, 2012). We will return to this issue and ways to dismantle institutional biases in American workplaces later in this chapter.

The subversive impact of modern sexism

In addition to institutional bias, evidence also points to persistent bias at a micro-level too. Experts agree that old-fashioned sexism, marked by explicit beliefs in the superiority of men over women, is far less prevalent in the US than it was in the 1960s and 1970s (Glick and Fiske, 2011; Twenge, 2011). And while this is certainly a positive development, modern sexism is not to be taken lightly either.

In contrast to old-fashioned sexism, modern expressions of sexism are far more ambiguous and difficult to pin down (Glick and Fiske, 2011; Swim *et al.*, 1995). Likely due to strong social and legal sanction in the US for failing to uphold egalitarian ideals, modern sexists endorse gender equality and vehemently decry sexism. Yet they simultaneously deny that sex discrimination still persists and reject policies that would help close gender gaps. Indeed, core to modern sexism is the notion that discrimination is a thing of the past, rendering further policy reform to promote equality unnecessary (Becker and Swim, 2012).

It is easy to see how modern sexism would stymie further progress towards gender equality. Modern sexism justifies the well-documented inequalities that still persist in the US, casting women's behaviors and/or characteristics as the "problem"—instead of sexism (Swim *et al.*, 1995). In other words, modern sexism gives its subscribers permission to turn a blind eye to gender gaps. Consistent with this view, Swim *et al.* (2004) showed that having modern sexist beliefs decreased the likelihood that individuals would detect sexist language. Other research by Swim *et al.* (1995) found that relative to those with low modern sexism scores, high scorers overestimated women's representation in traditionally male-dominated occupations. In sum, modern sexists are less likely to observe discrimination and routinely overestimate the progress that women have made in achieving parity with men.

But the effects of modern sexism go farther than complacency about gender gaps. Research suggests that modern sexism does in fact lead to discrimination. Swim *et al.* (1995) found the more individuals endorsed modern sexism, the more they favored male senatorial candidates over female ones. Moreover, other researchers (Klonis *et al.*, 2005) found that modern sexists inhibit their prejudices primarily to avoid social disapproval—not because they want to uphold personal egalitarian values. This finding suggests that in situations where their discriminatory behavior can be attributed to factors other than gender (and accusations of sexist behavior can be avoided) modern sexists might be especially apt to discriminate. Yet when we consider why progress towards gender equality has slowed, we must not only look at actions and behaviors of modern sexists. We must also consider how individuals *respond* to modern sexism.

In stark contrast to old-fashioned sexism, modern sexism often translates into behaviors that are far more subtle—often going undetected by both perpetrators and the targets of these sexist acts (Ellemers and Barreto, 2009). It is precisely this invisible quality of modern sexism that disempowers targets from responding to it in constructive ways. Research shows that compared to women who were exposed to old-fashioned sexism, those who witnessed modern sexism were less likely to respond with anger, and were less likely to engage in collective protest against perpetrators (Barreto and Ellemers, 2005). These findings suggest that modern sexism is far more likely than its traditional cousin to go unchallenged and unchecked—even by those most motivated to curb it.

Not only does modern sexism elude protest, but it also causes targets to behave in self-defeating ways that further contribute to gender inequality. For example, when targeted by modern sexism versus old-fashioned sexism, women are more likely to experience negative self-directed emotions, such as anger and disappointment. These emotions can in turn erode self-presentation and cognitive performance. In this way, experiencing modern sexism can ultimately cause targets to act in ways that confirm still persistent negative stereotypes about their competence (Barreto and Ellemers, 2005).

These self-defeating responses may be especially likely to occur in highly individualistic societies like the US. In individualistic cultures, many subscribe to the meritocratic ideology that people generally get what they deserve (Farmer, 2005). Thus when faced with modern sexism—where women *suspect* but aren't sure that they've experienced discrimination—meritocratic beliefs likely push them to attribute their outcomes to personal deficits instead of sexism. In the workplace, where no two candidates are exactly alike, it can be hard for a woman to discern whether she's been passed over for promotion because she lacked some qualification that her male counterpart had, or whether she lost out due to sexism. For racially/ethnically diverse women, there may be another layer of barriers and "what if" questions that could arise about perception of ones' abilities and qualifications. When faced with such ambiguity, meritocratic ideologies may cause US women to attribute their losses to personal failings. The fallout is a vicious cycle of response patterns on the part of both modern sexists *and* targets that perpetuate rather attenuate gender inequality. Over time, the effects of this cycle accumulate, accruing significant disadvantages to women and significant advantages to men. Over the course of a career, it's easy to see how modern sexism would issue "death by a thousand cuts," subtly reinforcing gender inequality and maintaining the disparities in women's access to leadership positions. Perhaps even more troubling is the fact that in addition to perpetuating gender disparities, contemporary forms of sexism at the same time diminish prospects for correcting that inequality.

Approaches to jumpstart progress

While the above trends are significant hurdles to be reckoned with, there is a way forward. Specifically, we argue that engaging men in advocacy for gender equality and institutionalizing inclusion are important strategies for accelerating the pace of change and building on the opportunities for change in the US.

Engaging men

As noted earlier, the dialing back of legislative or regulatory action from the federal government means that struggle for the equality will rely to a large extent on the voluntary, collective action of Americans. By virtue of the fact that men are over-represented in positions of leadership in business and government (Catalyst, 2015a; CAWP, 2015b), they are an influential and powerful stakeholder group whose advocacy for change is critical. As keepers of the societal institutions that help to maintain gender inequality, men's engagement in leading change—in partnership with women—is not just desirable but necessary. Men already disproportionately hold the positions of power and influence needed to change the institutional practices that stymie progress towards inclusion.

Notwithstanding, it also follows that if cultivating equitable gender relations is the ultimate goal, both parts of the gender equation—women and men—must contribute to realizing this end. Yet too often men continue to be overlooked, being viewed only as part of the problem and not part of the solution (Flood, 2015). However, contrary to this popular perspective, the benefits of men's involvement are multifold and offer a way forward in jumpstarting the pace of change in the US (and elsewhere).

One important benefit of engaging men is their increased investment in the struggle for gender equality. This is no trivial point as men often view gender equality initiatives as unnecessary at best, and adversely discriminatory towards men at worst (Davidson, 1999; Mor Barak *et al.*, 1998). Others see gender equality as a women's issue that is best left to women to address (Flood, 2015; Prime and Moss-Racusin, 2009). Yet when men are included in efforts to right gender disparities—alongside women—the odds are increased that they will not only develop greater awareness of inequalities but will also more readily recognize their own stake in changing the current gender order (Flood, 2015; Prime and Moss-Racusin, 2009). In this way, engaging men can be an important mechanism for curbing men's resistance to changes that challenge patriarchy.

As more and more men become visibly engaged in gender equality work, a tipping point can likely be reached far more quickly. This is yet another compelling reason to engage men. Research suggests that men may be more receptive to learning about gender from other men rather than from women activists (Carli, 2001; Drury and Kaiser, 2014; Prime and Moss-Racusin, 2009; Roy *et al.*, 2009). Concerns about breaking rank, and eliciting disapproval from male peers, often hold men back from championing equality (Prime and Moss-Racusin, 2009). Therefore, when men engage in activism and make clear that the struggle for equality is men's fight too, their voices can be particularly effective in diminishing resistance and legitimizing the cause of gender equality in other men's eyes. Engaging men as change agents may be one of the most powerful ways to generate a critical mass of men who are motivated to take collective action towards gender equality. In US society, where meritocratic, system-justifying ideologies, and modern sexism raise questions—especially among men (Jost and Hunyady, 2002)—about the very need for gender justice, amplifying the voices of influential men is paramount for motivating collective action among men accelerating the pace of change.

Clearly, gender equality will remain out of reach unless both the mindsets and behaviors of men shift. For this reason, men's perspectives and input are also necessary in designing practical interventions and solutions to effect change among men (Flood, 2015). Without cross-gender collaboration, women are far less likely to be effective in creating workable solutions for change that resonate with their male counterparts. Men's inclusion and input are vital. Indeed, as this reality becomes more widely embraced, a number of organizations are emerging with the goal of including men in gender equality efforts. Some prominent examples include the MenEngage Alliance, a global group of organizations working collaboratively to advance conversations and action around gender equality (MenEngage, 2015) and the UN's HeforShe initiative, which aims to build a solidarity movement among women *and* for gender equality (United Nations, 2015).

Promising workplace interventions: changing men's mindsets and behaviors

Clearly, the workplace is a critical frontline in the struggle to close leadership gender gaps. Increasingly, large corporations are implementing strategies they hope will enlist men's support and involvement in gender equity initiatives. Several are taking a multi-faceted approach, leveraging a variety of interventions ranging in formality and intensity, from leadership development programs and informal in-person and virtual convening to facilitate dialogue among, within and across gender, to employee resource groups. These approaches share common objectives including raising men's awareness of gender disparities at work, as well as motivating and equipping men to build more equitable and inclusive workplaces.

Lockheed Martin Corporation: building gender partnerships

An example of a leadership development program designed to engage men comes from Lockheed Martin. In 2007, Lockheed Martin launched a pilot program called Effective Leadership of Inclusive Teams (ELOIT), in partnership with White Men as Full Diversity Partners, to enlist the help of white male leaders in advancing diversity and inclusion (Catalyst, 2014c). In 2009, the program became mandatory for all vice presidents and above. ELOIT includes two learning labs, focused on creating a safe environment to explore diversity and inclusion (D&I) questions, challenges, and aspirations, as well as building partnerships across dimensions of diversity. One important strength of the ELOIT workshops is that they provide leaders with tools to effectively manage diverse teams and engage colleagues in difficult conversations about gender, race, and other dimensions of difference. Program participants are encouraged to share what they learned from these conversations and create action plans to help create more equitable and inclusive work climates.

Given ELOIT's success, in 2012 the company launched four pilot summits that provide early- and mid-career first-line leaders access to the program. Since then, summits have been held in multiple locations around the US and are championed by ELOIT executive alumni.

Men advocating real change

Other approaches include engaging men in ongoing communities of practice, like Catalyst's Men Advocating Real Change (MARC). MARC is a unique forum developed to convene professional men—both virtually and in person—who share a common commitment to building workplaces that are gender equitable and inclusive. Community members support and challenge each other's thinking and awareness of gender disparities at work, and share advice and best practices about ways to build more effective partnerships with women and men to effect change (MARC, 2015). Increasingly corporate leaders and professionals are turning to communities of practice, like MARC, for knowledge-sharing, leveraging a cross-company network of peers to accelerate learning about how to interrupt patterns of inequality, and build more equitable and inclusive work climates in partnership with women colleagues.

Building inclusive institutions

To accelerate the pace of progress, collaboration between women and men must focus not only on individual behavior but also on embedding equitable and inclusive *institutional* practices and structures. While most organizations appear to operate based on a set of gender-neutral practices, experts agree (e.g. Acker, 2006) that oftentimes these practices are in fact gendered, systematically perpetuating male privilege and female disadvantage. Compounding gender biases at the individual level, institutionalized career development practices systematically maintain gender hierarchies (Martell *et al.*, 2012). For example, in some organizations career advancement is governed by a tournament model (Freeman *et al.*, 2001; Martell *et al.*, 2012). Under this model, employees engage in series of competitions for advancement opportunities. Success or failure in early rounds of the competition then determine eligibility to compete for opportunities in succeeding rounds. Even with a slight evaluative bias favoring men, it's easy to see how the tournament promotion model would produce significant disparities in women's and men's access to leadership positions. Over time, increasingly lower proportions of women would be viewed as meeting the criteria to advance from one promotion round to the next. And much like we see in many organizations today, the tournament model would result in fewer and fewer women in the pipeline for the most powerful and prestigious positions. Although the tournament promotion model appears to be gender-neutral—with no express intent to create gender disparities—it nonetheless has the potential to produce dramatic patterns of vertical segregation (Martell *et al.*, 2012).

The same is true of the sponsored-mobility model, also common in many workplaces (Wayne *et al.*, 1999). Under this model, individuals are selected by a powerful leader and groomed for advancement. Those with sponsors get access to the most valuable resources and plum assignments—while those without sponsors do not benefit from these career-enhancing opportunities (Carter and Silva, 2010). On its face, the sponsor-mobility model, like the tournament model, seems gender-neutral. However, its impact is anything but gender-neutral. Since men predominate in positions of power in most organizations, more men than women have the positions of clout that would enable them to act as sponsors. Further, since sponsors tend to choose protégés with whom they share demographic similarities, the gender imbalance in positions of clout puts women at a disadvantage relative to men when it comes to being sponsored (Carter and Silva, 2010; Dinolfo *et al.*, 2012; Elliot and Smith, 2004). Via processes of homo-social reproduction, the sponsored-mobility model can maintain gender hierarchies in the workplace.

The effects of these promotion models can be further compounded by organizational norms and values. Perhaps especially in business contexts, competitive and agentic behaviors are valued and rewarded above others, and taken as indicators of leadership. While women and men are equally capable of these behaviors, research suggests that they are stereotypically associated with men. As a result of stereotypic biases, men are more likely than women to be seen as suitably qualified for business leadership. This is yet another example of the subtle ways in which seemingly gender-neutral practices and cultural norms reproduce gender bias.

Promising workplace interventions: changing work allocation practices

Changing gendered institutional practices is critical to making sustainable progress on the path to equality. In the corporate sector, promising examples of this approach include changing work structures and practices to include more collaboration and reduce hierarchy (Green and Kalev, 2008). Green and Kalev (2008) and others (e.g. Acker, 2006) have noted that organizational hierarchies tend to reinforce status differences and reinforce inequality between women and men. Given that women and men tend to hold a disproportionate number of top positions and women hold more of the lower status positions, cross-gender interactions are invariably unequal—right from the start. As a result, when women and men interact in hierarchical work settings, gender stereotyping and bias are more likely to occur, reinforcing and reproducing gender inequality (Acker, 2006; Green and Kalev, 2008).

However, by reducing hierarchy and organizing work around collaborative networks, this pattern can be interrupted, reducing stereotypic evaluations and discrimination. Consistent with this assertion, Smith-Doerr (2004) found that comparing companies with hierarchical structures, women fared far better in those with network-based structures. Specifically in the network-based firms, Smith-Doerr (2004) found that women were *eight times* more likely to attain supervisory positions than in hierarchical firms. In addition to inhibiting bias, network-based structures are also likely help to interrupt the sponsored-mobility model common in many large organizations. Instead of relying on sponsorship and recognition from higher-ups, employees in network-based settings likely rely far more on peer support and feedback to develop and advance.

In addition to changing the way work is organized, changes to talent development practices can also help interrupt the sponsored-mobility practices that disadvantage women. For example instead of relying on the homogenous networks of senior leaders—a practice that often disadvantages women (Carter and Silva, 2010)—organizations are taking a more systematic and less subjective way to identify employees development needs and assign opportunities. Such approaches include comprehensive talent review processes and tracking.

Concerted efforts are needed to jumpstart change

Jumpstarting progress on the path to equality means Americans must help generate the political will for change. Individual women *and* men, organizations, and governments— local, state, and federal—all have a role to play. Individuals and institutions must change, with hearts and minds won anew. If nurtured and embraced, efforts to engage men along with women in individual and collective action will hopefully place increasing pressures on employers and the government to remove the institutional barriers that keep gender equality firmly out of grasp in the US. Laissez-faire approaches and premature declarations about the end of inequality have proven counter-productive. Concerted efforts are needed to interrupt the self-perpetuating cycles of inequality that keep American women out of leadership roles.

References

Acker, J. (2006). Gender and organizations. In Chafetz, J. S. (ed.) *Handbook of the Sociology of Gender* (pp. 177–194). New York: Springer US.

Bagati, D. (2009). *Women of Color in U.S. Law Firms—Women of Color in Professional Services Series*. New York: Catalyst.

Barreto, M. and Ellemers, N. (2005). The burden of benevolent sexism: How it contributes to the maintenance of gender inequalities. *European Journal of Social Psychology*, 35(5), 633.

Becker, J. C. and Swim, J. K. (2012). Reducing endorsement of benevolent and modern sexist beliefs. *Social Psychology*, 40(3), 127–137.

Blackerby, C. (2013, December 5). The Equal Rights Amendment: The most popular never-ratified amendment [Blog post]. *Education Updates*. Retrieved from http://education.blogs.archives.gov/2013/12/05/the-equal-rights-amendment/

BLS (Bureau of Labor Statistics). (1995). *Table 14: 14. Employed persons in nonagricultural industries by age, sex, and race*. US Department of Labor. Retrieved from www.bls.gov/cps/aa1995/aat14.txt

BLS. (2014a). *Employed Persons in Nonagricultural Industries by Age, Sex, Race, and Hispanic or Latino Ethnicity.* US Department of Labor. Retrieved from www.bls.gov/cps/cpsaat14.pdf

BLS. (2014b). *Report 1052, Women in the Labor Force: A databook.* US Department of Labor. Washington, DC: Author.

BLS. (2015). *Families with own children: Employment status of parents by age of youngest child and family type, 2013–2014 annual averages.* US Department of Labor. Retrieved from www.bls.gov/news.release/famee.t04.htm

Bolzendahl, C. I. and Myers, D. J. (2004). Feminist attitudes and support for gender equality: Opinion change in women and men, 1974–1998. *Social Forces, 83*(2), 759–789. Retrieved from www.jstor.org/stable/3598347

Brown, J. K. (ed.). (2008). *Key Legal Cases for Women's Equality 1873–2007.* New York: Legal Momentum.

Carli, L. L. (2001). Gender and social influence. *Journal of Social Issues, 57*(4), 725–741.

Carter, N. M. and Silva, C. (2010). *Mentoring: Necessary but insufficient for advancement.* New York: Catalyst.

Carter, N. M. and Silva, C. (2011). *The Myth of the Ideal Worker: Does doing all the right things really get women ahead.* New York: Catalyst.

Catalyst. (2004). *The Bottom Line: Connecting Corporate Performance and Gender Diversity.* New York: Catalyst.

Catalyst. (2011). *The Bottom Line: Corporate Performance and Women's Representation on Boards (2004–2008).* New York: Catalyst.

Catalyst. (2014a). *Quick Take: Women in the United States.* New York: Catalyst. Retrieved from www.catalyst.org/knowledge/women-united-states.

Catalyst. (2014b). *Increasing Gender Diversity on Boards: Current index of formal approaches.* New York: Catalyst.

Catalyst. (2014c). *Practices: Lockheed Martin Corporation—Women Accelerating Tomorrow.* New York: Author.

Catalyst. (2015a). *Women in S&P 500 Companies.* New York: Catalyst. Retrieved from www.catalyst.org/knowledge/women-sp-500-companies

Catalyst. (2015b). *2014 Catalyst Census: Women board directors.* New York: Catalyst.

CAWP (Center for American Women in Politics) (2015a). *History of Women in the U.S. Congress.* CAWP, Eagleton Institute of Politics, Rutgers University. Retrieved from www.cawp.rutgers.edu/history-women-us-congress

CAWP. (2015b). *Women in Elective Office 2015.* CAWP, Eagleton Institute of Politics, Rutgers University. Retrieved from www.cawp.rutgers.edu/women-elective-office-2015

Cohen, N. L. (2013, April 24). Why America never had universal child care. *The New Republic.* Retrieved from https://newrepublic.com/article/113009/child-care-america-was-very-close-universal-day-care

Coltrane, S. (1988). Father-child relationships and the status of women: A cross-cultural study. *The American Journal of Sociology, 93*(5), 1060–1095.

Coltrane, S. (2004). Elite careers and family commitment: It's (still) about gender. *The Annals of the American Academy of Political and Social Science, 596*(1), 214–220.

Corbett, C. and Hill, C. (2012). *Graduating to a Pay Gap: The earnings of women and men one year after college graduation.* Washington, DC: AAUW.

Cotter, D., Hermsen, J. and Vanneman, R. (2014, July 30). Brief: Back on track? The stall and rebound in support for women's new roles in work and politics, 1977–2012. *The Council on Contemporary Families Brief Reports.* Retrieved from https://contemporaryfamilies.org/gender-revolution-rebound-brief-back-on-track/

Credit Suisse. (2012). *Gender Diversity and Corporate Performance.* Zurich, Switzerland: Credit Suisse.

Davidson, M. N. (1999). The value of being included: An examination of diversity change initiatives in organizations. *Performance Improvement Quarterly, 12*(1), 164–180.

Desvaux, G., Devillard-Hoellinger, S. and Baumgarten, P. (2007). *Women Matter: Gender diversity, a corporate performance driver.* New York: McKinsey & Company.

Dey, J. G. and Hill, C. (2007). *Behind the Pay Gap.* Washington, DC: American Association of University Women.

Dinolfo, S., Silva, C. and Carter, N. (2012). *High Potentials in the Pipeline: Leaders pay it forward.* New York: Catalyst.

Drury, B. J. and Kaiser, C. R. (2014). Allies against sexism: The role of men in confronting sexism. *Journal of Social Issues, 70*(4), 637–652.

Ellemers, N. and Barreto, M. (2009). Collective action in modern times: How modern expressions of prejudice prevent collective action. *Journal of Social Issues, 65*(4), 749–768.

Elliott, E. and Ewoh, A. I. E. (2000). The evolution of an issue: The rise and decline of affirmative action. *Policy Studies Review, 17*(2/3), 212–237.

Elliott, J. R. and Smith, R. A. (2004). Race, gender, and workplace power. *American Sociological Review, 69*(3), 365–386.

Farmer, B. (2005). *American Conservatism: History, theory, and practice.* Newcastle, England: Cambridge Scholars Press.

Flood, M. (2015). Men and gender equality. In M. Flood and R. Howson (eds), *Engaging Men in Building Gender Equality,* (pp. 1–33). Newcastle, UK: Cambridge Scholars Publishing.

Freeman, R., Weinstein, E., Marincola, E., Rosenbaum, J. and Solomon, F. (2001). Competition and careers in biosciences. *Science, 294*(5550), 2293–2294.

Frothingham, S. (2015, December 10). *Broader Paid Leave Would Provide Opportunity and Security for Millennial Caregivers.* Washington, DC: Center for American Progress.

Fullerton, H. N. (1999). Labor force participation: 75 years of change, 1950–1998 and 1990–2025. *Bureau of Labor Statistics Monthly Labor Review, 122*(12), 3–12.

Giscombe, K. (2007). *Women of Color in Accounting—Women of Color in Professional Services Series.* New York: Catalyst.

Glick, P. and Fiske, S. T. (2011). Ambivalent sexism revisited. *Psychology of Women Quarterly, 35*(3), 530–535.

Glynn, S. J. (2014). *Breadwinning Mothers, Then and Now.* Washington, DC: Center for American Progress.

Green, T. and Kalev, A. (2008). Discrimination-reducing measures at the relational level. *Hastings Law Journal, 59,* 1435.

Harrington, B., Van Deusen, F. and Humberd, B. (2011). *The New Dad: Caring, committed, and conflicted.* Boston, MA: Boston College Center for Work and Family.

Hegewisch, A., Williams. C., Hartmann. H. and Hudiburg. S. K. (2014, March). *The Gender Wage Gap: 2013. Differences by race and ethnicity, no growth in real wages for women.* Washington, DC: Institute for Women's Policy Research. Retrieved from www.iwpr.org/publications/pubs/the-gender-wage-gap-2013-differences-by-race-and-ethnicity-no-growth-in-real-wages-for-women

Jost, J. T. and Hunyady, O. (2002). The psychology of system justification and the palliative function of ideology. *European Review of Social Psychology, 13,* 111–153.

Kay, H. H. (2004). Ruth Bader Ginsberg, professor of law. *Columbia Law Review,* 2–20.

Klonis, S. C., Plant, E. A. and Devine, P. G. (2005). Internal and external motivation to respond without sexism. *Personality and Social Psychology Bulletin, 31*(9), 1237–1240.

Kovach, K. A., Kravitz, D. A. and Hughes, A. A. (2004). How can we be so lost when we don't even know where we are going? *Labor Law Journal, 55*(1), 53–61.

Leonard, J. S. (1989). Women and affirmative action. *Journal of Economic Perspectives, 3*(1), 61–75.

Livingston, G. (2014a, June 5). *Growing Number of Dads Home with the Kids: Biggest increase among those caring for family.* Washington DC: Pew Research Center. Retrieved from www.pewsocialtrends.org/2014/06/05/growing-number-of-dads-home-with-the-kids/

Local, The. (2015, May 15). Firms face penalties if boards not 'more female'. *The Local.* Retrieved from www.thelocal.se/20150515/employ-more-women-or-else-swedish-companies-told

MARC (Men Advocating Real Change). (2015). About. Retrieved from http://onthemarc.org/about

MenEngage. (2015). Homepage. Retrieved from http://menengage.org

Martell, R. F., Emrich, C. G. and Robison-Cox, J. (2012). From bias to exclusion: A multilevel emergent theory of gender segregation in organizations. *Research in Organizational Behavior, 32,* 137–162.

May, A. M. and Stephenson, K. (1994, January). *Women and the Great Retrenchment: The political economy of gender in the 1980s.* Paper presented at the annual meeting of the Association for Evolutionary Economics, Boston, MA.

Meyerson, D. and Tompkins, M. (2007). Tempered radicals as institutional change agents: The case of advancing gender equity at the University of Michigan. *Harvard Journal of Law & Gender, 30*, 303–322.

Miller, C. C. (2014, June 19). Women on the board: Quotas have limited success. *Upshot: The New York Times*, p. B4. Retrieved from www.nytimes.com/2014/06/20/upshot/women-on-the-board-quotas-have-limited-success.html

Mor Barak, M. E., Cherin, D. A. and Berkman, S. (1998). Organizational and personal dimensions in diversity climate: Ethnic and gender differences in employee perceptions. *The Journal of Applied Behavioral Science, 34*(1), 82–104.

Mosisa, A. and Hipple, S. (2006). Trends in labor force participation in the United States. *Monthly Labor Review, 129*, 35–57.

Mukhopadhyay, S. (2012). The effects of the 1978 Pregnancy Discrimination Act on female labor supply. *International Economic Review, 53*(4), 1133–1153.

National Center for Education Statistics, US Department of Education and the Institute of Education Sciences. (2014). *Digest of Education Statistics, Table 104.20, Percentage of persons 25 to 29 years old with selected levels of educational attainment, by race/ethnicity and sex: Selected years, 1920 through 2014.* Retrieved from https://nces.ed.gov/programs/digest/d14/tables/dt14_104.20.asp

OECD (Organization for Economic Co-operation and Development). (2015). LFS by sex and age – indicators. Retrieved from https://stats.oecd.org/Index.aspx?DataSetCode=LFS_SEXAGE_I_R

Pew Research Center. (2010). *Men's lives often seen as better. Gender equality universally embraced, but inequalities acknowledged.* Retrieved from www.pewglobal.org/files/2010/07/Pew-Global-Attitudes-2010-Gender-Report-July-1-12-01AM-EDT-NOT-EMBARGOED.pdf

Prime, J. and Moss-Racusin, C. A. (2009). *Engaging men: What change agents need to know.* New York: Catalyst.

Rosin, H. (2012). *The end of men: And the rise of women.* New York: Riverhead Books.

Roy, R. E., Weibust, K. S. and Miller, C. T. (2009). If she's a feminist it must not be discrimination: The power of the feminist label on observers' attributions about a sexist event. *Sex Roles, 60*(5–6), 422–431.

Silva, C., Carter, N. M. and Beninger, A. (2012). *Good intentions, imperfection execution? Women get fewer of the "hot jobs" needed to advance.* New York: Catalyst.

Smith-Doerr, L. (2004). Flexibility and fairness: Effects of the network form of organization on gender equity in life science careers. *Sociological Perspectives, 47*(1), 25–54.

Statistics Norway (2013, June). Table 2: Board Representatives, by gender, age groups, level of education, size groups and economic activity. Retrieved from www.ssb.no/en/virksomheter-foretak-og-regnskap/statistikker/styre/aar/2013-06-05?fane=tabell&sort=nummer&tabell=115398

Swim, J. K., Aikin, K. J., Hall, W. S. and Hunter, B. A. (1995). Sexism and racism: Old-fashioned and modern prejudices. *Journal of Personality and Social Psychology, 68*(2), 199–214.

Swim, J. K., Mallett, R. and Stangor, C. (2004). Understanding subtle sexism: Detection and use of sexist language. *Sex Roles, 51*(3), 117–128.

Thorpe-Moscon, J. and Pollack, A. (2014). *Feeling Different: Being the "other" in US workplaces.* New York: Catalyst.

Twenge, J. M. (2011). The duality of individualism: Attitudes toward women, generation me, and the method of cross-temporal meta-analysis. *Psychology of Women Quarterly, 35*(1), 193–196.

United Nations. (1948). Declaration of Human Rights. Retrieved from www.un.org/en/universal-declaration-human-rights/

United Nations. (2015). HeForShe homepage. Retrieved from www.heforshe.org/

United States Department of Labor. (n.d.). Family and Medical Leave Act. Retrieved from www.dol.gov/whd/fmla/

United States Department of Labor. (2013). Latest annual data. Retrieved from www.dol.gov/wb/stats/recentfacts.htm

United States Equal Employment Opportunities Commission. (2015). EEOC at 50. Retrieved from www.eeoc.gov/eeoc/history/50th/

United States Government. (2009, December 16). Code of Federal Regulations, Title 17: Commodity and Securities Exchanges § 229.407 (Item 407) Corporate Governance, sect. c (2) (vi); Securities and Exchange Commission, Proxy Disclosure Enhancements.

Valentin, I. (1997, August). Title IX: A brief history. *Women's Educational Equity Act (WEEA) Resource Center Digest*, 1–12.

Van Zandweghe, W. (2012). Interpreting the recent decline in labor force participation. *Economic Review*, Federal Reserve Bank of Kansas City.

Wayne, S. J., Liden, R. C., Kraimer, M. L. and Graf, I. K. (1999). The role of human capital, motivation and supervisor sponsorship in predicting career success. *Journal of Organizational Behavior, 20*(5), 577–595.

Wootton, B. H. (1997). Gender differences in occupational employment. *Bureau of Labor Statistics Monthly Labor Review, 120*(4), 15–24.

World Bank. (2015). *Women, Business and the Law 2016: Getting to Equal.* Washington, DC: World Bank.

World Economic Forum. (2015). *The Global Gender Gap Report 2015.* Geneva, Switzerland: World Economic Forum.

PART IV

Women in management

Australasia

12 Women in management in Australia

Phyllis Tharenou

Introduction

Informed by substantial and compelling evidence, Rodgers (2015) recently pointed out that it would take more than a couple of hundred years for Australian women to gain gender equality in the workforce; Rodgers's pessimistic forecast is consistent with that of the International Labor Organization (ILO, 2015a). Using the latest data, from 2011 to 2015, this chapter gives an overall picture of the presence of women in management and the professions in Australia, focusing on women's educational pursuits; their labor force participation; the proportion of women in management, on boards and in parliament; the gender pay gap; and initiatives in place to address this imbalance. A discussion of these issues enables an assessment of the progress of women in the period since Wood's analysis, given in the 2011 version of this handbook, and to make international comparisons.

Internationally, the *Global Gender Gap Report* measures the gender gap on four key areas of inequality (Bekhouche *et al.*, 2015): educational attainment; economic participation and opportunity; political empowerment; and health and survival. In 2015, Australia was ranked 36 of 145 countries (Bekhouche *et al.*, 2015), down from a ranking of 24 of 142 countries in 2014 (Bekhouche *et al.*, 2014), and a ranking of 15 of 115 countries in 2006 (Hausmann *et al.*, 2006). In 2014 and 2015, Australia achieved gender equality in only one area: educational attainment. Rankings for 2015, 2014, 2009 and 2006, respectively, indicate that Australian women experience poorer outcomes than men in economic participation and opportunity (32, 14, 19, 12), poorer and deteriorating outcomes on political empowerment (61, 53, 39, 32), and much poorer outcomes on health and survival (74, 70, 78, 57) (Bekhouche *et al.*, 2014, 2015; Hausmann *et al.*, 2006, 2009). From an international perspective, there is little evidence of gender equality in Australia, a developed and flourishing economy, apart from educational attainment.

Women pursuing education

Overall, Australian women have a higher educational level than men. While both men and women are equally likely to have a non-school qualification, they differ on the level attained (ABS, 2014a), with women more likely to hold a bachelor degree or a graduate diploma/ certificate in addition to being more likely to hold an advanced diploma/diploma or a certificate I/II qualification. By contrast, men are more likely than women to have attained a certificate III/IV qualification (ABS, 2014a). For their part, Indigenous women similarly are more likely to have attained an advanced diploma/diploma (8 percent vs. 6 percent) or a bachelor degree (8 percent vs. 4 percent) than Indigenous men, who are more likely to have attained a certificate III/IV qualification (ABS, 2014b). Consistent with their superior educational level, Australian women are undertaking some form of higher education program more often than men (57 percent vs. 43 percent), including a bachelor degree or above (34 percent vs. 25 percent) (ABS, 2015a).

Between 2001 and 2014 the proportion of women aged 20–24 years who attained a year 12/certificate II or above increased from 81 to 90 percent, indicating Australian women's educational improvement, while the corresponding figure for men was only 78 to 83 percent (ABS, 2015a). The increase for women is particularly noticeable in the 25–29 years age range, where the proportion of women who attained a bachelor degree or above increased from 29 to 42 percent; for men it increased only from 22 to 31 percent (ABS, 2015a).

Women and men also differ in non-school qualifications reflecting traditional gendered employment areas (ABS, 2014a). Women are more likely than men to have a qualification in health; education; management and commerce; society and culture; creative arts; and food, hospitality and personal services. Men are more likely to have a qualification in natural and physical sciences; information technology; engineering and related technologies; architecture and building; and agriculture, environmental and related studies (ABS, 2014a).

From an international perspective, Australia performs satisfactorily for female educational attainment, as indicated by its gender equality rating given in the *Global Gender Gap Report* (Bekhouche *et al.*, 2014, 2015), and its rank of five out of eight Organization for Economic Co-operation and Development (OECD) countries given in 2009 (OECD, 2011). Australia's female tertiary education rate (40 percent) is above the OECD average (30 percent) (OECD, 2011).

Labor force participation

Although approaching parity or better on educational attainment, Australian women are disadvantaged when it comes to labor force participation and advancement. Full-time employment statistics reveal women's disproportionately low representation in the labor force. In 2014 women comprised half of the total population of Australia (ABS, 2015b); nevertheless, from 2008 to 2015 they constituted 45–46 percent of the total workforce (ABS, 2011a, 2015c). A more detailed breakdown of the labor force participation of women reveals that they are also under-represented in full-time employment and over-represented in part-time employment (e.g. 36 percent of full-time workers, 70 percent of part-time workers), almost the same figures as given by Wood in 2011. In addition, women are less likely to have access to paid leave entitlements (i.e., annual leave and sick leave) than men (73 percent vs. 79 percent) (ABS, 2014d). Indigenous women, who also represent half the Indigenous population (ABS, 2015b), fare no differently, with a similar proportion in the workforce (45 percent in 2012–2013) (ABS, 2014b) and similar employment category proportions (e.g. 35 percent of full-time workers, 70 percent of part-time workers) (ABS, 2014b). This non-representative pattern of employment participation for women has changed only marginally since 2009 (ABS, 2011a, 2014d, 2015c).

Notwithstanding, the labor force participation rate of women is improving. Between 1993 and 2013, the rate of women aged 15 to 65+ increased from 52 to 59 percent, while that of men decreased from 74 to 71 percent (ABS, 2014c). The relatively low participation rate for all women (59 percent) (ABS, 2014c) becomes higher when the working-age population, of 15 to 64 years, is considered (71 percent) (OECD, 2015a). In 2014, a higher 71 percent of women aged 15–64 years and 76 percent of prime-age women, aged 25 to 54 years, participated in the labor force, being either employed or seeking employment. However, the figures for men are higher: 82 percent and 90 percent, respectively (OECD, 2015a). By contrast, the participation rate of working-age Indigenous women is much lower than that of Australian women in general, at 52 percent, as it is for Indigenous men, at 63 percent (ABS, 2012).

From an international perspective, in 2014 Australia was ranked 14 of 40 mostly OECD countries for the labor force participation of working-age women and ranked 28 of 40 countries for the participation of prime-age women (OECD, 2015a), the latter being an improvement on the 2010 rank of 20 of 22 countries for women in this age group (OECD, 2015a).

While female labor force participation in Australia is slowly increasing, it should be higher, especially for prime-age women, given the recent legislative changes aimed at improving gender equality in the workplace. For example, a government-funded paid parental leave scheme was introduced in 2011. Women's leave is also discussed later in this chapter.

In particular, age has a negative effect on women's labor force participation, with fewer older women participating than older men. The proportion (75–78 percent) of women aged 20–54 years who participate in the workforce drops at 55–59 years of age, to 65 percent; further at 60–64 years old, to 45 percent; and over 65 years drops markedly to 8 percent (ABS, 2014e). The labor force participation rate for men (82–88 percent) aged 20–54 years only falls to 81 percent at 55–59 years and, in contrast to women, men's participation rate only drops markedly when they reach 60–64 years of age, to 63 percent, and to 17 percent at 65+ (ABS, 2014e), demonstrating that older men are more likely to be employed than older women.

Despite the lower rate of participation of older women, in general their rate has increased. Between 2000 and 2014, the rate for women aged 55–64 years grew by 21 percent, from 35 to 56 percent; for older men the increase was a mere 11 percent, from 61 to 72 percent (OECD, 2015a). The rate for women aged 55–59 years increased from 47 percent in 2000 to 66 percent in 2014, and for women aged 60–64 years it leapt from 22 percent in 2000 to 45 percent in 2014 (ABS, 2015d). Nevertheless, despite the rise, in 2014 only 56 percent of mature-aged women (55–64 years) were participating in the labor force, fewer than the 72 percent of men (OECD, 2015a). This is only slightly higher than the 53 percent in 2009 (OECD, 2015a).

In summary, there has been a marked increase in the labor force participation rate of prime-age (25–54 years) and mature-age (55+ years) women, with the rate for prime-age men remaining constant, although increasing for mature-aged men. Despite a creditable increase, in 2014 Australia was only 16th in rank of 40 countries for the participation of mature-aged (55–64 years) women in the labor force (OECD, 2015a).

The increased pattern of labor force participation for prime- and mature-age women is attributed by Wilkins and Wooden (2014) to cohort effects (cf. Borland, 2011). Specifically, mature-age women are now better qualified and spend more time in paid work than their equivalents from previous generations and so are more likely to continue working until traditional retirement ages (Borland, 2011). Daley and McGannon (2014) see the increase in older women's participation between 1980 and 2010 as a consequence of better health, higher educational levels and partners who also worked until later in life (cf. Heady *et al.*, 2010).

A final aspect of the participation of Australian women in the labor force is their concentration in certain industries and occupations. In 2015, 78 percent of employees in the healthcare and social assistance industry were women, while the construction industry's share was 11 percent (ABS, 2015e). In 2015 (as for 2013–2014, WGEA, 2014), women were also over-represented in education and training, with men over-represented in wholesale trade, primary industries, manufacturing, logistics and utilities (ABS, 2015e).

The same ratios for gender in industries hold for the Indigenous labor force. Using the available figures (ABS, 2011b), in 2011, Indigenous women were also over-represented in healthcare and social assistance and education and training industries, whereas Indigenous men were over-represented in manufacturing and construction industries.

Occupations are also either female- or male-dominated. The occupation with the highest proportion of women in 2015 was clerks and administrators, whereas that with the lowest was machinery operators and drivers (ABS, 2015e). In contrast, men were over-represented as managers, laborers, technicians and trade workers, and machinists and operator drivers (ABS, 2015e). The pattern for Indigenous women follows that of non-Indigenous women; for example, in 2011, Indigenous women were over-represented as clerks and administrators, sales workers, community and personal service workers and professionals (ABS, 2012). The occupation category with the highest proportion of Indigenous women was clerks and administrators, at 79 percent, and the lowest was machinery operators and drivers at 9 percent (ABS, 2012).

Women in management and on boards

A manager in Australia is more likely to be a man than a woman (ABS, 2015e), with the proportion of women working in full-time management increasing only marginally since the introduction of the earliest Sex Discrimination Act 1984 more than 30 years ago (ABS, 2015e). In 2015 women constituted about a third (32 percent) of all full-time managers (ABS, 2015e), up from 25 percent in 1993 (ABS, 1993, 2015e), albeit an insignificant increase on the 2005 figure of 30 percent (ABS, 2015e). Indigenous women, however, are better represented among Indigenous managers, at 45 percent (ABS, 2012). The low proportion of women in management positions in 2012 (36 percent) meant that Australia was ranked a relatively low 42 of 126 countries on its proportion of female managers (ILO, 2015b).

Similar to their non-managerial colleagues, women managers are more likely to work part-time than men (8 percent vs. 4 percent) and thus of course less likely to work full-time (28 percent vs. 60 percent) (ABS, 2015d). However, women are better represented in management in the public sector, making up 40 percent of the senior executive service (SES) (APSC, 2014). Although an increase of only 2 percent from Wood's (2011) figure, the 40 percent represents a greater proportion of managers than the 35.9 and 36.5 percent in comparable private sector contexts (WGEA, 2014, 2015a).

Irrespective of sector, women are concentrated in lower levels of management, with progressively fewer women at higher levels (APSC, 2014; WGEA, 2014, 2015a). From 2002 to 2012, women in the Australian Public Service (APS) constituted about 58 percent of total employees and 67 percent of Indigenous employees (APSC, 2014). Indicating acceptable representation, women in general make up a slightly lower 55 percent of the top non-executive level (APS level 6), with Indigenous women at 64 percent, also only slightly lower than their overall representation. However, the real issue lies in the executive level, where only 36 percent of SES level 2 positions are filled by women, and Indigenous women are only 50 percent of Indigenous executive employees (APSC, 2014). Recent times have witnessed some improvement, however, with the percentage of women at SES level 3 rising by 8.5 percent in 2014, while the total number in all SES positions has increased by 2 percent on the level given by Wood in 2011 (APSC, 2014).

A negative link between managerial level and women's representation in management similarly appears to operate in the private sector. In companies of 100+ employees and which employed a total of one-third of Australia's workforce, women made up 35.9 percent of managers in 2013–2014 (WGEA, 2014) and 36.5 percent in 2014–2015 (WGEA, 2015a). However, as the management level increased, the proportion of women employed in ascending levels decreased. In 2013–2014 (WGEA, 2014) and 2014–2015 (WGEA, 2015a), respectively, at the first layer of management, women comprised 40 percent of employees, the numbers falling to 32 or 33 percent at the next level, that of senior managers. From this point, female representation steadily declined, with women comprising 28 or 29 percent of executive and general manager roles and 26 or 27 percent of key management personnel (WGEA, 2014, 2015a). Women held only 17 or 15 percent of positions at chief executive officer (CEO) level in private sector companies with 100+ employees in 2013–2014 (WGEA, 2014) and 2014–2015 (WGEA, 2015a). In 2012, women formed 12 percent of executive managers in the Australian Securities Exchange (ASX) 200 companies (i.e., the top companies listed on the Australian Stock Exchange) but only 4 percent of CEOs (ABS, 2015a), the latter signifying an increase of 2 percent from Wood's 2011 figure.

The increase in numbers of women in management positions in the APS—from 33 percent in 2005 to 40 percent in 2014 (APSC, 2005, 2014)—has not been replicated in the private sector, despite changes in legislation and other improvements (e.g. leave entitlements). In the ASX200 companies, female executive key management personnel increased from only 8 to 10 percent from 2010 to 2012, while from 2002 to 2012 the proportion of female CEOs increased by one percentage point to 3 percent (EOWA, 2012). Reflecting its very poor performance, Australia is ranked a lowly 32 of 44 countries on the proportion of women in senior management, at 22 percent (Grant Thornton, 2013).

Women managers are also concentrated in "feminine" industries, although even here they are generally employed at lower levels than men. In 2012, the industry with the highest proportion of women in executive key management positions in the ASX200 and ASX500 companies was in the pharmaceuticals, biotechnology and life sciences industry at 26 percent (ASX200 companies) and 22 percent (ASX500 companies) (EOWA, 2012). By contrast, the percentage of female employees as a whole was a meager 10 percent for ASX200 and 9 percent for ASX500 companies (EOWA, 2012).

As a consequence of there being so few women in executive positions, and because board members are traditionally drawn from executive ranks, Australian women are poorly represented on boards. In 2012, women held 12 percent of board directorships in ASX200 companies (ABS, 2015a), although this figure is 4 percent higher than that given by Wood in 2011. In 2013 women held only around 3 percent of board chair positions in Australia (Gladman and Lamb, 2013).

Following the establishment of targets, the number of women on boards in Australia has increased. In 2010 the Australian government introduced targets for women on its own boards and, by 2014, women made up 40 percent of appointments to Australian government boards and bodies, although they held only 31 percent of chairs/deputy chairs (ABS, 2015a). In the private sector, the proportion of female board directors in ASX200 companies increased from 8 to 20 percent between 2009 and 2015 (AICD, 2015a), a likely consequence of the targets set by the AICD in 2009 (AICD, 2015b). In 2015, in response to the ASX requirement for disclosure, via annual report, of measurable objectives for achieving gender diversity and progress towards achieving them, women comprised 30 percent of new appointments, up from just 5 percent in 2009 (AICD, 2015a).

Nevertheless, this substantial improvement comes off a low base. Despite compelling evidence that the proportion of women on corporate boards in Australia is positively related to employee productivity (Ali *et al.*, 2014), economic growth and social responsiveness (Galbreath, 2011), female board directors and chairs continue to be under-represented in the private sector in Australia. Hence, it is no surprise that Australia ranks poorly internationally. In 2013 Australia ranked 37 of 67 countries for the percentage of female directors on corporate boards (Terjesen *et al.*, 2015) and in 2014 ranked 10 of 20 countries (Catalyst, 2015).

Although there is no systematic evidence available, from examining their websites Australian business schools appear to have developed programs to attract more female students especially into MBA degrees by offering scholarships for women, partnerships with employers and mentoring (e.g. Curtin Business School, 2015; Macquarie University Graduate School of Management, 2015; Monash Business School, 2015; University of South Australia Business School, 2015; University of Wollongong, 2015). They also facilitate women's study once enrolled, for example through flexible study options for students with childcare responsibilities, career services specifically for women and women in management clubs (e.g. Melbourne Business School, 2015). The five business schools – Macquarie Graduate School of Management (MGSM), Curtin Business School, Monash Business School, UniSA Business School and Wollongong Business School – have formed a network to implement their WiMBA program. In particular, the program offers partnerships with employers to enable female employees with leadership potential to complete their MBA and financial, logistical and practical support, and mentoring. Indeed in 2015 the University of Sydney became the first business school in Australia to attract more women than men into its MBA program (University of Sydney Business School, 2015). There does appear to be an undergraduate pool of female students studying management. For example, in 2014, women represented 51 percent of management and commerce students (ABS, 2014a).

Moreover, Australian schools of science, technology and engineering have been trying for several decades to recruit more women students and support current students by providing financial, study and career support, networks and social events (e.g. Allen and Ravishankar, 2015; McDonald *et al.*, 2010), with little success. Women have only represented 40 percent of natural and physical sciences students, 25 percent of information technology students, and a very low 7 percent of engineering and related technology students (ABS, 2014a).

There is very little evidence available on what Australian science and engineering schools or business schools are doing to attract women faculty. A rare example is the University of South Australia's Business School, which partners with the Committee for Economic Development of Australia, to deliver a six-part series on women in leadership (WGEA, 2015d). Australian universities have implemented many gender equality initiatives in general to improve their representation of women faculty across their universities. The most common initiatives reported in the Workplace Gender Equality Public Reports have been strategic action plans/policies, mentoring programs, networking opportunities, leadership development programs and professional development programs (cf. WGEA, 2015d).

There are also a range of relatively new Australian professional women's organizations (e.g. Women on Boards, Australian Businesswomen's Network, Engineers Australia's Women in Engineering National Committee, Women in Science) seeking to attract into and support women in management and on boards and women in traditionally male occupations (Australian Businesswomen's Network, 2015; Engineers Australia, 2015; Women on Boards, 2015). The initiatives include professional development and networking, mentoring and coaching, and advocacy on behalf of women (Australian Businesswomen's Network, 2015; Engineers Australia, 2015; Women on Boards, 2015).

As an example, Women on Boards founded as an informal network in 2001 and as a company in 2006, aims to improve women's representation on boards and in other leadership roles, providing networking and professional opportunities, mentoring and coaching, and access to board vacancies. It seems to yield fruit (Women on Boards, 2015). More than 18,000

Australian women are registered with Women on Boards. The network has many experienced and highly qualified female executives, many of who are already in non-executive director roles or engaging in board work in conjunction with other career roles. Women on Boards has helped nearly 1,500 women to gain board positions since 2006.

Women in politics

Similar to their poor representation in management and on boards in the private sector, women are under-represented in federal and state parliaments in Australia. In 2015, women formed only 31 percent of Commonwealth parliamentarians, a figure 2 percent lower than that given by Wood in 2011 and one little changed from the 30 percent in 2009 (Inter-Parliamentary Union, 2015). From 1943 to 2015 the proportion of women has been higher in the Senate (38 percent) than the House of Representatives (27 percent) (Parliamentary Library, 2014). Smith (2010) argues that women have a similar chance of being elected to the Australian Parliament as men (about 14 percent in 2007), suggesting their under-representation may be linked to party pre-selection processes.

The Coalition federal government has a lower representation of women parliamentarians than the Australian Labor Party (ALP) Opposition (McCann and Wilson, 2014). In February 2015 women formed 17 percent of government ministers, 6 percent fewer than in Wood's (2011) chapter and 21 percent fewer than the 38 percent of Opposition shadow ministers (McCann and Wilson, 2014). The ALP currently has a quota system for pre-selection, of 40 percent for each gender, to increase women's participation (Wright, 2011), an approach that has proved to be successful. Labor's 1994 approach to pre-selection, where a 35 percent quota was adopted, meant that the number of women candidates increased from 15 to 36 percent by 2010 (McCann and Wilson, 2014). This is in stark contrast to the Coalition parties, none of which has established gender quotas for pre-selection (Loughnane, 2010; Mitchell, 2013), resulting in the lower representation of women among Commonwealth parliamentarians.

Women are also under-represented in state and territory parliaments. In 2014 and 2015 (McCann and Wilson, 2014), women constituted only about a third (32 percent) of state parliamentarians, although this figure ranged from a high proportion of 41 percent both in 2014 and 2015 in the Legislative Assembly of the Australian Capital Territory (2015) and 40 percent and 44 percent in 2014 and 2015 respectively in the Legislative Assembly of the Northern Territory (2015), to the low 25 percent in 2014 and 28 percent in 2015 in the Parliament of New South Wales (2015). The South Australian and Queensland parliaments were similarly low: 25 percent in 2014 and 26 percent in 2015 for South Australia and 21 percent in 2014 and 28 percent in 2015 for Queensland (Parliament of South Australia, 2015; Parliament of Queensland, 2015). Of the five bicameral parliaments, there is no consistent trend for women's higher representation in either house.

In the international context, between 2001 and 2011, Australia's ranking for the representation of women in parliament declined from 21 of 178 countries to 38 of 187 countries (Inter-Parliamentary Union, 2015). The situation deteriorated further in 2015, with Australia now ranked 43 of 190 countries, down 11 places from 2009, when the ranking was 32 of 188 countries (Inter-Parliamentary Union, 2015).

Women entrepreneurs

The available evidence demonstrates that Australian women are under-represented as entrepreneurs, comprising about 40 percent of such activity (Steffens, *et al.*, 2012), and are only 32 percent of small business owners (ABS, 2013). Women have increased their early-stage entrepreneurial activity, that is, starting or running a business fewer than three-and-a-half years old, but to a lesser extent than men. In 2010 men and women were equal, at 8 percent (Kelley *et al.*, 2011). By 2014, women, at 10 percent, were a poor second to men's 16 percent (Singer *et al.*, 2015). In 2010 and 2011 Australia was ranked first and second, respectively, of 22 and 23 innovation-driven countries, respectively, for female early-stage entrepreneurial activity (Kelley *et al.*, 2012), but by 2014 had dropped to third position of 29 innovation-driven countries (Singer *et al.*, 2015).

The low proportion of female entrepreneurs and small business owners in Australia cannot be attributed to Australia's financial system, with evidence indicating that women entrepreneurs and female small and medium enterprise (SME) owners are not discouraged from applying for finance, do not have a higher rejection rate, and are not discriminated against by financial institutions or sources of business finance (Van Hulten, 2012; Watson *et al.*, 2009)—although they may have lower growth aspirations and risk-taking propensity than their male counterparts, affecting the number of women taking on these roles.

Despite their fewer numbers, and irrespective of their lower business profit, investments in assets and annual salaries, female SME owners in Australia report higher levels of perceived success and attainment of their desired lifestyle than their male counterparts (Weber and Geneste, 2014). They also report shorter work hours and make a similar return on assets to their male counterparts and a comparable hourly pay rate (Weber and Geneste, 2014).

Gender pay gap

Although equal pay for women has been law for 40 years in Australia, women clearly do not receive salaries on a par with men, a situation that applies to most countries (Tharenou, 2013).

In 2014 in Australia, gender pay discrepancies reached their highest recorded levels, with the gap between male and female pay appearing unlikely to decrease (ABS, 2015f). Australian women who are full-time workers earned an average weekly income 22 percent lower than that of men, and 35 percent lower than employees in the workforce as a whole and not just fulltime (ABS, 2015f), the latter figure the same as that given by Wood in 2011. The gap begins with the first job, for example, graduates straight from university (Balasubramanian, 2014). At the graduate starting-salary level, Australian women in 2013 earned an average of 6 percent less than men—as they had in 2000 (Balasubramanian, 2014)—a figure 2 percent higher than in Wood's (2011) chapter.

Women in Australia earn less than men in every industry (ABS, 2015f) and occupation (ABS, 2014f), although some areas clearly have greater pay gaps than others. The largest by industry in 2014 were in financial and insurance services (a penalty of 30 percent for women); health care and social assistance (29 percent); rental, hiring and real estate services (29 percent); and professional, scientific and technical services (28 percent) (ABS, 2015f). The largest gender pay gaps by occupation were for technicians and trade workers (a 33 percent penalty); community and personal service workers (27 percent); and professionals (24 percent) (ABS, 2014f). The smallest gaps by industry were in public administration and safety (a 7 percent penalty); other services (8 percent); accommodation and food services (9 percent); and electricity, gas, water and waste services (9 percent) (ABS, 2015f). The smallest gaps by occupation were for sales workers (a 16 percent penalty); machinery operators and drivers (18 percent); and laborers (21 percent) (ABS, 2014f).

This discrepancy is more extreme for women managers (WGEA, 2015a, 2015b). High-level female management personnel (e.g. executives in charge of finance or operations) suffer a penalty of 28 percent (WGEA, 2015b). But when they are split by industry, women senior executives in administrative and support services receive an extraordinary 45 percent less remuneration; in arts and recreation services 35 percent; and in financial and insurance services 34 percent (WGEA, 2015b).

Research conducted around the world has found that the gender pay gap remains after gender differences in work and employee characteristics are taken into account (Tharenou, 2013). Compared with men, Australian women work in lower-paying industries (ABS, 2015f) and occupations (ABS, 2014f), are less likely to work full-time and in permanent jobs and have less continuous work experience (ABS, 2014d, 2015c), and are less likely to work in management positions (ABS, 2015e) and hold senior positions (APSC, 2014; WGEA, 2014). However, Australian research studies demonstrate that the gender pay gap remains even when many work and demographic factors (e.g. 14–18 factors) are controlled (e.g. Chzhen *et al.*, 2013; Coelli, 2014; Watson, 2010), especially for higher-paid workers (Bar n and Cobb-Clark, 2010). Scholars propose that the remaining 'unexplained' pay gap is due to direct and indirect gender discrimination (Tharenou, 2013; WGEA, 2015c).

Despite ongoing publicity about inequitable pay between Australian men and women, the gap is not shrinking, indeed from 1994 to 2014 it deteriorated only by 3 percent to 19 percent for the total workforce and to 22 percent for full-timers (ABS, 2015f), up half a percent from Wood (2011). In 2014, Australia had the eleventh largest gender pay gap of the 34 OECD (2015b) countries.

Country legislation

A number of pieces of legislation designed to improve women's advancement have recently been enacted by the Australian Parliament. Earlier federal acts to reduce discrimination included the Sex Discrimination Act 1984 and Affirmative Action (Equal Opportunity for Women) Act 1986. A lack of progress in this area saw the latter replaced by the Equal Opportunity for Women in the Workplace Act 1999. This was subsequently replaced by the Workplace Gender Equality Act 2012. The Act says that its aim is to promote gender equality in employment and the workplace; remove barriers to full and equal participation by women in the workforce; eliminate gender discrimination in employment; encourage discussion between employers and employees on gender equality in employment and the workplace; and improve the productivity and competitiveness of Australian business by achieving gender equality in employment and the workplace.

To address the barrier presented by childcare requirements, in 2011 the Australian government introduced government-funded parental leave for all Australian organizations. (Paid maternity leave was already available in the public sector through the Maternity Leave [Australian Government Employees] Act 1973.) Until 1990, Australia had been only one of four developed countries in the world without a paid maternity leave scheme (OECD, 2015c), supporting an unpaid scheme only since 1979 (Federated Miscellaneous Workers Union of Australia v ACT Employers Federation [1979] 218 CAR 2012 [Maternity Leave Test Case]). The Paid Parental Leave Act 2010 established a scheme for eligible parents and included parental leave pay. The Act provides financial support (a maximum of 18 weeks payment at the national minimum wage level) to primary caregivers of newborn and newly adopted children, regardless of whether they receive employer-paid parental leave. From July 2016, the scheme will only top up employer payments rather than provide an additional payment (Ireland and Wade, 2015). In 2013 Australia was ranked eight of 25 countries for the length of maternity leave offered and, like 11 others, covered 100 percent of pay (Terjesen *et al.*, 2015).

Nevertheless, work–family reforms have been criticized for failing to confront gender cultures in workplaces, households and social life that maintain gender inequality (e.g. Pocock *et al.*, 2013). With the objective of addressing these criticisms, the Fair Work Amendment Act 2013 extended the right to request flexible work arrangements to a wider range of employees, also requiring employers to consult with employees about family and/or caring responsibilities before making changes to rosters or hours of work.

Company initiatives to support the advancement of qualified women

The lack of progress in advancing Australian women in management, especially in the private sector, has prompted the recent introduction of several initiatives to improve gender equity in the workplace by company associations. In 2010, the ASX Corporate Governance Council (ASXCGC) amended its Corporate Governance Principles and Recommendations for companies listed on the Australian Stock Exchange to include gender diversity issues (ASXCGC, 2010). The associated guidelines suggested that listed companies should establish and disclose a diversity policy that includes setting measurable goals for improving gender diversity; disclosing goals and progress in achieving them; and disclosing the proportion of women in the organization at different levels (total, senior executive, board).

From 2010 to 2015, the Australian Institute of Company Directors (AICD) implemented several institute-specific initiatives (e.g. Chair's Mentoring Program, several Diversity Scholarship programs) and in 2015 proposed a number of measures to member companies (e.g. a target of 30 percent women on boards as directors, regular reports on progress) to improve the representation of female board directors in ASX200 companies by 2018, as well as in smaller and non-listed companies, although with no set time limit (AICD, 2015b). Since the introduction of the mentoring and scholarship programs in 2010 (as well as the diversity policy), the proportion of female board directors in ASX200 companies has increased from 8 to 20 percent (AICD, 2015a).

A number of Australian companies have responded to these initiatives by setting targets for gender diversity and increased women's representation in their management structures. By way of example, several measures have been implemented by the National Australia Bank (NAB) since 2011 to improve the representation of women in senior leadership roles. These include the Realise program, Board Ready program, the Women's Agenda Leadership Award from 2012 onwards, Group Diversity and Inclusion Policy, all of which establish measurable objectives for women in senior levels of management, flexible work arrangements and equal remuneration for men and women (NAB, 2015). The introduction of these initiatives saw female representation on NAB Group subsidiary boards increase from 14 to 32 percent by 2014 (NAB, 2014).

A further example is the electricity company Origin, which has also implemented several measures to improve the representation of women in senior leadership roles. The measures include a Diversity and Inclusion Policy that applies to all aspects of employment: flexible work arrangements; a paid parental leave scheme; the Working Parents program; and 'unconscious' bias training for recruiting and senior managers (Origin Energy Limited, 2015). In addition, Origin aims to have at least one woman on the selection panel and shortlist for all senior roles (Origin Energy Limited, 2015). Indicating some success, in 2014, 88 percent of selection panels and 30 percent of shortlists for senior roles included at least one woman (Origin Energy Limited, 2015). Indicating a successful increase in the proportion of women in management, the rate of appointment of women to senior roles increased by 33 percent and the turnover rate among women in senior roles decreased by 26 percent (Origin Energy Limited, 2015).

Progress in bridging the gender equality gap has been patchy, with several evaluations conducted since 2010 indicating that Australian organizations generally perform poorly on gender equality. KPMG (2014) found that in 2013 most companies listed in the ASX had complied with the requirement to establish a diversity policy (98 percent ASX200, 85 percent ASX201–500, 66 percent ASX501+), but a significant number outside the top 200 had not set measurable objectives in their annual reports for achieving gender diversity (86 percent ASX200, 56 percent ASX201–500, 53 percent ASX501+). Moreover, fewer ASX201–500 and ASX500+ companies had disclosed details on gender diversity than the top 200 companies (92 percent ASX200, 37 percent ASX201–500, 69 percent ASX501+). The compliance rate was clearly lower for companies outside the top 200 ASX companies.

A report by the Australian Government's Workplace Gender Equality Agency evaluating compliance by Australian companies with the Workplace Gender Equality Act in 2013–2014 revealed extensive problems (WGEA, 2014). The majority of employers who reported (4456 nonpublic sector employers with 100+ employees) had no policies in place to address key issues for women in the workplace, such as flexible working arrangements (52 percent), family and caring responsibilities (55 percent) and to boost paid parental leave to above that of the government scheme (51 percent) (WGEA, 2014).

Other evaluations suggest that recent private sector initiatives have not necessarily improved the participation and advancement of women in the workforce in Australia. The aim of the Women on Boards Traffic Light Index is to review how well ASX200 companies perform on gender equality issues in the workforce, including in relation to the Principles and Recommendations developed by ASXCGC (Women on Boards, 2013). The index assigns companies to one of three categories: red (shows little or no compliance with basic gender diversity principles), amber (needs to improve on gender diversity principles) and green (has truly embedded gender diversity principles). In 2013, 16 percent of companies were rated "red", a high 76 percent were rated "amber", and only 8 percent were rated "green" (Women on Boards, 2013). The banking sector outperformed all other sectors; 67 percent of banks rated "green," followed by 33 percent of food and staples companies. ASX100 companies rated better than ASX100–200 companies.

The future

Australian women have experienced some improvements in the workplace: they are better educated now and in general exceed men. Paid maternity leave provisions have prevailed in the private sector since 2011 to assist with labor force participation, and leave entitlements have increased. Legislation to create gender equality in the workplace has been replaced and strengthened.

Despite these improvements, women's advancement into management, especially in the private sector, has changed little since Wood's (2011) analysis, nor over the last 20 years. The exceptions are the increased proportion of women on boards (linked to the setting of targets by company associations) and the increased proportion of women pre-selected for the Australian Parliament (linked to the setting of quotas by the ALP). Australian women begin their careers as half of the total population and 45 percent of the working population (ABS, 2015b, 2015c) and they become 52–53 percent of professionals (ABS, 2015e; WGEA, 2014, 2015a). Sadly, as they move into management positions, their participation rates fall such that they constitute, on average, a mere third of managers (ABS, 2015e), further reducing to about

12–20 percent of executives (ABS, 2015a), and ultimately becoming a small 4 to 17 percent of CEOs (ABS, 2015a; WGEA, 2014). Recent times have seen women as a fifth of board directors (AICD, 2015a), but rarely do they become chairs (Gladman and Lamb, 2013). Women are almost invariably paid less for comparable work, a situation that deteriorates if they rise in the managerial hierarchy.

The current rate of progress clearly implies that gender equality in Australia will not be achieved any time soon—if ever. More effective regulatory change is one approach that has been suggested for dealing with this issue (Klettner *et al.*, 2014). There have been changes, such as setting gender diversity targets, which are currently voluntary and have been espoused and encouraged by some associations in Australia to produce good results in their individual member companies (e.g. increasing women's representation on boards) (AICD, 2015a). Another option is regulatory changes through the introduction of mandatory gender quotas, which have achieved effective and rapid results abroad, for example, in Norway, France and Spain (e.g. Klettner *et al.*, 2014; Wang and Kelan, 2013). Perhaps not surprisingly, 33 Australian top CEOs (31 men) are opposed to quotas but in favor of targets (Boyd and Smith, 2015). Irrespective of whether targets or quotas are used, regulatory approaches are needed for Australian women to achieve gender equality in management and the professions.

References

ABS (Australian Bureau of Statistics) (1993), *The Labour Force Australia,* Catalogue No. 6203.0, Canberra, Australia: Australian Government Publishing Service.

ABS (2011a), *Labour Force, Australia, February 2011*, Catalogue No. 6202.0, Canberra, Australia: Australian Government Publishing Service.

ABS (2011b), *Census of Population and Housing*, Catalogue No. 2068.0, Canberra, Australia: Australian Government Publishing Service.

ABS (2012), *Census of Population and Housing: Characteristics of Aboriginal and Torres Strait Islander Australians, 2011,* Catalogue No. 2076.0, Canberra, Australia: Australian Government Publishing Service.

ABS (2013), *Counts of Australian Business Operators, 2011 to 2012*, Catalogue No. 8175.0, Canberra, Australia: Australian Government Publishing Service.

ABS (2014a), *Education and Work, Australia, May 2014*, Catalogue No. 6227.0, Canberra, Australia: Australian Government Publishing Service.

ABS (2014b), *Australian Aboriginal and Torres Strait Islander Health Survey: Updated Results, 2012–2013*, Catalogue No. 4727.0.55.006, Canberra, Australia: Australian Government Publishing Service.

ABS (2014c), *Labour Force, Australia, April 2014*, Catalogue No. 6202.0, Canberra, Australia: Australian Government Publishing Service.

ABS (2014d), *Australian Labour Market Statistics, July 2014*, Catalogue No. 6105.0, Canberra, Australia: Australian Government Publishing Service.

ABS (2014e), *Labour Force, Australia, Detailed – Electronic Delivery, April 2014*, Catalogue No. 6291.0.55.001, Canberra, Australia: Australian Government Publishing Service.

ABS (2014f), *Employee Earnings, Benefits and Trade Union Membership, Australia, August 2013*, Catalogue No. 6310.0, Canberra, Australia: Australian Government Publishing Service.

ABS (2015a), *Gender Indicators, Australia, February 2015*, Catalogue No. 4125.0, Canberra, Australia: Australian Government Publishing Service.

ABS (2015b), *Australian Demographic Statistics, September 2014*, Catalogue No. 3101.0, Canberra, Australia: Australian Government Publishing Service.

ABS (2015c), *Labour Force, Australia, February 2015*, Catalogue No. 6202.0, Canberra, Australia: Australian Government Publishing Service.

ABS (2015d), *Labour Force, Australia, Detailed – Electronic Delivery, May 2015*, Catalogue No. 6291.0.55.001, Canberra, Australia: Australian Government Publishing Service.

ABS (2015e), *Labour Force, Australia, Detailed, Quarterly, February 2015*, Catalogue No. 6291.0.55.003, Canberra, Australia: Australian Government Publishing Service.

ABS (2015f), *Average Weekly Earnings, Australia, November 2014*, Catalogue No. 6302.0, Canberra, Australia: Australian Government Publishing Service.

AICD (Australian Institute of Company Directors) (2015a), 'Statistics', available at www.companydi-rectors.com.au/Director-Resource-Centre/Governance-and-Director-Issues/Board-Diversity/Statis tics (accessed 17 June 2015).

AICD (2015b), 'Boards should adopt 30 percent target for female directors', Press Release, 9 April 2015.

Ali, M., Y. L. Ng and C. T. Kulik (2014), 'Board age and gender diversity: a test of competing linear and curvilinear predictions', *Journal of Business Ethics*, **125** (3), 497–512.

Allen, Phillip and Jayashri Ravishankar (2015), 'A sustainable approach to attracting, retaining and supporting women in undergraduate electrical engineering', in *Proceedings of IEEE International Conference on Teaching, Assessment and Learning for Engineering: Learning for the Future Now, TALE 2014*, pp. 359–364.

APSC (Australian Public Service Commission) (2005), *State of the Service Report 2004–05: State of the Service Series 2004–05*, Canberra, Australia: Commonwealth of Australia.

APSC (2014), *Australian Public Service Statistical Bulletin: State of the Service Series 2013–14*, Canberra, Australia: Commonwealth of Australia.

ASXCGC (Australian Securities Exchange Corporate Governance Council) (2010), *Corporate Govern-ance Principles and Recommendations with 2010 Amendments* (2nd ed.), Sydney, Australia: Australian Securities Exchange.

Australian Businesswomen's Network (2015), 'About us', available at www.abn.org.au/baout-us/ (accessed 27 October 2015).

Balasubramanian, Bharat (2014), *Graduate Salaries 2013*, Melbourne, Australia: Graduate Careers Australia.

Bar n, J. D. and D. A. Cobb-Clark (2010), 'Occupational segregation and the gender wage gap in private- and public-sector employment: a distributional analysis', *Economic Record*, **86** (273), 227–246.

Bekhouche, Yasmina, Ricardo Hausmann, Laura D. Tyson and Saadia Zahidi (2014), *The Global Gender Gap Report 2014*, Geneva, Switzerland: World Economic Forum.

Bekhouche, Yasmina, Ricardo Hausmann, Laura D. Tyson and Saadia Zahidi (2015), *The Global Gender Gap Report 2015*, Geneva, Switzerland: World Economic Forum.

Borland, Jeff (2011), 'The Australian labour market in the 2000s: the quiet decade', in Hugo Gerard and Jonathan Kearns (eds), *The Australian Economy in the 2000s: Proceedings of a Conference Held in Sydney on 15–16 August 2011*, Sydney, Australia: Reserve Bank of Australia, pp. 165–218.

Boyd, T. and M. Smith (2015), 'What our top CEOs expect in 2015', *Australian Financial Review*, 6 January 2015.

Catalyst (2015), *2014 Catalyst Census: Women Board Directors*, New York, NY, USA: Catalyst.

Chzhen, Y., K. Mumford and C. Nicodemo (2013), 'The gender pay gap in the Australian private sector: is selection relevant across the earnings distribution?', *Economic Record*, **89** (286), 367–381.

Coelli, M. B. (2014), 'Occupational differences and the Australian gender wage gap', *The Australian Economic Review*, **47** (1), 44–62.

Curtin Business School (2015), 'Women in MBA scholarships now available', Press Release, 7 October 2015.

Daley, John and Cassie McGannon (2014), *Submission to the Productivity Commission: Inquiry on Childcare and Early Childhood Learning*, Carlton, Australia: Grattan Institute.

Engineers Australia (2015), 'Women in Engineering', available at www.engineersaustralia.org.au/ women-engineering (accessed 6 November 2015).

EOWA (Equal Opportunity for Women in the Workplace Agency) (2012), *2012 Australian Census of Women in Leadership*, Sydney, Australia: Commonwealth of Australia.

Galbreath, J. (2011), 'Are there gender-related influences on corporate sustainability? A study of women on boards of directors', *Journal of Management & Organisation*, **17** (1), 17–38.

Gladman, Kimberly and Michelle Lamb (2013), *GMI Ratings' 2013 Women on Boards Survey*, GMI Ratings.

Grant Thornton (2013), *Women in Senior Management: Setting the Stage for Growth*, Grant Thornton.

Hausmann, Ricardo, Laura D. Tyson and Saadia Zahidi (2006), *The Global Gender Gap Report 2006*, Geneva, Switzerland: World Economic Forum.

Hausmann, Ricardo, Laura D. Tyson and Saadia Zahidi (2009), *The Global Gender Gap Report 2009*, Geneva, Switzerland: World Economic Forum.

Heady, Bruce, John Freebairn and Diana Warren (2010), *Dynamics of Mature Age Workforce Participation: Policy Effects and Continuing Trends*, Melbourne, Australia: Melbourne Institute of Applied Economic and Social Research.

ILO (International Labour Organization) (2015a), *Women in Business and Management: Gaining Momentum*, Geneva, Switzerland: International Labour Organization.

ILO (2015b), 'Statistics and databases', available at www.ilo.org/global/statistics-and-databases/lang—en/index.htm (accessed 8 October 2015).

Inter-Parliamentary Union (2015), 'Women in National Parliaments statistical archive', available at www.ipu.org/wmn-e/classif-arc.htm (accessed 7 April 2015).

Ireland, J. and M. Wade (2015), 'Federal budget 2015: almost 50 percent of mums to lose government paid parental leave entitlements', *The Sydney Morning Herald*, 11 May 2015.

Kelley, Donna J., Niels Bosma and José Ernesto Amor s (2011), *Global Entrepreneurship Monitor 2010 Global Report*, London, UK: Global Entrepreneurship Research Association.

Kelley, Donna J., Slavica Singer and Mike Herrington (2012), *Global Entrepreneurship Monitor 2011 Global Report*, London, UK: Global Entrepreneurship Research Association.

Klettner, A., T. Clarke and M. Boersma (2014), 'Strategic and regulatory approaches to increasing women in leadership: multilevel targets and mandatory quotas as levers for cultural change', *Journal of Business Ethics*, 1–25. doi: 10.1007/s10551-014-2083-1.

KPMG (2014), *ASX Corporate Governance Council Principles and Recommendations on Diversity: Analysis of Disclosures for Financial Years Ended between 31 December 2012 and 30 December 2013*, Australia: KPMG.

Legislative Assembly of the Australian Capital Territory (2015), 'Current members', available at www.parliament.act.gov.au/members/current (accessed 27 July 2015).

Legislative Assembly of the Northern Territory (2015), 'Members by name', available at http://notes.nt.gov.au/lant/members/Members1.nsf/Members/By%20Name?OpenView&Start=1&Count=300&Collapse=18#18 (accessed 27 July 2015).

Loughnane, Brian (2010), *Liberal Party of Australia Federal Constitution*, Barton, Australia: Liberal Party of Australia.

Macquarie University Graduate School of Management (2015), 'Women in MBA program – partnering for leadership diversity', available at www.mgsm.edu.au/mba-and-graduate-programs/women-in-mbas-program/ (accessed 29 October 2015).

McCann, Joy and Janet Wilson (2014), *Representation of Women in Australian Parliaments 2014*, Canberra, Australia: Commonwealth of Australia.

McDonald, Jacquie, Birgit Loch and Aileen Cater-Steel (2010), 'Go WEST – supporting women in engineering, science and technology: an Australian higher education case study', in Aileen Cater-Steel and Emily Cater (eds), *Women in Engineering, Science and Technology: Education and Career Challenges*, Hershey, PA, USA: Engineering Science References, pp. 118–132.

Melbourne Business School (2015), 'Women at MBS', available at https://mbs.edu/about-us/women-at-mbs (accessed 27 October 2015).

Mitchell, Scott (2013), *National Party of Australia Federal Constitution*, Barton, Australia: National Party of Australia.

Monash Business School (2015), 'Business school brings Women in MBA program to Melbourne', Press Release, 12 August 2015.

NAB (National Australia Bank) (2014), *Dig Deeper 2014*, Melbourne, Australia: National Australia Bank.

NAB (2015), 'Corporate governance', available at www. nab.com.au/about-us/our-business/corporate-governance (accessed 22 April 2015).

OECD (Organization for Economic Co-operation and Development) (2011), *Education at a Glance 2011: OECD Indicators*, Paris, France: OECD Publishing.

OECD (2015a), 'OECD.Stat', available at http://stats.oecd.org/ (accessed 22 July 2015).

OECD (2015b), 'Gender wage gap', www.oecd.org/gender/data/genderwagegap.htm (accessed 7 April 2015).

OECD (2015c), 'OECD family database', available at www.oecd.org/social/family/database.htm (accessed 8 October 2015).

Origin Energy Limited (2015), 'Achieving gender diversity', available at https://originenergy.com.au/sustainability/material-aspects/achieving-gender-diversity (accessed 27 October 2015).

Parliament of New South Wales (2015), 'Browse members from both houses (by surname)', available at www.parliament.nsw.gov.au/prod/parlment/members.nsf/V3ListCurrentMembers (accessed 17 July 2015).

Parliament of Queensland (2015), 'Current members', available at www. parliament.qld.gov.au/members/current/list (accessed 27 July 2015).

Parliament of South Australia (2015), 'List of members', available at www.parliament.sa.gov.au/Members/Pages/List%20of %20All%20Members.aspx (accessed 17 July 2015).

Parliamentary Library (2014), *44th Parliament: Parliamentary Handbook of the Commonwealth of Australia 2014*, Canberra, Australia: Commonwealth of Australia.

Pocock, B., S. Charlesworth and J. Chapman (2013), 'Work–family and work–life pressures in Australia: advancing gender equality in "good times"?', *International Journal of Sociology and Social Policy*, **33** (9/10), 594–612.

Rodgers, S. (2015), 'Real equity "still hundreds of years away"', *The Australian,* 15 June 2015.

Singer, Slavica, José Ernesto Amor S. and Daniel Moska (2015), *Global Entrepreneurship Monitor 2014 Global Report*, London, UK: Global Entrepreneurship Research Association.

Smith, Tony (2010), *Candidate Gender in the 2010 Australian Federal Election*, Democratic Audit Discussion Paper 1/10, Melbourne, Australia: Democratic Audit of Australia.

Steffens, Paul, Michael Stuetzer, Per Davidsson and Neil James (2012), *Global Entrepreneurship Monitor National Entrepreneurial Assessment for Australia*, Brisbane, Australia: Australian Centre for Entrepreneurship Research.

Terjesen, S., R.V. Aguilera and R. Lorenz (2015), 'Legislating a woman's seat on the board: institutional factors driving gender quotas for boards of directors', *Journal of Business Ethics*, **128** (2), 233–251.

Tharenou, P. (2013), 'The work of feminists is not yet done: the gender pay gap a stubborn anachronism', *Sex Roles*, **68** (3), 198–206.

University of South Australia Business School (2015), 'UniSA joins other top business schools to boost female MBAs', Press Release, 11 August 2015.

University of Sydney Business School (2015), 'Business school leads Australia and the world in MBA gender balance', Press Release, 6 July 2015.

University of Wollongong (2015), 'Business school tackles gender imbalance in MBA study', Press Release, 10 August 2015.

Van Hulten, A. (2012), 'Women's access to SME finance in Australia', *International Journal of Gender and Entrepreneurship*, **4** (3), 266–288.

Wang, M. and E. Kelan (2013), 'The gender quota and female leadership: effects of Norwegian gender quota on board chairs and CEOs', *Journal of Business Ethics*, **117**, 449–466.

Watson, I. (2010), 'Decomposing the gender pay gap in the Australian managerial labour market', *Australian Journal of Labour Economics*, **13** (1), 49–79.

Watson, J., R. Newby and A. Mahuka (2009), 'Gender and the SME "finance gap"', *International Journal of Gender and Entrepreneurship*, **1** (1), 42–56.

Weber, P. C. and L. Geneste (2014), 'Exploring gender-related perceptions of SME success', *International Journal of Gender and Entrepreneurship*, **6** (1), 15–27.

WGEA (Workplace Gender Equality Agency) (2014), *Australia's Gender Equality Scorecard*, Sydney, Australia: Commonwealth of Australia.

WGEA (2015a), *Australia's Gender Equality Scorecard*, Sydney, Australia: Commonwealth of Australia.

WGEA (2015b), *Gender Composition of the Workforce: by Occupation*, Sydney, Australia: Commonwealth of Australia.

WGEA (2015c), *Gender Pay Gap Statistics*, Sydney, Australia: Commonwealth of Australia.

WGEA (2015d), *2014–15 Public Report Form Submitted by University of South Australia to the Workplace Gender Equality Agency*, Sydney, Australia: Commonwealth of Australia.

Wilkins, R. and M. Wooden (2014), 'Two decades of change: the Australian labour market, 1993–2013', *The Australian Economic Review*, **47** (4), 417–431.

Women on Boards (2013), 'WOB 2013 Traffic Light Index', available at www.women on boards.org.au/pubs/traffic-light/2013-traffic-lights/index.htm (accessed 22 April 2015).

Women on Boards (2015), 'About Women on Boards', available at www.womenonboards.org.au/about/social.htm (accessed 27 October 2015).

Wood, Glenice J. (2011), 'Women in management in Australia', in Marilyn J. Davidson and Ronald J. Burke (eds), *Women in Management Worldwide: Progress and Prospects* (2nd ed.), Farnham, UK and Burlington, VT, USA: Gower Publishing, pp. 225–245.

Wright, George (2011), *National Platform*, Barton, Australia: Australian Labor Party.

PART V

Women in management

Asia

13 Women in management in China

Fang Lee Cooke

Introduction

Despite the promotion of Chairman Mao's famous motto: 'women hold up half of the sky' as an egalitarian socialist ideology since the 1950s, and despite their high level of labor market participation, there remains a low proportion of women in political leadership and managerial positions in China. More precisely, in 2013 women made up just over 23.4 percent of all representatives to the National People's Congress of China (the highest state body and the only legislative house in the country) (NBSC, 2014). By 2007, only 17 percent of those in local government leadership positions were women (Nie, 2009). Only 1.2 percent of women worked as heads of organizations in 2013, compared with 3.1 percent of men who did so (NBSC, 2014). Only 2.6 percent of women were employers compared to 5.2 percent of men in the same category in 2013 (NBSC, 2014). This chapter analyzes the political, social, cultural and organizational barriers to women's advancement in their managerial careers against a context of high levels of education and labor market participation of women close to that of men.

Background of the country

As of 2013, China had a population of over 1.36 billion people, 48.68 percent of whom were women and 46.20 percent were rural residents (NBSC, 2014). The Chinese are a relatively homogenous population in terms of ethnicity. The *han* ethnic group makes up over 91 percent of the population, whereas the other 55 ethnic minority groups consist of less than 9 percent of the population (NBSC, 2014). Religion is not commonly practiced in part due to the continuous, albeit gradually relaxing, suppression of non-communist beliefs by the state (e.g. Gries and Rosen, 2004; Perry and Selden, 2011).

Since the founding of socialist China in 1949, significant progress has been made in achieving gender equality in education, employment, wage payment and social security provisions. This was mainly an outcome of strong state intervention. There has been a rising proportion of women participating in higher education and entering professional and managerial jobs at all levels in the last two decades (see below). Despite this progress, discrimination against women in recruitment is worsening, in part due to marketization and the rising level of unemployment amongst university graduates. Once recruited, women face formidable barriers to career advancement. This is particularly the case in government and civil service organizations where the macro-political processes continue to exert salient and often decisive influences (Zhao and Zhou, 2004) and individual performance may be more difficult to be measured as hard evidence for promotion.

Women's education level

In line with the world trend, Chinese women's education level has been rising steadily in the past three decades, with increases at the tertiary education level being more dramatic than that in primary and secondary education. According to the World Bank (2011), in 2009, females made up 48 percent of the students in secondary schools and 25.4 percent of women were enrolled in tertiary education compared with 23.8 percent of men of the same age group. However, it will take several more years for the educational attainment level of the female workforce as a whole to catch up with that of the male workforce because of the more significant gaps between the two amongst the older workforce. For example, in 2013, 46.1 percent of the women workforce, compared to 49.5 percent of male, had a secondary school level of education. Over 14.4 percent of the male workforce, compared to 13.8 percent of the female workforce, held a college or university degree qualification (NBSC, 2014).

A major problem encountered by women graduates is obtaining employment. The rapid expansion of the Chinese higher education sector since the early 2000s has led to a rising level of unemployment amongst university graduates (e.g. *Economist*, 2009). For example, the number of university graduates had grown from 2.12 million in 2003 to 4.95 million in 2007, 6.31 million in 2010, 6.99 million in 2013 and over 7 million in 2014 (China Education Online, 2014). Increasingly, employers only hire job candidates who have at least two years of work experience. Costs of training and retention problems are the main reasons for employers' unwillingness to employ university graduates without work experience (Cooke, 2009). While discrimination against women graduates in recruitment has long existed (Cooke, 2005), this problem has been exacerbated by the dramatic increase of university graduates since the early 2000s. A survey showed that 21 percent of female graduates, compared with 29.5 percent of male graduates, had signed employment contracts in 2011. Thirteen percent fewer women than men signed contracts with state-owned enterprises. Women graduates are also earning less than their male counterparts (Wu, 2011).

Women's employment patterns

In spite of the increasing difficulty for women graduates to find gainful employment, China has one of the highest women's labor market participation rates in the world that is characterized by full-time employment. In 2013, nearly 35 percent of the full-time workforce in urban units were women (see Table 13.1). The majority of working women work full time throughout most of their working lives, including those with childcare responsibilities. There are several related reasons for Chinese women's high participation rate in the labor market. One is that participation in employment is seen as an important indicator of women's liberation and independence by the state. Another reason is that the socialist state's economic policy that favoured full employment with low wages and low inflation, particularly during the state-planned economy period (1949–1978), necessitates dual wages to support a family (Cooke, 2005). The accessibility to extended family support networks and low-cost childcare services enable dual full-time working amongst couples with young children. The one-child policy enforced by the government since the early 1980s to control population growth has further reduced the amount of childcare required by working couples. A third reason is that most working women are in full-time employment because there are no established arrangements for part-time work in China to accommodate working mothers (Cooke, 2012).

It is worth noting that women's employment rate has been experiencing a small but steady decline since the 1990s. In 2000, women consisted of 38.0 percent of the national workforce

Table 13.1 Proportion (%) of female employment by ownership and sector in urban units and annual average wage for all employees in urban units (yuan)

Item	Total		State ownership		Collective ownership		Other ownership			
	2000	2013	2000	2013	2000	2013	2000	2013	2000	2013
National total	38.0	35.0	36.4	38.8	40.4	31.6	42.4	33.0	9,371	51,483
Farming, forestry, animal husbandry, fishery	37.9	36.9	38.2	37.0	27.7	26.7	34.9	36.2	5,184	25,820
Mining and quarrying	26.1	17.6	25.4	19.3	36.3	17.1	25.6	17.2	8,340	60,138
Manufacturing	43.2	39.4	38.6	26.7	48.9	40.2	45.8	40.0	8,750	46,431
Electricity, gas and water production and supply	32.1	27.1	32.3	27.4	31.9	29.9	30.9	26.8	12,830	67,085
Construction	18.5	10.1	20.3	12.4	17.5	11.8	14.4	9.7	8,735	42,072
Traffic, transport, storage and post	28.4	25.9	27.8	26.2	31.0	23.1	31.5	25.7	12,319	57,993
Wholesale and retail and hotel and catering*	45.7	50.1	43.6	35.3	45.5	40.2	52.5	52.8	7,190	50,308
		55.5		52.6		62.7		55.7		34,044
Finance	43.2	50.6	42.2	48.7	42.2	43.0	52.6	52.6	13,478	99,653
Real estate resident (community) services	34.1	35.9	34.6	35.9	33.9	35.3	33.0	35.9	12,616	51,048
and other services	—	40.5		33.7		39.4		44.1	—	38,429
Social welfare**	41.6	53.5	44.4	52.3	24.3	59.9	51.3	62.2	9,675	44,677
Healthcare**	58.2	61.8	59.0	62.1	52.0	56.7	59.3	63.6	10,843	58,355
Education**	44.4	52.0	44.4	51.6	45.8	58.6	45.8	57.3	9,069	51,950
Culture and art**	41.9	47.0	41.7	47.1	42.0	46.0	43.0	46.0	12,018	47,480
Governmental and party agencies, social organizations	24.4	29.7	24.3	29.7	42.7	37.5	43.0	35.8	9,978	50,528

Source: Compiled from NBSC (2001, 2014)

Notes: * Figures in 1995 were combined as one entry "Wholesale, Retail and Catering," but separated in 2007 as entries under "Wholesale and Retail" and "Hotel and Catering."

** Wage figures for the social welfare and healthcare sectors were in the same combined category in 1995 but separated in 2007. Wage figures for the education and culture and art sectors were in the same combined category in 1995 but separated in 2008. Figures contained in this table include only urban workers and not rural migrant workers working in the urban units. Gender statistics on rural migrant workers working in urban industries are not available. However, it is known that the majority of workers in the construction industry are male rural migrant workers, whereas the majority of workers in the catering industry tend to be female rural migrant workers. Also, women are specified by law to retire five years earlier than men of the same occupation. This partly accounts for their lower proportion in the total workforce in employment in the urban sector. This was reduced to 35.0 percent by the end of 2013 (NBSC, 2014). A key contributing factor to this reduction is the large-scale downsizing in the state-owned and collectively-owned enterprises since the mid-1990s where women had been disproportionately selected for redundancy (Cooke, 2005). Similar waves of downsizing also took place in recent years in the public sector and government organizations (Cooke, 2005), although the scale has been much smaller and with less damaging effect to women employees. For a number of reasons including age, education, skill portfolio and job preference, retrenched women workers tend to encounter more difficulties, and often discrimination, than men in regaining employment (Lu and Zhao, 2002; Cooke, 2005). As a result, an increasing proportion of women are engaged in informal employment with little job security, let alone career prospects.

Compared with countries where career interruptions and part-time employment are key features in women's labor market participation, particularly for those with family commitment (Stockman *et al.*, 1995; O'Reilly and Fagan, 1998; Rubery *et al.*, 1998; Cooke, 2010), gender segregation is relatively less pronounced in China. While women tend to be over-represented in certain industrial sectors such as education, healthcare, finance, wholesale, retail and catering (in part, because these jobs are traditionally seen to be more suitable for women), they are present in all sectors and occupations in a relatively even pattern (see Table 13.1). However, women tend to be under-represented in certain industrial sectors and types of organizations for very different reasons. For example, women are under-represented in the mining and construction industry due to the high risk and physically demanding nature of the jobs (employment law bans women from working in mines or in deep water). Similarly, women are under-represented in government and Communist Party organizations where power and control continues to be dominated by men (Cooke, 2009), as is the case in most countries. Government organizations are amongst those sectors that have the lowest proportion of women employees. The majority of women employed in government organizations are in administrative roles or work as officials in the lower ranks (Cooke, 2009). This is in spite of the fact that the education level of women is very close to that of men in this sector.

Women in management

A comprehensive set of statistics on women in management in China, including ethnic minority figures, is not available. But what is clear is that women continue to be under-represented in leadership and managerial positions, as indicated by a number of studies cited below. This is despite their significant advancement in educational attainments and a respectable inroad into professional and technical positions (see Table 13.2).

According to a recent study of women's careers in China (cited in Zhang, 2012), women made up less than 30 percent of the senior management in enterprises; in particular, women consisted of less than 10 percent of the senior management in large domestic corporate groups. The same study also revealed that the post-1980 generation of women are facing a tough choice of career or family commitment. In addition, they are encountering pressure of sexual harassment when dealing with clients/customers. According to the national statistics (cited in Shen and Xu, 2009), despite slight improvement from the statistics of 2003, women made up only 23 percent of the total civil servants, 10.3 percent of all government officials at or above the provincial level, and 11 percent of the government ministers in 2008. In addition, women made up 39.2 percent of the board of directors in enterprises in 2008, down from 46.8 percent in 2005.

Table 13.2 Occupational composition of urban employment by sex in China in 2013 (%)

Occupation category	Total	Male	Female
Total	100	100	100
Head of organization	2.3	3.1	1.2
Professional and technical personnel	9.9	8.9	11.2
Clerk and related workers	6.5	7.6	5.2
Commercial, business service personnel	20.7	18.7	23.1
Agriculture and water conservancy labor	36.1	30.9	42.5
Production, transport, equipment operators and related workers	24.2	30.4	16.5
Others	0.3	0.4	0.3

Source: Compiled from NBSC (2014)

To a small degree, differences in the education levels amongst the older workforce are accountable for the much smaller proportion of women than men in leadership positions, since the possession of a university degree qualification is the prerequisite for promotion in many organizations – in 2013, 14.9 percent of the male workforce held an undergraduate or postgraduate degree compared to 14.3 percent of the female workforce who did so (NBSC, 2014). However, Chinese patriarchal cultural values and gender discrimination at workplaces that reflects societal values are far more significant factors that have led to the low presence of women in management positions. Women are generally believed to be less likely than men to possess leadership qualities (e.g. Bowen *et al.*, 2007; Nie, 2009; Hu, 2012). The conventional family norm is for the husband to deal with external matters and the wife to look after home life. The husband's career also takes precedence, even though most couples are dual earners with similar educational backgrounds between husband and wife. It is not expected, or in some cases tolerated by the husband or his family, that a wife should be more advanced in her career than her husband (Cooke and Xiao, 2014).

If the dominance of the state sector and the direct intervention from the state during the state-planned economy period had led to significant achievements in gender equality at workplaces in the urban area (Liu *et al.*, 2000), then these achievements have arguably been eroded since the 1980s. As a result of the marketization, employers are granted greater autonomy in operating their businesses and human resource management (HRM) practices (Zhou, 2000). Discriminative practices widely exist in recruitment, job allocation, training, promotion, redundancy and retirement (Cooke, 2012). Organizations that violate equal opportunity regulations either deliberately or due to ignorance are rarely held accountable. Few organizations have an equal opportunity policy and/or a career development policy in place as part of their HRM policy. Where a clear career development and promotion policy is absent or ineffectively implemented, employees may have to rely more on the informal organizational career structure and networks outside the organization to advance their careers (Cooke, 2009). This presents additional barriers to women due to the patriarchal structure and gender norm.

Career advancement for women in government organizations is particularly difficult where promotion criteria may be more elastic and promotion processes less transparent, despite the existence of a standard set of promotion criteria and procedures nationwide (Cooke, 2009). In order to increase the number of women in leadership positions in government organizations, the government introduced an affirmative action policy in the early 2000s which specifies that there must be at least one woman in each management team at each level (Cooke, 2009). This does not mean that women will be lifted into the leadership position regardless of their competence. Rather, it creates a small opening for women in politics to advance their career through competition. Local government organizations typically implement the policy by the letter instead of in good spirit. In other words, women may be promoted to their leadership position for their symbolic value to fulfill the quotas imposed by the state (Tsang *et al.*, 2011). It is common that only one woman is appointed in the management team, who is usually put in the deputy position. Even when women have managed to gain the same official rank as their male counterparts, they are often placed in less lucrative departments with less organizational resources allocated to the posts. This further handicaps women's ability to network to obtain political and social capital within and outside the organization needed to perform their tasks and to gain further promotions (Cooke, 2009).

Bu and Roy's (2005) study of senior and middle managers in China that compared the composition and social exchange practices of Chinese male and female managers' career success networks (CSNs) found that most of the CSN ties formed by both male and female managers are with men, especially power ties. Bu and Roy's (2008, p. 1088) study further revealed that whilst Chinese male and female managers generally prefer to form CSN ties with individuals who are older than themselves, 'they are relatively more reluctant to include middle-aged or elder women in their CSN'. Gao's (2015) study of female school headteachers found that personal quality and competence, and support from superiors and subordinates were the most important factors in leadership development.

According to the Third National Survey of Women's Social Positions in China conducted in 2010, the level of party membership and the level of participation in decision-making and in management from women have increased since the previous study in 2000. However, survey respondents felt that gender discrimination in career progression persisted, and burdens of housework (67.5 percent), poor training and development and selection (60.5 percent) and social prejudice against women (57.6 percent) were attributed by the respondents to be the main reasons that accounted for the low level of women in leadership positions. Even for those in senior management positions, nearly 20 percent of them believed that gender was a barrier to their career advancement (Women's Studies Institute of China, undated).

Women entrepreneurs

The total number of women entrepreneurs in China is again unclear, due to the existence of different definitions and the lack of national statistics that are publicly available. Nevertheless, national survey statistics provide a snapshot of the demographic profile of Chinese women entrepreneurs. According to the 2006 survey on women entrepreneurs (cited in Shi, 2009), nearly 80 percent of women entrepreneurs registered their businesses after 1995. Their businesses were mainly in manufacturing (37.2 percent), wholesale/retailing trade and restaurants (28.2 percent) and social/community services (10.6 percent). In general, the education level of women entrepreneurs was higher than that of men entrepreneurs in that 32 percent and 15 percent of women entrepreneurs held college-level education qualifications and postgraduate degree qualifications respectively, compared to 28 percent and 10 percent of their male counterparts, respectively. The same proportion (26 percent) of male and female entrepreneurs held undergraduate degree qualifications.

The growth of women entrepreneurs can be attributed to a number of economic factors as a result of China's deepening economic reform. These include: government policy and financial support for entrepreneurship, the continuing growth of the private sector, particularly self-employed businesses; the continuing restructuring of China's industrial structure, with the resultant emergence of new service industries such as community work, tourism, healthcare and insurance; the accelerating rate of urbanization and the emerging development of the country's vast western region. For example, in 2000, 11 percent of the country's total workforce worked in private and self-employed businesses; this had increased to 28 percent in 2013. In 2000, 27.5 percent of the total workforce worked in the tertiary sector; this had increased to 38.5 percent in 2013 (NBSC, 2014).

Despite the increasing role of women's entrepreneurship in China's economic success, the development of women entrepreneurs is hampered by a number of factors similar to those encountered by women in political leadership and corporation leadership positions (e.g. Ouyang, 2006). In particular, role conflicts between being a good wife and mother on the one hand, and having a successful career on the other, is a key factor due to the competing demands for time and energy from both. Another key factor is the perceived negative public image of women entrepreneurs projected by the media. As Ouyang (2006) noted, media coverage about women entrepreneurs often focused on their hardship in setting up the business and the negative impact this had on their family life. The constant negative reporting of women entrepreneurship sends out a misleading signal about the huge opportunity cost of being a woman entrepreneur. This not only dampens women's enthusiasm to become entrepreneurs, but also affects the opportunity of them being accepted by society (also see below).

Legislation on gender equality

Since the founding of socialist China in 1949, Chinese governments have gradually established a regulative system that aims to promote gender equality and to protect women's rights and interests in their working, family and social lives (Cooke, 2005). This system consists of a series of legal and administrative regulations based on the Constitution of the People's Republic of China. In particular, several pieces of the legislation were introduced since the late 1980s when China underwent significant economic restructuring, resulting in large-scale downsizing in the state sector and the radical growth of the private sector. Major pieces of legislation passed include:[1]

*   Labor Insurance Regulations of the People's Republic of China (1953);
*   Announcement on Female Workers' Production Leave by the State Council (1955);
*   Female Employees Labor Protection Regulations (1988);
*   Regulations of Prohibited Types of Occupational Posts for Female Employees (1990);
*   The PRC Law on Protecting Women's Rights and Interests (1992);
*   The Labor Law of China (1994);
*   The Labor Contract Law (2007, amended in 2013);
*   The Promotion of Employment Law (2007);
*   The Social Security Law (2010).

In addition, China has agreed and signed up to a number of International Labor Conventions related to the protection of women and equal opportunities in employment, for example the UN Convention on the Elimination of All Forms of Discrimination Against Women; ILO Convention No. 45 concerning the Employment of Women on Underground Work in Mines of All Kinds (1935); and ILO Convention (1951) No. 100 concerning equal pay for men and women workers of equal value.

This framework of legislation is supported by a number of official policies for increasing the participation of women in employment. In drawing up the legislation and official policies, special attention was paid to protecting women both in finance and in working arrangements during pregnancy, maternity or while breast-feeding. The promulgation of the Program for the Development of Chinese Women (2001–2010) by the State Council also provided new goals, tasks and measures concerning women's development in the new century (ACWF, undated b).

Despite decades of equal opportunities legislation and administrative policies and more recently the introduction of affirmative action programs, women have not made significant inroads in political leadership and managerial careers. Two reasons explain why the impact of employment legislation on women's career advancement has been limited.

Firstly, the legal and constitutional recognition of gender equality was not followed by public campaigns for the furtherance of that equality in practice, especially in terms of career opportunities. In spite of the fact that labor laws clearly state that women should have equal employment rights and benefits with men in terms of pay and conditions, promotion opportunities, pay rises and housing, inequality abounds in practice as a result of ineffective law enforcement (Cooke, 2012).

Secondly, there is a strong element of gender bias in certain aspects of the employment legislation itself, particularly its promotion selection and retirement policies, which close off women's access to the top management ladder. Since the 1990s, the state employer has implemented an age-related policy for management training and development with the aim of injecting new blood into its vast management team. Young talent below 35 years of age is selected for management training as part of the succession plan. Potential candidates above the age of 35 may not be considered for first promotion. This means that women in their 30s who are ready for career progression when their child-rearing responsibility has eased off may not have the chance to progress as they have passed their 'sell-by date'. For those who are in the junior rank of management, once they are above the age of 40 for women and 45 for men, they will not be nominated for further promotions. This 'anti-ageing' policy of promotion to keep the management force young has resulted in the decrease of the proportion of women managers over 45 years old (see Table 13.3).

In addition, since 1951, China has followed a retirement policy in which female workers in general retire five years earlier than their male colleagues in the same occupations (at the age of 50 for blue-collar female workers and 55 for white collar). This legislative discrimination against women exists not only at the mass level, but also at the elite level where there is an obvious incentive for the state to amend the regulations. In order to retain and

Table 13.3 Age composition of heads of organizations by sex in urban employment in China in 2013 (%)

Age	Male	Female	Total
Total	100.0	100.0	100.0
16–19	0.1	0.2	0.1
20–24	2.9	4.4	3.2
25–29	7.5	12.9	8.9
30–34	14.6	18.5	15.6
35–39	15.2	18.0	15.9
40–44	20.0	18.5	19.6
45–49	17.4	14.9	16.8
50–54	12.1	7.4	10.9
55–59	7.7	3.5	6.7
60–64	1.9	1.6	1.8
65+	0.7	0.2	0.6

Source: Compiled from NBSC (2014)

utilise expertise more effectively, the Ministry of Personnel has, in the last two decades, issued a number of documents (e.g. Document 153/1983; Document 141/1983; Document 5/1990) which stipulate that professorial experts can carry on working until the age of 60 if they wish and their health permits. These documents also stipulate that a minority of female experts can carry on working after they are 60 if they are needed by their organization (Luo, 2000). Although these documents have provided legitimacy for intellectual and professional women to extend their working life, the opportunity to do so is largely controlled by their employing organizations.

According to three women government cadres interviewed by the author in November 2011, the situation is worse for female managers and cadres in governmental organizations who have to step down at the age of 55 (60 for men), whether they like it or not and irrespective of their rank. Those who are below a certain rank may have to retire at 55 (60 for men) while those who are above a certain senior rank can stay until they are 60 (65 for men). This means that few female managers and cadres can make it to the top level and if they do, they are not likely to stay there for long. Whilst there are signs of administrative policy change to equalize the age requirement for both genders, the implementation of this policy is determined by local government organizations through the elastic interpretation of the policy and local conditions. The reality is that older women cadres (those who are 55 years old or above) may not be able to benefit from the policy until age equality is legislated and effectively enforced.

Women's representing bodies

Two national non-government organizations (NGOs) – the All-China Women's Federation (ACWF) and the China Association of Women Entrepreneurs (CAWE) – have been set up to provide services and represent women's interests, including those of women managers and entrepreneurs. They champion the women's development cause through a range of initiatives, often in response to the state's direction. As Unger and Chan (1995) observed, the state forms unequal partnerships with these organizations which often act on behalf of the state and help implement government policies.

ACWF, established in 1949, is a semi-government organization as it is funded by the government and operates under its direction. Dedicated to the advancement of Chinese women of all ethnic groups in all walks of life, its mission is to represent and to protect women's rights and interests, and to promote equality between men and women through its participation, education, representation, service and liaison functions (ACWF, undated b).

Since the 1990s, defending women's equal employment rights became a priority of ACWF when women have been increasingly disadvantaged in the labor market as the economic reform of China deepens. For example, ACWF played a fundamental role in blocking the "women return home" proposal (Zheng, 2000) advanced by some (male) academics and economists in the 1980s:

> [U]sing unambiguous language of Maoist gender ideology drawn from Engels: [ACWF contends,] Women's employment must be linked with women's liberation. Economics is the foundation. Without participation in social production, women would have no economic status. This would in turn undermine the equality between men and women in politics, society and family.
>
> (Zheng, 2000, p. 68)

ACWF has also made a request to the National People's Congress several times to harmonize men and women's retirement age, an objective that has not yet been achieved.

Founded in 1985, CAWE is a group member of ACWF and the China Enterprise Confederation (CEC), which is one of the official employer associations that the state recognizes at the national level as the sole representative of employers interests. CAWE is the main official organization that organizes and represents women entrepreneurs. A registered association of the Ministry of Civil Affairs, CAWE is under the direct administration of the State Asset Supervision and Administration Commission of the State Council. By 2008, it had 46 group members from various provinces, municipalities and autonomous regions and more than 10,000 individual direct and indirect members who were successful women entrepreneurs, well-known government officials, company directors and managers (CAWE, undated a).

The mission of CAWE is to provide services to its members, to represent Chinese women entrepreneurs and to create a bridge between women entrepreneurs and the government and between women entrepreneurs and women from all walks of life, both within and outside China (CAWE, undated a). However, women in leadership roles in large businesses and government organizations make up the bulk of CAWE members. Women in small and self-employed businesses remain largely unorganized and unrepresented. Their voice may be less heard and needs less met. Yet, it is this group of women entrepreneurs who may need more support for their personal and business development. Since 2001, CAWE has been conducting its "Study of Chinese Female Entrepreneurs' Development" periodically, with the eighth report published in 2014 (CAWE, undated b). These reports highlight conditions, challenges, development and contributions related to women-run enterprises, particularly in the private sector. A general trend of findings of these studies has been that female entrepreneurs are becoming younger (mainly in their 30s–40s), more highly educated, more engaged with corporate social responsibility, and paying more attention to advanced technologies and innovations. However, the majority of the enterprises are small or micro in size, and difficulties in raising investment funds have been the main bottleneck for growth.

Initiatives supporting women's careers

Initiatives to support career progression of women in China have been limited to a number of state-sponsored high-profile public campaigns from time to time. In the 1950s and 1960s, Mao's motto 'women can hold up half the sky' was widely promoted, albeit based on the misconception of equal opportunities. Women were encouraged to perform strenuous tasks which were conventionally carried out by men, such as working at height, in mines and under cold water. Elite teams of women workers were formed and their achievements were dramatized in order to set examples for the once believing nation. This practice was stopped after the Cultural Revolution.

Another initiative includes the annual road show of "female model workers" on March 8 (Women's Day in China) when hard-working women role models are selected for the celebration ceremony. Less politically oriented initiatives have been that of "model husband" and "model family", which are essentially light-hearted social events aimed to encourage husbands to give more support to their working wives (often career women) by sharing (more) housework.

More practical initiatives to support working women come from company policies on childcare arrangements. Since the state-planned economy period, public sector organizations and state-owned enterprises have adopted a state-initiated policy to arrange their shift system to accommodate the childcare responsibilities for working couples with young children. For example, if one of the spouses has to work a night shift, then the other one will not be scheduled to work at night. Efforts have been made by the state to relieve the burden of housework for female workers through the subsidized provision of childcare facilities, often sponsored by and located in the organizations where the parents work. These company policies, however, have largely not been adopted in the private sector. Nor have the private companies promoted, according to public knowledge, gender equality initiatives to remove barriers to women's career progression. It should be noted that gender equality policies and initiatives adopted in the state-owned sector during the state-planned economy period have been eroded in the ensuing marketization period.

A number of high-profile (international) events have been held since the 2000s to showcase Chinese women's achievements and highlight future development needs and goals. For example, the Centenary Outstanding Women's Forum on Pioneering was held in Beijing in 2001. The forum was addressed by senior politicians and economists and was attended by more than 200 outstanding women entrepreneurs from 29 provinces. The theme of the forum was to help women entrepreneurs to grow their business and improve their business strategy in the light of the internationalization, informatization and capitalization of the market and China's accession to the World Trade Organization (ACWF, undated a).

A nation-wide Essays Competition on the Sustainable Development of Chinese Women Entrepreneurs was initiated by CAWE in 2008. The initiative was supported by the US-based Women's Network for a Sustainable Future and the Centre for International Business Ethics of the China Foreign Economy and Trade University. The intention of the competition was to give women entrepreneurs a voice in the sustainability debate, to raise their awareness of corporate social responsibility and to stimulate their motivation and creativeness. It must be noted that while these events create new inspirations and aspirations for women's development at the national level, they are largely symbolic and elitist occasions that fail to engage organizations at the local level to embed the equality culture necessary for women's career advancement on a larger scale.

In addition to episodic events to create renewed momentum for women's development cause, a number of initiatives are implemented by ACWF on a more regular basis. For example, in order to raise the number and proportion of women at the top decision-making level and the top administrative level, ACWF and its local branches have set up a talented women database and play a major role in training and developing women cadres and recommending outstanding women candidates for promotion to the government departments concerned (ACWF, undated b). Furthermore, in order to help Chinese women to broaden their knowledge base and develop their leadership and entrepreneurial skills, ACWF organizes (often in conjunction with government organizations and CAWE branches) women cadres and entrepreneurs for site visits in different parts of the country and overseas to learn good practices. Facilitating urban unemployed women and rural women to start up their own business is another function that ACWF branches provide. The services include, for example, disseminating government policy, providing training to develop women's entrepreneurial skills, lobbying for business loans and facilitating business applications' approval from the local government (ACWF, undated b).

A number of smaller women's professional associations, often as a branch of the main industry-based professional association, have been established since the 1990s to organize women professionals and facilitate their continuous professional development. These include, for example, the Chinese Women Geological Workers' Committee of the Geological Association of China (founded in 1990), the Women Mayors Chapter of China Association of Mayors (founded in 1991) and the China Women Scientific and Technological Workers

Association (founded in 1993) (ACWF, undated b). The existence of these associations may help enhance women's professional identity and provide a forum for women to communicate with and support each other. However, this kind of gender solidarity is gentle and largely formed on a professional and social basis outside the employing organizations. It is unlikely to develop into a political force to advance women's cause and certainly does not tackle, at least not directly, barriers to women's career advancement within their employing organizations.

One of the important gender development initiatives for women entrepreneurship in the last few years has been that of the 10,000 Women initiative launched in 2008 by the Goldman Sachs Foundation. This international initiative aims to educate women entrepreneurs in emerging economies including Brazil, India and China. The initiative was designed specifically to provide business education, access to mentors and networks, and links to capital for 10,000 underserved women operating small businesses (Babson College, undated). A total of 2200 of the 10,000 women were recruited from China and they are reported to have benefited from the initiative in terms of, amongst other things, business growth, confidence level and ability to serve the community (Chen, 2015).

Work–life balance issues and initiatives

Work–life balance is an important organizational initiative to support women's (and indeed men's) careers (e.g. Pocock, 2005; Haar *et al.*, 2008). Work–life/family-friendly initiatives, such as flexible working arrangements, have been promoted as good HRM practices in many developed countries to accommodate (women) workers who have family commitments and to reduce work–life conflicts of managerial/professional employees (e.g. Brough *et al.*, 2008; Burgess and Connell, 2008). This is despite the fact that the work–life balance discourse and its associated flexibility practices that have emerged from the European and North American politico-socio-economic contexts have attracted much critique (e.g. Fleetwood, 2007; Lewis *et al.*, 2007).

Work–life conflicts (WLC) in China derive from a range of sources that are different from those manifested in western societies and require different HR initiatives in the Chinese context. Whilst family commitment remains a key source of WLC, work intensity, including long working hours, appears to be the main HR issue amongst managers and professionals in multinational corporations and private firms in China (Cooke and Xiao, 2014). This is largely due to the heightened market competition and the rapid growth of firms, particularly those in the fast growing industries such as telecommunications, IT, consultancy, finance and real estate industries. Work intensification has led to health problems, retention issues and labor disputes (Cooke, 2012).

Xiao and Cooke's (2012) study of 122 chief executive officers (CEOs), managers and professional employees revealed that despite the fact that the one-child policy has led to the reduction of childcare work for married couples, childcare and elderly care responsibilities continue to fall upon women disproportionately. Therefore, women are more likely to feel the pressure of WLC than men. Outsourcing their housework and family care, drawing on family networks for assistance or domesticating one spouse, usually the wife, seem to be the coping mechanisms. For some career-oriented single women, their WLC takes another form – the difficulty in finding a spouse and the fear of starting a family at the expense of their career.

Xiao and Cooke's (2012) study further showed that Chinese organizational leaders and, to a large extent, workers tend to accept WLC as a fact of life without feeling the need for the organization to address it. Individuals adopt various coping strategies on their own. Whilst organizations are more likely to introduce HR initiatives to cushion the negative effect of long working hours on their key employees and their families, managers are far less sympathetic towards women's (and men's) childcare needs and are unwilling to introduce policies to accommodate family commitments.

Other research findings suggest that many women managers end up in their leadership position 'by accident' instead of through careful planning. They tend to take a passive attitude in their career battle and often adopt a non-confrontational and conciliatory style of leadership in order to gain acceptance (e.g. Cooke, 2009; Tsang *et al.*, 2011). Many of them are struggling to balance their career and family responsibilities and when a critical choice needs to be made, they will choose their family first and career second (e.g. Aaltio and Huang, 2007; Tsang *et al.*, 2011).

Conclusions

This chapter has provided an overview of the level of participation in education and employment by Chinese women. It has outlined the patterns of their political leadership, managerial and entrepreneurial positions and the provision of gender equality regulations and initiatives within the above political, economic, and cultural context. The chapter showed that whilst the level of gender equality is relatively high in China, measured by the education and employment level and the relatively mild gender segregation in industries and occupations, there remain formidable barriers to women's managerial careers. Moreover, gender equality achieved during the state-planned economy period is being eroded as marketization deepens and in the rise of post-socialist ideology pragmatism (Cooke and Xiao, 2014).

As such, women have made limited progress in mainstreaming into organizational leadership positions and the political arena in the last two decades. The existence of gender equality regulations serves more as a policy aspiration than an effective weapon to eliminate discrimination. It is worth noting that the level of gender discrimination is perhaps the highest in government organizations, a sector that should in principle play the leading role in implementing gender equality legislation and initiatives (Cooke, 2009). The unwillingness of the government to harmonize the retirement age between men and women through legislative change (despite rising demands from women's pressure groups) further disadvantages women in selection for career development and promotion.

Career development support for women managers comes mainly from professional associations external to the employing organizations. The low proportion of women in political leadership positions further prevents women from having sufficient voice to exert influence at the national level to advance the case for gender equality in career progression. The emphasis of state goals as the collective goals for the whole nation means that women's ultimate goal is "to serve the state and the people rather than to fight for gender equality as an end in itself" (Pittinsky and Zhu, 2005, p. 127). The supreme power of the state means that any real action to achieve gender equality needs to be initiated by the state without challenging its overall development agenda and those in power.

Finally, a new concern is that women university graduates are encountering growing difficulties in gaining meaningful employment. Although some measures are being taken by the government (for example, loans for university graduates to start up a business) and universities (for example, career advice and counseling for women students who are encountering employment problems) to address the problem, these measures are unlikely to tackle the roots of the cause – employers' discrimination. This problem, which is likely to persist for some time, is going to impact on the future stock of women candidates for political leadership and managerial roles. Effective policy intervention is therefore necessary to prevent present conditions from declining further and future prospects of gender equality being undermined.

Note

1   Year in the bracket after the law/regulation refers to the year when the law was passed, not enacted, which often takes place the following year.

References

Aaltion, I. and Huang, J. (2007). Women managers' careers in information technology in China: high flyers with emotional costs? *Journal of Organizational Change Management, 20*(2), 227–244.

ACWF (All-China Women's Federation) (ACWF) (undated a). ACWF. Retrieved from www.women. org.cn/english/english/whatisnws/07-25-01.htm, accessed on May 12, 2009.

ACWF (undated b). Brochure, Retrieved from www.women.org.cn/english/english/newsletter/ ACWF%20brochure.htm, accessed on December 19, 2011.

Babson College (undated). Investing in the Power of Women Progress Report on the Goldman Sachs *10,000 Women* Initiative. Retrieved from www.goldmansachs.com/citizenship/10000women/news-and-events/10kw-progress-report/progress-report-full.pdf, accessed on November 3, 2015.

Bowen, C. C., Wu, Y., Hwang, C. E. and Scherer, R. F. (2007). Holding up half of the sky? Attitudes toward women as managers in the People's Republic of China. *International Journal of Human Resource Management, 18*(2), 268–283.

Brough, P., Holt, J., Bauld, R., Biggs, A. and Ryan, C. (2008). The ability of work–life balance policies to influence key social/organisational issues. *Asia Pacific Journal of Human Resources, 46*(3), 261–274.

Bu, N. and Roy, J. P. (2005). Career success networks in China: sex differences in network composition and social exchange practices. *Asia Pacific Journal of Management, 22*(4), 381–403.

Bu, N. and Roy, J. P. (2008). Chinese managers' career success networks: the impact of key tie characteristics on structure and interaction practices. *International Journal of Human Resource Management, 19*(6), 1088–1107.

Burgess, J. and Connell, J. (2008). Introduction to Special Issue: HRM and job quality: an overview. *The International Journal of Human Resource Management, 19*(3), 407–418.

CAWE (China Association of Women Entrepreneurs) (undated a). CAWE. Retrieved from www.cawe. org.cn/xhjj.htm, accessed on May 14, 2009.

CAWE (undated b). Data center. Retrieved from www.cawe.org.cn/cawe/fore/dataCenterTwoInfos. action?dataCenterDTO.id=385, accessed on November 6, 2015.

Chen, Z. W. (2015). 10,000 women entrepreneurship: a dream fulfilled in China. *Social Innovation Review*, pp. 29–31.

China Education Online (2014). www.eol.cn/html/c/2014xbys/index.shtml, accessed on March 20, 2015.

Cooke, F. L. (2005). *HRM, Work and Employment in China*. London: Routledge.

Cooke, F. L. (2009). The changing face of women managers in China. In C. Rowley and V. Yukondi (eds), *The Changing Face of Women Management in Asia* (pp.19–42). London: Routledge.

Cooke, F. L. (2010). Women's participation in employment in Asia: a comparative analysis of China, India, Japan and South Korea. *International Journal of Human Resource Management, 21*(10–12), 2249–2270.

Cooke, F. L. (2012). *Human Resource Management in China: New Trends and Practices*. London: Routledge.

Cooke, F. L. and Xiao, Y. C. (2014). Gender roles and organizational HR practices: the case of women's careers in accountancy and consultancy firms in China. *Human Resource Management, 53*(1), 23–44.

Economist (2009). Chinese unemployment: where will all the students go? April 8. Retrieved from www.economist.com/world/asia/displaystory.cfm?story_id=13446878, access on May 12, 2009.

Fleetwood, S. (2007). Why work–life balance now? *The International Journal of Human Resource Management, 18*(3), 387–400.

Gao, J. (2015). A study of factors influencing female cadres' leadership. *Exploration*, *3*, 64–72.

Gries, P. H. and Rosen, S. (2004). *State and Society in 21st-century China*. London: Routledge.

Haar, J., Bardoel, A. and De Cieri, H. (2008). Work–life in Australasia. *Asia Pacific Journal of Human Resources*, *46*(3), 258–260.

Hu, Y. Y. (2012). A study of women managers' career development: from a leader–member exchange perspective. *Management*, *2*, 105–106.

Lewis, S., Gambles, R. and Rapoport, R. (2007). The constraints of a 'work–life balance' approach: an international perspective. *The International Journal of Human Resource Management*, *18*(3), 360–373.

Liu, P., Meng, X. and Zhang, J. (2000). Sectoral gender wage differentials and discrimination in the transitional Chinese economy. *Journal of Population Economics*, *13*(3), 331–352.

Lu, Q. and Zhao, Y. M. (2002). Gender segregation in China since the economic reform. *Journal of Southern Yangtze University* (Humanities and Social Sciences), 1, 22–48.

Luo, P. (2000). Retirement age and protection of women's employment rights. Paper presented at the International Seminar on the Legal Protection of Women's Employment Rights, April, Shanghai, China.

NBSC (National Bureau of Statistics of China) (2001). *China Labor Statistical Yearbook 2001*, Beijing: China Statistics Press.

NBSC (2014). *China Labor Statistical Yearbook 2014*. Beijing: China Statistics Press. Retrieved from www.stats.gov.cn/tjsj/zxfb/201501/t20150122_672472.html, accessed on February 3, 2015.

Nie, S. J. (2009). Reality of women leadership and development strategy. *Leadership Science*, November (first half), 51–53.

O'Reilly, J. and Fagan, C. (1998). *Part-time Prospects: An International Comparison of Part-time Work in Europe, North America and the Pacific Rim*. London: Routledge.

Ouyang, H. Y. (2006). Problems in the development of the Chinese women entrepreneurs. *Journal of Henan Normal University*, *33*(1), 199–202.

Perry, E. and Selden, M. (2011). *Chinese Society: Change, Conflict and Resistance*. London: Routledge.

Pittinsky, T. L. and Zhu, C. (2005). Contemporary public leadership in China: a research review and consideration. *The Leadership Quarterly*, *16*(6), 921–939.

Pocock, B. (2005). Work–life 'balance' in Australia: Limited progress, dim prospects. *Asia Pacific Journal of Human Resources* *43*(2), 198–209.

Rubery, J., Smith, M. and Fagan, C. (1998). *Women's employment in Europe: Trends and Prospects*. London: Routledge.

Shen, K. Y. and Xu, M. F. (2009). An empirical study of work–life conflicts of women entrepreneurs in Shanghai. *Shanghai Economic Studies*, 6, 99–106.

Shi, Q. Q. (2009). Overview of Chinese women owned businesses. Retrieved from https://docs. google.com/viewer?a=v&q=cache:jbuY5ah_-9oJ:pslforum.worldbankgroup.org/docs/WEConnect Event_090327_chinese.ppt+chinese+association+of+women+entrepreneurs&hl=en&gl=au&pid=b l&srcid=ADGEESj4SUOUimdj7mDw6FFLYgXTGSqkGDfWu72lQwmdVD3O-XHqChEl7 QueuoVmPaQ5OV2UIupsr8-vNvCTR92OLV6h92oY_X1hrFlgGUcb_cint2yUOGD 821jA90qoDB1CkIwHzSI2&sig=AHIEtbR7Xb3nxnfLMNdEzObun56S3isTyA, accessed on December 19, 2011.

Stockman, N., Bonney, N. and Sheng, X. (1995). *Women's Work in East and West: The Dual Burden of Employment and Family Life*. London: UCL Press Ltd.

Tsang, A. Y., Chan, P. S. and Zhang, L. (2011). Reconciling conflicts: the 'accidental' women leaders in contemporary China. *Affilia: Journal of Women and Social Work*, *26*(3), 314–326.

Unger, J. and Chan, A. (1995). China, corporatism and the East Asian model. *The Australian Journal of Chinese Affairs*, *33*(1), 29–53.

Women's Studies Institute of China (undated). Report of the Third National Survey of Women's Position in China, www.wsic.ac.cn/staticdata/84760.htm, accessed on November 3, 2015.

World Bank (2011). *World Databank of World Development Indicators and Gender Statistics*. Retrieved from http://search.worldbank.org/quickview?name=%3Cem%3ELabor%3C%2Fem%3E+%3Cem%3Efo rce%3C%2Fem%3E%2C+female+%28%25+of+total+%3Cem%3Elabor%3C%2Fem%3E+%3Cem

%3Eforce%3C%2Fem%3E%29&id=SL.TLF.TOTL.FE.ZS&type=Indicators&cube_no=2&qterm=labor+force, World Bank Group, Washington, DC, accessed on November 20, 2011.

Wu, L. F. (2011). 21% of Female Graduates Signed Employment Contracts. November 15. Retrieved from www.womenofchina.cn/html/report/135351-1.htm, access on December 22, 2011.

Xiao, Y. C. and Cooke, F. L. (2012). Work–life balance in China? Social policy, employer strategy and individual coping mechanisms. *Asia-Pacific Journal of Human Resources*, *50*(1), 6–22.

Zhang, J. (2012). An investigation of the application of the 'employees assistance programme' for stress management for the post-80 generation of professional women. *Enterprise Herald*, *21*, 180–181.

Zhao, W. and Zhou, X. (2004). Chinese organizations in transition: changing promotion patterns in the reform era. *Organization Science*, *15*(2), 186–199.

Zheng, W. (2000). Gender, employment and women's resistance. In E. Perry and M. Selden (eds), *Chinese Society: Change, Conflict and Resistance* (pp. 62–82). London: Routledge.

Zhou, X. (2000). Economic transformation and income inequality in urban China: evidence from panel data. *American Journal of Sociology*, *105*, 1135–1174.

14 Women in management in India

Neera Jain and Shoma Mukherji

Introduction

For a country as vast as India, generalization of behavior patterns is not easy. Society on the whole is collectivist. However, the urban–rural divide, social class affiliations, religious beliefs, education levels – all impact the feminine mind-set in India. On the one hand the outlook on life in general has been influenced by tradition, carefully constituted brick by brick by past generations. On the other hand, however, women have enjoyed the freedom of living in a more open society in the late twentieth century with the option of greater choices. In the last 40 years women have been entering the professional workforce in greater numbers and are even entering professions which have been traditional male bastions. Areas like banking, financial institutions, IT and IT services, healthcare, professional education, and engineering consulting have a large number of women professionals.

Urban Indian women are not denied education opportunities and significant progress has been made towards reducing the gender gap. In the matter of finding a work–life balance, the challenges and tensions faced by the urban professional woman in India have not been significantly different from those faced by their western counterparts. The differences which become evident are in two areas. The first is in the manner of response of urban Indian women in dealing with these challenges. The second difference, as described later in the chapter, manifests in the manner of support enjoyed by Indian working women. Most Indian women consciously focus on family but also find alternate avenues to give expression to occupational aspirations. The assertion of Indian women is covert rather than overt. Even if they have to take a step back, it is done consciously without any heart ache. The inherent faith in a divine cosmic order increases the ability to accept life as it comes. There is an underlying calmness which allows one to cope with challenges and come up with acceptable solutions.

A paradigm shift in how careers are developed, created, and shaped has occurred as a result of the "push" factor of technology, which has made work more adaptable and flexible, and the "pull" factor of individuals wanting to maintain more of a balance between their work and family lives. Although most scholarly writings show Indian society to be more gender-centric when compared to the west, the reality is that present-day Indian society has moved on (Chakrapani and Vijaya Kumar, 1994; Jung, 2000). Men are not necessarily considered the leader and provider and woman the idealized deity, submissive and subservient to the wishes of her family. Education leading to greater awareness has led to recognition of roles which are not stereotyped by gender, allowing men to recognize their femininity and women their masculinity. Globalization, fast-paced technological change and the internet boom are having large-scale impacts on Indian society. Women are juggling the traditional roles as homemakers and caregivers with the demands of meaningful careers. It is an exciting time for Indian women who are making conscious choices, not necessarily out of compulsion, for the ideal work–life balance. The challenges which rural Indian women face however are substantially different as the position of Indian women has always been paradoxical. While there has been growth in literacy and an increase in women's entry into professional fields, malpractices like child marriage, poor health conditions and discrimination are burning issues. If one side of the picture looks promising, there is also a side which is bleak.

Before we describe the status of women managers in India it is imperative to briefly review the historical perspective as this has a strong bearing on the current status of Indian women managers.

Women in India – a short history

From the Vedic Age to Mauryan rule and golden age of Guptas (circa 2000 BC to AD 1000), the Indian view of life has always been a search for the spiritual in the physical, the realization of the divine in the human. Ancient Indian texts espoused the four aims of life as moral behavior (*dharma*), attainment of wealth (*artha*), worldly pleasure (*kama*) and finally the highest ideal – salvation (*moksha*). In the Vedic times, women were educated and enjoyed equal status with men in all fields of life (Tharakan and Tharakan, 1975; Gupta, 1988). Co-education of boys and girls was the rule and women could conduct rituals independently.

Women in Vedic India were seen as residing at two ends of the spectrum – the ascetic (*brahmavadini*) seeking truth self-realization and spiritual well-being, while the domestically inclined *sadyovadhu* dedicated herself to the well-being of the family. It was not necessary for the *brahmavadini* to renounce the world, take a vow of celibacy and meditate in isolation. Similarly the *sadyovadhu* could find spiritual realization in the midst of domestic chores. What really mattered was that women had the freedom of choice and could choose the path on the basis of their ingrained ideals and inner inclinations. The Rig Veda contained hymns by 27 women seers (*brahmavadinis*). Ghosha, Lopamudra, Maitreyi, Gargi, Apala, Sasvati, Indrani and Chandramata were a few notable seers during this age.

Complementing the sacred texts of *Vedas*[1] and *Upanishad* were the *Puranas*,[2] which presented the philosophical doctrines through simple narrations. These too mention several accomplished women who were held in high esteem. In the period of *Smritis*[3] (codification of social laws), women were bracketed with the low caste (*sudras*) and lost the right to study the Vedas, utter Vedic hymns (*mantras*) and perform Vedic rites. The decline in women's education, the practice of pre-puberty marriage, the *sati* (burning of widows on the husband's pyre) and the ban on widow remarriages established the supremacy of the male over the female and pushed Indian women into dependency and subjugation. The essence is found in the Law of Manu which clearly states: "In childhood a woman must be subject to her father, in youth to her husband and when her lord is dead, to her sons. A woman must never be independent" (Tharakan and Tharakan, 1975).

The status of women went on a downward spiral thereafter. The Greek ambassador Megasthenes who visited the Mauryan kingdom of Pataliputra commented that while upper-class women were educated and accomplished in the arts, Brahmins normally were not keen on education for their wives, believing that knowledge and learning were not for females (Sharma, 1992). Under Asoka, as Buddhism flourished, women ascetics were allowed to enter the order and enjoyed the opportunity to study. Several women teachers went abroad to spread the teachings of Budhha. The position of women deteriorated further under the Gupta kings. Lowering of the marriage age affected education. There was a tendency to keep women indoors away from the prying eyes of invaders.

Muslim invasions

The Muslim invasions which began in the eleventh century AD further worsened the condition of women. Muslim culture looked at the woman as the property of her father, brother or husband without any will of her own. The imposition of the veil (*purdah*), practice of polygamy and unilateral right of divorce for men added to women's woes. Indians also wanted to shield their women from the invaders and thereby restricted their freedom of movement.

British rule

British rule in India coupled with efforts of reformers like Raja Rammohan Roy, Ishwar Chandra Vidyasagar and Mahadev Ranade saw the enactment of legislation for the abolition of *sati* and in favor of widow remarriage and the spread of education amongst women. Education and social reform led to Indian women being active participants in the freedom struggle. Women joined men in boycotting foreign goods and buying only *Swadeshi* (domestically produced) goods. Women were an integral part of Gandhi's non-violence movement. Even uneducated women sacrificed time and materials volunteering, campaigning, protesting, fasting and donating to the causes of freedom.

Post-independence period

Fast-paced urbanization and industrialization in the post-independence era brought social change, a rise in the employment of women and breakdown of the joint family system. There are women parliamentarians, Supreme Court judges, business tycoons and corporate heads. Yet, we hear of dowry deaths, female infanticide and stories of oppression and discrimination. Bumiller (1990) gives a succinct summation, "for every woman who sits in Parliament or has done a Ph.D. or goes to the Supreme Court to argue a case, you have thousands in the villages who don't even know about their basic rights." Speaking at a Incredible India@60 campaign at New York, the then HSBC India chief executive officer (CEO) Naina Lal Kidwai commented that "India lives in several centuries simultaneously and we have several challenges before us, such as maternal mortality, female infanticide, women having to grapple with poverty, livelihood and water issues" (Hindubusinessline.com, 2007).

A CII study of 149 companies showed the incidence of working women across companies at 6 percent (Bhattacharya, 2005) and women in senior managerial position at 4 percent. If there is no conscious discrimination being practiced by organizations, these figures are a cause for concern. The official Census of 2011 showed the population of 1.21 billion making India the second-most populous country in the world. The ratio of females per 1000 males stood at 940. Total literacy stood at 74 percent (male 85.1 percent, female 65.5 percent). India has one of the lowest female labor force participation (FLFP) rates (33 per cent) (typically measured as the share of women that are employed or seeking work as a share of the working-age female population) among emerging markets and developing countries (Das *et al.*, 2015). This implies that only 125 million of the roughly 380 million working-age Indian females are seeking work or are currently employed.

Education of women in modern India

The Constitution of India guarantees free primary school education for both girls and boys up to age fourteen. Though the urban child, irrespective of gender, has the opportunity of completing school-level education, the picture is not so rosy in rural areas. Parents often insist on girls learning domestic chores rather than attending school, keeping in mind their future as good daughters-in-law. They are also concerned about safety as schools are co-educational, may have male teachers and are often located at a distance. Parents are often unwilling to expose their daughters to the potential assault on their virginity that would ultimately result in an insult to the family's honor. Social sector programs like Sarva Shiksha Abhiyan (Education for Everyone) are promoting girls' education to equalize educational opportunities and eliminate gender disparities. Considerable progress has been made, from 5.4 million girls enrolled at the primary level in 1950–1951 to 61.1 million girls in 2004–2005, and 67.2 million girls in 2011. At the upper primary level, enrollment increased from 0.5 million girls in 1950–1951 to 29.9 million girls in 2011. The Indian government is making concerted efforts through initiatives like Beti Bachao Beti Padhao (Save the Girl Child, Educate the Girl Child), Swachh Vidyalaya (Clean Education Institute), various skills development progams and especially the National Digital Literacy Mission (NDLM), which is working towards enabling all to use IT and related applications and participate actively in the democratic process.

With the fall in dropout rates of girls from the education system, the net result is that besides having the world's largest number of professionally qualified women, India also has the largest population of working women in the world, and has more doctors, surgeons, scientists and professors than the United States.

Indian women are slowly recognizing their true potential. They have started questioning the oppressive rules laid down by society and are overcoming barriers. There is no arena which remains unconquered by Indian women, be it social work, politics, sports, entertainment, literature, technology, banking, finance, and even space. Ambition, competitiveness, and determination are helping women to prove themselves in their chosen professions. Enrollment in colleges and universities is on the rise, helping women enter into all kinds of professions like engineering, medicine, politics, teaching, and management.

The first Indian woman to earn a college degree was Kadambini Ganguly in the year 1883. She went on to earn a degree in medicine in 1886. It is a matter of concern that very few women have risen to a position of influence in the male-dominated Indian academic system. Of nearly 300 government-run universities in India, only about 6 percent have women as their vice-chancellors, 21 percent have women senior administrators and 10 percent have women heads of departments and principals of affiliated colleges. In the 62 institutes of national importance, including the Indian Institutes of Technology (IITs), there are only two women

Table 14.1 Number of girls per 100 boys enrolled by stage of education

Year	Primary (1–5)	Upper primary (6–8)	Secondary (9–10)	Senior secondary (11–12)	Higher education
1950–1951	39	19	NA	15	13
1960–1961	48	31	NA	26	21
1970–1971	60	41	NA	33	28
1980–1981	63	49	NA	45	36
1990–1991	71	58	NA	49	46
2009–2010	92	88	82	80	67
2010–2011	92	89	82	79	78
2011–2012	93	90	84	81	80
2012–2013 (provisional)	94	95	89	87	81

Source: Ministry of Human Resource Development, Government of India, 2014

directors — Dr. S. K. Pandey (director of NIT-Puducherry) and her counterpart in Rajiv Gandhi National Institute of Youth Development, Dr. Latha Pillai. Only two out of the sixteen national law universities have women vice-chancellors: Prof. Poonam Saxena (Jodhpur) and Prof. Rose Varghese (Kochi). In its over 65 years of existence, Viswa-Bharati University has never had a woman vice-chancellor. All India Institute of Medical Sciences (AIIMS), since its inception in 1956, has been headed by just one woman, Prof. Sneha Bhargava, from 1984 to 1990.

In the political arena however, women's leadership has been quite visible. Sarojini Naidu was the first Indian woman to become the president of the Indian National Congress and the first woman to become governor of Uttar Pradesh. Indira Gandhi was prime minister for three consecutive terms from 1966 to 1977 and then again from 1980 until her death in 1984. India has had a woman president (Pratibha Patil), and the post of speaker has been held by Meira Kumar (2009–2014) and Sumitra Mahajan (2014 to present). The current lower house of Parliament has 61 members, with 11.23 percent being women. The present BJP government is committed to ensure the passage of the Women's Reservation Bill which proposes to reserve one third of the Lok Sabha (lower house) and state assembly seats for women.

Women leadership at the grassroots level

Women have traditionally been ignored in villages and at grassroots level, their role being restricted to the domestic household. In recognition of the importance of the representation of women in the Panchayati Raj (local self-government) system, the 73rd Constitutional Amendment Act, 1992, enforced their political participation and decision making at the grassroots level by providing that one-third of the seats would be reserved for women. After taking the reins of villages as *sarpanches* (heads of village councils), hundreds of untutored women in India have led a silent gradual revolution, which has brought a paradigm shift in rural development (Sharma and Mukherji, 2011).

This shift has brought health and sanitation to the core of rural development. First-generation women leaders, who never even thought of opening their mouths in front of their men, have evolved dramatically. They are now talking about iodized salt, safe delivery of babies, clean drinking water, exclusive breast-feeding, sanitation and even safer sex to avoid HIV infection. Water management, wastewater disposal, toilets, solid waste disposal, domestic and environmental sanitation, personal hygiene, health education and communication, unconventional energy schemes, family welfare activities, community participation and innovative programs have become focal points on the agenda of the women *sarpanches*.

Women in the workforce

At around 33 percent in 2012, India has one of the lowest female labor force participation (FLFP) rates (measured as the share of women that are employed or seeking work as a share of the working-age female population) among emerging markets and developing countries (Das *et al.*, 2015). With an estimated 1.26 billion persons at the end of 2014, a FLFP rate of 33 percent implies that only 125 million of the roughly 380 million working-age Indian females are seeking work or are currently employed (Census of India, 2011).

Table 14.2 Women's workforce participation by sector

Sector	Percentage of women workforce
Farming	68.5
Manufacturing	10.8
Construction	5.1
Schools	3.8
Grocery store	2.1
Housework	1.6
Personal service	1.5
Healthcare	1.1
Bureaucracy	1.0

Source: Ministry of Statistics and Programme Implementation Report, 2014–2015

The glass ceiling in the Indian corporate world

On paper, corporate houses in India support the removal of the glass ceiling, the invisible barrier which keeps women from occupying the top echelons of management. In reality, much ground still needs to be covered. In a study by Jain and Mukherji (2010), it was established that though Indian men are in denial about the existence of a glass ceiling, the underlying stereotypes are well embedded. Women managers are not very vocal about having to strive harder than their male colleagues to reach the top. The Indian cultural legacy does not impose punitive restrictions on girl children but rather conditions them to accept differences in attitudes towards males as a reality of life. Thus women are used to finding ways around problems rather than rebelling. Socio-cultural as well as personal and organizational forces obstruct woman's rise in the corporate hierarchy. Talented women having self-confidence, perseverance, patience, the right kind of mentors and some amount of luck will enable them to crack through the glass ceiling. Sampath (2007) presents a very apt comparison to demonstrate how the actions of men and women are viewed differently on the basis of stereotypes, as shown in Table 14.3.

Table 14.3 Gender stereotypes: how we interpret behavior patterns

Comment	He	She
Has a family picture on the desk.	A responsible family man!	She places family before career!
Has a cluttered desk.	He is a hard worker!	What a disorganized person!
Is talking with co-workers.	Must be discussing business!	Must be gossiping!
Is not at the desk.	Must be at a business meeting!	Must have gone shopping or in the washroom putting on makeup!
Is getting married.	He will be settled now!	Her priorities will change!
Is having lunch with the boss.	He is on the way up!	They must be having an affair!
Was criticized by his boss.	He will improve his performance now!	She must be getting upset!
Is becoming a parent.	He needs a raise!	We should look at a replacement as she will most likely leave!

Source: Sampath, 2007

Women in the board room

India has also recently joined the bandwagon of countries like Norway by enacting the New Companies Act 2013, replacing the old 1956 Law. The objective of the Act is to bring more accountability and robust corporate governance by bringing in more women on boards. The New Companies Act requires every listed company and every public company (with a minimum paid up share capital of Rs100 crore or an annual turnover of at least Rs300 crore[4]) to appoint at least one woman director. The New Companies Act has already initiated changes in the corporate board rooms of India. In the five months that followed a Securities and Exchange Board of India (SEBI) board meeting in February 2014, 91 women were appointed to 97 directorship positions in 94 companies. Many Indian women may well be good success stories if they are able to demonstrate an actual change as a result of their presence at senior leadership levels.

Women in management

According to the *Global Gender Gap Report 2014* (WEF, 2014):

> the gender gap for economic participation and opportunity now stands at 60% world-wide, having closed by 4% from 56% in 2006 when the Forum first started measuring it. Based on this trajectory, with all else remaining equal, it will take 81 years for the world to close this gap completely.

The trials and tribulations of Indian women managers are no different from those of women around the world. The percentage of women in management in India is roughly 3–6 percent, with approximately 2 percent of Indian women managers in Indian corporations. The number of women at the entry level is 25 percent, decreasing to 16 percent in mid-level management, further reducing to 4 percent at senior management level (McKinsey, 2015). It is a general perception that women in the west are unshackled by restrictive social norms while Indian society is more conservative and thus more discriminatory towards women. This statement however does not hold true for twenty-first-century urban Indian women.

A woman is held responsible for home and hearth, be it in the US, Europe or India. While names like Indra Nooyi and Kiran Mazumdar Shaw are recognized the world over, there are several other women managers in India who have dared to challenge the stereotypes, change the rules of the game and are making their way into the list of powerful women in the corporate world. It is difficult to identify a corporate sector untouched by the leadership of the Indian woman. A look at the following section shows that from banking to software, biscuits to tractors, poultry to pharmaceuticals, healthcare to hospitality, women managers in India are making their mark as trailblazers.

Banking and finance

Banking, where pay is good and the work environment perceived to be safe, is one of the sectors where Indian women managers have been very successful in recent years. As per a report compiled by the Centre for Social Research in 2009 (CSR India, 2009), the combined share of women in public and private banks is 3.91 percent. A Standard Chartered Bank study (Community Business, 2010) found the financial sector performing best in terms of gender diversity. Nine of the eleven banks listed on the BSE-100 had a woman on their board, with two having female CEOs. Male domination existed in the Indian banking sector until the 1980s. With the opening up of the economy in the 1990s, the intake of women in the private banking sector rose. Public sector banks also made concerted efforts towards recruiting and developing women managers following the Khandelwal Committee report of 2010 (Financial Services, 2010) which stated that diversity management was getting inadequate attention.

The appointment of Zarin Daruwala, a chartered accountant who began her career with ICICI Bank in 1989 and worked in project finance, corporate banking and headed wholesale banking as chief executive of Standard Chartered's India operations, is the latest in a series of appointments of women to top spots in the country's banking sector. She joins Shikha Sharma (Axis Bank), Naina Lal Kidwai (HSBC), Kalpana Morparia (JPMorgan Chase), Kaku Nakhate (Bank of America Merrill Lynch), Vedika Bhandarkar (Credit Suisse India), Manisha Girotra (UBS Warburg India) and Falguni Nayar (Kotak Mahindra Capital).

When asked why more women bankers are able to move into the corner office, Swati Piramal, a non-executive director on the board of ICICI Bank commented that banking comes naturally to women as they are "more conservative, more structured, more careful about money, good leaders and better team players" (*Economic Times*, 4 October 2013). The chairman of Shriram Capital, Arun Duggal, himself a veteran international banker, confirmed this: "Banking requires sound instinct and intellectual capability to analyze businesses. I feel women are better at it than men" (*Economic Times*, 4 October 2013). He believes "women have the ability to judge a borrower situation instinctively and are able to make very sound judgements."

As there is no shop floor in banking, the problem of night shifts does not confront women. It must be noted that banks consciously began building diversity earlier than other sectors. Tarjani Vakil, who rose to the top spot in 1996 as chairperson of Exim Bank, was perhaps the first of her kind. She was followed by Ranjana Kumar who became chair and managing director (CMD) of Indian Bank in 2000. She managed a significant turnaround at the bank, before taking over as chairperson of Nabard (National Bank for Agriculture and Rural Development) in 2003.

Visionary leaders at ICICI Bank ensured that women got an opportunity to prove themselves, while according to Shubhalakshmi Panse, chairman and managing director of Allahabad Bank (cited in Naqvi, 2011), "Women who are at the top now are largely those who started their careers around that time and worked their way up." Puneet Singh, partner of Heidrick and Struggles, comments, "Women are successful in the banking sector as they are strong in external networking and more objective and performance-oriented in their roles."

Many banks have also proactively promoted women for fear of losing them to the competition. Thus it has now become possible for women to crack and penetrate through the glass ceiling in public sector banks also. Arundhati Bhattacharya has achieved the laudable feat of reaching the top slot in the country's largest bank, State Bank of India (SBI), through perseverance and hard work. As SBI's first woman chairperson, she orchestrated the jump of SBI's net profit by 20 per cent, deposits by 13 per cent, retail advances by 15 per cent, and a reduction in non-performing assets (NPAs) from 4.95 per cent to 4.25 per cent in March 2015. Other women who have broken through the male bastion in public sector banks and are holding the top positions are Archana Bhargava (United Bank of India), Vijayalakshmi Iyer (Bank of India), Shubhalakshmi Panse (Allahabad Bank) and Usha Ananthasubramanian (Bharatiya Mahila Bank).

Arundhati explains in an interview that her experience has shown that women managers drop out of the race as they have to make the choice between career and family for primarily three reasons: (1) to start a family; (2) to support a child during the last three years of school when she or he has to prepare not only for the board examination but also entrance examinations in professional courses like engineering, medicine or law; and (3) to look after parents or parents-in-law if they fall ill. Having herself experienced these pressures of work–life balance, Arundhati has been instrumental in introducing the facility of two-year sabbaticals to be allowed three times in the entire career of women executives of SBI. This enables successful women employees to carry on without making the difficult choice of falling away from their career path.

IT and IT enabled services

The other sector where women managers in India are making their presence felt is that of IT and IT enabled services. Of the 3,520,000 employees in this sector, 34 percent are women (NASSCOM, 2015). The Indian IT business process outsourcing (BPO) industry has been growing exponentially over the last 15 years, and it continues to be one of the fastest growing sectors in the Indian economy.

The National Association of Software and Services Companies (NASSCOM) is a not-for-profit Indian consortium established in 1988 to promote the development of the country's IT and BPO industries. It currently has 1200 members of whom about 250 are global corporations from Europe, UK, USA, Japan and China.

An excellent initiative known as Women in Leadership-IT (WIL-IT) has been taken by NASSCOM to promote networking and competency building through training and cross-company, cross-functional mentoring to enable women to assume leadership positions in the IT sector. Member companies are invited to identify two women employees within their company who have senior leadership potential and nominate them for the Mentoring Circle. The programme is conducted by recognized women and men industry leaders. Six sessions covering topics such as career management, negotiation skills, managing peers, matrix management, branding self and getting to the corner office are conducted by the mentors. Each session (one every month) is for about an hour and a half. The sharing and learning emanates from the mentors as well as from the peer group.

Five powerful Indian women in the technology sector are Vanitha Narayanan (managing director, IBM India), Neelam Dhawan (managing director, HP India), Kirthiga Reddy (head of office, Facebook India), Aruna Jayanthi (CEO, Capgemini India) and Kumud Srinivasan (president, Intel India). Each of these women have grown up in India and obtained higher management degrees from leading universities in the US. They have thousands reporting to them and are passionate about taking forward women leadership in the corporate world.

Srinivasan comments that "these companies have helped women to be geographically mobile and given them access to multiskilling, paving a road for them to evolve and grow. The work–life effectiveness initiatives, non-discriminatory policies, and equal employment opportunities have also contributed" (*Economic Times*, 25 October 2013).

A cause for worry creeps in however when one looks at the top five Indian companies in the IT sector: Tata Consultancy Services (TCS), Infosys, Wipro, HCL Technologies and Tech Mahindra. A survey reported by the Centre for Internet and Society in 2013 (CIS India, 2013) revealed that none of these companies were demonstrating their intent of encouraging women employees to reach the pinnacle of leadership in their respective organizations. There were no women chairpersons in any of these companies. Of a total of 66 board members, only four were women.

Table 14.4 Women on boards and in senior management in IT

	Total board members	Women board members	Total in executive management	Women in executive management
TCS	14	1	30	2
Infosys	15	1	14	1
Wipro	12	0	23	2
HCL Technologies	9	1	18	0
Tech Mahindra	17	1	13	1
Total	66	4	98	6

Source: Centre for Internet and Society, 2013

Nancy Thomas, vice-president, IBM Global Business Services, holds that diversity of background and ideas are key drivers of innovation. She urges women to

> learn when to stop consensus-building and make decisions for the team. Building credibility and authority is vital for leadership. Cultural factors do restrain women. But the real glass ceiling is the one we put upon ourselves. We women are our own barriers. Women must hone their capacity to handle opportunities and embrace them.
>
> (Info Change News, 2008)

Family business

Leading business families in India are really bringing in the winds of change and empowering their female progeny to take lead roles in their businesses. These women who have degrees from leading business schools are not mere figureheads but actively engage in decision making and day to day operations. Business families like Reliance, Godrej, Lupin, Thermax, Infosys, Cipla, Emami, Piramal, Sun Pharma and Wockhardt, among many others, are all walking the talk and ensuring important places for their women folk (*Business Today*, 31 August 2014).

Nita Ambani, who is married to Reliance Industries chairman and managing director, Mukesh Ambani, who also happens to be the richest man in India, has been chairperson of Reliance Foundation since its inception in 2010. Born in a middle-class family, she now manages India's biggest corporate social responsibility outlay of over Rs1,500 crore annually. The flagship program Bharat India Jodo (BIJ) aims to build capacity and develop rural areas, having touched over 4.5 million lives to date.

The Godrej daughters Tanya Dubash and Nisaba Godrej are key players in their family's business. "I have always considered them equal and anyone from the family who wanted to join the business was free to join if they were qualified," says their father Adi Godrej (*Business Today*, 31 August 2014). Lupin CEO Vinita Gupta, a pharmacy graduate from Mumbai University and an MBA from Kellogg Graduate School of Management, focuses on the company's business in the US, Europe and Japan. She and her brother took over the reins from their father in September 2014 and together are taking the company to new heights. Vinita Bali, former managing director of Britannia Industries, quadrupled Britannia's revenue from Rs1,615 crore in 2005–2006 to Rs6,342 crore when she exited the company in 2013–2014. She also made the company's biscuits more nutritious by fortifying them with minerals.

Women are literally walking in their father's footsteps and taking on the mantle of managing family-owned businesses. Most of them start something new and are change agents, giving the businesses new dimensions or complete makeovers. The chairperson of Thermax, Meher Pudumjee, has been driving her company's initiative into alternative energy solutions. Rather than making mistakes when moving into uncharted territory, Meher likes to carefully think things through, evaluate options, and then take the final decisions.

Radhika Piramal of VIP Industries says, "What I brought to the table was clear brand segmentation and a distinct portfolio strategy that targeted specific consumers." The four daughters – Suneeta, Preetha, Shobhana, and Sangita of founder chairman, Prathap C. Reddy, of the Apollo Hospitals group have taken varying responsibilities and ensured remarkable growth. Nearly two-thirds of Apollo's 40,000 employees are women and they are given ample growth opportunities under the leadership of the four sisters.

Sulajja Firodia Motwani, joint managing director of Kinetic Motors and managing director of Kinetic Finance, is responsible for Kinetic's transformation from a moped company to a manufacturer of great versatility. She has single-handedly designed and developed marketing strategies to spearhead the company's growth and has been selected as the Global Leader of Tomorrow by the World Economic Forum.

The entrepreneurial woman

More and more women are now striding out from the comfort of their homes to make a mark in the Innovation Next-Gen economy/business. Their success speaks highly of their shrewd business sense, a thorough understanding of the market and remarkable administrative acumen. Rashmi Bansal categorizes women entrepreneurs in India as (1) those who enlisted family support or are heirs (2) those who overcame hindrances and victimhood and battled hard for success and (3) educated women entrepreneurs who struck out on their own.

From humble beginnings to being the richest woman in the country, Kiran Mazumdar Shaw epitomizes the entrepreneurial spirit and never say die attitude of women in India. Having studied zoology at Bangalore University and brewing at Ballarat University, she started out as a trainee brewer at Carlton and United Beverages in 1974. Four years later she started her own company, Biocon, in her garage with an investment of Rs10,000. Financial institutions refused her applications as biotechnology was in a relatively nascent stage in India at that time. An unfavorable factor was that she was a woman with a company showing nil assets. It is relatively easy for women belonging to corporate families to set up new ventures, but here was a woman without any business background to help her in her endeavors. With sheer hard work and commitment, Shaw has transformed Biocon into one of the leading biopharmaceutical firms in India.

Shehnaz Hussain is one of India's most successful women entrepreneurs who has captured markets around the world. Her company Shehnaz Herbals is one of the largest manufacturers of herbal products in the world. Ekta Kapoor founded Balaji Telefilms and made it a household name and was instrumental in changing the face of Indian television. The soap operas made by her production house are always top of the charts. Finally, the story of Kalpana Saroj is both amazing and awe inspiring. Married at the age of twelve, she lived in a Mumbai slum with her husband's family. Unable to take the daily abuse she went back to her parents' village. Ostracized by the villagers, she attempted suicide. At sixteen, she returned to Mumbai and began working in a garment factory. Today she owns Kamani Tubes, has personal assets of over US$112 million, and is on the board of directors of the Bharatiya Mahila Bank.

The list of success stories of women entrepreneurs in India is long and varied. They are venturing into diverse fields like e-commerce, fashion attire, life-sciences, food products, healthcare, design and education. One must also note that there are nearly 3 million micro, small and medium enterprises with full or partial female ownership. Collectively, these women-owned enterprises contribute 3.09 percent of industrial output and employ over 8 million people. The services sector accounts for nearly 78 percent of women-owned enterprises. The small and medium size companies have developed through individual effort and a lot of sweat.

The support system

Family support has enabled women leaders of the large corporates to move forward and transform. Family and friends provide a safety net which helps professional women to cope with myriad challenges. Though the joint family system is disintegrating in the cities, family support is still available. Sons do not necessarily leave the family home after marriage. So children often have the care of grandparents. Even if the parents are living in a home of their own, they visit the son's family and daughters-in-law welcome visits from mothers-in-law as it means having someone with a watchful eye to supervise the domestic help. Parents are willing babysitters and always ready to provide support. Domestic help and drivers are also affordable. However availability of domestic help can be both advantageous and disadvantageous. There are reliability issues. There have been cases of ill treatment of children by domestic help. The risk of burglaries also exists. Even if full-time help is not preferred, part-time support is available in the form of cooks and maids. Without a support system at home, it is very difficult to focus on a career. SBI's chairperson Bhattacharya has commented that she was lucky to have good help at home who freed her from worrying about the daily domestic imperatives and enabled her to avoid the "double burden syndrome."

Collectivist society traits also result in another advantage. Women do not need to visit psychiatrists for every small dissatisfaction. Talking it over with friends provides the necessary outlet for coping with stress. Thus the incidence of broken homes is much lower. Naqvi (2011) lists a number of factors as crucial for the success of women managers. These include talent, management skills, ambitious nature, perseverance and self-confidence. She comments however that the overriding need is that of good family support.

The path ahead

The Indian woman's participation in the workforce has been increasing by leaps and bounds. It is necessary to come up with attractive policies in the workplace to retain the women workforce. Corporate houses in India, however, do not go out of the way to develop women-centric policies. Flexible working hours and supportive relocation policies are not the norm. Also organizations do not have supportive policies such as the provision of crèches, daycare facilities and reimbursement for childcare if the employee is travelling. Part-time work or opportunities for working from home are few and far between. Women often lose out on transfer promotions, being less geographically mobile than men. Regional development of industries, with mini headquarters in cities through the country, would facilitate the participation and promotion of women.

Call centers have introduced flexible work hours, but the concept of a 9 to 5 work regime needs to be changed in other sectors. Even in government offices and other organizations, staggered work schedules should be introduced. The concept of planned housing complexes with built-in daycare centers and elementary schools could also be feasible. Parents could then leave their children in daycare centers or at school within the residential complex, on their way to work. The children would be picked up at the end of the day, and dinner could be eaten in center and school cafeterias.

Good, cheap, efficient and safe public transportation is a necessity, as we are beginning to realize from an ecological standpoint. This is also true from the point of view of the woman who works, for she must be able to get to and from her place of business safely. The safety factor is a particularly important consideration for women, who are the most vulnerable members of a violent society. In the past it was assumed that a woman's safety was her problem, and that the solution was simple: she should stay home. Women are not staying at home any longer, and society's obligation is to protect its citizens.

Researchers (Kulkarni, 2002; Mehra, 2002) agree that women managers have certain key strengths which help them to be successful in the workplace. They are more sensitive in handling relationships with peers and subordinates, as compassion and empathy are inherent traits. They seem to have a sixth sense about situations and thus perceive complexities more effectively. Juggling a multitude of responsibilities in the home makes them adept at multitasking. Also women managers have a greater sense of loyalty towards their organizations and do not look for quick changes. Being empathic and intuitive enables them to handle crisis situations better.

Realizing the value of women managers and the need to keep them engaged and not allow them to drop out of their careers made Genpact introduce a novel gender diversity initiative named Career 2.0. It aims to feed the leadership pipeline and is meant for experienced women managers seeking to make a career comeback. The objective is to hire women mangers in mid to senior level roles across functions. Piyush Mehta, head of Global Human Resources comments:

> There are qualified women who perhaps do not know how to make a career comeback. We are more than happy to leverage their talent. Our approach is that through the use of Genpact policies, we give these women flexibility and full-time roles. Some want to work half-a-day, some can't work late in the evening. We want to offer flexibility to this set of super talented women.

Genpact genuinely believes that organizations with women in leadership roles have better results in the long run. Having more women in the senior management positions is thus a business imperative. Mehta continues: "Of our 68,000 employees, 38 percent are women. The percentage of women in the top 600 in the company is much lower, at 20 percent. This is exactly the challenge we want to deal with. We want to grow Career 2.0 joinees to this level."

It is indeed interesting to note that the company is using social media like Facebook to reach out to potential hires. Another notable initiative is that of "Tanmantra," which means potential in the ancient Indian language Sanskrit. This is a cross-industry women's leadership development program launched by Catalyst, IBM and IIM-Bangalore in 2014. The aim of this program is to leverage the best practical experience and research to advance women in the Indian business community. The first batch comprised 30 women across the pharmaceutical, retail, technology, and finance industries. They were nominated by their companies for the program, and many of them had attended leadership programs before. Vijayalakshmi, a nominee from IBM, comments that the curriculum is very useful as it is "tailored for Indian women": "The course really addresses the subtle nuances that hold women back at work. For me, it has been an excellent experience. Interacting with women who have faced similar situations has been wonderful."

Through case-based learning, the women managers are given practical challenges which they work on over a period of ten months. Inputs have to be collected from multiple stake-holders in their own organizations. The objective is to make them more assertive, interact with male colleagues, question them and thus develop levels of confidence.

Prabal Chakraborty, vice-president and managing director of Boston Scientific India, talks about the NARI program to nurture women's talent and prepare them for future leadership roles: "Women are a very important talent group for any organisation and giving them a workplace environment that nurtures talent, provides equal opportunity has now become critical. We started NARI initiative to focus on strengthening our women leadership pipeline in the organisation" (*Business Today*, 9 July 2015).

Flipkart rolled out its new maternity leave policy of 24 weeks plus an additional four months of flexi-working hours with full pay against the mandatory requirement of twelve weeks of maternity leave. The company is also offering a one-year career break without pay.

Another recent example is Citibank India which has announced its new policy of providing a childcare allowance over and above salaries worth up to Rs1.32 lakh a year. This aims at retaining employees who have recently become mothers, allowing them to pursue their careers uninterrupted. In 2008, the maternity leave of central government employees was increased to two years with full pay for two surviving children.

The government currently is focused on ensuring that change percolates down to rural areas and small towns. Social change however is difficult to achieve and cannot be brought about overnight. Societies have to find effective solutions consistent with their cultures and environmental conditions (Mukherji and Jain, 2009). It is now up to the people of India with support from the corporates to keep the momentum going and accelerate the process of change.

Notes

1   The *Vedas* are the ancient scriptures or revelation (*Shruti*) of the Hindu teachings. They manifest the divine word in human speech. Also known as *Samhitas* (collection of *mantras*, or chants) they are divided into *Rigveda*, *Yajurveda*, *Samaveda* and *Atharvaveda*. The Vedic Age, precipitated by the migration of the Aryan people, saw the development of agricultural activities on a large scale in the upper Gangetic plains of India. This period is known for its nature worship and formation of Hindu religious philosophy.

2   The *Puranas* are the most important or commonly used scriptural texts of the Hindus, serving as guides for the whole of life and society. Each of the eighteen major *Puranas* consist of various stories of the gods and goddesses, hymns, an outline of ancient history, cosmology, rules of life, rituals, and instructions on spiritual knowledge.

3   *Smritis* are the scriptures of lesser authority for Hindus. They contain mythological texts such as the epics – Mahabharata and Ramayana. Manusmriti is one of the texts of Hinduism that imparts ethics, morality, and codes of conduct.

4   Rs1 crore = Rs10 million + US$150,376 ($1 = Rs66.5).

References

Bhattacharya, P. (2005), "Attracting and retaining women employees", http://resources.greatplace-towork.com/article/pdf/attracting_and_retaining_women employees.pdf. Retrieved 5.12.08.

Bumiller, E. (1990), *May You be the Mother of a Hundred Sons: A Journey Among the Women of India*, Random House, New York.

Business Today (31 August 2014), www.businesstoday.in/magazine/cover-story/godrej-lupin-cipla-piramal-sun-pharma-wockhardt-tara-singh-vachani/story/209049.html. Retrieved 4.12.15.

Business Today (9 July 2015), www.businesstoday.in/opinion/perspective/india-inc-takes-baby-steps-to-break-the glass-ceiling/story/221520.html. Retrieved 5.12.15.

Census of India (2011), www.censusindia.gov.in/2011-common/census_2011.html Retrieved 22.7.16.

Chakrapani, C. and Vijaya Kumar, S. (1994), *Changing Status and Role of Women in Indian Society*, M.D. Publications, New Delhi.

CIS India (2013), http://cis-india.org/about/reports. Retrieved 16.4.16.

Community Business (2010), www.communitybusiness.org/images/cb/publications/2010/WOB_India.pdf. Retrieved 6.11.15.

CSR India (2009), www.csrindia.org/images/download/annual-report/2009-Annual-Report.pdf. Retrieved 6.12.15.

Das, Sonali, Sonali Jain-Chandra, Kalpana Kochhar and Naresh Kumar (2015), *Women Workers in India: Why So Few Among So Many?* IMF Working Paper, Asia and Pacific Department.

Economic Times (4 October 2013), http://articles.economictimes.indiatimes.com/2013-10-04/news/42718085_1_archana-bhargava-banker-magazine-kaku-nakhate. Retrieved 5.12.15.

Economic Times (25 October 2013), http://articles.economictimes.indiatimes.com/2013-10-25/news/43395544_1_vanitha-narayanan-intel-india-ibm-india. Retrieved 5.12.15.

Financial Services (2010), http://financialservices.gov.in/reports/HRIssuesOfPSBs.pdf. Retrieved 6.6.15.

Gupta, R. R. (1988), "Women in Hindu Laws", in Agrawal, S. (ed.), *Status of Women*, Printwell Publishers, Jaipur.

Hindubusinessline.com (2007), www.thehindubusinessline.com/2007/10/03/stories/2007100350530900.htm. Retrieved 6.12.08.

InfoChange News (2008), http://infochangeindia.org/women/features/new-vistas-for-working-women-in-indias-it-industry.html. Retrieved 7.12.15.

Jain, N. and Mukherji, S. (2010), The Perception of 'Glass Ceiling', in Indian Organizations: An Exploratory Study, *South Asian Journal of Management*, 17 (1), 23–42.

Jung, A. (2000), *Unveiling India: A Woman's Journey*, Penguin Books India, New Delhi.

Kulkarni, S. S. (2002), Women and Professional Competency: A Survey Report, *Indian Journal of Training and Development*, 32 (2) April–June.

McKinsey (2015), www.mckinsey.com/~/media/McKinsey/dotcom/Insights/Growth/The%20power%20of%20parity%20Advancing%20womens%20equality%20in%20India/MGI%20India%20parity_Full%20report_November%202015.ashx. Retrieved 5.12.15.

Mehra, P. (2002), *Women Managers: To the Top and Beyond*, Hindu Businessline, Saturday, April 27.

Mukherji, S. and Jain, N. (2009), Women Empowerment through Transformational Leadership: Case of Satya Jyoti, *Vision*, 13(4), 63–69.

Naqvi, F. (2011), Perspectives of Indian Women Managers in the Public Sector, *Indian Journal of Gender Studies*, 18 (3): 279–309.

NASSCOM (2015), www.nasscom.in/knowledge-professionals. Retrieved 5.12.15.

Sampath, V. (2007), "Breaking Barriers & Building Bridges", presented at Women Manager's Conference in Bangalore. www.mmachennai.org/ppt_2007/Ms%20Vijaya%20Sampath.ppt. Retrieved 14.1.09.

Sharma, L. P. (1992), *History of Ancient India*. StosiusInc/Advent Books Division, New Delhi.

Sharma, R. and Mukherji, S. (2011), "Women in India: Their Odyssey towards Equality", in Stefan Gröschlb and Junko Takagi (eds), *Diversity Quotas, Diverse Perspectives: The Case of Gender*. Gower Publishing Ltd., Surrey, England.

Tharakan, S. M. and Tharakan, M. (1975), Status of Women in India: A Historical Perspective, *Social Scientist*, 4 (4/5), 115–123.

WEF (2014), *Global Gender Gap Report 2014*, www3.weforum.org/docs/GGGR14/GGGR_Complete Report_2014.pdf. Retrieved 5.12.15

15 Women in management in Turkey

Hayat Kabasakal, Fahri Karakaş, Ceyda Maden and Zeynep Aycan

Introduction

The Republic of Turkey is located mainly in west Asia and partly in southeast Europe. It had 77.6 million inhabitants at the end of 2014 (TUIK, 2014a). The country has been a bridge between east and west throughout history. The analysis of women in society and in management positions conveys the simultaneous influence of eastern and western cultures in the Turkish context.

The Republic of Turkey was established upon the demise of the Ottoman Empire. After the defeat of the Ottoman Empire in the First World War, under the leadership of Mustafa Kemal Atatürk, Turks won the war of independence and established the new republic in 1923. As the president of the new republic, Atatürk guided a series of reforms in social, political, linguistic and economic areas, which were later referred to as the Kemalist principles. The Kemalist principles, which constituted the dominant state ideology, had important implications for the modernization and emancipation of Turkish women (Arat, 1999).

The reforms of the republic carried the values of secularism, nationalism and modernism which incorporated westernization into society. Women were assigned an important role in this modernization project and their progress was interpreted as a significant measure of success in reaching modernity, westernization and development of the nation (Arat, 1994; 1999). This state ideology upheld the value of gender equality in employment and elimination of discriminatory policies from the formal processes of public employment.

The cornerstones of emancipation of women in the Turkish republic were widely distributed through education, legislative and administrative reforms, political rights, public visibility and professionalism. The impact of the reforms was significant among middle- and upper-class families, while their influence was only partial among lower socio-economic groups and in rural areas. In the post-1980 period, however, two types of changes emerged to weaken the ideology of 'state feminism' (that is, advocacy of women's movement demands inside the state by women's policy agencies) (Kantola and Squires, 2008) that dominated the early republican era (Healy *et al.*, 2005). Firstly, change was related to the neo-liberal economic programme that had been applied since the 1980s and resulted in the weakening of government labour market regulations. 'This has diluted the traditional sex equality discourse of the republican ideology pursued by the state in all sectors' (Healy *et al.*, 2005: 254). Secondly, newly emerging political parties and economic institutions advocated gender segregation, which is considered to be against the principle of secularism. In contemporary Turkish society, these trends have created a duality between secularism on the one hand and religiousness and patriarchal Middle Eastern values on the other hand.

The changes in the post-1980 period have created some variations in social attitudes regarding the image of Turkish women: 'The image of republican Turkish women, expected to "self-sacrifice" and "pioneer" for the advancement of the nation, has lost its influence on a new generation of young women graduates' (Healy *et al.*, 2005: 254). Like women in other developed nations of the world, Turkish women started to perceive their careers from a standpoint of individualistic motivation rather than a collectivist sense of fulfilling a national duty.

In summary, despite the significant attempts at modernization of women as a dominant state ideology in the early republican era, some conflicting and traditional roles are simultaneously present in Turkish society, even among the middle and upper classes which have internalized these principles. With the changes that have emerged since the 1980s, 'state feminism' has weakened and attitudes favouring gender segregation have gained momentum. Traditional roles that are prevalent in parts of society and the right-wing executive power that has been dominant since early 2000s, promote segregation of gender roles, the role of women as mothers and wives and traits that are considered to be feminine. This chapter provides an analysis of existing gender segregation in Turkish society. It aims to portray women's general standing in society in terms of their contribution to the labour force as well as their position in specific areas, including management, politics and entrepreneurship. This chapter will also examine women's general well-being in terms of their income, educational and legal standing and attitudes towards them in society. It will summarize with positive initiatives that aim to support women and prospects for the future.

Labour force characteristics

Labour force participation

The Turkish labour force has gone through major changes since the 1950s (Özar, 1994) as a result of significant migration from rural to urban areas and the rapid growth of industrial and service sectors after the 1960s. As a result of these two trends, the agricultural labour force dropped significantly, leading to a steady decline in women's percentage in the total labour force.

Although women's labour force participation has been regarded as an important determinant of sustainable development, women's percentage in the total labour force is quite low. While women constituted 43.1 per cent of the total labour force in 1955, this ratio decreased to 30.3 in 2014 (Turkish Statistical Institute, 2007; TUIK, 2014b). However, men's labour force participation rate increased from 56.9 per cent in 1955 to 71.3 per cent in 2014. As a benchmark, participation of women in the total labour force in the Organization of Economic Co-operation and Development (OECD) and European Union-28 averaged 51.5 per cent and 51.8 per cent in 2014, respectively (OECD, 2014) (Table 15.1). Although women's labour

Table 15.1 Labour force participation rates (1990–2014) (%)

	Turkey			OECD	EU-28
	1990	*2000*	*2014*	*2014*	*2014*
Men	79.7	73.7	71.3	69.0	64.9
Women	34.1	26.6	30.3	51.5	51.8
Total	56.6	49.9	49.4	60.0	58.2

Source: TUIK, 2014a and OECD, 2014

force participation rates have started to rise in Turkey in recent years (Dayıoğlu and Kırdar, 2009: Taymaz, 2009: Uraz *et al.*, 2010), it revealed a declining pattern until 2007 and remains low over time (OXFAM and TEPAV, 2015).

According to previous studies and analyses, urbanization and agricultural job shedding have been the two major factors that contribute to the declining participation of Turkish women in the labour force. Turkey experienced high levels of migration from rural to urban areas in the 1980s. An important reflection of migration to women's labour force participation is the withdrawal of the migrant women from the labour force (from the agricultural sector) once they moved to urban areas. Agricultural shedding is also an influential factor in women's labour force participation. In Turkey, the participation of women in the labour force has been declining steadily from 34.1 per cent in 1990 to 23.6 per cent in 2007. As rural women are generally employed in the agricultural sector as unpaid workers, a decline in overall agricultural employment negatively affects their labour force participation.

The decline in rural female labour force participation is also related to the changing lifestyle preferences of an emerging middle class which pull them away from agricultural activities. The younger cohorts in rural areas are specifically becoming more educated and seeking better life and employment opportunities (Çelikoğlu *et al.*, 2009). Young men are rapidly moving from agricultural employment to better-paid jobs in other sectors. In addition, young women are married to men who no longer work in the agricultural sector. Accordingly, the family activities in rural areas depart from subsistence agriculture, which causes a withdrawal of women from the labour force.

Previous studies have suggested that the low participation in urban areas is the primary factor behind women's low labour force participation over the years (e.g., Dayıoğlu and Kırdar, 2009; Uraz *et al.*, 2010). According to Turkish Statistical Institute data[1] (TUIK, 2013), women's share in the labour force is quite low in urban areas (28 per cent in 2013) while it is significantly higher in rural areas (36.7 per cent in 2013). The total labour force participation of women (30.8 per cent in 2013) is closer to the urban average as the majority of working age population resides in urban areas (68.5 per cent) with the increasing effect of migration. Thus, in Turkey, the overall share of women in the labour force is mainly affected by the behavior and trends of female labour force participation in urban areas.

The low participation rate of women in urban areas is mainly a result of the low participation rates among poorly educated urban women. Although participation rates among educated women in urban areas (i.e., those who have attained tertiary education) are quite high (72.4 per cent in 2013), labour force participation rates among women who have completed only primary and secondary education are low, at 20.7 and 25.5 per cent, respectively (TUIK, 2013). Household Labour Force Survey statistics indicate that the main reason behind the non-participation of urban poorly educated women is their role as housewives (74 per cent in 2013), followed by the opposition of families to their working (8 per cent) (TUIK, 2013). Six out of 100 women are not in the labour force as they are disabled, sick or too old to work and the remaining 12 per cent are still in school or have other reasons for non-participation (e.g., seasonal worker, does not expect to find a job, not looking for a job but ready to work).

Indeed, there are also certain cultural and economic barriers that prevent labour force participation among poorly educated women in urban areas. Economic barriers mainly include the existing unfavourable working conditions for poorly educated women in urban areas. In 2013, 61 per cent of poorly educated women in urban areas worked in the informal sector in Turkey (TUIK, 2013) and received low salaries, had long working hours, and lacked affordable childcare. Besides, they are also faced with cultural barriers that relate to their societal role as caregivers and expectations of their husbands, extended families and others. Family pressure (from husbands, parents, and in-laws), pregnancy and childcare tend to be a particular constraint that decreases poorly educated women's intention to participate in the labour force in urban areas.

Along with the economic and cultural constraints, poorly educated women in urban areas may also experience an 'under-participation trap' (Booth and Coles, 2007; Çelikoğlu *et al.*, 2009; Taymaz, 2009). According to the under-participation trap, poorly educated women tend to work in the informal sector that generally offers them lower wages than what they would have to pay to hire someone else to do their domestic activities (e.g., childcare, cooking, cleaning). As a result, they are more likely to withdraw from the labour market. Low wages and low returns to education may also prevent families from investing in the education of girls as they think that women have little chance of participating in the labour force. This will contribute further to keeping wages low, which will subsequently keep labour supply low.

All in all, it is plausible to argue that various socio-cultural factors, education level and marital status and migration/urbanization trends influence women's labour force participation. The social roles of women and the norms of patriarchal society play an influential role in shaping women's decisions on labour market participation (Dayıoğlu, 2000; Dayıoğlu and Kırdar, 2009). Available literature argues that housework and childcare/eldercare are traditionally female duties that may preclude women from participating in the labour force (İlkkaracan and Acar, 2007). Women with young children find it even more difficult to participate in the labour force (Dayıoğlu and Kırdar, 2009). According to the analysis of Prime Ministry General Directorate on the Status of Women (2014), labour force participation rates of women (aged 29–45) with children (29.9 per cent) are significantly lower than those without children (45.5 per cent). This gap is even larger in the urban areas where women experience the increased burden of domestic work including childcare as they receive limited help from family members.

With respect to the effect of education, previous studies have shown that there is a positive relationship between the level of education and women's labour force participation (e.g., Aran *et al.*, 2009). Estimates reveal that having a higher educational degree increases the probability of employment from 3 per cent (primary school graduate) to 73 per cent (college graduate) for women (Çelikoğlu *et al.*, 2009). Finally, urbanization is an important trend that strongly influences women's labour force participation. The decline in agricultural production leads people to migrate to urban areas. Rural migrant women, who worked previously as unpaid family workers, find it more difficult to participate in the labour market in the urban setting due to their lower levels of education and insufficient skills. Besides, moving away from rural areas where the family support is substantial to urban centres often as a nuclear family may substantiate the burden of domestic work (e.g., childcare, care of the elderly and sick) on women.

Household Labour Force Survey statistics indicate a rise in women's employment over the period 2000–2014. This increase is primarily associated with the rise in service sector employment. Leaving its place to services, the agricultural sector is no longer the primary sector of employment for women. Although male workers continue to dominate the service sector (71 per cent in 2014), the number and percentage of women employed in the service sector more than doubled between 2000 and 2014 (TUIK, 2000, 2014a) (Table 15.2).

When we look at the employment status of women between 2000 and 2014, TUIK statistics reveal a positive change in women's engagement in economic and entrepreneurial activities. The employment status of women improved between 2000 and 2014 as women

Table 15.2 Employment by sector (thousands of people and %, population over 15 years of age)

	Agriculture	*Industry*	*Services*
Women			
2000	3,508 (45%)	763 (15%)	1,529 (18%)
2014	2,553 (41%)	1,235 (24%)	3,839 (29%)
Men			
2000	4,261 (55%)	4,411 (85%)	7,108 (82%)
2014	2,937 (59%)	4,079 (76%)	9,393 (71%)
Total			
2000	7,769 (100%)	5,174 (100%)	8,547 (100%)
2014	5,470 (100%)	5,315 (100%)	13,234 (100%)

Source: TUIK, 2000 and 2014a

moved out of agricultural and informal sector jobs to the formal economy. The percentage of women once working as unpaid workers dropped 21 per cent between 2000 and 2014 (TUIK, 2000, 2014a). There was a significant shift from unpaid employment to regular or per diem during the same period while there was no significant change in the proportion of women who were self-employed or who were job holders (Table 15.3).

In Turkey, being employed without being registered in any social security institution indicates working without any social protection. Despite the fact that the rate of employed women without social security somewhat improved between 2000 (70 per cent) and 2014 (48 per cent), half of women are still employed in the informal sector (TUIK, 2000, 2014a). The rate of employed women in agriculture without social security was particularly high (94 per cent), revealing that the decline in women's employment in agriculture did not substantially pull down the rate of employed women in the informal sector (TUIK, 2014a).

Unemployment and underemployment

Labour force indicators reveal that unemployment in both agriculture and non-agriculture sectors is higher for women than men. In 2014, the unemployment rate was 11.8 per cent for women while it was 9.9 per cent for men. Non-agricultural unemployment in Turkey, however, was higher than overall employment both for women (15.6 per cent) and men (11.0 per cent) (TUIK, 2014a).

Previous studies suggest that women are affected by unemployment more severely than are men, causing them to withdraw from the labour force. Tansel (2002) proposes that the

Table 15.3 Employment status by sex and by selected years (2000 and 2014) (%, population over 15 years of age)

	2000			*2014*		
	Men	*Women*	*Total*	*Men*	*Women*	*Total*
Regular/per diem employee	54	35	49	68	60	66
Employer	7	1	5	6	1	5
Self-employed	29	12	25	21	9	17
Unpaid family worker	10	52	22	5	30	12
Total	100	100	100	100	100	100

Source: TUIK, 2000 and 2014a

ultimate impact of unemployment on female labour force participation depends on the relative strengths of the "discouraged worker effect" and the "added-worker effect." The added worker effect implies that the labour supply of married women will increase when their husbands become unemployed. However, the discouraged worker effect suggests that the higher the unemployment rate the less likely women will be employed which, in turn, discourages women from looking for a job and causes them to withdraw from the labour force. Working with cross-sectional data from Turkey for the 2000–2010 period, Karaoğlan and Ökten (2012) report that married women whose husbands are unemployed or underemployed experience an 'added worker effect' and are more likely to enter the labour market and work more hours. However, worsening conditions of unemployment in a specific region are likely to have a discouraging effect on wives, decreasing their labour force participation. The rising share of female underemployment in total underemployment in recent years reveals that women are either pulling out of the labour market or settling for temporary or part-time work.

Gender differences in earnings

According to the *Global Gender Gap Report* prepared by World Economic Forum (2014), Turkey was ranked 87th in wage equality among 131 countries. Estimated earned income figures reveal US$10,501 for women and $26,893 for men with a respective female-to-male ratio of 0.39. Although these figure seemed to improve slightly over the years, Turkey is still behind most of the OECD and EU-27 countries in terms of wage equality (World Economic Forum, 2014).

In Turkey, there are two major wage-related concerns about the compensation of the female labour force. First, employment opportunities for women are generally concentrated in certain sectors paying low wage rates. Turkish women are mainly employed in labour-intensive and low-paying jobs, like textile and ready-made garment industries. Second, in most of the sectors they work and the occupations they choose women generally earn less than men (hierarchical segregation). Working without social security and with flexible hours decreases women's wages even further. When we examine the major occupational groups, in 2010, the largest wage gaps are observed for plant and machine operators and assemblers, professionals and craft and related trades workers (TUIK, 2010). The only occupational group where women were at an advantage with respect to wage levels compared to men was as managers, despite the fact that very few women reach such managerial positions (Table 15.4).

The gender pay gap does not change even taking education into account. In 2010, on the all education levels, men receive higher earnings than women although wages increase with the level of education for both men and women (Table 15.5). The highest wage differentials between men and women are observed in the vocational high school degree while the lowest differential is in the high school degree. The gender wage gap in vocational high school education may be related to the employment of women, with vocational school degrees in low-paying, low-status jobs in sectors such as garment production, catering and childcare.

Previous studies on wage differentials in the Turkish labour market have presented valuable findings regarding the role of education or human capital in the gender pay gap in Turkey. Using 1987 data from the Household Income and Expenditure Survey, Dayıoğlu and Kasnakoğlu (1997) found that almost 40.5 per cent of the variation in female earnings can be explained by basic human capital. In the same study, the authors report a 37.5 per cent wage gap in favour of men and point out that 36.2 per cent of this gap can be explained by human capital differences, while the remaining 63.8 per cent results from discrimination in the labour

Table 15.4 Average yearly (gross) wage rate based on gender and occupation and wage gap ratio (2010) (Turkish lira)

	Total	Men	Women	Wage gap* %
Managers	43,825	43,073	46,201	-7.3
Professionals	31,520	34,549	27,861	19.4
Technicians and associate professionals	22,082	22,536	20,865	7.4
Clerks	18,875	19,383	18,203	6.1
Service workers and shop and market sales workers	12,922	13,167	12,188	7.4
Skilled agricultural and fishery workers	14,091	—	—	—
Craft and related trades workers	15,278	15,586	13,004	16.6
Plant and machine operators and assemblers	13,336	13,851	10,518	24.1
Low-level occupations	12,075	12,449	10,713	13.9

Source: TUIK, 2010
Note: * Calculated based on total wages in 2010 [(male wages-female wages)/male wages*100]. 2010 year-end exchange rate: TL1 = US$0.6493

market. Tansel (2005) examines the wage differentials in the public and private sectors by using 1994 Household Expenditure Survey. The results reveal a female-to-male wage ratio of 77 per cent in the private sector in favour of men, while this ratio equals 84 per cent in state-owned enterprises. Examining the gender wage differentials based on 1988 Household Labour Force Survey data, Hisarcıklılar and Ercan (2005) argue that the wage gap between men and women cannot be explained by the differences between men's and women's human capital but by their differential treatment. In support of this argument, using 2003 Household Labor Survey data, İlkkaracan and Selim (2007) report that when personal characteristics such as education level, tenure, age, marital status, occupation, profession, part-time/full-time, firm size, working in an informal job and being a union member are controlled for, a 6 per cent gender wage gap is still observed in the public sector to the advantage of men. In the private sector, the corresponding difference is much higher, as high as 21.2 per cent. In a more recent study, Cudeville and Gürbüzer (2010) confirm the previous findings using 2003 Household Budget Survey data. The authors report that controlling the basic characteristics such as age, occupation and education, 76 per cent of the wage differences were due to outright discrimination. This form of discrimination amounts to a pay differential that occurs neither as a result of different productivity levels, nor as a result of the type of job or workplace, but merely due to the sex of the worker.

Table 15.5 Average annual (gross) wage rate based on gender and education and wage gap ratio (2010) (Turkish lira)

	Total	Men	Women	Wage gap* %
Primary school and below	13,099	13,526	11,065	19
Primary education and secondary school	13,043	13,505	10,949	19
High school	16,414	16,907	15,049	11
Vocational high school	21,280	22,195	17,109	23
Higher education	35,383	37,878	31,437	17
Total	19,694	19,683	19,728	-0.001

Source: TUIK, 2010
Note: * Calculated based on total wages in 2010 [(male wages-female wages)/male wages*100]. 2010 year-end exchange rate: TL1 = US$0.6493

In light of the empirical evidence above, it is plausible to argue that a significant portion of gender wage differentials in the Turkish labour market may arise due to unequal treatment against women in addition to differences in their human capital characteristics. İlkkaracan and Selim (2007: 59) state that 'part of the impact of this unequal treatment rewards men with higher payments but it mainly shows itself as lower wages for women'.

Education of women and men is one of the major problems in the way of the social development and modernization of Turkey. After the proclamation of the Republic of Turkey, Kemalist principles and state ideology that aims to improve women's position in society achieved some success in providing widespread education to Turkish women. Primary education is compulsory for both girls and boys and parents who do not send their children to school are liable to imprisonment.

In the early years of the republic, the rate of literacy was very low among women and over the years there was a significant increase in the numbers of literate women. In 1990, 67.4 per cent of women and 89.8 per cent of men were literate, and the literacy rate has increased gradually both for women and men, reaching 90.6 per cent and 98.1 per cent, respectively in 2013 (TUIK, 2014a). By a law enacted in 1997, compulsory education was raised from five to eight years, by combining primary and junior high school education as compulsory. In 2012 another law was enacted, which increased compulsory education to 12 years by a 4+4+4 structure of primary, junior and high school education as compulsory. Accordingly, the rights of girls to receive primary, junior and secondary (high school) education are put under state guarantee. In the 1997–1998 educational year, the schooling ratio for women was 78.9 per cent for primary education and 34.1 per cent for secondary education. In 2014–2015, for women the schooling rate in primary education reached 96.6 per cent whereas it was 94.3, 79.3 and 41.1 per cent for junior, secondary and higher education, respectively (Ministry of National Education, 2014–2015). Thus, there is no meaningful difference in the schooling ratio based on gender by the year 2015. This situation can be associated partly with the rise of private and public initiatives and campaigns that promote equal education opportunities for women (more information on these initiatives and campaigns provided below).

While years of schooling increased significantly for girls on the one hand, on the other hand gender roles are apparent in both vocational schools and university education, as there are distinct differences between the chosen subject areas of female and male students, which represent the cultural norms prevalent in society. Girls are frequently placed in vocational schools that teach subjects which are considered to be a part of the female role, such as home economics, child rearing and sewing, and boys are placed in schools that train them for jobs with a higher market value, such as electrician and carpenter (KSGM, 2015). At universities, female students constitute more than half of the students studying in non-technical areas such as language and literature (63.6 per cent in 2012–2013) and art (53.7 per cent in 2012–2013). Furthermore, their enrolment percentage portrays a gradual increase in the social sciences and applied social sciences, while the males' dominance in technical sciences is still prevalent (ÖSYM, 2007; TUIK, 2014a; YÖK, 2014–2015). In general, the employment of women with vocational school and higher education has increased significantly in recent years and as a general trend it can be stated that 'education' plays a primary role in improving women's position by increasing their employability in better-paid jobs with social security (Tan *et al.*, 2008).

Women in management

As part of the modernization project of the republic, the professionalization of women carried a significant importance. Beginning with the early years of the republic, middle- and upper-class families placed a high importance on the education of their daughters in highly prestigious professions. During the 1980s, Turkish women started their careers from a more individualistic motivation rather than as a duty for national development (Healy *et al.*, 2005) and continued to pursue education and careers in highly prominent professions.

The percentage of Turkish women in high-status professions can be considered to be high, even in comparison to many other industrialized western countries. In relation to some of the prestigious professions, for example, 42 per cent of architects, 40 per cent of lawyers and 43 per cent of academics were women in Turkey in 2014 (KSGM, 2015). As Table 15.5 shows, in 2014, in urban areas, 21 per cent of employed women were regarded as managers, professionals, technicians and associate professionals (TUIK, 2015), and this is an area where women are most concentrated (Tan *et al.*, 2008).

Nevertheless, the success of women in prestigious professional occupations is not reflected in the same proportions in decision-making positions. Only 2.4 per cent of women are employed in managerial positions and there are no statistics available on the demographic characteristics of these women managers or on minority women managers. While women frequently work in high-skill and technical professions, their representation drops sharply in high-level managerial positions (Kabasakal, 1998, 1999). The same situation is not observed for men. In 2014, 7.4 per cent of employed men worked in professional occupations and 6.6 per cent of them were regarded as managers (TUIK, 2015). In contrast, 13.9 per cent of employed women are professionals, but only only 2.4 per cent are in management positions. As seen in Table 15.6, a very high percentage of all professionals are women (45.4 per cent), while women constituted only 13.9 per cent of managers in 2014 (TUIK, 2015).

The trend is similar in the education sector where women have high representation rates. Although women make up 58.6 per cent of the primary school teachers, 53.9 per cent of the junior and 46.4 per cent of the high school teachers employed by the Ministry of Education in 2014, only 14.6 per cent of school principals are women (KSGM, 2015). Furthermore, only 2 of the 81 (2.5 per cent) provincial administrators of the Ministry of Education were women in the same year. In higher education, while 43 per cent of all academics are women, this rate decreases to 29 per cent among full professors and there are only 12 women rectors (6 per cent) in 176 universities (TUIK, 2015).

Women are not represented in decision making and discretionary power positions in labour unions, despite the fact that labour unions are institutions that examine the problems of female workers, propose strategies to eliminate discrimination, encourage participation of women in decision-making positions and promote equal opportunities (KSGM, 2008). In 2008, there were no female managers on the board of directors of workers' confederations and

Table 15.6 Percentage of employed population by occupation (2014) (population over 15 years of age)

	Managers	Professionals	Technicians and associate professionals	Clerical support workers	Service and sales workers	Skilled agricultural, forestry and fishery workers	Craft and related trades workers	Plant and machine operators and assemblers	Elementary occupations
Male	6.6	7.4	5.7	5.6	18.5	14.1	17.4	12.0	12.7
Female	2.4	13.9	4.7	9.5	17.9	22	5.5	3.1	21

Source: TUIK, 2014a

only 5 of the chairs of the 91 labour unions (5.4 per cent) and 32 of the 481 board of directors seats (6.6 per cent) were held by women. Labour unions in the public sector portrayed a relatively better situation; 5 of the chairpersons of the 51 labour unions (9.8 per cent) and 26 of the 325 centre managers (8.0 per cent) were women (KSGM, 2008).

Women managers in the public sector

In the Turkish bureaucracy in 2015, women constituted 36.5 per cent of all bureaucrats, yet only 9.8 per cent of upper-level decision-makers were women. Table 15.7 illustrates the percentage and number of women holding some managerial positions in foreign affairs and public administration in 2015. At the level of ambassadors, there are 32 women out of 229 (13.9 per cent), while women's representation in provincial public administration was almost non-existent. There are only two women assigned to the position of governors, 10 deputy governors and 17 district governors (KSGM, 2015). The representation of women in managerial ranks decreases sharply as they go up in the hierarchy from supervisory and middle levels to upper executive positions. While women constituted 13.5 per cent of department chairs and 10 per cent of deputy director generals, this rate dropped to 0.4 per cent among director generals in 2015 in the Turkish public sector. In addition, there was only one woman deputy minister (4.1 per cent) in the 24 ministries that exist in the Turkish bureaucracy in 2015.

Women managers in the private sector

Although there are no census data that portray the percentage of Turkish women managers in the private sector, there are some international reports which provide country comparisons regarding the situation of women in leadership positions. One of the prominent reports about worldwide gender equality is the *Global Gender Gap Report*, published each year after 2006. In the *Global Gender Gap Report 2014*, it is stated that Turkey has experienced a steady improvement of its overall score since 2011 and since 2006 all of its sub-index scores have improved. Yet Turkey is still the lowest performing country in the OECD on the overall index, with a rank of 125th among 142 countries in 2014. The country is part of the 20 lowest-ranked countries on the 'legislators, senior officials and managers' indicator (World Economic Forum, 2014). This is in line with the above finding that the relatively better rates of women's representation in professional jobs are not apparent when it comes to managerial and decision-making positions.

Several studies (Koca and Öztürk, 2015; Nalbant, 2002; Örücü *et al.*, 2007) show that factors related to low levels of women's representation in senior management positions reflect gender role stereotypes. In general, there is a perceived incongruity in society between the qualities associated with women and successful managers (Sümer, 2006). Sümer's study shows that

Table 15.7 Women in managerial positions in some occupations in the public sector

	Women	*Total*	*Women (%)*
Ambassador	32	229	13.9
Director general	1	156	0.6
Governor	2	81	2.4
Deputy minister	1	24	4.1

Source: KSGM, 2015

women are perceived to be lower on task-orientation and emotional stability than both men and successful managers, and these attributes may be among the factors that act as barriers to women's advancement to executive and strategic decision-making positions. Similarly, Koca and Öztürk's (2015) study in Turkish sport organizations show that management is stereotyped as a masculine domain and in line with role congruity theory it is perceived as requiring agentic characteristics. Consequently, employees working in sport organizations have a general preference for male sport managers and male employees in particular have negative attitudes toward female managers.

As part of the conflicting roles of women professionals, the role of mother and wife conflicts with career roles. A study compared 20 female and 20 male Turkish white-collar workers and found that marriage has a negative effect on women's careers (Kabasakal, 1998, 1999). Similar findings are reported by Aycan (2004), who suggests that men have more negative attitudes towards women in management (that is, believing that they are not suitable for managerial jobs) due to women's family-related roles and responsibilities. In her study among male and female managers working in several business organizations, Aycan (2004) found that societal attitudes towards women in management are slightly positive. Both male and female respondents are moderate in their beliefs about women's competencies to carry out work and family responsibilities with success and have doubts about women's assertiveness, intelligence and willingness to become successful business leaders. In addition, Aycan's study (2004) points to a discrepancy between the actual and the ideal, in such a way that while respondents doubt the competencies of women, they think that women's status in work–life and their advancement opportunities should be improved. This can be explained by system justification theory (Jost and Banaji, 1994) which suggests that women internalize societal values that disadvantage them to justify their low status.

For Turkish women in managerial and highly prestigious professions, the conflicting roles of wife, mother and career woman result in these women facing different dynamics compared to women in unskilled or semi-skilled jobs or to other career women in more developed countries. Turkish women in high-status jobs, and who come from a privileged background, are in a more advantageous position in reconciling the conflicting demands of their career and home duties by delegating the housework and child-rearing responsibilities to low-paid domestics. Given the fact that wages paid to domestics in developing countries are relatively low, professional women with a high socio-economic background can easily employ at least one domestic at home. In addition, Turkish society is characterized by high levels of family collectivism (Kabasakal and Bodur, 2002, 2007), where there is high interdependence between members of large families, and it is common practice that grandmothers and aunts take on part of the housework and child-rearing responsibilities.

In her study based on a series of in-depth interviews with top and middle level managers, Aycan (2004) indicates that respondents do not report any particular barriers (nor support) in their organizations because of their gender. Yet they indicate that they had 'to convince "themselves" first that it is okay not to personally fulfill domestic duties, but instead to get assistance from family or paid help' (Aycan 2004: 473). One of the most serious difficulties they face in their organizations is in getting into social and communication networks in male-oriented organizational contexts. Studies on the characteristics of the few women who are able to move up to senior managerial positions show that senior women managers come from a privileged background (Arbak *et al.*, 1998; Kabasakal, 1998, 1999). It is likely that the elite background of women helps in overcoming the lower status associated with femaleness and provides the prestige that is required for the execution of power and influence in executive positions (Kabasakal, 1998, 1999). That may be why women in executive positions report that they experience no major barriers in organizational contexts despite the fact that they experience many difficulties in getting into networks and convincing themselves and others that they can balance their work and home responsibilities (Aycan, 2004).

Women in politics

Turkey was one of the first countries to grant women the right to vote and to be voted for. Women were given political rights in the 1930s – the right to vote and to run in municipal elections in 1930 and in national elections in 1934. Turkish women were granted these rights much earlier than their counterparts in many industrialized western countries. However, in line with the above arguments that women are scarce in executive positions, the number of women elected to the Turkish Parliament has been very low. While the rate of women parliamentarians was below 5 per cent in all elections before 2007, in the 2007 general election it reached 9.1 per cent, 14.4 per cent in the 2011 election and in the 7 June 2015 election it was 17.8 per cent, the highest figure to date. One of the major reasons behind the significant jump in the representation of women in Parliament in the more recent elections can be attributed to the gender policy of one political party (the HDP), which has an ethnic-based, leftist orientation (Elmas-Arslan, 2014). HDP has provided women with substantial opportunities at all layers of the party, including the co-leader position. In the 7 June 2015 elections, 32 of the 80 parliamentarians from this party were women (40 per cent). However, the number of women in Parliament has recently decreased again (from 98 women to 76 women or 13 per cent) during the elections of 1 November 2015. The more traditional parties, including the governing party, have much lower percentages of women in Parliament, in line with the general attitudes and stereotypes prevalent in society about women's decision-making role.

Women parliamentarians in Turkey come mainly from an 'elite' background (Güneş-Ayata, 1994). An elite background is also common amongst women ministers who took posts in cabinets. The first women minister was assigned in 1971. There are no women presidents in the history of the Turkish republic, whereas there is only one prime minister, Tansu Çiller, who served in this post in the mid-1990s. In the 2000s, the cabinets included only one or two women ministers, which is the case for the cabinet in power in 2015, where there was only one woman minister who was responsible for issues concerning women and family.

Although political parties in Turkey have nominated more female candidates for the more recent 2009 and 2014 local elections, there has been little progress so far in the representation of women in local politics. Only 3 of the 30 (10 per cent) mayors of greater municipalities, and 40 of the 1381 mayors (2.8 per cent) elected in the 2014 local elections were women. Furthermore, just 10.7 per cent and 4.8 per cent of municipality council members and provincial general council members were women in Turkey in 2014. The reasons for the little progress made in local politics on the part of women include the huge expenses of standing as a candidate, male domination in politics and the prevailing cultural image of local administration as a 'man's business'. Another reason is that politics is associated in women's minds with lies (28 per cent), unfulfilled promises (27.3 per cent) and corruption (12.6 per cent), according to a survey conducted in Ankara (Özerkmen, 2008).

Women entrepreneurs

Turkey is a country where women are less likely than men to engage in entrepreneurial activities. Although TUIK statistics show that there was a significant shift from unpaid family work to regular work and self-employment between 2000 and 2013 for women (Table 15.3), the ratio of male to female entrepreneurs in Turkey is the one of the highest among the efficiency-driven economies. According to the Global Entrepreneurship Monitor's[2] (GEM) Total Entrepreneurial Activity (TEA) index (GEM, 2012), male TEA rates are 2.43 times higher than female TEA rates. This finding indicates that the measures taken to stimulate entrepreneurship in Turkey have not paid off for women as much as for men.

Previous research on entrepreneurship suggests that entrepreneurs may be motivated by two major factors while consider initiating a new business. Some start their business to take advantage of external opportunities (i.e., opportunity entrepreneurship) while others become an entrepreneur as they do not have other sources of income (i.e., necessity entrepreneurship) (Jennings and Brush, 2013). GEM (2012) data show that, in Turkey, 68 per cent of male and 64 per cent of female entrepreneurs start their business with opportunity motives (i.e., pulled by the business opportunities), whereas 30 per cent of male and 33 per cent of female entrepreneurs act from necessity motives (i.e., pushed into entrepreneurship). Empirical studies provide support for these figures by showing that women entrepreneurs in Turkey are affected by both pull and push factors in their self-employment decisions. These may include external factors such as gender discrimination and mobbing (i.e. the constant humiliation and downgrading of women at work that gradually weaken their confidence and self-esteem) (Özdemir, 2010) as well as personal preferences/expectations such as working independently and flexibly (e.g., Kutanis and Bayraktaroğlu, 2003; Maden, 2015), being productive and creating employment opportunities (e.g., Çetindamar, 2005; Maden, 2015), gaining a social status (e.g.,Yılmaz *et al.*, 2012), meeting family needs and having higher financial gains (e.g., Nayır, 2008).

With respect to the demographic profile of women entrepreneurs in Turkey, Household Labour Force statistics demonstrate that in 2013, 74 per cent of employer and self-employed women were married as compared to 90 per cent of men in the same employment category (TUIK, 2013). In addition, 18 per cent of women entrepreneurs were divorced or widowed, as compared to 2 per cent of men. These figures may reveal that divorced or widowed women are pushed to start their own business to make a living for their family (Özar, 2007). Household Labour Force statistics also show that women entrepreneurs were on average less educated than men (72 per cent attained only a primary school education or below). This figure contradicts Çetindamar and her colleagues' (2012) findings which demonstrate that except for graduate education (masters or PhD), women who attained a higher level of education are more likely to engage in entrepreneurial activity as compared to men.

The enterprises of women entrepreneurs are distributed across various sectors and differ in sizes and assets. Turkish women entrepreneurs have founded and managed enterprises in almost all industries including international trade, information technology, advertising and manufacturing (Cindoglu, 2003). However, in line with the international evidence revealing that (a) businesses led by women tend to be over-represented in the services sectors and under-represented in manufacturing, extraction and business services (e.g. Kelley *et al.*, 2011) and that (b) women entrepreneurs are more likely than men to establish hybrid ventures to achieve both social as well as economic objectives (Hechavarria *et al.*, 2012), women entrepreneurs in Turkey mostly operate in the service sector (Hisrich and Öztürk, 1999; Ufuk and Özgen, 2001a, 2001b;Yılmaz *et al.*, 2012) with hybrid ventures.

Women entrepreneurs cope with many difficulties in starting up and maintaining their business in Turkey. Entrepreneurial roles tend to be perceived as stereotypically masculine efforts in Turkish society, which causes women to suffer from both open and hidden discrimination (Karataş-Özkan *et al.*, 2010). Obtaining financial support is another important obstacle faced by women entrepreneurs in Turkey, again having connections with gender stereotyping and discrimination (Hisrich and Öztürk, 1999; Özar, 2007; Maden, 2015). The interaction between business and family life and the stress/anxiety that women suffer due to the conflict between their domestic and business lives act as an important 'personal' barrier for entrepreneurship (Maden, 2015). Many scholars suggest that the multiple roles of women entrepreneurs as a wife, mother, housewife and business owner (Karataş-Özkan *et al.*, 2011; Maden, 2015; Özar, 2007; Özgen and Ufuk, 1998) put extra pressure on them as they try to achieve a solution that satisfies the needs of all individuals involved (Ufuk and Özgen, 2001a).

Starting in the 1990s, Turkish governments and non-governmental organizations began to support women entrepreneurs by offering business set-up financing at reasonable rates, organizing training activities and providing business support services to those women who wanted to start up businesses. The Prime Ministry General Directorate on the Status of Women (KSGM) is one of the governmental units that conducts and funds research projects with a policy orientation; cooperates with other public institutions and women's associations; and increases awareness and consciousness through the mass media about women's problems. The Small and Medium Enterprises Development Organization (KOSGEB) is another organization that encourages women entrepreneurship by providing technical, managerial and marketing support to small and medium enterprises (SMEs). This organization organizes applied entrepreneurship training for general and specific target groups including women and charges no fees for this training (Maden, 2015).

Other organizations such as TUSİAD (Turkish Industry and Business Association) and TOBB (Union of Chambers and Commodity Exchanges of Turkey) draw attention to the important role of women entrepreneurs for the Turkish economy in different platforms. TOBB has a specific unit for women entrepreneurs, named Women Entrepreneurs Council, which sets general policies about women's entrepreneurship and provides advice. Finally, an important non-governmental organization that supports women's entrepreneurship is KAGİDER[3] (Women Entrepreneurs Association of Turkey). KAGİDER carries out a number of projects, provides incubation and mentorship support, and arranges training programmes for (potential) women entrepreneurs. KAGİDER also has close relationships with regional/international women organizations and has established sustainable project partnerships with different global institutions such as the World Bank and the International Finance Corporation (IFC).

Country legislation

Turkish women have enjoyed extensive social and political rights since the beginning of the Turkish republic. The principle of the equality of women and men has been adopted in the Constitution and in the early laws of Turkey. Over the last two decades, it has been realized that laws in practice are insufficient for ensuring the social and political rights of women in Turkey. Accordingly, there have been recent legal changes introduced to improve the social status of women in Turkey. Significant legal changes regarding women's equality took place in the Turkish Civil Code in 2002 and in the Turkish Penal Code in 2005 (Özden, 2006) to increase women's equal participation in social, economic and political life. Reforms to the Turkish Civil Code have granted women and men equal rights in marriage, divorce and property ownership. The amendments in the Constitution make up the most important part of the reforms directed towards women.

In addition to the laws that influence the general status of women in society, there are two sets of laws that cover employment-related issues of individuals in Turkish society (Zeytinoğlu *et al.*, 2001): the Constitution and Labour Law. According to the latest Turkish Constitution, which was accepted in 1982, all individuals are equal before the law, irrespective of language, race, colour, gender, political opinion, belief, religion and sect, or any such consideration. Under the Constitution, every individual has the right and duty to work and no one shall be required to perform work unsuitable for her/his age, gender or capacity. Minors, women and persons with disabilities shall enjoy special protection with regard to working conditions. Every individual has the right to work in public service and no criteria other than merit shall be taken into consideration for employment in the public sector.

Turkey has recently taken the equal opportunities for women in employment issue under legal guarantee by incorporating provisions regarding equal participation of women into the Labour Act. In the New Labour Act, effective as of 2003, employers must not discriminate, either directly or indirectly, against an employee in the conditions of her employment contract due to the employee's gender or maternity; and gender, marital status, family responsibilities and pregnancy shall not constitute a valid reason for termination of the contract (KSGM, 2009). In addition, provisions regarding sexual harassment in the workplace and part-time work are included in the Law for the first time. Turkey has also signed the Istanbul Convention (the first comprehensive international convention on reducing systemic violence against women) in 2011 and put it in action in 2014, which frames violence against women as 'part of a wider pattern of discrimination and inequality' and 'structural violence' and establishes comprehensive standards to eliminate gender-based violence. However, despite significant legal improvements, it is not possible to say that gender equality has been reflected completely in employment practices in accordance with these changes.

Initiatives supporting women in the workforce

In the last two decades, there have been a number of governmental, non-governmental and professional initiatives to support women in the areas of education, employment and entrepreneurship. Turkey has recently participated in many international conferences and has signed many international agreements to support women in the field of education. Some of the objectives regarding women are to increase the ratio of literacy among women to 100 per cent, to decrease maternal child mortality by 50 per cent and to remove the reservations included in the Charter for the Elimination of Discrimination against Women (CEDAW). Turkey, by increasing compulsory education to eight years, has taken a significant step to resolving girls' access problems in education, with a target to make the schooling rate reach 100 per cent for girls and boys. Since 2003, there has been a series of new initiatives and national campaigns by non-government organizations and these have been very successful in boosting the enrolment of girls (KGSM, 2009).

Since the 1980s there has been an increase in the number of voluntary women's institutions established in Turkey. Through the mobilization of the general public, these women's institutions have played a significant part in consciousness-raising endeavours on women's problems, opening more centres for helping women who are victims of violence or who are abused. The Foundation for the Advancement and Recognition of Turkish Women, the Women's Shelter Foundation of Purple Roof, the Flying Broom, the Association of Women's Rights Protection, Women's Solidarity Foundation and the Association for the Support and Training of Women Candidates are just a few names among more than 150 voluntary women's organizations working nationwide. The number of Women's Studies Centres set up in universities has reached 13 and a Woman's Library has been founded. Finally, a number of projects were put into practice by governmental and non-governmental organizations to support professional and entrepreneurial skill development for women, including the Project

Supporting Women Entrepreneurship, the Professional Development and Employment Project for Girls and Women, the Women's Professional Empowerment Project and the Microcredit Project for Women Entrepreneurs (KSGM, 2009).

Although these governmental and non-governmental initiatives have been quite effective in supporting women's labour, women in the private sector still need to overcome gender barriers in order to prove themselves successful in a male-oriented business culture. In order to understand whether private organizations in Turkey apply any policies to enhance the status of their women employees, interviews with managers of two management consulting firms were conducted by the authors of this chapter (Kabasakal *et al.*, 2004). These two consulting firms have a wide customer base and provide services in human resources applications. As reported by the interviewed managers, no firm among their customers was identified as providing any initiatives to enhance the status of women in management. Therefore, introducing positive discrimination policies to advance women to managerial positions seems a viable option for corporations to overcome gender barriers and the glass ceiling phenomenon in business.

There are a number of contemporary initiatives in Turkey that support women in the workforce. First, Turkey has set the target of increasing the percentage of women's labour force participation up to 41 per cent by 2023, outlining detailed strategies to achieve this in the report titled *National Employment Strategy: 2014–2023*. Second, the Equality at Work Platform was launched in 2012 as the biggest multi-stakeholder coalition on gender diversity in Turkey. Supported by most of the largest employers and civil society leaders, this taskforce has published the *Manual for Establishing Corporate Gender Equality* and has promoted 11 principles aimed at eliminating gender-based discrimination in the declaration of equality at work. Third, the minister of family and social policies has announced that the right to 16 weeks of paid maternity leave will be progressively extended to public servants.

The future

In general, laws that influence the general status and employment-related issues of women are gender-neutral. Many recent changes have been made in the Constitution, civil law and labour law in order to provide equal opportunities to women. Furthermore, there have been several governmental, non-governmental and professional initiatives to support women in the areas of education, employment, politics and entrepreneurship. Non-governmental organizations have been very successful in national campaigns geared towards improving the education levels of girls. Having said that, we suggest these initiatives and success stories are not a result of the women-friendly environment of Turkey, but rather as a result of women's creative capacities to overcome the multiple patriarchal mechanisms faced by them (McNay 2008).

The overall situation of women in Turkey does not currently portray a rosy picture. The *Global Gender Gap Report 2014*, published by the World Economic Forum, ranked Turkey 125th out of a total of 142 countries in terms of equality between men and women (Hausmann *et al.*, 2014). In the economic participation and opportunity sub-index, this rank falls even further to 132nd out of 142 countries, making Turkey one of the lowest performing countries in the world (Hausmann *et al.*, 2014). With women's labour force participation at 32 per cent compared to 76 per cent for men, Turkey ranks 128th on the labour force partici-pation gender gap. A recent UN report indicated domestic violence rates in Turkey were almost 10 times higher than in some European countries, and in 2014, 286 women were killed and there were 60,000 cases of reported violence against women in Turkey (Interpress Medya Takip Ajansi, 2014). Nevertheless, the women's movement of Turkey is very robust, resilient and adaptive. The long-term prospects of Turkish women's conditions at work and in their lives seem to be brighter as women of diverse backgrounds, ages and ideologies join forces and unite against all forms of injustice and oppression.

The political turn taking place in Turkey since 2010 has created a curious gender gap. While investing in the enhancement of women's presence in public life, the political figures of the ruling AKP have also made repeated statements about women's 'traditional' role in society, denying that men and women should be on 'equal footing' as this would be 'against their *fitrat*' (God-given nature/disposition). In recent work, Sehlikoglu (2015) discusses how anti-equality rhetoric echoes deeply ingrained attitudes within Turkish society about gender equality. Turkish women negotiate with not a single but multiple (nationalist, religious, secular and aesthetics) patriarchal mechanisms in their everyday lives as they try to participate in the workforce. Reflecting women's aforementioned creative capacities, in many cases, women's agencies under multiple patriarchal mechanisms may not always present themselves in the form of resistance (Sehlikoglu, 2016), but in the form of manoeuvring around their roles in society as traditional homemakers and mothers.

Sustainable positive change in working women's conditions in Turkey also depends on system-wide changes and institutional initiatives. Governmental and non-governmental organizations, as well as private organizations, need to be more active in promoting women's status in economic areas. Although some banks provide special credit targeted at women entrepreneurs, more advertising, less bureaucracy and improved conditions would help in extending credit to women entrepreneurs. Further, organizations can develop human resource practices targeted at employing and promoting more women under equal payment conditions. Private sector performance has been substandard in this matter and needs to be actively targeted as a social responsibility project. Improving the status of Turkish women in all areas of life would contribute greatly to the well-being of society and would pay back with maximum returns.

Notes

1   Starting from February 2014, the Turkish Statistical Institute reported Household Labour Force statistics without any 'urban' and 'rural' distinctions. The Institute announced that it would continue 'to report all related statistics in 'total' terms until the redefinition arrangements for 'urban' and 'rural' areas was finalized.
2   The Global Entrepreneurship Monitor (GEM) is an international research study that annually assesses entrepreneurial activity, aspirations and attitudes of individuals across a wide range of countries.
3   The discussion on KAGIDER was compiled from the information on the organization's website, www.kagider.org.

References

Aran, M., Çapar, S., Hüsamoğlu, D., Sanalmış, D. and Uraz, A. (2009) *Recent Trends in Female Labor Force Participation in Turkey* (Ankara: World Bank and Turkey State Planning Organization).
Arat, Z. (1994) Liberation or indoctrination: women's education in Turkey, *Boğaziçi Journal: Review of Social, Economic and Administrative Studies*, 8(1–2), 83–105.
Arat, Z. (1999) *Deconstructing Images of the Turkish Woman* (New York, NY: Palgrave).
Arbak, Y., Kabasakal, H., Katrinli A. E., Timurcanday, O. and Zeytinoğlu, I. U. (1998) Women managers in Turkey: the impact of leadership styles and personality, *The Journal of Management Systems*, 10(1), 53–60.
Aycan, Z. (2004) Key success factors for women in management in Turkey, *Applied Psychology: An International Review*, 53(3), 453–477.

Booth, A. L. and Coles, M. (2007) A microfoundation for increasing returns in human capital accumulation and the under-participation trap, *European Economic Review*, 51(7), 1161–1681.

Çelikoğlu, İ., Çapar, S., Hüsamoğlu, M., Okkalı-şanalmış, D., Yüksel, Y., Angel-Urdinola, D. F., Oral, I., Uraz, A., Aran, M. and Stamm, D. (2009) *Female Labor Force Participation in Turkey: Trends, Determinants, and Policy Framework* (Ankara: T. R. Prime Ministry, State Planning Organization and World Bank, Report No. 48508-TR).

Çetindamar, D. (2005) Policy issues for Turkish entrepreneurs, *International Journal of Entrepreneurship and Innovation Management*, 5(3/4), 187–205.

Cetindamar, D., Gupta, V. K. and Karadeniz, E. E. and Egrican, N. (2012) What the numbers tell: the impact of human, family and financial capital on women and men's entry into entrepreneurship in Turkey, *Entrepreneurship & Regional Development: An International Journal*, 24(1/2), 29–51.

Cindoglu, D. (2003) *Bridging the gender gap in Turkey: A milestone towards faster socio-economic development and poverty reduction*, Poverty Reduction and Economic Management Unit, Europe and Central Asia Region, OECD, <http://siteresources.worldbank.org/INTECAREGTOPGENDER/Resources/TurkeyCGA.pdf#page=115>, accessed 20 January 2013.

Cudeville, E. and Gürbüzer, L. Y. (2010) Gender wage discrimination in the Turkish labor market: can Turkey be part of Europe? *Comparative Economic Studies*, 52(3), 429–463.

Dayıoğlu, M. (2000) Labor market participation of women in Turkey. In F. Acar and A. Güneş-Ayata (eds) *Gender and Identity Construction: Women of Central Asia, Caucasus and Turkey* (Leiden: Brill).

Dayıoğlu, M. and Kasnakoğlu, Z. (1997) Kentsel kesimde kadın ve erkeklerin işgücüne katılımları ve kazanç farklılıkları [Differences in participation in labour force and earnings between men and women in urban areas], *METU Studies in Development*, 24(3), 329–361.

Dayıoğlu, M. and. Kırdar, M. G. (2009) *Determinants of and Trends in Labor Force Participation of Women in Turkey* (Ankara: Middle East Technical University Working Paper No. 5).

Elmas-Arslan, G. (2014) Türkiye'de çalışan kadın olmak ve kadın akademisyenler [Being a working women in Turkey and women academics], *Gazi Üniversitesi Öğretim Üyeleri, Derneği Akademik Bülteni*, 12(1), 36–40.

GEM (2012) *Global Entrepreneurship Monitor 2012 Report* (London: GEM).

Güneş-Ayata, A. (1994) Women in the legislature, *Boğaziçi Journal: Review of Social, Economic and Administrative Studies*, 8(1–2), 107–120.

Hausmann, R., Tyson, L. D., Bekhouce, Y. and Zahidi, S. (2014) *The Global Gender Gap Index 2014. The Global Gender Gap Report*. (World Economic Forum).

Healy, G., Özbilgin, M. and Aliefendioğlu, H. (2005) Academic employment and gender: a Turkish challenge to vertical sex segregation, *European Journal of Industrial Relations*, 11(2), 247–264.

Hechavarria, D. M., Ingram, A., Justo, R. and Terjesen, S. (2012) Are women more likely to pursue social and environmental entrepreneurship? In K. D. Hughes and J. E. Jennings (eds) *Global Women's Entrepreneurship Research: Diverse Settings, Questions and Approaches* (Cheltenham: Edward Elgar).

Hisarcıklılar, M. and Ercan, H. (2005) Gender based wage differentials in Turkey, *Bilgi*, 10, 45–62.

Hisrich, R. D. and Özturk, S. A. (1999) Women entrepreneurs in a developing economy, *Journal of Management Development*, 18(2), 114–125.

İlkkaracan, İ. and Acar, S. (2007) The determinants of female labor force participation in Turkey: Who caregives determines who participates and who does not. Paper presented at the Annual Conference of the International Association for Feminist Economics (IAFFE), July, Bangkok, Thailand <http://scholar.googleusercontent.com/scholar?q=cache:voWIZlxTRuAJ:scholar.google.com/&hl=tr&as_sdt=0,5> accessed 21 July 2015.

İlkkaracan, İ. and Selim, R. (2007) The gender wage gap in the Turkish labour market, *Labour: Review of Labour Economics and Industrial Relations*, 21(2), 563–593.

Interpress Medya Takip Ajansi (2014) Kadina Karsi Siddet Raporu [Press Report on Violence Against Women], *Interpress Basin Bulteni*, 2014.

Jennings, J. E. and Brush. C. G. (2013) Research on women entrepreneurs: challenges to (and from) the broader entrepreneurship literature? *The Academy of Management Annals*, 7(1), 663–715.

Jost, J.T. and Banaji, M. (1994) The role of stereotyping in system justification and the production of false consciousness, *British Journal of Social Psychology*, 22, 1–27.

Kabasakal, H. (1998) Top women managers in Turkey. In A. B. Mirzaoğlu (ed.) *75 Yılda Kadınlar ve Erkekler*, (İstanbul, Turkey: Tarih Vakfı, pp. 303–312).

Kabasakal, H. (1999) A profile of top women managers in Turkey. In Z. F. Arat (ed.) *Deconstructing Images of the Turkish Women* (New York, NY: Palgrave).

Kabasakal, H. and Bodur, M. (2002) Arabic cluster: a bridge between east and west, *Journal of World Business*, 105, 1–25.

Kabasakal, H. and Bodur, M. (2007) Leadership and culture in Turkey: A multifaceted phenomenon. In J. S. Chokar, F. C. Brodbeck and R. J. House (eds) *Culture and Leadership Across the World: The GLOBE Book of In-Depth Studies of 25 Societies* (NJ: Lawrence Albaum Associates, Inc).

Kabasakal, H., Aycan, Z. and Karakaş, F. (2004) Women in management in Turkey. In M. J. Davidson and R. J. Burke (eds) *Women in Management Worldwide: Progress and Prospects* (Aldershot, UK: Ashgate).

Kantola, J. and Squires, J. (2008) *From State Feminism to Market Feminism* (San Francisco, USA: International Studies Association Annual Convention).

Karaoğlan, D. and Ökten, Ç. (2012) *Labor Force Participation of Married Women in Turkey: Is There an Added or a Discouraged Worker Effect?* IZA Discussion Paper No. 6616.

Karataş-Özkan, M., İnal, G. and Özbilgin, M. (2010) Turkey. In S. Fielden and M. Davidson (eds) *International Handbook of Successful Women Entrepreneurs* (Cheltenham and New York: Edward Elgar Press).

Kelley, D., Brush, C., Greene, P. and Litovsky, Y. (2011) *The Global Entrepreneurship Monitor: 2010 Women's Report* (Wellesley, MA: Babson College & GERA).

Koca, C. and Öztürk, P. (2015) Gendered perceptions about female managers in Turkish sport organizations, *European Sport Management Quarterly*, 19(3), 381–406.

KSGM (Prime Ministry General Directorate on the Status of Women) (2008) *Women in Power and Decision-Making Policy Document*, Directorate General on Status of Women <www.ksgm.gov.tr/Pdf/kararalma_ing.pdf>, accessed 18 March 2009.

KSGM (2009) *Labor Act, Directorate General on Status of Women* <www.ksgm.gov.tr/kanun_4857_iskanunu.php>, accessed 2 March 2009.

KSGM (2015) *Women in Turkey*. Directorate General on Status of Women, <http://kadininstatusu.aile.gov.tr/uygulamalar/turkiyede-kadin>, accessed 24 August 2015.

Kutanis, R.O. and Bayraktaroğlu, S. (2003) *Female Entrepreneurs: Social Feminist Insights for Overcoming the Barriers* <www.mngt.waikato.ac.nz/ejrot/cmsconference/2003/proceedings/gender/Kutanis.pdf>, accessed 21 June 2014.

Maden, C. (2015) A gendered lens on entrepreneurship: Women entrepreneurship in Turkey, *Gender in Management: An International Journal*, 30(4), 312–331.

McNay, L. (2008) The trouble with recognition: Subjectivity, suffering, and agency, *Sociological Theory*, 26(3), 271–296.

Ministry of National Education (2014–2015) National Education Statistics <http://sgb.meb.gov.tr/www/mill-egitim-istatistikleri-orgun-egitim-2014-2015/icerik/153>, accessed 10 September 2015.

Nalbant, M. (2002) Kamu çalışanlarının kadın yöneticilerde liderlik davranışlarını algılamaları ve bir anket çalışması [Perceptions of public employees in understanding leadership behaviors in women managers and a survey study]. Basılmamış Yüksek Lisans Tezi, Unpublished Master Thesis (Ankara: Gazi Üniversitesi Sosyal Bilimler Enstitüsü).

Nayır, Z. D. (2008) İş ve ailesi arasındaki kadın: Tekstil ve bilgi işlem girişimcilerinin rol çatışmasına getirdikleri çözüm stratejileri, *Ege Akademik Bakis Dergisi*, 8(2), 631–650.

OECD (2014) *LFS by Sex and Age – Indicators: Labour Force Participation Rate* <http://stats.oecd.org/#>, accessed 20 June 2015.

Örücü, E., Kılıç, R. and Kılıç, T. (2007) Cam tavan sendromu ve kadınların üst düzey yönetici pozisyonuna yükselmelerindeki engeller: Balıkesir ili örnegi [Glass ceiling syndrome and obstacles which impede women's progress towards senior management levels], *Yönetim ve Ekonomi*, 14(2), 117–135.

ÖSYM (2007) *2006–2007 Higher Education Statistics*, Higher Education Council Student Selection and Placement Center, <www.osym.gov.tr/BelgeGoster.aspx?F6E10F8892433CFFA91171E62F0FF1533 D26410A22C2CA34>, accessed 18 March 2009.

OXFAM and TEPAV (2015) *Making Economies Work for Women: Female Labour Force Participation in Turkey* <www.c20turkey.org/uploads/OXFAM_TEPAV%20Report.pdf>, accessed 20 June 2015.

Özar, Ş. (1994) Some observations on the position of women in the labor market in the development process of Turkey, *Boğaziçi Journal: Review of Social, Economic and Administrative Studies*, 8(1–2), 21–43.

Özar, S. (2007) Women entrepreneurs in Turkey: Obstacles, potentials and future prospects <www.gender clearinghouse.org/Ar/Ar/upload/Assets/Documents/pdf/Comp%20I%20Prop%2043%20Full%20Dra ft%20Turkey%20copy.pdf>, accessed 15 January 2013.

Özdemir, A. A. (2010) Motivation factors of potential entrepreneurs and a research study in Eskisehir, *EgeAkademikBakis*, 10(1), 117–139.

Özden, Ö. T. (2006) *Women in Turkey and Turkish Civil Code* <www.allacademic.com/meta/ p_mla_apa_research_citation/1/2/1/1/9/p121196_index.html>, accessed 24 April 2009.

Özerkmen, N. (2008) Siyaset erkek işi midir? [Is politics a man's business?]. *Cumhuriyet*, 18 December <http://kitapdergi.cumhuriyet.com.tr/?im=yhs&kid=20&hn=24122>, accessed 26 March 2008.

Özgen, O. and Ufuk, H. (1998) Kadinlarin evde gerceklestirdikleri girisimcilik faaliyetlerinin aile yasamina etkisi [The impact of women's home-based entrepreneurship activities on family life]. In O. Çitçi (ed.), *20.Yuzyilin Sonunda Kadinlar ve Gelecek [Women and Future in the End of 20th Century]* (Ankara:TODAIE Press, pp. 285–302).

Prime Ministry General Directorate on the Status of Women (2014) *Labor Force Profile of Women in Turkey and Analysis of Statistics*, <http://kadininstatusu.aile.gov.tr/data/542a8e86369dc31550b3ac33/ T%C3%BCrkiye'de%20Kad%C4%B1n%20%C4%B0%C5%9Fg%C3%BCc%C3%BC%20Profili%20 ve%20%C4%B0statistikleri'nin%20Analizi%20(Nihai%20Rapor).pdf>, accessed 16 April, 2016.

Sehlikoglu, S. (2015) Public intimacies, intimate publics: Natural limits, creation and the culture of Mahremiyet in Turkey, *Cambridge Journal of Anthropology*, 33(2), 77–89.

Sehlikoglu, S. (2016) Exercising in comfort: Islamicate culture of Mahremiyet in everyday Istanbul, *Journal of Middle East Women's Studies*, 12(2), forthcoming.

Sümer, H. C. (2006) Women in management: Still waiting to be full members of the club, *Sex Roles*, 55, 63–72.

Tan, M., Ecevit,Y., Sancar-Üşür S. and Acuner, S.(2008) Türkiye'de toplumsal cinsiyet eşitsizliği: sorunlar, öncelikler ve çözüm önerileri [social gender inequality in turkey: problems, priorities and suggestions] <www.tusiad.org/tusiad_cms.nsf/LHome/30328AE15A0B0A61C225748700382F70/$FILE/KADI NRAPOR.pdf>, accessed 3 March 2009.

Tansel, A. (2002) Economic development and female labor force participation in Turkey: time series evidence and cross-province estimates. In T. Bulutay (ed.) *Employment of Women* (Ankara: Turkish Statistical Institute, No. 2594).

Tansel, A. (2005) Public–private employment choice, wage differentials, and gender in Turkey, *Economic Development and Cultural Change*, 53(2), 453–477.

Taymaz, E. (2009) *Growth, Employment, Skills and Female Labor Force* (Ankara: Middle East Technical University Economic Research Center).

TUIK (2000) *Labour Force Statistics*, Turkish Statistical Institute, <www.tuik.gov.tr/PreTablo.do? alt_id=1007>, accessed 2 August 2015.

TUIK (2010) *Earnings Statistics*, Turkish Statistical Institute, <www.tuik.gov.tr/PreTablo.do? alt_id=1008>, accessed 2 August 2015.

TUIK (2013) *Labor Force Statistics Dynamic Search – 2013*, <https://biruni.tuik.gov.tr/isgucuapp/isgucu. zul>, accessed 16 April 2016.

TUIK (2014a) *Turkey in Statistics*, Turkish Statistical Institute, <www.turkstat.gov.tr/IcerikGetir.do? istab_id=5>, accessed 24 August 2015.

TUIK (2014b) *Labour Force Statistics*, Turkish Statistical Institute, <www.tuik.gov.tr/PreTablo.do?alt_id =1007>, accessed 2 August 2015.

TUIK (2015) *Household Labour Force Survey Results*, Turkish Statistical Institute, <www.tuik.gov.tr/ Kitap.do?metod=KitapDetay&KT_ID=8&KITAP_ID=25>, accessed 19 August 2015.

Turkish Statistical Institute (2007) *Statistical Indicators 1923–2011*, Turkish Statistical Institute, www.turkstat.gov.tr/IcerikGetir.do?istab_id=158, accessed 2 August, 2015.

Ufuk, H. and Özgen, Ö. (2001a) Interaction between the business and family lives of women entrepreneurs in Turkey, *Journal of Business Ethics*, 31(2), 95–106.

Ufuk, H. and Özgen, Ö (2001b) The profile of women entrepreneurs: a sample from Turkey, *International Journal of Consumer Studies*, 25(4), 299–308.

Uraz, A., Aran, M., Hüsamoğlu, M., Şanalmış, D.O. and Çapar, S. (2010) *Türkiye'deKadınların İşgücüneKatılımında Son DönemdeGözlenenEğilimler [Recent Trends in Women's Labour Force Participation in Turkey]* (Ankara: World Bank and Turkey State Planning Organization).

World Economic Forum (2014) *Global Gender Gap Report 2014*, www3.weforum.org/ docs/GGGR14/GGGR_CompleteReport_2014.pdf, accessed 2 August 2015.

Yılmaz, E., Özdemir, G. and Oraman, Y. (2012) Women entrepreneurs: their problems and entrepreneurial ideas, *African Journal of Business Management*, 6(26), 7896–7904.

YÖK (2014–2015) Yükseköğretim İstatistikleri (Higher Education Statistics), <https://istatistik. yok.gov.tr>, accessed 10 August 2015.

Zeytinoğlu, I. U., Özmen, Ö. T., Katrinli, A. E., Kabasakal, H. and Arbak, Y. (2001) Factors affecting women managers' careers in Turkey, *Research in Middle East Economics*, 4, 225–245.

PART VI

Women in management

South America

16 Women in management in Chile

María Jose Bosch

Introduction

The massive entry of women into the workforce has led to changes for families, businesses and for society. It has impacted the way we organize ourselves as families and as a society, as well as the roles and the composition of the modern family. The model in which women looked after the children and the home and the man provided for the economic livelihood of the family is no longer the reality of many Chilean families. As these roles change, family dynamics also change. Many women today want to develop personally within the workforce, receive remuneration for their work and contribute to their homes at a personal level, but also in economic terms.

The change we have seen in female workforce participation in Chile has been large in scale but has not been as significant as expected, especially when compared with other countries where the level of female employment has been much higher. For example, Latin America reached an average of 54 percent in 2013 (INE, 2013a) and countries of the Organization for Economic Co-operation and Development (OECD), 63.8 percent (OIT, 2013).

The average difference in workforce participation between men and women in Chile is higher than the average of OECD countries by 15 percentage points. Despite this low level of participation compared with other countries, Chilean women are aggressively joining the labor market, however problematic are the conditions in which they are doing so. Most women who work are subject to subcontracting, thereby limiting some of the legal rights that Chile has made progress on.

Workforce characteristics

The incorporation of women into the workforce in Chile has led to great changes, not only in statistical indicators but also in terms of demographic change in organizations and the way in which we are organized as a society. There are more and more families that are economically dependent on both parents, and Chile is not exempt from this reality. Despite having one of the lowest rates of female participation in the region, it has been rising steadily in recent years.

Despite the steady increase in female participation over recent years, the difference between the participation of men and women remains significant. We are still far from the levels observed in other OECD member countries where female participation reaches 65 percent and in other Latin American countries reaches 53 percent.

In recent decades, the Chilean labor market has experienced an increase in its active workforce, from 4,888,590 in 1990 to 8,528,370 in 2015. One reason for this increase, apart from population growth, has been increasing female participation in the labor market. In the 1990s, the participation of women did not reach 30 percent, while in 2014 it was close to 50 percent.

Table 16.1 Workforce participation rate by gender (%)

Year	2010	2011	2012	2013	2014
Men	72.1	72.7	71.9	71.8	71.6
Women	45.3	47.3	47.6	47.7	48.4

Source: INE (2015a)

Of the total population of Chile, approximately 17.5 million people, 47.7 percent, are active in the workforce. The jobless rate is relatively low, reaching an average of 7.5 percent over the past 15 years. Most of the people employed in the workforce are salaried workers: 73.7 percent in the case of men and 64.6 percent in the case of women. The second largest category for both sexes is self-employment, at around 20 percent for both.

Amongst working women, the majority are involved in salaried employment (67 percent). The second group consists of women who are self-employed, accounting for 20 percent. An additional 9 percent of working women work in the area of domestic services, and finally, 2 percent are employers themselves and 2 percent are involved in unpaid family ventures.

Among salaried workers, we can make a distinction between those working in the private sector and those working in the public sector. In Chile, the majority (90 percent) of people work in the private sector.

The percentage of inactive women is particularly striking given that in Chile, even though 80 percent of women are over 15 years of age, that is, potentially active, a high percentage of these (51.7 percent) remain inactive. Of those women occupationally inactive, the highest percentage, at 37 percent, are dedicated to work at home. The second group, which is almost half that of the first at 18 percent, are retirees or pensioners. In addition, 18 percent are students, 11 percent do not work for reasons of health, 9 percent do not need to work, 2 percent have become discouraged from doing so, and 5 percent do not work due to other reasons.

In order to understand the low participation of women in the workforce, we must first understand how we organize ourselves as families and as a society. In Chile, a significant percentage of women do not enter the workforce because they do not have anyone with whom to leave those dependent on them. In Figure 16.3 we can see what percentage of responsibility women have in regards to those dependent on them: 51 percent of women have no dependents, 20 percent have at least one child under 6 years of age, 18 percent have at least one child between 7 and 14 years of age, 8 percent have dependents but who are not children, and 3 percent have children up to 14 years as well as other dependents (Banco Interamericano de Desarrollo, 2012). In summary, almost half of all women have dependents who require care by an adult.

Table 16.2 Distribution of employees by sex and category of work (%)

	Men	Women
Salaried	73.7	64.6
Self-employed	19.8	21.2
Domestic service	0.3	9.8
Unpaid family staff	0.8	2.1
Employer	5.5	2.4

Source: INE (2015c)

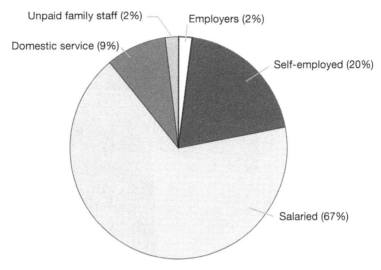

Figure 16.1 Distribution of the active female population
Source: INE (2015d)

The main reason that women give for remaining inactive is permanent family reasons (36.5 percent), unlike inactive men for whom only 1.6 percent is due to permanent family reasons. This shows that in Chile, the dominant pattern of distribution of roles is still one wherein women assume household responsibilities to a greater extent than their male peers.

This dependency has an impact on the opportunities and possibilities women have to join the workforce. For example, 50 percent of inactive Chilean women who have at least one child under 6 years old are under 30 years of age, of which 70 percent would be willing to work if they had a viable solution for the issue of childcare, which might include flexitime arrangements, telecommuting, salary increases in order to pay for good day care, etc. (OECD,

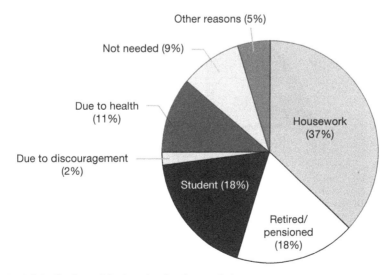

Figure 16.2 Distribution of the inactive female population
Source: INE (2015d)

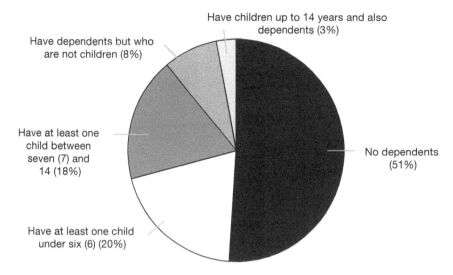

Figure 16.3 Dependent people in the care of women
Source: INE (2012)

2011). Also, 50 percent of inactive women, with at least one child between 6 and 14 are under 40, and 70 percent of them would be willing to work if they could deal with the issue of childcare in a satisfactory manner. In contrast, amongst inactive women with children between 6 and 14 but who are older than 50, the majority would prefer not to work (OECD, 2011).

For many women, work not only represents a means of personal development, but is also a family need. To understand this effect, we can analyze female participation in the workforce based on the marital status of the women in question. The female participation rate is, on average, 48.3 percent. If this is subdivided according to the civil status of women, we observe that the highest participation rate corresponds to divorced women (23 percent), followed by

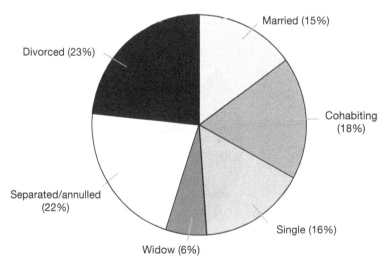

Figure 16.4 Female participation rate according to marital status
Source: INE (2013a)

separated women and those with annulled marriages (22 percent), while the lowest rate of participation corresponds to widows (6 percent), followed by married women (15 percent). This is directly related to the responsibilities that women have when entering the workforce.

In Chile, one's future pension is built up on an individual basis over time and therefore depends on the total number of years worked. According to OECD data (OECD, 2011), Chilean men retire with a pension equal to 64.3 percent of their average salary over the previous ten years, while women do so at a rate of only 49.9 percent. This difference occurs primarily because women have longer periods of unemployment or "gaps" that create periods of inactivity in their pension records, which in turn leads to a much lower monthly pension upon retirement than the salary they received during their working lives.

Another problem related to retirement evidenced as a difference between men and women is that they not only accumulate on average smaller amounts in their pension funds, but women also have a higher life expectancy than men, which affects the pension they receive from month to month. It is for this reason that the relevant institutions involved have continually attempted to devise benefits that seek to improve their retirement.

Some of these benefits are:

1   "Bonus per child" in which, through a recognition of motherhood, women who meet the requirements are eligible for a bonus for each live birth or adopted child, which amounts to US$493. The amount of this bonus is not given to the mother instantly or at one time, unless she makes use of it beginning at age 65, in which case it is incorporated into the amount of her monthly pension.
2   To order to improve the long-term pensions of women, it was possible to separate out disability insurance according to sex. Since 2009, all AFPs (Chilean pension system) together must tender for this insurance in order to achieve a more competitive price. As the cost for women is lower, and therefore entails a lower rate than that of men, the difference in monthly remuneration remains in their individual accounts therein constituting a greater contribution, which in the long term allows the balance of the account to increase and improve their pensions.
3   When a divorce or annulment takes place between a married couple, the judge may decide to make use of pension funds of one active affiliate as economic compensation. These funds are transferred to a "mandatory individual account" of the spouse to be compensated. The compensated spouse is normally the woman since in most cases she has postponed her paid work to attend to household chores and for this reason has ceased making contributions to her future pension, and once she is divorced or her prior marriage is annulled she can no longer make use of the benefits she had as a spouse.

In spite of all these legal benefits, it is important that women take certain actions to achieve a higher pension. Among the options they have in this regard are, for example, the option of postponing their retirement age, therein accumulating a larger fund total. Another option is to transfer a certain voluntary amount of money to an APV (voluntary pension savings) fund, in which the additional funds she has invested are divided up upon retirement and are thus added to her monthly pension.

Women pursuing education

Another impact that the massive incorporation of women into the workplace has had has been its impact on vocational training. Vocational training in Chile refers to degree programs lasting at least five years. The increase in the number of women in universities has been consistent through the years. In Chile, according to enrollment data, female higher education reached 51.8 percent in 2015, marginally surpassing men at 48.2 percent (MINEDUC, 2015). It is for this reason that six out of ten professionals that enter the job market today in Chile are women. Women also have better grades, take a year less to graduate, and are 10 percent less likely to drop out in the first year of higher education (MINEDUC, 2012). In addition, there are many women who continue postgraduate studies beyond these five years, either in the form of postgraduate degrees and certificate programs, specializations, masters and doctoral degrees, etc. This has allowed women to gain ground in the paid workforce, and means that they can occupy positions that were previously unthinkable for them. However, despite their preparation, the number of women in senior management is low compared to men.

What is clear is that the workforce participation rate of women increases with an increasing level of education. At the level of primary education, the workforce participation rate is 32.5 percent for women and 64.8 percent for men. At the highest level of education, namely, higher education plus additional studies, the percentage of workforce participation of women and men is similar, at 88.5 percent and 91.1 percent respectively (INE, 2014b).

Education in Chile is divided into four stages: preschool, primary, secondary and higher education. The first three stages are required. In the past five years, the number of people enrolled in one of these four phases increased by 0.79 percent (INE, 2014a).

Education levels also affect the composition of the workforce. There is a positive correlation between level of education and workforce participation. This is to say, the more educated the worker, the higher their workforce participation, both among men and women. Of course, this correlation is greater in women than in men.

At the level of primary education, female workforce participation is the lowest, reaching only 31 percent, while as the level of education increases, the level of female participation

Table 16.3 People enrolled in the educational system

Year	Total	Women	Men
2007	4,470,236	2,285,921	2,184,315
2008	4,488,254	2,293,900	2,194,354
2009	4,574,820	2,331,592	2,243,228
2010	4,635,250	2,355,503	2,279,747
2011	4,671,265	2,365,898	2,305,367
2012	4,676,329	2,359,476	2,316,853
2013	4,721,892	2,383,160	2,338,732

Source: INE (2014a)

Table 16.4 Employment rate by sex and education (%)

Education level	Men	Women
Primary education	62	31
Secondary education	69	46
Technical education	80	63
University education	72	59
Postgraduates/Masters/PhD	89	87

Source: INE (2013b)

increases as well. At the level of secondary education this reaches 46 percent, 63 percent in technical education and 59 percent in university education. At the level of postgraduate degrees and certificates, masters and doctoral degrees, the percentage of women is even almost the same as men, reaching 87 percent. There has been an increase of women with higher education entering the labor market during the last decade.

A worrying feature of the workforce in Chile is the level of education of those over 20 years of age: 45 percent of this population has an incomplete education, which is alarming since this group represents the lowest workforce participation rates and directly affects poverty levels and opportunities for our country, especially in the case of women. These data can be seen in the Table 16.5.

Women in management

In Chile, the gap in workforce participation between men and women is clear, but this gap is even greater in the case of managerial positions or positions of power. Globally, average female participation in senior management positions in the private sector reaches 24 percent. The highest percentages can be found in the Philippines (47 percent), Russia (42 percent) and Thailand (38 percent), while the lowest were found in Denmark (13 percent), Belgium (12 percent) and Japan (7 percent). In Latin America the figure stands at an average of 28 percent, while in Chile the figure reaches 24 percent, four percentage points below the Latin American average (Grant Thornton, 2009). This has to do with the low historical participation women have had in relation to other countries in the world and even to those of Latin America (INE, 2007).

According to a publication produced by the International Labour Organization (OIT, 2015), the presence of women at the upper and middle management level has insufficiently progressed in the last two decades. At the current rate it would take between 100 and 200 years to reach gender equality in the management of companies. The International Labour Organization conducted a survey of 1,200 companies from 39 countries in every region of the world. "The survey found that there were no women on boards in 30 percent of companies surveyed and in 65 percent of companies women represented less than 30 percent of all managers" (OIT, 2015).

In Chile, on average 24 percent of working women hold management positions (SER-NAM, 2011). Amongst different economic sectors, financial services employ a large number of women, reaching 46 percent of the workforce (CASEN, 2011). Less than 5 percent of this figure represents women on boards. This shows that even in sectors with a high percentage of women in the workforce, there are limitations that make it difficult for women to function at high levels of decision making and as members of boards.

In Chile the level of education of women has increased steadily, allowing them to continue to position themselves within the working world and in better condition to hold positions

Table 16.5 Female workforce participation rates by level of education (%)

Education level	(%)
Primary education or less	30
Incomplete secondary education	15
Completed secondary education	30
Higher education	25

Source: INE (2011)

within senior management, on boards, etc. In the long term, this will involve new challenges and commitments with companies and also with the family. The inequality that exists today in Chile regarding the presence of men and women in senior management is not a new phenomenon. All countries, even those where there is now a smaller gap, have started out this way.

In 2007, women in management and assistant management positions were aged mostly between 25 and 34 years (27 percent), and then between 35 and 44 years (22 percent) (SBIF, 2007). Work is time that women devote to themselves. Work not only provides them with information and financial resources, but also allows them to grow and develop personally and professionally.

Women in senior management

When we speak about women in senior management, women in Chile hold only 8 percent of these positions (SERNAM, 2011), even though this is more than those who hold positions on boards, and thus remains very low. According to a study conducted by SERNAM (2011), about half of the companies surveyed say they have at least one woman amongst the ranks of their top executives, and 90 of the 1,134 positions evaluated are held by women. Seventy percent of female top executives have an average of 13.5 years of experience, that is, the career path that allows them to take on a management position amounts to more than 10 years.

Of the companies evaluated in the study carried out by SERNAM, 31 percent of companies that have women in senior management are in the financial sector, followed by 29 percent in manufacturing, 24 percent in services, and 10 percent in commercial and distribution firms. Other companies represent the remaining 6 percent of the total.

While the rate of female participation in senior management positions is low, this increase in the exposure of female professionals is an example for other women to dare to apply for positions of greater strategic importance. It is also an incentive for women who are not yet professionals to dare to pursue careers that allow them to reach senior management positions or whatever else they might aspire to.

Women in decision-making positions bring a different vision to the company based on particular gender characteristics. They are better able to appreciate different points of view within a group that they are working in than their male counterparts. Some phenomena that take place when women are included in male workgroups are that they manage to bring about a warmer environment wherein more moderate vocabulary is used, different ideas are listened to and the different views of the participants are harmonized and taken into consideration (Debeljuh, 2013). That is, female managers are a complement to their male counterparts and represent a contribution to the organization.

According to a study carried out by PNUD (2009) and McKinsey & Company (2007), certain supposedly distinctive skills and characteristics tend to be associated with female leadership in relation to the distribution of women present. Figure 16.5 shows how women are distributed in senior management positions according to the business within companies. We can see that a higher percentage of women are found in the area of human resources (21 percent) and the lowest percentage are found in the area of sales (4 percent) (SERNAM, 2011).

Women on boards of directors

There is evidence that suggests that female participation in senior management is beneficial for companies. McKinsey (2008) studied the case of Latin America in 2013, assessing 345 listed

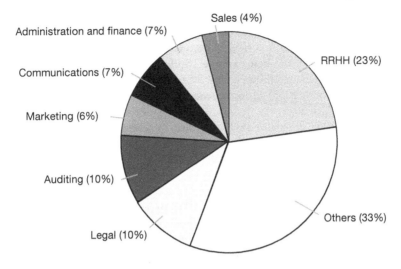

Figure 16.5 Women in senior management according to business area
Source: SERNAM (2011)

companies in six countries. The results showed that in companies with one or more women on their executive committees, yields on capital obtained 44 percent higher results, and margins before interest and taxes were 47 percent higher than for companies with committees made up of men only.

In spite of this evidence, the presence of women in senior management positions in Chile remains low. The percentage of women on boards represents only 3 percent of active women, in contrast to 97 percent of male managers. This percentage was calculated based on a study in which SERNAM (2011) analyzed 1,200 management positions in Chile. Of the 3 percent of working women in management positions, 43 percent belong to companies controlled by their families. As for the professions of these women, there is a great variety, but most (40 percent) belong to the commercial area. If we compare Chile with other countries, Chile's 3 percent is below the world average of 7.4 percent.

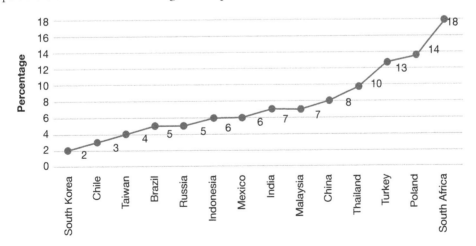

Figure 16.6 Percentage of women on boards worldwide
Source: GMI (2013)

The highest percentage amongst these 14 countries is South Africa, at 18 percent, that is, a 15 percentage point difference in comparison to Chile. While countries with higher participation rates are not those of Latin America, Chile is low compared to Brazil (5 percent) and Mexico (6 percent). If we take the best examples worldwide, we find Norway in first place (36.7 percent), followed by France (30 percent), Sweden (24 percent), Italy (22 percent) and Finland (22 percent) (Deloitte, 2015). However, the country with the lowest rate is Japan with just 1.3 percent (SERNAM, 2011).

If we differentiate participation on boards according to economic sector, the sector where most women in Chile are found is in financial companies at 52 percent, services at 12 percent, manufacturing companies at 11 percent, commercial and distribution companies at 11 percent, and 5 percent in other companies (SERNAM, 2011).

Amongst IPSA and IGPA companies, of a total of 82 companies, only 15 of them have incorporated women on their boards (SERNAM, 2011). In none of these is a woman the chair of the board. Internationally, country leaders in the percentage of women presidents of the board are Italy in first place (22 percent), then Norway (18 percent), Austria (9 percent), South Africa (8 percent) and Turkey (7 percent) (Deloitte, 2015). In Latin America, the countries with the highest percentage of female board presidents are Mexico and Brazil (INE, 2011).

Female entrepreneurship

There is no doubt that entrepreneurship is a key factor in a country's economic and social development, besides being an essential element in overcoming poverty. With this in view, in recent years Chile has developed a culture of increasing innovation and entrepreneurship, which in turn has impacted the female entrepreneurial ecosystem. According to Global Entrepreneurship Monitor (GEM, 2013), from 2005 to 2013, the 10 percent of economically active Chilean women who led a business venture increased to 26 percent.

In Chile, 38 percent of entrepreneurs are women (Ministerio de Economía, Fomento y Turismo, 2013). Most women who undertake a business venture in Chile are either married (42 percent) or single (22 percent). Their relationship with the head of the household is that most of them are in fact the heads of their respective households (41 percent) or are a spouse (37 percent). Another feature of these women that evidences few differences based on age level is the fact that we find entrepreneurs in every age group.

The education level of female entrepreneurs in Chile is very similar to that of their male counterparts. Most of them have finished high school (44 percent), and the second largest group has only finished primary education (29 percent).

At the level of prior work experience, 70 percent of them have had some kind of paid work, but left it mostly because they quit (35 percent), or because their work contract or

Table 16.6 Entrepreneurs by age group (%)

Age group	Men	Women	Total
15–24 years	3	4	3
25–34 years	9	12	10
35–44 years	17	20	19
45–54 years	30	28	29
55–64 years	24	25	24
65+ years	17	12	15

Source: Ministerio de Economía, Fomento y Turismo (2013)

agreement ended (16 percent), while 9.3 percent did so because they wanted to start their own businesses.

There are several reasons why women start businesses. The main ones are: to increase their incomes (31 percent), to have greater job flexibility (15 percent), to respond to a market opportunity (12 percent) and in order to make their own decisions (10 percent), among others (GEM, 2013). These alternatives are a good reflection of the reality of many women in Chile. There are very large and very clear wage gaps that cause women to seek out other employment possibilities. Additionally, the desire for flexibility and to reconcile work and family makes entrepreneurship an attractive alternative.

If we group the motivations listed by Global Entrepreneurship Monitor (2013), we can differentiate between the motivations men and women have to start their own businesses. Women do so mostly out of necessity (58 percent), while men do so out of necessity (43 percent) and because of opportunities (43 percent). Figure 16.7 shows the other categories and comparisons with men.

An important aspect of business ventures is their level of formality. In Chile, there is a difference on this point if we compare men and women. The business ventures of men tend to be more formal (54 percent) than informal (46 percent), while female business ventures tend to be more informal (52 percent) than formal (48 percent). In terms of levels of income, we also find differences between men and women. The incomes earned by women are lower than those of their male counterparts: 57 percent of women sell less than US$276 and 82 percent sell less than $860, while amongst men, 67 percent sell less than $860 and 84 percent sell less than $3,582.

Country legislation

Chilean law is considered one of the most supportive of a work–family balance in Latin America (Chinchilla *et al.*, 2011).

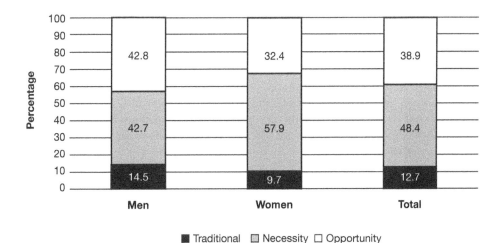

Figure 16.7 Sources of motivation for starting a business
Source: Ministerio de Economía, Fomento y Turismo (2013)

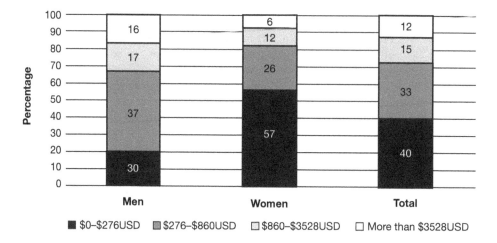

Figure 16.8 Levels of sales
Source: Ministerio de Economía, Fomento y Turismo (2013)

International agreements

The issue of compatibility between family responsibilities and work responsibilities has been the subject of regulation by international organizations, which have been ratified and are currently in force in Chile. The most relevant are the Convention on the Elimination of All Forms of Discrimination Against Women (CEDAW) and International Labour Organization Conventions (Bosch *et al.*, 2014):

1   Convention on the Elimination of All Forms of Discrimination Against Women (CEDAW): This convention was adopted in 1979 and entered into effect in 1981. It was born of the need for specific means to protect the human rights of women and avoid all forms of discrimination. CEDAW recognizes the contribution that women make to the welfare of the family and to the development of society, the social importance of motherhood and the role of parents in the family and in the education of their children. This convention requires state parties to prevent discrimination against women in different walks of life, and more specifically, refers to discrimination against women in employment. It establishes that for this purpose cultural patterns based on prejudice against women must be changed and an understanding of maternity as a social function and responsibility of men and women in this regard ensured.
2   International Labour Organization Convention: Workers with Family Responsibilities: These are international instruments that recognize for the first time that "to achieve full equality between men and women it is necessary to change the traditional role of both men and women in society and in the family." They aim to make work and family compatible and are based on the ideas of conciliation and social co-responsibility.
3   International standards for maternity protection
   a)   United Nations establishes in the Universal Declaration of Human Rights that "motherhood and childhood are entitled to special care and assistance."

b) CEDAW contains a special provision that deals with workplace discrimination against women due to motherhood.

c) The International Labour Organization has issued three conventions that promote a series of rights and privileges regarding motherhood. These conventions safeguard both working women and their children, and establish basic and general rights. They provide recommendations on the prenatal and minimum postnatal leaves that a female worker must have.

Chilean law

Relevant laws in Chile include:

1   Equality in remuneration: This law recognizes that both men and women have the right to receive the same salary if they perform the same work. This principle applies to both the private sector and the public sector.

2   Support for motherhood and fatherhood: Chilean law stipulates a maternity leave that can reach a total of 30 weeks divided into prenatal leave of 6 weeks before birth, postnatal leave of 12 weeks after birth and postnatal parental leave. After the first 12 weeks mothers may choose to take 12 full weeks or 18 weeks working part-time. This is an inalienable right.

3   Maternity leave: This is the protection given to pregnant women and aims to maintain a woman's employment so as to secure the source of her income. This leave extends from the time of pregnancy until one year after the expiration of the postnatal period (i.e., when the son/daughter is one year and 84 days old). The employer is prohibited from terminating her work contract without prior authorization of a judge.

4   Special leave: According to the Labor Code, when the health of a child under one year of age requires home care due to a serious illness, the working mother is entitled to a leave and subsidy for as long as needed. This must be documented by an official physician's order.

5   Feeding leave: Chilean labor legislation stipulates that female workers are entitled to have at least an hour a day to feed their children under two years of age. This right may be exercised at any time during the workday or by dividing up the time in two periods at the request of the mother. Finally, she may also delay or advance the start or end of the workday by half an hour.

6   Right to nursery: A working mother has the right to delegate the care of her child under two years of age to third parties in a nursery administered or funded by the employer. Only organizations with 20 or more workers of any marital status or age are required to provide nursery care. Therefore, not all Chilean female workers can exercise this right.

7   Bonus per child: This is a benefit that increases the amount of a woman's pension by means of a bonus for each live birth or adopted child. It is not paid at the time of childbirth, but is added to her pension at retirement. The amount of the bonus is established and begins to generate income from the date of childbirth and is equivalent to 10 percent of 18 minimum monthly wages (according to the year and month of the child's birth).

8   Third child bonus: This benefit is still awaiting approval by the Senate, but if approved, will pay a bonus to all women who are mothers starting from the birth of their third child. This initiative provides for a single payment of $143 for the birth of the third child of every mother, increases to $214 for the fourth, and will be $287 starting with a fifth child. However, these amounts may be modified depending on the debate surrounding the bill.

9   Shared responsibility: On August 4 2015, the Senate Working Committee approved the proposal to incorporate the principle of shared responsibility in the labor law, which establishes that both father and mother, living together or apart, can participate actively, equitably and permanently in the upbringing and education of their children. The purpose of this initiative is to improve conditions for workers with family responsibilities, thereby promoting the incorporation and permanence of women in the workplace.

Despite having rights related to motherhood, even above international standards, we still need to develop a culture wherein more fathers get involved in the care of the family. It is important in Chile to ensure that there is a consensus that women are part of the labor market and in the same way that men help with the housework. The roles between the couple should be complementary. We must ensure that both share responsibility, and that they complement and support each other. If we fail to do so, women will eventually interrupt or delay their careers to dedicate their time and efforts at home.

Company initiatives to support the advancement of qualified women

As we have seen throughout this chapter, in Chile women are the primary caregivers of a family with dependent people. As a way to promote the careers of women, various companies have begun promoting policies to reconcile work and family in order to enable them to progress in their careers without neglecting their responsibilities at home. Some of these policies are, according to Bosch *et al.* (2013):

*   Flexible working hours: Employees must work nine hours a day, but they can decide themselves what time to start and and what time to leave the company at the end of the day.
*   Part-time work: Reduction of working hours in exchange for lower wages.
*   Compressed week: People can work longer hours each day and in return have a day or half day off per week.
*   Job sharing: An agreement for the responsibilities of a full-time position to be shared between two or more workers.
*   Permission to leave work because of an emergency: Employees can leave their jobs to deal with an emergency situation without having to justify the absence in advance.
*   Flexible return after postnatal leave: This benefit seeks to make the time mothers leave work earlier during the days/weeks following their return to work, regardless of the mode of postnatal parental leave chosen (full or part time) as long as the mother resumes work on the day corresponding to that established for the leave.

Women in government and politics

In 2013, for the first time in Chile, there was a presidential runoff election wherein two women candidates were voted on at the polls. This was an important milestone in the rapid changes Chile has experienced in the participation of women in politics. Chile allowed women to join the political debate in 1949 when their voting rights were legally recognized.

Although men and women have the same political rights in terms of participation, in practice, the representation of women has not been equivalent and women still have a

Table 16.7 Women's suffrage

Year	Women (%)
1952	32
1958	35
1964	44
1970	49
1989	52

Source: Senate (2016)

minority presence in the various spheres of political decision-making. However, the turnout of women has gradually increased. Since 1984 women have represented around 52 percent of voters.

The first woman to join the Senate was María de la Cruz, in the legislative period from 1949 to 1953. She created the Women's Party, which represented 2 percent of the total composition of the Senate. However, she did not even manage to finish her term. In the same period, female representation in the House of Representatives was 0.6 percent. Some years later in the 1965–1969 legislative period, female representation in the House of Representatives stood at 4 percent and in the Senate at 7 percent (Senate, 2016). Female representation has not changed much. Although it has increased over the last 20 years, female representation in Congress remains low. The numbers of senators and representatives have failed to add up to more than 20 percent of the total representation (Senate, 2016).

In March 2014, at the start of a new legislature, 19 representatives (10 new and 9 re-elected) took office, which represented 16 percent of a total of 120 representatives, while in the Senate, women took 7 out of 38 seats, or 18 percent of the total. Compared to the previous period, there was an increase in female participation in both houses, 2 percent in the House of Representatives and 5 percent in the Senate. In addition to the two houses, in Chile 39 percent of ministers (executive) and 23 percent of those holding office in local government are women (13 percent mayors, 25 percent councilors). In comparison, the world average of women in the legislature is 22 percent, and it is 25 percent in the US (Senate, 2016).

In contrast to female participation in senior management, compared to South America, women's participation in the lower house is similar to that of Chile's neighboring countries.

Table 16.8 Women's participation in senior management in South America

Country	(%)
Ecuador	42
Argentina	37
Bolivia	25
Peru	22
Venezuela	17
Chile	16
Paraguay	15
Uruguay	13
Colombia	12
Brazil	9
Average for Latin America and the Caribbean	25

Source: MIMP (2014)

Table 16.9 Women's participation in politics

Area	(%)
Nordic countries	42
The Americas	24
Latin America and the Caribbean	24
Europe	23
Africa	20
Asia	18
Pacific	15
Arab states	13
World average	20

Source: OIT (2013)

If we compare participation in Latin America and the Caribbean (24 percent) with the rest of the world, this region is above the world average (20 percent), but at 16 percent, Chile still has a way to go in including more women in politics.

Examples of good news and bad news in Chile

Some bad news

> Article 62 bis – The employer must comply with the principle of equal remuneration for men and women for equal work, and objective differences in salaries must not be considered arbitrary but based on, among other reasons, skills, qualifications, appropriateness, responsibility or productivity.
>
> (Dirección del Trabajo, 2016)

While this law exists in Chile, a wage gap between men and women still exists. The wage gap between men and women is found at all levels and occurs independently of the level of education people have. With the same level of education women receive lower wages than men. While there is increasing economic participation of women in various sectors and there has been an increase in their level of education, there is still a significant wage gap. If we compare the average wages of men and women in Chile, the gap reaches 43 percent.

The wage gap between men and women exists in all occupational categories. Where we have a clear example of this is in the case of domestic workers where men who work in this sector earn on average more than 70 percent than women, which means that monthly they earn about $211 more than their female peers (INE, 2014c).

Figure 16.9 shows the comparison between the salary gap between men and women according to their level of schooling. It can be seen that the gap increases with increasing years

Table 16.10 Wage gap in Chile (US$)

Average male salary	Average female salary	Difference	Difference (%)
$704	$493	$211	43

Source: Fundación Sol (2015)

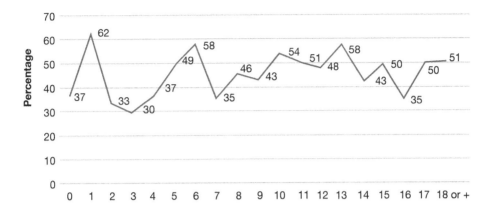

Figure 16.9 Salary gap
Source: INE (2015b)

of schooling. Where the greatest difference can be noticed is in the section of workers with 13 years of schooling, where a difference of 58 percent can be observed. This is followed by a 54 percent difference with 10 years of schooling, and finally for those with more than 17 years the difference reaches 50 percent. Where gaps are smallest is amongst those with fewer years of schooling, wherein a gap 29 percent persists for those with three years of schooling (INE, 2015c).

Another not very encouraging piece of news is that according to the latest Bicentenario UC-GfK Adimark survey (PUC, 2015), 53 percent of Chileans think that women who work outside the home are neglecting their responsibilities at home. This shows that a significant percentage of the population still believes that the woman is the primary caregiver at home, therein limiting her potential development outside of home.

Some good news

There is growing awareness of women's contribution in the workplace. Different organizations devote their energy and resources so that women can thrive in both the public and private sectors.

Some of these initiatives include:

1   SERNAM: the National Women's Service.
2   Comunidad Mujer: an independent, cross-sector organization that promotes the rights of women and actively contributes to the generation of public policies for greater equality, equity and participation of women in work-related and political spheres (for more information visit: www.comunidadmujer.cl/).
3   Mujeres Empresarias: an organization that supports women in business management, provides leadership for women business leaders, professionals and entrepreneurs through a wide and innovative network of contacts that allows for their inclusion in the economic and business worlds (for more information visit: www.me.cl/). It has numerous schemes, including the 100 Women Leaders Award to highlight women in the areas of business, professional, academic and public service; the Young Entrepreneur Award to encourage

women up to 35 years of age who make a contribution to the productivity of Chile with their business ventures; and Female Executive of the Year Award to highlight important executive women working in established and prestigious companies.

4   Fundación Chile Unido: a private, independent nonprofit institution that promotes the creation of a more humane country. It conducts a ranking of the best companies for parents.

5   ESE Business School: the business school of the University of the Andes in Chile. It has a Women's Lobby, which is an initiative that seeks to provide women managers with the training and tools they need to develop their talents from a humanistic vision enriched by a female perspective.

These are some of the public and private organizations that give visibility to many women who want to develop within the workforce of Chile, allowing the contribution women make in business to be appreciated, as well as giving visibility to many women in a predominantly male environment.

The future as I envision it

Chile still has a long way to go in terms of the development of women in the workplace. The way we organize ourselves as a society still assumes that the woman is the primary caregiver in the home and that an adult must be present at home in order to care for dependents, most of whom are women. This has placed limits on opportunities for the professional development of many women in Chile. However, I believe there are enough initiatives to change this reality in the medium term.

In terms of education, there are a large number of women who are now in universities and several studies have shown that the well-known Generation Y has incorporated new frameworks wherein men and women want to develop in family, workplace and personal spheres. I think generational change in addition to increased initiatives on the part of companies that want to promote the participation of women amongst senior management will accelerate these demographic changes, therein allowing more women to participate in the workforce and in positions of power.

References

Banco Interamericano de Desarrollo (2012): *Encuesta nacional sobre mujer y trabajo en Chile: Voz de mujer.* Santiago de Chile: BID.

Bosch, M. J., Cano, V., Riumalló, M. P. and Tarud, C. (2014): *Estudio percepciones y prácticas de conciliación y corresponsabilidad en organizaciones públicas y privadas.* Santiago de Chile: SERNAM.

CASEN (2011): *Encuesta de Caracterización Socioeconómica Nacional.* Santiago de Chile: CASEN.

Chinchilla, N., Las Heras, M. and Masuda, A. (2009): *Balancing Work–Family: No matter where you are.* Massachusetts: HRD Press.

Debeljuh, P. (2013): *Varón + Mujer = complementariedad.* Buenos Aires: LID Editorial Empresarial.

Deloitte (2015): *Women in the Boardroom: A global perspective.* Deloitte, www.global.corpgov.deloitte.com

Dirección del Trabajo (2016): *Código del Trabajo Artículo 62 bis.* Santiago de Chile: Dirección del Trabajo, Gobierno de Chile.

Fundación Sol (2015): *Mujeres trabajando: Una exploración al valor del trabajo y la calidad del empleo en Chile.* Santiago de Chile: Fundación Sol.

GEM (2013): *Global Entrepreneurship Monitor: Global report.* Babson, Universidad del Desarrollo & Universiti Tun Abdil Razak, Chile.

GMI (2013): *GMI Ratings' 2013 Women on Boards Survey*. GMI, www.calstrs.com/sites/main/files/file-attachments/gmiratings_wob_042013-1.pdf

Grant Thornton (2009): *Privately Held Businesses: The lifeblood of the global economy*. International Business Report. Grant Thorntonfile:///C:/Users/121141442/Downloads/IBR_2009_Global_overview_FINAL_Med_Res.pdf

INE (2007): *Mujer y trabajo*. Santiago de Chile: INE.

INE (2011): *Estadísticas de educación, cultura y medios de comunicación*. Santiago de Chile: INE.

INE (2013a): *Nueva Encuesta Suplementaria de Ingresos 2013*. Santiago de Chile: INE.

INE (2013b): *Estadísticas de educación, cultura y medios de comunicación*. Santiago de Chile: INE.

INE (2014a): *Compendio Estadístico*. Santiago de Chile: INE.

INE (2014b): *Empleo trimestral*. Edición No. 196. Santiago de Chile: INE.

INE (2014c): *Mujeres en Chile y mercado del trabajo: participación laboral femenina y brechas salariales*. Santiago de Chile: INE.

INE (2015a): *Género y empleo*. Santiago de Chile: INE.

INE (2015b): *Mujeres en Chile y mercado del trabajo: participación laboral femenina y brechas salariales*. Santiago de Chile: INE.

INE (2015c): *Participación laboral de las mujeres y equidad de género*. Santiago de Chile: INE.

INE (2015d): *Nueva Encuesta Nacinoal de Empleo*, nov2014-enero2015. Santiago de Chile: INE.

McKinsey & Company (2007): *Women Matter*, 2007. file:///C:/Users/121141442/Downloads/Women_matter_oct2007_english.pdf

MIMP (2014): *Participación Política de las Mujeres en América del Sur: En Busca de la Paridad*. Ministerio de la Mujer y Poblaciones Vulnerables, Perú.

MINEDUC (2012): *Serie Evidencias: Deserción en la educación superior en Chile*. Santiago de Chile: MINEDUC.

MINEDUC (2014): *Panorama de la Eudación Superior en Chile*. Santiago de Chile: MINEDUC.

MINEDUC (2015): *Servicio de Información de Educación Superior (SIES)*. Santiago de Chile: MINEDUC.

Ministerio de Economía, Fomento y Turismo (2013): *Emprendimiento y Género Tercera Encuesta de Microemprendimiento (EME)*. Santiago de Chile: Ministerio de Economía, Fomento y Turismo.

OECD (2011): *Mejores políticas para el desarrollo: Perspectivas OCDE sobre Chile*. www.oecd.org/fr/chili/mejorespoliticasparaeldesarrolloperspectivasocdesobrechile.htm

OIT (2008): *Informe sobre el trabajo en el mundo 2008*. Santiago de Chile: OIT.

OIT (2013): *Panorama Laboral America Latina y Cribe 2013*. Santiago de Chile: OIT.

OIT (2015): *Informe sobre el trabajo en el mundo 2014*. Santiago de Chile: OIT.

PNUD (2009): *Trabajo y Familia: Hacia nuevas formas de conciliación con corresponsabilidad social*. Santiago de Chile: Oficina Internacional del Trabajo y PNUD.

PUC (2015): *Encuesta Nacional Bicentenario Universidad Católica – GfK Adimark*. Santiago de Chile: PUC.

SBIF (2007): *Resultados segunda encuesta de antecedentes de género del sistema financiero chileno*. Santiago de Chile: SBIF.

Senate (2016): Noticias, www.senado.cl/mujeres-en-politica-los-derechos-con-corse-el-voto-femenino-y-su-participacion-en-cargos-de-poder/prontus_senado/2013-12-13/120728.html

SERNAM (2011): *Nueva Encuesta Suplementaria de Ingresos (NESI)*. Santiago de Chile: SERNAM.

17 Women in management in Peru

Kety Jauregui

Introduction

Peru has one of the fastest growing Latin American economies and it is one of the seven least poor countries in Latin America (ECLAC, 2015). With an average 6.1 percent gross domestic product (GDP) growth between 2005 and 2014, it has managed to cut its poverty rate from 55.6 percent in 2005 to 22.7 percent in 2013 (World Bank, 2015) through sound macroeconomic and fiscal policies in a context of favorable global commodity prices.

As a result of such sustained economic growth, Peru has risen from a middle-low income country to a middle-high income nation. It has also accomplished several of the Millennium Development Goals (MDGs), including reducing poverty, achieving universal primary education, fostering gender equality, reducing child mortality and improving maternal health (PCM y UN, 2013). Peru now ranks 82nd out of 187 countries in the United Nations Development Program's Human Development Index (0.737) (UNDP, 2015).

Nevertheless, despite strong economic results and social progress, Peru's accomplishments are not yet strongly reflected in improved population well-being. Poverty rates are still high in some Andean and Amazon departments (PCM y UN, 2013). On gender equality Peru ranked 45th out of 142 countries in 2014 (WEF, 2014). On the Gender Inequality Index (0.957) it placed in 72nd position among 187 countries in 2013 (UNDP, 2015). It is worth emphasizing that women account for 50 percent of the entire Peruvian population (INEI, 2015a).

This chapter discusses the condition of women in Peru. First, it examines the characteristics of the labor force and level of education. Next, it reviews women's share of board and management positions in both the political and business worlds, as well as women's overall participation in business. Then, it presents the domestic legal framework with regard to gender and reducing the remaining challenges, so that women can grow both professionally and in the family. Finally, it lists some recommendations on ways companies and government can support women's development.

Labor force characteristics

Women are increasingly present in the Peruvian labor market, to an even greater degree than in other Latin American countries (Jaramillo and Montalva, 2009). Since the 1970s, Peru has seen an increase in the number of women involved in some form of economic activity, from a participation in the total employed working population of 20.30 percent in 1972 (INEI, 1972) to 43.9 percent in 2014 (INEI, 2015b).

The larger share of Peruvian women in the domestic labor market is due to several reasons: growing education and professional training (MTPE, 2006; Blondet *et al.*, 1994) and the country's economic growth, as well as emerging women's movements (García, 2009) in the 1990s, together with the economic crisis Peru went through from the mid-1970s (Blondet *et al.*, 1994), and declining fertility rates since 2000 (Jaramillo and Montalva, 2009).

However, despite approximately 40 percent growth in the the number of women in the labor market between 1972 and 2014 (see Table 17.1), women still face various challenges: the differences between men and women in the labor market are still significant in 2014. Thus, women's activity rate reaches 63.3 percent, compared to 81.4 percent for men; women's employment rate reaches 60.8 percent compared to 78.7 percent for men, while women's unemployment rate is 4.0, compared to 3.4 for men (INEI, 1972; MTPE, 2015a). In 2014, women's participation in the non-economically active population (NEAP) reached 66.6 percent, of which 59.1 percent were engaged in household chores; 27.2 percent were studying, and the remainder were pensioners or sick (INEI, 2015b).

It is worth underlining that informality is the labor market's most serious issue, since 73.7 percent of the total employed population of working age works in the informal (non-official economy), of which 45.7 percent are women (INEI, 2015b). Additionally, non-registered employment is more frequent in certain industries, including agriculture, fisheries and mining (94.6 percent) and commerce (73.9 percent), where women's share is particularly high (INEI, 2015b). Moreover, the largest component of non-registered jobs is found in companies with less than 50 workers, where women's share is also high (INEI, 2015b).

In response to this market structure, Table 17.2 shows that the number of women working in industry and government rose by 45 percent and 16 percent, respectively, between 2001 and

Table 17.1 Main women's labor market indicators

Indicators	1972	1981	1993	2010	2014
A. Population (thousands of people)					
Working-age population (population 14 years and older) (WAP)	**13,508.90**	**13,741.00**	**18,727.10**	**21,223.50**	**22,668.60**
Women	6,742.10	6,893.70	9,455.60	10,649.60	11,381.20
Economically active population women (EAP)	**3,871.60**	**5,313.90**	**7,305.80**	**15,735.70**	**16,396.40**
Women	800.2	1,335.50	2,192.20	6,994.10	7,204.80
Working EAP	**3,653.00**	**5,027.90**	**6,778.80**	**15,089.90**	**15,796.90**
Women	741.6	1,208.90	2,025.30	6,664.10	6,915.90
Not working EAP	**218.6**	**285.9**	**527**	**645.8**	**599.5**
Women	58.6	126.6	166.8	330	288.9
Non-active population (PEI)	**9,637.30**	**8,427.10**	**11,421.30**	**5,487.80**	**6,272.20**
Women	5,941.90	5,558.20	7,263.50	3,655.50	4,176.40
B. Rates (%)					
Activity rate (EAP/WAP)	**28.7**	**38.7**	**39**	**74.1**	**72.3**
Women	11.9	19.4	23.2	65.7	63.3
Employment/population rate (employed EAP/WAP)	**27**	**36.6**	**36.2**	**71.1**	**69.7**
Women	11	17.5	21.4	62.6	60.8
Unemployment rate (Non-working EAP/EAP)	**5.6**	**7.4**	**13.6**	**4.1**	**3.7**
Women	7.3	9.5	7.6	4.7	4

Source: Adapted from MTPE (2015a); INEI (1972, 1981, 1993)

Table 17.2 Women's share of employment by market segment

Market segment	2001	2005	2014
Total employed population of working age (thousands of people)	11,862.20	13,120.40	15,683.60
Women			
Government	8.1	7.6	9.4
Company	22.3	23.4	32.4
From 2 to 10 workers	12.7	13.4	16.6
From 11 to 100 workers	6.1	5.8	8.1
101 or more workers	3.4	4.3	7.7
Independents	36.7	33.9	35.8
Non-wage-earning family workers	25.2	27	17.4
Household help	7.8	8	4.9
Relative total	100	100	100
Employed population of women of working age (thousands of people)	4,995.70	5,637.20	6,915.90

Source: Adapted from: MTPE (2015b)

2014. Meanwhile, the percentage of non-wage earning women and domestic help dropped by 2 percent and 30 percent, respectively. Moreover, despite an increase exceeding 100 percent among women employed by large private concerns between 2001 and 2014, only 7.7 percent of women work in private companies hiring more than 101 workers, a phenomenon that may be explained by their low level of employment in large companies that provide career opportunities. In 2014, most women (36.7 percent) worked first as independent workers, which may also be accounted for by the fact that women look for greater employment flexibility that allows them to combine their labor market and household work; second, in industry (34.7 percent) but particularly in companies employing between two and ten workers; and third, in government (9.4 percent). Women's participation in government employment has increased gradually since 2004 and currently stands at approximately 46 percent (SERVIR and PCM, 2015).

As regards employed women, as a share of the economically active population, by occupational group, the most women (26.1 percent) worked as sales people; 21.3 percent as farmers, livestock herders, and in fishing; 17.6 percent as service providers, and 13.4 percent as professionals, technicians, managers, administrators, or officials. Employment as office clerks and service workers has grown by 79 percent and 46 percent, respectively, in the last 13 years. Employment in farming, livestock herding, and fishing, as well as domestic service has dropped by 25 percent and 35 percent respectively (MTPE, 2015b). It is worth emphasizing that women have moved to other economic activities, leaving agriculture behind.

With regard to government positions, women's participation accounts for 53.3 percent of specialized careers, explained by the strong participation of women nurses in the health sector and women teachers in preschool and primary education, and a low participation in managerial and senior official level positions (28 percent). Among professionals, women's participation reaches 43 percent, while they make up 24.5 percent of assistants, where blue-collar workers and drivers are mostly men (SERVIR and PCM, 2015).

As regards work income, on average men received higher salaries, despite similar working conditions for women, reflecting strong wage inequalities for similar jobs (WEF, 2014). Significant gaps existed in 2001 for artisans (60 percent), sales people (44.5 percent), service workers (41.94 percent), and farmers (37.46 percent). By contrast, women working as miners and domestic maids earn more than men. In 2014, significant gaps still exist in positions such as artisans (57.6 percent), sales people (44.23 percent), farmers (44.81 percent), and service workers (43.22 percent). Significantly, the income gaps in certain occupations narrowed in the period 2001–2014 (MTPE, 2015c), including sales people – a position predominantly held by women, and women professionals and managers.

Studies carried out by consultancy firms Mercer and DNA Human Capital among their clients and published in the media show the compensation gap between male and female executives is about 2 percent for chief executive officers (CEOs) (general managers), and from 8 percent to 15 percent for functional management positions (Gestión, 2014). This variation may indicate that wage discrimination is disappearing as women climb the job ladder. In other words, the lower the labor skills, the greater the discrimination against women.

Women pursuing education

Regular and higher learning educational coverage has increased for more than a decade in Peru. However, the quality of education is still inadequate. In the 2012 PISA tests, Peru scored poorly among Latin American countries (Ministerio de Educación, 2013). In particular, enrolment rates are similar in pre-school (girls: 78.8 percent; boys: 75.6 percent), primary (girls: 91.3 percent; boys: 92.4 percent), high school (women: 82.8 percent; men: 81.8 percent) and university (women 48.9 percent; men 51.1 percent). However, more men (42.2 percent) complete their high school education compared to women (33.2 percent) and get a university degree (men: 17.2 percent; women: 14.5 percent) (INEI, 2015c; ANR and INEI, 2010). Women's higher dropout rates are mainly a consequence of economic issues (poverty, need to work), or pregnancy and marriage (World Bank, 2006).

Furthermore, 6.3 percent of Peruvians 15 years and older are still illiterate (INEI, 2015c), of whom 75 percent are women (United Nations Human Rights Council, 2015), even though the female illiteracy rate dropped from 15.3 percent in 2004 to 9.6 percent in 2014. Illiteracy is higher among older people. For instance, illiteracy is 21.1 percent among people 60 years and older, compared to barely 0.8 percent among 15 to 19 year olds (INEI, 2015c).

University careers favored by women, or for which they have enrolled in university, include teaching (20.5 percent), business management (12.1 percent), and economic and social sciences (12 percent). The least favored are zootechnics (0.03 percent) and nutrition (0.7 percent). Business management (men: 10.9 percent, women: 12.1 percent,), economic science (men: 11.6 percent, women: 12 percent), law and political science (men: 8.5 percent, women: 8 percent) enrolled similar numbers of men and women. It is important to mention that although teaching is still the most favored profession, it became less so between 2011 and 2014 (INEI, 2015c). The decline in preference for the teaching profession may be a consequence of lower wages paid to teachers compared to other professions, and limited opportunities for growth in the teaching career line (Saavedra and Díaz, 2000).

The most recent university survey shows only 12.4 percent of undergraduates eventually enroll in master's degree graduate programs (ANR and INEI, 2010) for reasons possibly including financial, academic, and time constraints. Women are more heavily represented than men in both master's and second specialization programs, where they account for 51.4 percent and 60.3 percent of total enrollments, respectively. In contrast to these figures, the participation of women in business master's is much lower than that of men, says the dean of one business school. Nonetheless, men's share (59.9 percent) of doctorate studies enrollment is still larger than women's (40.1 percent) (ANR and INEI, 2010).

Women in management

Although the share of women in positions involving higher responsibility and decision making in either industry or government has increased in recent years, men still largely predominate. In 2014, 30.8 percent of managerial positions (at first, second, and third levels) in industry and government were filled by women (INEI, 2015d); in 2012, the figure was 29.3 percent (ILO, 2015), up from 22.70 percent in 2008 (INEI, 2015d) and 14.12 percent in 2001 (Perú Top Ten Publications, 2011).

In particular, 29 percent of Peruvian companies include one or more women as owners, 6 percent of listed companies have women board members, and 14 percent of private companies include women in senior management positions (senior managers or corporate CEOs, and they may even be the company's owner, if they also work there as CEO), according to the latest *Global Gender Gap Report* (WEF, 2014).

A review of the number of women filling first and second level positions in Lima Stock Exchange-listed companies shows only 3.4 percent of women, compared to 93.4 percent of men chairing boards. Table 17.3 shows that women account for 8.7 percent of board members and 6.6 percent of CEOs.

The number of women filling management positions has increased gradually worldwide, but their share is still larger in fourth level positions than in first level jobs (ILO, 2015).

One of the reasons accounting for the differences between men and women in management positions is that certain companies do not give women the opportunity to ascend to positions of leadership. This is reflected in Peru's 3.9 score in the rating of women's ability to climb in corporate positions shown in the *Global Gender Gap Report 2014*, where 7 is the top score (WEF, 2014). Another consideration is that reaching first and second level positions requires experience in functional management (ILO, 2015) mainly as operations, commercial, or financial managers. However, the Perú Top Ten Publications (2011) report shows that 33.3 percent of female managers fill human resource management positions. Also, Cardenas *et al.* (2013) comment that the two main barriers to women's career advancement in Latin America are the balance between "work and family" and the ability to "develop skills."

As regards women's role in government, large differences remain between men and women in both national and local government levels in favor of men. At national government level, women's share reaches 37.3 percent while men's is 63 percent. Women's share of local government positions reaches 29 percent compared to men's 71 percent. In regional (state) governments, women's participation is higher (44 percent) given their stronger role in specialized careers in health and education (SERVIR and PCM, 2015), although men still hold 56 percent of those jobs.

Gender affirmative action (quota) laws and efforts during the present administration have also expanded the political role of women in senior positions in the various powers of the state. Currently, 31.6 percent of ministers are women, 4 percent are regional governors, 3.1 percent

Table 17.3 First and second level positions

	Number of women	(%)	Number of men	(%)	Total
Board chairman	9	3.4	259	96.6	268
Board member	114	8.7	1198	91.3	1312
CEO (general manager)	18	6.6	253	93.4	271
Total	**114**	**8.7**	**1198**	**91.3**	1312

Source: Lima Stock Exchange (2015)

are provincial mayors, and 2.7 percent are district mayors (Elecciones en Perú, 2014; Jurado Nacional de Elecciones, 2014, 2015). Table 17.4 shows details of women's participation in government positions.

Women entrepreneurs

Peru is one of the most enterprising countries in Latin America, according to Global Entrepreneurship Monitor (GEM) 2014 (Slavica *et al.*, 2015) and the second best for the entrepreneurial environment for women entrepreneurs in Latina America and the Caribbean, as reported by the Women's Entrepreneurial VentureScope (WEVentureScope, 2013). However, the GEM 2014 study points to a business failure rate of 8 percent in 2013, placing Peru among the countries most prone to business failure in Latin America (Slavica *et al.*, 2015).

Of all companies, 94.92 percent are microbusinesses, 4.11 percent are small companies, 0.2 percent are mid-sized, 0.4 percent are large and 0.36 percent are under state management (INEI, 2014a). Micro and small enterprises (MSEs) account for 99.03 percent of the country's economy, in particular from the standpoint of production structure and jobs. MSEs employ about 50 percent of the employed female working age or economically active population (EAP), either as out-of-payroll (unofficial) workers, or in private companies that hire between two and ten workers or employ non-remunerated relatives (Ministerio de la Producción, 2012). Men are 66.2 percent of small and medium enterprise (SME) owners compared to 33.8 percent who are women (INEI, 2014b). Most of these women business owners (67 percent) are between 25 and 49 years old, 27.1 percent are 50 to 64, 1.4 percent are 18 or younger, while 3.9 percent are 65 or older (MIMP, 2014).

Women's businesses are found mostly in commerce (54 percent), service including hotels and restaurants (39 percent), and light manufacturing (textiles) industries (34 percent). These industries typically provide low productivity jobs, less competitive wages, and scant social protection (MIMP, 2015a).

Table 17.4 Share of women in senior government positions

National government	Women		Men		Total	
Position	Number	(%)	Number	(%)	Number	(%)
Ministers	6	31.60	13	68.40	19	0.15
Vice ministers	7	20.60	27	79.40	34	0.27
Total	**13**	**24.50**	**40**	**75.50**	**53**	**0.42**
Regional (state) government						
Regional president (governor)	1	4.00	24	96.00	25	0.20
Deputy regional president (governor)	4	16.00	21	84.00	25	0.20
Regional (state) councilors	85	50.30	84	49.70	169	1.34
Total	**90**	**41.10**	**129**	**58.90**	**219**	**1.73**
Local government						
Provincial mayor	6	3.10	189	96.90	195	1.54
District mayor	45	2.70	1598	97.30	1643	13.00
Provincial and district councilors	4439	42.20	6087	57.80	10526	83.30
Total	**4490**	**36.30**	**7874**	**63.70**	**12364**	**97.85**
Global	**4593**	**36.30**	**8043**	**63.70**	**12636**	**100**

Source: Elecciones en Perú (2014), Jurado Nacional de Elecciones (2014, 2015)

Women entrepreneurs typically also hold a secondary school certificate (45 percent), post-secondary diploma (24 percent), but about 31 percent dropped out of high school or barely completed primary school (Serida *et al.*, 2015).

In the last eight years, Peru's entrepreneurship activity index (TEA) grew from 25.9 percent to 28.8 percent (Serida *et al.*, 2015). Despite some progress in the female TEA in recent years, it is still 28 percent compared to men's 29.65 percent (Slavica *et al.*, 2015). Factors accounting for the growth of female entrepreneurship include government, company, and non-government organization (NGO) technical assistance (capacity and skill building) programs for MSEs, access to business networks (business women's networking associations), funding opportunities, and a stable macroeconomic environment (WEVentureScope, 2013). Motivation is also a driving force to be taken into account. GEM classifies motivation entrepreneurs into two categories: those who identify a business opportunity and choose to go after it, and others who are compelled by their need to make a living (Serida *et al.*, 2013). Both male and female entrepreneurs are driven more by the opportunity (female opportunity TEA of 78.9 percent; men's, 86.97 percent) than by need (female need TEA of 20.24 percent compared to men's 12.63 percent). However, the women's need motivation was stronger than men's (Slavica *et al.*, 2015). In an interview, the minister for women said businesses generally start as a need, led by women household heads with children. No market surveys or training precede the business startup, giving their enterprises few chances to succeed (Slavica *et al.*, 2015).

Income from their businesses is intermediate to low: 51 percent earn an intermediate income, 33 percent earn a low income, and only 16 percent can be said to earn a high remuneration from their business (Sérida *et al.*, 2015; Romero, 2014). Microbusinesses owned by women also show lower rates of return then men's, with those of women earning US$273 compared to $373 for men in 2008 (GTZ, WB e IDB, 2010). This condition may be a consequence of inefficient management and the companies' smaller size, since the smaller the company, the smaller its revenues. Nonetheless, women-owned mid-sized and large companies show the same rates of return as those owned by men (GTZ, WB e IDB, 2010).

Country legislation

Since 1955, successive governments have introduced changes in Peruvian law, particularly in the constitutional, civil, and labor regimes, to accomplish gender parity. In that year, a law was enacted, replacing some articles of the 1933 Constitution so that women could become full citizens (Art. 84° and 86°, Law N° 12391) (CRP, 2013). Later, the 1979 Constitution acknowledged women's right to vote without any restrictions (Article 2, Constitution) (CRP, 2013). This, in turn, led to changes in the civil code in 1984, which suppressed certain situations of discrimination against women (CRP, 2013). Later, the 1993 Constitution, still in force, established the right to equality before the law without discrimination (Article 2, Constitution) (CRP, 2013). This is the law that underpins Peru's legal order.

The Municipal Election Law was amended in 2002 establishing a 30 percent quota for women in platforms to elect town councilors (Art. 10, Law N° 27734) (CRP, 2013). The same percentage share applies to the number of congressional candidates in each electoral district (Art. 116, Law N°26859) (CRP, 2013). Although these rules do not ensure that women will be elected to those positions, they do ensure their participation in elections.

In 2007, the Law for Equal Opportunities for Men and Women was enacted to create a regulatory and public policy framework to ensure men and women their rights to equality, dignity, development, well-being, and autonomy (Art. 1, Law N° 28983) (CRP, 2013). That same year, a mandatory supreme decree for government agencies was enacted to identify and establish national policies in various fields, including hiring of government workers and access to management positions; and access of women to executive and decision-making positions in society and government (Art. 2, Supreme Decree N° 027-2007-PCM) (CRP, 2013). Another supreme decree enacted in 2012 approved the third National Gender Equality Plan (Art. 1, Supreme Decree N° 004-2012-MIMP) (CRP, 2013).

As regards the labor field, Vinatea (2000) holds that women previously had the right to certain specific working conditions resulting from their gender, including protection from hazardous activities and access to certain benefits (indemnification for work accidents and unwarranted dismissal) different from those established for men. Most of those rights were eliminated in 1995, with a view to leveling equality rights for men and women (Vinatea, 2000). Several laws and supreme decrees were enacted in 2003, for example, pre- and post-labor maternity leaves; prohibiting dismissal of workers during and after pregnancy and labor; vacation after maternity leave; and breastfeeding time.

At the beginning of this last quarter, the Peruvian Congress enacted the International Labour Organization's (ILO) Agreement N° 183 on the protection of pregnant women. Toyama (2015) holds that this agreement introduces changes in existing regulations with regard to five issues: a) longer maternity leave; b) extension of a new pre-labor leave; c) enhanced protection against dismissal of pregnant women; d) guaranteed work positions, whether in the previous or similar position, with equal pay; e) prohibition of pregnancy tests or presentation of negative pregnancy medical certificates to get a job, unless required for a specific position.

Although the right to pre- and post-labor leave for pregnant women has been regulated since 1918, the length of such leave has changed from its previous 60 day duration to 98 days at present, in line with Agreement 183 of the ILO (ILO, 2000). Paternity leave was enacted in 2009, giving male workers in both industry and government the right to four paid, consecutive working days for child birth leave (Art. 2, Law N° 29409) (CRP, 2013), but not 45 days as in other countries.

The right to breastfeeding until the child's first year of age was also enacted in 1918 (Art. 21, Law N° 2851, CRP, 2013), but was repealed in 1995, only to be passed again in 2001 (Single Article N° 27403). Likewise, in 2012, a law was enacted mandating breastfeeding rooms in government and private organizations hiring more than 20 individuals of fertile age (Articles 1 and 2, Law N° 29896) (CRP, 2013). However, in 2014, the Cross-Agency Oversight Commission charged with ensuring compliance with Supreme Decree N° 009-2006-MIMDES (2014) found only 15.08 percent of government organizations and 37.86 percent of large private companies actually provided such breastfeeding facilities. Among other reasons given for failure to comply were lack of information and training on maternal breastfeeding, and insufficient space at agencies or companies. Moreover, some business leaders said that the mandate to provide breastfeeding facilities in companies or introduce gender quotas significantly hampered their "competitiveness," and that they should rather be "voluntary initiatives and companies should be rewarded for their efforts."

Another labor law, enacted in 1997, is the Single Unified Text for Legislative Decree N° 728, the Labor Training and Promotion Act (Art. 37, Supreme Decree N° 002-97-TR) (CRP, 2013), regulating special employment programs for women with family-related duties willing to work on a part-time or term contract basis. The Law on Labor Training Methods, enacted in 2005, also established certain guidance to encourage women who have responsibilities at home (Art. 17, Law N° 28518) (CRP, 2013). However, although these two regulations are fully in force, the programs implemented by the Ministry of Labor and Employment Promotion do not seek to enhance women's training if they have household responsibilities.

Another labor law, enacted in 1998, is the discrimination law (Law N° 26772) (CRP, 2013). This regulation also prohibits public and private schools from introducing discriminatory requirements to enroll in training and education programs and penalizes them if they do so. Moreover, the General Labor Inspection Law, amended in 2007, rates all sex-based discrimination violations as very severe infringements when related to hiring, compensation, length of workday, training, and promotion as part of the organization's practices (Art. 25, Supreme Decree N° 019-2007-TR) (CRP, 2013).

Initiatives supporting women in the workforce

There have been various initiatives from the public sector, international organizations and non-government organizations, and from companies have been taking action in order to promote the equality of opportunity between men and women and the equality of gender.

Since it was established in 1996, just one year after the Peruvian government signed the agreements reached at the Fourth World Conference on Women in Beijing, the Ministry of Women and Vulnerable Populations has been the governing body on national policies to ensure equal rights between men and women and protect the rights of women.

The government has signed most of the international and regional human rights instruments and the agreements of the ILO on equal payment, discrimination of workers holding household responsibilities, and maternity protection to create gender equality and social inclusion.

Four major national norms address issues of gender equality. First, the Constitution recognizes the right of all to equality before the law, prohibits discrimination against women, and guarantees full respect for human rights; secondly, the Law on Equal Opportunities for Women and Men; thirdly, a supreme decree that defines and establishes mandatory national policies on equality of men and women; and finally a supreme decree that approved the National Plan for Gender Equality 2012–2017 and established a cross-agency task force to oversee the implementation of the Plan through the National Information System of Gender Indicators. Within this framework of major rules, other more specific laws have been enacted to enhance the protection of women's rights and provide equal opportunities, such as laws to protect maternity and against discrimination in the workplace. Meanwhile, the regional (state) governments have adopted regional policies and resolutions on this subject, thus moving down the national framework to the regional government level.

The Ministry of Finance has ordered the ministries and public institutions to allocate part of their budgets to initiatives aimed at reducing the gender gap. The ministries of labor and employment promotion, transport and communications, foreign trade and tourism, agriculture, and production are preparing job training, entrepreneurship, SME management, and productive projects programs aimed at people at the base of the pyramid. Although not exclusively aimed at women, their participation in those programs is greater than 30 percent (MIMP, 2014).

The Ministry of Education has created mechanisms for public–private partnerships in education and works for taxes schemes in education to narrow the gap in school infrastructure, and thus provide access to education to the largest possible number of people (Ministerio de Educación, 2015). In addition, the Education Investment Promotion Law was enacted, which allows private universities to operate as companies (Díaz, 2005).

The Ministry of Women and Vulnerable Populations has also launched some initiatives to involve the private sector in efforts to achieve greater gender equality, such as the "Safe company, free of violence and discrimination against women" seal (MIMP, 2015b). Meanwhile, the "Good Labor Practices" competition organized by the Ministry of Labor and Employment

Promotion rewards efforts in several categories, including firms' efforts to create equal opportunities for men and women in the workplace, banish discrimination at work, and foster a better balance between work and family (MTPE, 2015d).

International organizations, nonprofit associations, and social enterprises also provide direct or indirect financial support to create equal opportunities for men and women, such as the Agency of the United States for International Development that funds Women Entrepreneurs Leading Development (Mujeres Empresarias Liderando el Desarrollo, 2015); the Association of Business Women of Peru (GTZ, WB e IDB, 2010), which aims at contributing to the development, growth, and professionalization of Peruvian women entrepreneurs; the Organization of Women in International Trade (OWIT), which seeks to promote the development of women in the workplace (OWIT, 2015); the Peruvian women's Manuela Ramos Movement to uphold the rights of women, human rights, and respect for democratic institutions (Manuela Ramos, 2015); Laboratoria, which trains young women without higher education as web developers through an intensive six-month course (Laboratoria, 2015); and WEConnect International, the main purpose of which is to facilitate inclusive and sustainable economic growth by empowering and connecting women business owners (WEConnect International, 2015), among many others.

The future

Significant improvements have been made in recent years to accomplish further equality between women and men. Women's participation in management positions grows. Progress has likewise been made in meeting international targets, particularly the MDGs and national policies on gender equality (UNDP, 2015).

Women in management's vision of the future is optimistic, though we are aware that a long road remains ahead. Government, companies, and women have been working on it for over 50 years, ever since women were given the right to vote and companies started to hire women for some business activities. Companies for their part are gradually introducing cross-cutting gender-oriented policies in human resource management, while government works on providing legal security to ensure gender equality. Women, meanwhile, are more effective and efficient in creating a better relationship with their environment while simultaneously growing personally.

The government has enacted many laws on issues of women' rights, violence against women, maternity leave, and discrimination. Nevertheless, to strengthen the legal framework aimed at ensuring gender equality, the departments of government charged with ensuring compliance must adopt an oversight approach. Meanwhile some of the regulations in force must be reviewed.

Companies are also adopting stronger women-inclusion policies in resource management, including balanced leadership, management and shop floor positions; recruitment, training, and education policies; career opportunities; compensation; and work and out of work–life options. The OWIT, and Aequales, a consultancy firm, prepared a list of the ten Peruvian companies showing the greatest respect for gender equality. Such initiatives do not reflect a cultural pattern as is clear from labor market statistics. The male employed working age population is higher than women's; the former's activity and employment rates are likewise higher than women's (INEI, 2015b). The grey labor market is still a major issue in Peru, since 73 percent of the economically active population works unofficially, with women accounting for 45.7 percent. Using stock exchange listed companies as an indicator of women's participation in the official labor market shows that they chair only 3.4 percent of boards, account for only 8.7 percent of directors, and make up only 6.6 percent of CEOs (Lima Stock Exchange, 2015).

Household responsibilities are one of the main challenges faced by women throughout their careers and these prevent them from filling board and first and second level job positions. Organizations and the country lose out when professional, well-trained women leave their jobs until their children grow, probably because no national gender regulations or corporate policies are in place to create a more flexible working environment or an appropriate infrastructure to provide childcare services. The male-dominated model of the successful business executive (who works 8 to 12 hours, travels constantly and is all-powerful) has become the stereotype of Peruvian leaders of business organizations, which does not help men or women to share their family responsibilities as they grow professionally.

Another challenge is posed by women's difficulty in pursuing master's degrees because of financial or time constraints, despite great progress made in accomplishing gender equality in access to university and regular schooling. Typically in a couple, men study for a master's degree while women will devote their time to work and their family duties, usually for longer than eight hours.

Nevertheless, women's university admissions have grown steadily and are now on a par with those of men. Preferred career options among women include teaching, business management, economics, and social sciences. The larger number of women in the professions and management classes is reflected in the greater share of third and fourth level positions they fill, but not in their number of board or first and second level jobs where higher academic degrees are demanded. A recommendation in this regard would be to insist on gender equality in university policies, including gender training across study programs, and making available grants and scholarships targeting women.

Although most women entrepreneurs have a level of secondary education, some women only have a level of primary education. The level of education of the owners of micro and small businesses is generally primary education. The micro and small businesses have difficulty in achieving adequate profit rates compared to intermediate and large companies. Microbusinesses face dire revenue, returns, and informality challenges compared to medium-sized companies. Given that microbusinesses owned by women account for some 45 percent of the entire business structure, their significant challenges become an issue of national concern. This is more so the case because these businesses are often established as a means of subsistence and making a living. Training can be the solution of the development of the microbusinesses owned by women.

Finally, women must develop a capacity for self-governing, setting their own priorities, managing risks, self-criticism, and other qualities that will allow them to build trust in their own capacity, decisions, opinions, and resolutions, because their success depends on no one but themselves.

References

ANR and INEI (Asamblea Nacional de Rectores e Instituto Nacional de Estadística) (2010) *Censo Nacional Universitario 2010 (II CENAUN 2010)*. [Tabla] Accessed: http://rpu.edu.pe/wp-content/uploads/2015/07/II-Censo-Nacional-Universitario.pdf

Blondet, C., Checa, C. M., Leau, Y. and Esquivel, R. L. (1994) La situación de la mujer en el Perú: 1980–1994. *Serie: Estudios de Género*, 1. Documento de Trabajo N° 68 (236 pp.) Lima: Instituto de Estudios Peruanos.

Cárdenas M., Eagly, A., Heller L., Salgado E., Jáuregui K. and Goode W. (2013) Claves para el ascenso de las altas ejecutivas en América Latina. *Incae Business Review*, 6 (7).

Congreso de la Republica (CRP) (2013) *Archivo Digital de la Legislacion del Peru.* Accessed: www.leyes. congreso.gob.pe/

Díaz, J. (2005) *Educación superior en el Perú: tendencias de la demanda y la oferta.* Accessed: www.grade. org.pe/download/pubs/analisis-2.pdf

ECLAC (Economic Commission for Latin America and the Caribbea) (2015) *Panorama Social de América Latina 2014.* Accessed: http://repositorio.cepal.org/bitstream/handle/11362/37626/S1420729_es. pdf?sequence=6

Elecciones en Perú (2014) *¿Qué se vota el 5 de octubre? ¿Cuántos cargos se elige?* Accessed: www.eleccione-senperu.com/informacion-electoral-que-se-elige-elecciones-municipales-regionales-peru-126.html

García A. (2009) *Mujeres Peruanas: Situación Nacional.* Lima: CEDAL.

Gestión (2014) *Los desafíos de las mujeres peruanas en el mercado laboral.* 6 de marzo, Accessed: http://gestion.pe/empleo-management/ines-temple-ricardo-herrera-carmen-cruz-lhh-dbm-hay group-dia-mujer-2090878.

GTZ, WB e IDB (GTZ, Banco Mundial, Banco Interamericano de Desarrollo) (2010) *Mujeres Empresarias: Barreras y Oportunidades en el Sector Privado Formal en América Latina y el Caribe.* Accessed: http://siteresources.worldbank.org/INTLACREGTOPPOVANA/Resources/840442-12608 09819258/Libro_Mujeres_Empresarias.pdf

ILO (International Labour Organization) (2000) *Convenio sobre la protección de la maternidad N°183.* Firmado el 7 de Febrero de 2002. Geneva: ILO.

ILO (2015) *La mujer en la gestión empresarial: Cobrando Impulso. Versión resumida del informe mundial.* Geneva: ILO.

INEI (National Statistics and Informatics Institute) (1972) *Séptimo Censo Nacional de Población.* Lima: Biblioteca Institucional del Instituto Nacional de Estadística e Informática.

INEI (1981) *Censos Nacionales 1981 VIII de Población y III de Vivienda.* [Tabla] Lima: Biblioteca Institucional INEI.

INEI (1993) *Censos Nacionales 1993 IX de Población y IV de Vivienda.* [Tabla] Lima: Biblioteca Institucional INEI.

INEI (2014a) *Perú: Estructura Empresarial 2014.* Accessed: www.inei.gob.pe/media/MenuRecursivo/ publicaciones_digitales/Est/Lib1262/index.html

INEI (2014b) *Resultados de la Encuesta de Micro y Pequeña Empresa 2013.* Lima: Depósito Legal en la Biblioteca Nacional del Perú N° 2014-03104

INEI (2015a) *Al 30 de junio de 2015 el Perú tiene 31 millones 151 mil 643 habitantes.* Nota de prensa. Accessed: www.inei.gob.pe/prensa/noticias/al-30-de-junio-de-2015-el-peru-tiene-31-millones-151-mil-643-habitantes-8500/

INEI (2015b) *Perú: Evolución de los Indicadores de empleo e Ingresos por Departamento 2004-2013.* Lima: Biblioteca Nacional del Perú. Accessed: www.inei.gob.pe/media/MenuRecursivo/publicaciones_ digitales/Est/Lib1200/libro.pdf

INEI (2015c) *Perú: Indicadores de Educación por Departamento 2004 al 2014.* Accessed: www.inei. gob.pe/media/MenuRecursivo/publicaciones_digitales/Est/Lib1293/libro.pdf

INEI (2015d) *Educación, cultura y esparcimiento.* Publicaciones digitales. Accessed: www.inei.gob.pe/ media/MenuRecursivo/publicaciones_digitales/Est/Lib1253/cap05/ind05.htm

Jaramillo, M. and Montalva, V. (2009) *Peru: Demographic Change and Labor Market Performance, 1997–2007.* Informe final. Lima: Grupo de Análisis para el Desarrollo.

Jurado Nacional de Elecciones (2014) *Más de 3 mil mujeres resultaron elegidas autoridades regionales y municipales.* [Tabla] Accessed: http://portal.jne.gob.pe/prensaypublicaciones/archivonoticias/Paginas/ M%C3%81SDE3MILMUJERESRESULTARONELEGIDASAUTORIDADESREGIONALESY-MUNICIPALES.aspx

Jurado Nacional de Elecciones (2015) *Una presidenta y 51 alcaldesas inician su mandato en todo el Perú.* [Tabla] Accessed: http://portal.jne.gob.pe/prensaypublicaciones/archivonoticias/Paginas/ UNAPRESIDENTAREGIONALY51ALCALDESASINICIANSUMANDATOENTODO-ELPERU.aspx

Laboratoria (2015) *¿Qué es Laboratoria?.* Accessed: http://laboratoria.la/

Lima Stock Exchange (2015) *Empresas con Valores Listados.* Accessed www.bvl.com.pe/mercempresas. html#

Manuela Ramos (2015) *Programas.* Accessed: www.manuela.org.pe/

MIMP (Ministerio de la Mujer y Poblaciones Vulnerables) (2012) *Plan Nacional de Igualdad de Género 2012-2017.* Depósito Legal en la Biblioteca Nacional del Perú. P. 73.

MIMP (2014) *VII Informe de Avances en el Cumplimiento de la Ley de Igualdad de Oportunidades entre Mujeres y Hombres, Ley N° 28983.* Accessed: www.mimp.gob.pe/files/direcciones/dgignd/informes/ vi_informe_avances_igualdad.pdf

MIMP (2015a) *Plan de Acción Intersectorial 2015 para el empoderamiento y la autonomía económica de la mujer.* Accessed: www.vivienda.gob.pe/banners/PLANpercent20DEpercent20ACCI percentC3percent 93Npercent20INTERSECTORIALpercent20-percent202015.pdf

MIMP (2015b) *Bases para el reconocimiento "Sello empresa segura, libre de violencia y discriminación contra la mujer": Segunda Convocatoria.* Accessed: www.mimp.gob.pe/webs/mimp/selloempresa_2015/bases. html

Ministerio de Educación (2013) PISA 2012: *Primeros Resultados. Informe Nacional del Perú.* Accessed: http://umc.minedu.gob.pe/wpcontent/uploads/2013/12/reporte_pisa_2012.pdf

Ministerio de Educación (2015) *Modernización.* Accessed: www.minedu.gob.pe/p/politicas-moderni-zacion-presentacion.html#

Ministerio de la Producción (2012) *MiPyme 2012: Estadística de la Micro, Pequeña y Mediana Empresa. Dirección General de Estudios Económico, Evaluación y Competitividad Territorial.* Accessed: www.produce. gob.pe/remype/data/mype2012.pdf

MTPE (Ministerio de Trabajo y Promoción del Empleo) (2006) *Informe Anual 2005: La Mujer En El Mercado Laboral Peruano.* Accessed: www.mintra.gob.pe/archivos/file/estadisticas/peel/documento_ mujer/inf_anual_mujer_2005.pdf

MTPE (2015a) *Perú: Principales Indicadores del Mercado de Trabajo, según sexo, 2001 – 2014.* Lima: Dirección de Investigación Socio Económico Laboral (DISEL). Accessed: http://mintra.gob.pe/archivos/ file/estadisticas/peel/estadisticas/oferta_laboral/sexo/2014/peru_total_sexo_001_2001-2014.pdf

MTPE (2015b) *Perú: Distribución De La Pea Ocupada, Según Sexo y Estructura De Mercado, 2001–2014.* Lima: Dirección de Investigación Socio Económico Laboral (DISEL). [Tabla] Accessed: http://mintra. gob.pe/archivos/file/estadisticas/peel/estadisticas/oferta_laboral/sexo/2014/peru_total_sexo_002_2 001-2014.pdf

MTPE (2015c) *Perú: Ingreso Laboral Promedio Mensual De La Pea Ocupada, Según Sexo Y Grupo Ocupacional, 2001–2014.* Lima: Dirección de Investigación Socio Económico Laboral (DISEL). [Tabla] Accessed: http://mintra.gob.pe/archivos/file/estadisticas/peel/estadisticas/oferta_laboral/sexo/2014/peru_tota l_sexo_011_2001-2014.pdf

MTPE (2015d) Concurso Buenas Prácticas laborales. Accessed: *www*.mintra.gob.pe/BPL/

Mujeres Empresarias Liderando el Desarrollo (2015) *Quienes Somos.* USAID Del Pueblo de Los Estados Unidos de América. Accessed: www.lideresempresarias.org/

Multisectorial Monitoring Committee Responsible for Ensuring Compliance with the Supreme Decree N° 009-2006-MIMDES (2014) *Informe Anual 2014.* Accessed: www.mimp.gob.pe/webs/mimp/ lactarios-institucionales/pdf/informe-anual-lactario-2014.pdf

OWIT (2015) *Quienes somos.* Accessed: www.owitperu.org/qsomos.shtml

PCM y UN (Presidency of the Council of Ministers and the United Nations) (2013) *Perú: Tercer Informe Nacional de Cumplimiento de los Objetivos de Desarrollo del Milenio.* Accessed: http://onu.org.pe/wp-content/uploads/2013/09/PNUD-LIBRO-PERU-web.pdf

Perú Top Ten Publications. (2011) *¿Quién manda a quién en el Perú?* Liderazgo y Desarrollo Ejecutivo. Primera Edición. pp. 17–18. Accessed: www.ptp.pe/pdf/muestra_coaching_liderazgo_desarrollo_ ejecutivo.pdf

Romero, G (2014) Presentación Primer diagnóstico e identificación preliminar de acciones/oportu-nidades para la incorporación de las mujeres en actividades productivas económicas. In: *Pasantía Promoción del empoderamiento y autonomía económica de las mujeres en las políticas, programas y proyectos de los gobiernos regionales y locales.* Lima, 27 y 28 de Octubre Organizadores: Ministerio de la

Mujer y Poblaciones Vulnerable y CEPAL. Accessed: www.mimp.gob.pe/webs/mimp/pasantia-empoderamiento/documentos/exposicion_romero.pdf

Saavedra, J. and Díaz, H. (2000) *La Carrera del maestro en el Perú: Factores Institucionales, Incentivos Económicos y Desempeño*. Documento de trabajo N°32. Lima: GRADE, Grupo de Análisis para el Desarrollo.

Serida, J., Nakamatsu, K., Borda, A., and Morales, O. (2013) *Global Entrepreneurship Monitor (GEM): Perú 2012*. Lima: Universidad ESAN.

Serida, J., Nakamatsu, K., Borda, A., and Morales, O. (2015) *Global Entrepreneurship Monitor (GEM): Perú 2013*. Lima: Universidad ESAN.

SERVIR and PCM (Autoridad Nacional de Servicio Civil y Presidencia Del Consejo de Ministros) (2015) *La Mujer en el Servicio Civil Peruano*. Accessed: http://filesservir.blob.core.windows.net/servicio-civil/Informe_La_Mujer_en_el_Servicio_Civil_Peruano_2015.pdf

Slavica, S., Amorós, J. and Moska, D. (2015) *Global Entrepreneurship Monitor (GEM): Perú 2014*. Accessed: www.babson.edu/Academics/centers/blank-center/global-research/gem/Documents/GEM percent202014 percent20Global percent20Report.pdf

Toyama, J., (2015) OIT: Licencias de maternidad en el Perú aún son conservadoras, *El Comercio*. Accessed: http://elcomercio.pe/economia/peru/oit-licencias-maternidad-peru-aun-son-conservadoras-noticia-1796521

UNDP (United Nations Development Programme) (2015) *Informe de Desarrollo Humano 2014*. Accessed: www.undp.org/content/undp/es/home/librarypage/hdr/2014-human-development-report/

United Nations Human Rights Council (2015) *Informe del Grupo de Trabajo sobre la cuestión de la discriminación contra la mujer en la legislación y en la práctica*. Accessed: http://daccess-dds-ny.un.org/doc/UNDOC/GEN/G15/134/54/PDF/G1513454.pdf?OpenElement

Vinatea, L. (2000) Discriminación laboral por razón de sexo en el Perú. Defensoría del Pueblo. Discriminación sexual y aplicación de la Ley, *Derecho Laboral*. Volume (2), 279–280.

WEConect International (2015) About Us section. Accessed: http://weconnectinternational.org/en/peru

WEF (World Economic Forum) (2014) *Insight Report: The Global Gender Gap Report 2014*, p. 395. Accessed: www3.weforum.org/docs/GGGR14/GGGR_CompleteReport_2014.pdf

WEVenture Scope (2013) *Índice del entorno empresarial para emprendedoras*. Fondo Multilateral de Inversiones (FOMIN). Accessed: www.weventurescope.com/en/Home/Ranking

World Bank (2006) *Por una Educación de Calidad para el Perú: Estándares, Rendición de cuentas y fortalecimiento de capacidades*. Accessed: http://cippec.org/mapeal/wp-content/uploads/2014/05/Por-una-educaci%C3%B3n-de-calidad-para-el-Per%C3%BA-estandares-rendici%C3%B3n-de-cuentas-y-fortalecimient-de-las-capacidades.pdf

World Bank (2015) *Peru: Panorama General*. Accessed: www.bancomundial.org/es/country/peru/overview

Women in management

Middle East

18 Women in management in Iran

Serena G. Sohrab and Rekha Karambayya

Introduction

In this chapter, we provide an assessment of the current status of Iranian women in workplaces. Since this is the first time that a chapter on Iran has been included in this series, we provide an overview on the status of Iranian women, their progress, or lack thereof, over the last ten years, and the challenges they face.

One key aspect of the progress made by Iranian women is their high levels of educational attainment. By any measure, women in Iran have surpassed men in post-secondary education, with 14.5 percent of women holding at least an undergraduate degree compared to 14.1 percent of men. Between 2002 and 2006, more than 50 percent of students in undergraduate programs were women. As a result, women who are currently in their late 20s or early 30s are more educated than their male counterparts (Majbouri, 2011). Despite rising levels of education among Iranian women, their labor force participation rate has demonstrated a steady decline over the last ten years, standing at 13.4 percent now. In addition, their unemployment rate has increased to 21.1 percent in 2015. As a result of the low participation and high unemployment rates, only 9.9 percent of all jobs are held by women, and a large share of these jobs are in the form of part-time work or unpaid contributions to family business in rural areas.

We begin this chapter with information on the educational attainments of Iranian women. Then, we share information on labor force characteristics and examine the structure of women's employment from various perspectives including the ratio of their employment in public and private sectors, their share of different job categories, and the ratio of part-time to full-time employment. This section is followed by a discussion around the relationship between women's education and employment. Next, we discuss women in leadership positions, including entrepreneurs, managers, and legislators. After a brief discussion on country legislation, we conclude by offering an overview of the major issues and our overall assessment of the current status of Iranian women.

Education attainment

Literacy rates[1]

Table 18.1 shows percentage of literate men and women (literate is defined as someone who can read a simple document and write) in different age groups in rural and urban areas. The first row in this table shows the literacy rate for the entire population. This rate is 82.4 percent for women and 90.8 percent for men. Although these numbers suggest a big gap between

Table 18.1 Literacy statistics (%)

Literacy statistics	Both sexes			Women	Men
	Entire country	*Urban*	*Rural*		
6 and older	86.6	90.2	77.2	82.4	90.8
6–9	96.2	96.2	96.2	96.2	96.3
10–14	99	99.2	98.5	99	98.9
15–24	97.8	98.6	95.9	97.4	98.1
25–64	85.8	90.3	72.6	80.4	91.3
65 and older	34.3	44.5	12	22.5	46.6

Source: Statistical Center of Iran (2014)

women's and men's literacy rates, it should be noted that, in recent decades, the government has placed a strong emphasis on enhancing literacy in both urban and rural areas. As a result, the percentage of literates in younger generations is very different from that in older generations. To get a better sense of the literacy rate in the younger population, it may be useful to examine younger age groups. In Iran, a child is usually six years old in order to start the first grade. Therefore, the 6-9 age group is not a good category to assess literacy rates in Iran. The literacy rate among 10-14 year olds is 99 percent and there is no difference based on gender. The literacy rate among 15-24 year olds is 97.8 percent, with female to male ratio equal to 0.99. So, based on these numbers, it seems to us that in terms of basic ability to read and write, there is no significant difference between girls and boys.

Higher education

Table 18.2 shows the highest level of education among people who are considered literate. The percentage of women and men with university degrees is comparable, with the percentage of women with an undergraduate degree slightly higher than men (12.6 percent versus 11.7 percent). Figure 18.1 shows female to male ratio at the undergraduate level in different disciplines since 1990. The dashed line shows the percentage across all disciplines. As illustrated in this graph, female presence at the undergraduate level has had a steady growth for 16 years (1990 to 2006). In fact, women's education level has increased to the extent that women who are currently in their late 20s or early 30s are more educated than their male counterparts (Majbouri, 2011).

Table 18.2 Highest level of education of literates (%), six years and older

	Both sexes	*Men*	*Women*
Diploma or less	78.9	79.3	78.5
College degree	4.5	5.1	3.9
Bachelor degree	12.1	11.7	12.6
Master	2	2.2	1.8
PhD	0.2	0.2	0.1
Uncategorized	2.2	1.4	3.1
Total	100	100	100

Source: Statistical Center of Iran (2014)

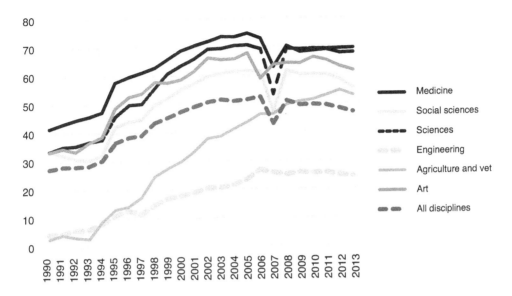

Figure 18.1 Percentage of women at undergraduate level in various disciplines (1990–2013)

Source: Retrieved from www.amar.org.ir

Note: Number of university students based on major disciplines and sex – time series. From 1990–1994, the graph
shows the percentage of female students in public universities. Starting in 1995, the graph shows the percentage
of female students in public and private universities

It should be noted that in Iran, all first-tiered universities are public and free, with students
paying no tuition. Admission to these prestigious public universities is based on an annual
national exam, which is organized by the National Educational Assessment Center. The exam
is based on multiple choice questions from a wide range of subjects studied at high school.
Due to the structure of the exam, the evaluation process is completely objective and a student's
mark in the exam depends only on her/his knowledge and ability to perform well in that
exam—particularly the ability to perform under stress. Once the exams are graded, each
student receives a mark that shows her/his ranking among all students who participated. Then,
students submit a form indicating their preferred program of study to the organizing agency.
Admission to public universities is based on a combination of test scores and student
preferences. Students who cannot get into their program of choice at public universities would
have the option to attend the private university system, including the Islamic Azad University,
Payam-e-Noor and many other smaller programs.

It is estimated that about 2 million candidates take the national university entrance exam
every year and only the top 5–10 percent are offered free admission to university. Historically
women have outnumbered men in universities in Iran. The number of women entering
university is evidence of their academic abilities and their desire to compete in a gruelling
entrance process. As shown in Figure 18.1, for five consecutive years—2002 to 2006—more
than 50 percent of first-year university students were female, with this percentage being the
highest in medicine at 74.82 percent and the lowest in engineering at 23.43 percent.

We speculate that the low presence of women in engineering programs is mostly driven by
the masculine image of the engineering discipline and associated work environments. Girls
who are interested in engineering might be factoring in the perception that they will have to

work in environments mostly comprised of men from the working class. In the Islamic culture, mingling of unrelated men and women is strongly prohibited and this principle seems to be most strongly practiced among people from the working class. Therefore, the presence of one or two women among a large number of men becomes both unusual and culturally inappropriate. In addition, there seems to be a widely held view that—due to strong patriarchal values of the society—these men would not accept a female boss or manager. We would like to mention that we do not believe that this difference is driven by any assumption regarding the ability of girls to excel in mathematics or the physical sciences. This is supported by evidence on the participation of women in education in the sciences.

In response to the increasing number of female students in universities, in 2002, the government started a plan to restrict women's presence in universities (Mehrkhane, 2014). For four years, these limitations were minor and were not publicly announced (Mehrkhane, 2014). In 2006, the newly appointed conservative government led by Mahmoud Ahmadinejad publicly announced its plan[2] and imposed severe restrictions on women's presence at public universities. While in some programs of study these restrictions were in the form of quotas (30 to 40 percent males – 30 to 40 percent females – the rest remaining competitive), in many other programs female students were not accepted at all (Mehrkhane, 2014).

The sharp decline in the percentage of female students in 2007 (overall presence dropped from 52.4 percent in 2006 to 42.93 percent) shows the impact of these restrictions. We have not been able to find any information that could explain why the percentage of female students recovered to 51.02 percent in 2008. Our research does not suggest any change in the restrictions in 2007. Since the data presented in Figure 18.1 show the percentage of female students in both public and private universities (before 1995, the graph shows data for public universities only), it is possible that women responded to these restrictions by attending less desirable private universities that did not face such restrictions.

In August 2013, Iran experienced a change in the government and the new Iranian president, Hassan Rouhani, who—compared to the previous government—advocates more liberal values, assumed office. A report by *Farhikhtegan* newspaper on August 6, 2014 announced the reversal of gender segregation at universities (*Farheekhtegan*, 2014). We have not been able to acquire information on the percentage of women in universities over the last two years, and are therefore unable to examine the impact of the new regulations.

The data presented in this section show that Iranian women have made significant progress in terms of education. The percentage of women with a university degree is closely comparable to men, resulting in a high percentage of educated young women. In the next section, we examine women's presence in the labor force.

Labor force characteristics

Table 18.3 shows labor force statistics for the population that is 15 years and older over the last ten years and Figure 18.2 illustrates participation rate, employment rate, and unemployment rate based on sex in urban and rural areas. As shown in Table 18.3, in 2015, only 13.4 percent of Iranian women were employed or were looking for a job and they face an extremely high unemployment rate of 21.1 percent. Comparison of these figures between women and men shows an enormous difference of 55 percent in their participation rate and that the unemployment rate of women is more than twice men's unemployment rate of 9.6 percent.

Examining the trends over the last ten years shows a steady decline in women's participation rate from 17.4 percent in 2006 to 11.2 percent in 2014. It should be noted that we also see a similar decline in men's participation rate from 72.5 percent in 2006 to 66.6

Table 18.3 Labor force statistics (%), 15 years and older population, 2006–2015

		2006	2007	2008	2009	2010	2011	2012	2013	2014	2015
Participation rate (%)											
Total	Women	17.40	16.70	15.40	14.10	13.40	14.00	13.10	14.10	11.20	13.4
	Men	72.50	71.10	68.80	68.00	67.70	67.80	65.70	66.80	66.60	68.30
Urban	Women	15.40	14.90	13.50	12.70	12.40	13.40	12.90	13.60	10.90	13.20
	Men	71.80	69.90	67.90	66.60	66.40	66.60	64.00	65.10	65.30	67.10
Rural	Women	21.60	20.60	19.80	17.60	16.10	15.80	13.50	15.70	11.80	14.00
	Men	74.20	73.80	71.20	71.70	71.10	71.20	70.60	71.70	70.30	71.70
Employment rate (%)											
Total	Women	14.40	13.90	12.80	11.50	10.90	11.10	10.20	11.30	9.10	10.60
	Men	64.50	63.20	61.40	60.30	58.80	58.80	57.50	59.60	60.60	61.80
Urban	Women	11.70	11.40	10.40	9.70	9.30	9.90	9.50	10.40	8.50	9.90
	Men	63.40	61.70	60.30	58.60	57.40	57.30	55.80	57.70	59.20	60.70
Rural	Women	20.00	19.30	18.50	16.00	14.80	14.30	11.90	14.00	10.50	12.40
	Men	67.10	66.70	64.10	64.60	62.50	62.90	62.60	64.90	64.50	64.90
Unemployment rate (%)											
Total	Women	17.30	16.90	16.80	18.50	19.20	21.20	22.40	19.60	19.00	21.10
	Men	11.00	11.10	10.80	11.30	13.20	13.30	12.50	10.80	9.10	9.60
Urban	Women	23.90	23.60	23.10	23.50	24.60	26.50	26.40	23.20	22.10	24.80
	Men	11.70	11.70	11.20	11.90	13.60	13.90	12.90	11.30	9.40	9.60
Rural	Women	7.20	6.40	6.70	9.50	8.40	9.30	11.70	10.90	11.10	11.30
	Men	9.50	9.60	10.00	9.90	12.20	11.60	11.30	9.60	8.20	9.40
Part time to total (%)											
Total	Women	5.1	4.1	3.4	4.9	5.4	4.2	4.5	3.9	4.6	4.3
	Men	10.6	9.4	8.9	12.1	14.3	11.7	11.5	10.2	11.9	11.9
Urban	Women	5.1	3.3	3.2	4.5	5.4	4.4	3.8	3.9	4.5	4.6
	Men	6.9	6.5	6.6	8.5	10.8	8.6	8.9	8.3	9.9	9.8
Rural	Women	5.1	5.1	3.6	5.4	5.6	3.9	6	4	4.8	3.4
	Men	18.5	15.7	14.1	20.6	23.1	19.5	18.2	15.2	17.1	17.5

Source: Statistical Center of Iran (2006 and 2014). Available from www.amar.org.ir

percent in 2014. Some analysts attribute this decline to a policy called the Subsidy Reform Plan introduced in 2010 by Ahmadinejad's government (*Shargh Daily*, 2014). Under this plan, each individual in a low-income household would receive a monthly payment equal to almost US$15. Even though this seems to be a very small amount, it could add up to a significant amount in a low-income family with several children at home. So, it could explain part of the observed decline in participation rate. However, examination of the percentage of decline shows a 35.6 percent decline in women's participation rate compared with 8.13 percent for men. Therefore, although we see similar trends for women and men, the decline in women's participation rate is much bigger than that of men. Another factor that might have contributed to the decline in participation rate is the steady increase in the unemployment rate, which could have discouraged job seekers from looking for a job and forced them to exit the workforce (*Shargh Daily*, 2014). Despite similar trends in data for men and women, the gap between women's and men's unemployment rate has widened, with the ratio of women's unemployment rate to men's unemployment rate increasing from 157 percent in 2006 to 219 percent in 2015.

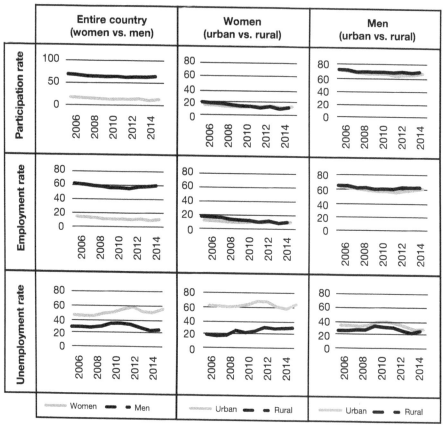

Figure 18.2 Labor force statistics (%) based on sex in urban and rural areas for population aged 15 and above (2006–2015)

Source: Statistical Center of Iran (2006 and 2014). Available from www.amar.org.ir

Urban versus rural areas

Comparison of labor force characteristics in urban and rural areas shows that for both men and women participation rates in urban and rural areas are comparable, with the rate being slightly higher in rural areas for both sexes. However, there are differences in the employment patterns of rural and urban women. While in urban areas, only 5 percent of women's employment is in the form of unpaid family work, 51.7 percent of rural women are categorized as involved in unpaid family work (compared with 5.9 percent of rural men) (Statistical Center of Iran, 2014). Comparison of unemployment rates between urban and rural areas shows a large difference in the unemployment rate of women in urban and rural areas, with the unemployment rate of urban women being more than twice that of rural women. The high share of unpaid family work among rural women might explain part of this difference between women in urban and rural areas.

The wage gap

According to the most recent *Global Gender Gap Report* published by the World Economic Forum in 2015 (Schwab *et al.*, 2015), the estimated earned income for an Iranian woman is

$4,787 compared to $27,744 for an Iranian man. As a consequence, Iran is ranked 142 out of 145 countries that were included in this report. According to this report, female to male ratio for wage equality for similar work is 0.59, which places Iran at 98 out of 145 countries. It should be noted this wage gap estimate is calculated based on a single-item question in the 2015 World Economic Forum's Executive Opinion Survey. In the survey respondents are asked to indicate their answer to the question, "In your country, for similar work, to what extent are wages for women equal to those of men?" (with answers ranging from 1 = not at all, significantly below those of men; to 7 = fully, equal to those of men) (Schwab *et al.*, 2015, p. 72). Therefore, this reported wage gap is somewhat subjective and might not represent the actual wage differences.

Figure 18.3 shows the income gap between men and women from 1991 to 2011. The data presented in this diagram were calculated by averaging the annual income reported in household expenditure reports of the Statistical Center of Iran (Alavian Ghavanini, 2011). These numbers show a similar pattern of income shifts for men and women over this time with a gender wage gap between 20 and 30 percent. As Alavian Ghavanini notes, since this diagram represents overall income, the observed difference could be due to difference in the number of working hours.

By analyzing household income and expenditure from 2005 to 2011, Alavian Ghavanini (2011) examined the wage gap between women and men. His research shows that different factors such as sector of employment and profession influence the wage gap. For example, he found a significant wage gap in the private sector but not in the public sector. In addition, his findings suggest that the wage gap varies across professions. For example, female to male wage ratio is 23.6 among technicians and associated professionals group, 65.4 among service and sales workers, and 98.4 among craft and related trades workers. Probably the most interesting finding of this research is that, among professionals as well as legislators, senior officials, and managers, the female to male wage ratio is 1.16.

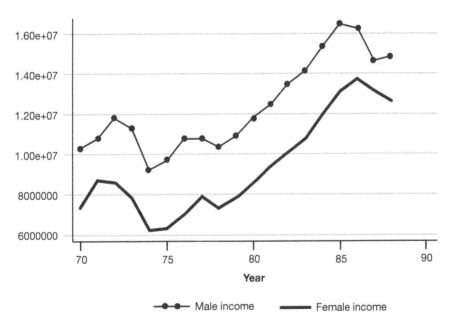

Figure 18.3 Income gap, 1991 to 2011

Source: Adapted from Alavian Ghavanini (2011, p. 3)

Note: Numbers on the horizontal axis show the year according to the Iranian solar calendar

Part-time employment

The definition of part-time employment reported in the Iranian Statistical Center seasonal reports is different from the definition of part-time work in other countries. In fact, the term used to refer to part-time work in Farsi is *incomplete work*. According to this definition, part-time workers are those who work less than 44 hours and are willing to work more. These are employed individuals who worked less than 44 hours due to economic reasons such as recession, inability to find work with more hours, or seasonal employment, and indicate a willingness to work more (Statistical Center of Iran, 2015). Based on this definition, the share of incomplete work among women is lower than men at 4.3 percent, compared with 11.9 percent in 2015 (Statistical Center of Iran, 2015).

If we use number of hours worked as a measure of part-time employment, similar to other countries such as Canada (see Sohrab *et al.*, 2011), the Netherlands (see Tijdens, 2011), and Spain (see Las Heras *et al.*, 2011), we find a very high rate of part-time employment among women. Table 18.4 provides information about number of hours that women and men work in a week. As shown in this table, more than 50 percent of employed women work less than 40 hours per week (58.87 percent compared to 24.26 percent of men). The percentage of women working less than 32 hours per week is 44.85 percent, which is noticeably higher than 16.03 percent of men.

Public and private employment

Table 18.5 shows employment in the private and public sectors over the last ten years. This table shows that, compared to men, women have higher levels of employment in the public sector. Over the last ten years, 26.1 percent of employed women have been employed in the public sector compared to 16.95 percent of men. This table also shows that in rural areas, the majority of employment—both men and women—is in the private sector. On average, over the last ten years, 93.3 percent of employment in rural areas has been in the private sector, which is noticeably higher than 76.19 percent in urban areas.

Employment in different sectors and occupations

In this section, we provide more detail on the structure and nature of women's employment. Figure 18.4 shows employment distribution in agriculture, manufacturing, and service sectors. As illustrated in this figure, compared with men, women have a higher involvement in service and agriculture sectors. We speculate that these differences are mainly influenced by socialized gender roles that assume manufacturing jobs are unsuitable for women. However, the overall distributions across these sectors are comparable.

Table 18.4 Hours worked per week (%)

Hours worked	Women	Men
16 hours or less	14.49	4.16
17–24 hours	16.36	5.42
25–32 hours	14.00	6.45
33–40 hours	14.02	8.23
41–48 hours	23.33	29.82
49 hours or more	17.80	45.92

Source: Statistical Center of Iran (2014)

Table 18.5 Employment in the public and private sectors (%), 2006 to 2015

		2006	2007	2008	2009	2010	2011	2012	2013	2014	2015
Women											
Rural and urban											
	Private	74.6	74.5	73.8	74.7	76.6	75	69.4	73.5	70.9	73.4
	Public	24.5	24.7	25.2	25.3	23.4	25.1	30.6	26.5	29.1	26.6
Men											
Rural and urban											
	Private	81	81.3	81.1	82.5	83.1	83.3	83.9	84.2	84.1	84.7
	Public	18.5	18.3	18.5	17.5	16.9	16.7	16.1	15.8	15.9	15.3
Both sexes											
Urban	Private	73	73.4	73.8	75.9	76.8	77.1	77	77.8	78.1	79
	Public	26.3	26.1	25.7	24.1	23.2	22.9	23	22.2	21.9	21
Rural	Private	92.9	92.8	92.4	92.8	94.1	93.8	93.8	94	93.1	93.6
	Public	6.9	6.8	7.1	7.2	5.9	6.2	6.2	6	6.9	6.4

Source: Statistical Center of Iran (2006 and 2014). Available from www.amar.org.ir

Note: For each category, the table is supposed to indicate the percentage employed in private and public sectors. However, the numbers in 2006, 2007, and 2008 do not add up to 100. This is a mistake in the official documents available on the website of the Statistical Center of Iran. We decided to report the numbers as presented in these documents

Figure 18.5 shows a more nuanced picture of women's employment and occupations based on the International Standard Classification of Occupations (ISCO-88) guidelines (Statistical Center of Iran, 2015). As illustrated in this figure, the employment distribution of men and women in different occupations is noticeably different. The distribution for women shows that three job categories (professionals, craft and related trades workers, and skilled agricultural, forestry, and fishery workers) form more than 50 percent of women's employment. In contrast, men's employment has a more balanced distribution across different occupations. In Figure 18.6, women's share in each of these job categories is illustrated. As shown in this figure, women have a very high presence (41.34 percent) in the professionals category which includes the following six occupation groups: science and engineering professionals, health professionals, teaching professionals, business and administration professionals, information and

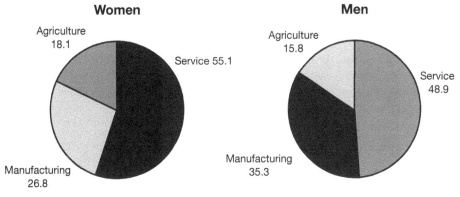

Figure 18.4 Employment distribution of 15 years and older population in different sectors
Source: Statistical Center of Iran (2015)
Note: Agriculture includes farming, hunting, forestry, and fishery

Women

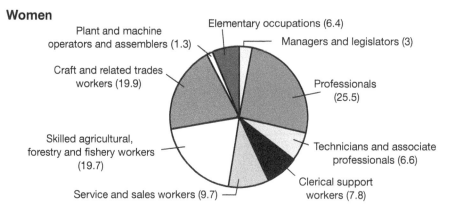

Plant and machine operators and assemblers (1.3)
Craft and related trades workers (19.9)
Elementary occupations (6.4)
Managers and legislators (3)
Professionals (25.5)
Skilled agricultural, forestry and fishery workers (19.7)
Technicians and associate professionals (6.6)
Service and sales workers (9.7)
Clerical support workers (7.8)

Men

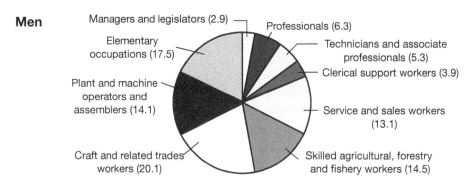

Managers and legislators (2.9)
Elementary occupations (17.5)
Plant and machine operators and assemblers (14.1)
Professionals (6.3)
Technicians and associate professionals (5.3)
Clerical support workers (3.9)
Service and sales workers (13.1)
Craft and related trades workers (20.1)
Skilled agricultural, forestry and fishery workers (14.5)

Figure 18.5 Employment distribution in different occupations (%)
Source: Statistical Center of Iran (2015)
Note: Numbers are rounded to one decimal place. Classification of different occupations follows the International Standard Classification of Occupations (ISCO-88)

communication technology professionals, and legal, social, and cultural professionals (ILO, n.d.). The second highest employment category for women is the clerical support worker category and the third is the skilled agricultural, forestry, and fishery category.

In sum, these numbers show an imbalanced distribution of employment across different occupations for Iranian women in that they reflect high representation in white-collar jobs that require university education and low representation in other categories. As Esfahani and Shajari (2012) point out, the patterns of women's employment reflect the high levels of education among women, suggesting that the university education has played a positive role in women's ability to enter the workforce. In the next section, we take a closer look at the impact of education on the employment of Iranian women.

Education and employment

Economists posit that increasing levels of education among women is expected to translate into higher level of female labor force participation. They argue that by enabling women to earn "higher income and social status through labor market participation, education increases the opportunity cost of homemaking" (Esfahani and Shajari, 2012, p. 9). Considering the rapid rise in the education levels of Iranian women, it is important to understand whether education has

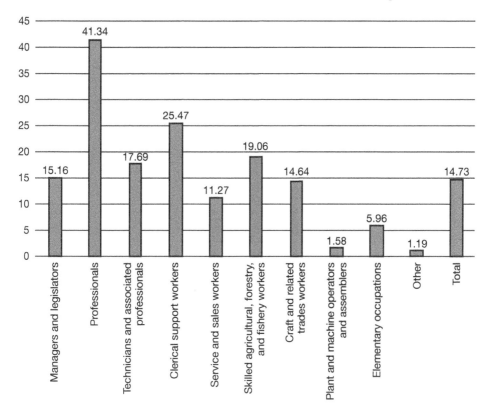

Figure 18.6 Women's presence in each occupation
Source: Statistical Center of Iran (2015)

had a positive impact on women's employment. Table 18.6 provides information on the participation rate and employment of women and men based on the highest level of education attained. The participation rate of men at all levels of education is above 54 percent and higher education does not increase that participation rate or employment. For women, however, higher levels of education are associated with higher participation rate and employment. This observation is consistent with examination of the relationship between education and employment data of the population aged 25–54 years old in 2006 by Esfahani and Shajari (2012) who observed that labor force participation "rises very fast with educational attainment for women, while displaying little variation among men" (Esfahani and Shajari, 2012, p. 14).

In order to understand the impact of education on women's participation rate, Esfahani and Shajari (2012) conducted a longitudinal analysis focused on the period between 1986 and 2006. During that time, the participation rate of women in both urban and rural areas increased. Esfahani and Shajari (2012) found that almost 60 percent of the rise in participation rate during that time period could be attributed to a decline in fertility rate and that education seemed to account for only 10 percent of the increase in women's labor force participation rate. These authors also note that, in addition to its direct impact, education has an indirect impact by reducing the fertility rate.

Figure 18.7 shows fertility rate in Iran from 1965 to 2013 (Google Public Data, 2015). As illustrated in this graph, the fertility rate during the period studied by Esfahani and Shajari has sharply declined from 6.02 births per woman (BPW) to 1.87. Since 2006, the fertility rate has

Table 18.6 Employment characteristics of 15 years and older population based on highest educational level attained or being attained

	Women			Men		
	Employed (%)	*Participation rate*	*Unemployment rate*	*Employed (%)*	*Participation rate*	*Unemployment rate*
Illiterate	8.28	8.37	1.14	52.34	54.22	3.47
Elementary school	9.13	9.48	3.77	74.57	79.20	5.85
Middle school	6.98	7.86	11.22	75.35	82.44	8.60
High school	7.04	9.15	23.03	56.93	63.34	10.12
College degree	20.59	27.14	24.15	52.29	59.40	11.96
Undergraduate	22.59	34.63	34.77	51.41	59.97	14.27
Graduate	36.08	46.93	23.13	63.28	69.47	8.91
Other	11.15	11.49	2.89	60.78	62.45	2.67

Source: Statistical Center of Iran (2014)

remained stable, with a slight increase to 1.92 BPW. Unlike the earlier period, over the last ten years both the fertility rate and higher education attainment level have remained stable and the participation rate has declined. Considering the stable fertility rate and high education attainment levels, we speculate that the impact of these factors on labor force participation has declined. However, a more comprehensive discussion of this pattern requires in-depth analysis that is beyond the scope of this chapter.

Education and income

We do not have detailed information on the relationship between education and income. However, Alavian Ghavanini's (2011) research on the wage gap in urban areas offers valuable insight into the relationship between education and the gender wage gap. This research reported a negative relationship between the gender wage gap and education. In other words, the wage gap was smaller in professions that require high levels of expertise and larger in low-skilled jobs. Alavian Ghavanini's study suggests that the wage gap disappears for professional jobs, and is sometimes even reversed. However, he found the wage gap to be significantly

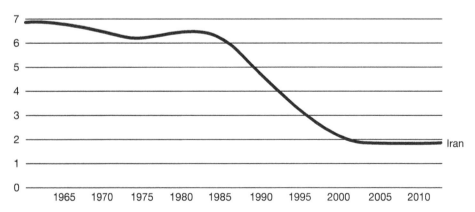

Figure 18.7 Fertility rate, 1960 to 2013
Source: Google Public Data (2015)

larger in the private sector. Considering that Esfahani and Shajari (2012) found educated women to be more likely to join the private sector, the impact of education on income and wage gap across the population becomes complicated.

In the next section, we take a closer look at some of the factors that seem to influence women's unemployment as well as their decision to leave the workforce entirely.

Understanding low participation rates and high unemployment rates of women

Figures 18.8 and 18.9 illustrate data on individuals' reasons for leaving their previous jobs—either voluntarily or involuntarily—in urban and rural areas. As shown in these figures, the main reasons for leaving the previous job are different for men and women in both urban and rural areas. For urban women, low income is the most important reason (25.57 percent), followed by a temporary job (14.95 percent), and family issues (13.46 percent). Urban men indicated temporary job (23.08 percent), end of military service[3] (17.22 percent), and low income (16.84 percent) as the main reason for leaving their job. In rural areas, seasonal job (24.63 percent), temporary job (21.25 percent), and low income (16.17 percent) are the top three reasons for women leaving their jobs. The top three reasons for rural men are temporary job (34.45 percent), end of military service (17.36 percent), and seasonal job (17.02 percent).

Figures 18.10 and 18.11 offer some information about women's and men's reasons for not looking for a job.[4] Both urban and rural women indicated personal or family responsibilities

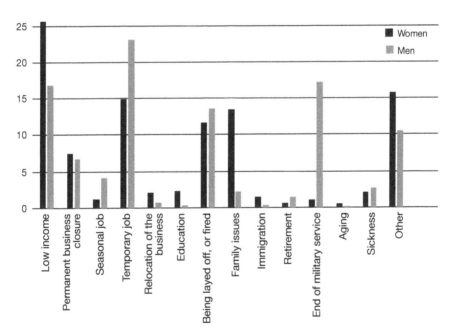

Figure 18.8 Reasons for leaving previous job (urban areas)

Source: Statistical Center of Iran (2015)

Note: This table shows that some women have chosen "end of military service" as their reason for leaving their previous job. Considering that women do not attend military service, it is not clear what this item means. It is possible that they have left their previous job because their husband's military service ended or that they misunderstood the question. The terminology used to refer to military service is very similar to end of employment contract. Therefore, that might be another explanation for this item.

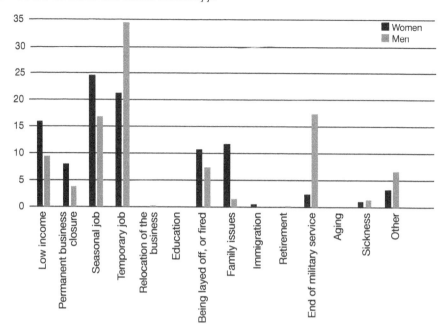

Figure 18.9 Reasons for leaving previous job (rural areas)
Source: Statistical Center of Iran (2015)

as the main reason for not looking for a job (69 percent of urban women and 72.95 percent of rural women). Both groups indicated education as the second reason for not looking for a job (22.02 percent for urban women and 17.67 percent for rural women).

Overall, low income and personal and family responsibilities seem to be two main factors that are driving women's unemployment. However, these categories are very broad and offer incomplete explanations for the problem. For example, although there is evidence that a wage gap exists, it is not clear whether low income refers to absolute income or the overall utility of the income, which could be influenced by other factors such as the high cost of childcare or transportation. Families, regardless of their income level, do not receive any government support for childcare. The daycare system is fully private and is not subsidized in any form. Some large organizations, mostly in the public sector, offer on-site daycare facilities, which are usually more affordable than private daycare; however, that option is available only to a limited number of working women. Similarly, "family issues" is a very broad term and it is not clear what kind of issues are inhibiting women from working.

In order to delve deeper into the reasons behind the high unemployment rate of women, we reached out to friends and acquaintances of the first author on social media and asked them to share their opinions on this issue. In the next section, we share some of the key themes that emerged from these conversations. Where possible, we use evidence from other sources to support and reinforce this anecdotal evidence.

We would like to note that the majority of people who shared their opinion on this issue have university education and have grown up in Tehran; therefore, their observations and understanding of this phenomenon represent the views of educated, urban professionals. Furthermore, while most of the people who shared their ideas live in Iran, some of them have been outside Iran for several years.

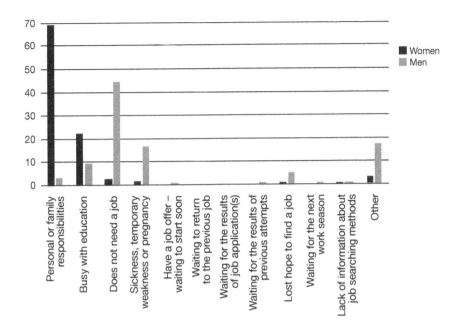

Figure 18.10 Reasons for not looking for a job (urban areas)
Source: Statistical Center of Iran (2015)

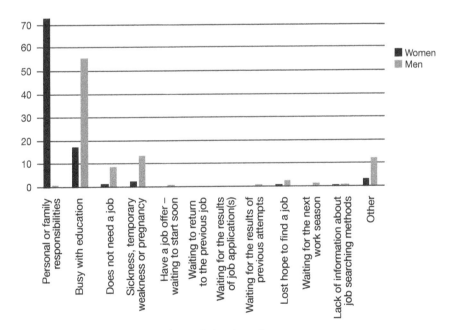

Figure 18.11 Reasons for not looking for a job (rural areas)
Source: Statistical Center of Iran (2015)

Discrimination in employment and lack of growth opportunities

Systematic exclusion of women from employment as well as lack of growth opportunities at workplaces form the main themes that emerged from our data. In October 2014, a bill was put forward to Parliament to inhibit the employment of single women as faculty members of public universities (Tabnak, 2014). Additionally, there is some evidence that women are likely to face hurdles in employment due to the application of gender-based quotas. A report by Al-Monitor (2015) indicates that the current government has imposed very strict gender-based quotas on its employment exams for different organizations in the government and public sector. The Iranian Ministry of Education announced on September 18, 2015, just prior to its nationwide exam for new job applicants, that of the 3,703 positions up for grabs only 630 would go to women (Al-Monitor, 2015). During the summer of 2015 the Iranian Central Bank advertised several positions open to university graduates. Of 47 vacancies 36 were reserved for men and 11 were available to both genders (Blair, 2015). These quotas appear unchanged despite a relatively moderate government and vocal resistance from women's groups.

In addition to these official reports, we have received abundant anecdotal evidence suggesting that women face overt discrimination and are systematically deprived of promotion and employment opportunities. While many of the factors that inhibit women from growth in organizations are similar to what women in other countries experience, our participants mentioned a factor that seems to be unique to Iran and to some extent legitimizes systematic discrimination against women. This factor is related to socialized gender roles, which see men responsible for breadwinning and women responsible for family care. As a result, a cultural expectation seems to have emerged that a woman's income is not expected to be used to support her family. One respondent shared his experience with a company that would not hire any women because the manager believed that by hiring a man he supports—and protects— a family, rather than an individual. Others shared stories indicating that employers and managers promote a less qualified man based on the argument that he is supposed to provide for his family and therefore he should be the one who is being promoted. Here is the story shared by a university professor:

> In our department, we have eight women and two men—this shows to what extent the number of educated women is higher that they have been able to take these positions— and one of these men is the chair of the department. At one point we needed to appoint a new department chair. The previous chair suggested that considering that female professors do not need money, they all vote for the other male professor—the chair position came with salary increase.

Another respondent shared her experience in the film industry. Although in her workplace they had very clear rules for promotion, she was denied promotion when she became qualified for the higher position. She explained that her manager told her she was not promoted because she is a woman and during the eight years of her tenure at this company, the manager did not promote any woman to that particular position.

Impact of childcare on women's employment

Another major theme that emerged from the data is childcare and marriage. Research shows that the birth of a child is a strong driving force behind a woman's—even highly educated ones—decision to leave their job and the workforce entirely (Esfahani and Shajari, 2012; Herr and Wolfram, 2009). Socialized gender roles that hold a woman responsible for family care and childbearing have a strong presence in Iran. Social pressure on women to stay home and take care of their children seems to play a substantial role. Women who shared their opinion suggested that "a mother who returns to work and leaves her baby at daycare is considered selfish and devoid of maternal instinct," and that "a woman who decides to leave her work to take care of her children is more valued by the society than a woman who decides to continue working in spite of all the difficulties." In addition to the social pressure, lack of high quality and trustworthy daycare combined with the high cost of daycare and the gender wage gap creates a setting in which women's employment does not seem an economically viable choice.

Marriage and means of wealth generation

Income and wealth generation seem to play an important and complex role in women's decision to work outside home. Independent generation of wealth through employment outside the home seems to be very difficult to achieve for Iranian women. As mentioned in a previous section, according to the most recent *Global Gender Gap Report* (Schwab *et al.*, 2015), there is a significant gender wage gap in Iran. This large disparity between men and women's ability to earn income seems to have influenced women's beliefs about their ability to earn a decent income.

On the issue of wealth generation, to our surprise, many of our respondents did not discuss the external factors that inhibit women from earning a high income and generating wealth. Instead, many of people who shared their opinions placed the responsibility squarely on women, blaming them for being lazy, lacking ambition, and relying on others to support them. In particular, many respondents argued that women do not value their jobs and their careers because they do not see their careers as a path to wealth generation. These respondents argued that higher education is seen as a personal asset that would enhance a woman's attractiveness for marriage and enhance their chance of marrying a man who can provide adequate financial support for her and their family. It was argued that once women get married to men who can provide for the family, they decide that they do not need a job and choose to stay at home. We would like to note that according to the data presented in Figure 18.10, while 44.59 percent of urban men indicated that they are not looking for a job because they do not need a job, only 2.46 percent of women chose this option as the reason for not looking for a job. Therefore, the claim that women do not work because they do not think they need to does not seem to be supported by these data.

A factor that adds to the complexity of this relationship is the cultural expectation that a man is responsible for providing for his family. In fact, not only is a man responsible for providing for his family, according to Islam, a man should pay his wife for her work at home and raising their children. Additionally, a man should pay his wife for breastfeeding. To the best of our knowledge, these laws are not commonly practiced in Iran. However, they shape the cultural expectation that a woman does not need to work to provide for her family. Some of our respondents shared stories of working women who invest their income independently of their husbands because they believe that their income belongs to them and they are not expected to share their income with the family or spend it on household expenses.

There is evidence suggesting that an unusual pattern has emerged among young and educated women—even among the upper class in Tehran—who seem to welcome the idea of staying home if their husbands can provide for them. Mehrkhane has conducted research asking three female bloggers to pose a question to their readers to inquire about possible reasons for women's decisions to leave their work (Mehrkhane, 2015a). Out of 120 responses to the questions, high workload and stress was indicated as the most popular reason (47 percent) followed by marriage and childbearing (31.67 percent), and preference to embrace their femininity at home (27.5 percent). In addition, several respondents mentioned that they would prefer to stay home if they have financial security.

Absence of responsibility for family financial support and the expectation of future wealth generation seem to influence young women and men. Iranian families expect their sons to work early on and plan for their careers, while they hold no such expectation for their daughters. As one respondent mentioned: "Most families do not see any problem with having an unemployed 25-year-old daughter; however, they would be *ashamed* to have a 25-year-old son who does not have a job." The interesting point here is that financial support from the family and lack of societal pressure seem to have created a setting in which girls have a *choice* to work with no financial obligation, an option that is not available to boys.[5]

Overall, Iranian girls seem to be in a setting in which their parents, their families, the political system, and the social system discourage them from pursuing work outside the home. They have grown to believe and accept that successful careers and wealth generation belong to men. In addition, we speculate that in the absence of successful role models and a period of stagnation for women, these young women are discouraged from investing in careers that do not promise an appealing future. The combination of all of these factors seem to have created a situation in which women are often complicit in a discriminatory system by exercising their "choice to not work." As one of our respondents said, discrimination is so widespread and overwhelming that women are not seen as having a responsibility for their lives and careers.

Women in leadership positions

We do not know the exact number of women in management positions in Iran. Based on the data presented in Figure 18.5, in 2015, 3 percent of employed women, compared to 2.9 percent of employed men, are categorized under the legislators, senior officials, and managers category. According to these data, women's share of these positions is 15.16 percent. This figure is in accordance with the 2015 *Global Gender Gap Report* (Schwab *et al.*, 2015) in which the percentage of women in this category in 2015 is reported at 17 percent.

Figure 18.12 shows the distribution of women and men based on status in employment. The first row of this figure shows the distribution of individuals listed as legislators, senior officials, and managers.: 60 percent of women, compared to 37.48 percent of men, who are listed under this category, are employed in the public sector, compared to 27.58 percent of women and 20 percent of men in the private sector. Considering that only 26.37 percent of working women are employed in the public sector, these numbers suggest that the public sector provides better opportunities for growth for women. In fact, these data show that 22.77 percent of employees in the public sector are women and 22.24 percent of individuals listed as legislators, senior officials, and managers in the public sector are women, suggesting better growth opportunities for men and women in the public sector. However, we find these numbers puzzling, as they are not compatible with information received from other sources. For example, as discussed below, only 3 percent of Parliament members are women and Iran has no female cabinet members. In addition, Al-Monitor reports that women hold only 1 percent of managerial positions in the Ministry of Education (Al-Monitor, 2015).

Considering that senior officials and legislators fall under the public sector, we can assume that the percentage of individuals listed under this category in the private sector would represent people in management positions. Using that assumption, these data suggest that in the private sector women occupy 11.43 percent of managerial positions. However, we should note that in 2015, several news agencies including *Shargh Daily* (2015) and the Iranian

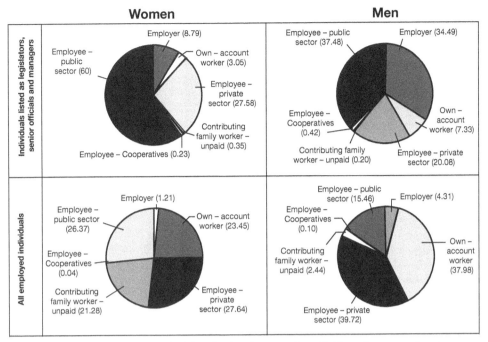

Figure 18.12 Distribution of individuals listed as legislators, senior officials, and managers based on status in employment

Source: Statistical Center of Iran (2014)

Students' News Agency (2015) reported on a public talk by Forough Azizi—a gender equality activist—at Rahman Institute. According to these news agencies, in this public presentation, Azizi indicated that women hold only 2.5 percent of decision-making positions. None of these news agencies provides details of Azizi's methodology and we could not locate a publication by Azizi herself. Therefore, the method of data collection is unknown and it is not clear what she meant by decision-making positions.

Women in Parliament and senior officials

Figure 18.13 shows the percentage of female members of parliament (also known as the Islamic Consultative Assembly) since the revolution. As shown in this diagram, although we see some progress in representation of women in Parliament, the overall percentage of women is very low at between 3 and 5 percent.

Since the Islamic Revolution in 1977, only one woman has been appointed to a cabinet. In the beginning of his second term as president, Mahmoud Ahmadinejad nominated three women to his cabinet. Only one of these women, Dr Marzieh Dastjerdy, was approved to become the head of the Ministry of Health. In the current government led by Hassan Rouhani men hold all cabinet positions. At vice president level, women hold 3 out of 12 positions.

Women entrepreneurs

We were not able to find published statistical data on the number of women entrepreneurs. However, recent research by Bahramitash and Esfahani (2014) offers very interesting insight

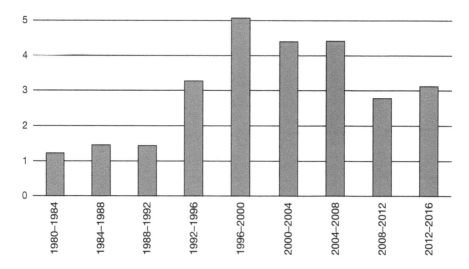

Figure 18.13 Percentage of women in Parliament

Source: HamshahriOnline (2012)

Note: Also known as Islamic Consultative Assembly

into women's entrepreneurship in Iran. Bahramitash and Esfahani found that female-owned firms tend to be relatively young, with a high percentage of them established in the early 2000s. During this period, the government developed policies to encourage private ownership and there was an increase in entrance of women with higher education into the labor force (Bahramitash and Esfahani, 2014). Research by Esfahani and Shajari (2012) shows that women with higher education, compared with those without a university education, tend to have a higher chance of joining the private sector as employers or self-employed. Therefore, the high percentage of women with higher education seems to have influenced patterns of women's entrepreneurship.

Bahramitash and Esfahani (2014) also found that women entrepreneurs seem to have higher representation in large firms compared to small and medium-sized enterprises. In fact, they found the percentage of female ownership of large firms was comparable to the rest of the world. In addition, they found that these large female-owned firms tend to be relatively young and that women entrepreneurs have a "high presence in the service sector, especially gender-segregated activities, as well as in some new and growing industries such as electronics and information technology" (Bahramitash and Esfahani, 2014, p. 1).

The census data offer some limited information about entrepreneurship among women. The data provided in the second row of Figure 18.12 provides information on individuals who are considered employers. According to the International Classification by Status in Employment guideline (LABORSTA, n.d.), employer refers to "a person who operates his or her own economic enterprise, or engages independently in a profession or trade, and hires one or more employees" (LABORSTA, n.d., para. 1). Therefore, according to this definition, an employer could be a small business owner or an entrepreneur. The percentage of working women categorized as employer is 1.21 percent, compared with 4.31 percent of working men.

Initiatives to support women as entrepreneurs

Historically, the concept of entrepreneurship and the role that it could play in economic development has not received much attention in Iran (Entrepreneurship Center of Qom University of Medical Sciences and Health Services, n.d.). Over the last two decades, however, the government has started various programs to promote and support entrepreneurship among men and women (Entrepreneurship Center of Qom University of Medical Sciences and Health Services, n.d.). We have identified several non-profit or government funded agencies that focus on women entrepreneurs. For example, the Association of Iranian Women Entrepreneurs was established in 2004 with the purpose of supporting women entrepreneurs, with a focus on education and consultation. In addition to ongoing workshops, each year, the association has organized a conference focusing on different aspects of women's entrepreneurship. The National Association of Women Entrepreneurs, Women, and Youth Entrepreneurship Development Foundation are two other examples of organizations devoted to the development and support of women entrepreneurs.

Another example of government support for women entrepreneurship is the International Exhibition and Conference on the Role of Women in Sustainable Development, which was organized annually over the last two years. The most recent conference focused on entrepreneurship and employment, was held in September 2015 in Tehran. The Best Woman Entrepreneur of the Year award and a collection of female entrepreneurs' profiles (in the form of a book) were among the highlights of the program (Iran Project, 2015).

Overall, in recent years, the notion of women entrepreneurs and the role they could play in economic development has received some attention from the government. The important question that remains to be answered is the effectiveness of these programs.

Country legislation

Under the Islamic Republic of Iran, a married woman needs her husband's permission to work and travel. In other words, a husband has the right to forbid his wife's work outside home at any point in time. In addition, if a woman needs to travel for her work, she would need her husband's permission to travel. We do not have any data to explore to what extent men exercise this right. Based on anecdotal evidence, it seems to us that not many men pursue legal actions to prohibit their wife's work. However, a significant number of men seem to demand that their wives quit their work and stay home after marriage.

Maternity leave

The duration of maternity leave in Iran is 270 days (9 months) and women receive 100 percent of their last salary and employment benefits during their leave. If a woman gives birth to twins, the duration of her maternity leave can be extended to 365 days (12 months) (Mehrkhane, 2015b). The duration of parental leave for men is 10 days—30 days in case of twins (Mehrkhane, 2015b). In addition to maternity leave benefits, women can benefit from a program called *breastfeeding time* or *breastfeeding leave*. According to this program, each working day a woman can reduce her hours by one hour to breastfeed her baby. This accommodation is available until the baby turns two years old (Mehrkhane, 2015b). Although according to the law all employers in the public and private sectors are obliged to offer breastfeeding time, more than 50 percent of employers do not follow the guidelines (Mehrkhane, 2015b).

Conclusion

This chapter has been an eye-opening experience for us and we hope that it will shed some light on the status of women in Iran. However, we found there were many sources of published data that challenged our original impressions of women in Iran. We also struggled to make sense of data that were sometimes contradictory and incomplete. For example, we found widely varying accounts of the gender wage gap, putting the gap at anything between 40 and 20 percent. Perhaps this requires a finer grained analysis, looking for differences across professional groups, part-time, full-time and seasonal work, government, private, and public sectors. We faced several unanswered questions and puzzling contradictions that we were not able to resolve. For example, why are highly educated women leaving the workforce permanently, and in large numbers? Why are women paying the "motherhood penalty" despite paid maternity leave that is more generous than in many other countries? We hope that this chapter will encourage others to look beyond the numbers to women's stories of life and work in Iran.

While women in Iran are often compared with other women in the Middle East living under *sharia* law, their situation is unique and somewhat paradoxical. Women in Iran achieved the right to vote in 1963, have been politically active, and were important participants in the Iranian Revolution of 1979. Women have demonstrated academic excellence, entering universities in large numbers, competing academically in a national system that is both demanding and highly selective. Despite several periods of conservative government, Iran has experienced socio-demographic changes that appear to improve the status of women. These changes include growing educational attainment, increase in the age of first marriage, lower fertility rates, and rising rates of divorce.

Most economic arguments would propose a positive effect of education on income. The data on Iran suggest just that pattern with women in professional jobs more likely to close the gender wage gap. However, women are still economically disadvantaged as demonstrated by lower levels of employment and higher levels of unemployment. Some experts attribute this to the shift from the private patriarchy of the family to the public patriarchy of the state (Moghadm, 2004). While women are required to seek permission from their fathers to marry and from their husbands to work and travel, there is little evidence that those restrictions are generally practiced. Meanwhile women are facing increasing restrictions on both employment and education, ranging from quotas in university admissions and employment to discrimination at work. These challenges have sometimes been referred to as "iron fences" rather than the glass ceilings faced by women in the Western world (Al-Monitor, 2015).

Women appear to be stuck in a vicious cycle in which their lower participation in the workplace is often used as an argument to reduce their access to publicly funded university education. Without access to education, they have even fewer options for employment, income generation, and egalitarian gender relations. When Iranian women choose to work outside the home they face overt discrimination at work, lower opportunities for advancement, lower incomes, and socio-cultural norms that force them to opt out when they become mothers. Also troubling is the fact that women are often blamed for their compliance with and lack of resistance to archaic gender norms that value their family roles at the expense of their paid employment. Shirin Ebadi, noted human rights activist and Nobel Peace Prize winner, has been quoted as saying, "Women are the victims of this patriarchal culture, but they are also its carriers. Let us keep in mind that every oppressive man was raised in the confines of his mother's home."

Women in Iran may be unable to claim gender equality until they achieve economic independence. They appear to be trapped in a gilded cage because the very factors that liberate them from having to be family breadwinners also restrict their access to fair and equal employment, forcing them to rely on men in their family for financial support and social status.

Notes

1   Literacy refers to the ability to write and read at elementary level.
2   It should be noted that, in 2005, the minister of higher education submitted a bill to Parliament to turn these restrictions into a law. This bill was never approved by Parliament and the minister of higher education pursued the original plan without the approval of Parliament (Mehrkhane, 2014).
3   In Iran, military service is compulsory for men and women cannot attend the service. After turning 18, each man is required to complete military service for a period of 21 months. For men who attend university immediately after high school (most students finish high school when they are 18 years old), military service is postponed until they finish their education.
4   The report does not clarify the length of unemployment for these people.
5   It should be noted that unlike Western countries, in Iran, girls and boys are not expected to leave their parents' home in their twenties. Both girls and boys are expected to live with their parents until they get married.

References

Alavian Ghavanini, A. (2011). Analysis of Gender Wage Gap in Urban Areas of Iran (Unpublished master's thesis). Sharif University of Technology, Iran.
Al-Monitor (2015). *Beyond Glass Ceiling, Iranian Women Face Iron Fence* (September 22). Retrieved from www.al-monitor.com/pulse/originals/2015/09/iran-women-employment.html
Bahramitash, R. and Esfahani, H. S. (2014). Gender and Entrepreneurship in Iran. *Middle East Critique*, 23(3), 293–312.
Blair, D. (2015). Iran's Big Woman Problem: All of the Things Iranian Women Aren't Allowed to Do. *The Telegraph* (September 21), Retrieved from www.telegraph.co.uk/women/womens-life/11875128/Irans-women-problem-All-of-the-things-Iranian-women-arent-allowed.html
Entrepreneurship Center of Qom University of Medical Sciences and Health Services (n.d.). *The History of Entrepreneurship in Iran and the World*. Retrieved from http://karafarini.muq.ac.ir/index.aspx?fkeyid=&siteid=123&pageid=776
Esfahani, H. S. and Shajari, P. (2012). Gender, Education, Family Structure, and the Allocation of Labor in Iran. *Middle East Development Journal*, 4(2). DOI: 10.1142/S1793812012500083.
Farheekhtegan (2014). *Complete Termination of Gender-Based Restrictions in 29 Universities* (August 6). Retrieved from http://farheekhtegan.ir/newspaper/page/1441/3/1127/0
Google Public Data (2015). Explore (October 16). Retrieved from www.google.com/publicdata/explore
HamshahriOnline (2012). *Table of the Number of Female Representatives in 9 Parliaments; Women's Share of the House of Citizens* (May 6). Retrieved from http://hamshahrionline.ir/details/169329
Herr, J. L. and Wolfram, C. (2009). Opt-out rates at motherhood across high-educated career paths: Selection versus work environment. *NBER Working Paper* 14717. NBER. Retrieved from www.nber.org/papers/w14717
ILO (n.d.). *Resolution Concerning Updating the International Standard Classification of Occupations*. Geneva, Switzerland: International Labor Organization. Retrieved from www.ilo.org/public/english/bureau/stat/isco/docs/resol08.pdf
Iranian Students' News Agency (2105). *Strategies against Female Managers* (December 7). Retrieved from http://isna.ir/fa/news/94021006117/

Iran Project (2015). *Iran to host Int'l exhibition on women's role: VP* (August 2). The Iran Project. Retrieved from http://theiranproject.com/blog/2015/08/02/iran-to-host-intl-exhibition-on-womens-role-vp/

LABORSTA (n.d.). *International Classification by Status in Employment (ICSE)*. Retrieved from http://laborsta.ilo.org/applv8/data/icsee.html

Las Heras, M., Chinchilla, N. and Leon, C. (2011). Women in Management in Spain. In M. J. Davidson and R. J. Burke (eds), *Women in Management Worldwide: Progress and Prospects*, 2nd ed. (pp.85–106). Surrey, U.K.: Gower Publishing.

Majbouri, M. (2011). Against the Wind: Labor Force Participation of Women and Economic Instability in Iran. Manuscript. Babson College.

Mehrkhane (2014). *The History of Gender Quotas at Universities since 61*. Family and Women News Analysis Database. (August 30). Retrieved from http://tnews.ir/news/811029737811.html

Mehrkhane (2105a). *Returning to Home; Choice of Some of Women in the Current Generation*. Family and Women News Analysis Database (January 20). Retrieved from http://mehrkhane.com/fa/news/14747/

Mehrkhane (2105b). *Implementation Complications of Working Women's Breastfeeding Leave*. Family and Women News Analysis Database (March 2). Retrieved from http://mehrkhane.com/fa/news/16093/

Moghadm, V. (2004). Women in the Islamic Republic of Iran: Legal Status, Social Positions, and Collective Action. Conference paper for Iran after 25 Years of Revolution: A Retrospective and a Look Ahead, organized by the Woodrow Wilson International Center for Scholars and the National Defense University, Washington, D.C., 16–17 November.

Schwab, K., Samans, R., Zahidi, S., Bekhouche, Y., Ugarte, P. P., Ratcheva, V., Hausmann, R. and D'Andrea Tyson, L. (2015). *The Global Gender Gap Report*. Geneva, Switzerland: World Economic Forum.

Shargh Daily (2014). *Statistical Center of Iran: Women's Participation Rate is 51 Percent Lower than Men* (April 15). Retrieved from http://sharghdaily.ir/?News_Id=31712

Shargh Daily (2015). *The 2.5 Percent Share of Women from Management Positions* (May 7). Retrieved from www.sharghdaily.ir/News/62319

Sohrab, G., Karambayya, R. and Burke, R. J. (2011). Women in Management in Canada. In M. J. Davidson and R. J. Burke (eds), *Women in Management Worldwide: Progress and Prospects*, 2nd ed. (pp.165–181). Surrey, U.K.: Gower Publishing.

Statistical Center of Iran (2006). *Labor Force Survey Results Winter 1384*. Tehran, Iran: Statistical Center of Iran. Retrieved from www.amar.org.ir

Statistical Center of Iran (2014). *Labor Force Survey Results 1392*. Tehran, Iran: Statistical Center of Iran. Retrieved from Retrieved from www.amar.org.ir

Statistical Center of Iran (2015). *Labor Force Survey Results Winter 1393*. Tehran, Iran: Statistical Center of Iran. Retrieved from www.amar.org.ir

Tabnak (2014). *Another Employment Restriction for Single Women* (October 4). Retrieved from www.tabnak.ir/fa/news/439439/

Tijdens, K. G. (2011). Women in Management in the Netherlands. In M. J. Davidson and R. J. Burke (eds), *Women in Management Worldwide: Progress and Prospects*, 2nd ed. (pp.55–67). Surrey, U.K.: Gower Publishing.

19 Women in management in Israel

Ronit Waismel-Manor and Ronit Kark

Introduction

In this chapter we present the current status of women in management and leadership positions in Israel. Although the advancement of women shows great progress, we present some of the challenges women holding elite positions face. To better understand women's advances in this domain we analyze the broader Israeli society and context, highlighting the historical, cultural, and socio-political developments and challenges that have shaped the scope and nature of women's representation in management. We begin with a description of recent trends in the women's labor force in Israel, and issues related to education. We then focus on three groups of women – managers, directors, and entrepreneurs – to illustrate the different challenges women face in the public and private spheres. The next section summarizes local initiatives aimed at facilitating social change and enhancing the role of women in the workforce. We conclude by considering the paradox of the duality of women's opportunities in management that arises when regional traditional-familial roles, norms, and expectations clash with the developed and Westernized culture, which both govern the Israeli society.

Labor force characteristics

Since the early 1980s, there has been a significant increase in the proportion of women in the civilian labor force (see Table 19.1). Women now make up close to 50 percent of the labor force in Israel and are more likely to be employed, stay employed during their lifetimes, and work full time. Israel, as well as other countries in Europe and North America, is commonly defined as a "work-oriented" country; that is, a country in which people are more likely to endorse women's paid work (and even full-time paid work) than are people in other countries (Treas and Widmer, 2000). Moreover, research indicates that more Israeli mothers of pre-school-aged children are in the labor force than their counterparts in many other industrialized nations (Mandel and Semyonov, 2006).

Despite its modern economy and western style of living, Israeli society is known for its "familialism" (e.g., Fogiel-Bijaoui, 2002; Remennick, 2006). The family and motherhood continue to be a central social anchor and expectation at both the individual and collective levels. This is evident in the rates of marriage and fertility, which are high relative to most countries in the developed industrialized world. One interesting expression of this perception of the cultural ideal toward working women can be seen in the way in which motherhood and work are integrated. For example, in Israel there is an extremely limited presence of childless women in high positions in different spheres (e.g., political, economic, and academic) (Frenkel, 2006; Herzog, 1999). A recent list of the 50 most influential women in the Israeli economy, drawn up by *Lady Globes Magazine* in 2015, included only three childless women.

Table 19.1 Women in the labor force in Israel (1980–2015)

Percentage of women in labor force (LF)	1980	2000	2007/8	2015
Women in LF as % of all women	36	48	51	59
25–54 year old women in LF	50	69	72	75
Working part time (<35 hrs/wk)	47	42	40	33
Women as % of total LF	37	46	47	45

Source: Central Bureau of Statistics (2001, 2008, 2015c); Statistilite (2009)
Note: Since 2012, the Central Bureau of Statistics classifies compulsory and career military personnel as part of the labor force

As a cultural code, familialism takes advantage of an unequal gender division of labor. The Israeli woman is typically viewed as both a wife and a mother, whose primary responsibility is to bear children and take care of her home and family. Her paid work is somewhat perceived as a secondary contribution to the family's budget (Fogiel-Bijaoui, 2002). Thus, in the past, the widespread gender division in Israel was based on the expectation that women will take part in the paid labor market and have a "job," but will not have a structured "career." Since the 1970s, however, Israeli public discourse is changing, and the issue of equal opportunities in different life domains is becoming increasingly important. Nonetheless, overall there has not been a notable change in the cultural ideal that stresses the need to integrate motherhood and paid labor (Frenkel, 2006; Kark, 2007).

There are also significant ethnic and national differences in the representation of women in the labor force in Israel. In 2013, among Jewish women, 73.5 percent of those born in Israel compared to 35.2 percent of those born in the countries of North Africa and the Middle East (referred to as "Easterners"), and 55.7 percent of those originating from Europe and North and South America (referred to as "Westerners") were in the labor force (Central Bureau of Statistics, 2014). These differences remained relatively stable over the past few years. Noteworthy is the dramatic increase in the employment rate of Ultra-Orthodox Jewish women, from about 50 percent between 2002 and 2011, to 68 percent in 2013 (Central Bureau of Statistics, 2015a). This change been encouraged and supported by governmental policy.

Comparing nationalities, 53.5 percent of Jewish women were in the labor force compared to only 24 percent of Arab-Israeli women.[1] With regards to religion, 41 percent of Arab-Israeli Christian women, 21 percent of Druze women, and only 16 percent of Moslem-Israeli women were employed in the labor force (Central Bureau of Statistics, 2011). The higher representation of Christian women in the labor force in comparison to the Moslem and Druze women can be explained by their higher level of education and their more modern lifestyle (Reches and Rodintzki, 2009; Yonay et al., 2015).

Labor force participation among Arab women is hindered by insufficient childcare facilities, poor educational facilities, limited transportation from their villages and cities to the workplaces, limited employment opportunities, limited knowledge of the Hebrew language, cultural norms that object to women working outside the home, and discrimination on the part of Jewish and Arab employers (Tzameret-Kertcher, 2014; Tzameret-Kertcher et al., 2015). These disadvantages are at their greatest where gender and other minority identities intersect (for example, ethnicity, class, nationality). Therefore, Eastern Jewish women, but much more so Arab women, may have a double disadvantage as workers and as applicants for managerial roles (Kark and Eagly, 2010). Still there are some encouraging trends, as over the last decade teen pregnancies went down, the average childbearing age rose, and more women are highly educated (Tzameret-Kertcher, 2014).

Women constitute over 65 percent of those employed by the state, with the vast majority employed in education, health and welfare, and public administration (Civil Service Commission, 2014). Studies have shown that women who are employed in the public sector are more likely than women who are employed in the private sector to work when they have young children and less likely to interrupt their employment (Okun *et al.*, 2007; Stier and Yaish, 2008). Furthermore, research has pointed out that women employed in the public sector appear to be subject to less pay discrimination than other women (Yaish and Kraus, 2003). In the private sector, individual employers have greater freedom to discriminate and the salary range between the bottom and the top is much greater than in the public sector where collective agreements and public scrutiny make it harder to discriminate and set a ceiling on salary levels.

Education remains a significant predictor of women's labor force participation. For example, in 2011, there was a very small difference in labor force participation among women with children under the age of four compared to other women (72 percent and 77 percent respectively were employed among women aged 25–45). However, only 26 percent of women with very young children and no high school diploma were in the labor force, compared to 42 percent of women without young children, while there is no such gap among women with an academic degree (87 percent among women with very young children and 88 percent among women without very young children) (Stier and Herzberg, 2013). This suggests that academic education can facilitate women's representation and integration in the labor force. The growing number of women in higher education (discussed below) re-enforces their attachment to the labor market.

Women pursuing education

Since the 1990s, there has been a rapid increase in the number of degree-granting academic institutions. This increase was absorbed primarily by newly established colleges that specialize in fields closely related to the labor market such as computer science, management sciences, and law (Council for Higher Education, 2014). As in many other Western countries, the percentages of educated individuals in Israel rose significantly over the last decades and more so for women than for men (Haim and Shavit, 2013). Women have continued to increase their investment in formal education as a means of improving job prospects in the labor market (Stier and Herzberg, 2013). In 1968 women constituted 43 percent of all university students, in 1990 they were 51 percent, and in recent years women surpassed men at all three academic levels. In 2013, women constituted 59 percent of all students in academic institutions (Central Bureau of Statistics, 2014; Statistilite, 2009). However, the numbers vary by field of study.

Table 19.2 shows that women are over-represented in the humanities, social sciences, biology, para-medical studies, and architecture. Women and men are equally represented in business, management, and law, occupations that lead to managerial positions. The number of women awarded different degrees in the exact sciences, such as in mathematics, statistics, and computer science is still very low.

Despite the fact that the percentage of women graduating from doctoral programs exceeds 50 percent, only 29 percent of university faculty members at all levels are women. Furthermore, the higher one climbs on the academic ladder the lower the number of women. At the highest rank (that is, full professors) the figure stands at 15 percent for university full professors and 10 percent for academic colleges (Council for Higher Education, 2015). Therefore, although it is widely accepted that human capital (for example, increased formal education)

Table 19.2 Percentage of women in the student population by degree and field of study, 2014

Field of study	Degree			Total
	First	*Second*	*Third*	
Total	59	60	52	57
Humanities	61	61	55	61
Social sciences	68	69	63	61
Business administration	52	48	50	51
Law	50	53	51	50
Medicine	54	55	69	55
Para-medical studies	82	86	76	83
Mathematics, statistics and computer science	29	28	24	28
Biological sciences	64	65	58	63
Physical science	37	36	39	37
Architecture	60	56	73	NA
Engineering	25	23	31	NA

Source: Council for Higher Education (2015)

contributes to enhanced opportunities for advancement, research in Israel suggests that women receive lower returns than men for their investment in education (Izraeli, 2004; Stier and Herzberg, 2013; Tzameret-Kertcher, 2014).

Women in management

Although women in Israel have more access today to managerial positions than at any other period in history, equal representation remains a distant goal. Nevertheless, the increase of women in managerial roles is substantial. In 1981 women constituted less than 9 percent of all managers but over 36 percent of the labor force. By 2014 they constituted 33 percent of all managers, 58 percent of the professionals, and 45 percent of the labor force (Central Bureau of Statistics, 2015b). However, these women are concentrated at lower and middle levels of management. Across all economic sectors, substantially more men than women occupy positions that constitute major decision-making authority and the ability to influence others' pay and promotions. While there are ample data about women managers in the public sector, regrettably, no official organization gathers systemic data in the private sector, and therefore we can only rely on sporadic private initiatives. In the public or government sector, women in Israel enjoy considerable representation and positions of authority, whereas in the private sector women's gains have been more limited.

Women managers in Israel adhere to the family imperative and combine family and work–life. Table 19.3 shows that the proportion of women managers who are married is higher than the proportion among non-managers, and the proportion of women managers who are single is significantly lower than the proportion among non-managers.

Table 19.4 indicates that men's and women's median years of schooling was similar in the year 2011, but women managers were more likely to have attended an academic institution than either men managers or women non-managers. They worked on average three hours a week more than women non-managers but seven hours less than men managers.

The overall proportion of women managers in senior positions (top three ranks) in the civil service increased gradually from 41 percent in 2004 to 46 percent of managers in 2012 (Tzameret-Kertcher, 2014). However, these numbers reflect a ranking system that

Table 19.3 Marital status by gender and managerial status, 2011 (%)

	Married	Separated	Divorced	Widowed	Single
Men managers	85.0	0.6	4.1	1.0	9.3
Women managers	72.0	0.7	10.5	2.2	14.6
Women non-managers	62.0	1.8	9.8	2.5	24.1

Source: Central Bureau of Statistics (2011)

automatically grants all attorneys in the civil service a managerial status. Excluding attorneys from these figures reveals that while there is some improvement across all top three ranks, only 33 percent of all managers are women (Civil Service Commission, 2014). The number of women in senior positions in the civil service who are employed under senior contracts increased from 25 percent in 2004 to 34 percent by 2012 (Tzameret-Kertcher, 2014).

In the Israeli governing body, the Knesset, women's representation is much lower. There were 29 female members in the 20th Knesset, elected in 2015 (representing 24 percent of the Israeli Parliament). This was the largest number of women ever in the Knesset. Given that in 2015 only three of the 31 ministers and one of the eight deputy ministers were women, men still tipped the scale. Unfortunately, there has been no progress in women's representation in local government. Although more women than ever ran for municipal government in the last local elections, in 2013, of the 191 local authorities where elections were held, only three women were elected mayor. In 2015 only four women were serving as mayors.

Notwithstanding, women have been recently represented for the first time in some influential roles. A woman served as the speaker of the 17th Knesset, and in the 18th Knesset a woman headed the largest political party after having served as vice prime minister and minister of foreign affairs in the 17th Knesset. Two women have served as president of the Supreme Court (former President Dorit Beinisch and current President Miriam Naor), and in 2013 a woman was appointed to the position of governor of the Bank of Israel for the first time (Karnit Flug).

Another important component of the public sector is the Israeli Defense Forces (IDF). In Israel, service in the armed forces is mandatory. Following high school graduation, men and women are drafted when they reach the age of 18. According to the most recent official update, 90 percent of all positions in the IDF are open to women, and between 2006 and 2012 the number of female officers increased from 49 percent to 57 percent (Israel Defense Forces, n.d.a). Female officers with the rank of colonel grew by 100 percent, from 2 percent in 1999 to 4 percent in 2015 (Israel Defense Forces, n.d.b). The percentage of female officers with the rank of lieutenant colonel grew by 70 percent in the last decade, from 7.3 percent in 1999 to 12.5 percent today. In 2011, Orna Barbivai became the first female major-general in the IDF (IDF's second highest) upon her promotion to the role of commander of the Manpower

Table 19.4 Managers and non-managers by gender, schooling, and hours worked, 2011

	Median years of schooling	Academic institution #	Hours/week
Men managers	15 yrs	53	55.6
Women managers	15 yrs	62	48.5
Women non-managers	14 yrs	40	45.6

Source: Central Bureau of Statistics (2011)

Note: # Proportion whose last school attended was an academic institution

Directorate. However, since her retirement in 2014 no other woman has been promoted to this rank.

Thus, there is clearly an under-representation of women in the highest ranks in the military. The strong link between military service and citizenship in Israel extends the effect of the military on women's status not only to the period of their army service, but to their status in Israeli civilian society as well. The advantages men in commanding positions obtain and derive from military service are converted into advantages in civilian life. Military elites shift easily into roles in civilian elites (for example, political, managerial, educational, and so on), thus contributing to the sustainability and reproduction of gender inequality.

In the private sector women rarely hold positions of power and control. In 2014, only 6 percent of companies in the TA-100 (which comprise Israel's biggest businesses as measured by market valuation) were run by women. This represents a slight decline from 7.5 percent in 2013 (Israel Women's Network, 2015). A survey of 20 leading private sector firms by a leading Israeli economic newspaper showed that although women were on the top management team of all of these firms, in most there were only one or two women and these women held specific professional managerial roles (for example, spokeswomen, legal adviser, and HR manager) (Parnet, 2009). These advisory roles (staff versus line roles) are usually the less senior ones in the top management team and usually command lower salaries. Thus, although women's representation in these top management teams is on the rise and is significant in and of itself, women's minority status and limited power create a framework in which their ability to influence is restricted.

There is a definite gender structure to the distribution of managers among fields of special- ization and economic branches in the private sector. According to a 2008 Dun & Bradstreet Israel survey of the 1,400 largest companies in Israel, women constituted 47.1 percent of the human resource managers, 16.6 percent of financial managers, and 15.3 percent of sales and marketing managers. Women were under-represented among managers at the senior levels of these business firms; namely, as chairpersons (2.2 percent) and in senior "masculine" positions such as operation managers (5.4 percent), and logistics managers (9.7 percent) (Dun & Bradstreet Israel, 2009).

In March 1993, the Knesset passed an affirmative action amendment requiring ministers to appoint qualified women to boards of the approximately 750 government companies in which women were not properly represented. Ministers initially did not comply with the amendment and in December 1993, the Cabinet approved the appointments of three male directors to two government-owned companies whose boards had no women directors. The Israel Women's Network, a feminist lobby, consequently filed two petitions to the Supreme Court demanding that the government and the relevant ministers explain why they had not appointed women directors as required by law. On November 1, 1994, the Supreme Court acting in its capacity as the High Court of Justice annulled the appointment of the men as directors and required the ministers to appoint women in their stead (High Court of Justice, 1994).

The strong position taken by the Court had an almost immediate impact on appointments to the boards of government-owned companies. Ministers sought women candidates and more women came to see themselves as potential candidates. Between the year 1993 and the year 2000, the proportion of women directors of government companies rose from approximately 7 percent to 38 percent, and the proportion of companies with women directors increased from 31 percent in 1993 to 78.5 percent in 1997 (Izraeli and Hillel, 2000). However, this positive development did not continue and the proportion of companies with women directors dropped to 67 percent in 2007. As a result, a government decision in March 2007 ruled that, within two years, ministers must appoint women to directorates of government companies until

50 percent representation is achieved. As a result, the proportion of women directors of government companies reached 38.5 percent in February 2008 and 43 percent in 2015 (Authority for the Advancement of the Status of Women, n.d.; Ministry of Finance, 2015).

Attempts by feminist organizations to introduce affirmative actions in the private sector have met with much greater opposition on the grounds that it is not legitimate to interfere with the market economy. In 2014, women directors comprised 18.2 percent of directors in the TA-100, a slight increase in comparison to previous years. Ninety two percent of the companies have at least one female director, but only 39 percent have more than one woman as board members (Israel Women's Network, 2015).

Women entrepreneurs

The changes which have taken place in Israeli society in the last few decades have resulted in a considerable increase in the number of new businesses. These changes include a push towards privatization of large government-owned sectors of the economy, and the growth of the private business sector. In addition, employers' preference to employ sub-contracted workers, along with technological changes which have facilitated setting up home-based freelance work, have also increased the extent of entrepreneurship. According to the latest Israeli national report by the Global Entrepreneurship Monitor (Menipaz *et al.*, 2013), which is a global longitudinal comparative study of entrepreneurship and economic growth, entrepreneurial activity in Israel is high relative to other innovation-driven (most developed) economies. Moreover, the rate of opportunity-driven entrepreneurship (individuals pursuing an opportunity) is higher than its necessity-driven counterpart (individuals with no other option for work): 77 percent of entrepreneurs at new enterprises chose to become entrepreneurs in order to take advantage of a business opportunity, compared to 17.4 percent who became entrepreneurs out of necessity.

In the 1990s, the government began to view entrepreneurship as an important vessel for the economic integration of some half million immigrants from the former Soviet Union who arrived between 1988 and 1993, and encouraged entrepreneurship through the funding of technological incubators, the Small and Medium Enterprises Authority, and a network of Centers for Promoting Entrepreneurship. Women were encouraged to take advantage of these opportunities by taking special training courses for future women entrepreneurs, through seminars for businesswomen and entrepreneurs, and through business clubs for women (Israel Small and Medium Enterprises Authority, n.d.). Some Centers for Promoting Entrepreneurship ran special training programs for women from specific sectors such as Arab women and Ultra-Orthodox women wanting to set up home-based businesses.

In 2011, only 7.2 percent of the female labor force could be classified as entrepreneurs, compared to 14.6 percent of men in the labor force. Of these entrepreneurs, 8.4 percent of the men and 5.6 percent of the women were self-employed; and 6.2 percent and 1.6 percent respectively were employers (Central Bureau of Statistics, 2011). Women's businesses are concentrated in a small number of economic branches including services and retailing and are under-represented in wholesaling, manufacturing, and big business in general. In the 2015 Female Entrepreneurship Index (FEI), which analyzes 77 countries to measure entrepreneurial environment ecosystem and individual aspirations on a scale of 0 to 100, Israel ranked 34, and is among the countries that scored in the middle on 23 gender-specific variables with a score of 47.6. Among the thousands of hi-tech start-ups that mushroomed during the 1990s, only a very small portion – less than 2 percent – were set up by women alone or in conjunction with others (Rosen-Genut, 2001).

Country legislation

Since the 1950s, Israel has been among the leading states in granting special protection to working women, and especially to working mothers. The issue of granting equal opportunity, beyond mere formal equality, however, is a more recent one that emerged only in the mid-1980s when women's groups called for legislation that would add protective measures to the concept of equal opportunity (Raday, 1995).

The 1988 Equal Opportunities in Employment Law combined the demand for formal equality with the recognition of the legitimacy of different provisions for men and women on the basis of biological differences and stipulated that such provisions do not constitute discrimination. Furthermore, the law put the onus of proof on the employer that s/he did not discriminate among employees or persons seeking employment on account of their sex or personal status in acceptance of employment, terms of employment, advancement, vocational training, or dismissal. The law also recognized sexual harassment as a form of prejudice. A 2004 amendment to this law protects pregnant women against discrimination in employment.

The 2000 amendment to the Women's Equal Rights Law (1951) was a key legislative development (Halperin-Kaddari, 2004). It requires that affirmative action measures be taken to ensure equality in areas that include housing, employment, health, and welfare. In 2005, the Law was amended again, making mandatory appropriate representation for women in all public bodies that determine national policy.

In 1995 the Knesset passed the Equal Pay Act which replaced earlier laws and requires equal pay and other remuneration for essentially equal, equivalent work, or work of comparable worth performed for the same employer in the same workplace. The Knesset's readiness to promote equal rights for women, however, stopped short of providing budgets required for their effective implementation. There are no agencies responsible for implementation and there have been relatively few cases of discrimination claims taken to court. The Equal Employment Opportunity Commission was only set up in 2008, its goals being to ensure equality at work and to generate public awareness regarding the importance of equality. Moreover, for the first time in Israel, there is now a governmental agency that has the authority to file civil suits in cases pertaining to discrimination at work.

In recent decades, the Supreme Court acting in its capacity as the High Court of Justice has had a powerful impact on establishing the principle of gender equality (Ziv, 1999). Its impact on the ground, however, has been curtailed by resistance to the principle of equality. In 1998, despite the Supreme Court ruling obligating the minister of work and welfare to search for a suitable female candidate for the position of associate director of the National Insurance Institute where all nine associate directors were men, the minister gave the job to a man from his political party. Similarly, in April 2009, the Supreme Court determined that the prime minister had to re-evaluate the pool of candidates for the position of the director general of the Anti-Drug Authority because his decision did not incorporate the principle of equal representation. Unfortunately, the male candidate was chosen once again.

Maternal rights such as the 14-week maternity leave with full pay covered by the National Social Security Institute have been transformed into parental rights (for fathers as well as mothers) while preserving the mother's privileged position. Men are entitled to share maternity leave with their spouse, starting from the seventh week after birth, as long as the mother is entitled to maternity leave and has chosen to shorten it and return to work. However, only several hundred fathers have availed themselves of this right to date.

Upon return from maternity leave, mothers can choose between public and private childcare options. The state subsidizes a national network of childcare services run by three large women's organizations, where cost is proportional to income. In addition, municipalities support childcare services and there are privately run kindergartens. According to the Compulsory Education Law 1949, children and youth, ages 3 to 17, have the right to free education. Although complete implementation of free education for children ages three to four has been deferred for budgetary reasons, as a result of the 2011 social protests education is now free from the age of three. The short school day enforced in Israel, in which first grade ends at noon and only extends slightly during the remainder of primary school, is a major constraint for women pursuing managerial careers.

Initiatives supporting women in the workforce and wider society

Two different kinds of initiatives to support the advancement of women have been taken: official initiatives sponsored by the government, and grassroots initiatives sponsored by individual feminists or women's organizations. The most significant government-sponsored body is the Knesset Committee for the Advancement of the Status of Women, established in 1992 and granted the status of permanent Knesset Committee in 1996. In August 2015, a new ministry was created, the Ministry for Social Equality, which will be responsible among other issues for gender and minority equality.

In addition, a narrower mechanism, the prime minister's adviser on the status of women, has operated since the early 1980s. The PM's adviser coordinates local advisers on the status of women in the municipalities and the local authorities. Although these advisers do not have a large budget and their power is limited, they represent many cities, towns, and regions in Israel and are able to form a country-wide network of over 230 advisers that can advance change within their organizations and in society as a whole. Furthermore, following hard work of grassroots women's organizations, the Israeli government announced that it is establishing a team to formulate a working plan to advance UN Resolution 1325 in Israel. This resolution calls for women's equal inclusion in all aspects of government decision making, especially around issues of peace and security (Heinrich Böll Foundation, 2015).

The Department for the Advancement of Women within the Civil Service, established in 1996, serves as an address for complaints from women, sponsors educational programs, and regularly collects and disseminates statistics on women's representation in the civil service. This department attempts to impact the different ministries by having a representative in each ministry who takes on an extra role as the adviser for the advancement of women in addition to her other professional duties. Here also a network of about 70 representatives has been formed that connects all the ministries and serves as a platform for actions that can lead to the advancement of women in the civil service. However, due to low funding and power resources, their influence is somewhat limited. Recently, there was a change in regulations and the women previously called the "representatives for women's advancement" were named "the representatives of gender equality." This is not merely a change in terminology, it also implies a change in role, authority, and strategy, suggesting that these representatives are now expected to hold events and training programs with both men and women, in order to advance gender equality. Furthermore, the representatives were instructed to change the "day for women" held in the ministries once a year to the "day for gender equality." A recent research report was published on the change in the role of the supervisor of the status of women in government ministries which traces the transition from a perspective of "equal opportunity" to a perspective of "gender mainstreaming" (for more see Steinberg, 2013).

The earliest private initiatives to promote the advancement of women include the establishment of the Senior Women Executive Forum within the Israel Management Center

(1986), and courses for training women in management (1988) and future women directors (1993). Towards the end of the 1980s forums were set up to enable women to acquire the "tricks of the trade" to become managers, entrepreneurs, or company directors. These forums emphasize personal transformation, skill acquisition, and networking among women as means to achieve goals and become independent and economically successful women. Although quite successful, these types of programs have been dubbed "fix the women" programs (for example, Ely and Meyerson, 2000; Kark, 2004), since they focus on changing and "fixing" women and not on changing society or the system. Thus, while resisting the male monopoly of the business world, these women's organizations do not challenge the gender structure of power within it. Currently there are many initiatives that have changed their focus and are aiming to challenge the wider status quo and affect the wider society, as well as organizations as a whole.

One such initiative is the "Equal Pay" initiative. Equal Pay is a three-year project that is activated as a collaboration between three non-governmental organizations (Shatil, Israel Women's' Network, the Adva Research Center, and the Equal Opportunities Commissioner), and is funded by the European Union. On average, women in Israel earn 30 percent less than men, in every sector and in every profession. Although the workforce consists of nearly 50 percent of women, the pay gaps are not decreasing. The goal of the project is to eliminate pay inequality by raising public awareness, providing workers and employers with knowledge and tools for action, and mobilizing decision makers towards more policy action. This initiative developed a novel tool: "the gender wage gap calculator," a computerized tool that allows employers to analyze salaries and benefits according to gender. Most recently, the Israel Women's Network hosted a conference at the Knesset on pay confidentiality and its impact on the wage gap (Israel Women's Network, n.d.).

Another notable recent initiative is the foundation of the Center for the Advancement of Women in the Public Sphere (WIPS), which was established at the Van Leer Jerusalem Institute in 2009. This center is committed to the idea of gender mainstreaming as an overall strategy for promoting gender equality in Israel. The center aims to advance the democratic and civil status of women from diverse social groups. Their perspective is transformational, by shifting the focus from understating gender inequality as a "women's issue," to viewing it as a wider social interest that relates to both men and women and to wider social structures at different levels and fields (e.g., legislators and decision makers). Some of the reports provided by this center include *The Gender Index: Gender Inequality in Israel* (Tzameret-Kertcher *et al.*, 2015), which provides an innovative tool to evaluate gender inequality in Israel across a spectrum of fields over time, thus allowing for an estimate of the depth of gender inequality and enabling a comparison between different domains of inequality (see www.vanleer.org.il/en/wips). These recent works demonstrate the changing perspectives in Israeli society towards ways in which women can advance into management positions due to changes in the wider organizational systems and social structure.

In the private sector, some companies have initiated "family-friendly" policies or programs to advance women. Those that have mainly permit flexible starting and ending times to accommodate working parents and mothers who have young children or are breastfeeding. For example, about 60 percent of the 103 organizations in the public and private sector whose human-resources professionals participated in an Internet-based survey, granted at least one flexible work arrangement, mostly flexible starting and ending times, and occasional work from home. However, most of the respondents also said that their organization expects them to always be available (Waismel-Manor *et al.*, 2015). There are quite a few recent novel initiatives in private sector organizations that aim to lead to higher levels of diversity and to the representation of women in elite positions. Several organizations have decided on quotas for women in management positions and have framed this as an organizational and managerial aim to be achieved. In order to do so they are initiating internal advocacy processes as well as specific training programs. For example, one of the firms that is taking a lead in this process is the Strauss Group, led by a woman chairperson of the board and by a male chief executive officer (CEO) (for their diversity and inclusion policy see www.strauss-group.com/sustainability/our-employees/diversit-and-inclusion/).

There have also been substantial actions taken by the grassroot women's organizations to advance women to management positions as well as actions taken by universities. Most of the universities in Israel have opened gender studies programs (for undergraduate and graduate students) in the last few years. One such interesting program is the Master's "Gender in the Field Track: Translating Feminist Theory into Social Action" (GIFT), which was established in 2005 within Bar-Ilan University's Graduate Gender Studies Program. The first and only program of its kind in Israel, it integrates two main bodies of knowledge: feminist theory and experiential knowledge from feminist activism, accumulated in local and global contexts. The GIFT programs' goal is to nurture feminist leaders who promote meaningful social change in different domains in Israeli society within non-government organizations as well as the public and private sectors. It does so by mentoring students to understand how theory and knowledge accumulated from academia and from thought and action in the field inform one another (see Kark *et al.*, 2016). The students that graduate from this program, as well as from the other recently founded gender programs in the different universities, acquire knowledge and tools to lead change in their varied workplaces, as well as lead change in lobbying, advocacy, education, legislation, and other means to bring about change.

Thus, the different programs run by feminist grassroots organizations in conjunction with their lobbying and legislation efforts have been fruitful in pushing the agenda of women's leadership in Israel and in providing political visibility. However, their ability to reshape the existing situation is restricted and is based on the strategy of small wins.

The future

Several years ago we suggested that Israeli women's opportunities and representation in management can be seen as a "paradox of duality," which reflects the characteristics of Israeli society. This duality is evident in the accumulation of disadvantages to women's advancement in management, but also to advantages and privileges working women attain (and mostly working mothers), which are not always apparent in other countries and contexts (Kark and Waismel-Manor, 2011). One of the most salient of these is the possibility to combine motherhood with a professional and managerial career, without being forced to give up one of these worlds. This paradox reflects the unique Israeli context as a country in the Middle East operating in a turbulent political, economic, and military environment, with strong ties nevertheless to the Western world and its norms. This duality is even sharper for various subgroups in Israeli society (for example, Arab women living in Israel, Ultra-Orthodox Jewish women, and so on). Individual women continue to excel and gain access to more senior positions, and for the majority of aspiring women the near future looks more promising than it did in previous years.

Note

1 Figures only include citizens of Israel and exclude foreign workers (legal and illegal) and Palestinian labor.

References

Authority for the Advancement of the Status of Women (n.d.) www.women.gov.il/MA/yetzug/ yetzug1/, accessed 2 August, 2009. In Hebrew.
Central Bureau of Statistics (2001) *Israeli Labor Force Survey*. Central Bureau of Statistics. In Hebrew.
Central Bureau of Statistics (2008) *Israeli Labor Force Survey*. Central Bureau of Statistics. In Hebrew.
Central Bureau of Statistics (2011) *Israeli Labor Force Survey*. Central Bureau of Statistics. In Hebrew.
Central Bureau of Statistics (2014) *Statistical Abstract of Israel*, no. 64. Central Bureau of Statistics.
Central Bureau of Statistics (2015a) *Selected Data from the 2013 Social Survey about employment, press release*, www.cbs.gov.il/reader/newhodaot/hodaa_template.html?hodaa=201519008, accessed November 10, 2015. In Hebrew.
Central Bureau of Statistics (2015b) *International Women's Day 2015 press release*, www.cbs.gov.il/reader/ newhodaot/hodaa_template.html?hodaa=201511057, accessed November 10, 2015. In Hebrew.
Central Bureau of Statistics *Israeli Labor Force Surveys Quarterly* (2015c) www.cbs.gov.il/webpub/ pub/text_page_eng. html?publ=69, accessed December 17, 2015.
Civil Service Commission (2014) *Committee's report for the advancement of women in civil service*, www.csc.gov.il/DataBases/Hozrim/Pages/naziv5-2014.aspx, accessed October 10, 2015.
Council for Higher Education (2014) The Higher Education in Israel, 2014. Planning and Budgeting Committee, http://che.org.il/wp-content/uploads/2014/05/%D7%9E%D7%A2%D7%A8% D7% 9B%D7%AA-%D7%94%D7%94%D7%A9%D7%9B%D7%9C%D7%94-%D7%94%D7%92%D7% 91%D7%95%D7%94%D7%94-%D7%91%D7%99%D7%A9%D7%A8%D7%90%D7%9C-2014.pdf, accessed December 13, 2015.
Council for Higher Education (2015) Committee's report for the advancement and representation of women in higher education, 2015, http://che.org.il/wp-content/uploads/2015/07/%D7% 93%D7%95%D7%97-%D7%99%D7%99%D7%A6%D7%95%D7%92-%D7%A0%D7%A9%D7% 99%D7%9D.pdf, accessed December 13, 2015. In Hebrew.
Dun & Bradstreet Israel (2009) *D&B Report Shows Minor Improvement in Women's Representation in Managerial Positions*, http://dundb.co.il/NewsShowHeb1.asp?idnum=453, accessed August 2, 2009. In Hebrew.
Ely, R. J. and Meyerson, D. E. (2000) Theories of gender in organizations: a new approach to organizational analysis and change, *Research in Organizational Behavior*, 22, 103–151.
Fogiel-Bijaoui, S. (2002) Familism, postmodernity and the state: the case of Israel, *The Journal of Israeli History*, 21(1–2), 38–62.
Frenkel, M. (2006) *Reprogramming Femininity: Gender Performance in the Israeli Hi-tech Industry between Global and Local Gender Orders*, Working Paper, Jerusalem, The Hebrew University
Haim, E. B. and Shavit, Y. (2013) Expansion and inequality of educational opportunity: a comparative study, *Research in Social Stratification and Mobility*, 31, 22–31.
Halperin-Kaddari, R. (2004) *Women in Israel: A State of Their Own* (Philadelphia, PA: Pennsylvania University Press).
Heinrich Böll Foundation (2015) *More Women Making Decisions in Israel*, https://il.boell. org/en/2015/01/06/more-women-making-decisions-israel, accessed December 10, 2015.
Herzog, H. (1999) *Gendering Politics: Women in Israel* (Ann Arbor, MI: University of Michigan Press).
High Court of Justice (1994) 453/94, 454/94, Israel Women's Network v. Government of Israel *et al.*, PD (5) 501. In Hebrew.
Israel Defense Forces (n.d.a) *International Women's Day: Facts You Need to Know About Women in the IDF*. www.idfblog.com/blog/2014/03/07/international-womens-day-facts-need-know-women-idf/, accessed December 13, 2015. In Hebrew.
Israel Defense Forces (n.d.b) Women of the IDF. www.idf.il/1589-en/Dover.aspx, accessed December 13, 2015. In Hebrew.
Israel Small and Medium Enterprises Authority (n.d.) www.asakim.org.il/english.php? pageid=0>, accessed August 12, 2009. In Hebrew.
Israel Women's Network (2015) Catalyst Census in Israel, www.iwn.org.il/site/upload/photos/ 143808825362415862a.pdf, accessed July 22, 2015.

Israel Women's Network (n.d.) *Our activities*, www.iwn.org.il/pages/our-activities, accessed December 13, 2015.

Izraeli, D. N. (2004) Women in management in Israel. In M. Davidson and R. J. Burke (eds) *Women in Management Worldwide: Facts, Figures and Analysis* (Burlington, VT: Ashgate Publishing Limited, pp. 294–310).

Izraeli, D. N. and Hillel, R. (2000) *Women's Representation in Boards of Government-owned Companies: 1993–97,* Unpublished Report, Ramat Gan: Bar-Ilan University. In Hebrew.

Kark, R. (2004) The transformational leader: who is (s)he? A Feminist perspective, *Journal of Organization Change Management,* Special issue on Transformational Leadership Research: Issues and Implications, 17(2), 160–176.

Kark, R. (2007) Women in the land of milk, honey and hi-technology: The Israeli case. In R. J. Burke and M. Mattis (eds), *Women and Minorities in Science, Technology, Engineering and Mathematics: Opening the Pipeline* (New York, NY: Edward Elgar, pp. 152–191).

Kark, R. and Eagly, A. (2010) Gender and leadership: Negotiating the labyrinth. In J. Chrisler and D. R. McCreary (eds), *Handbook of Gender Research and Psychology* (New York, NY: Springer, pp. 443–468).

Kark R. and Waismel-Manor, R. (2011) Women in Management in Israel. In M. J Davidson and R. J Burke (eds), *Women in Management Worldwide: Progress and Prospects (2nd edition)* (Aldershot: Gower Publishing).

Kark, R., Preser, R. and Zion-Waldoks (2016) From a politics of dilemmas to a politics of paradoxes: Feminism, pedagogy, and women's leadership for social change, *Journal of Management Education*, 40(3): 293–320.

Mandel, H. and Semyonov, M. (2006) The welfare state paradox: a comparative analysis of welfare-state policies and women's employment opportunities in 20 countries, *American Journal of Sociology,* 111 (6), 1910–1949.

Menipaz, E., Avrahami, Y. and Lerner, M. (2013) *National Report for Israel by the Global Entrepreneurship Monitor.* www.gemconsortium.org/country-profile/73, accessed October 7, 2015.

Ministry of Finance (2015) *Budget proposal*, www.mof.gov.il/BudgetSite/statebudget/BUDGET 2015_2016/MINISTERIESBUDGET/MinisteriesBudget/DocLib/Ozar_Prop.pdf, accessed October 10, 2015.

Okun, B. S., Oliver, A. L. and Khiat-Marelli, O. (2007) The public sector, family structure, and labor market behavior: Jewish mothers in Israel, *Work and Occupations*, 34(2), 174–204.

Parnet, T. (2009) Women in management survey, *Calcalist*, 5 March. In Hebrew.

Raday, F. (1995) Women in the labor market. In F. Raday, C. Shalev and M. Liban-Kobi (eds), *The Status of Women in Society and Law* (Tel Aviv, Israel: Shoken).

Reches, E. and Rodintzki, A. (2009) *The Arab Society in Israel,* The Abraham Fund Initiatives, Israel.

Remennick, L. (2006) The quest for the perfect baby; why do Israeli women seek prenatal genetic testing? *Sociology of Health and Illness*, 28(1), 21–53.

Rosen-Genut, A. (2001) Difficult to be a woman manager, *Status,* 24–26. In Hebrew.

Statistilite (2009) Women and Men in Israel (2009), no. 89, www.cbs.gov.il/www/statistical/ mw2008_h.pdf, accessed August 1, 2009. In Hebrew.

Steinberg, P. (2013) *From Equal Opportunity to a Perspective of Gender Mainstreaming: Transformations in the Role of the Representative for Women's Advancement Within the Ministries.* WIPS: The Van Leer Jerusalem Institute. In Hebrew.

Stier, H. and Herzberg, H. (2013) Women in the labor force: The impact of education on employment patterns and wages. In D. Ben-David (ed.), *State of the Nation Report – Society, Economy and Policy 2013.* Taub Center for Social Policy Studies in Israel. In Hebrew.

Stier, H. and Yaish, M. (2008) The determinants of women's employment dynamics: the case of Israeli women, *European Sociological Review*, 24, 363–377.

Treas, J. and Widmer, E. D. (2000) Married women's employment over the life course: attitudes in cross-national perspective, *Social Forces,* 78(4), 1409–1436.

Tzameret-Kertcher, H. (2014) *The Gender Index: Gender Inequality in Israel.* WIPS: The Van Leer Jerusalem Institute.

Tzameret-Kertcher, H., Herzog, H. and Chazan, N. (2015) *The Gender Index: Gender Inequality in Israel.* WIPS: The Van Leer Jerusalem Institute. In Hebrew.

Waismel-Manor, R., Rabenu, E. and Kaminka, S. (2015) *Flexible Employment Arrangements Survey.* Unpublished report, Netanya: Netanya Academic College. In Hebrew.

Yaish, M. and Kraus, V. (2003) The consequences of economic restructuring for the gender earnings gap, *Work Employment and Society*, 17(1), 5–28.

Yonay, Y. P., Yaish, M. and Kraus, V. (2015) Religious heterogeneity and cultural diffusion: The impact of Christian neighbors on Muslim and Druze women's participation in the labor force in Israel, *Sociology*, 49(4), 660–678.

Ziv, N. (1999) The disability law in Israel and the United States: a comparative perspective, *Israel Yearbook of Human Rights*, 28, 171–202.

20 Women in management in Saudi Arabia

Jouharah M. Abalkhail

Introduction

Saudi Arabia is the cradle of Islam, as it contains the holiest of sites within Islam and it is the location of the world's largest pilgrimage (the *hajj*) (Pharaon, 2004). It is also a country that has the largest proven oil reserves in the world, estimated at over 264 billion barrels, or 21 per cent of the world's total reserves (SAMIRAD, 2011). It has been characterized as a 'rentier state' which prospered almost exclusively from the rents received from the extraction and export of petroleum reserves (Al-Rasheed, 2010). The country views itself as the guardian of pure authentic Islam and it is governed according to Islamic law (*Sharia* law). At the same time it is a country in transition: a country in which successful economic growth has certainly changed its demographic and social structure. Since the 1970s, aided by its oil revenues, the Kingdom has undergone rapid development in many areas such as industry, education, transportation, health, social services and business. This rapid advancement of Saudi Arabia has provided more employment opportunities for men and women (Al-Khateep, 2007; MEP, 2014). This trend has gained further impetus from the government's commitment to ensuring that the Kingdom takes its place amongst the developed nations of the world; the desire to reduce dependence on foreign workers; and accession to the World Trade Organization (Budhwar and Mellahi, 2006). In this situation, the government has recognized that the key to the nation's further development lies in its human resources, and that women constitute a source of untapped potential.

In recent years, the education of women has undergone enormous and rapid expansion at all stages as a result of the Saudi government's generous public spending on education (World Economic Forum, 2014). The gender gap in education is narrowing at all levels (World Economic Forum, 2014). Women's participation in the labour force has also marked a major change in their traditional role in Saudi society. Increased economic resources and the availability of free education along with the continuous processes of urbanization and modernization have helped to create more job opportunities for women in both the private and public sectors (Al-Khateep, 2007; AlMunajjed, 1997; Al-Rasheed, 2010). However, women managers are grossly under-represented in Saudi Arabia organizations at all levels of management (Abalkhail, 2012). Generally, to date it seems that there is limited research on women in management in the Arab world (e.g. Jamali, *et al.*, 2005; Karam and Afiouni, 2014; Metcalfe, 2011; Mostafa, 2005; Singh, 2008; Tlaiss and Kauser, 2011), and this is specifically the case in relation to Saudi Arabia (e.g. Abalkhail and Allan, 2015; Abalkhail, 2012; Karam and Afiouni, 2014). Drawing on these studies, this chapter aims to look at the broader picture of Saudi women in education, in the labour force, in management and their entrepreneurial activities. It then examines legislation supporting women in management and current initiatives supporting employed women. The chapter concludes by exploring future avenues for the progress of women in the workplace.

Women in education

The oil boom of the early 1970s provided the means for Saudi Arabia to develop a broader economic and national infrastructure, which in turn, necessitated and generated desire for improvement in education (Al-Rasheed, 2010; Champion, 2003). In Saudi Arabia, formal education for boys began in the 1930s and for girls it began in the 1960s when King Faysal promoted female education (AlMunajjed, 1997). Boys and girls are in separate schools taught by teachers of their own sex, at all levels after kindergarten. Girls' and women's education at all levels – elementary, secondary, high school and some colleges – was under the Department of Religious Guidance until 2002, while the education of boys was supervised by the Ministry of Education (Hamdan, 2005). When it first began, women's education was under a different department in order to ensure that it conformed to its original purpose. The role of education was to make women good wives and mothers, and to prepare them for jobs such as teaching and nursing, which were believed to suit their nature (Hamdan, 2005). However, although education for both girls and boys is overseen by the Ministry of Education at the present time, the school curricula have not changed much (Hamdan, 2005).

The various five-year development plans in Saudi Arabia from 1970 to 2009 have increased the number of students (boys and girls) at all stages. For example, during the 1950s, there were only three secondary schools for boys in the country and the number of students was 54,000, whereas from 1970 to 1992 the total number of students in all stages rose from 547,000 to 2.9 million (MEP, 2014). In 2003, the number of government and private schools, apart from kindergartens, stood at 24,000, covering all geographic regions (2000–2004) (MEP, 2014). By 2010, the education system had dramatically improved, as a direct result of the government's generous public spending on education (MEP, 2014). The Saudi government has managed almost to close the gender gap in primary (84 per cent female and 85 per cent male) and secondary (76 per cent female and 70 per cent male) education. As in secondary, female students in higher education outnumber males (37 per cent and 23 per cent respectively) (see Table 20.1) (World Economic Forum, 2014). The literacy rate for Saudi women was reported at 80 per cent and for men at 90 per cent in 2009 (World Economic Forum, 2014).

This investment has significantly changed the supply, quality and profile of the labour force, especially for women (world Bank, 2014). In this sense, when compared with other countries of the Arab World, Saudi Arabia has been far more successful in closing the gender gap in education. Governments of the Arab world spend an average of 5.3 per cent of gross domestic product (GDP) on education, which is considered the highest in the world; however, gender gaps have been closed only in primary and secondary education in most Arab countries (World Bank, 2014).

Table 20.1 Gender gap in education attainment in Saudi Arabia

Education attainment	Female (%)	Male (%)	Female-to-male ratio
Literacy	80	90	0.90
Enrolment in primary education	84	85	0.99
Enrolment in secondary education	76	70	1.08
Enrolment in tertiary education	37	23	1.65

Source: World Economic Forum (2014)

The higher education sector comprises 21 government universities, three of which were established under the Seventh Development Plan (2000–2004) (MEP, 2014). The higher education institutions absorb about 57 per cent of all secondary school graduates. The total number of graduates at bachelor level during the first four years of the Seventh Development Plan stood at more than 199,000 students, of whom 66 per cent were female (MEP, 2014). Hence, the enrolment rates of girls and women at all educational levels have increased sharply, despite the relatively late start in female education. The average annual rate of increase in total female enrolment was 8 per cent during the period 1975–2002, compared to about 4.2 per cent for boys. Thus the gender gap in enrolment was closed at the primary level in 2003 and at secondary and university levels in 2002 (MEP, 2014). One significant achievement in this respect is that the gender ratio in enrolment in higher education institutions has now shifted in favour of females, to the tune of 1:1.4 in 2002, which could mean that between 2004 and 2020, there will be twice as many female college graduates as male (World Bank, 2005).

Education has a tremendous impact on both men and women; nevertheless it seems that the impact on women is greater. Mernissi (1993) argued that access to education seems to have an immediate and tremendous impact on women's perception of themselves, their reproductive and sexual roles, and their social mobility expectations. Supporting this argument, Al-Lamki (1999) reported that the primary indicator of women's status in a given society is their access to education and, as a result, it is the root of women's emancipation. For example, Saudi women are now marrying later in order to complete their education and their attitude toward marital relationships has changed to one based on sharing decisions (Al-Khateep, 2007).

Nevertheless, the education system has faced some difficulties recently. For example, in 2002, the total number of female higher education graduates (diplomas, graduate and post-graduate degrees) was 40,919, of whom 32,201 specialized in education and 3,162 in humanities; i.e., the two groups together accounted for 86 per cent of graduates (MEP, 2014). This is because women are not allowed to study certain disciplines such as political science or engineering. This practice contrasts with countries such as the UK in which law and policy do not prohibit women's entry to any discipline. Nevertheless, even in countries such as these, in practice education is experienced largely on gendered lines (Simpson *et al.*, 2004). For example, engineering faculties are still dominated by men, whereas nursing is still a predominately female discipline. In Saudi Arabia the concentration of women in certain areas of specialization does not help them to participate in economic activity because women are restricted to employment in government institutions, and in the education or health sectors. Thus, there is a mismatch between the needs of the labour market and the modern economy and the subject specializations of higher education students, which is particularly acute in the case of women (MEP, 2014). The Saudi government is well aware of this problem and its Eighth Development Plan aims to increase and widen the scope of women's specializations in higher education to enable them to play a more effective and diversified role in society and in economic activities (MEP, 2014).

Women in the labour force

The participation of Saudi women in the labour force is representative of a major change in women's traditional role in society; therefore it is important to give a very brief history of what has contributed to Saudi women's entrance to employment. During the early Islamic era, women were given the right to engage in public life and were very active members of society. Women worked in a variety of fields such as trade, education and politics (Mernissi, 2004).

After political divisions started in the period following Prophet Mohammed's death in 632 AD, women became less active in public spheres (Mernissi, 2004) such as the battlefield, the mosque and other social activities (Ahmed, 1992). Nevertheless during the eleventh to fifteenth centuries some elite women took part in politics and were active members in military campaigns and some of them took charge in directing state affairs (Afshar, 2006). Also, even with the existence of a system of segregation between men and women, some women managed to work within a female-only space, for example, reciting the Qur'an, or as midwives, bakers or female spies (Ahmed, 1992). From the fifteenth to the early nineteenth centuries, the lives of women seem to have been similar with respect to the degree and nature of their involvement in economic activities (Ahmed, 1992).

In the early nineteenth century, Arab societies began to undergo a fundamental social change, although in each country the pace of change differed. The social-economic and political transformations were the result of 'Western economic encroachment and domination in the nineteenth century, the response within the Middle Eastern countries. The economic and social changes that occurred were multileveled and intricate, as were the emergence and evaluation of the debate on women' (Ahmed, 1992: 127). The outcome of these factors was broadly positive because the social institutions and mechanisms that controlled women and kept them secluded and marginalized from the major spheres of activity were gradually dismantled (Ahmad, 1992).

In the early nineteenth century one development of unusual significance to women was their emergence as a central subject for national debate. This increased visibility was a consequence of the writing of Muslim male intellectuals, mainly in Egypt. For example, in *Tahrir Al-Mar'a* (The Liberation of Woman) published in 1899, Qasim Amin (1863–1908) called for women to be liberated from tradition and he insisted on equal civil rights for women and men (Ahmed, 1992, 2011). His reform programme was a turning point in how the problems of Arab women were perceived. The programme opened up the prospect of addressing women's subordination at all levels of Arab society (Ahmed, 2011). Amin's work has traditionally been regarded as marking the beginning of feminism in Arab culture (Ahmed, 2011). The Arab feminist movement was born in the early twentieth century. The most famous feminist was Huda Sha'rawi, founder of the Egyptian Feminist Union in 1923. Her movement impacted on other women in other Arab countries such as Nawal El-Saadawi and Fatima Mernissi (Ahmed, 1992; UNDP, 2005).

In the second half of the twentieth century, the role of women in Arab countries underwent an enormous change and transformation. The various state-led legal reforms in many Arab countries recognized the importance of women's development socially and economically. These reforms provided women with a wide range of rights and opportunities that allowed them to enter all fields and most professional work, including politics and business (Moghadam, 2004; Sidani, 2005), though not as judges or heads of state (Ahmed, 1992). In recent times access to education and employment has acquired the status of a fundamental right for all people in the Arab world (World Bank, 2005).

These significant changes in Arab societies were as important for women as they were for men and they have greatly influenced the Saudi government in its efforts to integrate women into the human resources development plans for the country (Al-Khateep, 2007; AlMunajjed, 1997). Economic resources combined with the continuous process of urbanization and modernization have enabled the Saudi government to play a major role in encouraging female employment through various initiatives, although the right of women to work was highly debated in Saudi society throughout the late 1970s and early 1980s. Attitudes ranged from extreme conservatism, which views the only appropriate role for women as that of wife and mothers, and the liberal view that insists on the emancipation of women to play an important role in the economy (AlMunajjed, 1997). The Saudi government has opened new employment opportunities for women and increased their number in economic activities in the five-year development plans. For example, the Sixth Development Plan (1995–1999) and Seventh Development Plan (2000–2004) aimed to increase the participation of women in employment within the framework of Islamic values and teachings (MEP, 2014). Nevertheless, the Eighth Development Plan (2005–2009) and Ninth Development Plan (2010–2014) seem to be the most important in terms of focusing on raising skill levels and developing women's capacity and improving women's position in society. It has a chapter dedicated to 'Women in Development', which aims to enhance the status of women by ensuring their participation in economic and social development. In addition, the recent development plan was intended to increase and diversify job opportunities for Saudi women. On 31 May 2004 the Council of Ministers approved a package of regulations and measures to enhance women's participation in economic activity (MEP, 2014). The implementation of this package will undoubtedly help to achieve the third of the Millennium Development Goals (MDGs), which is to improve the status of women through expanding opportunities in education, health and employment, thereby promoting gender equality and empowering women (MEP, 2014; UNDP, 2006).

Women in Saudi Arabia have been given the opportunity to work in both the public and private sectors. However, they are found predominantly in the public sector (96 per cent), and only in certain fields: education (85.8 per cent), health (6.1 per cent) and social work (4.4 per cent) (MCS, 2014a). The public sector has been the best available option for Saudi women, since it offers job opportunities in the fields of women's educational specialisms, and it exercises a sound policy of equal employment opportunities. There are a number of women who are accountants, lawyers, human resource (HR) managers and doctors. But the available statistics are only for doctors and nurses (see Table 20.2).

With regard to the subject of law for females, it is essential to know that the first law colleges for girls opened at King Saud University in 2006, at Taibah University in 2013, and at Sattam bin Abdulaziz University in 2015. The number of women students of law reached 3,222 in 2013 (Ministry of Higher Education, 2013). Saudi women who graduated from law school were previously employed as legal consultants, but were banned from practising law in the courtroom and were not given attorney status. They were also not allowed to own law firms. But later the Ministry of Justice granted Saudi female lawyers licenses to open their own law offices. Conditions to obtain the license are the same for men and women and include a university degree in law and three years of training. In addition, there are some women who have been appointed as HR managers within the public sector, yet these women are under the umbrella of the head office – the men's centre. With regard to doctors and nurses, the field of medicine is open to both male and female equally for study and work (see Table 20.2).

Table 20.2 Saudi females/males working in Ministry of Health hospitals in 2013

Category	Male	Female	Total
Physicians	5,373	2,161	7,534
Nurses	15,485	21,452	36,937
Pharmacists	1,093	1,080	2,173
Allied health professionals	24,848	6,141	30,989
Total	46,799	30,834	77,633

Source: Ministry of Health (2013)

328   *Jouharah M. Abalkhail*

According to the *Arab Human Development Report* (UNDP, 2009), the participation of women in economic activities in Saudi Arabia is very low, despite the narrowing gender gap in education between men and women and despite the increased level of female participation in employment. Table 20.3 therein shows that in Saudi Arabia female participation in the labour force is estimated to constitute less than 19 per cent and men 81 per cent of the total labour force (World Economic Forum, 2014). In addition, a woman's average earned income is less than a man's (PPP[1] US$19,763 and $40,000 respectively), and the gender pay gap between men's and women's salaries is 56 per cent (World Economic Forum, 2014), even though Saudi labour law prescribes wage equality for similar work (MCS, 2014b). Moreover, unemployment rates among men and women in Saudi Arabia, as in other Arab countries, are very high. However, the rate of unemployment in Saudi Arabia in 2014 is higher for women (13 per cent) than for men (4 per cent) (World Economic Forum, 2014). Thus the gender gap in economic participation and opportunity in Saudi Arabia is very large. The Global Gender Gap Index in 2014 ranked Saudi Arabia 130 out of 142 countries in terms of the gender gap in economic participation and opportunity (World Economic Forum, 2014).

Women in management

As shown above, in the last 20 years, there have been major and significant changes for women in Saudi Arabia. Women are now highly educated; they have entered the workforce and gained professional positions. Women have become visible in some managerial jobs and a very few of them have been moving up through organizational hierarchies (Abalkhail, 2012). Within the public sector, there are a number of women occupying different managerial positions such as director general, director of programming, head of college, head of department, research director, supervisor and dean at universities. Yet their number is very small and women managers in the workplace are generally supervised and subject to decisions coming from men's institutions. Consequently, they are excluded from decision making and have no access to important information or resources that would improve them professionally (Abalkhail, 2012).

This development is the result of the Saudi government's support through its development plans, particularly in the Ninth Development Plan (2010–2014). In addition, the United Nations Development Programme (UNDP) and the International Labour Organization (ILO) have been involved in gender equality measures. These measures have subsequently been integrated into the policies, programmes and resource allocations within organizations (UNDP, 2008). It can be seen from Table 20.4 that the proportion of women managers in Saudi Arabia is very low (7 per cent) compared to that in other countries, for example in the

Table 20.3 Gender gap in economic participation in Saudi Arabia

Economic participation	Female (%)	Male (%)	Female-to-male ratio
Labour force participation	19	81	0.25
Wage equality for similar work	–	–	56
Estimated annual earned income (PPP US$)	19,763	40,000	0.49
Legislators, senior officials and managers	7	93	0.08
Professional and technical workers	28	72	0.38
Unemployment rate	13	4	–

Source: World Economic Forum (2014)

Table 20.4 Women's share of legislator, senior official and management positions

Country	Women managers (%)
Australia	37
China	17
Egypt	11
Kuwait	14
Norway	31
Saudi Arabia	7
Sweden	32
United Arab Emirates	10
UK	35
USA	43

Source: UNDP (2013)

USA 43 per cent, in Norway 31 per cent and in the UK 35 per cent. In Arab countries, the percentage of women managers is also very low, for example 14 per cent in Kuwait and 11 per cent in Egypt.

However, research on women in management in the Arab world in general and specifically in Saudi Arabia seems to be very limited. Statistics obtained from the Saudi Ministry of Civil Service (MCS, 2014a) seem to be complicated and confusing at some points, since there are different occupational scales in different organizations within the Saudi public sector. Nevertheless, the general feature of employment distribution is that women are concentrated in the middle or at the lower end of the occupational scale, whereas men outnumber women on all occupational scales, particularly at the higher levels, and there are very few women, if any, present at the higher end of the occupational scales.

Moreover, other statistics on Saudi women managers that come from different sources such as the UN, World Bank or ILO tend to vary. Hence, to find out about women's progress in management in Saudi Arabia is difficult, given the absence of longitudinal data on women as managers, along with the variation in statistics on women that come from different sources. Even statistics on women from the UNDP or the World Bank can be confusing, due to different definitions of 'manager' in different countries (Wirth, 2004; World Economic Forum, 2014). Nevertheless, a common trend in these statistics is that the proportion of women as legislators, senior officials and managers in Saudi Arabia is extremely low when compared with that of other women worldwide, as shown in Table 20.4 (World Economic Forum, 2014). In addition, the proportion of women in politics is extremely low, e.g. in parliament 20 per cent, in ministerial positions 0 per cent and head of state 0 per cent, as shown in Table 20.5 (World Economic Forum, 2014).

Apart from labour statistics, very little is known about women in management in Saudi Arabia or in the Arab world generally, as there are few empirical studies. Although women in management have gained considerable attention among Western researchers, these studies have mostly been limited to Western (North American, Western European or Australian) settings and are not necessarily generalizable; and women in different cultural contexts have been given little attention. Yet a few reliable studies on women in management in Arab contexts have emerged recently, for example, in Jordan and Tunisia (Singh, 2008), in Lebanon (Jamali *et al.*, 2005; Tlaiss and Kauser, 2011), in the Gulf Cooperation Council (GCC) (Abalkhail and Allan, 2015; Al-Lamki, 1999; Al-Lamky, 2007; Metcalfe, 2011; Metle, 2002; Mostafa, 2005), and in the Arab Middle East (Karam and Afiouni, 2014).

Table 20.5 Gender gap in political empowerment in Saudi Arabia

Economic participation	Female (%)	Male (%)	Female-to-male ratio
Women in parliament	20	80	25
Women in ministerial positions	0	100	0
Years with female head of state	0	50	0

Source: World Economic Forum (2014)

Women entrepreneurs

Saudi Arabia is one of the best performing rapid-growth economies, particularly in terms of regulatory reforms related to entrepreneurship (World Bank, 2015). The country is aiming to diversify its economy away from its dependence on oil by encouraging entrepreneurs to build a more successful economic base (EY G20, 2013). In 2006, Saudi Arabia made it easier to start a business by simplifying processes at its Ministry of Commerce and cut registration time from 64 days to 39. The Saudi Arabian General Investment Agency (SAGIA) finalized agreements with 17 government agencies to remove impediments and introduce incentives for businesses. SAGIA also launched its 10/10 project, aiming to be among the top ten nations in the world by 2010 (World Bank, 2015). In 2007, Saudi Arabia ranked 13th globally and maintained its position of first place in the region on the ease of doing business, by scrapping the high minimum paid-in capital that used to be $124,464 and the fifth largest minimum capital requirement in the world, equivalent to 1057 per cent per capita income. Since its reform, the total number of businesses registered annually increased by 81 per cent (World Bank, 2015).

The Saudi government has played a crucial role in the social and economic development of the Kingdom, particularly in supporting women to join the workforce and working to the success of small and medium enterprises. This can be seen in the last four development plans, particularly the Ninth Development Plan (2010–2014) (MEP, 2014). Recently the minister of trade and industry granted women the right to participate in elections for the first time as board members of the Jeddah Chamber of Commerce, which has established a special centre for businesswomen to provide services and guidance and facilitate business opportunities for Saudi women. The Khadijah bint Khuwaylid Centre is a professional organization for women belonging to the local Chamber of Commerce in Jeddah (JCCI, 2015). The Centre's vision is to eliminate all obstacles that women face and support their participation in national economic development. This type of support has certainly contributed to the increase of women in Saudi Arabia owning small and medium businesses such as trading, simple manufacturing, nursery and private schools. Women in Saudi Arabia owned about 40 per cent of the Kingdom's real estate assets, 20 per cent of stocks and more than 18 per cent of bank accounts according to the National Commercial Bank in 2006 (Arab News, 2007). The number of commercial licences that were taken by women and registered in their own names in the big Saudi cities like Jeddah and Riyadh has reached more than 3,000 (Arab News, 2007). A study by the Khadija bint Khuwailid Businesswomen's Center at the Jeddah Chamber of Commerce and Industry reported that investment by Saudi businesswomen is, at about SR8 billion, equal to about 21 per cent of total investment (Arab News, 2007). Another supporting programme, the Prince Sultan Fund (PSF), was founded by Prince Mohammed bin Fahd in 2007, in Dammam, to support women's small enterprises nationally; as a financially independent non-profit organization, the fund provides technical and financial support to Saudi females and women's small existing projects (PSF, 2007).

In spite of the various attempts to support women entrepreneurs, challenges still remain. Saudi women are granted the right to control their finances: that is to hold accounts and make their own financial transactions without the intermediary of a husband, father or brother according to Islamic law (Hamad, 2005), yet, in practice, government officials often continue to implement old laws in this area (Alturki and Braswell, 2010). Also, there is only a small number of programmes to develop women's economic status (Danish and Smith, 2012). In addition, women have difficulties in getting financing and bank loans, locating advice and getting business information to develop their businesses (Ahmad, 2011). This explains why the majority of women-owned businesses tend to be small, and work on their own or with family members, relatives and close friends (Ahmad, 2011; Danish and Smith, 2012). What is more, there is a shortage of opportunities for market research and professional development (Arab News, 2007), as well as a lack of business-women associations which would facilitate networking (Sadi and Al-Ghazali, 2010). Furthermore, women in Saudi Arabia often have difficulty in fighting claims to their property, bank accounts and inheritances that emanate from male relatives and husbands. Until recently, Saudi Arabian women were only listed on the identity cards of their father, their husband or male next of kin (AlMunajjed, 2006; Hamad, 2005). What is more and although there are a number of women who are in the position of chief executive officer (CEO) or chair of the board, most companies are likely to be family owned. Lubna Olayan is an example. Most private companies are dominated by males in all their ranks. Females who are working in these big companies are usually working in customer care or sales with almost a zero chance of climbing up the ladder to a senior position (Arab News, 2012).

Country legislation

Saudi Arabia is an Islamic state where law is derived from *Sharia* law, 'a divine law above him and independent of his will' (Al-Rasheed, 2010: 49). Saudi Arabia is based on a monarchical system, which is led by the king and senior members of his family. The parliament, or the Consultative Council, *Majlis Al-Shura*, is ratified by royal decree, and acts in accordance with *Sharia* law.

Saudi labour law protects the rights of every employee, man and woman (MCS, 2014b). This is stated in Article 3: 'Work is the right of every citizen. No one else may exercise such right unless the conditions provided for in this Law are fulfilled. All citizens are equal in the right to work ... and when implementing the provisions of this Law', and in Article 4: 'When implementing the provisions of this Law, the employer and the worker shall adhere to the provisions of Sharia' (MCS, 2014b). Women employed in the public sector in Saudi Arabia formally enjoy the same benefits as their male counterparts in terms of wages, training and promotion (MCS, 2014b). Additionally, there is an entire section in the Saudi Labour Law dedicated to the employment of women. For example, Articles 149–160 clearly indicate the rights and working conditions of Saudi women. Articles 149 and 150 state that women can work in all fields which suit their nature in order to protect them from working in certain places or at certain times: 'Women shall work in all fields suitable to their nature. It is prohibited to employ women in hazardous jobs or industries; women's employment shall be prohibited or restricted under certain terms' and 'Women may not work during a period of night the duration of which is not less than eleven consecutive hours, except in cases determined pursuant to a decision by the Minister'. Articles 151–156 in Saudi Labour Law noticeably exhibit special advantages and support granted to working women in areas such as maternity and widowhood leave entitlements: six weeks paid and fifteen days paid, respectively. Working mothers who return to work while continuing to breastfeed are allowed to leave work an hour early each day for six months to feed their babies (MCS, 2014b). Yet, working women face explicit and implicit discrimination which involves excluding and restricting them from opportunities that would help their career development, mainly by individual interpretations of labour law that reflect cultural norms (Abalkhail, 2012).

Initiatives supporting women in the workforce

Economic wealth has transformed the social as well as the physical face of Saudi Arabia and it has become a more developed and modern state (Champion, 2003). The five-year development plans, first adopted by the Saudi government during the 1970s, have allowed for increasing levels of social change that are benefiting the whole population (Al-Khteep, 2007). For example, the focus in the Sixth (1995–2000), Seventh (2000–2004), Eighth (2005–2009) and Ninth (2010–2014) Development Plans is on the development of national human resources and the Saudiization of jobs. Yet the Ninth Development Plan (2010–2015) seems to mark a very significant change in Saudi Arabia, since the country is among the 189 members of the UN that signed the Millennium Declaration at the millennium summit, which was held by the UN in September 2000. Their aim is to achieve the eight MDGs. These are: to eradicate extreme poverty and hunger; achieve universal primary education; promote gender equality and empower women; reduce child mortality; improve maternal health; combat HIV/AIDS, malaria and other diseases; ensure environmental sustainability; and develop a global partnership for development (MEP, 2014; UNDP, 2006; UNPF, 2003).

The government of Saudi Arabia has been playing a significant role in accelerating social change, not only through the infrastructure of the country (its physical structures and basic social services such as schools and hospitals) but also through addressing the issues that concern the public in the national dialogue centre or Al-hiwar al-watani al-Saudi, established by King Abdullah in 2003. The aim of this centre is to bring together different members of society to discuss the various issues that relate directly to the development of the country. For example, there have been several assemblies regarding national unity and extremism (2003), women (2004), 'we and the other' (2005), education (2006), employment (2008) and health issues (2009 and 2010) (KACND, 2014). In 2004 the third National Dialogue was focused mainly on women's rights and duties. This marked an important step forward in the government's initiative. It involved 70 well-known participants, half of them female, who had reached prominent positions in professional fields such as university professors, physicians or leaders of social or religious foundations and associations. This showed that the Saudi government is aware of the specific challenges women face in society, which need to be discussed within state institutions (KACND, 2014); and is willing to support women's rights and duties and to encourage their full participation in economic activity; and it opened the first co-educational university, despite the protests of some religious authorities (Ali, 2009). Furthermore, in September 2011 King Abdullah of Saudi Arabia announced that women will be allowed to vote and to run in municipal elections (Al Hasni and Al Shaibani, 2011). Moreover, in 2013 King Abdullah issued two royal decrees: 1) granting women 30 seats on the 150-member advisory body; and 2) stating that women must always hold at least 20 per cent of the seats on the council (Aljazeera News, 2013). Thus, under King Abdullah's leadership, the Saudi government has allowed women greater visibility, for example, in education, in economics and in the social domain (Al-Rasheed, 2010).

As well as these efforts by the state, there have been initiatives in the private sector. One example is the large and influential company, Aramco, that has long been a regional leader in hiring women. In 1964 Aramco had only one Saudi woman leader, and in 2015 there were

84 Saudi women leaders. The number of women had risen in Saudi Aramco, yet it was slow. As such in 2010 they set up two initiatives to expand women's participation. One programme, Women in Business, targets younger people starting their careers. The second, Women in Leadership, is for senior employees. In the former, their focus is on the basic soft skills to build character, self-confidence, resilience, tolerance, flexibility, assertiveness and awareness and how to succeed in a male-dominated culture. In other words, the Women in Business programme aims to raise awareness and train women to speak up, to become visible.

The other programme, Women in Leadership, is for more senior women, both Saudis and expats. The programme includes two forums. The first shows participants how to lead themselves by discovering their own leadership style and approach, focusing on questions such as: Where do you get your energy? Who is in your network? What were formative moments in your career? Which strengths did you use to overcome obstacles? The second forum focuses on how to lead *others*. About 60 women have gone through the programme (McKinsey, 2015).

Also, Saudi Aramco launched the initiative 'Wa'ed' to encourage individuals to explore their entrepreneurial potential by providing expert guidance and tools to improve their business (Nieva, 2015). In addition, Saudi Aramco together with GE and Tata Consultancy Services (TCS) launched the first all-female business process services centre in Riyadh. The centre will be staffed by Saudi females with TCS and GE owning 76 per cent and 24 per cent equity in the new venture, which will initially serve Saudi Aramco and GE as anchor clients (TCS, 2013).

The future

It is evident from this chapter that the Saudi government is working toward promoting gender equality and empowering women through its recent development plan, as well as working on achieving the UN's third MDG. Saudi women today enjoy a similar level of education to their male counterparts. Not only that, Saudi women's human capital has exceeded the increase in men's human capital in recent years, to the tune of 1:1.4 in 2002, which could mean that in 2020, there will be twice as many female college graduates as male (World Bank, 2005). Women have participated in economic activities in both public and private sectors. Also, the number of female entrepreneurs has been growing in recent times. Women are now establishing and managing small- and medium-sized businesses, despite significant societal and institutional challenges. Furthermore, women are now holding a number of managerial positions, mainly at lower and medium management levels, due to Saudi labour law that exercises a sound policy of equal employment opportunities (Abalkhail and Allan, 2015).

However, these achievements have not led to a true level of gender equality in Saudi Arabia. Women's career progression is still impaired by a number of forces that preclude women from accessing higher managerial and other positions. The first force is the socio-cultural and traditional values that strongly shape perceptions of what constitutes an appropriate division of labour between the sexes in the family and public spheres within Saudi Arabia (Abalkhail and Allan, 2015; Norris, 2009). The value system within family institutions emphasizes the traditional gender roles of women (e.g. control over women, spatial segregation, veiling, the male breadwinner/female homemaker norm) (Abalkhail and Allan, 2015; Al-Khateep, 2007). Also, the social and cultural values encourage women to leave their jobs and care for their families and spouses when they marry (Abalkhail and Allan, 2015). These fixed traditional gender roles are employed to legitimate gender stereotypes (Mostafa, 2003; World Bank, 2005), which can have a huge effect on the types of work that are considered suitable for women and men (World Bank, 2005).

Also, in Saudi Arabia, despite the legal rhetoric of the labour laws that espouse the need for a greater economic role for women and measures for equal treatment, the culture and structure of the labour market emphasizes gender segregation and gender-based occupations. The idea of gender-segregation is guided by *urf* (custom and *Sharia* law), which reflects the need to 'protect' women from being subjected to sexual harassment, or being a source of *fitna* (temptation), which may create social disorder such as loss of morals and adultery (Mernissi, 2011; Tayeb, 1997); and hence the workplace is segregated to provide a moral work environment (Abalkhail, 2012). Thus, women work in separate places and they are required to wear the veil when in contact with men. Furthermore, occupations are typically gender based. For example, the labour market controls the types of jobs women may undertake, in that women are crowded in 'feminine' sectors and are not allowed to work as judges, or to hold senior leadership positions (Altorki, 2000; MCS, 2014b). Labour market law also controls the hours women may undertake; for example women are not allowed to work at night (MCS, 2014b). Thus, women will find it very difficult to gain access to a predominantly male environment, and their participation, opportunities for job mobility and career advancement to higher levels of management will remain limited, which will influence their socio-economic status, until the labour market is more engendered and addresses women's specific needs (World Bank, 2005).

Furthermore, there is a marked absence of mentoring programmes to facilitate the advancement of women's careers. Women tend to be isolated from their male colleagues, who often control valuable organizational information. Consequently, women managers frequently rely on their families for career support (Abalkhail, 2012; Abalkhail and Allan, 2015). In addition, women tend to gain support from other strong family connections, which help them to gain non-executive positions in organizations. Male family members and their connections play a major role in supporting and helping women to achieve success in the workplace. Thus, without the support of powerful family members, particularly male relatives, Arab women may find it difficult to access information and resources.

The low participation of women in the labour force and in management generally can also be related mainly to the structure of an oil-rich economy that reinforces the traditional value system. Generally speaking, according to Ross (2008) the income growth that comes from oil extraction is often unsuccessful in producing industrialization and thus hinders more equitable gender relations, which in turn diminishes women's role in the workforce and the political sphere. This gender imbalance will limit female opportunities to participate in political life and this, in turn, has an effect on the identities and perceptions of women; it limits access to formal and informal networks, and it means that governments lose their incentive to consider women's interests or to enhance women's status (Abalkhail, 2012).

The shortage of women in top management or in political life is therefore the result of the patriarchal culture and the petroleum patriarchy resource curse, along with the misinterpretation of Islam regarding the status of women, which continue to reinforce traditional values in the workforce and reduce the status of women in organizations. There is also a lack of organizational programmes to support women's careers (Abalkhail and Allan, 2015).

The issue of developing women's careers to break through the 'glass ceiling' (Davidson and Burke, 2011), or to navigate 'the labyrinth' (Eagly and Carli, 2007) in Saudi Arabia is a massive problem that extends beyond women themselves or organizations. Having said this, there are a number of strategies that could be adopted to help women's career progression. The empowerment of women needs to come from strong internal forces able to challenge patriarchal institutions. These strong forces come mainly from policy-makers in the government, who need to acknowledge that changing the male value system in the society needs an intensive programme through different institutions including the workplace, which requires working on changing senior managers' beliefs and perceptions, and the structure and culture of public organizations.

Also, I would suggest 'joined up thinking' between various institutions and researchers. For example, researchers from the leading universities in Saudi Arabia such as King Saud University, the Institute of Public Administration and the Saudi Majlis al-Shura (Consultative Council), should work hand in hand with government leaders to identify the research needed that would inform possible policy and programme initiatives. Likewise, these institutions should work together with leaders from leading private companies like Aramco to share ideas and plan strategy for developing women in management. Furthermore, organizations ought to work with professional associations (lawyers, educators, doctors, HR etc.) to develop ways forward, and to connect with schools of business at different universities to encourage them to recruit more female students, training them to build their confidence. Additionally, researchers within different organizations in Saudi Arabia should collaborate with scholars from other countries to further the research arena on women in management.

Empowering all Saudi women will help them to play an important role in the processes of social and economic transformation of the country. Thus, their visible presence in senior management will gradually create their own space in the conservative public sphere. Along with these, organizations need to facilitate Saudi women's career advancement through providing more professional training and development programmes, networking and mentoring (Abalkhail and Allan, 2015), all tailored to women's specific needs.

Note

1   Purchasing power parity (PPP) is a measure that is based on relative price levels of different countries (see World Economic Forum, 2010: 47–48).

References

Abalkhail, M.J. (2012), *Women in Management: Identifying Constraints on Progression into Senior Management in the Public Sector in Saudi Arabia*, PhD Thesis, Hull: University of Hull.

Abalkhail, M.J. and Allan, B. (2015), 'Women's career advancement: mentoring and networking in Saudi Arabia and the UK', *Human Resource Development International*, Vol. 18, No. 2, pp. 153–168.

Afshar, H. (2006), *Democracy and Islam*, London, Hansard Society.

Ahmad, S. Z. (2011), 'Evidence of the characteristics of women entrepreneurs in the Kingdom of Saudi Arabia', *International Journal of Gender and Entrepreneurship*, Vol. 3, Issue 2, pp. 123–143.

Ahmed, L. (1992), *Women and Gender in Islam: Historical Roots of a Modern Debate*, New Haven, Yale University.

Ahmed, L. (2011), *A Quiet Revolution: The Veil's Resurgence, from the Middle East to America*, London, Yale University Press.

Al Hasni, A. and Al Shaibani, M. (2011), 'A historical Royal decision: the woman is a member in Shoura and Municipality Councils', available at www.alriyadh.com/670324 (accessed 27 September 2015).

Ali, A. (2009), *Business and Management Environment in Saudi Arabia: Challenges and opportunities for multinational corporations*, New York, Routledge.

Aljazeera News (2013), 'Saudi women take seats in Shura Council', available at www.aljazeera.com/news/middleeast/2013/02/2013219201637132278.html (accessed 6 October 2015).

Al-Khteep, S. (2007), 'The oil boom and its impact on women and families in Saudi Arabia', in Alsharekh, A. (ed.) *Gulf Family: Kinship Policies and Modernity*. London, Saqi Books in association with the London Middle East Institute SOAS, pp. 83–108.

Al-Lamki, S. M. (1999), 'Paradigm shift: a perspective on Omani woman in management in the Sultanate of Oman', *Advancing Women in Leadership*, Vol. 5, pp. 1–18.

Al-Lamky, A. (2007), 'Feminizing leadership in Arab societies: the perspectives of Omani female leaders', *Women in Management Review*, Vol. 22, pp. 149–167.

AlMunajjed, M. (1997), *Women in Saudi Arabia Today*, Basingstoke, Macmillan.

AlMunajjed, M. (2006), *Saudi Women Speak: 24 Remarkable Women Tell Their Stories*, (1st ed.), Beirut, Arab Institute for Research and Publishing.

Al-Rasheed, M. (2010), *A History of Saudi Arabia*, (2nd edn.), Cambridge, Cambridge University Press.

Altorki, S. (2000), 'The concept and practice of citizenship in Saudi Arabia', in Joseph, S. (ed.) *Gender and Citizenship in the Middle East*, Syracuse NY, Syracuse University Press, pp. 215–236

Alturki, N. and Braswell, R. (2010), *Business Women in Saudi Arabia: Characteristics, Challenges, and Aspirations in a Regional Context*, Monitor Group, available at www.monitor.com/Expertise/BusinessIssues/EconomicDevelopmentandSecurity/tabid/69/ctl/ArticleDetail/mid/705/CID/2010 2207132025370/CTID/1/L/en-us/Default.aspx (accessed 20 July 2015).

Arab News (2007), 7 March, available at http://archive.arabnews.com/?page¼1&section¼0&article¼107594&d¼7&m¼3&y¼2008 (accessed 20 May 2015).

Arab News (2012), 'Saudi Arabia needs more women CEOs', available at www.arabnews.com/saudi-arabia-needs-more-women-ceos (accessed 20 May 2015).

Budhwar, P. S. and Mellahi, K. (2006), *Managing Human Resources in the Middle East*, London, Routledge.

Champion, D. (2003), *The Paradoxical Kingdom: Saudi Arabia and the Momentum of Reform*, New York, Columbia University Press, Cheltenham, Edward Elgar.

Danish, A. Y. and Smith, L., (2012), 'Female entrepreneurship in Saudi Arabia: opportunities and challenges', *International Journal of Gender and Entrepreneurship*, Vol. 4, Issue 3, pp. 216–235.

Davidson, M. and Burke, R. J. (2011), 'Women in management worldwide: progress and prospect: an overview', in Davidson, M. and Burke, R. J. (eds) *Women in Management Worldwide: Progress and Prospects*, Farnham, Gower, pp. 1–18.

Eagly, A. and Carli, L. (2007), *Through the Labyrinth: The Truth about How Women Become Leaders*, USA, Harvard Business School Publishing Corporation.

EY G20 Entrepreneurship Barometer (2013), 'The power of three', available at www.ey.com/Publication/vwLUAssetsPI/The_EY_G20_Entrepreneurship_Barometer_2013/$FILE/EY-G20-main-report.pdf (accessed 4 October 2015).

Hamdan, A. (2005), 'Women and education in Saudi Arabia: challenges and achievements', *International Education Journal*, Vol. 6, No. 1, pp. 42–64.

Jamali, D., Sidani, Y. and Safieddine, A. (2005), 'Constraints facing working women in Lebanon: an insider view', *Women in Management Review*, Vol. 20, No. 8, pp. 581–594.

JCCI (2015), The Khadijah bint Khuwaylid Centre, available at www.jcci.org.sa/Arabic/servicecenters/Pages/brief-about—KBK.aspx (accessed September 2015).

KACND (2014), 'King Abdulaziz Center for National Dialogue (KACND)', available at www.kacnd.org/ (accessed 20 December 2014).

Karam, C. and Afiouni, F. (2014), 'Localizing women's experiences in academia: multilevel factors at play in the Arab Middle East and North Africa', *The International Journal of Human Resource Management*, Vol. 25, No. 4, pp. 500–538.

McKinsey (2015), 'Women leaders in the Gulf: The view from Saudi Aramco', *McKinsey Quarterly*, available at www.mckinsey.com/insights/leading_in_the_21st_century/women_leaders_in_the_gulf_the_view_from_saudi_aramco (accessed 28 October 2015).

MCS (2014a), 'Statistical Year Book', available at: www.mcs.gov.sa (accessed 27 July 2015).

MCS (2014b), 'Civil Service Regulations, the Kingdom of Saudi Arabia', available at: www.mcs.gov.sa (accessed 24 March 2015).

MEP (2014), *The Ninth Development Plan (2009–2014)*. Riyadh, Ministry of Economy and Planning.

Mernissi, F. (1993), *The Forgotten Queens of Islam*, Cambridge, Polity Press.

Mernissi, F. (2004), *Women and Islam: An Historical and Theological Enquiry*, New Delhi, Women Unlimited.

Mernissi, F. (2011), *Beyond the Veil: Male–Female Dynamics in Muslim Society*, London, Saqi.

Metcalfe, B. D. (2011), 'Women empowerment and development in Arab Gulf states: A critical appraisal of governance, culture and national human resource development (HRD) frameworks', *Human Resource Development International*, Vol 14, No. 2, pp. 131–148.

Metle, M. K. (2002), 'The influence of traditional culture on attitudes towards work among Kuwaiti women employees in the public sector', *Women in Management Review*, Vol. 17, No. 6, pp. 245–261.

Ministry of Health (2013), Health Statistics Annual Book, Saudi Arabia, available at www.moh.gov.sa/en/Ministry/Statistics/book/Documents/Statistics-Book-1434.pdf (accessed 9 September 2015).

Ministry of Higher Education (2013), The Saudi Women in Higher Education, available at https://he.moe.gov.sa/ar/Ministry/Deputy-Ministry-for-Planning-and-Information-affairs/The-General-Administration-of-Planning/Documents/666.pdf (accessed 9 September 2015).

Moghadam, V. M. (2004), *Towards Gender Equality in the Arab/Middle East Region: Islam, Culture, and Feminist Activism*. Illinois State University, United Nations Development Programme.

Mostafa, M. (2003), 'Attitudes towards women who work in Egypt', *Women in Management Review*, Vol. 18, pp. 252–266.

Mostafa, M. (2005), 'Attitudes towards women managers in the United Arab Emirates. The effects of patriarchy, age, and sex differences', *Journal of Managerial Psychology*, Vol. 20, No. 6, pp. 540–552.

Nieva, F. (2015), 'Social women entrepreneurship in the Kingdom of Saudi Arabia', *Journal of Global Entrepreneurship Research*, Vol. 5, No. 11, pp. 2–33.

Norris, P. (2009), *Why do Arab States Lag the World in Gender Equality?* HKS Faculty Research Working Paper RWP09-020, Kennedy School of Government, Harvard University.

Pharaon, N. (2004), 'Saudi women and the Muslim state in the twenty-first century', *Sex Roles*, Vol. 51, No. 5/6, pp. 349–366.

PSF (2007), 'Prince Sultan Bin Abdulaziz Fund for Women Development', available at www.pmfhd.org/en/Support_Women_Project.aspx (accessed 9 September 2015).

Ross, M. (2008), 'Oil, Islam and women', *American Political Science Review*, Vol. 102, No. 1, pp. 7–123.

Sadi, M. A. and Al-Ghazali, B. M. (2010), 'Doing business with impudence: A focus on women entrepreneurship in Saudi Arabia', *African Journal of Business Management*, Vol. 4, No. 1, pp. 1–11

SAMIRAD (2011), 'Profile of Saudi Arabia, The Saudi Arabian Market Information Resource available at: www.saudinf.com/ (accessed 20 June 2011).

Sidani, Y. (2005), 'Women, work, and Islam in Arab societies', *Women in Management Review*, Vol. 20, No. 7/8, pp. 498–512.

Simpson, R., Sturges, J., Woods, A. and Altman, Y. (2004), 'Career progress and career barriers: women MBA graduates in Canada and the UK', *Career Development International*, Vol. 9, No. 5, pp. 459–477.

Singh, V. (2008), 'Contrasting positions of women directors in Jordan and Tunisia', in Vinnicombe, S., Singh, V., Burk, R. and Bidlimoria, D. (eds) *Women on Corporate Boards of Directors: International Research and Practice*. UK, Edward Elgar Publishing Ltd, pp. 8–122.

Tayeb, M. H. (1997), 'Islamic revival in Asia and human resource management', *Employee Relations*, Vol. 19, No. 4, pp. 352–364.

TCS (2013), 'TATA Consultancy Services Saudi Aramco, GE and TCS announce the first all-female services center for business processes in Saudi Arabia', available at www.tcs.com/news_events/press_releases/Pages/Saudi-Aramco-GE-TCS-first-all-female-services-center-business-processes-Saudi-Arabia.aspx (accessed 26 July 2015).

Tlaiss, H. and Kauser, S. (2011), 'Women in management in Lebanon', in Davidson, M. J. and Burke, R. J. (eds) *Women in Management Worldwide: Progress and prospects*, London, Gower, pp. 299–315.

UNDP (2005), *The Arab Human Development Report 2005: Towards the Rise of Women in the Arab World*. New York, USA, United Nations Development Programme (UNDP).

UNDP (2006), 'The Programme on Governance in the Arab Region (POGAR), UNDP', available at www.undp-pogar.org/ (accessed 26 July 2015).

UNDP (2008), 'Empowered and equal: Gender equality strategy 2008–2011', available at www.undp.org/women/docs/Gender-Equality-Strategy-2008-2011.doc (accessed 11 August 2015).

UNDP (2009), *Arab Human Development Reports: Challenges to Human Security in the Arab Countries, Regional Bureau for Arab States (RBAS)*, New York, USA, United Nations Development Programme.

UNDP (2013), 'United Nations Statistics Division, Statistics and indicators on women and men', available at http://unstats.un.org/unsd/demographic/products/indwm/statistics.htm (accessed 25 April 2015).

UNPF (2003), *Achieving the Millennium Development Goals, Population and Development Strategies, Series (10)*. New York, USA, United Nation Population Fund.

Wirth, L. (2004), *Breaking through the Glass Ceiling: Women in Management*, Geneva, International Labour Office.

World Bank (2005), *The Status and Progress of Women in the Middle East and North Africa, Social & Economic Development Group*, World Bank.

World Bank (2014), *The Status and Progress of Women in the Middle East and North Africa*, available at http://siteresources.worldbank.org/INTMENA/Resources/MENA_Gender_Compendium-2014-1.pdf (accessed 11 July 2015).

World Bank (2015), 'Doing Business 2015: going beyond efficiency – Saudi Arabia', available at www-wds.worldbank.org/external/default/WDSContentServer/WDSP/IB/2014/11/06/000477144_20141106135416/Rendered/PDF/921190WP0Box380audi0Arabia00Public0.pd (accessed 6 October 2015).

World Economic Forum (2010), *The Global Gender Gap Report*, Available at https://members.weforum.org/pdf/gendergap/corporate2010.pdf (accessed 20 August 2014).

World Economic Forum (2014), *The Global Gender Gap Report*, available at https://members.weforum.org/pdf/gendergap/corporate2014.pdf (accessed 20 August 2015).

21 Women in management in South Africa

Babita Mathur-Helm

Introduction

Many think that women in South Africa (SA) today have more freedom and opportunities than ever before (Kadalie, 2011). While equality legislation has created space for women to do exceptional things, SA society still struggles to actualise these legal ideals. Cultural ideologies and practices continue to subordinate women, who comprise over half of South Africa's unemployed.

March 2014 brought new hope for SA women struggling to get recognised in the workplace when the Women Empowerment and Gender Equality Bill was adopted in the National Assembly (Anonymous, 2015a). The Department for Women, Children and People with Disabilities tabled the document last year in an effort to eradicate gender bias in the SA job market (Anonymous, 2015a). The SA government demonstrated its commitment towards gender transformation by enforcing change in the workplace in support of women and speeding up the process of transformation (South African Government Communication and Information System, 2014).

This chapter gives an overview of women manager's experiences along with the changes SA society has gone through over the past 20 years. It examines labour market trends and women's status and contributions in the economy. It reflects upon and explores the current success factors and failures of women and points out how discrepancies based on different racial, cultural and ethnic backgrounds in SA impact on women's advancement in management and in business. The chapter also discusses how the barriers and constraints are overcome and curbed by the government, private and public sectors and by women themselves. It further gives examples of some success stories of women who have achieved success and have reached the top positions in their professions. It concludes by providing recommendations for future research and for the future success of SA women.

What does the Women Empowerment and Gender Equality Bill say?

Although gender laws are already in place, and South Africa has made efforts to achieve gender equality since the implementation of democracy in 1994, there is still a gender gap to address.

The bill comes at a time when gender transformation in corporate boardrooms continues at a much slower pace than in government (Williams, 2013). Nevertheless it calls for equal participation of women in the economy and for equal representation in decision-making in South Africa's private and public sectors. The Women Empowerment and Gender Equality Bill calls for business owners who do not comply with the new legislation to be fined or criminally prosecuted. The act also addresses educational opportunities for women.

Equal rights for women and men have already been put forth in South African legislation with the Commission on Gender Equality Act passed in 1996; the Skills Development Act passed in 1998; and the Promotion of Equality and Prevention of Unfair Discrimination Act of 2000. However, a gender gap of 25 per cent is still prevalent in South Africa's professional world. It is assumed that the bill will aggressively eliminate favouritism toward men in employment ratios (Budlender, 2011).

It further implies that in accordance with the new legislation, any public or private body with 150 members or more must comply with strict gender regulations on members. Half of employees in decision-making structures have to be women, leaving small and family-owned businesses with more than 150 employees in a predicament if they have a male-dominant boardroom. In the case of companies with less than 150 employees, the gender regulations take effect if their annual turnover exceeds a particular limit stipulated by the bill. This guideline was borrowed from the Employment Equity Act in order to maintain consistency.

The SA workplace is still predominantly male, with preference towards male employees and it shows in numbers and remuneration. Just like many other parts of the world, there is a pay disparity in jobs, and women in SA earn 35 per cent less than male counterparts (Anonymous, 2015a).

Labour force characteristics (position of women in labour market)

The SA population on average consists of 48.2 per cent men and 51.7 per cent women and continues to have slightly more women than men (Stats SA, 2011). Similarly in the labour force from 1995 to 2005, women's representation was 58 per cent, while men's was only 42.3 per cent (DOL, 2006).

The Labour Force Survey of 2014 reported a rise in the overall unemployment rate from 4.3 million or 22.5 per cent in 2008 to 5.1 million or 25.1 per cent in 2014. However, an increase in the numbers of overall employed was noted from 14.6 million to 15.1 million (Stats SA, 2015). Despite rising figures of unemployment and poverty, women's numbers have increased in paid employment and women continue to be over-represented in low-paid, less secure employment.

Currently, despite democracy in SA, women continue to experience high unemployment, lower incomes and less access to assets. SA society is reinforced and shaped by the disparity between race, class and gender. In addition, particularly, African black women continue to be subjected to the combined negative impact of both gender and race discrimination, and remain concentrated in the lowest status occupations (Mathur-Helm, cited in Davidson and Burke, 2011).

The percentage of women in employment rose from 39 per cent in 1995 to 44 per cent in 2014. However, this rise happened due to the inclusion of informal and subsistence activities as 'work'. Women's unemployment figures dropped from 55 per cent in 1995 to 49 per cent in 2014. Therefore, numbers of women in unemployment compared to men declined from 55 per cent in 1995 to 49 per cent in 2014 (Orr and Van Meelis, 2014).

Proof of an increase in women's labour force participation is a growth in women's labour force numbers from 49 per cent in 1995 to 64 per cent in 2005. The rate of unemployment for men has grown 14 per cent in 1995 to 24 per cent in 2014. This could be due to not enough new jobs being created, and also that jobs are lost faster than they are created (Orr and Van Meelis, 2014).

Furthermore, a relevant trend has emerged: while overall unemployment grew by 14 per cent and overall employment rose by only 10 per cent, women's labour force participation increased by 11 per cent (Stats SA, 2015). Possibly all women who entered the labour force were not able to obtain employment (Orr and Van Meelis, 2014). Further, in 2008, unemployment was at 21 per cent among men and 27 per cent among women. In addition, overall unemployment was even greater among young individuals, being 28 per cent for young men and 38 per cent for young women. It is clear that women experience higher levels of unemployment than men. However due to racial inequalities, unemployment remains higher among African black people than any other racial groups in South Africa.

Black women accounted for 55 per cent of the unemployed in 2003. This was over five times the rate for white women and approximately ten times more than white men. Moreover, African black women experienced the highest levels of unemployment in 1995, 2005 and 2014, while the beneficiaries of improved opportunities over time have been white women (Orr and Van Meelis, 2015).

African black women are primarily found in jobs such as domestic work, cleaning, clerical, sales and service occupations, or in teaching, social work and administrative jobs if they are in professional jobs. In contrast white men are largely placed in management and professional occupations. In addition, manufacturing, artisanal and elementary occupations are predominantly occupations for black men. These trends from South Africa's past still persist in the labour market (Stats SA, 2011, cited by Orr and Van Meelis, 2014).

Women pursuing education

There have been several efforts made by the government of SA to focus on girls' education. For example in 2003, the SA minister of education launched the Girls' Education Movement (GEM) (UNICEF, n.d.) in Parliament. Similarly, the National Department of Education rolled out GEM in South Africa's nine provinces (UNICEF, n.d.).

GEM is a highly successful project that enables schools to increasingly reach out to girls and address their needs. This project is aligned by the government of SA with a broader UNICEF vision for girls and it has created a Child Friendly School Plus (CFS+) programme. However since less emphasis is placed on girl's education, girls (especially from the disadvantaged groups) are raised to become home caretakers and child-bearers. Therefore, when girls perform well in subjects such as maths or science, they are not encouraged and nor do they have confidence to pursue careers that rely on these skills (UNICEF, n.d.).

Further to this, girls from disadvantaged and rural communities, between the ages of 15 to 18, are encouraged to make informed career and life choices by another interesting project called the Technogirls. This project is aimed at encouraging schools to focus on maths, science and technology subjects, and shows girls the professional benefits of choosing these subjects.

Students come from public schools and are selected on the basis of their scholastic potential. They are placed in corporate companies where they undergo a mentoring and skills development programme with opportunities for scholarships. Technogirls further builds on and supports the values of GEM in that it aims to tap into the value of young females and allows them to excel in the previously male-dominated fields of science and technology. Technogirls therefore has become the vehicle to realise the values of independence and girls' struggle to achieve their maximum potential in every arena of their choice (UNICEF, n.d.).

SA women make up the majority of enrolments in public higher education institutions almost every year. Findings on education from 2008 to 2010 reveal that women consistently made up more than 50 per cent of enrolments in higher education institutions across the country, with the figure of 57 per cent in 2010 (Shezi, 2015). Of the 900,000 students enrolled in higher education institutions in SA in 2011, 58 per cent were women (South Africa Department of Higher Education and Training, 2013); this was a more than adequate female intake.

The future looks promising, as the numbers of females enrolling for faculties previously filled by men such as accounting, engineering and information and communications technology have grown. However, many female students still lack confidence when choosing these courses. Males still tend to dominate in Master's and doctoral qualifications. Yet, 40 per cent of South Africa's scientists, engineers and technologists are female (Association of South African Women in Science and Engineering, cited by Shezi, 2015).

Figure 21.1 illustrates the fairly high graduate enrolment rates from 2010 to 2012, in undergraduate and postgraduate studies. Figure 21.2 illustrates the female share of tertiary graduates by programme/field for 2012. Together the figures indicate a consistency in the number of female graduate enrolments, of over 73 per cent, between 2010 and 2012.

Looking at the figures on job preferences among female graduates enrolled in 2012, service jobs were top at 79.3 per cent, with sciences at just under 50 per cent, and engineering with the lowest enrolment, at 28.5 per cent. This indicates that females are inclined towards gender-defined fields, and hence are graduating as nurses and/or healthcare workers, and female graduates preferred health and welfare as the third highest field of work, rather than entering fields with a high degree of specialisation (Shezi, 2015).

Can MBAs help in women's career advancement?

The MBA qualification has proven to be a breakthrough for women in increased pay and opportunities in business. It is assumed that an MBA raises self-confidence and career satisfaction among women (Milpark Education, n.d.). Numerous SA women believe that an MBA gives them the edge in business, and equips them with an in-depth knowledge of an organisation's core functions (Milpark Education, n.d.).

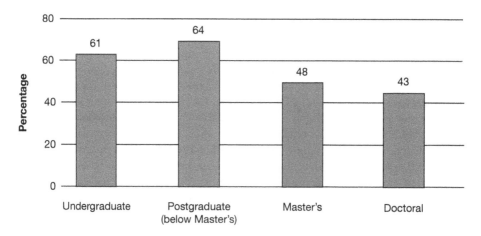

Figure 21.1 Female share of enrolment in public higher education, by qualification level, 2010–2012
Source: www.equaleducation.org.za

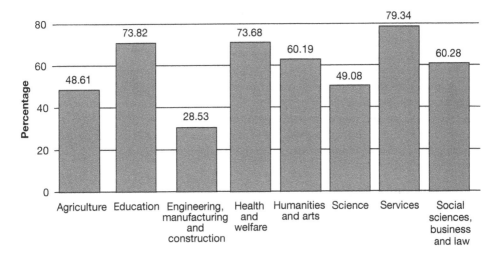

Figure 21.2 Female share of tertiary graduates by programme/field, 2012
Source: UNESCO Institute for Statistics (2015)

According to a salary survey conducted by MBA.co.za (Milpark Education, n.d.), an online resource and guide to MBA qualifications in South Africa, an MBA could enable graduates to achieve a pay hike from 32 per cent upon graduation to up to 42 per cent in subsequent employment. However, the question is how many women in SA are aware of the MBA program to enrol in it? The answer is very few and therefore not many of them benefit from the MBA qualifiaction.

Efforts made by business schools to attract more women students

Having an MBA is 'perceived by many as a passport to senior managerial roles and a fast track career tool' (Baruch and Peiperl, 2000). While a number of SA business schools see MBA qualifications as an effective way to attract more female candidates, there are however no extra efforts made to attract women candidates, such as bursaries, scholarships, subsidies and awards. Several businesses in SA that sponsor students or that value the MBA are male-dominated, including those in technology, mining, defence and management consulting (Drewery, 2012, cited by Finn, 2012).

An MBA may perhaps be seen as providing intrinsic (personal development) and extrinsic (career progression) benefits, however a graduate's choice and motivation to enrol for an MBA could be guided by numerous factors (Simpson and Sturges, 2007, cited by Ronnie and Wakeling, 2015). While there are women in SA who aspire to hold an MBA degree, there are those who also lack the confidence and motivation to be an MBA candidate, and therefore they do not pursue the MBA route. However, when they do, their salary expectations are significantly lower than that of men.

Some business schools in SA do target female applicants for the MBA, and to that end they have been continuously reviewing and improving on their marketing strategies. However there are others who do not directly promote women but instead focus on black people. Few business schools in the country are of the opinion that one of the strategies to attract more female applicants on the MBA programme could be to have more women academic staff on board, to develop more confidence amongst females. Other schools that have started to have more women academic staff have done so just to meet with the affirmative action targets, rather than particularly to attract more female applicants.

SA women face several obstacles besides lack of confidence and motivation to pursue not only postgraduate education but also an MBA. This is a substantially under-researched area, but there are some indications of inequalities by gender, race/ethnicity and socioeconomic background (Kelan and Jones, 2010; Montgomery and Anderson, 2007; O'Neil *et al.*, 2008; Schneer and Reitman, 2002; Simpson, 2005; Simpson *et al.*, 2004, all cited by Ronnie and Wakeling, 2015) that additionally affect women's postgraduate education.

Women in management

Several studies have raised concerns that without greater gender diversity at the top, SA companies might be less competitive than those in other emerging and developed nations (Maqutu, 2014). While men occupied 74.7 per cent of managerial positions in 2003, women occupied only 25.3 per cent of such positions (Mello and Phago, 2007). However, there was a marginal rise of 14.9 per cent in women's appointment to managerial positions from 1996 to 2000. This is massive progress, however it was within the context of the larger public service strategy. Currently in SA, women occupy 30 per cent of senior managerial positions (Statistics SA, 2015).

Interestingly, women's representation in positions of chief director is 39.2 per cent, deputy director general 33.5 per cent and director general 36 per cent. However women's representation in positions of director is rather more (Mello and Phago, 2007). The percentage of working women in senior management positions in SA is inadequate. In 2014 women's numbers declined by 2 per cent to 26 per cent in these positions and 21 per cent of local businesses were found to have no women senior managers (www.engineeringnews.co.za/article/amount-of-women-in-senior-sa-business-positions-down-2-2014-03-10). Grant Thornton (2014), cited by Klover (2014), found the percentage of women's positions in senior management statically fluctuating in the middle of their 26 per cent to 28 per cent range and remaining largely immobile over the past seven years (www.engineering news.co.za/article/amount-of-women-in senior-sa-business-positions-down-2-2014-03-10). Furthermore, on board positions, women form 15 per cent. Further to this, 34 per cent of SA businesses had female human resources directors and female chief financial officers, up from 32 per cent and 27 per cent in 2013 respectively (www.engineeringnews.co.za/article/amount-of-women-in-senior-sa-business-positions-down-2-2014-03-10). Meanwhile, only 52 per cent of SA's large and listed organisations support the idea of a women's quota for executives boards (www.engineeringnews.co.za/article/amount-of-women-in-senior-sa-business-positions-down-2-2014-03-10). Moreover, when asked whether they had strategies to hire and promote more women into senior management positions over the following 12 months, only 29 per cent of businesses had such specific strategies (www.engineer-ingnews.co.za/article/amount-of-women-in-senior-sa-business-positions-down-2-2014-03-10). The vast majority, that is 79 per cent of SA businesses, did not run a specific programme to support or mentor women and were not considering launching one (www.engine eringnews.co.za/article/amount-of-women-in-senior-sa-business-positions-down-2-2014-03-10).

According to the clause in the Women Empowerment and Gender Equality Bill of 2015, in future 50 per cent of all decision-making positions will go to women in designated public and private organisations (Klover, 2014). Although government can create conditions that favour women's career advancement, removing barriers to their success will remain the single most challenging task for human resource managers, which is why men still outnumber women in managerial positions.

The struggle for women in SA to progress in their managerial careers is still a challenge. Oosthuizen points out that companies with more women in senior leadership have proven to do better at bottom line performance, corporate governance and risk management (Milpark Education, n.d.). SA women in executive-level positions in all sectors persistently experience barriers such as social stereotypes and prejudices. Additionally, most career resistance happens in the middle-management level.

Efforts by the government to appoint more women into administrative jobs

The post-democratic government implemented legislation of affirmative action that provides women with employment opportunities (Mello and Phago, 2007). The 1996 Constitution, the Employment Equity Act, 1998 (Act 55 of 1998) and other policy documents, such as the White Paper on Human Resource Management of 1997 issued by the Department of Public Service and Administration, are all implemented to support women in getting hired; this was not the scene before 1994. All this forms the basis on which women can be advanced to managerial positions in the SA administrative and public services.

SA is the second highest ranked country in Africa in terms of women's representation and participation in parliament and politics (Anonymous, 2015b; Fick *et al.*, 2002 and Goetzee and Hassim, 2003, cited by Maseko, 2013) with the highest number of women in parliament globally. After the 2004 election there was a critical mass of 32.8 per cent women in parliament and 43 per cent women in 11 cabinet positions (Maseko, 2013).

Public service has various strategies to develop people, one being to develop human resources and to address challenges they face in public services (Department of Public Service and Administration, 2002, cited by Mello and Phago, 2007). These challenges include effective financial practices, integration of career and life goals, and the meaningful advancement of women and disabled people in public service and performance management systems. Disappointingly, the important issue of the meaningful advancement of women is not really addressed in the strategic objectives, key results and in the overall vision of the development strategy (Department of Public Service and Administration, 2002, cited by Mello and Phago, 2007).

There is much debate about whether increasing numbers of women in government is merely a legitimate exercise for the state or whether it aims to create a space for women to advance their needs and interests and to enable them to make policy retorts (Goetzee and Hassim, 2003, cited by Maseko, 2013). However it seems that the increasing presence of women in SA's parliament has already started to contribute to a change in the parliamentary culture by turning it into a more women-friendly institution, such as by creating childcare facilities, accepting a sexual harassment policy and changing the times of parliamentary meetings to suit women, also impacting on sexist language and jokes (Commission on Gender Equality, 2009 and Sadie, 2005, cited by Maseko, 2013).

The White Paper on the Transformation of the Public Service (South Africa, 1995) envisaged that within four years of implementing an affirmative action programme, at least 30 per cent of senior management in the public services should be women.

Examples of interesting and successful women in management research conducted in South Africa

Wendy Luhabe

A formidable and familiar face in South Africa's boardrooms, Wendy Luhabe (aged 55) is probably the most powerful and visionary businesswoman in the country, as well as a social entrepreneur and an author. Luhabe is a self-made woman, and has spent much of her career working to empower previously disadvantaged people, especially women.

Luhabe worked her way up at luxury brands Vanda Cosmetics and BMW. In 1992, she began her first foray into social entrepreneurship, founding a consultancy called Bridging the Gap, which helped prepare previously disadvantaged people for the business environment. She broke new ground in 1994 by founding the women's investment group Wiphold, which enabled tens of thousands of women to invest for the first time and was the first women-owned company to list on the Johannesburg Stock Exchange (JSE). She also started a private equity fund for women-owned businesses. She has been chair of, among others, the Vodacom Group, the Industrial Development Corporation and the International Marketing Council, and is the chancellor of the University of Johannesburg. Besides being the recipient of multiple awards and honorary degrees, Luhabe is also the author of *Defining Moments*, the profits of which go to a fund for women (Anonymous, 2015c).

Nicky Newton-King

Nicky Newton-King is the first woman to run the JSE, Africa's largest, in its 124-year history. Having been deputy chief executive officer (CEO) of the JSE for nine years, Newton-King stepped into the top spot recently. She was the obvious choice, considering she had been deputy and was an accomplished lawyer and manager. However, she was put through a stringent selection process. Newton-King, originally from Cape Town, is a graduate of Stellenbosch and Cambridge universities. Before she worked at the JSE, she was a partner at one of the country's biggest law firms Webber Wentzel Bowens, where she advised clients in the securities and financial services industry. In 1996, she joined the JSE to sort out an insider trading scandal, just as major changes began in the almost-bankrupt exchange. It was still very much a 'boy's club' then, but a time of transformation was beginning that Newton-King would lead.

Since then, she has been behind the writing of legislation, such as the Insider Trading Act, one of the only statutes in the world that compensates those negatively affected by insider trading. In addition to her normal duties, Newton-King also led the transformation process at the JSE, consulting with all staff about the implementation of employment equity. Newton-King has three law degrees, a fellowship at Yale and attended Harvard for a development programme (Anonymous, 2015c).

Nonkuleleko Nyembezi-Heita

Nonkuleleko Nyembezi-Heita is Forbes's 97th most powerful woman in the world. Since 2008, she has been CEO of a subsidiary of ArcelorMittal, the world's biggest steelmaker, owned by the Mittal family of India. Nyembezi-Heita grew up in Clermont, a township near Durban. She excelled at school and was awarded a prestigious scholarship from Anglo American that allowed her to study, a BSc in electrical engineering at the University of Manchester Institute of Science and Technology in the UK. She got her Master's degree at the

California Institute of Technology, where she was valedictorian. She began her career in 1984 with IBM in the US and SA. IBM groomed her for leadership and she headed its Windhoek division until 1998, when she became CEO of Alliance Capital Management. She then joined Vodacom as head of its mergers and acquisition division.

During Nyembezi-Heita's time at ArcelorMittal, the economic situation changed drastically as recession hit. The construction sector was particularly affected by the economic downturn and bought less steel, so Nyembezi-Heita has been steering her firm through tough times. She has faced these challenges with characteristic determination, with a thorough cost-cutting review. She has emphasised the need for the company to expand on its wider obligations in environmental, social responsibility and health arenas. She is the 2011 winner of the WBS Management Excellence Award (Anonymous, 2015c).

Maria Ramos

Maria Ramos is group CEO of the country's largest bank, Absa. Ramos was born in Lisbon, but migrated to South Africa with her family when she was six. Her family struggled financially, so she had to get a job straight out of school. She went to work at Barclay's Bank as a clerk. Ramos wanted to apply for the bank's university scholarship scheme, but was told it was only open to men. She persuaded the bank to give her the scholarship and went to Wits in 1984 to study for a B.Com, where as a student and later as a lecturer, she got involved in politics. When the ANC was unbanned, Ramos was involved in setting up its economic policy and in 1996 she became director general of the Treasury. In 2004, she became CEO of Transnet and embarked on an ambitious restructuring of the transport parastatal, making it profitable.

Ramos was named Outstanding Businesswoman of the Year 2009 at the African Business Awards, and serves on the executive committee of the World Bank's Chief Economist Advisory Panel. *Fortune* magazine ranked her as one of the most powerful women in international business for four years in a row, from 2004 to 2007 (Anonymous, 2015c).

Women entrepreneurs

According to GEM's *Women's Report 2013*, in most Sub-Saharan African economies there are fewer women than men in entrepreneurial businesses (Kelley *et al.*, 2013). However SA has equal percentages of women and men running established businesses. For the SA economy, the growth of female entrepreneurs is vital, as women entrepreneurs not only create jobs for themselves and become providers for their families, but they also employ others who become self-sustained. The continuous female involvement in the SME (small, medium enterprise) sector is a key contributor to economic growth, as well as job creation in South Africa (Business Partners, 2013).

SA's total entrepreneurship activity rate is rather low when compared to neighbouring African economies. Yet the government needs to create an environment of social entrepreneurship that will encourage females to embrace opportunities, develop successful businesses and see entrepreneurship as a viable career option. Nonetheless, SA women are venturing and entering into the domain of 'social entrepreneurship', and making huge contributions by supporting and creating opportunities for other disadvantaged individuals (Business Partners, 2013). Furthermore, there are women in SA who run models of excellence in service delivery (Kadalie, 2011), despite social and gender inequalities. They help deliver much-needed services in areas ranging from the environment, social justice, rural development, social welfare and the arts and education (Kadalie, 2011).

Stats SA's Quarterly Labour Force Survey estimates that women comprise 23 per cent of SA's total employers (Business Environment Specialist, 2013), and they are widely concentrated in the tourism sector, compared to manufacturing and business services (Business Environment Specialist, 2013). Due to higher entry requirements such as large capital investment and a requirement for specialised professional or technical skills, women-owned manufacturing and business service firms are a minority (Business Environment Specialist, 2013).

Since manufacturing has long been a male-dominated sector in SA (Business Environment Specialist, 2013), a small but significant presence of women entrepreneurs in this sector is encouraging, and these women provide valuable role models for SA women aspiring to start self-owned businesses in traditionally male-dominated fields (Business Environment Specialist, 2013).

SA women's motivation to start a business is twofold: either due to desperate conditions or an opportunity. For most disadvantaged people, including a majority of women in the country, informal entrepreneurship is the only option available to earn a living, rather than a positive choice (Business Environment Specialist, 2013). However for privileged people entrepreneurship becomes an opportunity for a better and fulfilling life. Furthermore, women entrepreneurs increasingly believe that conditions for them are less tough and it is easier to start up a business, while men business owners are finding the environment increasingly tough (Business Environment Specialist, 2013). This could be so because women are less hesitant to start an informal business, whereas men are more inclined to start a formal business. Comparative studies suggest that women are motivated to a higher degree than equally qualified men to become entrepreneurs, for family and lifestyle reasons (Business Environment Specialist, 2013), for career options that would allow them to balance work and family life and the desire to make a social contribution, which is found to be stronger in women and makes them less motivated than men towards wealth creation and career advancement (Business Environment Specialist, 2013).

SA women entrepreneurs do not regard cultural norms or family responsibility as an impediment to their business activities, however the ones who succeed are mostly those with a supportive family environment (Business Environment Specialist, 2013). Interestingly, SA appears to be increasingly accepting of women entrepreneurs. According to a survey done in one of the states, the Free State in 2012 (Business Environment Specialist, 2013), the attitudes of young people towards women's involvement in entrepreneurship were highly positive, and most did not believe that women should be constrained by their traditional roles (Business Environment Specialist, 2013). While it is true that societal attitudes towards women's place in the economy have historically limited women's entrepreneurship, it is also clear that this is changing profoundly (Business Environment Specialist, 2013) and therefore perceptions of discrimination are not a large issue.

The government wants to support and provide opportunities for women and to prompt their social and economic progress by eliminating the barriers they face resulting from prejudice, chauvinism and pervasive discriminatory attitudes (Business Environment Specialist, 2013). As a potential force for economic growth, women entrepreneurs are becoming stronger on their own. Firms owned by women tend to be smaller than their men-owned counterparts; nonetheless they are a pioneering community. Measures intended to benefit women, including the Women Empowerment and Gender Equality Bill, will expand the pool of women entrepreneurs in particular (Business Environment Specialist, 2013).

Women are educated, well-informed and demonstrate excellent results and growth prospects in their role as entrepreneurs. As a whole, they are showing a remarkably positive attitudes towards the future. It appears that the country's prospects for creating a growing pool of successful women entrepreneurs are very bright.

Country legislation

March 2014 brought new hope for women struggling to become recognised in the workplace when the Women Empowerment and Gender Equality Bill was adopted in the National Assembly (Anonymous, 2015a). The new Gender Bill makes provision for women to fill in at least 50 per cent of decision-making positions in the country. It wants to progress women's access to education, training and skills development (Botman, 2014).

For female entrepreneurs, the government has initiated a new national programme called Technology for Women in Business (TWIB). It is run by the Department of Trade and Industry's (DTI) Gender and Women Empowerment Unit, set up to ensure that the empowerment of women forms part of the broader mandate of the DTI. It aims to help move women from the sidelines to the mainstream of the economy through the innovative use of technology. They learn to apply scientific and technology-based business solutions to grow their businesses (Anonymous, n.d.). This initiative was first implemented in 1998 by the DTI and was renewed and has been modified since then.

TWIB offers tools, support and guidance to women to develop entrepreneurial skills to excel at all levels of business, from micro- to macro-enterprises. It also supports them in accelerating business growth through partnerships, education, mentoring and training. It offers a customised incubator programme, which encourages business development in a controlled and mentored environment.

TWIB's objectives are to:

- facilitate focused action by female entrepreneurs at all levels
- create successful role models
- unlock solutions to progressive approaches to doing business in a global economy.
- exploit partnerships with government, corporates and women-focused organisations (Anonymous, n.d.).

Company initiatives to support the advancement of qualified women

While in the western world today the daughters and granddaughters of bank clerks and locomotive dispatchers who started work in 1914 face a glass ceiling at a different level (Maqutu, 2014), for black women in SA, who are often the daughters of domestic workers, nurses and seamstresses (Anonymous, n.d.), the conditions are the same.

Several women executive board members in SA companies are voicing the opinion that company initiatives to support the advancement of qualified women should increase and that successful firms must advance the representation of women in managerial positions. 'Women bring a different perspective to issues and because diversity makes companies more representative of the world around them, it has profound implications for relationships with stakeholders', says argues (Maqutu, 2014). However while a few companies are focused on women's advancement and representation, numerous South African companies seem to be shying away from implementing the executive quotas. One of the requirements of the new bill includes listed companies to have 50 per cent of their executive positions filled by women. This was met with strong resistance from business and opposition parties. Business Unity South Africa described the bill's 50 per cent target as 'unrealistic and unattainable' (Maqutu, 2014). The bill was withdrawn earlier this year for further consultation.

Examples of what successful South African firms are doing to advance qualified women

Some of the examples of what successful SA firms are doing to advance qualified women are: Pick n Pay, a local retailer company that has adopted a model of granting women eleven months of maternity leave instead of four months. This comes as more women call for more time off work to bond with their children. Nine months of Pick n Pay's eleven months' maternity leave is paid leave. Perhaps more SA companies can follow this model.

Although schemes that are most essential for women are crèches at work and flexi working hours, they are not common in SA (Maqutu, 2014). Only 7 per cent of SA companies offer on-site childcare facilities (Maqutu, 2014). While this figures is low, it is 1 per cent more than the global figure. Also about 45 per cent of SA companies give working mothers access to continued professional development and education during maternity leave and reserve job roles for women for up to a year, found Grant Thornton (cited in Maqutu, 2014).

In 2014 the South African Institute of Chartered Accountants (CA) was recognised by the World Bank for its efforts to transform the profession through its Thuthuka bursary programme, as well as for upholding high standards in accounting and financial reporting in SA (Verduyn, 2015). Although it focuses more on racial advancement, it also focuses on gender development.

One of the largest black-owned accounting firms in southern Africa is Sizwe Ntsaluba Gobodo. One of the original founders of the firm, Nonkululeko Gobodo, became the first black female chartered accountant in the 1980s. The firm's management is just under 40 per cent female, with 18 per cent female representation at board level (www.gaaaccounting. com/the-advancement-of-women-in-accounting/#sthash.XuX3ht5T.dpuf). It sees women's empowerment as a business imperative. It is company policy that there should be at least 50 per cent female representation at all levels in the firm and it has successfully achieved this. It has also made progress in achieving equal representation of males and females at all levels in the business. The board of directors has seven members, four of whom are female and of the thirteen directors, six are women (Verduyn, 2015).

Another firm that supports transformation and women's empowerment and growth is Sekela Xabiso. It has developed Imbokodo Women's Forum, which supports and encourages up-and-coming female leaders (Verduyn, 2015). Yet another example is Grant Thornton, where 32 per cent of senior management positions are held by female executives and 54 per cent of its employees are female. The increasing number of females entering the profession can clearly be seen in Grant Thornton's annual intake of trainee accountants, which is now dominated by women nationwide (Bac, cited by Verduyn, 2015). The CA (SA) qualification, like an MBA, is helping in women's career advancement. The accounting profession has become an attractive choice for females and it bodes well for creating opportunities for women in leadership positions and has proved to be a good choice for potential CEOs, financial directors and most certainly for future audit partners (www.gaaaccounting.com/the-advancement-of-women-in-accounting/#sthash.XuX3ht5T.dpuf).

The right company culture can increase the number of females in an organisation, particularly those wanting to start families. Newton-King says over 50 per cent of the JSE 500 employees are women and the executive team comprises nine women and three men (Maseko, 2013). She argues that attracting more women to the stock exchange leads other women to look at it as a place where they might want to work (Maseko, 2013).

Women in government and politics

In 1994, prior to democracy, women's representation in parliament was a mere 2.7 per cent, however, presently in SA women's roles have increased through the implementation of new policies, organisational changes and organisations. All this is enabling women to progress (Anonymous, 2015d).

In Africa, only three countries, SA, Cape Verde and Rwanda, have more than 30 per cent women ministers in their cabinets. In absolute numbers, SA has the largest number of women ministers (Anonymous, 2015d). Presently in the cabinet, 47 per cent of deputy ministers are women, with 41 per cent women representation in the National Assembly and 41 per cent of all cabinet ministers being women (South Africa, 2015).

Women's representation in the SA legislatures is high, as strategies have been put in place to support and promote women within the structures of parliament and the legislature. Currently, both the speaker and the deputy speaker of the National Assembly are women, as is the chairperson of the National Council of Provinces (NCOP) (South Africa Parliament, n.d.).

The future

'My mother said it would be black women who would liberate white women', declares Sonja De Bruyn (Sebotsa, cited by Maqutu, 2014), founder of Identity Partners and former vice-president of investment banking at Deutsche Bank South Africa; 'And if we look back, that is true. There was no talk about gender before we dealt with issues of apartheid. By black women empowering themselves, they also empowered white women. However, there are probably more white women executives than black women executives'. This is a very powerful and insightful statement.

Since 1994 and the transformation of society in SA, racial matters have taken priority over gender issues and gender empowerment. Society is still divided in two: the affluent and the deprived. Hence, people live in the two worlds at the same time: one with a first-world lifestyle and the other with third-world living standards. The life experiences of individuals are divided between these two. This however leads to further divisions within the experiences of women, with huge divides between the affluent and the middle class and the disadvantaged women. This means that their experiences of challenges and opportunities are unique to some extent. However in general, all women in SA, whether educated, affluent or disadvantaged, go through common discrimination experiences. The reason for this is that SA society is still male dominated and socially hierarchical. While the younger generation of men are more accepting of empowered and successful women, older men are still stuck within the old paradigms.

The future for SA's women looks promising with legislative measures put in place by the government and private sector organisations, however corporate organisations could implement strategies and policies to improve working conditions for both women and men at low cost and with minimal impact on productivity. Policies and legislation in isolation will not improve women's retention, development and empowerment. More broad-based acceptance of women in professional careers and the empowerment of women within SA's wider society are essential.

References

Anonymous (2015a) *South African Women Demand Equal Opportunities in the Workplace: Proposed New Legislation,* http://southafrica.smetoolkit.org/sa/en/content/en/56266/South-African-women-demand-equal-opportunities-in-the-workplace-%E2%80%93-proposed-new-legislation, accessed 14 December 2015.

Anonymous (2015b) SA 2nd on list of African countries with most female MPs, *Mail and Guardian,* 13 March. http://mg.co.za/article/2015-03-13-sa-2nd-on-list-of-african-countries-with-most-female-mps, accessed 14 December 2015.

Anonymous (2015c) South Africa's 30 wonder women, *Leader,* 16 August, www.leader.co.za/article.aspx?s=51&f=1&a=3890, accessed 14 December 2015.

Anonymous (2015d) South Africa's women in politics, *Media Club South Africa,* 27 August, www.media clubsouthafrica.com/democracy/4333-south-africa-s-women-in-politics#ixzz3u0YEfZGp, accessed 14 December 2015.

Anonymous (n.d.) *Technology for Women in Business,* www.southafrica.info/about/science/twib.htm#.Vm6QaUp96Uk, accessed 14 December 2015.

Baruch, Y. and Peiperl, M. (2000) Career management practices: An empirical survey and implications, *Human Resource Management,* 39(4), 347–366, http://onlinelibrary.wiley.com/doi/10.1002/1099-050X(200024)39:4%3C347::AID-HRM6%3E3.0.CO;2-C, accessed 14 December 2015.

Botman, H. (2014) Universities' role in the struggle for women's rights, *Rektor se Blog/Rector's Blog,* 11 March, http://blogs.sun.ac.za/rector/2014/03/11/universities-role-in-the-struggle-for-womens-rights/, accessed 14 December 2015.

Budlender, D. (2011) Gender equality and social dialogue in South Africa, *ILO Working Paper,* 2/2011, www.ilo.org/wcmsp5/groups/public/—-dgreports/—-gender/documents/publication/wcms_150430.pdf, accessed 14 December 2015.

Business Environment Specialist (2013) Understanding women entrepreneurs in South Africa, *Issue Paper,* 3, www.sbp.org.za/uploads/media/SBP_Alert_-_Understanding_Women_Entrepreneurs_in_SA.pdf, accessed 14 December 2015.

Business Partners (2013) *Growth in Female Entrepreneurship Vital for SA's Economic Prosperity,* www.businesspartners.co.za/media-room/posts/growth-in-female-entrepreneurship-vital-for-sas-economic-prosperity-1218/, accessed 14 December 2015.

Davidson, M. J. and Burke, R. J. (2011) *Women in Management Worldwide: Progress and Prospects.* Surrey: Gower.

DOL (Department of Labour) (2006) *Annual Report 2006.* DOL, South Africa, www.labour.gov.za.

Finn, W. (2012) MBA women: Breaking down barriers at business school, *Telegraph,* 22 November, www.telegraph.co.uk/education/educationadvice/9683856/MBA-women-breaking-down-barriers-at-business-school.html, accessed 14 December 2015.

Kadalie, R. (2011) World Press Freedom Day, 5 May 2008, *Global Media Journal African Edition,* 2(1), http://dx.doi.org/10.5789/2-1-42, accessed 14 December 2015.

Kelley, D. *et al.* (2013) *Global Entrepreneurship Monitor 2012 Women's Report,* www.babson.edu/Academics/centers/blank-center/global-research/gem/Documents/GEM%202012%20Womens%20Report.pdf, accessed 14 December 2015.

Klover, L. (2014) Number of women in senior SA business positions down 2%, *Engineering News,* 10 March, www.engineeringnews.co.za/article/amount-of-women-in-senior-sa-business-positions-down-2-2014-03-10, accessed 14 December 2015.

Maqutu, A. (2014) Women in business: Slippery top floor, *Financial Mail,* 28 August, www.financialmail.co.za/coverstory/2014/08/28/women-in-business-slippery-top-floor, accessed 14 December 2015.

Maseko, T. I. (2013) A comparative study of challenges faced by women in leadership: a case of Foskor and the Department of Labour in Mhlathuze Municipality. Doctoral dissertation, University of Zululand, http://196.21.83.35/handle/10530/1338, accessed 14 December 2015.

Mello, D. and Phago, K. (2007) Affirming women in managerial positions in the South African public service, *Politeia,* 26(2), 145–158, http://reference.sabinet.co.za/sa_epublication_article/polit_v26_n2_a4, accessed 14 December 2015.

Milpark Education (n.d.) *Should More South African Women Pursue MBAs?* www.mba.co.za/infocen-trearticle.aspx?s=48&c=10&a=4624&p=3, accessed 14 December 2015.

Orr, L. and Van Meelis, T. (2014) *Bargaining Indicators, 2014: Twenty Years – A Labour Perspective* (Woodstock, South Africa: Labour Research Services), www.lrs.org.za/docs/BI2014-lowres_Chapt3.pdf, accessed 14 December 2015.

Ronnie, L. and Wakeling, P. (2015) Motivations and challenges: The South African Masters in Business Administration (MBA) experience, *International Journal of Teaching and Education*, 3(1), 45–63, http://iises.net/international-journal-of-teaching-education/publication-detail-85?download=4, accessed 14 December 2015.

Shezi, L. (2015) *SA Women Less Likely to Pursue Engineering and Science, Study Says*, www.htxt.co.za/2015/08/12/sa-women-less-likely-to-pursue-engineering-and-science-study-says/, accessed 14 December 2015.

South Africa (1995) *White Paper on the Transformation of the Public Service*, www.dpsa.gov.za/dpsa2g/documents/acts&regulations/frameworks/white-papers/wpstoc.pdf, accessed 14 December 2015.

South Africa (2015) *Women's Month 2015*, www.gov.za/womens-month-1-31-aug-2015, accessed 14 December 2015.

South Africa Department of Higher Education and Training (2013) *Statistics on Post-School Education and Training in South Africa: 2011* (Pretoria: Department of Higher Education and Training), www.saqa.org.za/docs/papers/2013/stats2011.pdf, accessed 14 December 2015.

South Africa Government Communication and Information Systems (2014) *South Africa Yearbook, 2013/14*, www.gcis.gov.za/content/resourcecentre/sa-info/yearbook2013-14, accessed 14 December 2015.

South Africa Parliament (n.d.) *Representivity and Public Participation*, www.parliament.gov.za/live/content.php?Item_ID=305, accessed 14 December 2015.

Stats SA (2011) *Census 2011: Gender Distribution*, http://mobi.statssa.gov.za/census2011/Gender.html, accessed 14 December 2015.

Stats SA (2015) *Labour Market Dynamics in South Africa: 2014 Report*, www.statssa.gov.za/?p=4445, accessed 14 December 2015.

UNESCO (2015) *UNESCO Institute for Statistics*, Montreal, Canada, www.uis.unesco.org.

UNICEF (n.d.) *Girls' Education Movement: South Africa*, www.unicef.org/southafrica/SAF_resources_gembrief.pdf, accessed 14 December 2015.

Verduyn, M. (2015) The advancement of women in accounting, *GAA Accounting: Journal of the Global Accounting Alliance*, www.gaaaccounting.com/the-advancement-of-women-in-accounting/, accessed 14 December 2015.

Williams, P. (2013) Celebrating our women's liberation, *South African Government Blog*, 30 July, www.gov.za/blog/celebrating-our-womens-liberation, accessed 14 December 2015.

Index